The *Theatres* Trust

Guide to British Theatres
1750~1950

Chatham, Theatre Royal (Christopher Brereton Collection)

The *Theatres* Trust

Guide to British Theatres
1750~1950

A Gazetteer

Edited by
John Earl & Michael Sell

A & C Black

Dedication

To Kathleen Barker (d. 1991) and Christopher Brereton (1941–1992)

This book is dedicated jointly to two important theatre historians. Without Christopher Brereton's pioneering work, the 1982 book would have taken years longer in preparation. A generous bequest from Kathleen Barker paid for a substantial part of the work on this edition.

Special thanks must be given to the Rufford Foundation for their generous financial contribution towards the editorial work.

Front cover Lyceum Theatre, Sheffield (photo: John Walsom/Arts Team)
Spine Lyceum Theatre, London (photo: David Crosswaite)
Back cover Edinburgh Festival Theatre (photo: Law & Dunbar-Nasmith)

First published 2000
A & C Black (Publishers) Limited
35 Bedford Row, London WC1R 4JH
ISBN 0–7136–5688–3

© 2000 The *Theatres* Trust

An updated, expanded and retitled version of *Curtains!!! or A New Life for Old Theatres* published 1982 by John Offord (Publications) Ltd.

A CIP catalogue record for this book is available from the British Library.

Printed and bound in the United Kingdom by Biddles Ltd, Guildford and Kings Lynn.

Contents

Foreword by Sir Donald Sinden

As a young actor in the 1940s and 1950s, every play I was in embarked on a long tour and I was very fortunate to perform in many of the great provincial theatres. I have never got over the excitement of arriving by train (none of us owned a car in those days) in a new town and first finding my way to my digs. I always took the precaution of arranging my accommodation well in advance, unlike dear old Cecil Winter, who would merely knock at a likely door and enquire 'A little sustenance and somewhere to lay my head?' It never failed.

I am surprised how many actors do not know that James Boswell mentions somewhere, that during a visit to a London Coffee House he encountered an actor who most interestingly had compiled a list of theatrical landladies. The actor's name was West Digges (1720–1786) and his compilation became known as Digges' List – which became essential for every actor.

On Monday morning I would set out to find the theatre where I gazed in awe at the (usually) colonnaded facade. If it was called the Theatre Royal; The Grand; The Opera House; The Kings or The Queens I was overjoyed – so much nicer names than the prosaic Streatham Hill Theatre. Then round the corner down a cobbled alley into (usually) a market place, where fruit and vegetables encroached on The Stage Door... I knew my history: through those doors had gone Henry Irving and Ellen Terry, John Martin Harvey and Nina de Silva, Fred Terry and Julia Neilson, Johnston Forbes Robertson and Gertrude Elliott, Beerbohm Tree, Frank Benson, etc. etc! In a cupboard sat the Stage Door Keeper: 'Good morning, my name is Sinden'. 'No letters, Sir – you're in number 15'. Then up four floors with my suitcase to my dressing room (I would unpack later). Then down again to sneak a look at No. 1 and No. 2 to see where my illustrious predecessors had left their ghosts, and then onto the stage... ohhhh! Just look... I peered out into the empty auditorium and felt goose bumps as I feasted my eyes on the great arc of the gilt enriched circles – how many? two – three?, the painted ceiling and, sometimes, the great chandelier. And then to the boxes supported by gilded caryatids and, above my head, the sweep of the proscenium arch. Gilt everywhere. Baliol Holloway had once told me that 'when a great actor walks out onto the stage the gilt lights up'.

The seats were covered in plush, the walls and ceiling made of wood and plaster – perfect acoustics. Last week's theatre seated 750; this week's 1800 but a whisper could be heard in either. Mentioning this to a musician friend, he replied 'But, of course – have you ever heard of a concrete violin?'

I always made my way through the Pass Door and explored the Front of House: the foyer, the bars, the secret staircases and, from the back of the circle, looked down at the stage. For a week it was my stage and my home.

I was brought up in a Sussex village, some eight miles from the coast, and our Mecca was Brighton, where before the last war there were seven professional theatres. The Theatre Royal in the 1930s had its own Repertory Company and in the '40s and '50s, it housed all the number one tours. All the great actors of the day appeared there – my first visit was to see John Martin Harvey in 'The Only Way'. I saw Marie Tempest, Irene Vanbrugh, Sybil Thorndike, Edith Evans, John Gielgud, Donald Wolfit, Ralph Richardson, Alec Guinness, John Clements, the Lunts, Peggy Ashcroft, Marie Lohr, Tom Walls, Ralph Lynn, The Vic Wells Ballet, The Anglo-Polish, Ballet Joos and so many others.

Next door was the Dolphin Theatre. It had gone through many changes of name and at that time it took in all the number two tours of the West End plays.

The Hippodrome was the number one variety (music hall) house where I saw George Robey, Max Miller, Harry Tate, Billy Bennett, Anne Ziegler and Webster Booth. It was there that I saw Ivor Novello and Roma Beaumont in 'The Dancing Years'.

The Imperial was a very large modern theatre which had just been built by Jack Buchanan and there I saw nearly all of Gilbert and Sullivan with Martyn Greene in the lead. (In 1934 I had seen the great Henry Lytton in 'The Yeoman of the Guard' at the Theatre Royal).

The Grand Theatre housed the number two variety shows such as 'Strip, Strip Hooray' and 'This Is The Show', the latter advertised with the initial letters six feet high and the rest six inches high.

The Palace Pier and the West Pier both had theatres where each had a summer season of a repertory company, and at Christmas each mounted a pantomime. The Pavilion Theatre housed small-scale shows and was the venue for festival performances.

Now there are only the Theatre Royal and the Pavilion left in use. All the others have either been pulled down or turned over to bingo. The Imperial is about to be destroyed – the last venue in the town and for many miles around for large-scale opera, ballet or musicals. Every city in the country has suffered the same vandalism, which started in the 1950s and still hangs, like the Sword of Damocles, over many wonderful theatres.

Fortunately we still have The Theatres Trust to record the theatres that are left and to alert us to the dangers hovering over others such as the Tunbridge Wells Opera House, the Festival Theatre in Cambridge, the Theatre Royal, Portsmouth, the Theatre Royal, Chatham, the Tyne Theatre in Newcastle and Aberdeen's Tivoli – to say nothing of the more modern ones such as those in Leatherhead, Salisbury and Farnham. This book – the fruit of many people's labours and love over many years – is another 'Digges List', essential for every actor and for everyone who cares about our theatrical heritage. It has brought back many memories for me, and will be a trusted friend in the future. I commend it to you, in the hope that it will help us to stop the iconoclasts before it is too late and (as Shakespeare said in Richard II)'... child, child's children, cry against you – "Woe".'

Donald Sinden
June 2000

Preface by the Director of The Theatres Trust

Producing a book like this takes time and teamwork, and the accumulated experience of several people's lifetimes. It was our great fortune at The Theatres Trust to be able to harness such a resource, and an important part of my role here is to pay tribute to all concerned.

For some of us – including many of our readers – this is our second outing on this circuit, for we were involved as producers or as users of its predecessor. *The Theatres Trust Guide* is a totally new book, but it was in *Curtains!!! or A New Life for Old Theatres* published back in 1982 that the task of recording and analysing our theatrical heritage started. Eighteen years have passed since then, and attitudes to old buildings and the nature of our task have changed. The Theatres Trust was in its infancy then, fine theatres were still being needlessly lost, and the case still had to be made for considering what already existed before building new ones from scratch. Now we can quote two or three dozen examples of ësleeping beauty' theatres being returned to life, and we have the splendid *Encore: Strategies for Theatre Renewal*, a series of case studies written by Judith Strong and published by the Trust.

The Theatres Trust Guide – the title reflects the Trust's role in co-ordinating and facilitating it – is, therefore, more a volume of record than its predecessor. We have been able to reduce the polemic, to give more space to the architects and other background information, and to extend the dateline to 1950. We have also been able to include many more buildings which will never return to their original uses, but are nevertheless of architectural or historic interest in their own right. Most of them are still capable of fulfilling a useful purpose and add distinction or interest to the townscape. If this guide encourages more people to look at and appreciate a remarkable and often under-rated building type, it will have fulfilled an important part of its purpose. For those of us who work in theatre planning, or in building conservation, or who otherwise care for our built heritage, this should also be an essential guide and working tool – the demand for which has continued ever since its predecessor went out of print.

Sir Donald Sinden, one of Britain's most distinguished and best loved actors and a Life Friend of the Trust, pays tribute to our theatrical heritage in his Foreword, and we are most grateful to him. His love of architecture and his practical experience of working in most of our finest theatres (and some of the others) make him ideally qualified for this task.

The decision to produce a new and more comprehensive book was taken in 1991. As previously, the initial site visits and assessments were undertaken on a voluntary basis, but it soon became clear that the Trust's input would have to increase and that some paid help would be needed. The Trust decided to create a database, which it would hold and which could be easily updated and made more generally available once the book had appeared. Financial support for this bigger project came initially from funds held by the Trust as part of the Kathleen Barker Bequest, and then from a most generous grant over three years from the Rufford Foundation. This enabled us to employ an architectural editor for the database entries and to co- ordinate the process of data collection. We are most grateful to the Rufford Foundation for providing help at a crucial moment in the project. Financial contributions have also been made by the Asolo Centre for the Performing Arts in Florida, the Equity Trust Fund, the Department of the Environment and the Olivier Foundation.

Our special thanks go to the team of volunteer compilers. The core members of this group have very different backgrounds, but they have all had a long association with the Trust and have been among our most loyal and valued helpers. Ted Bottle, formerly a science teacher, covered the Midlands; Ian Grundy, who runs an hotel in Scarborough, and Dr David Wilmore of Theatreresearch generally operated in the North of England; Dr Terence Rees, who has a scientific background as well as a theatrical one, did Wales; Ken Woodward, who has notched up fifty years' experience on the amateur stage and a career in the insurance business, covered much of East Anglia and Kent and helped fill in many of the gaps elsewhere; while Sally McGrath, who started her career as a performer and moved into theatre management, travelled far beyond her base in the South West and unearthed many buildings that would otherwise have escaped our notice. These, our regular helpers were joined for this exercise by Bruce Peter, a lecturer in architecture with a particular interest in entertainment architecture , who dealt with Scotland, and Robert McKinstry an architect with theatre experience – who surveyed Northern Ireland . Others who helped with compiling include Elain Harwood, Jim Lee and John Muir. We were also able to draw extensively on the records of the late Christopher Brereton, one of the main compilers of the original book.

Christopher Brereton's name must stand alongside that of Kathleen Barker, as one of four dedicatees without whose input this book and the associated database would never have appeared. The third name is that of Iain Mackintosh. Iain was the inspiration and the driving force behind the original Curtains!!! project. He established the methodology and set the high standards that we have endeavoured to follow, and has probably done more than anyone in the last thirty-five years to reawaken interest in our theatrical heritage and to demonstrate how it can be adapted for modern use. But it is to the Trust's former Director, John Earl, that pride of place must go. Like Iain Mackintosh, John was a central member of *Curtains!!!* team twenty years ago, and for this book he has again compiled the London entries. But he has also taken the key role of architectural editor and author, and pulled together the work of the volunteer team of inspectors. This book reflects the fruits of a distinguished career in building conservation and a forty year study of theatre building. Si monumentum requiris.....

Our co-author, Michael Sell has also made a life long study of theatres and was co-editor in 1982 This time he has edited the book entries and selected the photographs, and compiled many of the database entries. We have all benefitted greatly from his objective eye and vast knowledge of buildings throughout the United Kingdom.

From The Theatres Trust staff we owe a huge debt of gratitude to Paul Connolly, who took over the administration of the database and then masterminded and oversaw our end of the book production process. Jean Sedley and Sally McGrath provided particular help with the meticulous tasks of data entry and checking everything, while Fiona Nichols has coped uncomplainingly with the large volume of extra work generated in the office over the last nine years. I am most grateful to all of them for their help in making order out of chaos and for keeping calm under pressure.

Photographs have come from a number of sources including the Trust's own archives – we owe particular thanks to Ian Grundy, who has been supplying us with professional standard images over many years, and to all those who waived reproduction fees and granted consent for us to use their material. Credits will be found attached to each photograph.

Our publishers, A & C Black have proved willing collaborators, sharing our enthusiasm, while adding a professional and objective eye to our labours. We are particularly grateful to Tesni Hollands and Anne Watts.

Many other people have helped and encouraged us in various ways – they will know what they have done, and I hope they will understand if I simply list their names in alphabetical order: the late David Anderson, Sir Geoffrey Cass, Nick Charlesworth, David F. Cheshire, Graeme Cruickshank, Denis Corble, Sir James Dunbar-Nasmith, Richard Gray and his colleagues at the Cinema Theatre Association, G. Laurence Harbottle, Michael Holden, Paul Jones, Frank Manders, John Middlebrook, Sherie Naidoo, Ian Newman, John Offord, Robert Reilly, John Rotheroe, Colin Sorensen, Ken Sutcliffe, Keith Todd, and the late Bob Williamson. I should also like to thank the Trustees of The Theatres Trust – past and present – for their patience and continued support for this project through what turned out to be a far longer and more difficult task than any of us envisaged. There will be others who we have forgotten and to whom we now owe an apology as well as our thanks.

Finally, our thanks must go to all those building owners and managers who allowed us to visit and answered our questions, and to the many museums, libraries and theatre collections who have assisted in the collection of this information. Almost without exception, we were treated with courtesy and our enquiries evoked enthusiasm once our intentions were understood. Inevitably, there will be errors and omissions, and the passage of time will already have made some of our description and reports out of date. We intend to update and extend the database at the Trust's office, and to make it more easily accessible. We would welcome comments, corrections and suggestions from our readers so that these records can be improved and kept up to date. In that way we can ensure that even if this volume has to be the last word between printed covers for the foreseeable future, the work of those who made it possible will be continued.

Peter Longman
June 2000

Introduction

The Scope of the Survey

The *Curtains* Gazetteer revised

This book, production of which has been co-ordinated by the Theatres Trust Charitable Fund (TTCF), is the successor to *Curtains!!! or a New Life for Old Theatres*, published in 1982. Times have changed since that pioneering book was published. It is now generally recognised that theatres are a scarce national resource and that the best of them need to be jealously protected, whether or not they are currently being used for their designed purpose and whether or not they are listed buildings. Much of the polemical material in the opening chapters of the first edition has, therefore, been dropped. Insofar as the advice contained in those chapters is still needed, it is contained in leaflets readily available from (and frequently updated by) The Theatres Trust.

Curtains!!! proved to be a valuable tool in the hands of theatre preservers, historians, officials concerned with the listing of historic buildings and (not least) The Theatres Trust itself. For some years, however, it has been obvious that it needed to be brought up to date, corrected and extended. In particular there was a growing need for information about buildings later than 1914, the cut-off point adopted in the 1980s. The new book was obviously going to be bigger than the 1982 edition, but the temptation to make it into a two-volume work had to be resisted. The trustees of TTCF were determined to have a single volume and, furthermore, one which could be carried in the hand or kept in a glove compartment, since portability was seen as a prime reason for the success of the original *Curtains!!!* Decisions about the extent of coverage had to be taken with this limitation in mind.

Limits of the Survey

The choice of 1950 as the new cut-off was not arbitrary. It was felt unwise to embrace very recent theatres, especially those of the 1960s and 1970s generation, argument over whose qualities and faults can still generate more heat than light. To include reactions to even later buildings would have changed the character of the book. This is a reference book. It is packed with opinions, but it tries to avoid making immediate judgements over highly topical issues where views, including our own, may change with experience. A terminal date of 1950 — a grey postwar year when the building of new theatres had hardly started and the demolition of old ones was about to become a massacre — seemed practicable and defensible. It would allow reasoned judgements to be made in a fifty-year historical perspective and seemed a chance that they would be accepted by our readers as sensible and useful. In this way, we have been able to take in the very first post-war theatres while leaving the assessment of the 'concrete civics' to our successors. Sadly, by adopting this approach, we have also had to omit from the book some very fine post-war theatres, but they will be duly considered in the 2020 and 2040 editions.

The exception we have had to make to our own rule is a fairly obvious one. Where 'old' theatres (i.e. pre-1950 buildings) have undergone alteration, restoration or major refurbishment in more recent times (up to shortly before publication) we have included a brief description and critical assessment of these works in our review. The extent to which later interventions — of which there may have been a whole series — have succeeded in preserving or enhancing the qualities of the original theatre is vital to an appreciation of the architectural and theatrical qualities of the building today. Hence, you will see nothing in this book about the 1995 replacement for Glyndebourne, since what is there now is, for all practical purposes, a post-1950 building — but you will find, to take just two examples, appreciations of the 1983 works to the Old Vic and the 1994 transformation of the Edinburgh Festival Theatre.

The Database and the Book

It was decided early on that a computerised database should be created into which all relevant material coming to hand concerning theatres of all ages, extant and demolished and including those only recently built, could be recorded. The database will be continually enriched and updated. Its principal purpose will be to provide a service to The Theatre Trust and a basis for future editions of the gazetteer, but as soon as it contains sufficient checked and corrected material it will be made available to assist research by others. This is likely to be some time after the publication of the present volume.

Extent and style of coverage

Errors and omissions came to light in the first *Curtains* gazetteer, as might reasonably have been expected in a book which was packed with facts never before assembled in such a form. The gazetteer, nevertheless, quickly gained a reputation as the most comprehensive and reliable survey ever attempted of the theatre population.

The descriptions and assessments, brief as they were, carried authority because they were based on actual inspections made by a small but highly experienced group of historians. The members of the team were well known to one another, met frequently, shared a common architectural vocabulary and came to a broad consensus of views about architectural and theatrical values. Without the initials after each entry it would often have been difficult for the reader to guess who wrote what.

Few members of the original team were available to undertake the new work. Chris Brereton, in particular, who was the author of the majority of the 1982 regional entries, had died at a tragically early age in 1992. The new team was composed of experts in a variety of fields who gave freely of their time and knowlege, but their dispersal throughout the country made frequent meetings impractical. There was no longer a shared language of description and their literary styles varied from the telegraphic to the discursive.

However good the material that our compilers provided,

editing was inevitable if the text was to be made consistent in style, coverage and relative evaluation. The initials, therefore, now refer to the compiler or compilers who did the work on the ground, inspected the building and submitted their findings in manuscript. Where work by earlier contributors has been incorporated in the published text, their initials are also given. All original submitted material is kept on file unedited and is available for study, but the words that appear in the book and in database entries have often been modified by the general editor, Michael Sell, and the architectural editor, John Earl. The result of this editing is that there is usually more information in the filed manuscripts — sometimes a great deal more — than appears in either the book or the database, but the editors have rarely interfered with the compilers' qualitative judgements.

The extended coverage itself introduced new problems. By bringing the cut-off date forward to 1950 we obviously had to deal with a far greater number of surviving theatres, but we also had to grapple anew with the question of what, precisely, constitutes a theatre. Everyone knew what a 'real' theatre of pre-First World War date looked like. The first team's discussions of borderline cases mostly concerned the less ambitious private theatres, early concert rooms and flat-floored halls designed to serve too many purposes for us to label them confidently as theatres or music halls. The contentious cases were not numerous and the solution was a simple one. If more than one of the team felt passionately that a particular building could absolutely not be left out — it went in!

The new survey was faced with a population quite different from those of the pre-1914 period. Problems were more numerous and choices far more difficult. After the First World War there was a brief surge in theatre buildings, mostly in London, between the mid 1920s and the mid 1930s, but new, dedicated, purpose-designed theatres were otherwise uncommon. Those that were built reflected the theatrical uncertainty of the time, by ceasing altogether to conform or even approximate to a single classic architectural type. Far more numerous and, in some ways, more consistent in their architectural development, were the inter-War cinemas, many of which, over the whole period, had stages for live performance.

The new survey had to deal with countless ciné-variety houses, ranging from little tunnel-shaped electric palaces with vestigial stages and miserably cramped dressing places ('dressing rooms' would be too grand a term) to giant super cinemas with proper fly towers and technical facilities to make the local Empires and Hippodromes look hopelessly ill equipped.

Selection not only had to be made. It had to cut deep. We attempted to lay down logical rules and these are set out hereafter, but borderline cases were numerous and arbitrary decisions sometimes followed. There will inevitably be many instances where others would have made different decisions, but to those who complain of the omission from the book of particular theatres we can only say — nothing is lost. If we have received information, it is on our manuscript files and it will eventually be added to the database, if it is not there already. If we do not have information we will be delighted to consider what is sent to us for inclusion in the database.

Finally we draw attention to the specialised knowledge of the Cinema Theatre Association (CTA). Ideally we would wish to look forward to a time when the CTA could be funded to create its own parallel database, providing a much more comprehensive account of ciné-variety houses than this project could ever attempt. Our own database entries, simply provide a gloss on the theatrical potential of a minority of such buildings.

Rules governing selection for the Gazetteer

For a theatre to be included in the book, it must have been active at sometime between 1750 and 1950.

Extant theatres

Pre-1914 buildings All buildings described in the 1982 *Curtains!!!* have full entries in the new gazetteer unless they are now known to have been demolished. In a few cases, fragmentary remains described in the earlier book have been reassessed and treated as demolitions, but otherwise, all complete buildings and substantial remains of public theatres, classic music halls, variety palaces, and important private theatres are described. They include a number of pre-1914 theatres located since 1982. An effort has been made to include some information, however brief, on all substantial remains earlier than 1850 (see Appendix 1 below, Early Theatres).

Post-1914 buildings Those of undoubted theatrical status are included, with the exception of amateur houses with no professional potential. Cinemas with stages, fly towers, dressing rooms and a history of consistent use for variety or other live use are usually included. The smaller ciné-varieties are excluded unless they appear to have been historically important in the theatrical history of the town or they are potentially useful theatrical resources in towns now otherwise poorly provided (see Appendix 3 below, Ciné-Varieties).

Demolished buildings

In order to give a rounded picture of the theatrical life of each town, we have included lists of demolished buildings. As many as possible of the identifiable substantial theatres and music halls active at some time between 1750 and 1950 and known to be demolished are noted with (where known) authorship and dates of live theatre use and demolition. We have not intentionally included any theatre totally demolished before 1750. The rules for inclusion and exclusion follow, so far as possible, those set out above for extant theatres. Demolished buildings of earlier and later dates are included in the database only (see also Appendix 2 below, Early Theatres).

Unexecuted projects

These are not generally included in the book but may be admitted to the database as information comes to hand. The lists in the biographical section include unexecuted works, where known.

Style and Content of Entries in Gazetteer

Town With continual fragmentation of local government structures and changes to county boundaries (and in some cases the total abolition of counties as administrative entities) the name given after the town is based upon the existing new county/unitary authority administrative area.

In some instances, where it is felt that the administrative area given may not aid the reader in locating a town geographically, the (old) county or metropolitan area is also provided. Where the administrative area is the same as the town, the name is not repeated. In the case of London entries the borough is given after each theatre name.

Name The first name given is usually that by which the theatre is currently or has been best known. Other names, where known, are listed with dates of use.
Examples: Where a Hippodrome was, briefly before closure, the Grand Picture House and has now become a supermarket, neither the cinema name nor the name of the supermarket would be helpful as finding references. It will be listed as Hippodrome.
Where the Hippodrome spent its last thirty years as the Grand Picture House, it is more likely to be remembered locally by that name. It will be listed as Grand. If the building displays a name in prominent, permanent lettering, that name may be preferred here, even if it was later changed.

Dates Dates given for original design and subsequent alterations are, so far as possible, those of opening or reopening of the theatre. There may be discrepancies (usually not more than year or so) between these dates and those given in books and papers by architectural historians, who more often refer to dates of design or construction.
We have admitted some broad datings where precision is not achievable, e.g. 1880s or 1930s but have avoided 1800s, etc. as ambiguous, preferring 'before 1810' or 'c. 1800–10' (if that is meant) or, when referring to the whole century, C19.

Architects The names of architects or designers (they were not always architects) are given where known for both the original building and significant subsequent alterations.

Statutory listing of theatres The process of listing helps to project buildings of 'special architectural or historic interest'. Buildings can be listed because of age, rarity, architectural merit and methods of construction, and are graded to show their relative architectural or historic interest. Grade I buildings are of exceptional interest; Grade II★ are particularly important buildings of more than special interest; and those listed as Grade II are of special interest. It should be noted that the system of grading operating in Scotland differs slightly, and here Grades A and B are adopted, with Grade A equating to I and II★ categories and B to Grade II. It should be noted, however, that, whatever the grade, a building is listed in its entirety, including its interior.
An Advice Note on Theatre Preservation, available from The Theatres Trust, explains the effects of statutory protection so far as it affects theatres. An offical guidance note, called simply *Theatres*, is also available free on application on English Heritage.
Listing is a continuing process and although late checks have been made wherever possible, some new listings or upgradings may have occurred since the relevant entries were written.

Capacity Figures seen for dates before the Second World War, although recorded in the database, should be treated with reserve, since they were often rounded up for publicity purposes and were inconsistent as to the inclusion or exclusion of standing capacity. Before about 1890 they have practically no value for comparative purposes. They invariably assumed that pit and gallery benches and all standing spaces would be tightly if not dangerously crowded, while stalls seating would be supplemented with loose chairs in every gangway. The only reliable early figures are those taken from licensing records.
Present-day managements do not overstate licensed capacities. The tendency for the last forty years has been for genuine capacities to fall, not only because the regulators have demanded it, but also because of the comfort expectations of theatregoers.

Dimensions Dimensions in both gazetteers and database are provided to give some impression of scale and should not be used for any other purpose without checking. Where we have been able to obtain technical data sheets from active theatres, we have relied on them. In a number of other cases (not a majority) measurements have been taken on site by our compilers. Metric measurements have been given priority but Imperial equivalents are given. Dimensions in metres are given to two places of decimals (I.e. 9.02m not 9m 2cm and not 9020mm) but where these have been converted from unchecked Imperial figures a false impression of precision may result).
The only abbreviations used are:
m   for metre(s)
ft   for foot/feet
in   for inch(es) (no fractions)
c.   For circa

Definitions

The following meanings are to be applied to recurrent terms, except where the context clearly implies otherwise.
Extant   Some substantial part of the building survives complete or nearly complete.
Facade   The body of the theatre, or the greater part of it, has been demolished but the street facade can be readily identified and is worth a full description.
Fragment   The theatre has been largely demolished but enough significant old fabric remains visible (or has been incorporated into a successor building) to be worth noting briefly.
Demolished (D)   The building no longer exists or such fragments as remain are too insignificant to be worth identifying.
Current uses   'Theatre' is used only where live entertainment — drama, opera, ballet or variety are predominant. Music venues, whether for 'serious' or popular concerts, are described as such and not as theatres. The current use given is normally that seen at the time of the compiler's inspection, which may have been some time before publication.
Dark   Means the building has recently been an active theatre but is now disused (i.e. no change of use has occurred).
Disused   Refers to a theatre building whose use has changed before it fell into disuse or one which has been too long disused to be described as 'dark'.

Derelict Normally used only where condition is visibly so poor that it must be a major issue in any consideration of the future of the building.
Replaced Completely new theatre built on the site of an earlier, demolished theatre.
Rebuilt   Existing theatre largely reconstructed (e.g. 'rebuilt internally' meaning nothing of old interior remaining).
Renovated or modernised Brought up to a more satisfactory standard without substantial rebuilding.
Restored   Faithfully restored to original architectural design, wholly or in part.

Star rating

On the line below the name will be found the rating of the theatre. These ratings are quite independent of whether or not the building is currently in use as a theatre, although it should be noted that nearly every starred theatre, if not now in use, is restorable.

We have generally adopted the system used by our predecesors in the 1982 Curtains gazetteer; unless subsequent developments or new information demand otherwise we have not sought to change those ratings. And in considering post-1914 theatres we have tried to work in the same spirit as our predecessors. However, we have no longer applied stars where only a façade or a completely gutted shell now remains, and we have not attempted to apply ratings to certain buildings which not strictly theatres but have been included for their historic interest or relevance. Nor have we attempted to give ratings when the building that exists today is entirely post 1950 and shows no visual evidence of its predecessor on that site. But where any part of a pre-1950 theatre still remains we have applied a star rating on the basis of what is seen today, thus taking account of any subsequent works.

Many of the buildings which feature in this book were designed after 1914 for a dual use as a cinemas or a flat-floored and multi-purpose halls. Some of these buildings are of considerable importance in their own right and may be statutorily listed. However, in applying our ratings we have considered them solely for their theatrical quality, with the result that many of them do not merit any stars. This should not be taken to imply that the buildings concerned are of no value or do not fulfil a useful purpose.

★★★   A very fine theatre, etc., of the highest theatrical quality.

★★   A fine theatre, etc., which is an excellent example of its type.

★   A theatre, etc., which is of some interest or quality.

no rating Of lesser interest — it may be half complete, irretrievably altered, or a complete but unremarkable theatre. This category also includes buildings which have some theatrical quality but were primarily intended for other purposes. There are also a few which occupy pre-1950 sites but have been wholly reconstructed since and are thus outside the scope of this book.

Key to Compilers of Gazetteer

Initials indicate the compiler(s) who actually inspected the buildings (see *Extent of Coverage* above, regarding editing of submitted work). Some entries are unattributed having been composed by the editors from several sources, including some material from informants, who were not members of the regular team but made occasional contributions.

TB	Ted Bottle
CB	Christopher Brereton (d 1992)
GC	Graeme Cruickshank
JD–N	James Dunbar-Nasmith
JE	John Earl
IG	Ian Grundy
VG	Victor Glasstone
EH	Elain Harwood
JL	Jim Lee
IM	Iain Mackintosh
JM	John Muir
RMcK	Robert McKinstry
SM	Sally McGrath
BP	Bruce Peter
TR	Terence Rees
MS	Michael Sell
DW	David Wilmore
KW	Ken Woodward

London, The Old Vic

The Gazetteer

ABERAMAN
Rhondda Cynon Taff

Grand ★
Cardiff Road
Other names
    Poole's Palace
Original architect
    1908   Unknown
Later works
    1930s Unknown: converted to cinema
Current use Bingo

Built as Miners' Public Hall and Institute – a type common in South Wales (e.g. Mountain Ash, New Theatre), but more of a landmark than most. Institute on ground floor with auditorium above. Fully equipped stage – 6.4m (21ft) proscenium, 8.5m (28ft) depth and 11.9m (39ft) grid. Shallow balcony on three sides. Altered on conversion to cinema in 1930s. Impressive, five-storeyed, red brick facade surmounted by Flemish gable above a big mullioned and transomed arched window. The ground floor has three large, arched and pedimented entrance doors. Small fly tower projecting above main roof.   CB/TR

ABERCRAVE
Powys

Adelina Patti Theatre ★★★
Craig-y-Nos Castle
Original architect
    1891   Bucknall and Jennings

Abercrave, Patti Theatre

Listed   Grade I
Current use Theatre (in occasional use)
Capacity   158

Added by Dame Adelina Patti and her husband, the tenor Nicolini, to the existing neo-Gothic house. The most ambitious of the few private theatres in Britain, and still intact. Like Chatsworth, it also functioned as a ballroom but has a proper stage with fly tower, and also original machinery and scenery, including a spectacular act drop of Patti as Semiramide, attributed to Hawes Craven. The stage has a slight negative rake. The small, rectangular auditorium has a coved and panelled ceiling and the walls are richly articulated by giant, fluted Corinthian columns. The proscenium, flanked by columns, has a central pedimented tablet with the names of Verdi, Rossini and Mozart. There is no fixed seating. The flat floor can be tilted downwards towards the stage to form a raked auditorium and a sunken orchestra pit opened up. The main house was for many years used as a hospital, later converted to a hotel.

The theatre continues to be used at intervals for performances of opera and the fabric is well maintained. There was a proposal to turn it into an Opera Study Centre with occasional public performances but this has so far made no progress. There has been, however, an annual opera season for some years. The proscenium is 6m (20ft) wide and the

stage has a depth of 6.46m (21ft).
This is one of the most important private theatres in Britain and deserves exceptional effort to see it restored and brought back to use.   TR

ABERDARE
Rhondda Cynon Taff

Hippodrome
Canon Street
Other names
    Temperance Hall
    Palladium
Original architect
    1858   Unknown
Later works
    1920s Unknown: converted to cinema
Current use Bingo
Capacity   est. 700

Built as a temperance hall for concerts, meetings, etc., it was renamed Hippodrome early in the twentieth century when music hall performances were given. It was converted to a cinema in the late 1920s, for which use the auditorium was altered. It has a decent, chapel-like, two-storey stucco front with a pedimented gable to a slated roof. The ground floor is channelled with an altered central entrance of vaguely Po-mo character. Five windows at first floor, the centre one glazed and pedimented, the others blind.   TR

ABERDEEN

Alhambra
Guild Street
Original architect
    1794   Unknown: as a church
Later works
    1881   Unknown: converted to theatre
    c.1907 Unknown: converted to retail
            units
Current use Retail

Dull granite box with a pitched roof. Gable broken into by shop display windows.   BP

Beach Pavilion
Original architect
    1882   Unknown
Later works
    1928   Unknown: rebuilt

1963 Unknown: converted to restau-
      rant
Current use **Restaurant**

A wooden pavilion in use from 1882 was replaced by the present multi-purpose building in 1928. Single-storey sprawl of brick and stone clad in buff faience, in nondescript style of contemporary municipal swimming baths, fronting hexagonal hall with steeply pitched red tile roof capped by lantern. The venue was constructed to host tea dances, summer concert parties and such seaside fare, but became famous for variety.   *BP*

Capitol ★★
Union Street
Original architect
   1933 A.G.R. Mackenzie of
         A. Marshall Mackenzie, Son
         and George
Listed   **Grade B**
Current use **Dark**
Capacity   **(was) 2080**

The Capitol is an outstanding intact survivor from the era of the super cinema. It is also among the first British cinemas in the Moderne style. It was always considered to be Aberdeen's most prestigious cinema with annual pantomime seasons and other regular live shows. It has hosted concerts since the 1950s and is presently unused, except for the former café which functions as a bar.

Throughout, Mackenzie's innovative design was heavily influenced by contemporary European cinemas and theatres, such as the Savoy in London. The dignified facade is of classical proportion and is in unadorned dressed granite, eight bays wide with three tall windows in the centre, soaring above the entrance canopy to a simple pediment, which originally carried the name in neon letters. Neon was also used to outline the roof line and the facade was floodlit in white, an early use of German-inspired 'Night Architecture' in Britain. The entrance, flanked by shop units, has a V-shaped canopy and doors in mahogany with bold half-circular glasses and stainless steel inlays. Each set of doors closes to form a dramatic 'target' design. The remainder of the structure is faced in plain brick with a pitched slate roof.

Within, the building was originally decorated throughout in modish pale blue with silver leaf (reflecting Aberdeen's status as the 'silver city by the sea'). Following protests that it appeared too cold, it was quickly redec-

orated in the present pink and gold scheme. The outer foyer has elegant full-height wood veneered walls and terrazzo flooring with typically enigmatic abstract patterns of mosaic. Grand staircases with chromed balustrades sweep up to the lofty circle and stalls foyers, complete with tinted mirrors and contemporary wall and ceiling light fittings. The powder room in the ladies' toilet is pure Hollywood, with a swirling carpet, bevelled mirrors and fluted make-up tables in black, cream and mint green. Nothing has been radically altered since the 1930s.

The auditorium has one balcony with truncated slips fairing into the side walls, which are splayed to the rectangular proscenium. To either side, there are elegant organ and ventilation grilles and tableau panels with stylised foliage. Otherwise, the space is largely unadorned and relies on an extensive scheme of concealed Holophane lighting for its effects, one of the first and best installations of its kind. Today, it glows seductively in orange. The organ is a Compton. The ravages of time and excessive use by drinkers and rock concert patrons have exacted their toll, but the seats and carpets are genuine 1930s' patterns. This makes the Capitol unique, particularly in view of its size and city-centre location.

The Capitol is an outstanding building which deserves a full restoration. Although the stage is of restricted depth and a road behind would preclude its enlargement, it has good acoustics and sightlines and could host stand-up comedy and folk or rock concerts.   *BP*

His Majesty's ★★★
Rosemount Viaduct
Original architect
   1906 Frank Matcham
Later works
   1933 D. MacAndrew: 'sight lines
         improved'
   1982 City architect: modernised,
         refurbished and stage facilities
         improved
Listed   **Grade A**
Capacity   **1456**

His Majesty's is a grand touring theatre in Matcham's later, restrained idiom. Its prominent site, above Union Terrace Gardens and flanked by the imposing court house and a church, called for a monumental approach in Kemnay 'white' granite. The individual elements have impressive intention, yet Matcham's erratic adoption of early Georgian mixed with free Baroque – rusticated arches, giant pilasters with a central bay that breaks forward on two attached Ionic columns and a curved gable above the parapet – appears more appropriate for a place of entertainment. The idiosyncratic composition is capped by a copper-covered dome (carried on a drum of columns) reflecting the dome of the church to the left of the theatre.

The front-of-house spaces are commodious by the standards of the time, with many fine fittings. The dress-circle bar is circular with a marble counter. The auditorium is remarkably intimate for its more than 1400 seats (originally over 2300!), achieved by three closely stacked balconies which curve round to meet an elaborate composition of superimposed boxes flanking the proscenium.

THEATRE AND WALLACE STATUE, ABERDEEN

Aberdeen, His Majesty's (John Earl Collection)

The plasterwork is uncharacteristically chaste for Matcham and is in Roman classical idiom. The ceiling is flat and divided into panels by heavy beams with egg and dart moulding There is a frieze by W.H. Buchan with robed figures in relief above the pink marble proscenium frame. The interior is elegantly decorated in ivory, pale blue and gold with crimson upholstery and drapes.

A fine theatre. The 1982 refurbishment cost over £3 million, a remarkable sum for its time. Good stage with 9.16m (30ft) proscenium opening.   *BP*

Palace
Bridge Place
Original architect
  1898   John Rust
Later works
  1931   Marshall and Tweedie
         (Newcastle): interior rebuilt as
         cinema
Listed   **Grade B**
Current use **Nightclub**

The Palace was built following destruction by fire in 1896 of the People's Palace on the same site. The interior of the new Palace, originally with two tiers and of vigorous oriental appearance, was completely gutted to the shell tanks in 1929 and rebuilt, reopening as a cinema with one balcony in 1931. The four-storey asymmetrical granite facade survives largely intact, but this is a crude design of industrial quality – plain with a pediment over the three central bays and three large doorways with thin broken segmental pediments.   *CB/BP*

Tivoli ★★★
Guild Street
Other names
  1872   Her Majesty's Theatre
Original architect
  1872   C.J. Phipps and James
         Matthews
Later works
  1897   Frank Matcham: auditorium
         altered
  1909   Frank Matcham: auditorium
         reconstructed
Listed   **Grade A**
Current use **Dark**
Capacity   **est. 800**

The Tivoli is one of Britain's most important Sleeping Beauties still awaiting recall to life. It would make an excellent second theatre for Aberdeen, being smaller in scale than His Majesty's, and thus more appropriate for variety, drama and chamber lyric theatre.

It presents a delightful polychromatic Italian Gothic facade to the street, the main building being of three storeys and seven bays with the windows in each storey united by a series of parti-coloured arches. Deep bracketed eaves and hipped roof over. To the left, a lower, gabled bay. The rear wall, to Wapping Street, rendered with slightly recessed arcaded bays, bears an accidental resemblance to an older type of music hall.

The main facade is of 1872, but the intimate auditorium owes its present character to Matcham's reconstruction of 1909. Two balconies – the first of nine rows and a gallery above of ten padded benches. Two superimposed boxes on each side of the proscenium, stepped down in level from the balcony fronts and flanked by tall Ionic columns. The upper boxes have canopies surmounted by cartouches set in front of characteristic shell hoods.

The rectangular proscenium is framed by slender, garlanded colonnettes which carry scrolled brackets. On either side are fine female figures carrying lamps. Above is a tympanum with rounded corners framing a cartouche. The most splendid feature of the auditorium is the opulently decorated circular ceiling, incorporating four painted panels. By

present standards the auditorium would seat approximately 800 and, although last used for bingo, has suffered very few alterations.

There is considerable local interest among local amateur groups in acquiring and reopening this theatre. Apart from the obvious need for modernisation of stage and seating, the main problem will be in improving the cramped front of house accommodation. The acquisition of a small adjoining property could open up new possibilities in this respect.   *CB/JE*

ABERGAVENNY
Monmouthshire

Borough
Cross Street
Original architect
  1890s?   Wilson and Wilcox (Bath)
Later works
  1990   Unknown: stalls raked
Listed   **Grade II**
Current use **Theatre**
Capacity   **338**

The theatre is situated on the top (3rd) floor of the Town Hall. This part of the building has been devoted to public entertainment from the very beginning, but no part of the external architecture

Aberdeen, Tivoli (Steve Mackie)

suggests the presence of a theatre within. It was possibly created in the 1890s.

There was originally a flat-floored auditorium with a single balcony but the most recent alterations, dating from 1990, have introduced steeply raked seating, the back row of seats reaching a point just below the sinuous front of the balcony which still carries the original decorative plasterwork. Internal alterations continue.

The stage has no fly tower and there is no sub-stage machinery. There is no significant flying height – all cloths must be rolled. An orchestra pit is available on removal of the first two rows of seats, but it is only 0.3m (12in) below the level of the first row. The stage extends 1.5m (5ft) before the line of the house curtain. *TR*

ABERYSTWYTH
Ceredigion

Coliseum ★★
Terrace Road
Other names
   Philips' Coliseum
Original architect
   1905   Arthur Jones
Listed   Grade II
Current use Museum
Capacity est. 800

Remarkable for its well-preserved auditorium which has the appearance of a mid C19 music hall, although built much later. Neither past cinema nor present museum use has damaged its character. This is at first-floor level with shops below and would have a capacity today of approximately 800. Slightly raked

main floor with iron columns supporting two shallow balconies – semi-circular at the rear and extending with straight arms of three rows along the side walls to meet a simply framed, elliptically arched proscenium. The balconies have elaborately fretted cast-iron balustrades with Art Nouveau-inspired decoration. Plain, flat ceiling subdivided by thin plaster ribs running between cast-iron roses. Small music-hall stage and low grid. Exuberant facade to Terrace Road which, although vulgar, is stylistically more of its time than the auditorium. Three-bay, gabled centre with two unequal levels of windows above the altered ground floor, divided by debased Ionic pilasters. Symmetrical flanking bays with semi-circular oriels boldly projecting at first-floor level and surmounted, above the cornice, by cupolas. TR

Royal Pier Pavilion
The Pier
Original architect
   1896   Marks
Current use Bingo

A typical aisled pier pavilion with a semi-circular roof. The end gable is fully glazed with ornamental glazing bars, in the manner of an elaborate Georgian fanlight. Lower ellipsoidal roof on either side with little gothic-arched gables to the aisles. The original railings and kiosks on the street front have now gone and the facade has been modified by the addition to either side of an ice-cream parlour and a hot-dog stall. The auditorium has been converted to a penny arcade. No fly tower. *TR*

AIRDRIE
North Lanarkshire

Hippodrome
Hallcraig Street
Other names
   1856   Corn Exchange Hall
   1908   Hippodrome Theatre
   1929   Rialto cinema
   c.1965   Rialto bingo
Original architect
   1856   James Thompson
Listed   Grade B
Current use Bingo/amusement arcade
Capacity   (was) c.1000

Harled gushet building of two storeys, entrance signified by diapered pilasters rising to support a central pediment with the town crest grandly aloft, flanked by chimneys. A most attractive piece of Scots borough architecture by a respected and prolific local architect. The interior has been altered many times, most recently for bingo. *BP*

ASHBOURNE
Derbyshire

Empire
King Edward Street
Other names
   1960   Empire Ballroom
Original architect
   1912   Unknown
Later works
   1960   Unknown: converted to ballroom; floor levelled with stage; new stage built on top
Current use Multi-purpose hall
Capacity   (was) c.500

Opened as a ciné-variety in 1912, it was converted to a ballroom in 1960 and a bar and refreshment room later added on stage right.

Two-storey facade with rendered ground floor, boarded above, with a two-storey projection containing the entrance and projection room over. The original main structure was of corrugated iron but the stage is now partly enclosed by brickwork. The interior has been altered for ballroom use with a dance floor level with the original stage and new stage built on top. The ceiling was originally pitched and boarded and has been replaced by a curved slatted lining. Proscenium arch with fibrous plaster ornamented frame. The present chandeliers (and the piano) came from the Derby Albert Ballroom.

An interesting ciné-variety house. It is

Aberystwyth, Coliseum (Ceredigion District Council)

a pity that so much of the original interior has been obliterated. *TB*

ASHBY-DE-LA-ZOUCH
Leicestershire

Lyric
Lower Church Street
Original architect
  n.d.   Unknown: as public house
Later works
  1912   Unknown: converted to cinema
  1922   Unknown: exterior altered
Current use Function room

The Wagon and Horses public house was converted to the Lyric cinema in 1912, with stalls and small balcony and stage, the roof of which was 0.53m (21in) above roof of auditorium. In 1992, after a long period as a warehouse, the exterior was altered. The former entrance from Lower Church Street was bricked up and a new entrance in alleyway on right-hand side facing building opened. Floor of hall is now level and used as a Function Room. Small balcony at rear is not original. Former stage area occupied by kitchens. This part is raised from the main hall the steps leading being a few feet in from the beginning of the low fly tower. Wooden (pine) ceiling, said to be original. Little otherwise remains of the original interior and exterior. *TB*

ASHTON-UNDER-LYNE
Tameside

People's Opera House
Stamford Street/Booth Street
Other names
  1855   Oddfellows Hall
  1863   People's New Concert Hall
          Booth's Theatre
          Oddfellows Hall Cinema
Original architect
  1855   Unknown: as Oddfellows Hall
Later works
  c.1863   Unknown: converted to theatre
Current use Disused

Opened in 1855 as Oddfellows Hall. Brick building of three storeys in classical style with stone dressings and deep bracketed stone crowning cornice. The name ODDFELLOWS HALL remains above a niche over the main entrance which is set between contemporary shop fronts. After conversion by W. Revill for concert entertainment, and later for music hall, it was given the title of People's Opera House, though it is thought only the D'Oyly Carte Company appeared in 1884. It concluded its enter-

tainment days as a cinema, possibly c.1910–50. No interior description found. Hall gutted, probably after conversion to a pub and more recently to a club. Now disused and for sale. *SM*

Tameside Hippodrome
Oldham Road
Other names
  1904   Empire Hippodrome
  1933   New Empire
  c.1963   ABC
  1976   Tameside Theatre
Original architect
  1904   J.J. Alley
Later works
  1933   Drury and Gomersall: convert-
          ed to cinema; auditorium and
          foyers redesigned, removing
          balcony and boxes; organ
          installed
  1935   Drury and Gomersall: facade
          redesigned
  1976   Unknown: refurbished; organ
          removed
  1983   Unknown: refurbished
Current use Theatre
Capacity 1262

Plain, red brick facade, typical of Alley, with sparse yellow brick relief and broad gable, remodelled and part-rendered when the theatre became a cinema in 1933. Canopy altered at the same time. The original frontage incorporated two shops.

Previously a three-tier auditorium with boxes, but auditorium completely reconstructed in 1933; clean lines with one balcony, in plain Art Deco style. Stage retained with dressing rooms and stage facilities. Altered foyers; former cafeteria at circle level now a theatre bar.

The adjacent Palais de Danse, also a Broadhead house, was constructed later than the theatre. The Pavilion Cinema in Old Street, located almost to the rear of the property, was also part of the Broadhead empire. *SM*

AYR
South Ayrshire

Gaiety ★
Carrick Street
Original architect
  1902   J. McHardy Young
Later works
  1904   Alec Cullen: reconstructed
          after fire
  1935   Unknown: facade remodelled
  1955   Unknown: reinstated after fire
  1995   Unknown: annexe added
Listed   Grade B

Ayr, Gaiety (Paul Iles)

Current use Theatre
Capacity   584

Facade, originally red brick with stone dressings and industrial in character, was remodelled in 1935 in cream and black faience resembling contemporary cinema design. Intimate auditorium in florid Baroque style with two balconies – the first of six rows and the second now only of three rows after reconstruction following a fire in 1955 when the capacity was reduced to 570. Single boxes tied into each balcony, framed by pilasters and surmounted by broken segmented pediments with large cartouches. The proscenium is strangely low in relation to the auditorium – the top of the frame being level with the underside of the upper boxes. Above is a wall, decorated with a heavy, segmentally arched panel. Saucer-domed ceiling undecorated apart from cornice mouldings with cartouches at intervals. Garish pink and gold paintwork.

Annexe of dubious merit added in 1995, containing an enlarged box office, café, administration and backstage facilities. This breeze-block addition resembles nothing so much as a social security office, being neither memorable for its modernity nor complementing the existing theatre. Within, it is coarsely detailed with horrid suspended ceilings and 1980s' style shopping centre decor. The extra space, however, has been most welcome and has enabled the theatre to expand its activities, thus attracting more customers. *BP*

Green's Playhouse ★
Boswell Park
Original architect
  1924   John Fairweather

Current use **Bingo**
Capacity   **Originally c.3100**

Green's Picturedrome of 1911 was a conversion from a roller-skating rink. The Picturedrome became the (original) Playhouse in 1922 and was destroyed by fire the following year. The present building was erected in 1924. It became a bingo house in 1965.

Crude and dominating harled brick edifice typical of its period of stylistic transition, incorporating elements of earlier building. Symmetrical facade with debased classical details and large pediment concealing projection box. As with many ciné-variety venues, it is the interior which delights.

The foyers are solidly classical with weighty Ionic pilasters and white marble floors and balustrading. The auditorium has one enormous balcony. On either side, giant Ionic orders with superimposed boxes soar triumphantly to the heavily beamed ceiling. Wide stage. *BP*

Pavilion ★
The Green
Original architect
    1911   J.K. Hunter
Listed   **Grade B**
Current use **Nightclub/community uses**
Capacity   **est. 600**

Simple harled red sandstone hall with tall elegant Italianate towers at each corner and set amid promenade gardens. A long, narrow auditorium. Flat main floor and one horseshoe balcony. Plain barrel-vault ceiling. Indeed, the only decoration in the entire hall is a scroll with acanthus leaves over the proscenium. Showing wear because of nightclub use. *CB/BP*

Theatre Royal
Fort Street
Other names
post
    1860   Queen's Hall
Original architect
    1815   Unknown
Listed   **Grade B**
Current use **Baptist Church**

Modest rectangular hall of sandstone rubble with a two-storey facade of five bays, clad in cement stucco. Five arched windows to first floor with pediment containing infilled ocular window. Inevitably, the interior has been radically altered, although it is still possible to identify the original layout. The auditorium was decked over at circle height

(a half storey up from ground level). The former pit, excavated to a depth of 3m (9ft 10in), became the crypt. The church is an unadorned rectangular space with a flat ceiling and one balcony with truncated slips. All evidence of the proscenium and stage has gone. *BP*

BABBACOMBE
Torbay

Babbacombe Theatre ★
Babbacombe Downs
Other names
    1939   Babbacombe Downs Concert
           Hall
Original architect
    1939   Unknown
Current use **Theatre**
Capacity   **604**

There has been a tradition of concerts and entertainments on the site of the present Babbacombe Theatre since Victorian times and in 1920 a roofed bandstand was built. This was replaced by the present Babbacombe Downs Concert Hall which was built in order to extend the season for musical concerts. Opened in 1939, it was equipped for outside broadcasting. During the war, the auditorium became a lecture hall for aircrew trainees, as well as being used for ENSA shows and RAF Flying Training Command Band Concerts.

The building is very plain, of brick and timber, single-storey, resembling a cinema, on a small grass down on top of the cliffs. The foyer is small and austere. The auditorium is raked, with excellent sightlines, and the ridged plaster is reminiscent of a cinema. Seating 604, is popular amongst entertainers, possibly because of the atmosphere and the comfortable stage (although wing space is extremely limited), but more probably because of the strong tradition of good shows and broadcasts, following its popularity during the war.

It is well maintained and well run, being one of the few summer theatres to stay live all year. It is privately owned, and leased to the local authority. *SM*

BACUP
Lancashire

Empire
Rochdale Road
Other names
    Royal Court Theatre
    New Court Theatre
    Court Theatre Picture Palace
    Art Picture Palace

Original architect
    c.1850   Unknown: as an Iron Works
Later works
    1892   Unknown: converted to the-
           atre
    1948   Unknown: upper circle
           removed
Current use **Amateur theatre**
Capacity   **485**

Situated away from the town centre on the side of a steep slope with entrance at upper level, through a completely plain and featureless exterior. The building was originally constructed c.1850 as the Henrietta Street Iron Works. The factory was plagued by fires, one occurring in 1867 and another in 1886 when the building was gutted and became dangerous. It was eventually bought in 1892 by John Walters and W.A. Love who resolved to turn it into a theatre.

It opened in 1893, incorporating some of the external walls of the foundry. The back wall of the stage still has the derelict window frames of the gutted factory. Internally it originally had two balconies, the upper split into gallery and upper circle. However, in 1948 an architect's report suggested that a pillar supporting the upper circle was unsafe (this turned out to be incorrect!) and the upper circle was removed and the circle tier continued up to the back of the theatre.

Today the interior of the theatre is heavily altered from its 1893 form, the obvious remnants being the cast-iron columns that support the dress circle. The decorative finish of the auditorium is very dark and 'pseudo-1930s', probably the result of many unco-ordinated alterations, the main one being almost certainly in 1948. *DW*

BANBURY
Oxfordshire

Grand
Broad Street
Original architect
    1911   Unknown
Later works
    1930s   Unknown: rebuilt
    1968   Unknown: converted to bingo
Current use **Bingo**
Capacity   **(was) 500**

The Grand opened in 1911, reputedly constructed by the roofing-in of a builder's yard. It was rebuilt after a fire in the 1930s in 'faintly Egyptian style'. A charming, intimate house. Balcony intact, and stalls now converted to bingo. Could be a venue for live theatre in Banbury. The dressing-room area would no doubt need renovation in such an event, but the popularity of bingo has certainly preserved the auditorium and, indeed, the theatre. *SM*

BANGOR
Gwynedd

The County ★
Dean Street
Original architect
  c.1850 Unknown: as a chapel
Later works
  1912 Unknown: converted to theatre
Current use Nightclub
Capacity est. 800

Former Tabernacle chapel of c.1850, converted to a theatre in 1912. This was done by adding a brick fly tower to one side of the square-shaped stone chapel and a small stuccoed foyer, etc., on another side. The auditorium was square in plan and had an unusual five-sided balcony which may have survived from the chapel, with six steeply raked rows of seating. A short central section facing the stage linked by canted sections to side arms at right angles to the proscenium. The proscenium was an elliptically shaped arch with a cartouche above the centre. Original flat chapel ceiling. After some time as a cinema and later a bingo hall The County was converted to a night club, 'The Octagon', which specialises in such spectacular lighting effects that it was necessary to install a separate generator. This is housed in an extension at the right side of the facade and extends across the forecourt. *CB/TR*

BARNSLEY

Theatre Royal ★★★
Wellington Street
Original architect
  1898 Walter Emden with Herbert Crawshaw
Later works
  1942 Dyson Cawthorne and Coles: partly rebuilt after stage house gutted by fire
  1996 Unknown: converted to nightclub
Listed   Grade II
Current use Cabaret nightclub
Capacity est. 900

Delightfully intimate auditorium with two well-curved balconies of six rows

each, terminating in boxes linked vertically by superimposed columns. Rectangular proscenium with a curved sounding-board above and a domed ceiling. Richly modelled Baroque plasterwork.

Although very successful theatrically the auditorium lacks the sophistication of Emden's metropolitan interiors at the Duke of York's and the Garrick to a degree that cannot entirely be put down to comparative lack of funds. It may be that the local architect, Crawshaw, was rather free in his interpretation of Emden's intentions. Good three-storeyed, five-bay stone facade. Rusticated, arched entrance doors and pedimented first-floor windows. Triangular pediment over the three central bays with 'Theatre Royal' carved on a scroll in the tympanum.

The overall layout of the building is similar to Emden's Duke of York's Theatre, London. Notable similarities include a separate dressing-room block, attached to the stage tower by a service staircase, yet nevertheless an independent structure. Also the domed ceilings of the auditorium are set tightly into a small pitched roof structure, providing little or no loft access above.

The damage caused by the fire in 1942 removed the decorative fibrous plasterwork from all the box fronts,and the timber panelling around the proscenium may also date from this time. The original decorative work carried out by Jonas Binns and Son of Halifax. has now been virtually obliterated by many decoration schemes, and latterly a repaint for the film You're a good man, Bert Rigby which was shot in the theatre. Originally the auditorium ceiling contained Italian figure paintings representing Comedy, Tragedy, Music and Drama in four main panels, and, in the other four panels, Spring, Summer, Autumn and Winter with floral and other decorations in harmony with the subjects. The central ventilation grille in the ceiling still contains the remains of a sunburner, which has had a primitive electrolier inserted into it in later times. The sunburner appears to be almost identical to the one at the Buxton Opera House.

There is virtually nothing left of the 1898 stage. It was completely reconstructed in 1942 and is framed with concrete and laid with timber.The reinforced concrete is now badly corroded and would have to be replaced prior to any re-use. A single concrete fly floor is positioned on either side of the stage.

Barnsley, Theatre Royal (Ian Grundy)

The grid is constructed of steel channel and is probably re-usable. The safety curtain, also dating from 1942, is a single-piece rigid asbestos-clad curtain with two counterweight cradles diverted onto the rear wall of the stage. The get-in door is located stage right, with a small scene dock area before the stage proper.

Access from the small foyer to the stalls, located below street level, is by a staircase terminating externally on the stage left side of the building effectively down an alleyway. At the end of this alley was/is the stage door entrance providing direct access to the dressing-room block.

One of Britain's most important surviving medium-sized theatres which are no longer in use as such. Restoration is highly feasible and would give back to Barnsley and its neighbourhood a real theatre in place of the present civic hall/theatre. Sadly, the theatre has recently been converted to a nightclub. *DW*

BARNSTAPLE
Devon

Queen's ★★
Boutport Street
Other names
  1855 Music Hall (in Corn Exchange)
  1897 Albert Hall
  1940s Civic Hall
  1952 Queen's Hall
Original architect
  1855 R.G. Gould: as Corn Exchange

Barnstaple, Queen's (Sally McGrath)

Later works

1897   Owen Davis: redecorated and refurbished to form Albert Hall

1941   Unknown: converted to British Restaurant after fire destroyed interior

1952   B.W. Oliver: interior reconstructed as theatre with ball-room

1994   Burrell Foley Fischer: interior extensively modernised; new stage facilities, dressing rooms, etc.

Listed   Grade II
Current use Theatre
Capacity   688

The Music Hall formed part of the Corn Exchange, built under Barnstaple's Markets Scheme in 1855, the large first-floor room being so used. In 1897 the hall was redesigned with a stage and organ from Broadgate House, opening as the Albert Hall. The seating was removable for dances. It was used as a concert hall, theatre and cinema. During the Second World War, quantities of food were stored on the ground floor and in 1941 these caught fire and destroyed the interior. A roof was built over the ground floor and it became a British Restaurant for the remainder of the war. A stage was added later, and it was used as a Civic Hall.

As part of the Festival of Britain celebrations, it was completely rebuilt internally, the whole forming The Queen's Hall – a theatre and ballroom. The auditorium had a flat dance floor and a raked balcony with fixed seating.

It became the largest municipally owned venue in the South West. Externally the frontage designed by Gould 100 years previously was retained and topped by a modern green-tiled roof. The main entrance doors were given by the architect B.W. Oliver in commemoration of his Mayoralty (1931–32). A hospitality suite was built and named in memory of the town's famous John Gay.

The Queen's is an impressive three-storey stucco Italianate building with two-storey wings; round arched windows to ground floor; bracketed cornice, all well restored in 1994. The interior is now that of a modern theatre, with permanently tiered seating; the stalls are raked; the walls enlivened with panels of cherry and maple. A new box office, exhibition area and bar complete the modernisation. *SM*

BARRY
Vale of Glamorgan

Theatre Royal
Broad Street
Other names
1907   Theatre Royal and Hippodrome
1910   The New Theatre Royal
Original architect
1907   W.E. Knapman
Later works
1909   Winship and Knapman: rebuilt
1930   Unknown: converted to cinema; stage removed
Current use Cinema
Capacity   over 2000 (prior to sub-division)

The present building is successor to an earlier Theatre Royal. Frontage block, of three and a half storeys, in red brick and stucco debased classical style, with taller pedimented centre. Converted into a cinema in the 1930s when the stage was removed and absorbed into the auditorium which was completely reconstructed with one balcony. More recently the auditorium has been divided into upper and lower levels by the insertion of a floor; only the upper level is in use. The canopy above the main entrance has been removed. The building is in a good state of repair. *TR*

BASINGSTOKE
Hampshire

Haymarket ★★
Wote Street
Other names
   Corn Exchange

1913   Grand
Original architect
1865   Salter and Wyatt: as a Corn Exchange
Later works
1910   Unknown: converted to roller-skating rink
1913   Unknown: converted to ciné-variety
c.1926   Unknown: converted to theatre following fire
1940   Unknown: foyer and bar added
1982   Unknown: new front-of-house areas constructed behind Lesser Market facade
1993   RHWL: improved and refitted
Listed   Grade II
Current use Theatre
Capacity   456

In 1865 a Corn Exchange was opened in Wote Street. The Basingstoke Fire Department kept their fire engine in the basement from 1890. By 1910 it was used as a roller-skating rink. It was reopened in 1913 as a ciné-variety house with a raked floor and a stage. It was then known as the Grand. A fire devastated the building in 1925, following which it was reinstated, with the interior remodelled as a theatre. The Town Council repaired and redecorated the building in 1940, adding a small foyer and bar at the back of the hall. In the following years a repertory company was established and the theatre was also used by touring companies. Extensive renovation was completed in 1993. The old Corn Exchange has been transformed into a lively and intimate theatre. The accommodation within the Exchange was demolished, including the roof over the stage and the main entrance stair. The stage was deepened by moving the proscenium wall forward, widened on stage right by extending into the Haymarket Yard and heightened with a new box-shaped flying loft breaking through the original pitched roof. The stage house has an enlarged acting area with modern suspension structure. An elevator provides a forestage extension, an additional two rows of stalls seating or an orchestra pit, and, at its lowest level, a goods elevator to get in heavy scenery. The iron curtain is in two halves, with a painted view of Basingstoke. The original internal elevations of the Corn Exchange have been left intact, the new balcony being supported on an independent steel structure. The walls in the auditorium with their classical pilasters, cornice and

Basingstoke, Haymarket

round-arched windows, have been restored.

The main elevation is in seven bays with big windows. The frontage to the street has taken in the Lesser Market's three shop fronts, and the resident scenic designer has painted a mural on the Corn Exchange facade to depict the history of the building.

The get-in is difficult: the dock doors are 3.5m (11ft 6in) above the Haymarket Yard which approaches at a steep gradient. *SM*

BATH
Bath and North East Somerset

Forum
St James' Parade
Original architect
    1934 W.H. Watkins (Bristol)
Later works
    1960s Unknown: converted to bingo
    1986 Unknown: retail units created
            at street level
    1988 Nicholas Stubbs: interior
            restored and auditorium
            improved
Listed   Grade II
Current use Evangelical services/festival
            productions and concerts
Capacity   1600

With a 1930s' Art Deco interior and a classical stone exterior, the Forum was built as a theatre/cinema in 1934. Its architect, W.H. Watkins, was responsible for many 'super' cinemas such as those at Plymouth, Coventry and Exeter. It had no fly tower and a fairly shallow stage,

but was nevertheless used for live shows. In the 1960s the building was converted to bingo, but closed around 1966. Empty for some years, planning applications were submitted in 1986 for conversion to part dance hall and part retail. The exterior has been preserved, except at street level where there has been some change to accommodate retail outlets. The interior has been well restored, and stage and acoustics improved to form a performance venue, not only for evangelical use, but for stage/concert and festival productions. Other rooms allow the whole to be hired for seminars, etc. A dancing school occupies rooms at the top of the building for classes. *SM*

Little
St Michael's Place
Original architect
    1934–35 Unknown: from foundations of
                1726 house
Later works
    1979 Unknown: scene store and
            lounge converted into second
            screen
    1989 Unknown: refurbished and
            improved
Listed   Grade II
Current use Twin cinema
Capacity   c.220 (prior to subdivision)

The Little Theatre was built in 1934–35 by Consuelo De Reyes and her stage-designer husband Peter King. She had run an experimental theatre in Citizen House next door, in Westgate Buildings, and organised summer schools in drama

which brought students from all over the world. The flood of visitors was stemmed by the Second World War, and an accidental fire destroyed Citizen House. The present theatre building dates from 1726 and was originally a large town house. The new Little theatre was designed to function also as a cinema. In addition to the main auditorium there was a roof garden theatre, a tea and coffee lounge, and access to dressing rooms in the adjacent building.

Miss De Reyes formed a partnership with Jim Fairfax-Jones of the Everyman Theatre, Hampstead, and productions were exchanged for a short time. In 1936 the Little reopened as a cinema. In 1979, the original scene store and lounge were converted for a second screen and thereafter the building was used wholly as a cinema. Ten years later a major refurbishment programme was carried out, and some decorative features of 1930s' character were reintroduced. Meanwhile, the roof garden theatre had become a separate office suite.

The freehold of the building is still owned by the family. *SM*

Palace ★
Sawclose
Other names
    1886 Pavilion
    1895 Lyric Theatre
    1903 Palace
    1956 Regency Ballroom
    1980 Zetters
    1986 Gala
Original architect
    1886 Unknown
Later works
    1895 Wylson and Long: converted
            to theatre
    1930s Unknown: balconies altered
    1956 Unknown: converted to
            Regency Ballroom
    1969 Unknown: converted to pub
            and cinema
Listed   Grade II
Current use Bingo
Capacity   est. 800

Opened as Pavilion Music Hall on the site of the old Hay and Straw Market. Renamed Lyric in 1895 and Palace in 1903. Auditorium completely altered with one straight-fronted balcony in 1930s. In 1956, on conversion to a ballroom, the stage and boxes were removed and the balconies extended. The facade of 1895 survives intact – a handsome music-hall front of one wide bay only, recessed at first-floor level

Bath, Palace (Sally McGrath)

Bath, Theatre Royal, Old Orchard Street
(Sally McGrath)

and were contained within a coursed rubble, pitched-roofed structure which still exists. Between this and the street is a shallow range, formerly containing lobbies, staircases, etc.The ashlar facade has three storeys and seven bays of plain sash windows – hardly distinguishable from adjacent houses. Former doorways to pit, boxes and galleries now removed and replaced by windows. Present pedimented entrance dates from conversion to Freemasons' Hall.

Called Theatre Royal from 1767 – the first provincial theatre to be given a patent. Closed in 1805 after the owners had built the present Theatre Royal in Beaufort Square. Became a Catholic Church in 1809 and a Masonic Lodge in 1866.   CB/SM

behind a balustraded balcony, flanked on each side by single giant Corinthian pilasters carrying a bracketed cornice. Pyramid roof.

From 1966–68 there was a revival of 'old-time music hall revues'. In 1969, the auditorium was styled for bingo. The saloon bar was converted to a pub, with a small cinema in the circle bar above, the main entrance being halved. Today the main auditorium remains as a bingo hall, with a pub in the old bars areas, and a garage to the side which was presumably once stables. The auditorium is now plain, all decoration removed. The pillars and other original features are covered in. The original character is retained in the pub.   SM

Theatre Royal (i) ★

Old Orchard Street
Original architect
  1750 John Hippisley/John Palmer
          (after a design attributed to
          Thomas Jelly)
Later works
  1767 John Palmer: auditorium
          remodelled
  1775 Unknown: altered
  1809 Unknown: converted to church
  1866 Unknown: converted to
          Masonic Lodge
Listed   Grade II
Current use Freemasons' Hall

The interior has been substantially rebuilt for its present purpose, but the shell and front to Orchard Street are basically intact. The axis of the auditorium and stage lay parallel to the street

Theatre Royal (ii) ★★★

Sawclose
Original architect
  1805 George Dance the Younger,
          with John Palmer
Later works
  1863 C.J. Phipps: rebuilt after fire on
          old foundations, retaining
          Dance facade
  1864 Unknown: box office enlarged;
          interior redecorated
  1902 Unknown (? Verity): additional
          staircase to upper circle; new
          entrances/exits; fireproof curtain installed
  1981 Dowton and Hurst: stage

Bath, Theatre Royal, Sawclose

C19, seven windows wide, three storeys in classical style with stucco dressings and clearly not a theatre of any date. Part of the Fisher theatre was reputedly incorporated into the bank, but the common belief that it is within the main building is unlikely to be correct. A seemingly older and lower structure at the back, incorporated in 1945 is, very possibly, the shell of the theatre, but it is doubtful if the wooden pilasters, referred to in *Curtains*, 1982, still survive. Further investigation is needed. *JL*

BEDFORD

Royal County
147 Midland Road
Original architect
   1893   Unknown: as auction house
Later works
   1898   Unknown: converted to
           Central Hall
   1899   Henry Young: converted to
           theatre
   1957   Unknown: fascia altered;
           Victorian features removed
   1964   Unknown: converted to bingo
Current use Church
Capacity (was) c.680

Converted in 1899 from Central Hall. Facade altered on conversion to bingo hall in 1964, although there is still some ornamentation surviving over the stage door in Grafton Road. Originally debased classical, red brick with stone dressings. The interior retains an altered stage which has been cut right back from the proscenium which is now merely a feature (and perhaps holds up the roof!) with a promenade between the back of the proscenium and the stage. The auditorium is like a 1930s' cinema theatre conversion with one balcony and boxes, but interestingly the rear of the circle is like a separate space with rows of lesser length (cf Phipps's Exeter design). *MS/SM*

BELFAST

Grand Opera House ★★★
Great Victoria Street
Other names
   1904–9
           Palace of Varieties
Original architect
   1895   Frank Matcham
Later works
   1913   Mugrave's Foundry: cast-iron
           canopy extended
   1914   J. St. J. Phillips: dressing rooms
           extended

rebuilt; steel grid and counter-weights installed; auditorium restored
   1997   Tektus: improved further; Ustinov Studio Theatre added
Listed   **Grade II***
Current use **Theatre**
Capacity c.950

The principal facade of Dance's theatre is to Beaufort Square, on the long axis of the auditorium/stage. Fine restrained Neo-Classical design in ashlar with three-storeyed, five-bay centrepiece. Panelled pilasters above ground floor, with masks carved in relief in the frieze over the tops of each pilaster and linked by swags. Large Royal Arms with two lyres each side, set on parapet above cornice. One of the most important surviving examples of Georgian theatre architecture. Entrance moved to Sawclose when theatre reconstructed in 1863. Phipps added an Italianate three-bay arcaded entrance in front of the ground floor of a fine early C18 house.

The auditorium was Phipps's first theatre commission; it survives largely intact, with two lyre-shaped balconies carried along front edge by iron columns. Delicate plasterwork. Superimposed stage boxes framed between slender colonnettes with foliated capitals supporting a flared elliptical arch, repeated on either side above what were formerly the gallery slips (since removed). Saucer-domed ceiling, now lacking its original painted decorations (these were paintings by Casali, removed from Fonthill).

The Theatre was taken over in 1981 by a trust and a second non-profit trust was formed to run the administrative side. The theatre was restored, and reopened in late summer 1982. The stage was flattened and actually lowered slightly on the front edge which impaired sight lines from the upper levels. Unfortunately much historic stage machinery and equipment was also lost in the rebuild of the stage.

The Ustinov Studio was added at the rear in 1997. There are plans for further improvements, including the reseating of the auditorium. *CB/SM*

BECCLES
Suffolk

Theatre
Sheepgate Street
Original architect
   1814   **David Fisher**
Current use **Part of a bank**

The building now on the site is a bank. As seen from the street it is of the mid

1932 Samuel Stevenson: seating and furnishings improved
1950 Henry Lynch Robinson: dress circle, bar and entrance remodelled
1961 J. McB. Neill: converted to cinema
1980 Robert McKinstry and Melvyn Brown: completely restored and upgraded
1991 and 1993 Robinson and McIlwaine: bomb damage repaired
Listed **Grade II**
Current use **Theatre**
Capacity **1001**

Used as a cinema for many years then closed after bomb damage. Reopened as a theatre in 1980 after undergoing a splendid scheme of renovation and restoration. The magnificent auditorium is probably the best surviving example in the UK of the Oriental style applied to theatre architecture – largely Indian in character with intricate detail on the sinuously curved fronts of the two balconies and an elaborate composition of superimposed boxes surmounted by turban-domed canopies. The ceiling, which is divided into several richly framed, painted panels that have been exquisitely recreated by artist Cherith McKinstry, is supported on arches above the gallery slips, with large elephant heads at springing level. Proscenium 12m (39ft 8in), stage depth 13.71m(45ft), grid increased to 18.28m (60ft) from 15.84m (52ft). Large new orchestra pit, the sharp single radius curve of the orchestra rail providing the

only slightly jarring note in this superb auditorium.

The exterior, of brick and cast stone, is in a free mixture of Baroque, Flemish and Oriental styles – typical of Matcham's earlier work. He made good use of the corner site by building up the composition of his design in stages, linked by strapwork scrolls, to the triangular-pedimented central gable which is flanked by domed minarets. The new projecting glass extension to the previously cramped first-floor bar is quite in the spirit of Matcham's architecture (cf Theatre Royal, Portsmouth). In 1982 it was made complete by the addition of the visually important column supports. In 1991 and 1993 the theatre was damaged by terrorist bombs. This necessitated considerable rebuilding of the Glengall Street dressing-room block, stage door and get in. Fortunately the auditorium suffered only superficial damage.

Now a touring theatre and Ulster's only venue for major opera and dance companies. *CB/IM/RMcK*

Ulster Hall and Group Theatre
Bedford Street
Original architect
  1862   W.J. Barre
Later works
  1978   Unknown: refurbished
Current use **Concert hall and theatre**
Capacity **220 (Group Theatre)**

A mid-Victorian hall, situated in the centre of the city close to the City Hall. The

exterior, which has been altered, is dignified in its use of five arched windows and Corinthian columns at first-floor level (concealing the Group Theatre) with a projecting lower storey fronted by an iron and glass canopy across the pavement. The date 1862 and the Ulster Hall name appear above the central arched window. On the right-hand side there is a set-back entrance to the Group Theatre.

The main auditorium, the Ulster Hall, is at ground and first-floor levels, with a high ceiling taking it to the full height of the second floor. There is a single balcony, supported on cast-iron columns with unusual foliate caps. The balcony, along three sides of the room, has a plain front, relying on an elaborate painted pattern for decoration – the only plasterwork being raised square panels over the columns. There are four rows of seats on each side of the balcony, fixed and stepped. Above the balcony the walls are divided into tall arches with windows down each side and plain plaster infills at the end; the arches are divided by pilasters topped with acanthus leaf capitals, above which are circular shields. The ceiling is wooden panels, mainly flat but heavily coved at the edges of the hall.

The stalls floor is flat with loose linked chairs which are often removed for pop concerts. The stage (concert platform) is flat with raised choir stalls behind. It is dominated by a magnificent Hill organ with open pipes. It is the main home of the Ulster Orchestra, although some concerts are now given in the Waterfront Hall, and also presents pop concerts, some dance events and boxing. The acoustics are considered excellent and the hall is often used for recordings.

The Group Theatre is above the main entrance foyer at the front of the building behind the five arched windows and can be reached from the main foyers of the Ulster Hall and from its own separate entrance and small foyer. It appears to be original to the building but was remodelled in 1978 after a bomb attack.

It is a small space with twelve rows of seats in the stalls, the front eight rows being flat, the rear four raised, and a dinky flat-fronted balcony of four rows giving a total capacity of 222. The balcony is supported on plain cast-iron columns and has a simple panelled decoration. The ceiling is flat and plain and the proscenium is a utilitarian rectangular opening, framed on the top and sides and with a comedy/tragedy mask painted above the centre. The entire auditorium is

Belfast, Grand Opera House

currently painted black with gold relief to the proscenium arch, balcony front and ceiling cornice.

The stage is smallish and has no flying or orchestra pit. Disabled access is limited.

The facade was badly damaged by a bomb and as a consequence the arched windows were filled in and a plain false wall constructed down the side of the theatre. This was a temporary measure that is now giving damp problems.

It is extensively used for amateur performances by groups across the city. Major improvements are planned for 2000. *IG*

BEXHILL-ON-SEA
East Sussex

De la Warr Pavilion ★
The Marina
Original architect
1935   E. Mendelsohn and
         S. Chermayeff
Later works
1993   Troughton McAslan: restoration strategy
Listed   Grade I
Current use Theatre
Capacity 1016

The de la Warr Pavilion was the result of an open competition run by the RIBA at the request of the Borough Council in 1932. The selected design resulted in the building of one of the first big welded steel-framed structures in Britain. It is now regarded as one of the icons of the inter-War International Modern Movement, described by Sir Nikolaus Pevsner as 'Mendelsohn's magnum opus during the short time that he lived in England' and 'as exhilarating today as it was when it was new and a revolution for the English seaside'.

In a prominent position on the front, its rectilinear, unornamented and imperforate walls toward the sea make a dramatic contrast with its generously projecting staircase tower, whose decks penetrate curving glass walls.

Years of seaside exposure took their toll as severe damage to the concrete facings was caused by rusting steel. In 1989 a structural survey was undertaken and a programme of repair recommended. A Pavilion Trust was then created to assist the Council with necessary fund raising. By 1994 over £1 million had been spent on repairs and a campaign to remove damaging internal alterations and restore the original architects' design intentions was commenced.

The auditorium is capable of

Bexhill, De La Warr Pavilion (Peter Cook/VIEW)

improvement as a theatre space. It is flat-floored, surrounded on three sides by fixed seating. The stage has 20 hemp lines with space for a further 12, a trap and a carpet cut.

The Italianate Colonnade with domed end pavilions, which formerly had a bandstand at its centre, predates the Pavilion. It was built in 1911 to the designs of J.B. Wall. *KW*

BILSTON
Wolverhampton

Odeon
Lichfield Street
Other names
1921   Wood's Palace
1936   Palace
later   Cascades Bingo, Imperial
         Palace
Original architect
1921   Hurley Robinson
Current use Multi-purpose venue
Capacity c.1400

The Odeon opened in 1921 as Wood's Palace, with full stage facilities. In 1937 it became an Odeon and was later used for wartime concerts. It closed as a cinema in 1964 and reopened the following year as a bingo hall.

The two-storey frontage in Lichfield Street is now faced with faience incorporating two shops to the left. There is a tall fly tower and a three-storey dressing-room block. The auditorium floor has been levelled with the stage. The decorative plasterwork to the ceiling is now entirely concealed by a false ceiling at circle front level. The walls have some traces of original decorative plasterwork.

Although the stage house is generous for its day, any reversal of the alterations, in order to reinstate as a major theatre venue, would be difficult and expensive. Nevertheless, following the cessation of bingo, the building did reopen as a multi-purpose venue in November 1999 with an evening of variety. It is difficult, however, to see the Odeon competing with Phipps's Wolverhampton Grand, only a few miles distant. *TB*

BIRMINGHAM

Alexandra ★
Station Street
Other names
1901–02 Lyceum
Original architect
1901   Owen and Ward
Later works
1935   Roland Satchwell (Birmingham) and Ernest Shaufelberg: almost completely rebuilt
1967   Unknown: exterior bridge and new foyer created
1983   Unknown: renovated
1988   Unknown: front of house renovated
1990   Seymour Harris Partnership: auditorium and backstage refurbished; white cladding boards removed to expose original proscenium arch
Current use Theatre
Capacity   1347

Most of Owen and Ward's Lyceum building was demolished and rebuilt in 1935, except for the plain brick dressing-room wing flanking the auditorium and stage.
The present entrance is in a separate (1960s) block, some distance from the original, quite decent, black and cream faience facade, which is now somewhat drastically interfered with by a link bridge penetrating it at first-floor level.
The auditorium, by contrast, has been stripped of later, dismal alterations and partly restored and partly sympathetically reinvented. It can now be seen as a handsome room of its period, with rippled plaster ornament over the ante-proscenium. Two balconies. Splendid, deep-coved, enriched proscenium arch in Art Deco style. The total effect is, in some ways, reminiscent of the much smaller London Whitehall. Metal- clad fly tower. *TB*

Birmingham Hippodrome ★★★
Hurst Street
Other names
1899   Tower of Varieties and Circus
1900   Tivoli Theatre of Varieties
1903–24 Hippodrome; Barrasford's Hippodrome; Hippodrome Theatre of Varieties; Tivoli
1925   Birmingham Hippodrome
1965   Birmingham Theatre
Original architect
1899   F.W. Lloyd

Later works
1900   F.W. Lloyd: auditorium rebuilt and stage enlarged
1917   Bertie Crewe: altered internally
1925   Burdwood and Mitchell: auditorium rebuilt
1963   Edwin M. Lawson: tower and part frontage demolished; main facade redone; altered internally
1981   J. Seymour Harris Partnership: major alterations and improvements
1984   J. Seymour Harris Partnership: stage extended; other alterations
1986 J. Seymour Harris Partnership: exterior clad in glass fibre coloured facing
1990   J. Seymour Harris Partnership: Birmingham Royal Ballet HQ built
1992   J. Seymour Harris Partnership: stalls rake increased; other improvements

2000   Associated Architects/Law and Dunbar-Nasmith: completely refurbished; second theatre space created; new facade constructed
Current use Theatre
Capacity   1887

Opened in 1899 as the Tower of Varieties and Circus, a music hall with a circus ring which could be flooded. It had a tall Moorish tower. Interior completely reconstructed in 1925, with a fine neo-Classical auditorium with one very deep fan-shaped balcony, twelve boxes and seating accommodation for over 2000.
In 1963 the foyer and main facade were completely refurbished and the tower was demolished. Further major alterations in 1980/1 improved the dressing rooms to accommodate 100 artists, raised the grid from 15.25m (50ft) to 22m (72ft), and redecorated and reseated the auditorium to excellent effect. With later improvements, the

Birmingham, Hippodrome

Hippodrome is the major regional touring house for opera and ballet in the Midlands and, since 1990, the home of the Birmingham Royal Ballet.

The main facade and part of the returns were clad in 1984 with coloured glass fibre material in a sort of post-modern classic.parts of the 1899 theatre remain visible externally. The auditorium design appears to be in line of descent from Manchester Palace (1913) and Drury Lane (1922) with three bays of boxes set between fluted Ionic columns on either side of the proscenium opening. There is a single balcony, with a long curving front, reflecting later, cinema-influenced styles.

The annexe built in 1990, on land newly acquired to provide the Birmingham Royal Ballet with its headquarters, is a self-contained unit, but linked to the theatre. It has a brick facade with mirror glass windows and contains offices and four spacious studios.

A further major extension and improvement project in 2000 included a complete overhaul of the theatre's public and backstage areas, the adddition of a 200 seat studio theatre, a centre for the treatment of dance injuries and a striking new facade, carried round the Hurst Street/Thorp Street corner. *TB*

Coutts

Park Street

Other names
1863   London Museum Concert Hall/Music Hall
1890   Canterbury
c.1893   Pavilion
1895/6 London Music Hall
1897   Coutts Theatre (briefly as Palace of Delight)
1912   Bull Ring Cinema
Original architect
1863   Unknown
Later works
1912   Unknown: converted to cinema
n.d.   Unknown: converted to restaurant and karate club
Current use Restaurant, etc.
Capacity   c.480 (after 1912 cinema conversion)

Built in 1863 behind the Royal George Tavern, it was said to have been designed after the fashion of the London concert rooms of the time. It reopened in 1890 as the Canterbury with 'new scenery and decorations', became Coutts in 1897 and fell into disuse in 1901. In 1912 it became the Bull Ring Cinema. Now a restaurant and karate club.

The interior has been gutted and sub-divided, with the loss of all original features (a great pity, since so little is known of the physical nature of music halls of this early date outside London). Exterior survives almost intact in the form of a plain, rectangular brick structure with a pitched roof. Street elevation is one of the long sides, in six rendered bays, relieved by a blind arch in each bay. *CB/TB*

Old Rep ★★

Station Street

Other names
1913   Birmingham Repertory Theatre
1972   Old Repertory Theatre
Original architect
1913   S.N. Cooke
Later works
1914   Unknown: adjacent building incorporated
Listed   Grade II
Current use Theatre
Capacity   378

Historically important as first purpose-built repertory theatre in Britain. Design influenced by Munich Kunstlertheater of 1908. Built on narrow site with steeply raked stalls, one straight-fronted balcony (Barry Jackson would have chosen a bigger single tier had it not been for the small site) and plain panelled side walls. Flat coffered ceiling. Simple, corniced proscenium with chaste classical details. 6.7m (22ft) proscenium opening. Convertible orchestra pit.

Good 3½ storey neo-Georgian brick and stone facade in three bays, the outer bays narrow and rising to square attics, the centre bay wider with giant Ionic pilasters supporting a full entablature, parapet and balustrade above. Ground-floor ashlar faced with cantilever canopy extending the full width. *CB/TB*

Windsor

Bearwood Road/ Dunsford Road
Original architect
1930   Horace Bradley

Birmingham, Old Rep (Ian Grundy)

Later works
    1963   Unknown:converted to skating
            rink
    later   Unknown: converted to
            snooker hall
Current use Snooker hall
Capacity   c.1750 (prior to subdivision)

This has been an interesting building but its present state is disappointing. Built in 1930 as a ciné-variety, it has suffered a succession of alterations over the last three or four decades, mostly to its detriment. It operated mainly as a full-time cinema until 1946, when it became a variety theatre. In 1957 it was a repertory theatre but closed in 1960, to reopen three years later as a skating rink. It is now a snooker hall.

Built on the corner of Bearwood Road and Dunsford Road it is faced with brick and stone. There is a short tower on the corner, which contains the entrance. Stage with fly tower. Auditorium now has a flat floor and is divided horizontally by a false ceiling. Above this, the single balcony still exists, as does the oval-domed ceiling.

Re-establishment of live theatre, if the demand arose would no doubt be possible, especially if the stage could be extended over land at the rear.   *TB*

BISHOP AUCKLAND
Durham

Hippodrome *
Railway Street/Union Street
Other names
    Essoldo
Original architect
    1909   J.J. Taylor of Darlington (? with
            G.F. Ward)
Later works
    1909   R.F. Braithwaite: unspecified
            alterations
    1917   Unknown: renovated and
            redecorated
    1920   W. Stockdale: unspecified
            alterations
Current use Bingo
Capacity   est. 800

Intact inside and out. Auditorium has two almost straight balconies, each with long slips parallel to side walls. Consoles forming panels on front of first balcony, but no other enrichment, and no plasterwork on second balcony. A single, bow-fronted box with semi-circular arched corniced hood at first balcony level flanking either side of the rectangular framed proscenium. The flat ceiling, panelled with simple geometrical design

Bishop Auckland, Hippodrome (Ian Grundy)

is now concealed above a false ceiling at upper balcony level. Stage floor lowered to stalls level. Plain facade in brick with cast stone dressings. Arched windows in upper storey with the name 'Hippodrome' on panel. Brick side elevations with fly tower.

A modest but pleasing Edwardian theatre, in good condition. Restoration to theatre use would be feasible.   *JD-N/CB/IG*

BLACKPOOL

ABC
Church Street/King Street
Other names
    1895–
    1900   Empire
    1900   Hippodrome; King's (briefly)
    1963   ABC
    later   Cannon, MGM
Original architect
    1895   John Dent Harker
Later works
    1900   Unknown: converted to circus
    1910   Unknown: arena removed;
            main floor raked
    1963   C.J. Foster: almost totally
            rebuilt
Current use Disused
Capacity   c.2000 (prior to subdivision)

Built as a large ballroom/music hall called the Empire with a flat floor, gallery round three sides and shallow stage. Converted to circus in 1900 and renamed Hippodrome. In 1910 the arena was removed and the main floor raked for cinema use, with seasonal variety. After use as a TV theatre for live

variety shows in the 1950s and early 1960s the theatre was almost totally rebuilt in 1963, leaving very little of the Hippodrome. The outer side, front and rear walls follow the footprint of the old theatre and are probably three-quarters height of the original. Designed by C.J. Foster (chief architect for ABC), it consisted of stalls and a deep single balcony with a combined capacity of 1934. The ceiling was lit by hundreds of small individual lamps set in gold moulded panels concealing ventilation and sound. After many years of theatre usage the auditorium was split into three cinemas. The stage, orchestra pit and original (1963) proscenium and front stalls and dressing rooms all survive behind the screens of 2 and 3, but are nothing to excite. The cinema closed in 1998.   *CB/IG/SM*

Grand ★★★
Church Street
Original architect
    1894   Frank Matcham
Later works
    1910   Unknown: pit incorporated
            into stalls; circle enlarged
    1977   John Wyckham (consultant):
            interior refurbished (while still
            a bingo house)
    1980–98 MacKeith Dickinson and
            Partners: extensively restored
            and improved; entrance
            canopy reinstated; studio theatre created; gallery reseated
Listed   Grade II*
Current use Theatre
Capacity   1215

The auditorium of this theatre, built as a

Blackpool, Grand

drama house in 1894, is one of Matcham's finest creations, combining intimacy with a sense of imposing spaciousness. He achieved this by stacking the audience vertically in three closely spaced, relatively shallow, balconies which curve well round the sides, separated from the proscenium by only one box on either side at dress circle level. The boxes are each surmounted by an elaborate arched and pedimented canopy rising above the level of the gallery front. Splendid high round-arched proscenium frame, with open plasterwork decoration on the inside of the arch and large oval painted panels in the spandrels, by Binns of Halifax. Magnificent oval ceiling incorporating six painted panels of composers. Opulent plasterwork on balcony fronts, boxes, proscenium and ceiling. One of the best surviving examples of the astonishing density of 'art decoration' in a Matcham house of the 1890s. The only slight disappointment is the rather aggressive colour of the post-1980 house tabs.

Exterior in plain brickwork, apart from the Baroque corner entrance in stone, with spirited, cheerfully 'incorrect' details, topped by a jolly copper fish-scaled dome rising behind scrolly gables with finials and crowned by a colonnetted lantern.

All has been progressively and sensitively restored since the Grand survived a threat of demolition in 1973. The battle for its survival was one of the earliest of a series of events which eventually turned the tide of post-war destruction of theatres (cf London, the Granville, Waltham Green, demolished in 1971, leading to the immediate listing of many Victorian and Edwardian theatres, and the Lyric Hammersmith, demolished c.1970 and recreated in 1979).

The Grand is now owned by a Trust which has run it as a successful touring house since 1981. Their recent reinstatements, additions and backstage improvements (including an 80 seat studio) have greatly enhanced the potential of this magnificent theatre. *JE/CB*

North Pier Pavilion

The Promenade
Original architect
    1874 R. Knill Freeman
Later works
    1922 Unknown: reinstated after fire

    1939 Unknown: rebuilt after fire
Listed   **Grade II**
Current use **Theatre**
Capacity   **1529**

The Blackpool Pier Company opened the North Pier in 1863, but the Pavilion was not built until 1874. This was known as the Indian Pavilion, referring to its style of decoration. An inscription read 'The Hearing Falls in Love before the Vision'. No architectural description has so far been found but top-quality artistes appeared there.

The Indian Pavilion suffered severe fire damage in 1921, was reinstated and reopened in 1924, only to be destroyed by another fire in 1938. A replacement was quickly erected, opening 1939. Several changes in ownership have since occurred. The last change was in 1998 when Leisure Parcs took over.

The present building is a fairly basic box covered with corrugated sheeting, with some recladding in plastic-covered steel. Seating is on one level. Sparse internal decoration in vaguely Art Deco style. Broad, shallow barrel vault ceiling; wide, low proscenium arch with inconsequential decoration. Minimal front of house; ample dressing rooms; orchestra pit to accommodate twelve musicians.

Plans to build a 2000-seat replacement have been discussed but no action has followed.   *SM/IG*

Theatre Royal

Talbot Square
Other names
    1868 The Arcade and Assembly Rooms
    1907 Tivoli Electric Theatre
Original architect
    1868 Unknown
Current use **Public house**
Capacity   **(was) c.800**

The building opened in 1868 as the Arcade and Assembly Rooms, said to be 'magnificent'. It contained a basement arcade of elegant shops, refreshments and a billiard-rooms, together with a spacious hall with a gallery on three sides, and a stage for theatricals and entertainments. Becoming the Theatre Royal, the plays were of the highest quality, and at one point, there was a stock company. It was one of the first places in Blackpool to show animated pictures and, by 1907, it became the Tivoli Electric Theatre.

Exterior basically intact on a triangular site at the junction of two streets. Low, octagonal tower on corner,

Blackpool, (former) Theatre Royal (Ian Grundy)

side elevations subdivided by piers, framing recessed panels and crowned by a modillion cornice. First floor at corner now has glazed conservatory.

After cinema and bingo use, it became a 'wine lodge', with live entertainment, often of music-hall style with local entertainers. The former theatre space is much altered.   *CB/IG/SM*

Tower Ballroom ★★★

Tower Buildings
Original architect
    1899   Frank Matcham
Later works
    1956   Andrew Mazzei: reconstructed
           after fire
Listed   Grade I
Current use Ballroom
Capacity   up to 3000

Although not a theatre, the Tower Ballroom makes use of the repertoire of theatre architecture and is one of Frank Matcham's most important works. The Tower buildings were designed by Maxwell and Tuke in 1894. Matcham was called upon to redesign the original ballroom in 1899.

The interior conveys an impression of quite staggering opulence. Two tiers of shallow balconies run round three sides of the hall, divided into broad bays by square piers. The upper balcony takes the form of slightly bowed boxes, each of one bay's width. The end facing the stage has three balconies. The prosceni-um frame to the orchestra platform is flanked by onion-domed boxes, stylistically related to some Matcham theatres designed about this time but, as always with this architect, given an individuality which belongs to this particular building, rather than to an habitual style. The richly ornamented, segmentally arched ceiling is divided into framed painted panels rising from a false-galleried cornice, bowed forward in each bay and supported on winged term caryatids. The dance floor has been reduced in size by a broad strip of carpet to mark the sitting out areas on three sides (but it is still vast). The stage has a Wurlitzer organ and a modern Yamaha 130X.

The Ballroom suffered a seriously damaging fire in 1956. Remarkably for that time, when appreciation of this kind of architecture was at its lowest ebb, a careful reinstatement was carried out by Andrew Mazzei. As now seen, it is comparable with the finest late Victorian rooms in Britain.   *CB/JE/KW*

Tower Circus ★★★

Tower Buildings
Original architect
    1894   Maxwell and Tuke (probably

Blackpool, Tower Ballroom (Ian Grundy)

with Frank Matcham)
Listed   **Grade I**
Current use **Circus**
Capacity   **1600**

This circus interior is probably by Frank Matcham. Stylistically it could certainly be his work. Fitted in between the four giant legs of the Tower itself, this gorgeous interior and the Great Yarmouth Hippodrome (qv) are the only surviving complete examples in Britain of the once popular purpose-built circus/hippodrome building type which was common throughout Europe in the C19 (other British examples, like the Brighton Hippodrome and Liverpool Olympia, have been converted to non-circus uses).

The Tower Circus has ceased to use animals. Circuses occur only occasionally, as do other entertainments requiring the flooding of the ring.

The space remains virtually unchanged. The seating is on two levels, with the upper level in the form of four balconies, set within four great semi-circular arches formed within the tower legs. Wonderfully fanciful Alhambresque plasterwork enrichment everywhere. *CB/VG/JE/KW*

Winter Gardens Complex
Church Street
Original architect
    1875   Thomas Mitchell of Oldham
Later works See entries for individual elements
Listed   **Grade II***

The Winter Gardens, together with the Tower and its attendant buildings (including the Tower Ballroom and Circus, qv) established Blackpool as the premier brash seaside resort – the one that the others could only aspire to be. Its success owed much to the management of William Holland, appointed in 1887.

It is interesting to note that Pevsner wrote in 1969: 'The Ministry...has issued no list for Blackpool, which means that there are no buildings of architectural or historic interest in the town. It depends of course what you mean by historical and by architectural.' It does indeed! To be fair, the listing investigators have more recently paid careful attention to Blackpool, recognising that it has its own outstandingly important social history and something in the way of quite special architecture.

The Winter Gardens is a vast entertainments complex containing a number of individual elements built round a pre-existing house (still just discernible) over

a long period between 1875 and 1939. The first part opened was an outdoor skating rink in July 1875. Grand opening of the complex was in July 1878.

The parts of the Winter Gardens we have found to be of particular interest are described separately following this item.

The Winter Gardens has a complicated history, traced by Brereton and Slinn in a 1984 Theatrephile article. It contains other components of lesser but still noteworthy interests. The exotic Indian Lounge has, regrettably, gone but the Spanish Hall (by Andrew Mazzei, c.1929), Baronial Hall and Renaissance Room remain and have a kind of impermanent 'atmospheric cinema' quality which goes well with this kind of exhibitionistic entertainment building.

It has to be said that parts of the complex come fully to life only during conferences. *JE*

Winter Gardens Pavilion
★★★
Other names
    1878   (Grand) Pavilion
            Winter Gardens Theatre
Original architect
    1878   Thomas Mitchell
Later works
    1889   Thomas Mitchell of Oldham: converted to theatre
    1896-7 Wylson and Long: auditorium rebuilt
    1982   Mackeith, Dickinson Partners: stalls rake removed; converted for multiple use/conference hall
    1986   Mackeith, Dickinson Partners, auditorium reopened to ambulatory
Listed   **Grade II***
Current use **Conference hall**
Capacity   **c.1500**

The Grand Pavilion was built as a glass-domed winter garden, giving the complex its name, and converted to a theatre (the original design having proved acoustically disastrous) by Thomas Mitchell in 1889. The present auditorium of 1896-97 is by Wylson and Long. It is no longer a theatre, the proscenium stage having been blocked off, the stalls levelled and a restaurant formed in the stage house, but it is still a most impressive space and a nationally important home for major conferences. The vestigial forestage must now be entered through the auditorium doors.

It is surrounded by a wide, encircling

arched ambulatory, linking it to the rest of the complex. A splendidly opulent apsidal-ended music hall interior, it has two balconies, supported on iron columns, running round three sides, first with nine rows in the centre, the second with twelve rows, set back to the line of the sixth row of the balcony below. The sides curve round to meet superimposed stage boxes framed between giant enriched composite columns surmounted by segmental pediments. Richly decorated ceiling over the whole space with caryatids rising through the perimeter cove to support a centre divided into deeply coved panels ornamented by garlands.

The alterations made could, if the opportunity were to arise (it is to be hoped that it will), be restorable. As a theatre or concert hall it would seat perhaps 1200. Theatre use seems unlikely in a town now so well provided, but it would be a pity if its present completely acceptable conference use were to leave it for ever with a 'blind' proscenium. *JE/CB*

Winter Gardens Empress Ballroom ★★
Original architect
    1897   Mangnall and Littlewood
Listed   **Grade II***
Current use **Ballroom and conference hall**
Capacity   **up to 3000**

The Empress Ballroom may seem marginal for inclusion in this gazetteer, but it is a splendid room with a marked theatrical flavour, providing an interesting comparison and contrast with Matcham's Tower Ballroom. It was, in fact, built (like the less successful Winter Gardens Ferris Wheel) to answer competition from the Tower complex. The Empress adopts the alternative ballroom plan, where the orchestra is placed, perhaps more logically, at the centre of the length, rather than at the end. This arrangement was also adopted in one or two early music halls and more often in flat-floored concert rooms where good theatre sight lines were not essential (as, for example, in Bassett Keeling's 1864 Strand Musick Hall in London).

The room is divided into eleven bays in its length and five in its width, defined by iron fluted columns which rise from faience tiled pedestals to support the semi-circular, 22.85m (75ft) span, arched beams of the ceiling. The ceiling is divided into 77 square panels from which are suspended 15 crystal chandeliers. There is a single balcony (two at the ends) with fronts bowed between the columns. Outside the columns is a promenade extending all round the room, including behind the orchestra. The orchestra takes the form of a semi-domed recess framed by an elaborate proscenium with four frisky caryatid supporters and a big crowning cartouche with a great deal to say for itself. All the plaster surfaces are moulded and enriched. The room once had a mighty pipe organ.

Occasionally put to its original purpose for dance festivals, etc., it is also used for conferences. Tiered seating can be brought in. *JE/KW*

Winter Gardens Opera House ★★

Other names
  Her Majesty's Opera House
Original architect
  1889 Frank Matcham
Later works
  1911 Mangnall and Littlewood:
        reconstructed
  1939 C.H. MacKeith: reconstructed
        after fire (a new building)
Current use Theatre and conferences

Capacity   c.2920

The Opera House has had an unusual history. Few Matcham theatres are ever handed over to lesser architects for improvement, but, in this case, his fine early design (1889) with its simple geometry but richly crusted ornament, was rejigged in 1911 by Mangnall and Littlewood. Their theatre was burnt down in 1938 but its white faience facade and foyer (both altered) survive.

The 1939 theatre, by Charles MacKeith is quite unlike its predecessors, a confident essay in 1930s' geometric ciné-design, with a series of sinuous arches, originally emphasised by coloured bands, bridging the auditorium. Surface ornament is limited to the proscenium arch, which is enlivened with a broad band of angular relief in Deco manner. Two plain-fronted balconies, a little altered. A canopied box was added in 1950 for a Royal Variety Performance.

The Opera House was designed for the mounting of spectacular shows and can handle major tours. *JE*

BOGNOR REGIS
West Sussex

Pier Theatre

Other names
  1976 Ocean Bars
  1986 Sheiks Night Club
Original architect
  1912 G.C. Smith
Later works
  1977 Unknown: fly tower removed
  1992 Unknown: false floor introduced at balcony level
Listed   Grade II
Current use Nightclub
Capacity (was) 1400

The theatre is situated at the shore end of the pier, which itself dates from 1865. Although only a modest example of its genre, the rendered exterior goes some way toward relieving the bleakness of the length of the promenade.

As now seen, the front takes the form of a cross wing with pediments at either end, ornamenting otherwise plain flanks. A central segmental pediment is flanked by two short square towers, but the architectural effect is lessened by single-storey forward extensions.

Originally the main roof had what was described as a 'handsome dome' at the centre (the stump of the drum is still visible). The fly tower, said to be unsafe, was demolished in 1976. A false floor (theoretically removable) was inserted in 1992 at circle level to provide a dance floor. *MS*

BO'NESS
Falkirk

Hippodrome ★★
Hope Street
Original architect
  1912 Matt Steele
Later works
  1916 Unknown: converted to
        cinema
  1960 Unknown: converted to bingo
Listed   Grade B
Current use Derelict
Capacity est. 900

Circular hippodrome with entrance pavilions at either end in typically Scottish debased Art Nouveau style. Harled exterior with cornices round shallow domed roof. First floor of main entrance with dome is a later addition. Interior is an amphitheatre with ring, altered to a cinema about 1916 then, from 1960s, to a bingo club. A remarkable and fascinating survivor which

Blackpool, Winter Gardens Opera House (Ian Grundy)

Bo'ness, Hippodrome (Bruce Peter Collection)

deserves to be restored as a matter of urgency, but restoration should certainly aim to strip away the redesign aberrations which have spoilt the building's purity of form.

Given that Bo'ness, with its successful steam railway and heritage centre, is promoting itself as a tourist mecca for West Lothian, the Hippodrome could surely find use as a multi-cultural venue-cum-theatre or a cinema, facilities which the town presently lacks. *BP*

BOSTON
Lincolnshire

Shodfriars' Hall
South Street
Original architect
    1874 J. Oldrid Scott (?)
Later works
    1905 Unknown: new proscenium
    1915 Unknown: redecorated and
            reseated; new proscenium;
            new entrance in Shodfriars
            Lane
    1929 Unknown: converted to bil-
            liards room
Listed   **Grade II**
Current use **Snooker hall/restaurant**
Capacity **800 (prior to 1929 conversion)**

The Shodfriars Hall comprises two different buildings of contrasting styles. At the front is a C15 'L'-shaped timber framed structure, with jettied storeys at first and second-floor level; the remainder consists of additions made, presumably to the designs of J. Oldrid Scott, when he carried out a radical restoration of the old building in 1874. The hall opened following these works.

The former theatre is housed in a red brick Gothic-style construction. It has a high pitched roof with the stage forming a separate projection, the roof of which is not as high as that of the main auditorium. The theatre being on the first floor made for an awkward 'get in'. The wooden doorway halfway along the stage left wall is 5m (16ft 6in) from the street and above the opening is a hoist with a block and pulley and rope attached.

The altered auditorium has a flat floor. The circle is now disused and the space is used as a darts room. The balcony front has turned wooden balusters. The stage proscenium rises well into the roof but the space over the stage provides insufficient room for flying.

The Shodfriars Hall is an historically interesting building and its massively tall auditorium is impressive but, even before alteration, it cannot have been a satisfactory theatre and it became a billiards room in 1929. A proposal to convert it into an arts centre in 1944 proved abortive. The town is infinitely better served by the Blackfriars Theatre (1966). *TB*

Theatre
Market Place
Original architect
    1777 Unknown
Later works
    1820 Unknown: converted to ware-
            house
Current use **Warehouse**

Reportedly erected 'at the expense of the Corporation' and used by the Lincoln circuit of the Robertson family. In use as a seed warehouse after 1820. Interior gutted. Three-storey facade, three windows wide with pedimental gable. The gable has a recessed roundel inscribed '1820'. Ground floor much altered with restaurant shop front. *SM/JL*

BOURNEMOUTH

Hippodrome
(Opera House) ★★★
The Royal Arcade, Christchurch Road, Boscombe
Other names
    1895 Boscombe Grand Pavilion
            Theatre
    1905 Boscombe Hippodrome
            Royal Ballroom
            Tiffany's
    1982 The Academy
Original architect
    1895 Lawson and Donkin
Later works
    1910 Unknown: paired boxes created
            on both sides of proscenium
    1982 Unknown: flat floor inserted
            for nightclub use
Listed   **Grade II**
Current use **Nightclub**
Capacity **originally 2000**

Opened as the Grand Pavilion Theatre, renamed Hippodrome in c.1910. Built as part of a development including the spacious Boscombe Arcade (intact) and Salisbury Hotel. The theatre front, in brick with stone dressings, is subservient to that of the arcade, and difficult to identify separately from the shops and former hotel on either side. It consists basically of three very tall, mullioned and transomed windows, each surmounted by a Flemish gable. The auditorium is most unusual and interesting, with the character of an early music hall. Above the flat main floor is a shallow balcony carried on iron columns with a semi-circular end and straight side arms and an openwork iron balustrade incorporating acanthus leaf decoration. Tall, slender iron columns rise from the front edge of the balcony to support a curved ceiling and lateral arcade, with florid openwork spandrel decoration. A wide promenade runs round the rear of the balcony, above which, carried on a further ring of columns, is a second, shallower balcony set back behind the arcade. The galleries originally ran straight up

Bournemouth, Hippodrome, c.1910 (John Earl Collection)

to the proscenium wall, but in 1910 a range of paired boxes was put in either side, flanked by giant composite columns and decorated with Baroque plasterwork. At the same time the proscenium was reconstructed – a tall plaster frame, straight-headed with rounded corners. Proscenium 8m (26ft), stage depth 11.25m (37ft), grid approximately 15.25m (50ft).

In December 1982 it reopened as The Academy nightclub. The floor is now flat but the stage and flying facilities remain in place. Concern is felt over redevelopment of adjacent land which might affect get-in arrangements.

Apart from some fittings used in connection with the present purpose, the auditorium and stage are intact and could be restored to theatrical use. The style of entertainment is more that of floor show/nightclub, also alternative revue. Sources say that help was enlisted from students from the Bournemouth College to restore the interior, and so it was freed from the Mecca purple and sympathetically painted inside. By present standards it would seat approximately 800. *CB/SM*

Pavilion ★★
Westover Road
Other names
   1929   Concert Hall
Original architect
   1929   G. Wyville Home and Shirley Knight
Later works
   1934   Unknown: concert platform converted to stage house; flying system, revolve and lift to stage installed
   n.d.   Unknown: Compton Organ installed
   1950s Unknown: further remodelling
   1980s Unknown: foyer areas improvements
Listed   **Grade II**
Current use **Theatre**
Capacity   **1518**

The Pavilion was first proposed in 1876. The second of two competitions assessed by Sir Edwin Cooper led to the design by G. Wyville Home and Shirley Knight being selected. This had been modified by the time it was executed in 1928–9.

The complex consists of a theatre/concert hall (originally designed for the Municipal Orchestra, with a fly tower added in 1934) a ballroom and restaurant. Brick and Empire (cast) stone elevations in Beaux Arts manner, partly two, partly three-storey with the central block

flanked by pavilions and with later additions in matching style. The main entrance is set in a shallow portico with square columns in antis. Hipped, pantiled roofs, that to the main theatre block being in the form of a shallow pyramid crowned by a low cap, somewhat reminiscent of the roof of the Tower of the Winds.

The auditorium is approached through a cross-vestibule containing principal circular staircases to left and right, and a 'silence' corridor. The auditorium is square on plan with a domed ceiling and is decorated in a restrained Grecian manner. It has raked stalls and at high level there is a promenade on three sides behind the perimeter columns; simply decorated front to dress circle. The proscenium is plain, supported by two square columns with reeded anteproscenium housing the organ pipes. The Compton organ is on a lift at the side of the orchestra pit.

The Pavilion, when listed in 1998, was described as 'an excellent example in good condition of a purpose-built multi-purpose entertainment venue built to serve a major seaside resort. Other resorts do not have such a complete and complex example of this style and period.' The Pleasure Gardens which surround the Pavilion are on English Heritage's Garden Register. *SM/JE/JL*

Playhouse ★

Hinton Road/Westover Road
Other names
    Palace Court Theatre
    Little Theatre
Original architect
    1931   Seal and Hardy
Later works
    1939   Unknown: redecorated;
            orchestra pit added
    1970   Unknown: totally refurbished
Current use Church
Capacity 595

The Playhouse was the last theatre to be built in Bournemouth and has stood in its present form since 1971. It owes its existence to the Bournemouth Little Theatre Club for whom it was opened in 1931 as the Palace Court Theatre.

Through the 1930s, 1940s and 1950s it was a focal point for drama in Bournemouth. At this time there were administrative offices and accommodation facilities alongside the theatre in what are now the staff quarters of the Palace Court Hotel. By 1966, rising costs made it obvious that amateurs could no longer afford the Palace Court Theatre. Louis Michaels bought the theatre in 1970 and created the Galaxy cinema in the old Green Room downstairs. During the next eight years the Playhouse was a repertory theatre.

Like most such theatres the Playhouse suffered falling audiences and for a time went over completely to film. In 1983 it

returned to live theatre but, on the death of Louis Michaels, it was put on the market and sold to the Assemblies of God who had been hiring it for Sunday services. A change of use to a church was allowed on appeal, but the use was made personal to the present owners so that, on any change of ownership, permission would lapse. The stage areas, etc., have, since then, remained virtually untouched, though the Galaxy cinema has been stripped and is a lecture room with kitchen.

The first Seal and Hardy design published c.1930 had a vaguely Egyptian cinema-style facade but, as built, it was a frank paraphrase of the Portland stone facade of Stone's London Whitehall Theatre. Inside is a fairly plain, typically 1930s interior with single balcony. The acoustics are excellent for the spoken word, and it is the only theatre in Bournemouth fully suitable for plays, the Pier Theatre being against the elements of the sea and weather, and the Pavilion far too big.   *SM*

Shelley ★

Boscombe Manor, Beechwood Avenue, Boscombe
Original architect
    1866   possibly Joseph Peacock, with
            Sir Percy Florence Shelley
Listed
Current use Private theatre/lecture room
Capacity c.200

Bournemouth, Playhouse

One of two private theatres built by Sir Percy Florence Shelley, son of the poet. The other, behind his town house in Tite Street, Chelsea, was demolished many years ago.

Sir Percy carried out major building and alteration works at Boscombe Manor between about 1850 and 1879. Around 1850, he built a temporary theatre in the garden and this was replaced in 1866 by the present room. His favourite pastimes were theatricals and painting and he doubtless had a hand in the detailed design and decoration of the theatre. Descriptions of the scenes for various productions make it apparent that an ambitious standard was achieved. Much of the scenic painting and musical composition was carried out by Sir Percy himself.

Nearly all private theatres were built with flat floors so that they could double as ballrooms or grand dining rooms. Once a wonderfully colourful room whose walls were lined with mural paintings. Now absent, these are said to have been removed for safe keeping during the Second World War, but no evidence has yet been found to confirm this. The raked stage had wood machinery, but this was destroyed in later years to make space for a boiler room. An 'archaeological' investigation of the floor structure is needed to establish its nature so that it can be properly restored if the opportunity arises.

The proscenium arch is now blocked and the swagged pelmet and tabs as well as the painted act drop representing Poole Harbour are lost. An interesting curiosity is a window in the rear wall from a bedroom on the other side, from which, it was said, Lady Jane Shelley could enjoy the presentations in privacy and comfort.

Even in its altered condition, the Shelley remains a valuable example of a mid-Victorian private theatre which would merit restoration and more appropriate use.   *JE/SM*

Theatre Royal ★

Albert Road
Other names
    New Theatre Royal
Original architect
    1882   Kemp, Welsh and Pindar
Later works
    1887   Unknown: converted to Town
            Hall
    1892   Unknown: refurbished (with
            fittings from Her Majesty's
            Theatre, London)
    1909   Unknown: large foyer added

*Bournemouth, (former) Theatre Royal
(Sally McGrath)*

1962   Unknown: converted to cinema
1971   Unknown: twinned
c.1985   Unknown: converted to casino
       (downstairs)
Listed   **Grade II**
Current use **Casino/part disused**
Capacity   **(was) 800**

Described as 'a handsome and well-appointed Theatre' the Theatre Royal, Bournemouth, opened in 1882, in the heart of the town in Albert Road. It cost £10,000 and seated 800, between stalls, dress circle, upper circle, pit, gallery and private boxes. In 1887 it was converted to a Town Hall but reopened as a theatre in 1892 after refurbishment.

During the Second World War years, the theatre became a services club. It suffered fire damage in 1943 and was reconstructed. In 1949, it reopened as the New Theatre Royal. In July 1962, the theatre was converted to the Curzon cinema and bingo club, and in 1971 'twinned' as the Tatler cinema club.

The theatre has a good stuccoed facade of four bays and four storeys with giant Corinthian pilasters embracing the upper three storeys. A casino now operates in the lower part, whilst the (balcony) cinema closed in 1982 and has been for sale ever since. The grid area and flying system remain intact. *SM*

Winter Gardens ★
Exeter Road
Original architect
1937   Uncertain, thought to be
       Borough Architect
Later works
1940s   Unknown: converted to con-
       cert hall
1959   Unknown: redeveloped and
       refurbished; café bar and ter-
       race added
1960   Unknown: exterior renovated
Current use **Occasional concert use**
Capacity   **1818**

In 1937, the new Winter Gardens, red brick and solid, was opened as an indoor bowling green. War intervened, and it was decided to convert it to a concert hall. Not built for music it had by chance a brilliant acoustic, which became famous. Alterations took place in the 1950s to improve the theatrical facilities. Well dressed, the very wide proscenium stage platform is an attractive setting for variety shows and concerts, the audience capacity being greater than anywhere closer than the Southampton Mayflower. Two-thirds of the theatre seating is raked, giving excellent sight lines.There is no fly tower, but the stage offers ample space for sets and rolled cloths. The dressing-room facilities are excellent. The hall is in a pleasant gardens setting, with a long terrace outside the bar and café areas.

In 1992, the Friends of the Winter Gardens was formed and an appeal launched. As a result, the Council has agreed to fund the venue, but attempts to present first-class entertainment have been discouraged, as it would be in opposition to the newer Bournemouth International Centre. At time of writing Bournemouth University, Bournemouth Borough Council and the Winter Gardens Trust were embarking upon the joint development of an Arts Centre incorporating the concert hall. *SM*

BRADFORD

Alhambra ★★★
Morley Street
Original architect
1914   Chadwick and Watson
Later works
1986   RHWL (Christine Leyland and
       David Wright): refurbished,
       restored and extended
Listed   **Grade II**
Current use **Theatre**
Capacity   **1464**

An outstanding example of a theatre in what had appeared to be terminal decline re-established as a touring house of regional significance. The old city of Bradford had damaged itself severely in post-war years but the restoration of the theatre signalled (as it has elsewhere) a return of civic pride and confidence. It is sobering to think how recently its prominent site was seen as an ideal spot for a city centre car park.

Chadwick and Watson's design could almost have been the work of two distinct hands. The exterior took maximum advantage of the triangular site with a rather coarsely handled classical composition in faience. A corner entrance tower with a smooth semi-circular dome carried on a drum of giant coupled Composite columns stood well in advance of a symmetrical front with square corner towers topped by two more rather hesitant domes. These main elements were linked by lower blocks which looked like architectural afterthoughts. The auditorium, by contrast, was a delightful design, comparable with the best of its time and, in fact, of rather Sprague-ish character.

The 1986 works, for which all praise to the City of Bradford Metropolitan Council (aided by EC funds), made quite radical changes to the exterior. A stronger link was made to the left of the corner tower (which no longer contains the entrances) with a facade matching the pilastered treatment of the street flank of the auditorium. To the right, an interestingly patterned glazed addition rises to the full height of the principal cornice to contain new and generous front-of-house facilities. In advance of this, a single-storey block continues (perhaps a little too continuously) the channelled treatment of the tower base. The drum of the tower itself has full-height glazing behind the columns to display a new grand staircase serving all levels. The dome now looks, if anything, even more overweight than it did when there was masonry and a dark upper void between the columns, but this is a small price to pay for a highly successful replanning of the front of house and the total effect is a dramatic event in the townscape.

The auditorium has been superbly restored. It has two deep, slightly curving balconies, a rectangular proscenium frame, opening nearly 11m (c.36ft), with an elliptical-arched, painted tympanum over, flanked on each side by paired superimposed boxes framed by Composite columns and surmounted

Bradford, Alhambra (Martin Charles)

above 2nd-balcony level by a broad semi-circular arch between telamons. The centre of the ceiling rises to a high octagonal dome. The original, finely modelled de Jong ornament and allegorical paintings had survived in remarkable condition and have now been complemented by a sensitive colour scheme. The stage has been doubled in depth and the grid raised to 21.3m (70ft).

The adjoining Majestic cinema was acquired and incorporated to permit major backstage improvements. It also provides a separate 200 to 400-seat auditorium for smaller-scale productions, rehearsals and events. This auditorium is rectangular with a balcony on all four sides.   *JE/IG*

Odeon
Princes Way
Other names
   New Victoria Theatre
   Gaumont
   Odeon Film Centre
Original architect
   1930 William Illingworth
Later works
   1969 Gavin Peterson and Sons: subdivided into bingo and two smaller cinemas
Current use Cinema/part disused
Capacity originally c.3300

Built as a ciné-variety theatre, the former New Victoria, now disused, occupies most of a large island site. The vast seating capacity was split between stalls, mezzanine circle and balcony.

There were twelve dressing rooms, a fully equipped fly tower and an orchestra pit. Also contained in the building were a ballroom and a restaurant. The auditorium was dominated by a huge dome and coved rectangular proscenium. A frieze ran round the auditorium below the ceiling. A curious feature here was that the balcony, whilst quite separate from the circle, did not overhang it.

At the end of 1968, the theatre, by then hopelessly too large, closed for subdivision. Two large cinemas were created in the circles whilst bingo took over in the stalls. The conversion work effectively destroyed all decoration in the theatre. The stage, however, remained intact in the bingo hall. Later a third screen occupied the ballroom. Before this subdivision, the stage was regularly used for live shows, popular concerts and broadcasts.

The exterior is still an impressive landmark, brick faced, stone ground floor, entablature and parapet. Octagonal towers on two corners with copper domes. *IG*

Priestley Centre for the Arts
Chapel Street, Little Germany
Other names
   Civic
   Playhouse and Film Theatre
Original architect
   1937 Eric Morley
Later works
   1997 David Quick of VJQ Ltd: stage rebuilt; auditorium reinstated after fire
Current use Theatre
Capacity 291

Bradford Playhouse Company was established in 1929, playing in the Jowett Hall. This was a Temperance Hall of 1837, converted to a cinema in 1910. It burned down in 1935. A new theatre on the same site, named for J.B. Priestley who had donated royalties, was opened in 1937 by Barry Jackson. It was, from the beginning, a dual-purpose theatre and cinema. A fire in 1996 destroyed the stage and damaged the auditorium and foyers. The theatre reopened after restoration with a rebuilt stage in 1997.

The facade in Chapel Street is very simple, a little reminiscent of the London Whitehall but with applied metal ornament. Small foyer, spacious bar in the basement. Plain auditorium. Balcony of eight rows under barrel-vault ceiling. Balcony front, which is flat with horizontal ribbed ornament, projects at ends. Ceiling over stalls slopes down toward proscenium, which is rectangular, flanked by fluted quarter-columns without caps or bases. *IG*

BRIDGWATER
Somerset

Arts Centre
11 and 13 Castle Street
Original architect
   after 1723 Unknown: as a house

Later works
1930s   Unknown: theatre added at rear
1982   Unknown: adjoining property incorporated; balcony extended

Listed   Grade I
Current use Theatre and arts centre
Capacity   196

The Bridgewater Arts Centre is a three-storey Georgian merchant's house of affluent style, now united with its neighbour and forming part of a terraced street, built from 1723 onward. The theatre was built behind the house in the 1930s, extending over the length of the garden. In 1946, the whole became the first arts centre in Britain.

In 1982, with the adjoining house, the theatre was extended sideways to accommodate a balcony, the stage being down one side, and the entrance to the side of the auditorium. The theatre is small with fixed seating only in the balcony. Proscenium stage, no flying facilities. used for music, drama and cinema presentations.   *SM*

Palace
Penel Orlieu
Other names
1916   Empire Theatre
1917   Albany Ward's Palace
Original architect
1916   Samson and Colthurst
Later works
1917   Unknown: converted to cinema
1939   Unknown: converted to Barracks Theatre
1950   Samson and Colthurst: refurbished
Current use Disused
Capacity   c.700

Slightly Moorish in style, the entrance had shops either side and a café above. The facade rendered brick; the central entrance has a large rounded window and above that a short tower and cupola. The words PALACE THEATRE emblazon the front on either side of the central tower, above the first-floor windows.

Beyond the entrance porch with two doors was a vestibule with central paybox. The interior was said to be grandly decorated, and included reeded columns and a pair of angels which looked down from the proscenium. The balcony had 200 seats arranged in curved tiers and a refreshment lounge at rear (in addition to cafe below).

It was difficult to make the theatre

pay, and it was sold to Shipman and King, who were in turn taken over by Gaumont-British. Revues and pantomimes continued until 1929, but films were gradually introduced for the main part. It was closed in 1938. It soon reopened after improvements to means of escape and during the Second World War it was very popular as a Barrack Theatre entertaining troops. Theatre use probably finished in the late 1940s.

It was refurbished and the proscenium altered in 1950 to accommodate wide-screen films. Now disused, the original features from the 1950 reburbishment survive. There is a movement to reopen it, the theatre having survived demolition so far.   *SM*

BRIDLINGTON
East Riding of Yorkshire

3B'S Theatre
Leisureworld, The Promenade
Other names
1937   Grand Pavilion
Original architect
1937   P.M. Newton
Current use Multi-purpose hall, including theatre
Capacity   900

Very bland exterior, now bounded on three sides by the equally bland Leisureworld complex of swimming pool/exhibition hall/café, etc. No theatre name, just some small plain lettering 'Theatre Entrance' above the central of three pairs of doors with windows in openings 2 and 4. Minuscule foyer with box office.

Given the plain exterior, the Art Deco interior is quite a surprise. Largely intact and unaltered, it resembles an Odeon. The decoration consists of two broad bands running from the back to either side of the wide plain proscenium arch. These bands, approximately five metres wide, contain ribbed plaster and concealed lighting - there was no direct lighting anywhere in the hall. The front stalls are much wider than the rear and originally had seating with appalling sightlines at the sides, as a result of which, within two years, the capacity was reduced by 160. Between the two bands in the centre of the ceiling is a third band, curved in front of the stage, and containing a narrower lighting trough. The front stalls area was always flat floored to allow for other uses and was designated the 'lower hall'. The 'upper hall' was stepped and had permanent seats. The

steppings have now been altered to allow for tables, with two rear corners built up to form a café and bar area. The plaster either side on the proscenium arch has been clumsily cut to house speakers (now replaced with more modern units free standing in front of the arch).

There are two dressing rooms. The stage is very wide with a low proscenium arch and a full tower with a 25-line hemp system. Direct stage access has been lost in the expansion of the site.   *IG*

Spa
South Marine Drive
Original architect
1896   S. Dyer: original theatre
Later works
1907   W.S. Walker of Brodrick, Lowther and Walker (Hull): rebuilt following fire
Current use Theatre
Capacity   1031

An earlier theatre burned down in 1906. The replacement theatre is basically intact today. The interior, in Italian Renaissance style, consisted of a pit (with separate entrance), now seated, and a single balcony, returned to the proscenium wall and divided into three areas: grand, upper and back circle.

The proscenium arch is almost square with a central cartouche containing a female mask. In the ceiling is a round saucer dome with four relief plaster leaf-scrolls and four smaller swags dividing the dome. The whole is surrounded by a moulded cornice. In the main part, above the stalls, there is an octagonal raised cornice. The balcony, supported on plain columns, has a panelled front with rich plaster scrolls. The walls at both levels are simply decorated with panels. The balcony is now divided into two areas separated by a barrier approximately 0.6m (2ft) high.

The entrance on South Marine Drive gives access to a good-sized foyer nearly at circle level with the former main entrance on the Esplanade at stalls/pit level. There is a small first-floor balcony above the old entrance.

In January 1932 the adjacent Royal Hall was gutted by fire. The Spa suffered minor smoke and water damage. An insurance settlement allowed rapid repair and full redecoration, the theatre reopening at Easter 1932. It remained open whilst the Royal Hall was reconstructed.   *IG*

Bridlington, Spa (Ian Grundy)

swept away and replaced with a rather dull cinema auditorium. Most of the stage was incorporated into the enlarged auditorium – the tower is of greater depth outside than the space now existing behind the present plain proscenium. There is no trace of the original layout of the Albert nor any features surviving from the theatre. Further changes have been wrought since the cinema closed and bingo took over. A staircase has linked the stalls with the circle, adjoining properties have been purchased and incorporated, etc.

The theatrical significance of the Albert has been much reduced but given its location, close to Halifax, it should not be written off without careful consideration of its potential.   *IG*

BRIGHTON
Brighton and Hove

BRIDPORT
Dorset

Palace
High Street
Other names
    Electric Palace Cinema
Original architect
    1926   Frederick Cooper and Sons,
        Bridport
Listed   **Grade II**
Current use **Disused**
Capacity   **407**

The Palace, which was opened in 1926, was the brainchild of local Brewery owner J.C. Palmer. He was interested in the local operatic society, but realising that he could not fill a theatre six nights a week in Bridport, equipped the building as a cinema with stage and dressing rooms. The simple auditorium was rather archaic in architectural design, but was enlivened some time after 1936 with murals of rural scenes painted by local artist George Biles (who painted almost all of Palmer's Pub signs). The murals in the Foyer are all that is left of his work at the Palace, the auditorium walls having been painted out.

J.C. Palmer's dream of a small opera house was realised every April when the local Operatic Society took the Palace over for its annual production. A very successful pantomime ran every January from 1950.

In 1999, the Palace closed as structural work was deemed necessary. A Friends group was immediately formed with a view to raising money for the

necessary works in order to reopen. The building was at this time spot-listed.   *SM*

BRIGHOUSE
Calderdale (West Yorkshire)

Albert Theatre and Opera House
Huddersfield Road
Original architect
    1899   Sharp and Waller
Current use **Bingo**
Capacity   **(was) 1200**

Built in 1899 at a cost of £4000, the theatre seated 1200 on three levels. Provision was made for electric lights and the act drop depicted a scene from Constantinople. In the 1930s this was all

Brighouse, Albert (Ian Grundy)

Dome, Concert Hall and Pavilion Theatre ★★
Church Street and New Road
Original architect
    1804-8   William Porden: as stables and
        riding school
Later works
    1867   P.C. Lockwood: converted to
        concert hall
    1935   Robert Atkinson: concert hall
        interior reconstructed; supper
        room/concert room construct-
        ed
    2000   RHWL: major refurbishment of
        entire complex
Listed   **Dome and Concert Hall Grade
        I/Theatre Grade II**
Current use **Concert hall, theatre and
        multi-purpose room**
Capacity   **Concert hall 2102/Theatre 230**

The complex surrounding the Dome conveys the impression of being the product of a sustained building campaign in consistent style, but it is actually the work of a number of different hands and periods.

The Dome itself (not so called until the mid-1850s) was a rotunda stable, designed by William Porden in 1804 in the 'Hindoo' manner, and built to serve the Prince Regent's Brighton residence, the Pavilion. It was this stable building which set the Islamic style, later to be adopted in spectacular fashion for the remodelling of the Royal Pavilion itself. Alongside was a Riding School, now the Corn Exchange. The Museum and Library which make up the remainder of the complex, were added by Philip Lockwood in the 1860s and 1870s, and

Brighton, Dome

modified and extended by Francis May in 1901–2.

The stables were converted into a concert hall with a magnificent polychrome Saracenic interior by Lockwood in 1867, but the whole of his work was lost or obscured when Robert Atkinson removed an inner ring of columns and constructed a new interior in ciné-modern style in 1934-5. Atkinson also built a new Church Street entrance for the Corn Exchange (by this time used for a multiplicity of purposes) and a supper room doubling as a concert room (now the Pavilion Theatre) on the south-west, New Road, corner of the site.

As seen now, the complex contains three performance spaces: the Dome Concert Hall, the Corn Exchange and the Pavilion Theatre. The least altered is the Corn Exchange, still a flat-floored multi-purpose room, recognisably Porden's Riding School, a fine space with an elliptical roof in one span without tie beams. A gallery entrance to the Pavilion Theatre was added near the south end by Atkinson.

The Dome Concert Hall is much as Atkinson left it, a circular domed interior, interesting of its date but now inadequate in both its stage dimensions and its acoustic performance. May's magnificent tiled entrance remains in altered condition.

Atkinson's Pavilion Theatre presents a simply massed facade to New Road, with minimal ornament faintly echoing the Islamic style of its neighbours. It is disappointing in having no public entrance from the street, where it could have intensified evening activity in the vicinity of the nearly opposite Theatre Royal. The auditorium is a flat-floored multi-purpose room, decent enough, but not

Atkinson at his best.

The 1999-2000 works to the complex include radical improvements to the Dome. *JE*

Hippodrome ★★★

Middle Street

Original architect

1900   Frank Matcham: conversion of
            older building

Listed   **Grade II***

Current use **Bingo**

Capacity   est. **1400**

A magical conversion of an 1897 ice rink. Long, low and very restrained stuccoed facade to Middle Street. Central entrance flanked by square Italianate towers with pyramid tiled roofs. The reticent exterior is scant preparation for the

huge, opulently decorated, near-circular auditorium. Originally a dual purpose circus/variety theatre and now possibly the finest surviving example of its type in Britain. The arena was soon given over to permanent seating facing the proscenium. There is only one balcony (with seven rows) curving with the walls to meet the single, large onion-domed boxes which flank each side of the wide, low proscenium.

The most spectacular feature of the auditorium is the vast ceiling in the form of a panelled tent which covers the whole space and is richly decorated with boldly modelled Baroque plasterwork. At the centre is a balustraded gallery, reminiscent of (but not the same as) the one at the London Hippodrome before it was altered.

The 'Palm Court' is an impressive separate room with paintings which appear to date from the original 'art decorations', but the room with its false bridge has undergone some alteration, not entirely to its architectural advantage. The body of the theatre is intact, with only superficial alterations (the levelling of the auditorium, for example, which 'submerges' part of the lower boxes). It could be readily restored to use. However, owing to the great size of the auditorium it would be most suitable for spectacular dance productions, opera and possibly orchestral concerts. The circus sight lines would permit the use of the former arena as an additional performance area. In such use it will be vitally important to retain rear vehicle access. *CB/JE*

Brighton, Hippodrome

Imperial ★★★

North Street

Other names

    1948   Essoldo
    1964   Essoldo Bingo Club
    Ladbroke's Social Club
    Top Rank Bingo
    Top Rank Hot Shots

Original architect

    1940   S. Beverley (of Verity and
            Beverley)

Later works

    1996   Unknown: converted to bowl-
            ing alley and amusements

Current use Disused

Capacity c.1875 (prior to removal of
    balcony in 1996 conversion)

Designed before the last war, with foundation stone laid by Ralph Lynn and Jack
Buchanan in July 1939. Opened in April
1940. After 1945, intermittently in live
use, but mainly a cinema. Became
Essoldo cinema in 1948, then bingo.
Following use as a bowling alley and
general entertainment centre the building (at the time of writing) is disused
and the site threatened with redevelopment.

    Externally, as might be expected of
the period, it has the apprearance of a
super-cinema. Long, plain brick flank to
Windsor Street. Entrance facade on
North Street, brick with stone dressings
with 3-light bow window, recessed
between tall, narrow, plain-faced wings,
the three elements linked by a cill band
at second-floor level and a simplified
crowning entablature.

    The original interior might be seen as
a final fling for its 1930s' eclectic manner: Art Deco in feeling but with a mildly classical flavour. The organ grilles
flanking the proscenium had an overall
scalloped pattern with superimposed
marine motifs. The boxes, two over
three on each side, with double-height
draped boxes next the proscenium,
were prow-like projections, set between
square piers with Ionic-derived capitals
featuring swagged shell features and
supporting an abbreviated entablature
and crowned by scallop shells. The per-
forated valence below the boxes was
decorated with motifs like palmettes.

    This fine interior had suffered alter-
ation in bingo use and more recently
and radically (by the removal of a balcony) in the change to bowling alley. It
was a great misfortune, in theatrical
terms, that Brighton Corporation, as
freeholders, were unable to prevent
these works. The building, as it was previously, would have been capable of pro-

viding the South Coast with a lyric theatre of regional significance (even more
so with the development of the land at
the rear reserved by the Corporation for
the express purpose of allowing for an
increase in stage size and ancillary backstage accommodation). However, there
still remains the potential for future
reclamation for live theatre use.   JE/JM

Playhouse

Sudeley Place, Kemp Town

Other names

    Kingscliff
    Picture Playhouse
    Metro
    Continentale

Original architect

    1891   Unknown: as chapel

Later works

    1920   Denman and Matthew
            (Brighton): converted to cine-
            ma

Current use Residential

Always clearly showing its chapel beginnings, the Playhouse had six high arched
windows down the side of the corner
site and a tiny entrance of double doors
into a small foyer. Either side of the
entrance was a largely bricked-in smaller
arched window with a range of windows
at first-floor level, two outer rectangular
and two central arched, and a superimposed projection box at second-floor
level - well into the eaves of the sloping
tiled roof.

    Inside, the roof had the original open
timber trusses and the arched window
openings were highlighted for decorative effect with dummy arches down the
wall adjoining the neighbouring property. There was a single balcony. Little else
in the way of decorative features, but the
auditorium had a certain innate charm
and a vibrant intimacy. It is not certain if
the stage was part of the 1920 conversion (probable) or a later addition, but
for the size of the theatre it was quite
spacious.

    A professional weekly repertory com-
pany was established in 1947 for
Playhouse Productions Ltd. Over sixty
productions were staged before the
building reverted to a cinema in 1949. In
1986 the death of the owner (Miles
Byrne) forced a sudden closure. This was
only a few months after a complete
refurbishment.

    After lying empty for many years,
during which time a return to stage use
as a home of the National Youth Theatre
was discussed, the Continentale was sold
to developers who retained the exterior

walls and roof whilst turning the auditorium into three town houses with a
fourth on the site of the former stage
and dressing room block, which were
completely demolished.   IG

Theatre Royal ★★

New Road

Original architect

    1807   Unknown

Later works

    1866   C.J. Phipps: auditorium and
            stage rebuilt; facade
    altered
    1894   C.E. Clayton: exterior recon-
            structed
    1927   Sprague and Barton: auditori-
            um partly redecorated
    1999   Jaques Muir and Partners:
            refurbished

Listed   **Grade II**

Current use **Theatre**

Capacity   **951**

The scene door in Bond Street looks as if
it could belong to the early C19 theatre.
When the first building was extended
and reconstructed by C.J. Phipps in
1866, the original structural walls and
colonnade were retained. The height
was, however, increased and a glazed
extension added at first-floor level.
Internally the stage area was updated
and a typically intimate 'Phippsian' auditorium was constructed, shaped like a
squeezed horseshoe, with three closely
spaced, steeply raked balconies supported by iron columns. The 1866 colour
scheme was purple, cream and buff.

    Unfortunately, in 1927, most of the
auditorium plasterwork was redone in
French neo-classical style by Sprague
and Barton. All that survives of Phipps'
scheme of decoration is a deep frieze of
'Jacobean' strapwork above the proscenium. The boxes at 1st and 2nd balcony
levels are framed by twinned, fluted
pilasters above extremely attenuated
consoles flanking omnibus boxes. Flat,
circular ceiling over the well of the balconies.

    In 1894 C.E. Clayton replaced the
original facade with a new design in red
brick with stone dressings. It is very reticent; distinguished only by small octagonal flanking turrets with ogee domes.
This provided entrances only to the pit
and upper levels of the auditorium; the
main entrance being to the left, in the
end pavilion of a terrace of 1807, giving
access to pleasant foyers and staircases
decorated with pilasters above a
mahogany dado.

    Contemporary with the 1894 front is

Brighton, Theatre Royal (Ian Grundy)

a colonnade of small coupled columns with bulbous bases, which extends, on a slightly larger scale, in front of the main entrance. The theatre is privately owned and run as a touring theatre for drama. A reopened Hippodrome would certainly be complementary to the Royal, being on an entirely different scale.   *JE*

West Pier Theatre ★

Original architect
    1893–1916
    Unknown: pier buildings
    added throughout this period
Listed   **Grade I**
Current use **Derelict**
Capacity   **est. 1000**

The West Pier is the only pier in the United Kingdom listed at Grade I. Designed by Eugenius Birch, it opened in 1866, was partially closed in 1965 and has been completely inaccessible to the public since 1975, since when parts of the structure have been demolished for safety reasons. Like the old Palace Pier theatre, the theatre on the West Pier was a fine example of its kind, a music hall with cast-iron galleries on three sides, but remodelled after the war. Externally, it is a festive pavilion, a pile with two main storeys, and a domed roof in two stages and corner towers with domes. It is now marooned at the end of the severed pier and has been in a derelict state. Work started, however, on the repair of the pier in 1999 and is intended to continue until the pier and its buildings are restored and reopened.   *JE*

BRISTOL

Hippodrome ★★★

St Augustine's Parade
Original architect
    1912   Frank Matcham
Later works
    1948   Unknown: fly tower partially
            rebuilt with better flying facili-
            ties
    1964   Unknown: exterior refur-
            bished; globe and pavilion
            roof removed; facade radically
            altered
    1980   Unknown: dressing rooms
            improved
    1987   Unknown: new bars and box

office in adjoining premises
    1998   Thomason Partnership (engi-
            neers): stage reconstructed to
            remove rake; orchestra pit
            enlarged
Listed   **Grade II**
Current use **Theatre**
Capacity   **1981**

A Stoll theatre, second only to his flagship, the London Coliseum, this is Matcham's last major work and is in scale typical of the largest variety theatres built in the decade before the First World War. Well-designed auditorium - wide, though not too deep, somewhat in the manner of the London Palladium. The stalls have an unusually good rake, made, as at the London Coliseum, by a series of steps. The two big cantilevered balconies do not have the oppressive overhangs from which some theatres of this date suffer. The elliptically arched proscenium is set in a deep, panelled reveal with niches at the sides. At the ends of the balconies are ranges of six boxes, three on each level, divided by giant fluted Doric columns which carry the second balcony slips. The ceiling is in the form of large saucer dome, the 'eye' of which is (or was) capable of being slid open for summer-time ventilation. Baroque in style, the geometry is less complex and the ornament less dense than in Matcham's earlier theatres, producing a slightly sparse appearance, further accentuated by the loss of original painted decoration on the pendentives below the dome, on the dome itself and at the sides of the proscenium.

The   stage,   like   that   of   other

Bristol, Hippodrome

Hippodromes of the period, was built so that the front section could be withdrawn to reveal an immense tank for water spectacles. Like most of Matcham's later designs, the theatre was designed with projection equipment.

The foyer (originally intended to be the full width of the building but reduced before construction) had elaborate painted decoration and illuminated coloured glass panels. The narrow entrance front rose to a square tower with a tall pavilion roof surmounted by a metal sculptural group - deliberately so designed by Matcham in order to make maximum impact. The upper levels of the tower are now removed, leaving a disappointingly bland front which provides no preparation for the grandeur of the interior.

The Hippodrome is now a touring theatre, excellent for opera, ballet and big musicals, though too large for drama. The interior would benefit from a thorough restoration and appropriately opulent redecoration in the Matcham manner, including the reinstatement of draperies (photographs of the original interior exist). The facade cries out for restoration.

The present owners have, in fact, instituted a rolling programme of improvements, front and back of house. *CB/JE/SM*

People's Palace
Baldwin Street
Other names
　1930s　New Palace Cinema
　1947　Gaumont
since 1980s
　　　Ritzy
Original architect
　1892　James Hutton (Dundee)
Later works
　1912　Unknown: converted to cinema
　1928　Frank Verity: rebuilt
Listed　Grade II
Current use Nightclub

Opened in 1892, as a music hall, built by the Livermore Brothers, the People's Palace was said to be a replica of the People's Palace, Dundee, by the same architect. It became a cinema in 1912 and was rebuilt by Frank Verity in 1928. In 1947 it became a Gaumont. A proposal to demolish and redevelop the site was turned down in 1974 and the building subsequently became a nightclub. The facade survives almost intact. *SM*

St Monica Home Theatre ★
Cote Lane, Westbury-on-Trym
Original architect
　1925　Sir George Oatley
Listed　Grade II
Current use Theatre/events
Capacity　originally c.1000

St Monica Home lies on the site of Cote House, purchased by Harry Wills in 1920, overlooking the Durdham and Clifton Downs. It was founded by his wife, Mary Monica Cunliffe Wills, to provide a home for elderly gentlewomen in reduced circumstances and in need of medical care.

The buildings, set in landscaped gardens, form a spacious symmetrical composition in a mix of extravagant Jacobean and Elizabethan styles, with timbered gables and tall chimneys, and dominated by a Gothic chapel, built in local pink Pennant stone. Sir George Oatley had, early in his career, designed mental institutions in Croydon and in Lancashire. St Monica Home included a theatre.

The main building is entered through a canted projecting porch of three arcaded bays between unfluted Doric columns. Here there is access to two levels; the theatre is on the upper level, but at the end of the building which is built into a slope, the exits and the get-in are virtually at ground level.

The auditorium has a barrel-vaulted ceiling with plaster bands, between which is some plaster decoration, ending in massively ornate corbels. Square proscenium, plain, except for the founders' initials in a central cartouche, all very understated. Portraits of Harry and Monica Wills hang on either side. A panelled dado encircles the interior and stage front, broken only by mullioned and transomed windows. At the rear of the flat-floored hall is a wooden dais on two levels. The small end balcony, also in wood, is without seats and reserved for wheelchairs. The room is multi-functional (as are many institutional theatre halls) to allow for dances and parties for staff, residents and visitors. The stage is raked, generously deep and equipped with a small grid. *SM*

Theatre Royal ★★★
King Street
Original architect
　1766　Thomas Patey
Later works
　1790　Thomas French: ceiling raised; boxes newly lined and theatre redecorated

　1800　James Saunders: facade altered; further tier added in auditorium
　1853　Unknown: refurbished, redecorated, painted and gilded; new act drop
　1881　C.J. Phipps and T. Pope (City Architect): auditorium altered, cutting back stage 5 feet; 'Phipps Patent chairs' installed; star-studded ceiling and new ventilator enclosed in heavy gilt moulding; painting/scenery stores and dressing rooms at rear; understage machinery overhauled and upgraded
　1903　W. Skinner: new facade and iron portico; new dressing rooms, secondary lighting system (gas) installed; new fire curtain installed and proscenium modified
　1943　J. Ralph Edwards: repaired and redecorated
　1944-48　J. Ralph Edwards: new seating system; upper circle bar removed; new box office
　1949　Unknown: new exits created
　1951　Unknown: reseated and re-raked
　1973　Peter Moro: stage house rebuilt; new entrance made through Coopers' Hall; facade replaced; studio theatre built behind new facade
Listed　Grade I
Current use Theatre
Capacity　668

Bristol, Theatre Royal (Coopers' Hall entrance)

A theatre of oustanding historic interest, occupied by a company of national stature. The auditorium is a remarkable survival of an C18 city theatre, with similar dimensions to those of the contemporary Theatre Royal, Drury Lane. Whereas it is thought that Drury Lane may have had a slightly fan-shaped auditorium with tiers facing the stage on a shallow curve, the balconies at Bristol are fully semi-circular in the centre and very nearly parallel at the sides. Stage-boxes are framed between giant Corinthian pilasters. The stage originally projected as far as the outer pilasters, but has long been cut back to the inner pair, and the crucial Georgian proscenium doors removed. As first built, the theatre had a stalls circle of boxes and one tier above. In about 1800 a further tier was added with a deep gallery in the centre. The ceiling slopes steeply upwards from the line of the outer pair of pilasters to the back of the gallery. The tier fronts are supported by slender fluted columns at 2.75m (9ft) centres. Most of the delicate gilded filligree decoration on tier fronts, pilasters and ceiling dates from the early and mid-C19 rather than C18.

In 1972 the whole structure of the C18 stage house with its splendid Victorian machinery was demolished, an incredibly destructive act, and rebuilt with an inappropriately flat stage instead of the raked stage that the form and sight lines of the auditorium demand. Surprisingly, the opportunity to restore the original apron and proscenium arch doors was not taken. A sad memorial, a model of the stage machinery, was put on display in the theatre foyer in 1981. In 1972 W. Skinner's mediocre 1903 entrance front was demolished to allow the building of a new studio theatre by Peter Moro, the New Vic, itself now of interest as an important work of its time. A new entrance was made through the adjacent imposing mid C18 facade of the former Coopers' Hall. The opportunity was lost at this time to make use of the fine hall at first-floor level as the main saloon for the theatre. It now forms the well and landing of a staircase leading from ground floor to first-balcony level.

The time is ripe for improvements to be made for the Bristol Old Vic Company which has been in occupation since 1946 and this should be made the occasion for a new look at ways in which the auditorium in particular might be sensitively restored. *CB/SM*

BRIXHAM
Torbay

Brixham Theatre
Bolton Square
Other names
  (New) Market Buildings
Original architect
  1887 Unknown
Current use **Theatre (occasional)**
Capacity **280**

The new Market Building opened in 1887 at a cost of £3000. Over the Magistrate's room and offices for the Harbour Commissionaires was a large upper hall for public meetings, concerts and theatre, originally seating 800. The theatre use now is mainly amateur and there are plans to offer cinema presentations to help viability. *SM*

BUNGAY
Suffolk

New ★
Broad Street
Original architect
  **1828 Unknown (for the Fisher
          circuit)**
Listed   **Grade II**
Current use **Warehouse**

A rare survival. Bungay Theatre was built in 1828 as one of the Fisher circuit playhouses in which use it remained until 1844. It was then converted into a corn hall and subsequently served as a furniture store, a laundry, a cinema and a warehouse.

Bungay, New (Jim Lee)

The overall plan dimensions of the theatre are c.10.7m (35ft) wide on Broad Street and c.24.4m (80ft) long. The building is the equivalent of two storeys high, generally in red brick but with a handsome stuccoed facade enriched in the classical manner with four full-height Tuscan pilasters carrying an entablature topped with a small, central pediment. A central entrance, marked by a large blind, round-headed arch, is flanked by probably later subordinate entrances each with a window over. On the left-hand pilaster there is a plaque commemorating the theatre. The building has a slated roof with the ridge at right angles to the road. Internally, a later floor has been inserted overall at ground level. Also of later date are the balcony and the three large roof lights. The surviving original fabric of the building appears to be confined to the envelope walls, possibly the roof trusses and some vestigial remains beneath the ground floor: the lower courses of the curved rear wall of the pit and of the front wall of the stage, two pit access stairs leading up through cottages and some stone benching along the walls (laundry?). Although the basement is much as it was when inspected by Richard Southern after the last war, the building has only recently been fully surveyed and may still call for further archaeological investigation before major works are undertaken. A feasibility study into the possibility of reopening as a theatre was undertaken in 1998 but the group formed to acquire the building for this purpose was overtaken by a commercial purchaser. The building continues in warehouse use. *JL*

BURLEY-IN-WHARFEDALE
Bradford

Scalebor Park Theatre ★
Scalebor Park
Original architect
  c.1901 J. Vickers Edwards of Wakefield
Current use **Disused**

A small theatre built about 1901 within the complex of a psychiatric hospital and probably contemporary with the adjoining Lodge House. The theatre can also be approached via a glazed walkway of similar date, from the 'stage right' side of the building.

Internally a flat-floored ballroom auditorium, with oval leaded lights at high level depicting various flowers. The 'stage left' side of the auditorium is equipped with a small bow-fronted box or minstrels' gallery at high level. The main entrance to the auditorium is on the 'stage right' side and has a mahogany surround with a scrolly broken pediment. The rectangular proscenium with scroll-bracketed upper corners is flanked on each side by mahogany pilasters, part fluted and cabled, which are repeated round the auditorium, dividing the walls into panelled bays. The ceiling is divided into ribbed panels, rising from the deep cove over the cornice.

The stage has primitive fly floors and a small timber grid. Proscenium 5.5m (18ft).

Externally the theatre is built of sandstone and the simple pitched roof is of small red tiles. The dominant Lodge House elevation is divided into three bays, the central one surmounted by a large lead-clad and timber clock tower crowned by an open cupola. The windows in all three bays are mullioned, the whole presenting an imposing presence in the grounds. The auditorium of the theatre is fitted externally with a leaded ventilator, surmounted by a dome which matches that of the clock tower. *DW*

BURNLEY
Lancashire

Empire ★★
St James Street
Other names
   Empire Music Hall
   Empire Theatre of Varieties
   New Empire
   Gala Bingo
Original architect
   1894 G.B. Rawcliffe
Later works
   1911 Bertie Crewe: auditorium
           reconstructed
   1938 ?Lewis and Co. of Liverpool:
           converted to cinema
Listed   Grade II
Current use Disused (last used for bingo)
Capacity   est. 1200

When bingo moved out of this theatre in 1995 there were fears that it would be vulnerable to neglect and vandalism. The disused upper level already shows signs of fairly extensive water penetration. The more immediate risk seemed, however, to be that it would be sold for some highly profitable non-theatre activity, removing a splendid building from any prospect of a return to its designed use. There was much local pressure for the opportunity for reopening to be grasped, and the local authority and The Theatres Trust contributed to the cost of a feasibility study.

Narrow, altered facade. The auditorium is unelaborate but pleasing. As reconstructed by Crewe in 1911, it has two slightly curved wide and deep balconies, terminating in superimposed stage boxes framed between Corinthian columns. Segmentally arched proscenium, now with a false ceiling inserted halfway over stage. Flat, panelled ceiling with circular centre panel. Restrained plasterwork on balcony and box fronts. Three boxes and the upper balcony have been partitioned off, but could easily be reopened.

The theatre could be readily restored to use, but the narrow stage would need to be extended back over a narrow stream at the rear. Front of house would need improvement. Not a cheap return to use, but the possibilities could be excellent for a town with no large theatre, serving a quite extensive area. It would complement Burnley Mechanics (1986) perfectly, to the benefit of both. *CB/IG/DW*

BURTON-UPON-TRENT
Staffordshire

New Theatre and Opera House (Hippodrome)
George Street
Other names
   The Hippodrome (only for variety
      dates)
   1868 St George's Hall
   1887 St George's Hall and Theatre
   1902 Opera House
   1906 Opera House and Hippodrome
   1935 Ritz

Burnley, Empire (Ian Grundy)

   1957 Gaumont
   1968 Odeon
Original architect
   1868 Essex, Nicholl and Goodwin
           (Birmingham)
Later works
   1888 Adams: enlarged theatre; new
           stage; new scenery (by T.H.
           Hall of Birmingham Royal)
   1902 Essex, Nicholl and Goodman
           (formerly attributed
           E. Forshaw)
   1906 Unknown: converted to music
           hall
   1935 Thomas Jenkins and John
           Fairweather (Glasgow): rebuilt
           as a cinema; building turned
           round 180°; new entrance in
           Guild Street
   1974 Unknown: tripled
Current use Dark
Capacity   c.1350 (prior to subdivision)

Opened in 1868 as St George's Hall, essentially a concert hall with two levels of seating. Enlarged 1888 to become the St George's Hall and Theatre and rebuilt as a theatre in 1902, remaining in theatrical use until 1930. Again rebuilt in 1935, in enlarged form, as a cinema. Tripled in 1974.

All that remains of the former theatre buildings are a section of wall of the 1860s on the right flank and the former front of 1902, now at the rear and of little interest. The latter is in two storeys, originally described as 'in Jacobean style', brick and terracotta in three main bays, each of three small arched windows at first-floor level.

It was operated for a number of years by the Robins cinema chain but closed at the end of 1999. Its future remains uncertain. *TB*

BURY

Art Picture House ★
Haymarket Street
Original architect
   n.d. Unknown: as Baptist Chapel
Later works
   1911 Albert Winstanley: converted
           to theatre
   1922 Albert Winstanley: completely
           rebuilt
Listed   Grade II
Current use Bingo
Capacity   c.1200

An elaborate and complete example of an early 1920s' cinema, exceptionally theatrical in its plan and decoration. The first theatre on the site was a conversion of a Baptist chapel which had become a warehouse. It had a minimal stage, 1.83m (6ft) deep, and a long 'winter garden' glazed foyer added along the length. This theatre was demolished in 1922 and replaced by the present building, also by Winstanley. It had stalls, a pit and a twelve-row circle. The ciné chamber, unusually, was at the rear stalls, not the circle. The first floor café was not completed until 1923.

Main three-storey elevation is symmetrical in five major bays, the wide centre crowned by stepped pedimental parapets, all in white faience. The outer bays were originally crowned by elaborate arches with large keystones now replaced by stepped parapets above the third-floor circular windows.The ground floor has been altered with modern tiling around the main entrance.

Internally, a two-level auditorium with two boxes on either side of the proscenium, having extended rounded fronts between Ionic columns. Proscenium 9.14m (30ft) wide. The L-shaped café was known originally as the Oriental or Indian Lounge. *IG*

BURY ST EDMUNDS
Suffolk

Theatre ★
Cornhill
Other names
  Early C18 Market Cross
Original architect
  1734   Unknown
Later works
  1774   Robert Adam: exterior redesigned
  1819   William Wilkins the Younger: upper floor converted to concert room

Bury St Edmund's, Theatre

Listed   **Grade I**
Current use **Art gallery**

In 1774 Robert Adam proposed new elevations for the old Market Cross (like most of its kind it also served as a Town Hall) which had been in use as a theatre since 1734 by the Duke of Grafton's Comedians (The Norwich Company) and the Grammar School. In 1819 William Wilkins the Younger converted the first floor into a public concert room and transferred all the fittings to his new theatre in Westgate Street (see Theatre Royal).

No trace of theatrical activity or evidence as to the layout of this small playhouse remains. The public room has been restored as an art gallery. Fine exterior with piano nobile, complete with Venetian arches under pediments on all four sides flanked with niches and windows, over a heavily rusticated ground floor. It is in excellent condition and conforms to the original drawing by Adam of an end elevation (the drawing is still in the possession of the Corporation). *CB*

Theatre Royal ★★★
Westgate Street
Original architect
  1819   **William Wilkins the Younger**
Later works
  1906   **Bertie Crewe: alterations, mainly to auditorium**
  1965   **Ernest Scott: partially restored**
  1974   **Norman Westwater: further improvements**
  1994   **Purcell, Miller and Tritton: single-storey extension at rear**
  1995   **Purcell, Miller and Tritton: facade improved; forecourt lowered to 1819 level; foyer and auditorium ceiling redecorated**
Listed   **Grade I**
Current use **Theatre**
Capacity   **352**

The Bury Theatre is unusual in that it is one of the few existing C19 theatres built by major but non-specialist architects – others being the Royal Opera House, Covent Garden, the Grand, Leeds, and the Theatre Royal, Drury Lane.

The younger William Wilkins was, for all his distinction as leader of the Neo-Classical movement (his work includes Downing College, Cambridge, and the National Gallery, London), a man of the theatre. He followed his father, the William Wilkins, as proprietor of the East Anglian circuit, which included the for-

mer Barnwell Theatre in Cambridge (see Cambridge Festival Theatre). They had rebuilt all their theatres before William the Younger decided to erect 'a theatre of ample dimensions and elegance' in Westgate Street, Bury St Edmunds.

The auditorium is on four levels and originally held 800. The pit is surrounded by a double horseshoe of boxes, the lower tier having four rows of tip-up seats, in the centre where once there were boxes. The upper tier, which is supported by 16 slender cast-iron pillars on the forward edge of the tier below, consists of an unbroken sweep of 15 boxes with no pillars to obstruct the view. This is achieved by the setting-back of the gallery above a canopy, an effect that gives the whole a grace and an elegance which one might associate more with a European court theatre than an English country playhouse. The auditorium walls are deep salmon pink which allows the eye to dwell on the upper-tier front with its sphinxes and winged griffins in gold on ochre and the lower tier with its crimson screen panels, also in flat painting, on a grey ground.

The proscenium is rectangular in shape, 7.3m (24ft) wide and 5.5m (18ft) high, and is flanked by pairs of marbled classical piers between which are curved and panelled proscenium arch doors. The line of the present forestage, which is also convertible into an orchestra pit, dates not from 1819 but from 1906 when the theatre was redecorated by Bertie Crewe. Other C20 solecisms that jar include the plush velour seats in the pit, the centre gangway inserted in 1965, and the removal of the stage boxes which linked the lower tier to the outer proscenium pilasters. A 1906 improvement which pleases is the breaking-open of the screen wall behind the upper tier of the boxes.

The exceptionally large stage, 12.2m (40ft) wide by 12.2m deep had been removed between 1925, when the theatre closed, and 1962 when it ceased to be a barrel store for the neighbouring brewery. The theatre was restored by a specially formed Trust who employed Ernest Scott as architect assisted by Iain Macintosh as consultant. The modern stage surface is unfortunately flat where once it was raked. Although the walls and the main roof trusses are original, the scenic suspension system is modern and depends on a tubular structure introduced in 1965 to take the load down onto concrete pads in the basement below.

The theatre is built of red brick and

Bury St Edmunds, Theatre Royal: reopening night 10 Dec 1906

presents an attractive small-scale classical facade to Westgate Street. Above the porte-cochère, now glazed, is the windowless circle bar, introduced in 1906 and extended in 1974 to include additional escape stairs from the gallery. The theatre is freestanding save for an uneasy connection with the adjoining house, reputedly by Wilkins himself on land he sold off to pay for the theatre. If this house could be brought back into the same tenure and united with the Royal, the improvement and further restoration of this rare and precious theatre would be greatly assisted.

For a full analysis of Wilkins's design, which is geometrically disciplined in a way that his father's Cambridge (Festival) Theatre is not, see Axel Burrough's paper 'Theatre of Proportion' (*Architectural Review*, Sept 1988).

The theatre is now used as a medium-scale touring and amateur theatre by a charitable company, while the head lease has, since 1975, been in the hands of the National Trust. It was the first theatre to be acquired by that body. *IM/JE*

BUXTON
Derbyshire

Opera House ★★★
Water Street
Original architect
  1903 Frank Matcham
Later works
  1928 Unknown: auditorium reseated; pit benches removed; two gangways replaced by a central aisle
  1979 Arup Associates (Derek Sug-

den): completely renovated
Listed   **Grade II***
Current use **Theatre**
Capacity   **937**

This is the most striking element in a Spa town complex, which also includes the Pavilion Pleasure Gardens (1871), Winter Gardens and Octagon Hall (1876), and Playhouse (1889). It was built over the old entrance to the Gardens, adjoining and modifying the Winter Gardens entrance.

The Opera House is a masterpiece of Edwardian theatre architecture, completely intact and repaired and redecorated in 1979 to reopen as a theatre after many years use as a cinema. Stone exterior with entrance facade flanked by twin, leaded domes on low, columned drums.

White marble was used extensively in the foyer. Superbly intimate auditorium with opulent Baroque plasterwork by de Jong. Two balconies with a gallery as a continuation of the 2nd balcony, box divided from it by a parapet. Small box at each end of 1st balcony framed between columns supporting a little plaster canopy. Superimposed stage boxes, stepped-down in level, with upper box backed by characteristic niche flanked by terms. Curved head of proscenium carried on heavy scrolled console. Splendid oval saucer-domed ceiling set with six original, richly framed, oval painted panels, which were fortunately not obliterated during the cinema years.

The old gas plate survived the change to electricity (Grand Master installed

1938) as did the gas sunburner in the centre of the ceiling. This was restored to working order in 1979 and is an extremely rare example of a once common method of lighting and ventilating auditoria.

This is a Festival theatre run by a trust. It is a touring theatre and a home for amateur productions for the remainder of the year. *CB/TB*

Playhouse (Paxton Suite)
Pavilion Gardens, St Johns Road
Other names
  1889 Entertainment Stage
  1889 Pavilion
  1903 The Old Theatre (popular name)
  by 1912 Hippodrome
  1928 The Palace Theatre and Hippodrome Cinema
  c.1935 Playhouse
  1979 Paxton Suite
Original architect
  1889 W.R. Bryden
Later works
  1894 Unknown: extra dressing-room accommodation (2 rooms) added
Listed   **Grade II**
Current use **Multi-function room**
Capacity   **250**

Part of the Pavilion Gardens, Winter Gardens and Opera House complex, it was known popularly as 'the old theatre' after the Opera House, which it immediately adjoins, opened.

Long, low stone street facade running the full 59m (193ft) length of auditorium and stage, the four centre bays divided by rusticated pilasters with finials. Elaborate Baroque gable at left-hand end (right wall of stage). Pitched roof overall, with no visible fly tower (but limited flying is possible).

The auditorium is, at first sight, heavily altered, but without, in fact, much loss of original fabric. A sloping false ceiling rises from the curving front of the balcony, which now forms a storage space, from which it is still possible to see a painting over the proscenium. The main floor has been raised in a series of terraces off the old raked stalls.

This is now a multi-function room. There is no fixed seating. The stage is complete but is rarely used, apart from the flat, shallow forestage where there was once an orchestra pit. It would not be difficult to restore the Playhouse to its original appearance, but a return to theatrical use seems rather unlikely. *CB/TB*

CAMBRIDGE
Cambridgeshire

ADC ★
Park Street
Original architect
    1860   Unknown: a set of rooms in a
            larger building
Later works
    1866   Unknown: gallery added
    1888   Unknown: structural improve-
            ments and gallery
            demolished
    1935   Harold Tomkinson with W.P.
            Dyson: largely rebuilt after fire
Current use Theatre
Capacity   227

Cambridge, Arts (Richard Davies)

In the early C19 a series of University Dramatic Societies existed in Cambridge (e.g. The Garrick Club 1834-42). The Amateur Dramatic Club (ADC) was founded in 1855, the oldest University dramatic club in the country, operating the oldest amateur-run theatre. In the first decade of the C20 it was still described as 'confined to members of the University who undertake both male and female parts'.

The club started in two rooms leased at the back of the Hoop Hotel in Jesus Lane. In 1860, a larger set of rooms was hired which was purchased in 1882. Structural improvements were required in 1888 and the gallery (built in 1866) was demolished. In 1933 part of the theatre was burned down and was rebuilt in 1935. At that time the Manchester Guardian wrote: 'All the seats are good. The bare grey undecorated walls are certainly rather chilly in effect, but these new theatres disdain that cultivation of a jovial atmosphere which was once the first concern of the theatrical architecture.'

The theatre has recently been reseated and recarpeted but it still cannot be described as having a particularly warm auditorium. Seating is in a single rake. The forestage lifts off when the orchestra pit is to be used. There is a fly tower with double-purchase counterweight lines and a number of hemp lines, the fly gallery being stage left. The large trap in the stage is used only as a get-in for scenery. There are two workshops. The theatre has always been mainly used for student productions. Nowadays it does occasionally book small-scale professional shows.   *KW*

Arts ★★
6 St Edward's Passage
Original architect
    1936   George Kennedy

Later works
    1996   Bland, Brown and Cole: exten-
            sively rebuilt
Listed   Grade II
Current use Theatre
Capacity   671

In the historic centre of Cambridge, close to the colleges, built in 1936 on land leased from King's College. More land recently acquired has made possible a number of major improvements, but the theatre still forms part of the old and intricate development pattern.

The 1996 works, which amounted to a major rebuilding, effected massive improvements both front of house and backstage, but the attractive 1930s' character of the auditorium has been successfully maintained.   *JE/KW*

Festival ★★★
Newmarket Road
Other names
    Theatre Barnwell
    Theatre Royal, Barnwell
Original architect
    1814   William Wilkins the Elder
Later works
    1926   Edward Maufe for Terence
            Gray with Harold Ridge and
            Norman Marshall: reconstruct-
            ed, retaining most of old audi-
            torium
Listed   Grade II*
Current use Buddhist Centre
Capacity   est. 450

The Festival Theatre is a remarkable and rare survival, comparable with and a few years earlier than the Theatre Royal in Bury St Edmunds, by the same archi-tect's more distinguished son, William Wilkins the Younger, architect of Downing College and the National Gallery. Its C20 history, however, added a layer of special interest (and complication) which is absent in Bury.

The future treatment of the Festival will call for a sensitive balance to be struck between the restoration of its late Georgian character and the retention of its historically significant later works. The theatre survives today almost intact mainly because it was used for many years as a workshop and wardrobe administered by the Cambridge Arts Theatre Trust (founded in 1936 to run Cambridge's only remaining professional theatre, the Arts).

The Festival, as it has been known since 1926, was purchased by the Trust in 1946. It provides remarkable evidence of two periods of theatre architecture: the late Georgian playhouse (in that its three-level horseshoe auditorium is intact) and the open-staging techniques pioneered in the 1920s. In 1926 Terence Gray assisted by Edward Maufe, Harold Ridge and Norman Marshall totally removed the old proscenium and created a space stage complete with revolve, fixed cyclorama and Schwabe lighting according to the ideas that had been propounded by Gordon Craig for the preceding 25 years but had not been put into practice elsewhere in the UK.

William Wilkins the Elder is known to have built a new Barnwell theatre in 1808, but this was on the opposite side of the Newmarket Road on a site next to the Sun Inn. The present building is a new construction of 1814. There was never an imposing entrance, the theatre

Cambridge, Festival

Original architect
mid C19 Unknown
Later works
   c.1860   Unknown: balcony added
   Listed   **Grade II***
   Current use **Live music venue**
   Capacity **c.250**

Front to Northgate entirely domestic in appearance - an altered C17 house with shop windows inserted at ground-floor level. Auditorium added to rear, probably of mid-C19 date. A very simple, very small music hall - the overall dimensions being only 5.5m (18ft) wide x 10.7m (35ft) long. Flat main floor and balcony round three sides, straight across the rear and wide enough for only one row of seats. The balcony is believed to have been added in 1860. Its fronts are decorated with 38 paper panels painted in somewhat naive manner, most of them with pictures which seem to form part of a dramatic narrative. The pictures look rather earlier than the hall and are traditionally said to have come from a pleasure garden. Whatever the truth of the matter may be, they are clearly rare and precious and their condition gives some cause for anxiety. Flat ceiling with exposed timber beams. Miniature proscenium with a plain (probably modern) elliptical arch. Tiny lean-to stage house.

Theatrical use probably ceased between 1898 and 1903 and the building has been in a variety of shop and store uses. It has served as a restaurant, a small variety hall (failed by 1989) and more recently as a blues music venue. A proposal was made in 1999 to turn it into a 'theme' pub.*CB/JE*

being originally reached down an alley where the 1926 foyer now stands alongside a still-surviving house by Wilkins.

The theatre is rectangular in shape and of solid brick construction, containing a horseshoe-shaped auditorium on three levels, two tiers of boxes with gallery over. The upper levels are supported by slender iron pillars on the leading edge of the box tiers, continuing up to the ceiling except in the centre of the gallery. The gallery side slips were always blind. The rear walls of the boxes are intact and the original box doors remain. On the face of the tiers the 1926 decoration and later over-paintings have been partially removed and traces of an early C19 decorative scheme can be seen, together with Biblical texts which date from the period between 1878 and 1920 when the theatre was a mission hall.

The removal in 1926 of the proscenium arch and doors was neatly achieved, the already curved ends of the tiers being simply returned to the side walls. On the face of a massive over-stage lighting bridge the painted pediment was refixed as a reminder of the width of the original 7.3m (24ft) proscenium. The stage itself was completely reconstructed in 1926 and is now an important and unique relic of the development of the open stage. It has a hand-operated

wood revolve. The 1926 plastered cyclorama also survives.

The Barnwell theatre, originally built outside the City boundary because of the virulent opposition in a University City to theatres in general, has for a century been in the 'wrong' part of the now larger city of Cambridge. In 1996 there appeared to be a good prospect that the Festival would return to active theatre life as the experimental 'research and development' house for the Arts Theatre Trust. A major repair to the roof was carried out and an expert conference was held on the manner in which the theatre should be restored, but financial difficulties aborted the project. The theatre has been sold to a Buddhist organisation which intends occasional theatre use. *JE*

CANTERBURY
Kent

Alexandra Music Hall (Penny Theatre) ★★
30/31 Northgate
Other names
   Princess Alexandra Theatre
   Canterbury Music Hall
   Regency Theatre
   1845–61 Royal George
   1861–65 The Cannon
   1865–1903 Princess Alexandra Music Hall
   1989   Penny Theatre

Marlowe ★
The Friars
Other names
   1933-38 Friars
   1955-81 Odeon
Original architect
   1933   Alfred and Vincent Burr
Later works
   1982   P. Jackson, City Architect: converted to theatre/concert hall
Current use **Theatre**
Capacity **993**

The first Marlowe Theatre in St Margaret's Street closed in 1983. Canterbury City Council acquired the former Odeon as a replacement as part of a planning gain arrangement.

The cinema was converted to a theatre and concert hall and reopened in 1984. The old Odeon facade, itself

Canterbury, Marlowe

something of a architectural oddity, with six tall first-floor windows above the entrance canopy, three balustraded panels below the cornice and a tall stepped parapet, was little altered. The foyer, too, is almost untouched. The auditorium is seated in two raked stages separated by a cross gangway, the new rake reaching to the height of the former balcony. The new chandeliers can be lowered to form a 'light curtain' reducing capacity to 600. The roof is now open to the auditorium. The stage house was totally rebuilt with a proscenium opening of 13m (42ft 8in), a stage 11.5m (37ft 10in) deep, and with an orchestra pit for up to 60. *KW*

New
Orange Street
Other names
  Building is now known as 'Theatre House'
Original architect
  1790   Unknown
Current use **Offices**

Good facade to Orange Street of c.1820 - stuccoed, of three bays and three storeys. Tall windows in piano nobile with inward-sloping jambs of 'Egyptian' character, fashionable at the time, e.g. Egyptian Hall, Piccadilly, and Egyptian House, Penzance. The entrance of the theatre was earlier to the rear of the building, from Dancing School Yard. This is now a completely plain brick wall with modern windows. Theatrical use ceased in 1859 when the structure was

said to be unsafe.
  A warehouse until 1960 when the interior was completely gutted and subdivided for office use. Internal evidence of former theatre use has been obliterated, but the exterior (which shows signs of interest, e.g. blocked openings) could be worthy of close study. *CB/KW*

CARDIFF

New ★★
Park Place
Original architect
  1906   Runtz and Ford
Later works
  1970   and 1976 John Wyckham Associates: new stage built;

(continued top right) orchestra pit enlarged
  1988   RHWL: major external and internal improvements
Listed   **Grade II**
Current use **Theatre**
Capacity **1159**

Rather low-key exterior apart from the curved corner entrance facade in red brick and stone, set between the two stuccoed flanks. This has a high-level, shallow loggia with coupled Ionic columns, supporting a curved entablature and balustrade, set between short, domed octagonal turrets.
  The 1988 works replaced the rather tatty main-entrance canopy with an architecturally appropriate iron design with lanterns. The major internal structural alteration was the scooping-out of the narrow entrance lobby and staircases in the corner rotunda and the creating of a grand staircase to serve all levels. An alabaster tablet which recorded the opening of the theatre in 1906 by Sir Herbert Beerbohm Tree seems to have disappeared.
  As designed, Runtz and Ford's auditorium was rather cool, with a stretch of blank wall separating the upper balcony front from the proscenium boxes. The 1988 works effected a great improvement in this respect by extending the upper balcony with side slips. The rectangular proscenium has no frame as such, being contained by the two bays of side boxes in two tiers, set between fluted giant Ionic columns rising from tall pedestals, with a straight entablature over. The box fronts themselves (the upper ones iron-balustraded) have an interesting undulating, rather than simply bowed form. Flat ceiling. The orna-

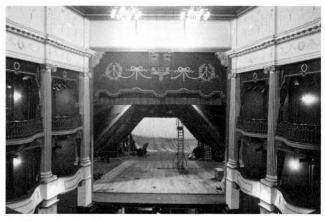

Cardiff, New (Ian Grundy)

mental plasterwork is restrained, but the total effect is intimate and pleasing. JE/TR

Palace and Hippodrome
9-10 Westgate Street
Other names
    1904 King's
    1907 Grand Palace and Hippodrome
    1913-32
         Hippodrome Picture Palace
Original architect
    1887 J.P. Jones and Messrs Waring
         and Sons
Current use Furniture salesroom

Lively stuccoed front of three storeys with three central bays slightly recessed between flanking, one-bay pilastered pavilions. Ground and first floors altered. Tall windows in upper storey with Corinthian pilasters and steep pediments. Balustraded parapet. Interior completely gutted.   CB

Philharmonic Hall ★★
St Mary Street
Other names
early 1880s
         Morrella's Palace of Varieties
    1886 Philharmonic Theatre
    1892 Stoll's Panopticon
    1918 Pavilion Picture Theatre
    1997 The Square (pub)
Original architect
    1877 Jackson and Son (builder?)
Later works
    1997 Inside Out Design Partnership:
         converted to pub
Listed   **Grade II**
Current use **Pub**
Capacity est. up to 700

Cruelly altered but important example of a music hall of the rarest early concert-room type (cf Wilton's of 1859; City Varieties, Leeds of 1865). The main facade with a triangular pediment over the three central bays is of particular importance as part of a group extending from the corner of Wood Street to the end of St Mary Street.

The Philharmonic had a characteristic auditorium – a rectangular hall with a slightly raked main floor and originally with a balcony round three sides (the centre section later increased in depth to the rear). Permission was unfortunately given for the balcony slips to be altered in the 1980s and the centre balcony was again extended forward, both alterations being detrimental to the balance of the building. The balcony sides, supported on slender iron

Cardiff, Philharmonic Hall (Ian Grundy)

columns, had a serpentine configuration, having probably been divided originally by low partitions to form boxes. Balcony fronts of bombé section were enriched with foliated plaster work. The narrow proscenium was framed by well-modelled, coupled Corinthian demi-columns on pedestals. There was a shallow apron stage, cut back in the 1980s, by which time the back wall had been brought forward and the wings walled off. The side walls of the auditorium, above balcony level, were articulated by Corinthian pilasters. Flat ceiling originally divided into panels.

Capacity, seated to modern standards, might be approximately 600-700. This theatre could have been a significant addition to the range of auditoria available to performing arts in Wales's capital city. The foyer is still quite splendid but, so far as the original spirit of the hall itself is concerned, the most recent alterations have amounted to brutal murder. Nearly all significant traces of its architectural character have been destroyed or obscured. Restoration would require heroic effort and can now be regarded only as a remote possibility. The Philharmonic represents a dismal failure of the historic buildings control system due, it would appear, more to ignorance than to any lack of scope for compromise. Let it be a warning. CB/TR/JE

Prince of Wales ★★
Wood Street and St Mary Street
Other names
    1878 New Theatre Royal
    1920 The Playhouse

Original architect
    1878 Waring and Sons and W.D.
         Blesslay
Later works
    1920 Willmott and Smith: auditorium reconstructed
    n.d. Willmott and Smith: new elevation to St Mary Street
    1988 and after Unknown: sequence of internal alterations for multiple uses
    1998 Lawrence Tring: partially restored and converted to public house
Listed   **Grade II**
Current use **Pub**
Capacity c.1000 (prior to radical alterations in 1988)

Opened as the New Theatre Royal. A good, three storeyed, Gothic, painted facade to Wood Street - traceried windows, canopied niches, etc.Later entrance now round the corner in St Mary Street (adjacent to the Philharmonic Hall), where one bay of the shop buildings, originally reflecting the Gothic style of the theatre, was rebuilt in Greek Revival style – giant columns in-antis above the ground floor linked by a triangular pediment, open below and having a square-headed niche containing a statue.

The auditorium was recontructed in 1920 in the same distinctive Greek style. Three straight balconies with slips, imposing proscenium flanked by giant fluted Ionic columns carrying a big triangular pediment (open below as at entrance) with a bas-relief Grecian frieze above. Flat panelled and coffered ceiling. This interior was, for all practical pur-

Cardiff, Prince of Wales (Lawrence Tring Architects)

poses, obliterated after 1987, following the grant (on appeal) of consent for multiple use; this made radical changes inevitable and a return to theatre use a distant prospect. Such architectural benefits as followed from the new occupation were all external. The three separate street facades were stripped of old advertisement hoardings and the stonework cleaned and repaired. The rose window, high in the Great Western Lane facade, was reopened and reglazed. The roof was reslated with decorative ridge tiles and the haystack above the stage rebuilt. The main entrance canopy was, however, removed. Internally the spaces were divided to form a slot-machine arcade, a computer games parlour, etc., and the intention was that there should also be a fast-food restaurant and bar. The auditorium was horizontally divided at two levels. Some created spaces remained for a long time unused. The stage was dismantled but the grid remained.

This has been a dismal recent history, not unlike that of the Philharmonic adjoining. However, the building was converted to a pub in 1999. Some of the damaging alterations have been removed and the move away from divided use has, to an extent, revealed the quality of the interior, unseen since 1988. *TR*

Victoria Music Hall
90 St Mary Street
Other names
   Victoria Hall
Original architect
   1871   Unknown: conversion of auc-
          tion house
Current use **Offices**

Originally a small music hall at first-floor level. Interior gutted and subdivided. The building appears to have been an 1871 conversion to music hall from the former Victoria Sale and Public Rooms (auction rooms). In 1881, it reopened and was run in conjunction with the Philharmonic Music Hall. By 1883 it was a touring house. In 1885 it was occupied by Monsieur D'Arc's waxwork and marionette exhibition, with a part used by a wine merchant. The waxwork exhibition remained until the Second World War. All that now remains is the entrance, to one side of the ground floor of a plain, painted brick facade – double doors in a tall frame with arched fanlight. Remains of paybox on staircase.

CARMARTHEN
Carmarthenshire

Vint's Electric Palace
Blue Street
Other names
   The Palace
Current use **Fragment**

The shell of the building survives but the interior has been gutted and is now occupied by two shops. All Vint's establishments offered ciné-variety in their early years. *TR*

CHATHAM
Medway

Theatre Royal ★★
102 High Street
Other names
   1938   **Royal Hippodrome**
Original architect
   1899   G.E. Bond
Later works
   1900   G.E. Bond: rebuilt after fire
   1938   Andrew Mather: redecorated
Listed   **Grade II**
Current use **Disused (partly derelict but
               secure)**
Capacity   **est. 1500+**

The recent history of this theatre puts it in the 'Perils of Pauline' category - a sleeping beauty, abused, cast out, mutilated and tortured, but always just surviving at the end of each instalment. It remains to be seen whether the Theatre Royal Chatham Trust, which has battled for years against all odds, can now stop the hurtling express (or the circular saw) from dealing the death blow, but the Trust and its professional team certainly deserve every success.

The Royal was built as a theatre and

variety house by a well-known local architect. The entrance facade has an Italianate loggia in four (2 + 2) semi-circular arched bays. Above this, a central blind attic rises above the parapet and is crowned with a broken pediment. On either side, small towers were originally capped with onion domes.

In the early 1980s, a furniture showroom occupied most of the foyer areas and used the auditorium, whose floor had been levelled in concrete, for storage. After a fire gutted the stage house in the 1960s, the proscenium opening was filled with brickwork and the damaged boxes were removed, but the enriched tier fronts and ceiling remained almost intact. When shop use ceased, neglect and vandalism led to further deterioration. When the 1982 *Curtains* description was written the Royal was thought to be 'probably too far gone to make restoration economically feasible'.

The possibilities opened up by the National Lottery have changed the economic climate for the restoration of well-sited traditional theatres like Chatham Royal. What was improbable in the late 1980s may be possible in the late 1990s.

The Trust which now has tenure of the theatre and an adjoining building (needed to improve front of house spaces) has cleared out the rubbish, opened the staircases, made the premises secure and arrested decay. The foyer and auditorium are now cleaned up and presentable, and recent work by volunteers, helped by the prison service, has shown that some of the tiled walls and mosaic facings, thought to have been lost, are still recoverable.

Progress was frustrated for some years by the fact that the Council held possession of the stage area and showed little inclination to release it, thus depriving the theatre of an element essential to its functioning. The impasse was resolved in 1997 when the new unitary authority for the Medway Towns determined to support the Theatre Royal Chatham Trust. This is a most promising move toward the eventual reopening of Chatham's only remaining purpose-designed theatre.

Although Central Hall in Chatham has a good record in providing a variety of entertainment, it is far from ideal for theatrical productions. If restored, the Royal would provide an excellent theatre of the right size for the Medway Towns and it would be well located to fill a gap in theatre provision in North Kent. *JE/IM/KW*

Chatham, Theatre Royal: supporters of the theatre are tireless in their efforts to return it to live use

CHATSWORTH
Derbyshire

Chatsworth
Private Theatre ★★
Chatsworth House
Original architect
　1830　Wyatville
Listed　Grade I
Current use Store and workroom for textile conservation

The private theatre of the Duke of Devonshire. A rare example of a theatre of a kind more common in central European palaces, in this case on the first floor of a tower at the north end of a long wing added by Wyatville to the ducal palace of Chatsworth from 1820–27.

It was designed as a multi-purpose ballroom, flat-floored, with windows along the side walls, a central doorway at one end flanked by two large, slightly raised boxes and a small gallery above for servants.

It has a fine ceiling with panels to form frames for late C17 painting by Cheron and Thornhill. The most notable feature theatrically, however, is the proscenium which, although flat, is painted in trompe l'oeil to give the illusion of a florid plaster frame with richly tasselled drapes. The proscenium divides the original room, with the cornice continuing over the stage. There is a splendid act drop (no longer hung, but kept in a roll) depicting the Elizabethan Chatsworth. The stage is shallow with no grid but with original pulleys, wings, borders, etc.

Not open to public view.　*CB*

CHELMSFORD
Essex

Regent ★
Moulsham Street
Other names
　　　　Regent Theatre
Original architect
　1913　Francis Burdett Ward
Later works
　1935　A.E. Wiseman: foyer altered;
　　　　new staircases inserted
　1975　Unknown: converted to bingo
　1997　Unknown: converted to pub
Listed　Grade II
Current use Pub
Capacity　est. 1000

An early ciné-variety house, and rare survivor. Handsome stuccoed facade in three two-storey bays with a wide, recessed balustraded balcony at first-floor level above the entrance. Central segmental pediment has been removed leaving only tympanum decoration of an oval with plumes, festoons and swags above, within a high stepped parapet. Shallow fly tower, with small rounded windows at rear.

Foyer, partly rebuilt in 1935, echoes the Rococo style of the interior. Stairs to balcony at either side, with iron balustrade. The auditorium has richly decorated plasterwork, with reliefs and modelled figures, including round ceiling, curved splay walls and balcony front. Balcony is terminated by pavilion boxes. Marble-flanked proscenium. Deep stage and dressing rooms.

The Regent, which was still described as 'theatre' rather than simply cinema in the 1946 *Stage Guide*, was converted to bingo in 1975, closing in 1993. It is now a pub, retaining most of the original features.   *CB/SM*

CHELTENHAM
Gloucestershire

Coliseum
Albion Street
Other names
    1913   Gilsmith's Hippodrome
Original architect
    1913   H.R. Rainger (retaining an earlier facade)
Later works
    1931   Unknown: modernised for cinema
    1974   Unknown: converted to bingo
Current use Snooker and club
Capacity   c.880 (before 1974 conversion)

The building was opened in 1913 on the site of the old Conservative Club, retaining the facade of that building. It operated as a theatre until 1931, when it was modernised for cinema,with the original arched design replaced by a new square proscenium; a lounge bar, a new canopy and external neon lighting was added. For a time, c.1922–31, when both the Opera House and Winter Gardens were engaged in full-time cinema, the Coliseum served as Cheltenham's only theatre.

Two-storey building with attic, facade plain, now rendered, with pitched roof, originally designed to carry flagpole. Remainder of the building is brick. The balcony has now gone and little remains of any other original internal features. It was a bingo house for some time. Horizontal subdivision in recent years for dual operations has rendered any return

to theatre use unlikely, but the town is well served by the Everyman (formerly Opera House). The stage house is thought to remain.   *CB/SM/KW*

Everyman ★★★
Regent Street
Other names
    1891–1960 New Theatre and Opera House
Original architect
    1891 Frank Matcham
Later works
    1984–86 Unknown: new stage house; front of house renovated
    1995 Christopher Richardson: front of house improved
Listed   Grade II
Current use Theatre
Capacity   658

Believed to be the oldest surviving complete Frank Matcham theatre. Opened as the New Theatre and Opera House, renamed Everyman in 1960. Very low-

key painted brick facade, merely part of the frontage of a very minor street and altered to its architectural disadvantage. Excellent intimate auditorium similar in scale and character to Matcham's Lyric Hammersmith. Two slightly curved balconies of seven rows each, the upper one subdivided by a raised parapet to form a small gallery. Both balconies continue as slips along the side walls to meet large boxes, one either side of the proscenium, with splendid Rococo canopies carried on slender turned colonnettes.   Semi-circular   arched proscenium as at Hammersmith and Blackpool, but without their Rococo valences. Beautiful saucer-domed ceiling with eight painted panels in rich Rococo frames, encircled by a flat border with smaller oval paintings. The stage house is entirely new (i.e. post-1960). Modern alterations to front of house are not as sympathetic as might have been wished for in such a fine Matcham house, and neighbouring

Cheltenham, Everyman

developments were not used as an opportunity to improve access to the stage house.

The theatre is owned by the local authority. *CB*

Playhouse
Bath Road
Other names **Civic**
Original architect
   1806   Unknown: as baths
Later works
   1945   Unknown: converted to theatre
Listed   **Grade II**
Current use **Amateur theatre**
Capacity   **228**

Discovery of mineral springs in 1718 turned a market town into a Spa. The Montpellier Baths opened in 1806 and was an extensive establishment for its time. As now seen, it is a classical building with three Doric entrances.

The Corporation purchased the baths in 1898. Changes then made included a swimming pool, but its popularity waned and in 1945 the building was converted to a theatre for amateur use.

The floor of the auditorium was built over the swimming pool, originally as a flat-floor venue, the seats not being fixed. More recently the auditorium has been raked. Part of the former swimming pool provides the orchestra pit and the remainder is used for storage. The old reception lounge of the baths, with its stained-glass windows remains in use as the theatre lounge. The stage has 14 hemp lines. There are five dressing rooms, and a quick-change room, the largest dressing room doubling as a green room.

The adaptation of two adjacent cottages provided a large workshop area, with five rehearsal rooms of varying sizes, two wardrobes and stores for lighting equipment and curtains. *KW*

CHESTER
Cheshire

Music Hall
St Werburgh Street/Northgate Street/Music Hall Passage
Other names
   1777   **Theatre Royal**
   c.1915   **Music Hall Pictures**
Original architect
   1280   Abbot Simon: as a chapel
Later works
   1777   Unknown: converted to theatre
   1855   James Harrison: converted to concert room

   1921   E.J. Muspratt and G.E. Tonge: reconstructed and modernised for cinema
   1961   Unknown: reconstructed for retail use
Listed   **Grade II**
Current use **Store**
Capacity   **820 (prior to 1961 conversion for retail use)**

A remarkable building with a long and complex history. It was originally the Chapel of St Nicholas, built in 1280 on Cathedral land. After various uses, including that of a wool hall, it was converted into the Theatre Royal in 1777. A second conversion in 1855 by James Harrison was as a concert room and it is as this that it is best remembered, being still referred to as the Music Hall. Another internal rebuild in 1921 saw modernisation for cinema.

The visible mediaeval fabric (probably of 1488) is on the south side. The base of the building is of local red stone, coarsely hewn and weathered. Above, the later additions including the stage house, rise in red brick with many variations in the brickwork, blocked-in windows and doors, etc., which reflect changing uses over the centuries. The entrance on St Werburgh Street is advanced at ground-floor level, with steps up to the entrance. The mid-C19 Gothic front is by James Harrison. The rear of the property on Northgate Street is of plain modern stone in run-of-the-mill post-modern style, dating from 1993. The get-in door and some exits have been replaced within the last two or three decades.

The interior has been radically altered, suspended ceilings and new wall linings obscuring all the older fabric; no evidence of theatre fittings remains. No description of the theatre interior has been found, but it is known that, as a music hall, there was a single balcony, approached from the narrow foyer by a single stairway.

The building has been converted to retail use from about the time of its closure as a cinema in 1961. *SM*

Royalty
City Road
Original architect
   1882   B.E. Entwistle
Later works
   1958   Unknown: altered internally
Current use **Disused/club**
Capacity   **c.960**

The Royalty was built in 1882 on the site of a wooden structure used for circuses,

etc. At that time it was the only theatre in the city.

The exterior is plain, painted brick on City Road side, two storeys with windows of domestic scale on first floor. There is evidence that a long canopy covered the entrance. The theatre is entered at the side, through an ante-building containing foyer, stairs, bars, refreshment areas, etc., and it is this area which is currently run as a nightclub. The theatre lies lengthways behind this, with a fly tower, and good access to scene dock from a road the other side of the building.

Accommodation is stalls, circle and gallery supported by pillars; there were originally two round-fronted boxes at circle level on each side of the proscenium, removed during cinema days. Interior is now plain with proscenium stage which was altered in 1958 for variety/pop entertainment, since when the seats have been removed. It was converted for bingo in 1960, closing in 1966. The auditorium is at present disused and the fabric of the building appears to be on the decline. *SM*

CHESTERFIELD
Derbyshire

Pomegranate
Corporation Street
Other names
   1879   **Stephenson Memorial Hall**
   c.1904   **Corporation Theatre**
   1949   **Civic Theatre**
Original architect
   1879   Smith and Woodhouse (Manchester)
Later works
   1898   W.H. Wagstaff: large stage and dressing rooms added at east end
   1910   Unknown: auditorium floor raked; orchestra pit formed
   1949   Chesterfield Corporation (E. Bonsall): improved
   1990   Chesterfield Corporation (David Botton): major repairs to roof and trusses
   1994   Unknown: reseated and recarpeted
Listed   **Grade II**
Current use **Theatre**
Capacity   **546**

Built in 1879 as the Stephenson Memorial Hall, it was enlarged in 1898 and given a proper stage. In 1910 the hall achieved its present dimensions, with a raked auditorium. The original hall was intended for a multiplicity of uses, public concerts, etc., but was poorly equipped for theatrical performance. By 1910, theatre use was fully achievable but was still one of many uses. Since the further improvements carried out in 1949, it has operated as a theatre, financed by the borough council.

Gothic exterior in brick and stone. The stage extension with its low fly tower, built in 1898, employed matching materials. The local museum is to be found in the same complex.

The auditorium as now seen is the result of a series of past alterations. The fine trusses of the 1879 hall are still present, supported on corbels. Straight balcony front with relief ornament; plain walls; proscenium framed by square columns supporting a low-arched tympanum. Raked stalls; orchestra pit for sixteen players. There is evidence of the former existence of wood stage machinery, but none remains.   *TB*

Chichester, Theatre

CHICHESTER
West Sussex

Theatre ★
43 South Street/Theatre Lane
Original architect
   1791   Thomas Andrews (of St
            Pancras, Chichester)
Later works
   1850   Unknown: converted to brew-
            house
Listed   Grade II
Current use Shops

Built in red brick with a tiled, hipped roof with eaves along Theatre Lane. To the two-storey entrance facade on South Street, however, there is a parapet incorporating a pediment over the slightly advanced central three bays. At first-floor level the advanced section contains two tall windows either side of a central, smaller blind opening. A similar blind window is in each of the flanking bays. The ground floor is marred by a modern, full-width shop front.

Replacing an earlier theatre on the same corner site, the present building formed part of a circuit which included Southampton, Winchester, Portsmouth and Newport (I.O.W.). It survived until 1850 when it was sold at auction to become variously a brewhouse, gymnasium, library, furnishers, a box office for the Chichester Festival Theatre (1962) and, latterly, shops. Although nothing of the theatre remains internally the shell and roof are original making it a rare and important example of a small, late C18 theatre.   *SM/JL*

CHORLEY
Lancashire

Little
Dole Lane
Other names
    Empire
Original architect
   c.1900 Unknown
Current use Amateur theatre
Capacity   238

Thought to be a late Victorian or Edwardian Music Hall, adapted for cinema, perhaps ciné-variety, in 1912.

The main facade forms the entrance to the backstage areas, suggesting that it formerly fronted owner's/manager's accommodation, or a company office. It stands on the curve of Dole Lane, at an angle towards the auditorium, which lies on a U-bend of the Lane. This front is heavily pseudo-Georgian, stone-faced, with EMPIRE in gable. The present entrance-front is at the other end of the Lane and is quite plain.

Through the public entrance is the original paybox, with stairs to shallow balcony at one side, stairs to projection room at the other. A door at either side leads to the raked stalls area. The roof is pitch pine with cast-iron stancheons. The radiators and fittings are original. The seats were bought from (Bolton?) Theatre Royal when it closed. Two prosceniums, one from theatre days and a second from cinema times may be seen, set about 1m (3ft 3in) apart.

The Chorley Amateur Dramatic

Society acquired the building in 1959 for £2000 and moved the stage halfway down the body of the building, creating a bar/green room behind. Films are screened when theatre is not in progress.   *SM*

CIRENCESTER
Gloucestershire

Theatre
27 Gloucester Street
Original architect
   1799   Fisher
Later works
   1820   Unknown: front of building
            converted to pub
   later   Unknown: auditorium subdi-
            vided
   1955   Unknown: converted to resi-
            dence
Listed   Grade II
Current use Residence
Capacity   originally c.500

The theatre was built in 1799 by Fisher, who acquired a row of ten cottages for the enterprise. All but one of the cottages were gutted, and the theatre was constructed using some retained walls as a basis. It has a handsome, three-bay, stone-dressed facade onto Gloucester Street, a part of the town with many remaining Georgian buildings; round-headed central entrance with fanlight, (formerly with cartouche above) and sash windows to ground and first floors. The front was originally parapeted with a central pedimental hump and blind lunette. The slated roof now has shallow eaves. Accommodation was pit, tiers of private boxes and gallery. The interior was decorated with floral wreaths and gilding. The retained cottage was at the right-hand side and its outline can be seen in the side wall today.

In 1808, a primitive Methodist Chapel was erected to one side, set back from the street, for which the cottage was demolished. In 1820, the front part of the building was converted to a public house, the Loyal Volunteer. The theatre's fortunes were by then in decline, mainly after John Boles Watson's death, since neither son nor grandson possessed his flair and business acumen. By c.1840 it was used as a store for beer. Later, the auditorium was subdivided. However, many features were retained and could be seen until the Methodists succeeded in closing the pub by 1955, when it was converted into a residence. Damage by flooding and by fire occurred in the 1930s and 1950s. The shell of the building, however, survives, the facade little changed.   *SM*

CLACTON-ON-SEA
Essex

Operetta House
Rosemary Road
Other names
1936–38   Tivoli
1938   Savoy
Original architect
1894   J.W. Chapman
Later works
late 1930s   Unknown: reconstructed
with new frontage and auditorium (as cinema)
Current use Nightclub
Capacity est. 700

Theatre on first floor of the old town hall buildings. Renamed Tivoli in 1936. Reconstructed in late 1930s and renamed Savoy, with new frontage and remodelled auditorium. Later altered to bingo and now a nightclub. In spite of all these changes, the outline of the theatre clearly remains. In particular, the circle is still in use, albeit as a bar and drinks area. This is now linked by parallel walkways to the main staircase to the dance floor, which is now accessed from the middle of what was the proscenium. Little of the original decoration remains but the stairway is very reminiscent of 1930s' cinema architecture.   *MS*

Pier Pavilion and Ocean Theatres
Other names
by 1962 the Pier Pavilion was renamed The Jolly Roger
Original architect
1892/3   Unknown
Current use Part derelict
Capacity Pier Pavilion: originally 900/Ocean Theatre: not known

The Pier was built in 1873 to allow steamship passengers who embarked at Fresh Wharf, London, to land. It was extended in 1890 and the pier head pavilion added c.1893. It was oval on plan and, like most pier pavilions, in concert-hall style with concert party stage. Rectangular proscenium with rounded top corners. An Ocean Theatre was added in 1932 when the landward end of the pier was widened and mounted on concrete pillars. The Ocean had its weatherboarding replaced by aluminium cladding in 1962, at which time it was being used by Gordon Henson's concert party. It was later converted to an amusement saloon. Following storm damage in 1977 the Ocean closed and the Pier Pavilion began to fall into dereliction.   *KW*

Prince's
Town Hall, Station Road
Original architect
1926   Sir A. Brumwell Thomas
Listed Grade II
Current use Theatre
Capacity 816

Good, brick classical town hall of 1930, incorporating, immediately behind the facade, the Princes Theatre. The town hall's main entrance vestibule serves as a generous theatre foyer. This is a flat-floored multi-purpose venue with bleacher seating and an end balcony. Segmental vaulted ceiling, plaster-panelled side walls and tongue-fluted flat balcony front. Proscenium with broad moulded frame and segmental arch. Very limited wing space. Fly tower with 20 sets of counterweights. Cyclorama. Four dressing rooms.   *KW*

West Cliff Theatre
Tower Road
Original architect
1894   Unknown
Later works
1928   G.W. Gould: rebuilt
Current use Theatre
Capacity 590

Low-built with no fly tower; hipped mansard roof behind a single-storey frontage building with stucco-ornamented entrance. The auditorium is a big, rectangular single-raked space of little architectural distinction, but much loved by its mainly amateur users.

Opened in the same year as the Ocean Theatre on the pier, it replaced a temporary building on the same site. Initially the building was used only in the summer, but it opened all year round from 1934. A fire in a loft in 1950 destroyed the grid and stage furnishings. When Clacton UDC purchased the building, the floor was reconcreted and the stage extended over the orchestra pit. From 1989, the theatre again became an all-year-round venue.   *KW/MS*

CLEETHORPES
North East Lincolnshire

Empire
Alexandra Parade
Other names
Alexandra
Original architect
?1896   J.R. Withers
Current use Amusement arcade
Capacity originally c.800

The building appears sound, if a little run down, in its present guise of amusement arcade. Inside it is an open area of false ceilings and black featureless walls both garishly decorated with pink and blue neon. Its opening date has been given variously as 1889 and 1896. It was later run in tandem with the Theatre Royal, with the Empire possibly getting the better shows. Seasons of variety, repertory, even opera featured on its stage.

An old undated photograph shows a simple proscenium arch framed by pillars and with arches on either side. The balcony (only one can be seen but there was probably a second) was possibly square – the slips were certainly straight with two rows of seats at right angles to the stage. The proscenium opening was not wide and probably did not survive into cinema days. The sight lines from the slips must have been poor.

Apart from windows being blanked out the exterior has changed little, being an unremarkable Victorian facade with seven windows on each of the first and second floors. A central gable is framed by vaguely Moorish pillars. A canopy extends along the width of this and other properties in the terrace. At the rear is a small, low, fly tower in brick.   *IG*

Pier Pavilion
Promenade
Original architect
　　1875　Unknown
Later works
　　1907　Unknown: rebuilt nearer land-
　　　　　ward end
Current use Disco
Capacity　(was) 500

The present building is a replacement of the original 1875 pavilion at the seaward end of a longer pier, which was partly demolished after the Second World War, leaving the present theatre at the end of a short, unimpressive stump of a pier.

It was a flat-floored hall, barrel-roofed with no flying facilities. It had been modernised and added to over the years – together with long periods of disuse. It is now a disco and unrecognisable as a former theatre.

Very exposed site – structure in need of repair at time of inspection. *IG*

CLEVEDON
North Somerset

Curzon ★
Old Church Road
Other names
　　1920　The Picture House
　　1945　Maxine
Original architect
　　1912　Victor Cox
Later works
　　1913/14　Unknown: enlarged
　　1920/22　Victor Cox: built new cinema
　　　　　　over old
　　later　Unknown: box fronts and
　　　　　organ removed
Listed　Grade II
Current use Cinema
Capacity　c.420

The first cinema, constructed in 1912, was built by Victor Cox. It seated 200, enlarged eighteen months later to seat 389.

Between 1920 and 1922, a new cinema with a tearoom was constructed over the old one, also at first floor. Later, a parade of shops was designed underneath, incorporating much of the first cinema space. The cinema had stage facilities, a dressing-room block at prompt side, with connecting door, fly gallery and grid.

Modern alterations have concealed, rather than removed, the old finishes. The auditorium and its balcony are intact, save for the box fronts and the organ which were removed some years ago. A false ceiling now extends from

the balcony front to the proscenium. From the fly gallery, approached from the passageway which served the side boxes, can be seen the stage and extent of the proscenium. The deading cleats establish the position of the original bars. The grid survives. It should be possible to restore to theatre use.

The interior decoration is extremely uncommon in that all of what appears to be plaster decoration, including the ceiling, is comprised of pressed metal plates of various dimensions. This type of decorative lining, common in North America, is rarely found in Britain. Only one other fragmentery surviving example (a cinema) is known.

Good main elevation with five-bay centre, looking rather like a market hall with broad gabled outer bays, boldly arched at first floor.   *SM*

COALVILLE
Leicestershire

Regal ★
Jackson Street
Other names
　　1910-33　Olympia
　　1963　Casino Bingo
　　1992　Flutters Bingo
Original architect
　　1910　Thomas Ignatius McCarthy
　　　　　(Coalville)
Later works
　　1933　Archibald Hurley Robinson:
　　　　　completely rebuilt as ciné-vari-
　　　　　ety
Current use Bingo
Capacity　est. 800

The Regal's predecessor was the Olympia which opened in 1910 as a skating rink but within three months stage shows were being presented.

Having a flat floor, it was capable of serving a dual role. Many professional and amateur companies played there during its 23 year life. It had a small squat fly tower.

No trace of the old Olympia now remains. The present brick-faced building dates from 1933. It consists of a square tower on the right-hand side, the top of which is higher than the rest of the rectangular block. The auditorium is parallel to the street. The stalls are steeply raked, giving very good sight lines. Wide proscenium opening 11.2m (36ft 8in). The stage, used frequently by local amateurs until the 1960s, and occasionally by professional artists, is shallow with a recess in the rear wall. There is no grid as such. A series of pulleys hang from beams about two feet below the stage roof. Two dressing rooms occupy the upstage part of each wing. The Regal still has the ambience of a theatre, although it needs much backstage improvement. It is unlikely to host stage shows again in the immediate future, despite the fact it is the most suitable building in the area for this purpose, which seems a pity when local organisations are pressing for a civic theatre of some kind. One cannot imagine there being sufficient private or public cash to provide a new building with proper stage facilities.   *TB*

COCKERMOUTH
Cumbria

Grand
Station Road
Original architect
　　1915　Unknown
Current use Veterinary surgery/retail
Capacity　originally c.750

Cockermouth, Grand (Ian Grundy)

The facade is in excellent condition. Three major bays, all channel-rusticated, the outer slightly advanced as pavilions flanking the pedimented centre with the name 'Grand Theatre' in Art Nouveau lettering. Ground floor with shopfront glazing. No fly tower. The interior is now subdivided. Circle steppings remain (6–7 rows) but floor at balcony level inserted. Proscenium arch remains (plasterwork stripped) and stalls floor levelled, orchestra pit filled and stage levelled. Original barrel-vault ceiling with ornate ventilation ducts intact. Judging by photographs taken during conversion to shop, the stage was deep, but no flying. Orchestra pit. Four dressing rooms.   *IG*

COLCHESTER
Essex

Hippodrome ★★★
131 High Street
Other names
    Grand Palace of Varieties
    Grand Theatre of Varieties
Original architect
    1905   J.W. Start, possibly with Ben Kirk
Later works
    1987   Stanley Bragg Partnership: converted to leisure centre/retail
    1988   Stanley Bragg Partnership: new entrance canopy
Listed   **Grade II**
Current use **Discotheque**
Capacity   **est. 900**

The suggestion that this building is on the site of an 1880s' theatre rebuilt by Frank Matcham after a fire in 1889 cannot at present be confirmed, although he is known to have worked on theatres in Colchester. Built in 1905 by local architect J.W. Start, possibly with Ben Kirk and with Paul Hoffman as consultant.

Despite later alterations as a cinema, a mixed-use leisure centre and, in 1995, a startling redecoration as a discotheque, including much intrusive lighting, the building survives as an exceptionally fine example of a medium-sized Edwardian theatre. A fire damaged the stage area in 1972, ending cinema use. This area behind the proscenium now houses a bar, with restaurant above and kitchens behind.

The intimate auditorium has two well-curved balconies of nine and ten rows each, partly supported on slender cast-iron columns. Each balcony terminates in two bow-fronted boxes on either side.

The boxes are divided by squat columns linked by arches - ogee at the lower level and elliptical above. The rectangular proscenium has a moulded frame richly decorated with foliated plasterwork. Over the top of the proscenium is a big cartouche supported by reclining female figures. This forms the focal point of the remarkable ceiling which is in the shape of a huge shell, its ribs radiating outwards and upwards from the cartouche.

The busy Edwardian Baroque facade makes a pleasing contribution to the varied frontages of the fine High Street. It is in red brick with ample stone dressings and of an oddly asymmetrical design - three main bays and three storeys, with a centrepiece surmounted by a curved pediment with the name 'Grand Theatre' in the tympanum, above three blind oeil-de-boeuf openings. Three windows to each of the first and second floors, divided by pilasters. But the bays flanking this centre, although of broadly similar design, are of unequal width - the bay to the right being a squashed-up version of that to the left.

Although a repertory theatre (the Mercury) has been built in Colchester, the Hippodrome is, nevertheless, still capable of restoration, and could well house medium-scale touring productions, concerts, amateur groups, etc.   *CB/JE/SM*

Odeon
Crouch Street
Other names
    1931–74   Regal
Original architect
    1931   Cecil Masey
Later works
    1974   Unknown: tripled
Current use **Multi-screen cinema**
Capacity   **c.1200 (prior to subdivision)**

One of the earliest atmospheric designs in the UK, in Mediterranean style, the auditorium was given the romantic appeal of an Italian courtyard. As in the Walthamstow Granada design, the facade has a central entrance bay, with high arched window above (and in this case a very high, almost Gothic apex) and side bays at either side in Italian style with balconied windows and shops at ground-floor level.

The theatre was fully equipped with stage facilities and dressing rooms, café and bar areas. Fire in 1944 closed building for three months, after which it was refurbished. It was tripled in 1974, ending stage use.   *SM*

Playhouse ★
St John's Street
Other names
    1929   Garrison Theatre
    1962   ABC
    Coral Bingo
    Gala Bingo
Original architect
    1929   John Fairweather
Later works
    1932   C.J. Foster: gallery removed; balcony enlarged; reseated and redesigned for cinema
    c.1981   Unknown: converted to bingo
    1994   Tuffin, Ferraby and Taylor: converted to (Wetherspoon's) pub
Current use **Pub**
Capacity   **est. 975**

The Playhouse opened in 1929 as a garrison theatre and originally had a three-tier interior. The building is on the slope of St John's Street on a corner site, so that exits and small foyer on the lower side form almost an additional half level. The theatre is three storeys high, red

Colchester, Playhouse

brick faced. The entrance elevation on St John's Street is symmetrical with stucco or stone-faced ground floor, the entrance bay emphasised and rising above the height of the wings with a stone entablature and brick parapet. The centre is advanced with paired windows at first and second floor. At first-floor level to the right of the entrance is a large semi-circular window. The doors and windows at entrance and exit level seem to date from 1932.

In 1932 the interior was redesigned in two tiers and modernisation took place for cinema. Recently sympathetically converted to a pub, it is this interior which may be enjoyed today. Huge ceiling dome with decorative centrepiece. The balcony is deep with curved front ending in two round-headed boxes at each side which look almost directly into the auditorium, their fronts all decorated with matching wreath medallions and anthemion ornaments. A deep decorative frieze is supported by four pilasters at either side of the balcony, and this continues over the proscenium which is plain and square, with a slightly fluted cove moulding and a small coat-of-arms at the centre. This frieze, however, continues only to the rear of the circle, leaving the ceiling to the former third tier plainly panelled, suggesting a previous partition for projection/lighting, or a bar area here. The stalls area is now flat to accommodate dining, etc., but the stage remains and is decorated with a set, as if for a play.

Reconversion to a theatre would be possible if pub use ceased, but any future plan to reopen a proscenium theatre in Colchester would have to consider the Hippodrome first. *SM*

Repertory

High Street
Other names
   Albert Hall
   Corn Exchange Cinema
Original architect
   1845   Rafael Brandon: as Corn
          Exchange
Later works
   1925   Borough Architect?: converted
          to assembly hall and art
          gallery
   1937   Duncan, Clarke and Beckett:
          converted to small theatre
Current use Co-operative Bank
Capacity   est. 360

The Corn Exchange was built with a public hall (St George's Hall) at rear, used as a lecture hall. In 1925, the main space, now known as the Albert Hall, was converted to an assembly room for concerts, etc., and art gallery. When Robert Digby founded the local repertory company, the hall was converted to a small theatre, incorporating the rear hall for stage space, etc. This arrangement lasted until 1972 when the repertory company moved to the new Mercury Theatre. The building now houses a bank.

The facade is in Classical style, single storey with attic. Central bay of three-arched entrance doors with two Doric columns between; outer bays, each with tall round-headed window. *SM*

COLNE
Lancashire

Pendle Hippodrome ★
Newmarket Street
Original architect
   1914   R.S. Pilling
Current use Theatre
Capacity   500

Built as a ciné-variety house, at first with much stage entertainment, but gradually dominated by cinema use until closure in mid 1960s. Subsequently used for bingo until 1975, when it was taken over, in very poor condition, by a group of amateur societies who have painstakingly repaired, restored and improved it. Since reopening, they have presented over 250 performances a year with volunteer staff. They receive more requests for hiring than their limited resources can cope with.

In a side street, near the Town Hall. Simple ashlar-gabled facade with two round-arched, rusticated entrance doorways. A long, narrow auditorium with single end balcony of six rows. Circle front with fibrous plaster swags, shields and flowers. Three panels on side walls each side carry 'crossed flaming torch' light fittings rescued from the Palace Hippodrome, Nelson. Vaulted ceiling panelled in wood. Deep proscenium with adequate stage and flying facilities.

A remarkably successful effort by a local group which has already rebuilt the dressing-room block and acquired the stable range from the next-door pub to provide workshops and storage. *CB/IG*

Colne, Pendle Hippodrome (Ian Grundy)

COLWYN BAY
Conwy

Theatr Colwyn
Abergele Road
Other names
  1890s Public Hall
           Rialto
           The Repertory
  1959 Prince of Wales
Original architect
  1895 Unknown
Current use Repertory theatre
Capacity 443

Early use was as a minstrel or concert-party hall, now a producing theatre. Built in red brick with the principal facade on the Abergele Road, the entrance to the theatre lobby takes up most of the width of the narrow central bay of this facade, sheltered by a small glazed modern canopy. Above, at first-floor level, is a large central window beneath a gable in the centre of which is a small panel of decorative brick in which the words PUBLIC HALL appear in relief. The two broader, outer bays each contain at ground-floor level what appears to have been a shopfront beneath a shallow arch.

The auditorium is raked with no balcony. There is a shallow, arched ceiling. The upper border of the proscenium is curved. Flying height is limited to 4.27m (14ft) and cloths are either rolled or tumbled. Wing space is severely restricted by the passage beneath the stage of as many as four staircases, the bulkheads above them taking up a great deal of space. The two downstage sets of stairs lead to emergency exits: the two upstage sets to sub-stage dressing rooms. *TR*

CONSETT
Durham

Empire
Front Street
Other names
  Empire Palace
Original architect
  1912/3 Jos W. Wardle
Later works
  1920 Howard Hill: new circle
           installed
  1929 Murray and Hurd: operating
           box installed
  1966 Unknown: converted for cine-
           ma and bingo
Current use Theatre and cinema
Capacity 535

The Empire was probably a ciné-variety from about 1912 to the late 1920s, thereafter a cinema. It is now owned by the local authority and again has mixed use as a cinema and theatre.

Pleasant, rather domestic-looking, rendered facade with three bay centre piece of two storeys, articulated by slender, superimposed Doric demi-columns. Pedimental gable over. Intimate auditorium with one balcony. No fly tower. *CB/DW/IG*

Globe ★★
Front Street
Other names
  New
  Theatre Royal Picture House
  Theatre Royal Cinema
Original architect
  1895 William S. Shell
Later works
  1915 J. Eltringham: gallery removed
           and circle altered
  1916 Murray and Hurd: operating
           box installed
  1956 Unknown: pub extended into
           ground floor
Current use Working Men's Club
Capacity c.600 (prior to 1956 conversion)

Replaced the Theatre in Trafalgar Street. Accommodation: stalls, dress circle, pit, circle gallery and amphitheatre. Gallery removed in 1915 and circle improved. Boxes removed and replaced by two canted alcoves with panelled sides and tops in a pagoda style. Reopened in 1916 as the Theatre Royal Cinema, but was not a success and after a few months closed to reopen as the Globe Theatre. Continued until c.1926

Local rifle and small-arms shooting range set up in auditorium until 1947 when troops were billeted there. In 1956 Vaux breweries extended the Freemasons Arms next door, underdrawing the circle with a ceiling and removing the stage to create a dance and banqueting room. Above this false ceiling the Globe Theatre remains. *DW*

COVENTRY

Coventry Theatre ★★
Hales Street
Other names
  1937 New Hippodrome
  1979 Apollo
  1981 Gala and Hippodrome
  1985 Granada
Original architect
  1937 W. Stanley Hattrell and
           Partners (Coventry)

Later works
before 1954 Unknown: seven extra
           dressing rooms added
  1986 Gould Singleton and Partners
           (Birmingham): converted to
           bingo
Current use Bingo
Capacity c.2100

This large variety theatre was constructed as a replacement for and almost next to the 1906 Hippodrome whose name it took, with Trinity Street separating the two.

The exterior is a plain almost windowless stucco-faced box. The interior is still theatrical in character, but all stalls seating has been replaced with tables and chairs and a wide stairway has been constructed on stage right wall of the auditorium to allow access from the stage to the dress circle. The upper circle overhangs the last six rows of the dress circle. The gallery is now disused. The sight lines in all parts of the house are very good.

The interior is rather bland. The ceiling curves down towards the top of the proscenium. A fluted pattern surrounds the proscenium opening and this design is repeated along the two balcony fronts. Originally there were two boxes each side, which were little more than extensions to the sides of the dress-circle balcony front. The two on stage right have now been incorporated in the walkway approach to the new stairway linking the dress circle with the stage and stalls. Although many alterations have taken place, including the obliteration of the

Coventry Theatre (Bruce Peter Collection)

dress-circle boxes on stage left, this is still essentially a theatre and it would be possible to reconvert it. Large touring companies are unable to use the Belgrade and, plain though it is, this building could be resurrected to house such productions.   *TB*

CRADLEY HEATH
Worcestershire

Royal
High Street/ Bank Street
Other names
   Royal Electric Theatre
Original architect
   1913   Unknown
Later works
   1918   Unknown: new stage and
          dressing rooms added
   1938   Unknown: original auditorium
          decor covered by cladding
Current use Disused
Capacity   est. 500

Opened as the Royal Electric Theatre. Present stage and dressing rooms added in 1918. The interior was substantially altered in 1938.

A ciné-variety with its original broad gabled red brick front to Bank Street relieved with sparse terracotta ornament; 'Royal Theatre' in panel at first-floor level; above this, four oval windows in thin pedimented surrounds; thin bands across gable and lantern finials at springings and apex.

The auditorium is subdivided and its original features are no longer discernible. The stage is used for works to motor vehicles. A modest and unpromising survival but it is interesting to reflect that this is one of the few purpose-built theatres left in the Black Country. It has the benefit of a deep stage and full flying.   *TB*

CREWE
Cheshire

Lyceum ★★★
Heath Street
Other names
   1900   The Opera House
   1909   Opera House/Opera Scope
   1910   New Theatre
   1960s   Crewe Theatre
Original architect
   1889   Alfred Darbyshire
Later works
   1893   Darbyshire?: redecorated and
          modernised (unspecified
          works)

   1911   Albert Winstanley: interior
          rebuilt after fire
   1994   RHWL: modernised and
          extended
Listed   Grade II
Current use Theatre
Capacity   693

The Lyceum Theatre, Crewe, is the only surviving pre-First World War theatre in Cheshire.

In 1881, Henry Taylor, a printer and a keen amateur dramatist, went into partnership with Thomas Cliff, a local farmer and landowner who had previously acquired the old Catholic Church in Heath Street. Together they converted this into the first Lyceum which opened in 1882. The Crewe Lyceum Theatre Buildings Company (Ltd) was formed in 1885 to build a new theatre on the church site and the adjoining graveyard. This theatre built to designs by Alfred Darbyshire opened in 1889, accommodating 1250. It suffered a serious fire in 1910 and was substantially rebuilt by Albert Winstanley, went into partnership with Thomas Cliff, a local farmer and landowner who had previously acquired the old Catholic Church in Heath Street. Together they converted this into the first Lyceum which opened in 1882. The Crewe Lyceum Theatre Buildings Company (Ltd) was formed in 1885 to build a new theatre on the church site and the adjoining graveyard. This theatre built to designs by Alfred Darbyshire opened in 1889, accommodating 1250. It suffered a serious fire in 1910 and was substantially rebuilt by Albert Winstanley. It is his interior which is seen today.

In 1994 major improvements were made by taking in an adjoining site to the left. This provided extensive new facilities, including a large foyer, restaurant, kitchens and bars. The 1994 addition also incorporated English Touring Theatre's headquarters.

The facade of the old theatre is not much altered. It is quite plain, in red brick, a broad semi-circular arch filling the gable, with the tympanum carrying the date 1911 and the name of the the-

atre. To the left, the new wing is also quite plain, but rendered with a channelled base and a simple cornice below the parapet. The main feature of the old facade is echoed in a full height, semi-circular arched, glazed bay containing the new main entrance under a sharply tilted, shaped glass canopy. The name LYCEUM is repeated in bold serifed letters in the parapet band. The interior of the new wing is crisp and undemonstrative, with ceiling troughs containing lighting.

The pleasing, intimate qualities of Winstanley's auditorium have been well displayed in the 1994 refurbishment. It comprises stalls, dress circle and gallery with slips to two superimposed stage boxes topped by onion-domed canopies, flanked by little Jacobean-style obelisk finials. Unusually generous high-relief moulded plasterwork (cartouches with reclining maidens and musical instruments) on box and balcony fronts. The elliptical proscenium arch has plasterwork of similar quality. The safety curtain, based on an earlier design ('for thine especial safety') is also inscribed with the name of the theatre. A rare example of a gas sunburner can be seen at the centre of the circular, deeply coved ceiling which is decorated with heavy scrolled brackets and garlands. The old benched gallery has been reseated with tip-up seats. A forestage lift provides an orchestra pit when required.

At the time of writing further improvements were being proposed, including the raising of the fly tower.
CB/KW/SM

Crewe, Lyceum

CROMER
Norfolk

Pier Pavilion
Cromer Pier, Promenade
Original architect
   1901   Douglass and Arnott (engi-
            neers)
Later works
   1905   Unknown: roofed over
   1912   Unknown: stage built
   1969   Unknown: front of house
            enclosed
Listed   Grade II
Current use Seasonal variety theatre
Capacity   443

The Pavilion was built first in 1901 as an open-topped area with a bandstand, then roofed over in 1905, as seen today. About 1912, a stage and proscenium replaced the bandstand. In 1969, a front of house was created by screening off rear of auditorium; in 1978 the present seating arrangements were installed.
   The Pavilion is built off the main pier structure with the uniquely located Cromer lifeboat station upon a separate structure immediately seaward. The Pavilion itself appears to be, in its essentials, the original of 1905. It is an iron framework of three bays by three bays, having lower perimeter stanchions and four taller internal columns. Between these inner and outer members are segmental quarter trusses with the main roof formed by flat lattice trusses between the main columns, incorporating a large central clerestory. The extent of the building is enlarged by shallow, single-storey extension standing beyond the framework thereby widening the auditorium, providing for ancillary accommodation and forming part of the entrance foyer. The four corners of the building are cut back on the diagonal. The curved lines of the roof affirm the fin-de-siècle (despite the date) origins of the design.
   Externally the walls are now rendered and the roof is covered with a propri-etary lead-like material; internally, the walls are plastered and the roof is lined above the exposed ironwork with matchboard. The rear six rows of seating are raked and along the side walls are what appear to be original timber benches. The entrance foyer and bar area have been formed by a screen wall run across the rear of the auditorium. The stage is simple with a segmental proscenium arch. The auditorium is dec-orated predominently in a red terracotta which makes it warm and intimate.   *JL*

Town Hall Theatre
Prince of Wales Road
Original architect
   1890   George J. Skipper
Listed   Grade II
Current use Hall disused (retail in front
            block)
Capacity   c.750

The term 'town hall' in this instance is equivalent to 'village hall' rather than local government premises. Built in 1890 in red brick in Queen Anne style, it is a free-standing building, comprising a front block of two storeys and an enter-tainment hall at the rear. The front block is entered by a central arched doorway within a slightly advanced pedimented pavilion bay which is flanked by single-window bays. Between first and ground floors a band of carved brick coats of arms. The hall is a single-storey structure at the rear, its eight bays marked by but-tresses and covered by a pitched tiled roof. Each bay contains a tall window. Flat floor within; a balcony approached from the front block; a flat ceiling with boldly compartmented ornamental plas-terwork.
   It is said that the stage was removed at some time during the hall's commer-cial life. Owned by wine merchants 1963–85; bought by Cromer Property Corporation 1991 and let to Co-op, who moved out in 1997. Building restored externally 1994 with English Heritage grant aid. A handsome building much appreciated locally when it was in enter-tainment use.   *JL*

CROOK
Durham

Empire
12 South Street (Market Place)
Other names
      Empire Palace
Original architect
   1910   Henry Gibson and Pascal J.
            Stienlet
Current use Shop
Capacity   est. 700

Facade divided in three bays, the central bay flanked by rusticated pillars with Ionic capitals, contains the entrance. Semi-circular window at first floor. The outer bays each contain double doors. The ground and first floor are now painted whilst the second storey, appar-ently added at a later date, is plain brick.
   Internally a barrel-vaulted ceiling with single curving balcony with no boxes. The balcony front still intact with car-

touche and scrollwork. The small prosce-nium still retains its fibrous plasterwork, the arch gently curved with a central car-touche. The bingo equipment remains on the stage; the front of house is an autoparts shop. The balcony tier is intact though damaged, and the whole could be restored though it would require a great deal of work, and is probably too isolated geographically to make such a proposition likely.   *DW*

DARLINGTON

Civic ★★★
Parkgate
Other names
      New Hippodrome
      Hippodrome
      Palace Theatre
Original architect
   1907   G. Gordon Hoskins (built
            under the supervision of
            G.F. Ward of Owen and Ward)
Later works
   1990   Unknown: major extension;
            gallery restored to use
   1994   Unknown: conservatory bar
            added at stalls level
Current use Theatre
Capacity   901

When built, this theatre curiously carried two names – Hippodrome on the Borough Road frontage and Palace Theatre on the Parkgate/Borough Road corner. It became the Civic Theatre in 1966, having been acquired by the local authority some years earlier.
   The principal front is practically as built, red brick with terracotta dressings in a carefree Baroque manner, the entrance pavilion symmetrical, with Ionic pilasters at first-floor level, carry-ing a scrolly gable and semi-circular lunette with exaggerated voussoirs. Over the gable, a pyramidal roof with iron cresting. At the rear, the 1990s extensions are in plain brick with light brick dressings and a corner tower, like a bastion.
   The auditorium has two balconies with delicate plaster ornament and a sin-gle pedimented box on either side at 1st balcony level. Rectangular proscenium with a thin spirally enriched roll mould-ing and a central cartouche. Circular ceiling set in a square with good plaster ornament in the corners.
   The reopening of the long-isolated gallery and the extensions containing bars, etc., have greatly improved this well-preserved theatre. The present, aggressively contrasty decorations and

Darlington, Civic (Ian Grundy)

the rather mean pelmet and drapes in the auditorium, however, fail to make the best of a very pleasing interior. *CB/JE*

DEAL
Kent

Astor
Stanhope Street
Other names
   1909   Stanhope Hall
   1911   Winter Gardens
Original architect
   1909   Unknown
Later works
   1945   Unknown: extended
Current use **Multi-purpose hall**
Capacity   c.275

A multi-purpose flat-floored venue with a shallow proscenium. The floor area was increased in 1945 by more than 50% when an extension was built to one side. It is used for amateur productions, bingo, concerts, dances, aerobics and youth theatre. *KW*

Globe ★
Royal Marines Barracks, Canada Road
Original architect
1862 or 1863 Unknown
Current use **Disused**
Capacity   c.450

This is a mid-Victorian garrison theatre, free-standing at the extreme south-west corner of the Royal Marines Barracks and bearing the same name as its sister RM theatres in Plymouth and Portsmouth. It was built in the early 1860s, probably as

a more convenient replacement for the playhouse of 1798, which stood in High Street and was converted to a shop (demolished c.1912).

It is rectangular box with gables at either end and a loft and lantern over the stage. It has a restrained but handsome front in stock brick with red brick bands and steps up to five segmental arched openings of which nos 2 and 4 are wider and contain the main entrances. The narrow outer openings are set between brick piers which rise the full height of the front and are linked at the top by semi-circular red brick arches with keystones. Three flat-headed sash windows at centre first-floor level and above them, in the step-corbelled gable, a big circular window with four keystones.

Auditorium with end balcony with plain face and wood soffit supported on iron columns. Raked stalls with plain side walls and shallow curved proscenium arch springing from console brackets. The side walls splay in at the stage end

Deal, Globe (John Earl Collection)

and it seems possible that there was originally a deep apron to the stage with doors in the splays on either side. The auditorium has certainly suffered some alteration, but it would be easy to restore and would look a great deal more attractive with sympathetic redecoration. There is good head room under the stage.

The theatre has been caught up in, and has consequently been threatened by, the uncertainties over the future of the (now vacated) Royal Marines School of Music. Its position would, however, make it perfectly possible to separate it from the rest of the complex and exploit its theatre potential. *JE*

Royal
King Street
Other names
   Oddfellows Hall
   Theatre Royal
Original architect
   1890   Unknown
Later works
   1934   H.W. Coussens: interior remodelled
   1981   Unknown: subdivided
Current use **Amusement arcade/snooker hall**
Capacity   c.500 (prior to subdivision)

Built as an Oddfellows Hall for the Palmerston Lodge. Used as a theatre from 1892 and later given the name Theatre Royal. In 1934, the Hastings architect H.W. Coussens remodelled interior, replacing the wooden balcony with steel and concrete, and covering the open roof trusses with fibrous plaster. Later in use as a cinema, it became a bingo hall between 1961 and 1963, before reverting to cinema.

In 1981, the interior was subdivided, the stalls area converted to an amusement arcade and the extended circle area to a snooker hall. At this time, the stage with set of substage machinery was removed. The building remains in good condition and some original features (and many from 1934) remain. *KW*

DERBY

Grand
Babbington Lane
Other names
   1959   Tiffanys
   1992   Ritzy
Original architect
   1886   Oliver Essex: original building and rebuilding after fire

Later works
1892 Unknown: safety curtain
installed; whole of proscenium
strengthened to take weight
1893 Frank Matcham: new entrance
canopy; auditorium altered
1900 Frank Matcham: auditorium
reconstructed; other improvements and additions
1959 Unknown: auditorium rebuilt
as dance hall
Current use Facade only

Only the main 1886 facade survives. The remainder was completely reconstructed as a dance hall in 1959. A symmetrical design, stuccoed, and of nine bays and three storeys with an attic storey above the entablature. Wider end bays have giant Corinthian pilasters to first and second floors framing tripartite windows. Three central bays also articulated by pilasters with oeil-de-boeuf windows above in the attic.

The 1959 dance hall has subsequently been converted to a 'themed' pub. *CB/TB*

Hippodrome ★★
Green Lane
Original architect
1914 Marshall and Tweedy
Later works
1930 Unknown: converted to cine-
ma
Listed Grade II
Current use Bingo
Capacity est. 1800

A large variety theatre. Red brick with terracotta dressings. Advanced end bays, with recessed banded corners. Corner entrance. Slated hipped roof. Stalls below street level with two, deep, slightly curved balconies above. The 1930 alterations seem to have been fairly limited, mainly the small single boxes on either side at 1st balcony level. They are framed by giant pilasters carrying a serpentine pediment. Rectangular proscenium surmounted by a big segment-headed panel framing a garland. Flat ceiling with concentric circular moulded panels in rectangular frame. Rich Baroque plasterwork on balcony fronts, proscenium, ceiling, etc., rather coarse in detail.

A theatre with real potential, well situated in the city centre, it could be readily restored to provide Derby with a touring theatre. Listed in 1996 after a long delay in reaching a decision. *CB/TB*

Derby, Hippodrome (Ted Bottle)

Theatre Royal ★
Bold Lane
Other names
1865 became Gospel Hall
Original architect
1773 Unknown
Listed Grade II
Current use Disused
Capacity originally c.600

Converted from a former malthouse in 1773. The theatre declined in the face of competition from other entertainment houses and closed in 1864, reopening as a Gospel Hall in 1865, with an intermediate floor inserted. At this time the Green Room fireplace was said to be one of the last relics of the old theatre. Later became a magistrates court, but disused and shabby by 1992.

The basic brick shell and pitched roof remain largely intact. The stuccoed facade of three wide bays and two storeys has been altered - the three arched entrances removed and replaced by a strip of plate glass windows, and the arched windows above lengthened downwards. Straight cornice and parapet. Although now much pulled about, this is nevertheless a valuable surviving example of an C18 playhouse. *CB/TB*

Trocadero
London Road
Original architect
1934 W.E. and W.S. Trent
Later works
1974 Unknown: tripled
1983 Unknown: altered for bingo,
retaining circle for cinema

Current use Disused
Capacity est. 2400

Built as a big Gaumont Palace with full stage facilities, a 13.4m (44ft) proscenium and nine large dressing rooms. As late as 1960–72, it was staging one-night pop concerts and occasional touring productions but it was tripled in 1974.

Three-bay facade, the outer bays red brick with horizontal ribs, the centre bay with narrow faience pilasters. Top storey has sculptured reliefs of harlequinade characters by Newbury A. Trent. Fly tower.

The auditorium floor has been levelled with the stage. Some good Art Deco ornament, but now completely concealed by a false ceiling. The original size of the auditorium would make it suitable only for large-scale musicals and, for this purpose, the stage is too small. If another theatre is envisaged in Derby it is far more important to rescue the former Hippodrome. *TB*

DERRY

Artillery Street Theatre
Artillery Street
Original architect
1795 Unknown
Later works
1838 Unknown: converted to church
1879 Unknown: converted into
Synod Hall
Current use Synod Hall

The site of the 1795 theatre is on the corner of London Street and Artillery Street just inside the city walls and close to the Protestant Cathedral.

The theatre (the first in Derry) was converted into a Presbyterian Church in 1838 with a plastered and pedimented facade to Artillery Street (which may have been the entrance side of the theatre) which is still standing.

In 1879 the church was made into the Synod Hall for the Church of Ireland with the hall on the first floor. Part of original theatre shell may still remain as part of the present structure but it is impossible to trace anything definite. *RMcK*

St Columb's Theatre ★
Orchard Street
Original architect
1886 Croome and Toye
Later works
1990 Martin O'Kane of H.M.D.
Architects: restored and refur-
bished

Listed   **Grade B**
Current use **Theatre and community centre**
Capacity   **872**

The building, originally a Temperance Hall with reading and recreation rooms, is situated on the steep hill below the city centre: therefore the two floors at the front slide down into three floors at the back. The imposing Italianate three-bay entrance front is faced in ashlar sandstone and the centre bay breaks forward, fronted by the balconied portico which extends over a wide flight of steps. Walls at ground-floor level are rusticated, the tripartite windows each side of the entrance are pedimented and all of the first-floor windows, set between Corinthian pilasters, have semi-circular heads. Above a heavy frieze cornice and balustrading is a pedimented centrepiece with statues of Erin, Temperance and Vulcan perched on top (sculptor C.W. Harrison, Dublin).

The fine entrance hall has an air of belonging to a civic building: plaster panelling on the ceiling, marbled Corinthian pilasters, marble paving, oak doors and dado. Through the entrance hall is the way into the auditorium and a wide staircase leads up to a foyer restaurant, a reception room and the entrances to the curved balcony.

The auditorium floor has a slight rake and removable chairs are laid out with a central aisle. Five tall, semi-circular headed windows on each side wall are set between Corinthian pilasters supporting a frieze and cornice. The springing at each end of the segmental barrel-vaulted ceiling terminates in quarter-circle coving. Generally the decorative plasterwork is of a high quality. Worthy of note is the Adamesque screen with delicate pilasters and panels round the segmental-headed proscenium opening, over which is a large inset painting of St Columb preaching from a boat. Single iron-fronted balcony. The pleasant colour scheme is of warm grey with off-white details and the centre of the ceiling is terracotta. Glass chandeliers and crimson curtains with well-designed pelmets and ropes introduce a welcome theatrical swagger.

The small stage has a neat little orchestra pit and there is a proposal to increase the stage area by moving the proscenium wall forward by one bay. All the dressing rooms are behind the stage on three floors with a service lift. At ground level there is a large bar/coffee room and a small cinema (120)

with its own entrance.

Derry with its much acclaimed dramatic and musical tradition does need a theatre like St Columb's and may still continue to do so after the long-awaited Civic Theatre becomes a reality. *RMcK*

DEWSBURY
Kirklees (West Yorkshire)

Playhouse
Crackenedge Lane
Other names
    ABC
Original architect
    1931   Robert Cromie
Current use **Disused**
Capacity   **est. 1850**

A vast cinema situated in a side road of the town centre. The Playhouse had a large stage and featured quite extensive professional use until closure in 1970. Latterly this was mainly pop concerts, but initially many variety stars did odd nights or full weeks here.

The wide facade is in three major bays, the centre one over the small entrance canopy, and, above this, a blind, fluted attic.The outer bays have tall narrow windows lighting the stairs. Above the stairs, windows are masks looking rather like a combination of comedy/tragedy and lions! The side elevation is bland.

Stage access and dressing rooms are at the rear of the building in a minor road and, because of the slope of the land, are at a high level, maybe second floor.

The auditorium, on two levels, is sparsely ornamented. The ceiling contains grilles and the rectangular proscenium is stepped down in four ribbed stages. On either side of the ante-proscenium is a rectangular recessed niche, which probably contained modelled figures originally.

After many years of bingo the Playhouse is now boarded up and unused although it appears secure and in good condition. *IG*

DINNINGTON
Rotherham

Lyric
Other names
    Picturedrome
Original architect
    1910   Unknown
Current use **Theatre**
Capacity   **300**

Red brick, three-bay facade with gauged brick and terracotta crowning balustrade. Central entrance with flanking shops; residential flat over. Built in 1910 as a music hall, complete with fly tower (removed during the last war). Seating on one level only but balconies on three sides for technical staff. Open roof trusses and wooden panelled ceiling. Elaborate proscenium arch with Corinthian pilasters and a broken pediment over the flattened arch in the manner of the Dunfermline Opera House. The top part of the arch and the wooden ceiling are now hidden, but undamaged, by a false ceiling dating from the mid 1960s. The floor is now flat; a sprung dance floor was installed c.1920 but rostra are laid to form a rake for stage productions.

The Lyric had many ups and downs (including prosperity as a dance hall, closure, then use as a Salvation Army citadel) until 1962 when it was purchased by the local council. Since then many improvements have been made. In 1980 the Milner Lounge was added, used as a bar, meeting room and dressing room! It is now in need of further updating. Proposed improvements include new extended stage with tower, restoration of original ceiling and proscenium arch, disabled access and facilities, new dressing rooms, etc.

It is currently used for professional and amateur productions. *IG*

DONCASTER

Civic
Waterdale
Other names
    1922   Arcadia Cinema
    c.1949   Arts Centre
Original architect
    1921   Wilburn and Atkinson
Current use **Theatre**
Capacity   **500**

Originally built as a sports hall but, while still new, was redesigned by Edgar Wilburn and opened in 1922 as the Arcadia Cinema, used for ciné-variety. The raked auditorium is quite plain. Raked stage. There is no fly tower but 14 hemp sets. Never a particularly satisfactory theatre and generally accepted in 1990s as being near the end of its useful life. *KW*

Grand ★★

Station Road
Other names
  1899   New Grand Theatre and Opera
         House
Original architect
  1899   J.P. Briggs and Chapman
Listed   Grade II
Current use Disused
Capacity   est. 500

A decent and potentially valuable theatre that has been to the brink of the
abyss without, as yet, falling over.
  The Grand, built in 1899, may incorporate parts of the shell of an older (possibly circus) building. As originally built it
stood on a prominent site in a shopping
street facing the main railway station.
Old-fashioned (but comparatively
recent) city centre 'improvements' have,
however, robbed it of any sensible context. It is no longer in a street but on

Doncaster, Grand (Bob Williamson)

what now looks like the backlot of an
inward-looking shopping precinct. It still
faces the station but is separated from it
by a busy inner ring road which comes
so close that it has actually snipped off a
lower corner of the stage house. The
approach from the station (to the town
as well as the theatre) is now by way of
a repellent subway. It is a wonder that it
has survived at all and it was, in fact,
threatened with demolition even after it
was listed in 1994.
  An energetic local campaign eventually led to the reversal of a decision to
permit demolition, but the future
remains uncertain. There seems to be a
desire to strengthen the pedestrian link
from the railway station to the town and
a public transport interchange may be
created at this point, giving opportunities for improving both the public face
and the environment of the theatre.
  The facade, which, with an improved
setting, could again become a local
landmark, is three-storeyed, Baroque in
treatment with a complex rhythm of
bays articulated by coupled and single
pilasters and groupings of arched windows and doorways. There is a broken
segmental pediment over the three central bays.
  Intimate auditorium. Two well-curved
balconies with good plasterwork on fronts,
the upper gallery benched (some of the
least useful seating areas could be colonised
to improve front-of-house facilities). Single
pedimented boxes in otherwise plain side
walls, flanking a rectangular-framed 7.9m
(26ft) proscenium.
  Provided any replanning of the surroundings allows for the get-in and

other needs of the theatre, the Grand
could quite readily be restored and
reopened and would be infinitely better
than the present Civic Theatre. It could
serve both amateur and professional
drama and musical productions, small-
scale touring and other activities.
CB/JE

DONHEAD ST MARY
Wiltshire

Donhead Hall

Watery Lane
Original architect
  probably late C18 Unknown
Listed   Grade II
Current use Private theatre
Capacity   c.180

Donhead Hall is a manor built in the
early C18 for Godfrey Huckle, later Sir
Godfrey Kneller (died 1781). It is symmetrical in design, of two storeys with
attic and basement, in local greensand
ashlar, and set on a hillside in acres of
parkland with a lake, woods, etc.The Hall
has been attributed to Thomas Archer.
To the side of the house is a private theatre, probably of a later date. This building is faced with dressed limestone with
a tiled roof. It is single storey, in nine
bays with round-headed leaded iron
windows on one face and entrances
through high double round-arched
planked doors. A fireplace, since
removed, once dominated the opposite
wall. The theatre is flat-floored with a
platform stage (no traps) at one end
with a removable forestage. The rear
stage wall is panelled with two openings

for entrance/exit and a small rear-of-
stage leading to dressing rooms. The
ceiling is a panelled wood barrel-vault
with a void above, which allows house
lighting to be maintained. When gas
was replaced by electricity, lighting was
redesigned, with a series of small lights
in rows over the audience area.
  Under the ownership of Charles
McVeigh, who acquired Donhead Hall
c.1990, the theatre has undergone
restoration. Built for family theatricals
and for strolling troupes by invitation, it
is still much in use for family and estate
functions, private parties and for entertainment. Donhead Hall has always been
in private ownership and this historically
important survival has, therefore, hither-
to attracted little attention. *SM*

DOUGLAS
Isle of Man

Empire

Regent Street
Other names
  Empire Picture Hall
  Mona Theatre
  Bijou Theatre
Original architect
  1893   Unknown
Later works
  1913   George Kay and Sons: convert-
         ed to cinema
Current use Shops

In 1896, W. Rennison's submitted plans
show an auditorium at first-floor level,
consisting of a simple horseshoe tier supported by columns. Structural walls
remain with interior completely altered.

The large two-level space at first floor must have been part of the auditorium. *VG/DW*

Gaiety ★★★

Harris Promenade
Other names
pre 1893 Marina
    1893 Pavilion
Original architect
    1893 W.J. Rennison (as the Pavilion)
Later works
    1900 Frank Matcham: new theatre built within old shell
    1978 Victor Glasstone: major refurbishment
Current use Theatre
Capacity 896 (upper circle closed)

One of the best and most exciting of Matcham's surviving theatres. Excellent stuccoed facade – busy and festive. Three-storeyed towers with low pyramid roofs and Dormer pediments on each face, flanking a two-storeyed centre section with a columned loggia at first-floor

level, surmounted by a curved gable. Higher curved gable to rear wall of auditorium rising behind, with a small pediment on top.

Splendidly opulent auditorium, fitted by Matcham into the narrow shell of Rennison's 1893 Pavilion (and the even earlier Marina). Matcham incorporated the Marina's Belfast roof truss construction into the Gaiety reconstruction, as well as re-using a number of pieces of architectural ironmongery, including the supporting cast-iron column at the rear of the stalls. The reorganisation of the volume is masterly, producing an exquisite and well-equipped theatre from these old and extremely unpromising beginnings. Having never 'benefited' from a destructive modernisation programme the theatre is being methodically restored back to its original specification. Victor Glasstone's sympathetic refurbishment in 1978 started a process of restoration which has continued to an exemplary standard.

The theatre's stucco facade was

restored in 1995 and the words 'Gaiety Theatre and Opera House' highlighted in gold leaf. The original front canopy was restored to include leaded lights and four large lanterns mounted on the supporting columns of the canopy (lanterns very similar to the ones on the Buxton Opera House canopy).

The auditorium has two balconies, set well back from the stage, the lower one running into a range of three boxes either side with half-domed plaster canopies over, projecting beyond the face of the straight slips of the upper balcony. Rectangular proscenium opening set within a segment-headed frame. Painted tympanum with figures of putti. Magnificent ceiling with painted panels of the four seasons. The whole thickly encrusted with richly modelled Baroque plasterwork.

Since Glasstone's work, which included the re-creation of the rich box hangings and the fine printed wallpapers, the stalls barrier that once separated the front stalls from the pit has more recently been faithfully restored. The rare painted act drop by William Hemsley was restored in 1992 and is used on a regular basis. The 16-segment stained-glass rosary laylight, centred round the original gas sunburner, forms the central feature of the auditorium ceiling. It was restored in 1992 after the discovery of one of the shattered glass petals in the roof space above the auditorium. Lit from above, and enhanced with simulated gas effects from the sunburner, this feature completes one of the finest auditorium ceilings in the British Isles.

Outstanding restoration works include the gallery (which was retiered for cinema use in the 1950s) and front-of-house areas, e.g. dress-circle bar. The continuing restoration of the substage machinery is scheduled to be complete for the year 2000. It will include 2 bridges, 2 cuts with sloats, 2 corner traps, 1 grave trap and (uniquely) a fully working Corsican trap – once a common feature of the C19 English wood stage but now everywhere destroyed.

The theatre is owned by the Manx Government whose commitment to faithful restoration is particularly commendable. *DW/CB*

Villa Marina ★

Harris Promenade
Other names
    1913 The Villa Marina Kursaal
    1914 The Royal Hall

Douglas, Gaiety

Original architect
1913   Percy Robinson and W. Allen
Jones
Current use Civic Centre
Capacity   Main hall 1573/Garden room
320

The building, first known as the Kursaal, was commissioned by Douglas Corporation and was the subject of an architectural competition assessed by Professor Adshead of Liverpool University, opening in 1913. The Kursaal name was dropped at the start of the First World War and the main auditorium rechristened, The Royal Hall.

The main auditorium was originally designed for orchestral concerts, but was also intended as a multi-use space. It has an octagonal footprint, the auditorium being 30.46m (100ft) in diameter and 20.1m (66ft) up to the central pinnacled lantern, which provides light for the daytime activities. One side of the octagon contains the comparatively small stage and the stage house adjunct. There is a small apron downstage of the proscenium arch, the arch formed by a wide plaster moulding, with upper corners gently curving - but not at all fussy. The plasterwork in the auditorium is generally restrained, if a little uncertain. There are Edwardian echoes but no definite suggestion of a new style - rather more a dilution of a previous age.

The main stalls area is a flat sprung maple ballroom floor with removable seats, six rows round the periphery of the dance floor. Above these six rows is a balcony supported at intervals along the perimeter by broad plain columns. This has six further rows of seats on seven sides of the octagon. Behind these upper six rows the auditorium wall is punctured at regular intervals by large arched openings, some containing doorways, others simply with handrails opening onto an ambulatory, in the true traditions of the Kursaal style. The coffered ceiling rises on all eight sides of the octagon to the central pinnacled lantern, detailed with cornices and dogtooth ornamentation.

The Marina Gardens were not completed until 1931, long after the Villa Marina had opened. The landscape architect for this scheme, which linked the Villa Marina and the Gaiety Theatre, was F. Prentice Mawson of Thomas H. Mawson and Sons of Lancaster. Later accretions include, notably, the 'Garden Room' of the 1970s which is wholly out of keeping with the general character of the Villa Marina.

Externally, the Villa Marina has the appearance of a small continental permanent circus building, with a wigwam-like form, rendered and pebbledashed in a most unbecoming manner. The small stage house forms a small rectangular box which abuts abruptly onto the Harris Promenade.

It is an important survivor of its genre now a rare form of seaside architecture.   *DW*

DUDLEY

Hippodrome *
Castle Hill
Original architect
1938   Hurley
Later works
1973   Unknown: stage removed and
new circle erected in its place
to form an amphitheatre
Current use Bingo
Capacity   c.1500 (prior to 1973 conversion)

The Hippodrome, built as a 'twice-nightly' theatre in 1938, next door to the Plaza and opposite the Odeon Cinema, replaced the Opera House, destroyed by fire in 1936, on the same site. Externally like a super cinema of the time, in buff brick. At the centre, above the canopy, there were originally glazed, now blind, panels between the brick end bays, divided by two tall brick mullions. Above this a deep brick attic is divided by five horizontal bands. The name HIPPO-DROME in a central panel has been removed. Plain flank. Fly tower.

Small foyer. The fan-shaped auditorium has not been destructively altered for bingo use. Stalls rake rises to a rear terrace. Single, steeply raked, deep balcony. Square proscenium with

moulded architrave. Ceiling and walls with simple moulded ornament. Major adaptations have been made within the stage house.

The building is well maintained and the interior still has a theatrical 'feel'. It would be possible to return it to live use, but it would be necessary to remove the structural steelwork inserted in the fly tower. The stage is quite shallow, but there is open land at the rear.   TB

DUMFRIES
Dumfries and Galloway

Theatre Royal*
66-68 Shakespeare Street
Other names
Electric Theatre
Original architect
1792   Thomas Boyd
Later works
1876   C.J. Phipps: auditorium excavated and extended within existing walls; new front of house and facade added
c.1920   Unknown: auditorium partitioned horizontally – circle retained for cinema, stalls converted to roller skating rink
1959   Unknown: renovated as amateur theatre
Listed   Grade B
Current use Theatre
Capacity   219

The basic pitched-roofed shell of 1792 survives. Dignified two-storey stucco facade by Phipps, with central doorway flanked by arched openings, which originally accessed the pit and balcony. Five small windows, divided by pilasters, under the eaves. In Phipps's delightful auditorium of 1876, the pit was at basement level. This was decked over at

Dudley, Hippodrome (Ian Grundy)

dress-circle height around 1920 and the balcony rebuilt with a straight front, re-using the foliated iron balustrade of Phipps's dress circle. The side walls now are plain, except for some frames added in 1959. The former pit is now used to store costumes, props and scenery. *BP*

DUNDEE

King's ★★
Cowgate
Other names
  1941-45 Garrison Theatre
  1950-73 Gaumont
  1973-82 Odeon
  1982-95 County Bingo
Original architect
  1909 James Thomson
Later works
  1955 Lennox Paterson: converted to
        cinema
Listed **Grade B**
Current use **Pub**
Capacity **originally 2227**

This is important as the only surviving large touring theatre in the Dundee area. The dour ashlar facade of three storeys, rusticated to ground floor, has an almost industrial solidity with no obvious ornamentation. Within, the the-atre was originally luxuriously decorated with commodious front-of-house spaces, lined in mahogany and teak, and a very opulent auditorium in the Edwardian manner. The two tiers faced the stage squarely with the boxes iso-lated between decorative panels. The plasterwork was in a free mix of Baroque and Rococo with a fine saucer-domed ceiling with frescoes and a marble proscenium frame. Following post-war restoration, this scheme was unneces-sarily mutilated in 1955 through the partial demolition of the balcony and the insertion of a false ceiling above the circle. The side walls and original proscenium were covered over. After it failed as a bingo hall, much archaeology took place and it was established that enough of the original (including the ceiling) remained intact to enable the theatre to be restored. If this had happened, the handsome King's could have become a great asset to the City of Dundee which badly needs a capacious proscenium touring house, but per-mission was given to convert the building to a music bar. The interior is now so radically changed in appearance that it would be difficult, without prior knowledge, to identify it as a theatre. *BP*

Theatre Royal
Castle Street
Original architect
  1810 Samuel Bell
Listed **Grade B**
Current use **Offices and retail**

Only the handsome restrained ashlar facade remains after 1888 fire. Three storeys and seven bays, the three central bays topped by a pediment containing a bust of Shakespeare in a recess, the only visible clue that this was once a play-house. *BP*

Whitehall
Bellfield Street
Other names
  State
  1928 Alhambra
Original architect
  1928 Frank Thomson
Later works
  1984 Unknown: stage extended
Current use **Theatre**
Capacity **742**

Former ciné-variety venue of quite paralysing dullness. Totally unadorned two-storey cream-painted stucco-on-brick facade with asbestos-roofed brick hall looming behind. Stadium plan audi-torium seating with simple pilastered side walls and flat beamed ceiling. Commodious stage with fly tower and extensions housing bar, café and green room. *BP*

DUNFERMLINE
Fife

Alhambra ★
Canmore Street and New Row
Original architect
  1924 John Fraser
Listed **Grade B**
Current use **Bingo**
Capacity **est. 1000**

A mighty pile of red facing brick dwarfs the modest three-storey entrance block of three bays with red sandstone dress-ings to Canmore St. A soaring castellat-ed fly tower casts its shadow across New Row. The foyer is lofty with composite columns and pay booths flanking a high arch.

The auditorium is spacious and the-atrical in form and decoration (similar to Milburn and Milburn designs of the same period). A single large fully can-tilevered balcony meets stacks of super-imposed stage boxes with enriched pilasters and broken pediments, two

each side. The proscenium arch is curved with egg and dart moulding and flank-ing pilasters. Above is a deep frieze with cartouches and a flat panelled ceiling. The stage is very large and now put to good use as the no-smoking section of the bingo club. Having lost the Opera House, Dunfermline presently lacks a theatre. However, the Alhambra is a very large building and may be difficult to fill, although the town has a large hinter-land. It is well cared for as a bingo club. *BP*

EASTBOURNE
East Sussex

Devonshire
Park Theatre ★★★
Compton Terrace, Devonshire Park
Original architect
  1884 Henry Currey
Later works
  1903 Frank Matcham: redesigned
        auditorium, inserting four
        stage boxes and redesigning
        proscenium
Listed **Grade II**
Current use **Theatre**
Capacity **936**

The Devonshire Park Theatre was built by Henry Currey, architect to the 7th Duke of Devonshire (and designer of St Thomas' Hospital in London) as part of a complex designed on land given by the Duke in 1874. The Winter Garden was built in 1876, the theatre in 1884 and the Indian Pavilion in 1891, all by the Devonshire Park and Baths Company, of which the Duke was the main shareholder. The three-tier theatre is entered from the main foyer at 1st balcony level. The low white stuccoed facade is flanked by two Italianate tow-ers with pyramid roofs. These house fire-proof stairways, and originally held water tanks at the top – the ultimate fire protection.

The foyer has mirrors, delicate iron-work features and light fittings, paybox-es either side and a ceiling dome richly decorated in delicate gilded plasterwork. Entrance to the stalls is via the balcony; the gallery is entered separately along doors at either side. The intimate audito-rium originally had a straight balcony and gallery, delicately decorated with plasterwork and supported by iron columns. It had a saucer-domed ceiling. In 1903, Frank Matcham redesigned the interior. Currey's balconies were extend-ed to the proscenium, adding two boxes at either side, with panelling supported

Eastbourne, Devonshire Park

by pilasters above, and plasterwork in more flamboyant style decorating the balcony and gallery fronts. The proscenium was redesigned to be rectangular with heavy corner brackets, similar in design to Buxton Opera House, with a tympanum embellishment of fans, scrolls and pendentives on either side. The domed ceiling of 1884 was enhanced by Matcham with radiating panels, delicately painted and embellished with garlands and figures, and with decorative light fittings. It is this charming interior which is seen today, with the 1903 colours of white and gold and Rose du Barri furnishings. *SM*

Pier Theatre
Pier
Other names
   Dixieland Showbar
Original architect
   1901   Noel Ridley
Current use Show bar
Capacity   originally c.2000

The Eastbourne Pier Company was formed in 1865 and the pier, designed by Eugenius Birch, built in 1870. The theatre, constructed mid-pier, was completed in 1901 and replaced an earlier pavilion built in 1888 at the seaward end. It had cantilever balconies and a camera obscura on the roof. No further description found. In 1970 fire gutted the stage house and the theatre was rebuilt as a show bar. The camera obscura may be restored. *MS*

Royal Hippodrome ★★
Seaside Road
Other names
   1883   Theatre Royal
   New Theatre and Opera House
Original architect
   1883   C.J. Phipps
Later works
   1990   John D. Clarke, of Richard
          Crook: progressive restoration
          of ornament
Current use Theatre
Capacity   643

Originally called the Theatre Royal. Restrained but good symmetrical stuccoed facade with shops flanking the entrance and eleven bays of rectangular windows at first-floor level, subdivided by small Corinthian pilasters. A seven-bay upper storey with Tuscan pilasters and a shallow hipped roof

above the cornice.

The breadth of this facade, 26.8m (88ft), gives the impression of a large theatre. In fact the auditorium is small and intimate. Two horseshoe balconies, supported by slender iron columns, curve round to meet stage boxes originally framed between giant Corinthian columns carrying a deep, flared, elliptical arch. 'Omnibus' boxes at stalls level. Flat circular ceiling with deep panelled coves at the sides, characteristic of Phipps. There is an arcade at the rear of the 1st balcony, smaller in scale but similar to that of the Lyceum, Edinburgh. In general shape the theatre has much in common with the Theatre Royal, Nottingham.

When built the balcony fronts were enriched with delicate, scrolled plasterwork, but in the 1970s this was callously removed, together with the Corinthian columns flanking the boxes. The result was an unadorned, 'basic-form' Phipps auditorium. Fortunately a Royal Hippodrome Eastbourne Restoration Fund was founded locally and has been active in setting about restoration to the original designs, aided by workers on Government training schemes. The programme will continue as funds become available. The theatre is owned by the local authority. *CB/MS*

EASTWOOD
Nottinghamshire

Empire
Nottingham Road and King Street
Original architect
   1912   A.G. Wheeler (Eastwood)
Later works
   1950   Unknown: repaired and
          reopened after fire damage
Current use Shop

Eastbourne, Royal Hippodrome

The Empire opened with ciné-variety in 1912. It is now a Woolworth's store and has been massively altered, but the ashlar facade (which originally had heavy shields and lions' heads) is still discernible, as is a stage house which also contained a scene painter's studio. The interior has been completely gutted. *TB*

ECCLES
Salford

Crown
Church Street/Mather Road
Other names
  1899   Lyceum
  later   Grand Theatre and Opera
          House
  1907   Crown
  1955   Crown Cinema
Original architect
  1899   Campbell and Horsley
Later works
  1955   Unknown: adapted for
          Cinemascope
  1963   Unknown: converted for bingo
Current use Disused
Capacity   c.2500

The Crown opened in 1899 as the Lyceum Theatre. The intention was to provide a luxury theatre for Shakespeare productions and drama as well as revue.

The facade is of moulded red brick of five storeys with terracotta dressings to three high arched windows at first floor. Asymmetrically placed short corner tower. This once had a roof with balcony.

The auditorium was designed with three balconies, supported by four columns. The ornamentation of the proscenium comprised an allegorical representation of Shakespeare's 'Seven Ages of Man'. The act drop was a facsimile of Beverley's noted work for the opening of the Theatre Royal (Manchester) in 1845 – a Grecian subject painted by Mr Keith.

Becoming a cinema in 1932, it was later adapted for Cinemascope, ending stage use. In the late 1980s it was reported to be falling into disrepair internally. The exterior is largely intact, apart from the stage house which has been partly demolished. *SM*

EDINBURGH

Capitol
Manderston Street, Leith
Other names
  1928   Capitol Theatre
  1961   Top Rank Club
Original architect
  1928   J.A. Ross and J.M. Johnson
Current use Bingo
Capacity   originally c.2600

Externally, this is a ciné-variety venue of unspeakable ugliness. Entrance is gained through an arch in the railway viaduct with the vast bulk of brick auditorium on the far side of the (now disused) tracks. The entrance portico, projecting from the arch, has a Doric order and the interior is a Roman classical fantasy on a grand scale. One balcony without slips faces a wide proscenium with curving splay walls with organ and plenum grilles. Above is a heavy cornice with panelled ceiling coves and a beamed central section. The interior has been altered for bingo with new raised seating wings and a typically garish colour scheme. *BP*

Edinburgh, Festival

Festival ★★★

13–29 Nicolson Street
Other names
1892-
  1990s Empire Palace; Empire
Original architect
  1892 **Frank Matcham: new theatre
built on site of earlier circus
and performance halls**
Later works
  1911 **Frank Matcham: stage house
rebuilt and theatre reinstated
after fire**
  1928 **W. and T.R. Milburn: new theatre built**
  1994 **Law and Dunbar-Nasmith:
front of house/stage house
rebuilt; Milburn auditorium
restored**
Listed   **Grade A**
Current use **Theatre and opera house**
Capacity **1913**

Edinburgh, King's (Ian Grundy)

There was a series of circuses and performance halls on this site from the 1820s
(Ducrow's, etc.) and a music hall from
about 1860 (Alhambra, Queen's, etc.).
Frank Matcham built the very first Moss
Empire (the Empire Palace) here in 1892
and also carried out its reinstatement
after a destructive fire in 1910. The 1892
theatre had a circus-theatre interior of
almost barbaric magnificence.

In 1928 the Matcham house was
demolished and a new theatre built by
W. and T.R. Milburn, who were amongst
the most competent theatre designers of
their time (see, e.g., London Dominion,
Liverpool Empire and Southampton
Mayflower). The Edinburgh auditorium
is arguably their best surviving work. The
subsequent transformation of the
Empire into the Edinburgh Festival
Theatre by Law and Dunbar-Nasmith
(Colin Ross) completed in 1994 was
(until the Royal Opera House reopening)
perhaps the most radical make-over of
an old theatre undertaken in Britain in
modern times.

Edinburgh's long drawn-out quest for
an opera house, which spawned a number of abortive new-build projects over
the years, had become a standing joke
by the 1980s. Theatre Projects
Consultants, with Law and Dunbar-
Nasmith, identified the Empire as a
prime candidate for conversion for this
purpose as early as 1975, but it was to
be nearly twenty years before their sensible idea was followed up. When it was
eventually done, there was no penny-
pinching.

The undistinguished facade and front
of house were demolished and, with the
acquisition of additional space, rebuilt
on spacious modern lines, with a curved,
transparent facade, visible distantly as a
glowing landmark in Nicolson Street.
The back of house, too, was totally
demolished and a new stage house built,
together with dressing rooms and a
generous staircase, described as a 'vertical green room'. The stage itself is
immense at 25m x 18m (82ft x 59ft),
plus huge wing space on stage left and a
rear scene dock which can be opened up
for deep vistas.

The retained Milburn auditorium has
become the splendid filling in a modern
sandwich. Like most of the Milburns'
designs, it owes more to contemporary
North American models than to the
Matcham school. Two balconies with
slips meeting a deep-splayed ante-
proscenium with pairs of boxes stepping
down on either side. Rectangular
enriched proscenium frame with a flaming urn at the centre. Ceiling divided
into panels with a central dome. Three
forestage lifts. Sighting throughout is
excellent.

The stalls (altered for bingo) have
been re-raked to work with the now flattened stage, which has thereby been
raised at the front edge and has thus
improved sight lines from the unaltered
circles. Necessary changes of this kind
have been easily absorbed. The architects did not lose their nerve (as so often
happens with so-called restorations)
over matters of detail. The seats, for
example, are either 1928 originals or
careful reproductions. The decorations
are not an exact re-creation of the
Milburn scheme, which was rather
skimped, but a convincing essay in the
manner of the period with sensitively
applied patina glazes to avoid an over-
bright appearance. *JE*

King's ★★★

Leven Street
Original architect
  1906 **J.D. Swanston and James
Davidson**
Later works
  1951 **Unknown: top balcony demolished and upper circle extended back to form large
amphitheatre**
  1985 **City Council architect's department: theatre renovated**
Listed   **Grade B**
Current use **Theatre**
Capacity **1336**

One of Britain's most opulent touring
venues. The exterior, by Davidson, is in
the Coatbridge architect's typical
'Lanarkshire municipal' style. The four-
storey symmetrical ashlar sandstone
facade presents a dour solid mass which
could easily be mistaken for the Glasgow
offices of an insurance company and
seems strangely at odds with
Edinburgh's refined classical propriety.
That said, it makes an impressive fore-
taste for the wonders housed within.

The extensive foyer spaces have a
solid civic grandeur with parquet floors,
mahogany panelling, marble staircases,
heavily modelled architraves, lofty gilded
ceilings and marvellous amoebic patterns of bevelled Art Nouveau-inspired
stained glass. The auditorium is a space
of operatic magnificence – a glorious
extravaganza of lush Viennese Baroque.
On either side, there are massive stacks
of superimposed boxes – nine each side
with three at each level – with astonish-

ingly three-dimensional plasterwork – delicately modelled terms, cornucopias, scrolls and cartouches – making a wonderful frontispiece for the stage. Alas, the ends of the two tiers appear to slam into the boxes quite arbitrarily and the demolition of the top balcony in 1951 has left vast expanses of bare side wall, made more obvious by the present all-ivory decoration. Also, the rear seats in the consequently enlarged upper circle feel remote from the action on stage.

These are minor criticisms for, since its 1985 renovation, the King's has become one of the most comfortable traditional theatres. It has modern pedestal-mounted high-backed seating for all, wide aisles and good sight lines. Now owned by the local authority as a touring venue, it has recently been somewhat overshadowed by the reopened Festival Theatre. A venue rich in theatrical lore, it continues to be an asset to the city, especially during the busy Edinburgh Festival Season.   BP

New Victoria/Odeon
Clerk Street
Original architect
    1930   W.E. Trent
Later works
    1982   Unknown: tripled
    **1989   Unknown: screens 4 and 5
        converted from front stalls**
Listed   **Grade B**
Current use **Multi-screen cinema**
Capacity   **c.1780 (prior to subdivision)**

Originally a very large and luxurious city centre super cinema with a café, organ, orchestra and full stage facilities. The facade of five bays in faience has four Doric columns in antis above the entrance canopy with French windows opening on to a balcony for the café. The interior was (and still is) commodious, the grand marble-floored foyers with high mahogany dados in Roman classical style.

The auditorium, with one tier facing the proscenium, was a distinctly Germanic interpretation of the 'atmospheric' style, then popular. Below a blue plaster 'sky' ceiling, the side walls contained five top-lit niches featuring the muses of art, music and drama (the work of a sculptor called Beattie) interspersed with slender, fluted engaged Ionic columns. The proscenium was pedimented with a coffered frame and the safety curtain was painted with a scene from a Roman forum. Although repainted, this interior survives substantially intact behind the structure and cladding

of the present five-screen arrangement. The truncated original design is still visible from the former circle, although, throughout, the building is full of the tat associated with modern cinema use.   BP

Playhouse ★★
18-22 Greenside Place
Original architect
    1929   John Fairweather
Listed   **Grade B**
Current use **Theatre**
Capacity   **3056**

The Playhouse is truly a great monster of a theatre – in every sense. This vast enterprise started life as a 'super' cinema with full stage facilities and a café, all the work of Fairweather, designer of several such giants in the 1930s. The inspiration was American - the architect went to the United States to study the latest trends. The Playhouse makes clever use of a sloping site, the vast brick bulk of the auditorium rearing up behind the clumsy symmetrical sandstone facade of eleven bays in debased classical style. A proscenium frame recess denotes the entrance between flanking shop units.

Within, it is the scale which impresses most of all. There are commodious foyers with fine terrazzo floors and a partially glazed barrel-vaulted ceiling in the inner foyer. The decor is heavyweight classical with torchbearers flanking the stairways and giant cornices everywhere.

The auditorium has two massive fully cantilevered balconies, each seating over 1000. These curve to meet single stage boxes below organ grilles with fanlights,

flanked by giant pilasters. Above the upper circle, truncated pilasters rise to the heavily beamed ceiling. The entire interior is decorated in Apollo Leisure's standard lipstick red and gold. Remarkable as a cinema, the Playhouse is perhaps the least beautiful of Edinburgh's major theatres. It is, however, among the most commercially effective, its large capacity and well-equipped stage, c.13m (42ft 8in) deep, being put to good use with short runs of touring West End musical sensations.   BP

Royal Lyceum ★★★
Grindley Street
Original architect
    1883   C.J. Phipps
Later works
    **1977   Edinburgh District Council
        architects: renovated**
    **1986   RHWL: glazed porch added to
        entrance foyer**
Listed   **Grade A**
Current use **Theatre**
Capacity   **658 (top balcony disused)**

A charming and beautiful survivor of a once vast body of theatres by Phipps, the Royal Lyceum is an imposing stuccoed edifice in French classical style which successfully attempts to emulate the civic pomp of contemporary European designs. The three central bays have attached Corinthian columns and flanking pilasters rising to a triangular pediment, and the entire composition is topped by a steeply pitched mansard roof. A fully glazed entrance porch, which runs the entire length of the building, was successfully grafted on in 1986, much improving the circulation

Edinburgh, Playhouse (Ian Grundy)

Edinburgh, Royal Lyceum (Ian Grundy)

space without compromising the theatre's inviting appearance.

Notwithstanding the garishly unsuitable powder blue and gold decor of 1977, which still refuses to go away, the auditorium is a delight with three shallow horseshoe tiers, supported on slender iron columns. These are ornamented with complex delicate plasterwork scrolls and panels. Three stage boxes to each side of the dress circle are separated by small composite columns with bulbous bases.

The proscenium is rectangular, intricate with filigree plasterwork and topped with an elliptical tympanum with a painted panel of the muses. Above, the elegant circular panelled ceiling rises over richly ornamented coves. The Royal Lyceum is now run by a trust and leased to the highly successful Royal Lyceum Company. It is a firm favourite with lovers of the drama from Edinburgh and beyond, not least during the annual Edinburgh Festival.   *BP*

FALKIRK

Grand
Vicar Street
Other names
   Opera House
Original architect
   1903 **Alex Cullen**
Current use **Cinema**
Capacity   originally **2200**

Only the remarkable tenement block containing the main entrance and frag-

ments of one side wall survived the demolition in 1932 of Cullen's massive enterprise. The designer of a clutch of sadly long-lost theatres, he was a leading exponent of Art Nouveau and the Grand's facade is typically enigmatic.It consists of four storeys in sandstone with arched windows at first floor, rising to tall bay windows at either end. The centre bays consist of broad chimney breasts with fanlights and slender pilasters between. The bay containing the main theatre entrance was to the right, culminating in a dome carried on a drum of columns containing a lantern with flanking pinnacles. The building makes an interesting landmark and the old theatre entrance now leads to the café of the ABC cinema which replaced it in 1934.   *BP*

FARNHAM
Surrey

Castle
Castle Street
Original architect
   1939 **Unknown: converted from a barn**
Current use **Restaurant**

Originally a barn converted to a theatre; large, high ceilinged foyer with wooden beams, staircase and gallery. Small auditorium. Stage area larger than auditorium, 6.4m (21ft) by 2.4m (8 ft). Upper-level rehearsal room, property room, wardrobe and residential flat. Approached under an archway in Castle Street leading to its own courtyard, the building is much in keeping with the surrounding old buildings of the town. It was sold when the Redgrave Theatre was built and was then converted to a restaurant.   *SM*

FELIXSTOWE
Suffolk

Spa Pavilion
Sea Front
Other names
   Floral Hall
Original architect
   1910 **Harry Clegg, county surveyor**
Later works
   1938 **Unknown: totally rebuilt as theatre**
   1950 **J. Sharman: reconstructed after war damage**
   1960 **Unknown: seaview lounge added**
Current use **Theatre**
Capacity   **919**

An ornamental bandstand with open-air seating for 400 existed on the site by 1907. In 1910, the Floral Hall was erected, incorporating the bandstand and with sides which could be opened to enable passers-by to see in and hear the music.It seated 700. The Spa Gardens, surrounding the building, opened in 1928.

The Floral Hall closed in 1938 and was demolished. Its replacement, the Spa Pavilion, was designed primarily as a theatre rather than a concert hall. It was bombed in 1941, rebuilt and reopened as a theatre in 1950. A seaview lounge was added in 1960. Raked auditorium floor with proscenium stage.   *KW*

FLEETWOOD
Lancashire

Albert Music Hall
North Albert Street
Original architect
   1863 **Unknown**
Current use **Flats/offices**

Totally unnoticeable as a theatre from the front, consisting of a pair of doors in the centre of a terrace. The rear is more easily identifiable with three original arched windows and a very tall door. A balcony on cast-iron pillars ran round three sides of the room and it would seem that the theatre itself was at ground and first-floor levels. A near contemporary of the Alexandra Music Hall, Scarborough, but on a smaller, less impressive scale. Now converted to shops and flats/offices it was not possible to view inside but it is believed to have retained at least some of the iron columns, and therefore the form of the Music Hall may still be discernible. In use until at least March 1887, it may well have closed when the Queen's Theatre (now demolished) in Adelaide Street opened at the end of that year. It has been used, before its most recent conversion, as a furniture repository which survived until around 1979 with the hall supposedly more or less intact.   *IG*

Marine Hall
Esplanade
Original architect
   1935 **William Melville, engineer**
Later works
   1967 **Unknown: foyer extended**
Current use **Multi-purpose hall**
Capacity   **636**

Opened in 1935 the Marine Hall is set in the corner of an L-shaped colonnade in the Marine Gardens along the North Promenade. It is constructed of brick and reinforced concrete with structural steel framework to the auditorium. The external finish is Portland cement relieved with faience bands. There is a central reinforced concrete dome.

The auditorium design originally incorporated flush panelled walls veneered to a height of six feet with Australian Walnut with horizonal bands of black Macassor Ebony, eggshell finished in cellulose. The sprung floor was polished maple with dark walnut borders. The ceiling had extensive fibrous plaster ornament in an Art Deco style with the dome at the centre glazed with coloured leaded lights. Galleons and the Borough Arms featured at eight points on the circle of the dome. Above the walnut panelling were ornamental panels and, at either side of the rectangular stepped proscenium was a clock (left) and an act number indicator (right).

Today the auditorium is substantially intact, although the walnut panelling has been replaced in a more prosaic wood and the upper walls have been curtained. The dome remains and although it looks splendid, it causes acoustical problems.

In 1967 the foyer was extended by the incorporation of part of the colonnade. At the same time a series of small rooms was swept away and the building enlarged over the car park to form the Viking Bar. Further improvements are proposed. *IG*

FOLKESTONE
Kent

Leas Cliff Hall ★
The Leas
Original architect
   1927   J.L. Seaton Dahl (to design of 1913)
Later works
   1980   Unknown: alterations
Listed   Grade II
Current use Multi-purpose hall
Capacity   825 (seated)

Resolutely calling itself a hall, this may be regarded as a theatre. Although designed in 1913 it was not built until 1927. It is a four-storey building, reinforced concrete-framed with brick infill, and partly faience faced, with iron balconies. It is set into the side of the cliffs, at the top of which is the parade known as The Leas. The box-office building on the Leas was replaced in 1980 by one which resembles a pagoda. A fine

double staircase leads down to the hall. A balcony runs round three sides. Movable stalls seats on a polished, sprung dance floor. There are sightline problems because the hall is about twice as wide as it is deep, the stage being in the middle of the longer wall, opposite the staircase. A variable sized proscenium arch can be created and rostra are available to provide forestages of differing sizes. Backstage there is a band room, rehearsal room, green room and six dressing rooms.

At the time of writing there are plans to extend and refurbish the building. *KW*

Leas Pavilion ★
The Leas
Other names
   1994   Leas Club
Original architect
   1902   Unknown (as a restaurant)
Later works
   1910   R.A. Pope: converted to concert party venue
Current use Club
Capacity est. 425

The Pavilion was converted in 1910 from a restaurant to become a concert party venue. Further minor works of conversion were carried out in 1929, after which it was in continual use for repertory seasons until the mid-1980s. The restaurant atmosphere was still marked in the 1960s when the balcony held tables and chairs, and teas could be taken during matinee performances.

Now a club, the building lies below street level and is reached by a few steps. In front is a paved area on which tables

and chairs can be placed in good weather. Apart from the absence of stalls seats, the interior appears the same as it was in the 1970s. There is a balcony round the three sides where there are now billiards and pool tables. The proscenium arch remains, covered by ruched tabs, silver in colour and of a reflective material. The conversion does not appear to have altered the basic structure of this unusual theatre. *KW*

FRAMLINGHAM
Suffolk

Theatre
Fore Street (behind no. 20, facing a backland yard)
Original architect
   late C18/
   early C19 Unknown
Current use Unused barn

A late C18/early C19 brick barn known as 'the old theatre' by strong local tradition. Overall dimensions c.8.75m x 11m (24ft x 36ft) with a simple pitched roof supported by principal rafters with collars and tie beams. This has four constructional bays, reinforced with longitudinal iron tie rods. Gable to entrance or west elevation of horizontally boarded timber construction. An upper hayloft door, within a once larger opening above the main door, covered by a latter-day sliding door. In the opposite gable a small circular window. Internally, an intermediate timber floor reached by a (derelict) staircase against the west wall with two nicely turned Doric newels which are the only evidence of any earlier polite use. Ground

Framlingham, (former) Theatre (Jim Lee)

floor of brick/cement/earth with latter-day stub brick walls to form storage bins. General condition of building not good.

Two playbills in Framlingham Castle Museum of 1835 advertising Framlingham Theatre (they give no address) describe it as having boxes, pit and gallery seats. It is not possible to conclude whether that building was originally purpose-built or merely served as a fit-up: Elizabeth Grice certainly considers the Framlingham venue to have been of the latter type. *JL*

GAINSBOROUGH
Lincolnshire

King's
Trinity Street
Other names
1885 Albert Hall
1891 Royal Albert Hall
        Albert Theatre
Original architect
1885 Unknown
Later works
1891 Unknown: proscenium brought forward; balcony lowered; other alterations and additions
1904 Unknown: proscenium front enlarged; private boxes added next to proscenium; fibrous plaster decorations on proscenium and new balcony front
1908 Unknown: auditorium altered
1927 Unknown: reconstructed; new dome-shaped roof replacing former flat one
1988 Unknown: stage removed to provide space for a bar
Current use Bingo
Capacity est. 1000

Opened as Albert Hall with stalls and balcony. Ballroom attached. After a series of improvements it was gutted by fire in 1927, reopening as a theatre in the same year. Stage removed about 1988.

Three-bay gabled facade with a cheerful mixture of classical details, facing Trinity Street. The central bay is set forward and framed by superimposed orders of coupled columns supporting an open segmental pediment at the apex of the gable, above which is a pedestal carrying a lion. Within the pediment tympanum is an oeil-de-boeuf. Brick flank wall of nine bays divided by piers. Next to the stage, right end, is a long low building, now the Liberal Club, but which could have been the original Ballroom of 1885.

Internally the ground floor has been levelled throughout. There is a deep 'U'-shaped balcony supported by iron pillars, which may be a survivor of the 1927 fire. The ceiling is barrel vaulted with Greek key guilloche on the longitudinal and cross beams. The original position of the stage is clearly visible. The grid is hidden from view. There is external fly tower. *TB*

GLASGOW

Athenaeum ★
Buchanan Street
Other names
   Part of the former Royal Scottish Academy of Music and Drama
Original architect
1893 Sir J.J. Burnet and J.A. Campbell
Listed Grade A
Current use Disused
Capacity c.345

A narrow frontage vertical composition exploiting contemporary innovations in structural technology to enable better use to be made of Glasgow's Georgian house plots. Its two-part asymmetrical composition is a strikingly enigmatic fusion of Scots baronial, Indian and European Art Nouveau styles. A stair tower rises to a cupola to the right of the six-storey main section. This has superimposed bay windows framed within an arch and surmounted by a steep gable, broken by an aedicule and flanked by small minarets.

The interior consists of a shallow raked stalls with one semi-circular balcony with straight slips. The ceiling is flat with moulded panels and a circular centre. Presently disused, but for the time being unaltered, this important building is threatened with retail use, which would be an unfortunate fate for a pleasant and intimate performance space. *BP*

Britannia Music Hall ★★★
109–121 Trongate and 9 New Wynd
Other names
1860 Campbell's Music Saloon
1860 Britannia Hall
1869 Britannia Music Hall
        The Trongate
        Hubner's Cinematograph Hall
1904 Britannia Music Hall (again)
1905 Britannia Theatre of Varieties
1906 Britannia and Grand Panopticon
        Pickard's Waxworks
1907 Panopticon Carnival and Roof Gardens
1908 Noah's Ark in the Panopticon
        after 1922
        Tron Cinema
        Panopticon Pictures
        'Pots and Pans' (local nickname)
Original architect
1857 Gildard and MacFarlane (incorporating an earlier building)
Later works
1869 Hugh Barclay: new front stair and vestibule
1893 James Thompson: means of escape improved
1906 Boswell and McIntyre: stairs altered
1938–
c.1950 Unknown: series of alterations including amalgamation of ground-floor spaces into a single shop, removal of front stair and vestibule and insertion of fully glazed shopfront
1968 Unknown: ground-floor facade altered
Listed Grade A
Current use Disused and dilapidated (former stalls area used for storage)
Capacity est. 350 max.

The Britannia is of outstanding importance as the only early 'supper room' style music hall now surviving in Scotland. The history of the building is complex. There was a four-storey commercial building on this site, with cottages at the rear, by, at the latest, 1840 and the shell of the present building incorporates a large part of this earlier fabric (visible on New Wynd). In 1857,

Glasgow, Britannia Music Hall

the facade and part of the return to New Wynd were rebuilt in a pleasing Italianate style to the designs of Gildard and MacFarlane. It is fairly certain that the music hall was inserted at first- and second-floor levels at this time, although it may not have opened as such until about 1860.

In the normal way for this kind of music hall, the Britannia hall was an adjunct to a pub which, in this case, was on the ground floor. The hall was given its own vestibule on the street front, together with an improved access staircase, in 1869. Over a long period it presented music, variety turns, freak shows and tableaux. By 1922 it was primarily a cinema but variety acts continued until it closed in 1938. Almost the whole of the ground floor was subsequently cleared to form a single shop, the vestibule and front staircase were removed and the upper floors fell into disuse. The music hall was divided by a pitched roof-like construction just below balcony level. Beneath this division, the stalls area has been used for storage, while above, the music hall, still substantially intact, has become sadly dilapidated. A construc-

tion containing toilets intrudes into the stage area.

The building, as now seen, is at once a source of delight and concern. The painted ashlar facade, rusticated at first-floor level, has nine bays of arched windows in the two storeys above the shop front, with two bays returning to the west. The top floor has a pretty arcade of recessed windows (5 + 4 + 6) to Trongate, with the four-bay centre slightly advanced and a pediment over. The facade is crowned by a deep frieze and cornice.

The hall itself, despite past alterations and its flimsy horizontal subdivision, is a remarkable survival, a relic of both mid-C19 music hall and early C20 cinema. The seated area of the auditorium is about 14m (46ft) wide by 15.3m (50ft) deep with a single U-shaped balcony of three rows on three sides. The stalls probably had tables and chairs, a benched area and an encircling promenade at first, giving way later to seating in fixed rows. The balcony seating is divided, row from row, by low, boarded partitions which presumably served as bench backs and drink rests. The deep, upper foyer or promenade on the Trongate front now

houses a lightly built projection room. The original positions of the bars and services are not now obvious. The hall ceiling is flat panelled with a deep cove and enriched cornice. The high stage, about 3.65m (12ft) deep, is typical of a small, early music hall. The proscenium is of wood and there are only the simplest suspension arrangements. The storey within the roof, above the hall, was used to accommodate dressing rooms and public displays of various kinds.

The Britannia is of such rarity and interest in a national context, that a full physical and documentary investigation needs now to be undertaken prior to a full restoration for some appropriate public use. At the very least, urgent repairs need to be put in hand to arrest further decay. *JE*

Citizens ★★★

119 Gorbals Street
Other names
    1878 **Her Majesty's**
    1879 **Royal Princess Theatre**
Original architect
    1878 **Campbell Douglas with James Sellars**

Glasgow, Citizens (Ian Grundy)

Later works
1989 BDB Architects: new facade and foyer
Listed **Grade B**
Current use **Theatre**
Capacity **605**

A fine theatre with a well-deserved national reputation for the quality of its work over many years. Located in Gorbals, a once densely populated inner-city area which has suffered drastic redevelopment, the Citizens formerly had a magnificent facade (by James Sellars) with a giant order of Tuscan columns. This was unfortunately destroyed in 1977 together with the adjacent Palace theatre. In 1989, the present undistinguished yellow brick frontage was added which externally resembles social work offices. The theatre is entered beneath a fully-glazed pediment, especially effective when illuminated at night. Within, it is spacious and decorated with statuary and terms rescued from the Palace.

The fine auditorium retains its dark allure. Two lyre-shaped balconies with fine plasterwork are supported by slender columns with large capitals. Superimposed stage boxes are surmounted by caryatids. The proscenium opening is framed by the inner pilasters of the boxes. The ceiling is flat and plain with deep panelled coves round the perimeter. In 1989 an adjacent studio theatre was added as part of a major renovation and the existing Victorian auditorium was renovated with modern Pullman seats.

There is still a remarkably well-preserved set of Victorian wood machinery below the stage, the best survival of its kind in Scotland. *BP*

Coliseum

Eglinton Street
Other names
ABC Coliseum
Coliseum Cinema
County Bingo Club
Original architect
1905 **Frank Matcham**
Later works
1931 W.R. Glen: proscenium dismantled and stalls seating extended into stage area
1963 Leslie C. Norton: upper circle partially demolished; suspended ceiling inserted and Cinerama equipment installed
Current use **Bingo**
Capacity **c.3100 (after 1963 conversion)**

This somewhat industrial-looking effort from Matcham is in a 'big brick box with a bit of architecture tacked on the front' mode - not inappropriate in Gorbals. The comparatively small ashlar frontage to Eglinton Street is presently covered by a corrugated metal frontispiece. The octagonal balcony stair tower has a carved stone frieze and a steeply pitched roof. The entrance was through a high archway with a loggia above and a steeply pitched pavilion roof. The pit and balcony entrances were at various points around the block and the theatre's name is spelt out on large carved panels. The interior has been devastated by consecutive rebuilds. The proscenium was demolished in the 1930s and the remainder was irretrievably altered for Cinerama use in the 1960s when the top tier was partially demolished. The building was further altered as a bingo hall and the numbers game is played within an inner envelope inside the original auditorium. The investigator was not permitted to make a detailed inspection, but according to plans lodged in Glasgow City Archives, the original ceiling and other Matcham fragments remain. *BP*

Granada ★

Duke Street
Other names
1971 **Mecca Granada Bingo**
Original architect
1934 **Lennox and McMath**
Current use **Derelict**
Capacity **est. 2200**

A vast ciné-variety venue with full stage facilities - one of several built for the proprietors of the city centre Metropole Theatre of Varieties (demolished). Located in a densely populated working-class area in the East End, the Granada had a white stucco entrance portico with a pediment and fin-shaped name pylon in the form of a skyscraper with flanking poster hoardings, now truncated and re-clad in corrugated metal sheeting. The auditorium is some way behind and of brick with corrugated roofing. Lofty foyers with polychromatic mosaic and terrazzo flooring led to a cavernous auditorium with one straight cantilevered balcony. The decor is a riot of sunbursts, waves and zigzags, the plenum grilles modelled on skyscrapers. Dark since 1995 and now in dilapidated condition. *BP*

King's ★★★

Bath Street
Original architect
1904 **Frank Matcham**
Later works
1912 **Unknown: upper foyers improved**
Listed **Grade B**
Current use **Theatre**
Capacity **1785**

In designing King's, Matcham made the most of a prominent site, designing two show facades in Dumfries-shire red sandstone. The elevation to Elmbank Street fronts the plush lounges to the rear of the auditorium. The fascinating symmetrical Bath Street elevation has overtones

Glasgow, King's (Ian Grundy)

of the Baroque and Art Nouveau but, as with everything Matcham did, it is truly an enigmatic mixture of styles and influences. Two-storey pavilions at each end contain the main foyer and stage access. When seen from a distance, the whole composition, topped by ball finials and statuary (now missing) looks prosperous and inviting – everything one could want of a theatre. The entrance is disfigured by an inappropriate modern canopy with dot-matrix signs.

The entrance hall still makes a wonderful impression on today's audiences. The heavy, mahogany doors with their bevelled glass and lustrous brass, the warm pink-grained marble-lined walls and a splendid barrel-vaulted ceiling with statues gazing benignly down from the corners, adequately prepare one to witness one of Matcham's boldest auditorium designs.

The auditorium is magnificently opulent in a free mix of Baroque and Rococo. There are three generously curved balconies which engage with complex arrangements of boxes. The dress circle meets pairs of boxes with banded Ionic columns. The tier above runs over the first box to larger stage boxes with elaborate half-domed canopies. At this level, columns are set forward along the flank walls to support a triplet of shell canopies. Above, there is a magnificently decorated twelve-sided ceiling, the panels of which radiate from a single rose. The proscenium has several heavily modelled frames topped by a giant cartouche and angels. One's senses are assailed by a feast of gilding, flock wallpaper, marble, plum velvet plush and embroidery. *BP*

Odeon (Paramount)
Renfield Street
Original architect
   1934   Verity and Beverley
Later works
   **1970   Dry-Halasz-Dixon Partnership:
        rebuilt as triple cinema**
Current use **Multi-screen cinema**
Capacity **c.2750 (prior to subdivision)**

One of a small group of once large and luxurious ciné-variety theatres developed by Paramount in Britain's provincial cities and designed by Verity and Beverley. The former Paramount occupies an entire block between Renfield and West Nile Streets and has an imposing Art Deco frontage in moulded reconstructed stone. The facade has now been beautifully restored and is bathed in neon and floodlighting at night. The remainder is of well-mannered dark red facing brick and the large fly tower to the rear is still very conspicuous. The interior was completely gutted in 1970 and replaced by the present multi-screen arrangement. It is proposed (1998) to subdivide the auditorium further to give a total of nine screens, but to restore the exterior. *BP*

Olympia
Orr Street
Other names
   1963   ABC Cinema
   1987   County Bingo Club
Original architect
   **1911   George Arthur with Frank
        Matcham and Co**
Later works
   **1936   Charles J. McNair: converted
        to cinema**

Listed   **Grade B (facade only)**
Current use **Furniture warehouse**
Capacity **c.1690 (following conversion
      to cinema)**

Only the imposing landmark ashlar facade of the theatre survives, the interior having been rebuilt as a cinema in the 1930s in streamline mode. Cleverly occupying a fan-shaped site, the principal external feature is the curved corner entrance with giant attached Ionic columns above the first floor and a dome with four ocular windows round its base rising from the parapet above. To the right, five bays with giant pilasters are flanked by two-bay rusticated ends. The building lies marooned in a twilight neighbourhood and was neglected after it failed as a bingo hall. Recently reopened as a furniture warehouse with the cinema interior intact. *BP*

Pavilion ★★★
121 Renfield Street
Original architect
   1904   Bertie Crewe
Listed   **Grade B**
Current use **Theatre**
Capacity **1449**

Unlike many grand variety palaces, the Pavilion is still gloriously alive and has now been entertaining Glaswegians for over ninety years. Like much of its famously Francophile architect's work, the Pavilion is an interesting essay in French Renaissance style. The prominent corner site is clad in buff terracotta. The long frontage to Renfield Street has three main bays, each consisting of three subordinate bays, with elliptical pediments and oeil-de-bœuf windows at the fourth storey. The facade to Renfrew Street (the rear of the auditorium) is flanked by stair towers with pointed roofs.

Foyer spaces are robust rather than luxurious, but distinguished by ornate terrazzo flooring. The entrance hall is circular with a heavy cornice. Dingy bars and waiting rooms are squeezed into unlikely corners, adding greatly to the theatre's period charm.

Despite its capaciousness, the auditorium is remarkably intimate with two wide and deep serpentine-fronted balconies. Single boxes on each side at 1st balcony level are framed by composite columns carrying a wide elliptical arch, enriched with scrolls, over the unfortunately altered proscenium. The side walls above the upper tier have blank arches carried by terms and rising to the ceiling

Glasgow, Pavilion (Ian Grundy)

coves. The ceiling is divided into panels with a sliding roof. Vigorous Rococo plasterwork is liberally applied to every surface, yet the decoration presently looks half-finished as the drapes, pelmets, gilding and fresco panels are missing and need to be replaced. The Pavilion is nonetheless a remarkable survivor as a commercial theatre. *BP*

Theatre Royal ★★★
282 Hope Street
Other names
   1867 Royal Coliseum
Original architect
   1867 George Bell
Later works
   1880 C.J. Phipps: rebuilt after fire
   1895 C.J. Phipps: rebuilt after further fire
   1975 Arup Associates (Derek Sugden): restored and modified as opera house
   1997 Law and Dunbar Nasmith: enlarged orchestra pit and redecorated
Listed   **Grade A**
Current use **Theatre and Opera House**
Capacity   **1547**

This Cinderella of theatres was famously rescued from use as a TV studio in 1975 and transformed into a magnificent venue for grand opera and ballet. This is the largest and among the finest theatres by Phipps to survive. The painted stone exterior is of little merit, the entrance being inserted into a long row of mediocre existing three-storey properties which the theatre has annexed progressively through the years. It was once distinguished by a tower with a dome and a glazed full-length canopy, long-since removed.

The foyers mainly date from the 1970s but are an elegant pastiche of the Phipps manner. It is the auditorium which makes the Theatre Royal such a delight. Three balconies - each of about eleven rows - the first with a serpentine front and the upper two horseshoe, were originally fully supported by iron columns, some of which have been removed and cantilevers inserted. The balcony slips meet superimposed stage boxes set between pairs of giant Corinthian columns with enriched shafts. The entablature continues the line of the 3rd balcony front and has a richly decorated frieze which returns above the rectangular proscenium frame. The tympanum takes the form of a deep elliptical arch. Coves above carry a stately panelled circular ceiling with

Glasgow, Theatre Royal (Ian Grundy)

fine gilded decoration. Indeed, the whole space positively glows with gilt on ivory and rich blue upholstery. The ornament on the balcony fronts is a delicate combination of Renaissance strapwork and Rococo and is of exceptional quality. The 1997 redecoration was a well-researched essay in the manner of Phipps. The Theatre Royal feels like a miniature version of grand European opera houses and has fulfilled its role very well. *BP*

Zoo, Hippodrome, Circus and Grand Variety Theatre
New City Road
Other names
   1911 Bostock's Joytown and Grand Variety Theatre
   The Joytown Grand Electric Theatre
Original architect
   1897 Bertie Crewe
Current use **Supermarket/restaurants/ snooker hall**

A vast warehouse-like iron-framed structure with a partially glazed roof of industrial proportions and originally containing a zoo, roller skating rink and hippodrome under one roof. The remarkable enterprise, a fully enclosed entertainment centre, was the brainchild of the circus magnate and showman, E.H. Bostock. The exterior was originally clad in brick with stone dressings with twin towers and onion domes at the entrances. Today, it is entirely re-clad in corrugated metal and the once-ornate interior has long since been removed, so that only the frames remain original. *BP*

GLOUCESTER
Gloucestershire

Palace
Westgate Street
Other names
   1791 Theatre Royal
   New Theatre and Opera House
Original architect
   1791 Unknown
Later works
   1857 Unknown: rebuilt
   1897 J.P. Briggs: rebuilt
Current use **Fragment**

The Theatre Royal was opened in 1791 by John Boles Watson. No description found, but accommodation was probably pit, gallery and private boxes. Gas lighting was installed in 1835.

In 1857 the theatre was acquired by John Blinkhorn, a railway contractor, who reconstructed it internally with two horseshoe-shaped balconies and a gallery supported by iron pillars. All decorated with ornate plasterwork; William Beverley painted the act-drop which depicted an Italian landscape. The stage facilities included a vampire trap and two star traps. Again rebuilt in 1897.

Bought at auction by Poole (of Poole's Diorama) in 1902, after which ciné-variety, theatre and cinema were presented. The building was dismantled in 1922 but a doorway and a bust of Shakespeare remain in Westgate Street, and, below ground level, a door in the Theatre Vaults Public House adjoining was the former pit entrance. *SM*

GOOLE
East Riding of Yorkshire

Theatre Royal
Adam Street
Original architect
1841 Unknown
Current use **Store**
Capacity **est. 800**

A small provincial theatre that seemed to struggle to survive throughout its life. It opened in 1841 as a simple hall with a shallow balcony at the rear and slips to either side of the proscenium arch. A central sunburner coped with lighting and ventilation. In the early C20 electricity was introduced. Despite its ups and downs some major companies – D'Oyly Carte among them – came to the Theatre Royal.

By the outbreak of the First World War two cinemas had opened and the centre of gravity of the town had shifted, leaving Adam Street in an unfashionable part. The theatre was often closed and in 1916 it was severely damaged in a gale. The theatre later became a public hall, a warehouse, then a garage and is now a builder's store.

The balconies have been removed but their line on the walls can be seen and plaster pillars and panels survive. The proscenium arch has been bricked up but at upper levels the wooden beam also survives. The stage area is now incorporated into a plumber's shop and storeroom. The ceiling contains the extraction flue from the sunburner, a large circle shows a former decoration and the ceiling contains eight decorative plaster roses which may date from the post-1916 repairs. Used 1881-83 as a church. A house, probably for the manager/owner is just beyond the Cross Street doors. Stage access seems to have been in Chapel Street.

Given the remains extant, it might be possible to reconstruct this early theatre. *IG*

GOUROCK
Inverclyde

Cragburn Pavilion
Esplanade
Original architect
1935 James Carrick
Current use **Community centre**

Competition-winning design for a multipurpose concert venue, ballroom and theatre for summer shows. A chunky great white tomb of three storeys in cement stucco-clad brickwork with black cornicing. The long side frontage, facing the Clyde estuary has six tall windows (now bricked in) interspersed with vertical fluting and a veranda for sunbathing. The interior has lost most of its period fittings and the structure now looks sad and neglected and present potential for theatre use (although it retains a stage) must be minimal. *BP*

GRAVESEND
Kent

Gem Picture House
New Road
Other names
1934 Regal
1968 Coral Bingo
Gala Bingo
Original architect
1910 Unknown
Later works
1968 Unknown: converted to bingo
Current use **Bingo**
Capacity **est. 600**

Probably opened as ciné-variety but no record seen of how long (or if) live use continued. Recessed arched entrance from New Road. The building is well to the rear of this, occupying a site on a corner of Barrack Row, from which it can be seen to have an octagonal roof, rather suggestive of a cattle auction ring. It has a pleasant auditorium with a single balcony and looks as if it might make a tolerable playhouse, but the stage is very small and the site gives little scope for enlargement. *JE*

Tulley's Bazaar
Windmill Street and South Street
Other names
1848–56 Bayne's Bazaar
1859 Milton Hall
Original architect
1835 Unknown
Later works
1859 J.B. Cooper: major alterations
Current use **Flats and Workshop**

Gravesend's entertainment history is only now being fully researched. Tulley's Bazaar was popular in the mid-C19, when Gravesend was both a fishing port and a favourite Cockney excursion resort. Actor and singer Donald King referred to it affectionately (almost certainly remembering an earlier period) in his musical lecture about the Thames in the mid-1850s.

Many well-known performers appeared at Tulley's Bazaar and Concert Room, including Charles Sloman, J.A. Cave, the Caulfields and the Great Mackney. It existed as Tulley's from 1835 until 1848 when financial disaster forced the proprietor (who also had short-lived bazaars in High Holborn, Newington Causeway, Maidstone, Margate and Rosherville) to sell to local printer Godfrey Baynes, who almost completely discontinued the entertainment side. After some rebuilding in 1859 it was named Milton Hall, used as a drill hall by volunteers and also for amateur dramatics.

It is a long, narrow corner building in greybrick with stucco classical ornaments. In Tulley's time it had a platform stage with a curved front and a mirrored back wall. It has recently been divided horizontally with flats over a workshop. No identifiable features, therefore, survive internally. The front was altered at some time to insert a shopfront, but the exterior is otherwise probably much as it would have appeared in 1859. *JE*

GRAYS
Thurrock

State ★
George Street
Original architect
1938 F.G.M. Chancellor
Listed **Grade II**
Current use **Dark**
Capacity **2200**

The State Cinema is one of the most completely preserved and 'theatrical' of late 1930s' cinemas. It has a striking exterior, with a faience-clad tower over the entrance facade, but it was for the quality of its interior that it was listed. This comprises a large but relatively simple auditorium, with rather standard mouldings either side of the proscenium, behind pleasant Art Deco entrance foyers. However, it retains its original Compton theatre organ and projectors and in the late 1970s and early 1980s its qualities were enhanced by the showmanship of its manager and the support of the Friends of the State Cinema. Additional features included an extra set of curtains (making three in all) that swept open in sequence at the start of each film, an automatic piano linked to the organ, and a brenograph that cast coloured light patterns across the curtains as the organist played. The building has a 4.57m (15ft) stage which has been used for occasional live shows since its construction, and has three dressing rooms. It has also featured in a number of advertisements and music videos, and, most famously, in *Who Framed Roger Rabbit?* (1988).

The State closed in October 1990 following the sudden death of its manager and the opening of rival multiplex cinemas at the nearby Lakeside shopping development. It was acquired by a Guernsey-based entrepreneur and the foyer was used briefly as a bar. The building is now in poor condition, and is being closely monitored by the local authority, who have already served one repairs notice. It is hoped that a new development on an adjoining site will regenerate interest in reviving the State as a mixed arts venue. *EH*

Great Yarmouth, Gorleston Pavilion (Ken Woodward)

GREAT YARMOUTH
Norfolk

Empire ★
Marine Parade
Other names
  Bourbon Street New Orleans
Original architect
  1908   A.S. Hewitt
Listed   **Grade II**
Current use **Theme bar and disco**
Capacity   est. **800**

Early in the C20 Great Yarmouth and nearby Gorleston were quite elegant resorts. Several of the old entertainment buildings are architecturally pleasing. Alongside the Empire are two small arcades, at right angles to the sea front, one bearing the date 1902, the other 1904.

The Empire itself is architecturally imposing for a narrow-fronted ciné-variety of such an early date. The terracotta facade is framed by giant fluted and cabled, coupled Ionic columns rising from pedestals with tall blockings over; the centre is taller with a shallow, segmentally arched recess above the entrance, containing a triple-arched balcony. Cornice and blocking over. The brick flank walls are blind-arcaded.

The auditorium has raked stalls and a single balcony and barrel-vaulted ceiling. The circle ends very close to the proscenium arch, and extends back towards the front of the building, occupying about two-thirds of the length and forming an elongated horseshoe. The sides of the balcony take a single line of seats – strangely these are not angled. It is clear that the high proscenium arch was originally flanked by Corinthian columns of which only the caps remain. There is a fly tower, with the grid and two fly rails

still in position. Although now disused, this was once a fine auditorium with excellent plasterwork on the balcony fronts in the form of a series of cartouches supported by cherubs encircled with laurel wreaths. There are dressing rooms and a band room under the stage. *KW*

Gorleston Pavilion ★
Pier Gardens
Original architect
  1898   J.W. Cockrill (Borough Engineer)
Later works
  1919   Unknown: new proscenium
Current use **Theatre**
Capacity   **400**

The exterior promises more than the interior now delivers, but this is still an impressive late-Victorian seaside pavilion. Red brick with single-storey entrance block in front of a two-storey concert hall with an advanced centre flanked by short towers with domes. Brick cornices, terracotta balustrades and decorative panels, with much stained glass, all in an exuberant Art Nouveau manner. Unsympathetic modern entrance canopy. The flat-floored, relatively plain concert hall interior has a three-row end balcony and iron arched girders. The 1919 proscenium arch is decorated with nymphs and garlands. No fly tower and limited wing space. This handsome building is in need of investment to reverse its decline. *KW*

Hippodrome ★★★
St George's Road
Original architect
  1903   R.S. Cockrill
Listed   **Grade II***
Current use **Circus**
Capacity   **1200**

A building of outstanding importance. There are only two purpose-built permanent circuses in Britain still in full working order and probably only four or five operational pre-1950 circuses in the world. The type was once common across Europe but is now rare everywhere. Those that survive are normally in other uses or are used infrequently for their designed purpose (e.g. Cirque d'Hiver in Paris, the Koninklijk Theater Carré in Amsterdam and Brighton Hippodrome).

The Yarmouth example, like the Blackpool Tower Circus, is a true Hippodrome, whose traditional sawdust ring can be flooded for water spectacles. Its terracotta front is of three bays, defined by two short outer towers and two taller, domed inner towers with Art Nouveau ornament. It has a big lunette window to each bay. Cockrill had clearly absorbed something of the Matcham manner. The interior, however, does not reflect the splendour of Matcham's Hippodromes or his Blackpool circus. This is a traditional, unadorned circus with arena seating round a 12.8m (42ft) ring, covered by a shallow arched roof.

Animal circuses are expensive to run and (apart from equestrian shows) tend

Great Yarmouth, Hippodrome (John Earl Collection)

to be against the tide of opinion of the present time, but circus now comes in many guises and it should be a matter of priority to keep this exciting arena with its water transformations at work. Apart from its mainstream uses, it has excellent acoustics for orchestral concerts (although the circus itself no longer has its own band). The stables and outbuildings are all intact. This is in many ways the most important entertainment building of any kind in (and for many miles around) Great Yarmouth. *JE*

Regent ★★

85-87 Regent Road
Other names
    Regent Ciné Theatre
Original architect
    1914   Francis Burdett Ward
Later works
    1982   Unknown: converted to bingo
    1990   and 1996 Unknown: further
            alterations
Listed   **Grade II**
Current use **Bingo**
Capacity   **est. 1650**

Amongst the surprising theatre riches of Great Yarmouth, the Regent is worthy of special attention.

This is an unusually well-preserved ciné-variety of 1914. Free classical facade with a giant order of Ionic pilasters above ground floor. Semi-circular central entrance arch rising above a projecting canopy into the first-floor level. In the centre bay, the pilasters are replaced by giant Ionic columns carried on console brackets. They originally supported an entablature, now absent. Relief frieze below parapet.

The interiors have most of their fine

original plasterwork which, in the rectangular auditorium, is concealed at one end only by a modern false proscenium. There are boldly projecting, bow-fronted boxes, four on either side, each carried on a single, slender iron column. Between the boxes, at balcony level, are free-standing columns carrying a five-bay arcade of elliptical arches. The balcony and box fronts have elaborate full-relief ornament. The upper walls are ornamented with consoles over the columns, scrolly arch keys and treillage panels and, above this, a frieze with garlanded oeil-de-boeuf motifs, then a cove with rococo mouldings and a flat ceiling with shallow-domed centre.

Alterations for bingo have been made sensitively, without compromising the possibility of future theatre use. There is sufficient space at the rear of the site to

permit construction of an enlarged stage house. *KW*

Royal Aquarium

Marine Parade
Other names
    Royalty
    Royalty Theatre and Cinema
    Little Theatre
    Hollywood Cinema and Rosie's
        Nightclub
Original architect
    1876   Unknown: as an aquarium
Later works
    1883   Bottle and Olley: converted to
            theatre
    1925   Unknown: Little Theatre creat-
            ed
    1970   Unknown: converted to cine-
            mas (later cinema/theatre)
    1984   Unknown: main auditorium
            reconverted for use as season-
            al theatre
    later   Unknown: division into four
            screens and nightclub
Current use **Four cinemas and a nightclub**
Capacity   **was 1242**

Built, as the name suggests, as an Aquarium, the thick glass tank fronts are said to exist still, behind the drapes in the main auditorium.

The Aquarium was converted to a theatre in 1883. The Little Theatre was created under the same roof in 1925. Both theatres became cinemas by 1970, but the main house was adapted in 1984 to serve as a seasonal theatre.

A large structure on a permanent island site, in red brick with arcading and panels on the main south front. Internally, the main auditorium (theatre

Great Yarmouth, Regent

and Cinema I) is largely as it was after cinema conversion. A false ceiling obscures the original, presumably barrel-vaulted form. The projection room, follow-spot positions and sound and lighting desks are believed to occupy the remaining part of an original horseshoe-shaped balcony. The stage has an extraordinary complex rake.

The Little Theatre (Cinema II) has a barrel-vaulted ceiling and good ornamental plastering on the walls, but all now 'painted out'. Restoration of the complex to anything resembling an 'original' form now seems a remote prospect. *KW*

Wellington Pier Theatre
Marine Parade
Other names
    Wellington Pavilion Theatre
Original architect
    1903   Unknown
Later works
    1960   Unknown: auditorium reconstructed with balcony
Current use **Summer theatre**
Capacity   **1248**

A summer theatre of original design with an Art Nouveau flavour, now diluted by unsympathetic alterations. In 1903 the theatre had octagonal turrets at four corners and a big cupola on the top. There was an internal reconstruction in 1960 which produced the present, rather plain auditorium, with a single balcony. *JE/KW*

Windmill ★
Marine Parade
Original architect
    1911   A.S. Hewitt
Listed   **Grade II**
Current use **Waxworks exhibition**
Capacity   **est. 800**

A ciné-variety similar in scale to the Empire and of similar architectural ambition. Terracotta front in three bays, the outer bays slightly advanced as towers in three stages with generous ornament. Modillioned cornice below the top stages, which are crowned by square ogee domes with fish-scale copper covering and globe finials. The gabled centre has a balcony at second floor with a rotating illuminated windmill feature.

The present small cinema is the original theatre balcony and today has a somewhat oppressive atmosphere. The front of the balcony was walled up and is fronted by the screen. The stalls area of the building has been rendered

almost unrecognisable by the installation of a semi-permanent exhibition which occupies more than one level but has been installed in such a way that everything could be removed. The auditorium had heavily enriched ceiling ribs and walls with medallions supported by cherubs. Most of this ornament survives, although partly obscured. The proscenium arch is original, and on either side are the rectangular frames which displayed the illuminated numbers during a variety bill.

There was never a fly tower but dressing rooms can still be seen under the stage. *KW*

HALESWORTH
Suffolk

Rifle Hall
London Road
Other names
    Theatre
Original architect
    1793   Unknown
Later works
    1864   Unknown: converted volunteers' drill room and lecture hall
    1892   Bottle and Olley (Great Yarmouth): altered
    1968   Unknown: modernised
Current use **Community hall**

Built by Joseph Hounslow of Bedford for £300, the theatre was by 1796 owned by the Warde family and leased to the Fisher circuit. David Fisher bought the copyhold in 1844 and the property was auctioned. Andrew Johnson, who then acquired it, gave it to the town under a charitable trust for use as a drill hall and lecture room. Since 1968 it has been owned by Halesworth UDC.

Although there are some areas of exterior brickwork which could well be of C18 date – and thus the main side wall alignments – the building appears to contain little, if any, original theatre fabric. The handsome front and associated rooms were added in 1892 by Bottle and Olley of Great Yarmouth and the local council extensively modernised the hall on becoming its owners. It is entirely of brick although there are freestone enrichments to the 1892 front. There is a continuous pitched roof. In the 1892 extension there is a balcony above the entrance and side rooms. At the time of writing the recent threats to the building seem to have been withdrawn. *JL*

HALIFAX
Calderdale (West Yorkshire)

Playhouse
King Cross Street
Other names
    Hanover Methodist Church
Original architect
    1949   Messrs Pickles
Listed   **Grade II**
Current use **Theatre**
Capacity   **291**

The theatre was inserted into a C19 Methodist church in 1949. The original interior of the church was gutted save for the retention of the decorative plaster ceiling, the rake of the stalls and the stage house being created within the original envelope. The building is used essentially for drama and is part of the Little Theatre Guild.

The auditorium is a single raked bank of seating with no central aisle. Three small bays of seating (known as alcoves) are also situated at the rear of the auditorium. The side walls are plain, save for houselight fittings dating from 1949. The proscenium, which is relatively low, given the overall height of the auditorium ceiling, is heavily surmounted by a large concrete lighting bridge cosmetically concealed behind hardboard panelling. This feature is highly reminiscent of Harold Ridge's alterations to the Festival Theatre, Cambridge. Further research has revealed that he was closely associated with the Halifax Thespians in 1949 and the stage arrangements must surely be by Ridge, in collaboration with the local architect, Pickles.

The stage is flat with a small apron forestage. The stage house is equipped with one fly floor at each side, and all flying is by hemp and hand winch. There is no grid, and all suspensions are made from three I-beams. A small orchestra pit can be created with the loss of seats at the front of the auditorium. The front of house was originally the vestry of the chapel, and this has in recent years been extended to provide a wheelchair ramp access from the side street.

Externally the front elevation of the chapel forms the rear wall of the stage. This is unfortunate, since it makes the central grand entrance to the chapel effectively redundant.

The owners recognise the shortcomings of the building and a 'stage one' Arts Council funded feasibility study was in progress at the time of writing. *DW*

Halifax, Theatre Royal (Ian Grundy)

Theatre Royal

Southgate
Original architect
   1905   Richard Horsfall and Son
Later works
   1930s Unknown: converted to
          cinema
Listed   **Grade II**
Current use **Disused**
Capacity originally c.1700

Designed by Richard Horsfall and Son of Halifax and very similar externally to the Palace and Hippodrome in Burnley, also by Horsfall.

Excellent Edwardian Baroque ashlar facade, unusually formal for an English theatre. Three main storeys with an attic. Flanking bays surmounted by open segmental pediments enclosing enriched circular windows. Three central bays above the arched entrances emphasised by giant Ionic pilasters, and a triangular pediment set against the attic storey. An additional bay to the right provides access via an archway with a large set of iron gates bearing the words 'Theatre Royal' to the stage door.

The auditorium was gutted in the 1930s for cinema use and the proscenium wall demolished to allow the new auditorium to be extended into the stage house. However, the proscenium wall was retained at high level in order to support and retain the grid. Access can still be gained into the original stage tower, which has one timber fly floor on each side of the stage. All the grid and pulleys, etc., are still intact.

Proposals for redevelopment have envisaged keeping no more than the facade. *DW*

Victoria (Civic) ★★

Commercial Street and Wards End
Other names
   Victoria Hall
Original architect
   1901   Clement Williams
Later works
   1964   Unknown: fly tower built
Listed   **Grade II**
Current use **Theatre**
Capacity **1505**

Built as a concert hall called the Victoria Hall. The platform was set behind a permanent proscenium frame and was, from the beginning, intended for occasional theatrical use. Following the purchase of the hall by the local authority a

fully equipped fly tower was built in 1964. It became the Civic Theatre, then the Victoria Theatre, though still used for concerts, etc.

The fine auditorium has a European opera house look about it, with a semicircular rear wall and two semi-circular balconies extending along the sides to the wide proscenium. Panelled ceiling with deep, enriched cove. Flat main floor. Spacious and elaborately decorated entrance foyer and main staircase with stained-glass dome. Good, free-classical, ashlar exterior on an important site at the junction of two roads. Imposing curved entrance facade with first floor windows divided by coupled columns and square flanking-towers surmounted by tall cupolas.

At the time of writing a feasibility study was being conducted into the future potential of the building. *CB*

HAMILTON

South Lanarkshire

Granada

Quarry Street
Other names
   1887   Victoria Hall
   1909   Playhouse
Original architect
   1887   Andrew Downie
Current use **Shop**
Capacity originally 1500

Symmetrical ashlar facade to Quarry Street survives unaltered above ground floor. Two-storey bay windows with corbelled gables, flanking a five-bay central

Halifax, Victoria (Ian Grundy)

section with big mullioned and transomed windows at first-floor level.
Smaller windows above, divided by coupled pilasters and a large tripartite
arched window in the centre surmounted by a small gable. Despite a capacity
of 1500, it was a cramped theatre with
inadequate facilities.

The interior has been decked over to
make storage space, but is still recognisable. *BP*

HARROGATE
North Yorkshire

Empire
Cheltenham Mount
Other names
1930-31   Gaiety Theatre
Original architect
1872   Unknown: as a chapel
Later works
   **1910   Unknown: converted to
       theatre**
   **1970s   Unknown: converted to restau-
       rant**
Current use **Restaurant**
Capacity **(was) c.1000**

The building was originally constructed
in 1872 as a Primitive Methodist Chapel
and converted to a theatre in 1910. It
finally closed as a theatre in October
1931. It was used for a number of retail
purposes and, by 1948-49 as a garage.
The front-of-house area was converted
to a restaurant in the 1970s and in the
1980s this was enlarged to incorporate
the original auditorium. Previous to this
the auditorium and stage had been used
as a scenic workshop by the Harrogate
Repertory Company, located immediately across the street from the Empire.

Externally the upper part of the building, above the shopfronts, remains
much the same as it was conceived for
the Primitive Methodist Chapel. Four
windows wide, cill band, semi-circular
arches with imposts and keystones and a
crowning cornice and parapet.

Internally the original proscenium
arch, which is carved timber rather than
fibrous plaster, has been restored. New
cast-iron balcony fronts have been
installed round the original line of the
single balcony. New floor levels have
been inserted at stalls level, and original
cast-iron columns, supporting the balcony, have been boxed in.

The stage area is also used for dining,
and the stage house has been under-
drawn with a false ceiling. The theatre
suffered a fire in 1996, that was caused
by a fire bomb sent to an adjoining shop
by animal rights activists. This caused
significant fire damage to the stage area.
The proscenium and auditorium survived, although water damaged. *DW*

Georgian Theatre
Church Square
Other names
The Theatre
Original architect
1788   Samuel Butler (?)
Listed **Grade II**
Current use **Residential**

The central portion of a domestic
building, now known as Mansfield
House, thought to have opened as
Harrogate's first theatre in 1788. It
must later have undergone a number
of significant changes as nothing
remains internally to identify this building as a theatre. However, a recently
discovered map indicates that there
was a theatre on the site and the footprint suggests the theatre was orientat-
ed with the stage at the south end,
abutting what is now the Empress
Hotel. This would suggest that the
entrance to the theatre was gained
along the side of the auditorium.

The property presents a handsome
front to the Stray. Stone-faced in seven
two-storey bays, the centre three slightly advanced and with a prominent pediment. Centre doorway, wood surround
with Doric attached columns. Slated
roof. Commemorative plaque. *DW/SM*

Harrogate Theatre ★★
Oxford Street
Other Names
Grand Opera House
Original architect
1900   Frank Tugwell
Later works
**1972   Roderick Ham and Partners:
      refurbished**
Listed **Grade II**
Current use **Theatre**
Capacity **500**

Harrogate, Theatre (Ian Grundy)

A delightfully intimate theatre, very well suited to its present role as a repertory playhouse in this attractive Victorian Spa town. The site is wedge-shaped at the acute-angled junction of two streets. The stage is at the wide end, with an irregularly shaped rear wall, and the side walls of the auditorium converge towards the back. There are two serpentine-fronted balconies and two boxes either side at each level, divided by delicate pilasters and surmounted by broken scrolled pediments. Balcony and box fronts richly decorated by cartouches supported by putti, garlands, etc.rectangular acanthus leaf bracketed proscenium surmounted by a central cartouche containing a lyre. Central part of the ceiling carried up into a dome. Intimate foyer with richly modelled plaster frieze by F. Darlington depicting the development of arts through the ages ('The rehearsal of a Mystery Play', 'The Invocation of Terpsichore', etc.)

In 1972 a major scheme of refurbishment was carried out by Roderick Ham and Partners, including reseating and the reduction of the gallery to two rows. The total capacity was reduced from 797 to 475. At the same time, front of house and dressing rooms, etc., were reorganised and updated.

The exterior has a four-storeyed octagonal tower at the apex of the site, with the steeply pitched roof and illuminated leaded light cupola bearing the inscription 'Grand Opera'. The 1972 scheme is now in need of further review. The theatre would benefit from a thorough restoration both front of house and backstage. The house light fittings are a less than pleasing (post-1972) addition to the auditorium. The upper circle has been damaged by the unsympathetic insertion of a control room, but with some careful planning this could be improved, and the auditorium reseated to provide a superb small playhouse ideally suited to the present repertory company.

The theatre still possesses many of its original front-of-house fixtures and fittings, all too rare a feature today. The intimacy of the foyers gives the place an almost domestic quality which is endearing and worthy of sensitive restoration. DW

Royal Hall ★★★
Ripon Road
Other names
   Kursaal
Original architects
   1903   **Robert J. Beale and Frank Matcham**

Later works
   1960s   **Unknown: public bar area modified and modernised**
   c.1980   **Unknown: original canopy removed and new canopy erected**
   1997   **Unknown: entrance canopy reinstated to original design**
Listed   **Grade II***
Current use **Multi-purpose venue**
Capacity   **1275**

Although a multi-purpose hall rather than a theatre, the Royal Hall's inclusion here is justified by its use of many of the elements of theatre architecture, as outstanding of its type and a well-cared-for example of Frank Matcham's architecture of entertainment.

It is quite unlike any other piece of extant work by Matcham. He was originally appointed by the Harrogate Corporation to be the judge of an architectural competition to design a new place of entertainment within the town. The winning entry was submitted by Robert Beale and the designs appeared in *The Builder*. The final building bears little resemblance to these drawings and much more to the direct involvement of Frank Matcham.

The Royal Hall has a richly decorated rectangular auditorium. There are six boxes on either side, below three bow-fronted sections of the single balcony. The stalls area is, in truth, a flat-floored ballroom accessed from marble staircases at the front of the stalls and oak staircases at the rear. A major contribution to the ambience is provided by the conscious admission of daylight into the auditorium. Six clerestory windows at upper-circle level, originally glazed with leaded lights, a central auditorium dome (in some ways reminiscent of the

London Hippodrome, qv) and a sliding glazed lantern at the rear of the upper circle, all provide opportunities for natural daylight. The corporation employed a full-time orchestra, and in its early days the building was used expressly for entertainment during the day, whilst its patrons promenaded and 'took the waters'.

The stage house is very small, particularly for a building (not theatre) which seats today 1275. It was originally equipped with choir stalls and a pipe organ, the stage forming a restricted 'D' shape expressly for this purpose, with no flying height. Subsequent alterations and improvements have created a stage of increased technical capacity, but it will always be restricted. The stage and the auditorium are encircled by a 360° promenade, which effectively isolates the stage and makes technical expansion almost impossible.

The auditorium has been little altered since its construction, although the original fresco panels by Jonas Binns of Halifax, which once adorned the large rectangular panels flanking the proscenium were over-painted in the 1950s, the original (it was said) having 'faded away'. Similarly the triangular panels at each corner of the ceiling have been over-painted, having once contained the heraldic shields of the Borough of Harrogate and the Duchy of Lancaster.

Shortly after the building opened, a biograph box was installed behind the elevated and raked seating area to the rear of the hall. This was removed in the 1930s, but a new technical control room has been constructed in the same location, copying the footprint and style of the original.

Future restoration work is anticipated. DW

Harrogate, Royal Hall (Tennant Brown)

HASTINGS
East Sussex

Gaiety

Queen's Road
Other names
   Gaiety cinema
   Cannon cinemas
Original architect
   1882   C.J. Phipps (with Cross and
          Wells)
Later works
   1932   Unknown: converted to cinema
   1972   Unknown: tripled
Current use Cinema
Capacity   c.1600 (prior to conversion to
             a cinema)

Given the local history of extreme antipathy to the theatre from both the churches and the magistrates, Phipps was a wise choice as architect.

The external treatment is, if anything, more restrained than that of the Council offices, nearly opposite. At ground level a restaurant was incorporated to the left of the inconspicuous main entrance, and a shopping arcade (still open) to the right.

The theatre became a cinema in 1932 and was converted into a multi-screen in 1972 which completely obliterated the original interior, but there is an excellent painting of the auditorium in the local museum.

Hippodrome

Pelham Place
Other names
   1912   Royal Cinema de Luxe
          Empire Theatre
          Royal Marine Palace of Varieties
Original architect
   1899   Runtz
Later works
   1978   Unknown: rebuilt internally at
          ground-floor level
Current use Amusements
Capacity   originally c.1500

Prominent seafront site, wedged up against the face of the cliff on which stands Hastings Castle. Apart from the insertion of a floor at the level of the 1st balcony front, the essential features of the auditorium survived until 1978 when it was finally wrecked. Although in need of maintenance and marred by a crude modern canopy the enriched terracotta exterior is basically intact. The facade lies along the axis of the auditorium/stage and is flanked at each end by imposing domed pavilions with Arts and Crafts octagonal turrets at their front corners.

Hastings, Hippodrome (Ian Grundy)

The pavilions are linked by four large semicircular-arched windows at first-floor level and a loggia (now glazed) of squat coupled columns below the eaves of the pantiled roof. Here the style is vaguely Spanish Renaissance, reminiscent of the Middlesborough Empire. *CB/MS*

White Rock ★

White Rock
Other names
   White Rock Pavilion
Original architect
   1927   C. Cowles Voysey
Later works
   1985   Unknown: auditorium altered
Listed   Grade II
Current use Theatre and concert hall
Capacity   1165

A handsome building on the seafront, built in Spanish Colonial style. Rendered facade with brick band at second-floor level, where the windows are grouped to give the impression of an open loggia, above which is a deep entablature and overhanging eaves to Roman tiled roof. Tall arched entrance approached by steps and flanked by lower, square-headed entrances. Above the outer entrances are well-modelled coloured faience roundels, a motif carried along the flank elevation.

The auditorium was refurbished and redecorated in 1985. It is very wide, of concert hall proportions giving strained sight lines from the sides both at stalls and circle level. The circle overhangs the stalls by 8 rows of seats. The plain walls have medallions, as added decoration. *MS/JE*

HEBDEN BRIDGE
Calderdale (West Yorkshire)

Picture House ★

New Road
Original architect
   1921   Unknown
Listed   Grade II
Current use Cinema and occasional live
              shows
Capacity   c.500

A 1921 cinema, intact inside and out. It now often presents a live show on its original (very small) stage, especially of music and stand-up variety and during the annual Arts Festival. The building is of great charm and is an interesting survivor of its period. The stone frontage (cleaned and restored in 1978) is in an unusually pure classical style in three bays, defined by channelled quoins, the centre bay recessed with a Doric portico in antis. In the outer bays are good original shopfronts. Only the disproportionately small windows over the shops dilute the effect.

The original paybox remains in perfect condition, but has been superseded by an internal box in the small main foyer. Dressing rooms and stage access are at the rear of the building which backs onto the canal. The building has been the subject of regular recent improvements: a general refurbishment in 1978, stage and dressing-room upgrades in 1985, new sound system and a new electric roll-up wide screen in 1993 (to facilitate more live shows). *IG*

HENLEY-ON-THAMES
Oxfordshire

Kenton
New Street
Other names
   The Theatre
   The New Theatre
Original architect
   1805 William Parker of Henley
Later works
   1816 Unknown: converted to school
   1930s Unknown: altered internally
   1957 John Piper: new painted
           proscenium
   1967 Maurice R. Day and Assocs:
Current use Theatre
Capacity 245

Built in 1805 in light brown brick with red brick flat arches. Three storeys with a tiled hipped roof behind parapets. There is an extended facade, the frontage building being three windows wide in front of the actual theatre plus having an offset tier of windows and a wide segmental arched opening to the right indicating a separate (but originally associated?) property. The extent of the theatre is marked at ground floor by a semi-circular arched doorway at either end and by stuccoing. There is a modern canopy and theatre entrance beneath the first two window bays.

After closing in 1813 the theatre became successively a chapel, a school, a parish hall and a scenery workshop. In the mid 1930s it reverted to theatre use. The consequent alterations together with a further series in the 1960s appear to have left of the original fabric only the shell of the building. The double curved balcony probably dates from the 1967 remodelling which left only the earlier windows, the balcony front and the central ceiling mount for a sunburner. The present auditorium is in domestic neo-Georgian style. *SM*

HEREFORD
Herefordshire

County
Berrington Street
Other names
   1887 Beethoven Hall
   1913 Picture House
   c.1919 Palladium
   1957 County Ballroom
   1962 Regal
Original architect
   1787 or 1790 Unknown: as a church

Later works
   1887 Unknown: converted to piano
           showroom
   1913 H. Skyrme: converted to ciné-
           variety
   1957 Unknown: converted to ball-
           room
   1962 Unknown: again converted to
           cinema
   1964 Unknown: converted to bingo
           hall
Listed   Grade II
Current use Bingo
Capacity c.500

The present auditorium is the relic of a building of c.1790 which started life as a church of the Countess of Huntingdon's Connexion, became a piano showroom and was converted to the Picture House (ciné-variety) in 1913, incorporating cottages on the Berrington Street front. It is not known whether the fly tower was added at this time. By 1939-46 stage use was occasional only, but in 1946 it became a full-time repertory theatre. By 1957 it was a ballroom and further uses included roller-skating rink and warehouse. It reopened as a cinema in 1962 but became a bingo house in 1964.

Six-bay asymmetrical rendered two-storey front; sandstone third bay slightly advanced with pedimented gable and a Venetian window over wide entrance; semi-circular headed windows with sandstone surrounds, imposts and keyblocks; sashes with thin glazing bars, curved at head to form Gothic panes. Pitched slated roof. *TB*

HERNE BAY
Kent

Bijou
75 High Street
Other names
   Cinema de Luxe
   Coliseum
   Red Lantern
Original architect
   1911 probably J. Wilson
Later works
   1912 J. Wilson: alterations
Current use Retail outlet

Opened in 1911 and altered in 1912 to reopen as the Bijou Theatre. High concave entrance set in short tower with cupola, with shops either side, the auditorium lying at the rear of the shops. No interior description found.

The theatre was used for concert parties and variety, until acquired for use as a cinema in 1926. In 1936, it was pur-

chased by Union, but never reopened. It was used as an auctioneer's and later the auditorium was subdivided for retail use at street level and office use above, which use continues. Today the entrance is unmistakable, with original glazing intact. *SM*

HIGH WYCOMBE
Buckinghamshire

Intimate Theatre
The Tower, Frogmore
Original architect
   1893 Unknown: School of Science
           and the Arts
Later works
   1946 Jack Stone (builder): converted
           to theatre
   1984 Geoffrey Hawkins (for Crest
           Estates): rebuilt internally as
           offices
Current use Offices

A two-storey detached Victorian building of Queen Anne Revival style, with imposing brick elevations; the entrance built at the base of the clock tower which, with cupola and weathervane, is the dominant feature. The building was erected in 1893 as the School of Science and the Arts. Between the wars it became a swimming pool and later a skating rink. In 1946, it was converted to a theatre by four ex-servicemen with repertory experience. It would seem the conversion was a fairly makeshift affair due to postwar restrictions on building work. The auditorium floor was raked and seated 'by a London firm of theatre furnishers'. There was no balcony. The stage was built incorporating a series of electric lifts. There were a workshop and a café. Over the years a laundry, effects room and club room were created, and later the company ran a drama school. Financial difficulties forced closure in 1957. The building fell into disrepair and was converted to offices in 1984. *SM*

HINCKLEY
Leicestershire

Regent
Rugby Road/Lancaster Road
Other names
   1955 Gaumont
   1967 Classic
   c.1980 Zetters
   1980 Rainbow Club
Original architect
   1929 H.G. Bradley (Birmingham)
Current use Bingo
Capacity c.920

The Regent was built in 1929 to accommodate films, variety and orchestral concerts. It opened with a live show given by the local Operatic Society, but seems to have become a full-time cinema soon after. It closed in 1968 as a cinema and reopened as a bingo house.

The building lies parallel to Rugby Road. It is brick faced in two storeys, with the entrance set in a row of shops. The height of the stage house does not reach the apex of the main roof, so it can hardly be said to have a fly tower in the ordinary sense. Conversion to bingo has made access difficult to some parts of the house. The stalls floor still has a good rake. A false ceiling has been inserted at the level of the top of the balcony front, allowing the plaster ornament to be seen. From the now isolated circle the top of the proscenium is visible, with lattice and rose ornament. The wooden grid does not extend to the full depth of the stage. There is no evidence of a safety curtain (which may have been of roller type).

It would not be impossible to return the Regent to live performance use if the need arose, but the existence of a better-equipped theatre, the Concordia (1972), albeit with a smaller stage, makes this unlikely. *TB*

HINTON ST MARY
Dorset

Theatre
Manor House
Original architect
   C15   Unknown: as a tithe barn
Later works
c.1929-
   1939   George Pitt-Rivers: converted
             to theatre
Listed   Grade II*
Current use Theatre

C15 tithe barn converted to theatre c.1929 by George Pitt-Rivers. Ashlar and cob, with two entrances with sconces at side. Gable-ended tiled roof. Appearance is that of a long flat-floored hall with square proscenium stage with small apron. Later roof of collar-braced trusses on vertical wall posts supported on corbels.

Family portraits line walls and a large stone fireplace with stone panels, in keeping with early appearance of the building, has been inserted halfway down hall. Seating on loose stacking chairs. Low grid, with curtains, etc., hand-drawn.

Also used for political rallies and union meetings – Sir Oswald Mosley once addressed audiences here. Now serves mainly local theatricals, concerts, meetings and, latterly, weddings and parties. *SM*

HOLMFIRTH
Kirklees (West Yorkshire)

Picturedrome
Eldon Yard
Other names
   Valley Theatre
Original architect
   1912   P.M. Brown and Co.
Current use Cinema and theatre
Capacity   200

The Picturedrome reopened in 1998 as a cinema/theatre. Originally opened in 1912 as a ciné-variety theatre; the proscenium is a typical Edwardian gilt affair with a central cartouche above the flattened top. The stage is 5m (16ft 5in) deep and 7m (23ft) wide. Limited flying. The single flat-fronted balcony is returned to the wall on the right-hand side only, facilitating an emergency exit to the rear of the building. The front of the circle is decorated with well-modelled plasterwork. The ceiling is a coffered segmental barrel vault executed in pressed tin – a very rare survival for Britain (more common in North America – see Clevedon Curzon).

The revamped auditorium uses the front stalls area only, the rear stalls having become a large bar area. The balcony, reached by a single staircase with a tiled lower portion, has recently become a picture postcard museum (Bamforths who produced cards in the town operated the cinema and also produced many films 1913–15).

The exterior, with its pitched gable following the line of the slate roof is typical of a cinema of this period. It has two pairs of glazed entrance doors with a window either side and four windows at

Holmfirth, Picturedrome (Ian Grundy)

first-floor level. The date of the building is above the two central upper windows.

The fly tower is not raised above the roof line. Stage access doors are now slightly restricted by a modern hotel built to the rear of the theatre - but still accessible. *IG*

HORSHAM
West Sussex

King's Head Assembly Rooms
King's Head Hotel, East Street
Other names
   Theatre
early
   1900s King's Hall
   1919   King's Theatre
Original architect
   n.d.   Unknown
Current use Part of hotel

The King's Head (Hotel) is an old coaching house. It is an accretive building whose history is not easily read from superficial inspection. Assembly rooms were built in the C18 which were visited by Thomas Trotter in the early C19 and referred to as 'the Theatre' (presumably a regular fit-up). Pantomimes were presented there for many years. A building attached at the rear can probably be identified with this room. The use continued until after the First World War, by which time it had shown 'animated pictures'. Tip-up seats were installed and from 1919 it was known as the King's Theatre. It was eventually made obsolete by the opening of the Capitol theatre in the late 1920s (now demolished).

In 1869 there was a 'music hall' attached to the hotel. This was not the same as the assembly rooms and may be the present function room. *SM*

HUDDERSFIELD
Kirklees (West Yorkshire)

Hippodrome
Queensgate
Other names
   Tudor Cinema
Original architect
   1905   W. Cooper: converted from
             older building
Later works
   1928   Unknown: auditorium
             enlarged and new stage built
             on added land
   1960s   Unknown: rebuilt as cinema
             after a fire
Current use Cinema
Capacity   originally c.2000

The Hippodrome was the result of the conversion of an 1846 riding shed into a theatre in 1905. The auditorium (now a cinema) contains none of the original theatre interior, all having been destroyed in a fire in the 1960s. The stage house was originally annexed to a scenic workshop at the rear of the stage, now a heap of rubble. The connecting door has been bricked up but is still visible. Fly tower is intact, one fly floor per side and grid still present. A small second screen has been inserted on the stage. Dressing rooms originally under the stage, now very derelict.

The external walls of the auditorium were lowered significantly after the fire, though what remains is millstone grit and must date from the Hippodrome's original construction. The auditorium side of the fly tower clearly shows where the original auditorium roof abutted the stage house at a much higher level than today. Externally to Queensgate the front of the building is clad with Westmorland slate in a modern style.   DW

Hull, New (Ted Bottle)

HULL
Kingston upon Hull

New ★
Kingston Square
Other names
    Assembly Rooms
Original architect
    1834   R.H. Sharp: as Assembly Rooms
Later works
    1939   W.B. Wheatley and Robert Cromie: converted to theatre
    1966-8   Unknown: auditorium and stage improved
    1980s   Hull City Council: entrance portico glazed in to provide additional front of house facilities
Current use Theatre
Capacity   1189

The building was originally constructed as Georgian Assembly Rooms. The foundation stone was laid on 28 June 1830. In 1924 an amateur theatre group formed the Hull Repertory Theatre and secured the use of an old lecture theatre. The success of the group attracted them to the Assembly Rooms next door, and a deal was made which allowed the city to extend the Fire Station (!) into the site of the Lecture Theatre (then known as the Little Theatre) which in turn allowed the theatre group to acquire the Assembly Rooms which now adjoin the Fire Station.

Architects W.B. Wheatley and Robert Cromie were appointed to draw up the conversion plans for the building. Externally they appear to have blinded most of the Georgian windows and demolished two elegant pediments over handsome Ionic porticos on Kingston Square and Jarrat Street.

Internally the Assembly Rooms were gutted to allow a complete new scheme to be executed. The results were not strikingly successful. A single straight balcony abuts harshly the side walls and one large and oversized box is 'hung' on each side of the auditorium. The functional elements of a theatre auditorium are all present but in an uneasy relationship. The wide, sprawling auditorium has no true point of command and the balcony is a long way from the stage. The plaster ornament is sparse. The moulded rectangular proscenium arch is surrounded by a decorative metal grille which probably served a ventilation duct.

Some improvements were made in 1966 and 1968: the auditorium was reseated, the orchestra pit enlarged and, most significantly, the stage was deepened. In the 1980s the front portico was 'glazed in' to provide additional front-of-house facilities and, at the same time, the foyers were remodelled.   DW

HYDE
Tameside

Theatre Royal ★★
Corporation Street/Henry Street
Other names
    1902   New Theatre Royal
    1914   New Royal Cinema
    later   Theatre Royal
Original architect
    1902   Campbell and Horsley (Manchester)
Later works
    1972   Unknown: second cinema screen incorporated in stage area
Listed   Grade II
Current use Disused
Capacity   c.650

The Theatre Royal was opened in 1902 as a replacement for the first Theatre Royal which had stood in Frank Street; this was owned by the Hyde Theatre Company Limited who secured the land for a newer and better theatre in 1901. It opened as the New Theatre Royal in 1902 and seated 1000.

The facade to Corporation Street was a flat but not unpleasing composition in red brick, three storeys high, in three major bays, the centre having an arched, shallow central recess with a semi-circular arched head and pilasters rising from corbels to support a triangular pediment, richly decorated with moulded brickwork.

In 1914, the theatre was leased for cinema use and called the New Royal Cinema, but the name of Theatre Royal was soon in use again for the regular pantomimes, variety and local shows. In 1950 it became a repertory theatre for two years and thereafter reverted to cinema, with Christmas pantomime and occasional shows, until the 1960s when it was used largely as a cinema. The last show was staged in October 1972. The stage area was then converted into a

Hyde, Theatre Royal (Sally McGrath)

second cinema. It finally closed on 17 January 1985.

Good intimate auditorium with two balconies curving round to meet the altered proscenium. Despite prolonged disuse, this remained undivided and with much of its theatrical atmosphere. The flies, grid and 13.4m (44ft) deep raked stage also remained and conversion back to live use would probably have been feasible. The theatre is well situated in the town centre, adjacent to the architecturally inferior Festival Theatre (ironically the converted Alexandra Cinema and Billiard Hall) now used by the amateur companies, who transferred their productions when the Royal lost the stage area.

Although consent for demolition was given in 1999 and a redevelopment scheme, including plans for a pub on the site, approved, the building was spot-listed in April 2000 and, therefore, the threat of demolition has effectively been removed. A viable future for the theatre still needs to be found but, at the time of

writing, interest had been expressed in re-opening it as a cinema to serve the local Asian community. *SM/CB*

ILFRACOMBE
Devon

Alexandra
Market Street
Other names
  Alexandra Hall
  Palace?
Original architect
  1900 Unknown
Current use **Nightclub/bar**
Capacity **(was) 1400**

The theatre was built on the hill between Market Street and Avenue Road on more than one level to accommodate the steepness of the slope. The lower part of the building contained the flat-floored Alexandra Theatre. It presented drama, concerts, revue and seasonal variety. During the Wars it was used as a Garrison Theatre. In 1965 a fly tower

was added, and stage and dressing rooms improved. In the early 1970s the interior was gutted to accommodate a (roller?) skating rink.

The building has been altered and reopened as a nightclub/bar. *SM*

Gaiety
Sea Road/Wilder Road
Original architect
  c.1900 Unknown
Later works
  1963 Unknown: interior reconstruct-
    ed as an amusement arcade
Listed **Grade II**
Current use **Amusement arcade**
Capacity **c.390 (prior to 1963 recon-**
    struction)

A seaside theatre at the end of a terrace of shops facing the sea. It is now listed, a charming incident in the street with its turret and weathervane. Closed in 1963 after failing to meet safety requirements which would have reduced its capacity, the theatre became a amusement arcade. *SM*

ILKLEY
Bradford

King's Hall ★
Station Road
Other names
  Assembly Hall
  Assembly Room
Original architect
  1907 William Bakewell (Leeds)
Current use **Theatre and multi-purpose hall**
Capacity **484**

Part of a larger development including the Town Hall and Carnegie Library, the King's Hall is the right wing of a symmetrical block in Arts and Crafts style. The design was the winning entry from over forty submissions in a competition. Stone under a pitched slate roof. The Town Hall is the central block and the library the left-hand wing. The Winter Garden was a later addition, in a different style, opening in 1933.

The auditorium of the King's Hall (originally called the Assembly Room) is a delight and consists of a small balfronted balcony of four rows with five bow-fronted boxes down each side with glazed rear panels and doors. Both the balcony front and boxes are richly decorated with busts of famous authors and composers. There is a barrel-vaulted and ribbed ceiling with a lay light in three sections. The proscenium arch is elliptical and richly decorated with a Yorkshire

Rose design and a bust of Edward VII in an ornamental frame at the centre. The stalls floor is flat and on the right-hand side is linked with the Winter Garden.

The stage is deep and extremely steeply raked (1:10). Dressing rooms are below the stage. Orchestra pit is now boarded over and unused. The rear wall of the stage is gently curved with a high access door in the centre. There are twenty-five hemp sets.

The Winter Garden is a handsome rectangular room with an iron balcony with curving fronts on three sides approached by a staircase on the fourth side. Cove rises to large rooflight with ornamental aprons. *IG*

IPSWICH
Suffolk

Regent ★
3 St Helen's Street
Other names
   1952   Gaumont
   1980   Odeon
Original architect
   1929   W.E. Trent
Later works
   1991   RHWL and Borough Council: improved and refurbished
Current use Theatre
Capacity 1783

While basically a steel frame construction with precast concrete floors and brickwork, the entrance front is a trim neo-Georgian exercise two storeys high with a hipped roof over the front-of-house accommodation. The central section comprises three first-floor windows set in brown brickwork all surmounted by a lead-dressed and enriched stone cornice; the entrance doors beneath are reached by the customary full-width flight of stone steps protected by a canopy. This section is flanked by rather narrow stone pavilions each topped by a pair of urns; each pavilion has a first-floor window and a display recess in the ground-floor rusticated work. To the left is a two-storey single-bay extension of the same style and date, originally the entrance to the cheaper seats.

Acquired by the Borough Council as part of a wider redevelopment project, the theatre was reopened in 1991 for live entertainment. Attendant works included reversing a number of alterations made during Rank's tenure, provision of a new get-in and four new dressing rooms, the general repair, redecoration and re-equipping of backstage areas. The grid is tight to the fly

tower roof. The public areas were also overhauled although, at the time of writing, Rank's interior colour scheme remains. Apart from the loss many years ago of the Wurlitzer organ, its grilles set either side of the proscenium, and the light fittings, the auditorium retains so much of its original form and fabric that a faithful restoration could be achieved fairly easily. *JL*

KENDAL
Cumbria

Shakespeare ★
Highgate
Other names
1829–30 New
Original architect
   1829   John Richardson
Later works
   1834   Unknown: converted to ballroom
   later   Unknown: gutted and converted to store
Current use Church

Sited at the end of the long narrow yard of the Shakespeare Hotel, the theatre closed in 1834 when it was converted into a ballroom. Later the interior was gutted and it became a store.

A simple rectangular building of stone with a pitched roof. Three-bay gabled front with a central arched doorway reached by a flight of five steps and flanked by plain sash windows. Single doors similarly flank the steps at basement level. A single square window in the gable above which there is, remarkably, a chimney stack. *MS*

KILMARNOCK
East Ayrshire

King's
Titchfield Street
Other names
   1904   King's Theatre
   1934   Regal
   1964   ABC
   1987   Cannon
   1996   ABC
Original architect
   1904   Alec Cullen
Later works
   1934   Charles J. McNair: rebuilt internally as cinema
Current use Dark

Imposing French Renaissance ashlar facade of four storeys, disfigured by modern cinema tat at ground-floor level. The three central bays at first-floor level have large round-arched windows; high above, under the projecting cornice, three square-headed windows, now bricked up, are subdivided by small attached columns on brackets. The flanking bays, containing staircases, have lunette windows in the upper storey, framed between elongated composite pilasters. The composition is capped by polygonal turrets with steeply pitched roofs. The 1930s' interior was destroyed by fire in 1975.

The cinema closed in 1999 following the opening of an Odeon multiplex nearby. There are plans to convert the building to retail and restaurant use with a smaller cinema on the second floor. *BP*

Kendal, Shakespeare (Ian Grundy)

Palace

9 Green Street
Other names
    1863   Corn Exchange Hall
    1903   Palace Theatre
Original architect
    1863   James Ingram: as a Corn
            Exchange
Later works
    1903   Steele?: converted to music
            hall
    1927   James Miller: annexe hall
            added
    1979   Unknown: rebuilt after fire
    1985   Unknown: refurbished
Listed   **Grade B**
Current use **Theatre**
Capacity   **503**

Formerly a public hall in the Corn Exchange, built 1862. A robust two-storey Victorian classical exterior with a tall campanile over the entrance. Converted to a variety theatre with a fully equipped stage in 1903. The auditorium is long and narrow and the balcony is isolated from the stage by blank side walls. The modern interior is comfortable but nondescript.   *BP*

KING'S LYNN
Norfolk

Guildhall of St George

29 King Street
Original architect
1410–20   Unknown
Later works
    1766   Unknown: converted to play-
            house
1950–51 Marshall Sisson: repaired and
            restored
Listed   **Grade I**
Current use **Arts Centre**
Capacity   **349**

A Guildhall of 1410–20 with a complex later history. End on to the street, a tile-covered brick building 32.6m (107ft) long by 9.1m (30ft) wide forming part of a probably unique mediaeval complex on a long tenement strip running between King Street and the Great Ouse. The hall/theatre is at first-floor level above an undercroft and a wide service passage on the south side. The roof is of closely set scissor-braced trusses with high-set collars and modern metal tie rods every fifth truss. Four-centred traceried windows to each side and entrance front in freestone.
    The Guild used the hall for only a little over 100 years. It was subsequently used variously as a warehouse, a court-

King's Lynn, Guildhall of St George

house, a Civil War powder store and a painted scenery storehouse. It was also used as a theatre at intervals from its beginnings until the early C19, by the guild for nativity plays and by travelling players of the Norwich circuit as a fit-up. In 1766 it was converted into a permanent theatre which was in use until 1814 when another theatre was built in St James Street (burnt down 1936).
    By 1945 the Hall was so dilapidated that demolition was only averted by private acquisition (plaque on inside of south wall) enabling the Hall to become the theatre of the present arts centre. In 1948 sufficient remained of the 1766 playhouse which had been built within, for Richard Southern to make a complete reconstruction in model form, but the new theatre of 1951 was not a restoration of the Georgian form. The works of repair and adaptation carefully retained the archaeology of the original building although the new timber stage masks the one remaining hammerbeam truss. Open to the magnificent roof, the proportionally long auditorium is raked and is gained by a seemly new timber staircase set beneath the great east window to the street. The stage curtain is grey, the walls are whitened, the tip-up seating is red as are the window curtains. The 1951 works provided a new back-of-house extension. *JL*

KIRKCALDY
Fife

King's

High Street
Other names
    1904   King's Theatre
    1916   Opera House
    1937   Regal
    1963   ABC
    later   Cannon, MGM, ABC
Original architect
    1904   J.D. Swanston and William
            Williamson
Later works
    1937   Charles J. McNair: rebuilt as
            cinema
Listed   **Grade B (facade only)**
Current use **Triple cinema**

Ashlar sandstone street front and end wall, only, survive from 1904 building with entrance through a rusticated arch (now overclad) between shop units and two floors of flats above. Projecting corner turret with dome. The interior was once similar to Swanston's magnificent King's in Edinburgh. It was gutted in 1937 to be rebuilt in streamlined cinema mode (now three cinemas). Fragments are said to survive above modern ceilings. *BP*

LANCASTER

Grand ★★

St Leonardsgate
Other names
    1782   The Theatre
    1803   Theatre Royal
    1848   Music Hall
after
    1860   Athenaeum
    1884   Athenaeum Theatre
Original architect
    1782   Unknown
Later works
    1848   Edmund Sharpe: converted to
            concert hall; added dwellings
            to front
    1857   Edmund Sharpe: extended to
            rear and installed organ
    1884   Unknown: staircase improved,
            galleries and stage altered
    1897   Frank Matcham: remodelled,
            rebuilt stage with small fly
            tower
    1908   Albert Winstanley: reinstated
            after fire gutted the building
    1931   Unknown: projection box
            added, minor alterations to
            front of house
1978 and later
            Unknown: various improve-
            ments

Lancaster, Grand (Ian Grundy)

Listed   **Grade II**
Current use **Theatre (mainly amateur)**
Capacity   **468**

An early theatre, remarkable in that, although it has been through a succession of alterations and extensions at various times over a period of 200 years, much of the basic stone shell of the original building survives.

It opened in 1782 with pit, upper and lower boxes and gallery and a capacity of about 500. It was managed from 1791-94 by Stephen Kemble and enjoyed a Sarah Siddons season in 1799. Edmund Sharpe, a local architect, acquired it in 1843. He extended and reopened it in 1848 as a concert hall with added dwellings and a museum for the local Literary and Natural History Society. The Georgian stage was probably removed at this time and windows opened in the outer walls. He later extended it to the rear and installed an organ. From 1860 it was owned by the Lancaster Athenaeum Company but was closed as unsafe in 1882. A new owner, Henry Wilkinson, improved the staircases, altered the galleries, rebuilt the stage and reopened in 1884 as the Athenaeum Theatre. It was altered by Frank Matcham in 1897 and given a new stage with a small fly tower. Unfortunately, all this was lost in 1908 when a fire gutted the building. A new interior, designed by Albert Winstanley, was constructed within the Georgian shell and the theatre reopened, renamed the Grand, in the same year.

Subsequent remodellings have not been radical. The building as now seen is still recognisable as a partly C18 structure externally, with Winstanley's Edwardian, four-bay stucco facade and his pleasing interior. The auditorium has one balcony with rich plasterwork on its front, curving round to stage boxes flanking an arched proscenium. Flat ceiling with raised, moulded frame and restrained ornament. Wedge-shaped stage. The theatre is an amateur producing house owned by the Lancaster Footlights Club. *DW*

Hippodrome
Dalton Square
Other names
   1859   **Palatine Hall**
   1931   **County Cinema**
Original architect
   1902   **Unknown: converted from
          temperance hall of 1859**
Later works
   1931   **Unknown: rebuilt as a cinema**
   1980   **Unknown: gutted and convert-
          ed to offices**
Current use **Facade only (offices behind)**
Capacity   **(was) 2000**

Converted from a temperance hall of 1859, itself a conversion of an R.C. chapel of 1799.

Interior completely reconstructed as a cinema in 1931 with one balcony and the small stage incorporated into the auditorium. Ashlar front to Dalton Square, which forms the end of a handsome terrace of houses. The side walls show the arched windows of the former chapel/temperance hall. In 1980/81 the interior was gutted for offices, the facade restored, the arches in the side elevation unblocked and windows inserted. *DW*

LARGS
North Ayrshire

Barrfields Pavilion
Coast Road
Original architect
   1929   **Unknown**
Current use **Viking museum and leisure
          centres**

Blocky white stucco-clad structure with pitched roof, set in landscape gardens. Recently extended and rebuilt to house a museum and cinema, the building is now almost unrecognisable as the former theatre and concert hall which hosted so many popular variety revues. *BP*

LEAMINGTON SPA
Warwickshire

Loft Theatre
3 Victoria Colonnade
Other names
   Victoria Pavilion
   Victoria Grand Circus
   1909   **Olympia Skating Rink**
   1910   **Colonnade Theatre**
   1927-32 **Colonnade Cinema Theatre**
Original architect
   1871   **Unknown: as a circus**
Later works
   1909   **Unknown: converted to skat-
          ing rink**
   1910   **Unknown: rebuilt as a theatre**
   1945   **Unknown: new proscenium,
          dressing rooms and temporary
          stage erected**
   1968   **James A. Roberts (of Stanley
          Sellers): refurbished following
          fire**
   1974   **Unknown: storage facilities,
          dressing rooms and bar
          lounge extended**
Current use **Amateur theatre**
Capacity   **200**

In 1871 a domed building was erected on the site of an old drill shed and used as a circus. The dome was removed in 1900. Opened as a skating rink in 1909. Rebuilt as Colonnade Theatre in 1910. Became the Loft Theatre in 1945 and rebuilt in 1968 as, for all practical purposes, a new theatre.
The building fronts the river Leam. In addition to the main auditorium there is a rehearsal room which occasionally doubles as a studio theatre. The main auditorium has ten rows of seats in a single rake. There is a squat fly tower and one fly gallery. *TB*

Theatre in Clemens Street

Clemens Street
Original architect
 n.d.   Unknown: as a chapel
Later works
 **1848   Unknown: converted to
            theatre**
 1993   Unknown: facade altered
Current use **Shops**

Closed as a theatre in 1866. The much altered two-storeyed stuccoed facade and pitched roofed brick shell survive but the interior has gone. The ground floor has lost its five arched entrance doors and three-bay, square-columned porch. In 1993 some unsightly alterations to the facade were made good, but the ground floor is now shops.   *TB*

LEATHERHEAD
Surrey

Leatherhead Theatre

High Street
Other names
 pre 1885 ? Victoria Hall
Original architect
 1880s Unknown
Current use **Disused**
Capacity **c.470**

Opened as the Victoria Hall, the building became the Leatherhead Theatre, which outgrew the tiny premises and was the reason for the conversion of the Crescent Cinema to the Thorndike Theatre nearby. It was in entertainment use pre-1885, and staged tableaux vivants, concerts, pantomimes and plays for many years.

The entrance is set within a large semi-circular glazed opening with stone surround surmounted by a cartouche sitting upon a console keystone. At first-floor level a wood balustrade is prominent behind the glazed arch. It has a tiny stage with a corrugated iron roof. The building is well preserved, except possibly for makeshift added dressing rooms, etc., at the rear, where there has been development. As rear access is no longer available, there seems little possibility of a return to theatre use.   *SM*

Thorndike ★★★
Church Street
Other names
 1939–69 Crescent Cinema
Original architect
 **1939   A.E. Richardson, C. Lovatt Gill
          and A.P. Starkey: as a cinema**
Later works
 1969   Roderick Ham, with Ronald

Spacious foyer at Leatherhead, Thorndike

     **Bayliss, David Hancock and
     Colin Bex: converted to theatre**
Listed   **Grade II**
Current use **Theatre (disused)**
Capacity **530**

The striking brick and stone 1930s' cinema facade, now seen best at first-floor level, is by Richardson, Gill and Starkey. The Crescent, built on the site of the Manor House in 1939, was a purpose-built cinema, but had stage use throughout, even in 1941, when it became the HQ of the fire service. In 1969, it was internally gutted to build the Thorndike Theatre and Casson studio, by Roderick Ham. The entrance leads through a narrow passage to the box office and spacious foyers, which lend themselves to exhibition space, and are well used. The auditorium, which is warm and intimate, is bricklined and has a fan of 530 raked seats with side aisles. The theatre was built to continue the Leatherhead Theatre in quarters larger than the little High Street Theatre (ex Victoria Hall). It is well equipped with dressing rooms, green room and band room. It is now rightly recognised as one of the best theatre designs of its time.   *SM*

LEEDS

City Varieties ★★★
The Headrow and Swan Street
Other names
 before 1865 The White Swan Inn
 **1865   Thornton's Varieties
          Stansfield Varieties**

City Varieties Music Hall
Original architect
 1865   G. Smith
Later works
 **1885   W.H. Beevers: improved; pre-
          sent staircase to circle created**
 1888   Jas Charles and Son: altered
 **1893   Thos Winn: altered at ground-
          floor level**
 1900   Thos Winn: pub altered
 **1903   Thos Winn: altered internally;
          ground-floor warehouse inte-
          grated into backstage accom-
          modation**
 1904/5 Thos Winn: various alterations
 **1954   Kitson, Ledgard and Pyman:
          various improvements**
Listed   **Grade II***
Current use **Variety theatre**
Capacity   **531**

The early history of this hall cannot yet be fully researched owing to the inaccessibility of the pre-1876 records in Leeds archives.

It is believed that there was a White Swan Tavern singing room in existence as early as 1762 and it is known to have been active in the mid-C19. It is possible that a multi-purpose music hall was built before 1865 over the old buildings in Swan Street. In that year, a hall was either newly built or radically reconstructed by George Smith for Charles Thornton (who also built the neighbouring Thornton's Arcade). A music and dancing licence was granted in 1867.

This was a three-tier hall (pit or 'area' plus two balconies), but it would appear that the upper tier originally took the form of an end balcony only, the side slips being added in the 1880s. A flat supper-room-style floor was probably converted to a rake at about the same time. The box divisions at 1st balcony level were made between 1885 and 1887.

What is seen today would appear to be the 1865 hall, possibly incorporating earlier fabric, and still more or less in its modified 1888 form. It is, thus, one of the most important early grand music hall survivals, comparable in rarity and completeness with London, Wilton's and Hoxton Hall, and the Glasgow Britannia.

The auditorium is rectangular with two balconies, straight at the rear with slips along the side walls. The box subdivisions at the lower level are formed with slender colonnettes. The lower balcony is supported on iron columns, but the upper side slips are suspended from rods, which pass through the ceiling to hang on the roof trusses, a curious ad

Leeds, City Varieties (Ian Grundy)

hoc arrangement.

The ceiling is flat with simple ornament of gaslight roses (now with electric pendants) linked by flat bands, as seen in engravings of supper room music halls of the 1850s and 1860s. Good plasterwork on balcony fronts with festoons and other decoration.

The three-centred arched proscenium may possibly be a later insertion, as at Wilton's. Shallow stage with apron and low flies, the stage left fly floor having a flat fretted wood balustrade, an unusual place to find even so simple an ornamental feature, and quite unlike anything to be seen elsewhere in the theatre. Low loft. Rolled safety curtain. The Tobin tube ventilators in the body of the hall seem to be early examples of their kind (they were invented in Leeds).

The original brick and rendered entrance facade, facing the narrow Swan Street, bears the evidence of successive alterations. An escape staircase to the Headrow, formed in 1888, later became the main entrance. This entrance had a bold, once fashionable illuminated canopy but is otherwise almost invisible having become an escape exit again.

This theatre merits significant investment and the exercise of meticulous care in its long-overdue restoration and improvement. It must, however, be said that Henry Joseph's disposal of the ground-floor pub to Tetley's as a separate entity in the early 1950s gravely reduced the scope for replanning. Reintegration of the ground floor should be seriously considered if the opportunity ever arises. *JE*

Civic ★★
Cookridge Street
Original architect
1865   Cuthbert Brodrick: as Mechanical Institution
Later works
1949   R.A.H. Livett (City Architect): converted to theatre with fixed proscenium installed
1983   RHWL (Nick Thompson): major alterations
Listed   **Grade II★**
Current use **Theatre**
Capacity   **521**

An important but lesser-known work by Cuthbert Brodrick, the architect of Leeds

Town Hall. Opened as the Leeds Mechanical Institution and Literary Society or the Leeds Institute of Arts and Science but by the early part of C20 the Albert Hall lecture room was primarily used as a theatre. It did not gain a fixed proscenium until 1949 when a brutally rectilinear arch was constructed in a style totally divorced from the hall. A dressing room was also constructed on each side taking up precious wing space.

In March 1983, RHWL restored the auditorium, removing the inserted proscenium, regilding and rehanging the sunburner and stripping the decorative tile dado of years of paint. The stage dressing rooms were removed and a new elliptical proscenium arch was constructed of timber and plasterboard, successfully reflecting the character of the 1865 hall.

It is now a delightful auditorium with much of the original detail intact. Circular in plan, there is a particularly fine open wrought-iron balcony front; the shallow balcony of four rows is supported on slender cast-iron columns with bracketed caps. A series of windows at a high level is continued in a trompe l'oeil painting across the flat proscenium wall. The saucer-domed ceiling is painted blue with a decoration of stars executed in gold leaf. Although there is no raised tower the height of the hall allows full flying of scenery. A large trap in the stage connects to an extensive workshop below the auditorium. Dressing rooms are behind the stage.

The exterior is monumental. It was said to have been influenced by the Bibliothèque Ste Geneviève in Paris.

Leeds, Coliseum (Ian Grundy)

Ashlar stone in one tall storey above a channelled basement, it has a full-height arched central entrance set between robust piers; segmental pediment above this with enriched tympanum and a pavilion roof over. On either side, ranges of six windows whose arched heads with shell tympana form an arcade, above which are small oeil-de-boeuf windows, a panelled band, dentil cornice and parapet with vases. Flank walls in red brick with stone dressings.

The size of the exterior leads one to expect a larger theatre but until 1997 the building was shared with a college. There now exists a chance to expand into the former college space to improve the cramped buffet, bar and foyers which are all of utilitarian design (except the main foyer which consists mainly of steps). *IG*

Coliseum ★
Cookridge Street
Other names
  Gaumont
  Norwood Studios
  Town and Country
Original architect
  1885 Unknown (? W. Bakewell): as a concert hall
Later works
  c.1895 Unknown: converted to theatre
  1938 W.E. Trent, W.Sydney Trent and Daniel Mackay: converted to cinema
  1992 Unknown: converted to music venue
Listed Grade II
Current use Music venue
Capacity 1800

Opened as a concert hall in 1855, with two balconies and arched timber trusses. Concert platform with choir stepping and an organ on a balcony above. After less than ten years the concert hall was converted to a theatre, with a false ceiling above and two balconies, perhaps partly those of the concert hall but with raked side slips on lower balcony. Deep elliptically arched proscenium with boxes on either side framed by Corinthian columns. Stage with full flying.

Like the concert hall, the theatre was not a great success and in 1905 it became a cinema without noticeable alteration. In 1928, Denman/Gaumont took over and, in 1938, reconstructed the auditorium with a single balcony. The cinema closed in 1961 and was later used as rehearsal rooms, scenery work-

shop, film and TV studios and, briefly, for bingo.

Town and Country reopened it as a popular music venue in 1992, removing much of the cinema interior and extending the auditorium to the rear wall, regaining the original volume. The stalls floor was levelled, but the removal of the false ceiling revealed the trusses as they had appeared in 1885. It has proved to be a successful and conspicuous addition to entertainment facilities in Leeds.

Through all these changes the exterior was barely altered. George Corson's Grand Theatre had already set a precedent for a Gothic theatre in Leeds. The Coliseum has a big, gabled stone Gothic facade with plate-traceried windows and a central rose window and portal. It has recently been cleaned and attractively floodlit. *IG*

County Arcade and Cross Arcade
Briggate
Other names
  Empire Palace (adjoined)
Original architect
  1898 Frank Matcham
Listed Grade II*
Current use Shopping arcades

Although not itself a theatre, the County Arcade must be included here as one of Matcham's finest contributions to public architecture and the remnant of a unified city block development which included his splendid Empire Palace Theatre.

The Empire was demolished in 1961 but the arcade remains complete in itself. The undistinguished building which replaced the theatre has now itself been replaced (1996) by a building which makes a rather better job of healing the gash in the townscape.

The County Arcade is one of the most impressive of its kind in Britain, in opulent Victorian Baroque manner in terracotta, iron, glass and coloured mosaic. A secondary arcade which crosses it at a right angle (Cross Arcade) forms the approach to what has been at various times a ballroom and a restaurant.

The traces of the Empire are now slight, but the arcades are in sparkling condition. The unique concentration of arcades of different periods in Leeds has recently been joined by an entirely new one, formed by roofing over the next street off Briggate and named after the vanished Empire. *JE*

Leeds, County Arcade

Grand Theatre and Opera House ★★★
46 New Briggate
Original architect
  1878 George Corson
Listed Grade II*
Current use Theatre and Opera House
Capacity 1550

Well described by Christopher Brereton as 'a one-off theatre for the architect, but probably the finest of its size in Britain', the Grand is a building of metropolitan stature, conceived to a scale rarely even planned, let alone executed, on this side of the English Channel. Originated by local industrialists it cost the immense sum of £62,000 to build. It occupies a three-quarter acre site and originally included a concert hall (the Assembly Rooms) and a row of shops, producing a facade 49.4m (162ft) long. To the north it adjoins the northernmost of the Leeds arcades. The Assembly Rooms (actually one long room with a foyer) became the Plaza Cinema under separate lessees but has now been reinstated as part of the Grand complex.

Externally, the main facade, in hard red brick with stone dressings, is in a highly eclectic and romantic mixture of styles in which Romanesque and Gothic predominate. The entrance block has three major bays expressed at ground-floor level with round arched openings, the centre one divided by a column supporting two contained arches; at first-floor level there are 1 + 3 + 1 round arched windows. The bays are divided

Leeds, Grand (Ian Grundy)

by shafts crowned by conical-roofed tourelles. A central gable with traceried rose is flanked by pyramidal slate-roofed turrets. To the right the long flat facade is in similar style but lower key. Originally the shopfronts were set within a Gothic arcade, of which two arches only are at present visible. The right-hand corner block takes the form of a squat tower with pyramidal roof, the ground floor being occupied by the separate arched entrance to the Assembly Rooms (this originally matched the central arch to the theatre entrance but was altered when cinema took over).

The internal spaces, front and rear of house, are unusually generous and the public areas, with a spacious main staircase rising in one flight and returning as two, have a sense of occasion noticeably absent in most commercially driven

Victorian theatres.

The auditorium is magnificent and stylistically unique in Britain, an opulent high Victorian invention with clustered Gothic shafts framing the proscenium. The saucer-domed, richly encrusted ceiling is carried on four pendentives of fretted fan-vault form which flow into depressed peripheral arches. The three sweeping horseshoe balconies are supported on iron columns. The 1st and 2nd balconies have their arms divided into eight boxes (four over four) on each side. The 3rd balcony is divided by a parapet into gallery of nine rows rising behind an amphitheatre of four rows which extends into side slips. Above is a fourth level of upper slips.

The balcony fronts are splendidly decorated with deeply undercut plasterwork, incorporating imaginatively

designed foliated scrolls, bosses, etc. The proscenium, flanked by two projecting superimposed boxes in a pedimented, modelled frame flanked at upper level by female figure sculpture, has a grand, semi-circular inner frame with richly scalloped decoration. The present powerful colour scheme, completely appropriate to the architectural style, is by Clare Ferraby.

The installation of an orchestra pit elevator in 1975 resulted in the removal of the front edge of the stage, making it appear too abruptly cut off. Apart from this, it is a tribute to Corson's skill that very little significant alteration has taken place. The only really regrettable and irreversible change was the removal of the unique and wonderfully complete complex of substage machinery in the 1970s. This was an early example of mixed wood and iron construction, complete with traps, bridges, cuts and sloats. Given the lavish space available backstage compared with nearly every other major theatre in Britain, this loss of historic fabric was tragic and unnecessary, attributable, surely, to ignorance rather than need. The accommodation gained could have been created elsewhere.

The first-floor Assembly Rooms are in a completely different but pleasing classical style, the present appearance resulting from C20 alterations to an originally taller room. There is now a shallow arched ceiling, somewhat reminiscent of a mid C19 concert room but with a deep, serpentine-fronted balcony at one end. The flat floor extends into a shallow orchestra recess framed by little kiosks with niches.

This amazing theatre complex has been the home of Opera North since 1978. It is to be hoped that proposals, currently in formation, to carry out a restoration and development scheme worthy of its national importance, will soon be brought to fruition. *JE*

LEEK
Staffordshire

Grand
High Street / Field Street
Other names
  1909 **Grand and Hippodrome**
  1915 **Hippodrome**
Original architect
  1909 **Unknown**
Later works
  1912 **Unknown: theatre altered and capacity increased**
  1931 **Unknown: balcony reconstructed with straight front;**

Leigh, Grand: prior to recent refurbishment (Ian Grundy)

auditorium reseated; floor
covered with cork linoleum
late 1960s Unknown: converted to
twin cinema
Current use Disused
Capacity   c.1750 (prior to subdivision)

Opened 1909. Major alterations were
made in 1931 when the balcony was
reconstructed and the proscenium
altered. Unaltered brick exterior. The
building has been empty since the mid
1980s and is in very poor condition.   TB

LEICESTER

Little
Dover Street
Original architect
    1930   Unknown
Later works
    1958   Frank Brown and A.L. Sharpe:
            stage rebuilt after fire
    1967   Unknown: foyer altered
    1974   Unknown: auditorium re-
            raked; new forestage/orches-
            tra pit
    1989   Jonathan Smith and Partners:
            auditorium altered
Current use Amateur theatre
Capacity   349

Opened as a theatre in 1930, converted
from upper part of a C19 Rechabite
(temperance) Hall - originally a Baptist
chapel.
    It has been much altered over the
years (including after a fire in 1955), but
still looks like an old chapel (gravestones
in yard at rear) with added red brick fly
tower. Auditorium single-raked with flat
ceiling.   TB

LEIGH
Wigan

Grand Theatre and Hippodrome
Leigh Road
Other names
    1920s Hippodrome Cinema
          Odeon
          Classic
Original architect
    1908   Prescott and Bold (Wigan)
Later works
    1939   Gray, Evans and Crossley
            (Liverpool): completely mod-
            ernised
    1969   Unknown: twinned
    1999   Unknown: converted to music
            venue
Current use Music venue

Externally little altered except at ground-
floor level since opening in 1908, the
Hippodrome has a four-storey
Edwardian Baroque facade, in red brick
and buff terracotta. Symmetrical, in five
bays, the outer two slightly advanced as
short towers with segmental gabled
tops. The altered central entrance has a
broad semi-circular arch with exaggerated voussoirs forming a sunburst effect.
This contained a charming stained-glass
window, now boarded up. Three mullioned windows above divided by rustic-
banded pilasters. Slate roof with a small
cupola on the ridge.
    In 1939, the theatre closed for radi-
cal modernisation which had little
effect on the external appearance. The
auditorium was remodelled in Art Deco
style. In early 1955, after thirty-three
years as a cinema, the Hippodrome
returned to live entertainment as a variety theatre but was sold in 1956 to the
Rank Organisation, who redecorated
the interior and reopened it as an
Odeon cinema. It was twinned by
Classic in 1969.
    Following the closure of the cinema,
the building reopened for a short time as
a Laserquest centre in the late 1980s.
After a long period of closure when the
building became very derelict, some
refurbishment was undertaken and the
venue reopened in late 1999, presenting
live music.   IG

Theatre Royal and Opera House
Lord Street
Other names
    Theatre Royal
    Casino Ballroom
    Ruebens Nightclub

Original architect
    1885   J.C. Prestwich
Later works
    1955   Unknown: stalls levelled
    1966   Unknown: gutted
Current use Nightclub
Capacity   originally c.900

The Theatre Royal opened in 1885
replacing an earlier wooden structure
which closed the previous year. The
ground floor was divided into orchestra
stalls and pit. A single horseshoe circle
and four boxes were at first-floor level.
The theatre was not a success and closed
a few months later. Extensive alterations
took place to correct defects. New
entrances were constructed, seats
replaced and the auditorium totally
redecorated.
    Despite occasional weeks of films the
Theatre Royal was basically a live entertainment venue until 1954 when it
closed. In August 1955 it reopened,
apparently little changed, as the Casino
Ballroom. Balcony and stage were
retained, the stalls levelled and a sprung
maple dance floor laid at stage level. In
March 1966 the building was gutted to
form a nightclub.
    As seen now (and despite its grand
name) it is not a particularly distinguished building, the gabled front and
flank being divided into pebbledashed
panels by cement pilaster strips. The
brick stage house could be later. A
plaque on the facade reads THEATRE
ROYAL A.D. 1884, with oak leaf decoration.   IG

LETCHWORTH
Hertfordshire

St Francis' Theatre
St Francis' College
Other names
    1924-34 Saint Christopher Theatre
Original architect
    1924   C.M. Crickmer (Letchworth)
Current use School theatre
Capacity   300

The theatre lies north of the main school
block and forms a complex with a gymnasium, etc. From the school, an arcaded walk with iron gates leads to the
entrance. Separate gates from the road
also give access to the same entrance,
through a private courtyard and under
an ornamental arch. Another courtyard
beyond gives access to the OP rear stage
get-in. The outside of the building is rendered.
    The auditorium is raked and originally

seated 600. It is single-tier, with the exception of a convex-fronted box to seat possibly six or eight at first-floor level. Above this is a gallery for spots, etc.The ceiling is very high, plain-banded barrel vault. A series of round-headed mullioned windows are set high on the walls each side, and are covered on the outside by wooden shutters to obscure the light. The only ornaments are three corbels each side, which carry coved lighting, each bearing the face of a muse. The proscenium arch is square and plain.   *SM*

LINCOLN
Lincolnshire

Theatre Royal ★★
Clasketgate
Other names
  1806 New Theatre
  n.d.   County Theatre
  1893 New Theatre
Original architect
  1893 Bertie Crewe and W.G.R.
        Sprague: replacement for an
        earlier theatre
Later works
  1945 Unknown: entrance front
        rebuilt
Listed   Grade II
Current use Theatre
Capacity   482

There was a theatre (the New Theatre) on the site in 1806, built over a former burial ground. Replaced by the present theatre in 1893.

Delightful and intimate auditorium. Two slightly curved balconies with short slips to superimposed boxes flanking

proscenium. Good Rococo plasterwork on balcony and box fronts and proscenium, now in need of repair. Plain ceiling. Proscenium 6.5m (21ft 6 in), stage depth 7.8m (25ft 6 in). The dull exterior of 1945 presents an unappealing outward image and the theatre would greatly benefit from a similar scheme to that carried out at York Theatre Royal. Owned by Local Authority. Formerly the theatre of a resident repertory company who planned first a new theatre and second a renovation of the existing building, before going bankrupt in the mid 1970s. Now used as a touring house, this delightful theatre would benefit from a careful and sympathetic renovation.   *TB*

LIVERPOOL

Empire ★★★
Lime Street
Other names
  1866 New Prince of Wales Theatre
        and Opera House
  1867 Royal Alexandra Theatre and
        Opera House
  1895 Alexandra Theatre
  1896 Empire
Original architect
  1866 Edward Solomons
Later works
  1867 C.J. Phipps: minor work (gas
        lighting)
  1896 Frank Matcham: major alter-
        ations
  1925 W. and T.R. Milburn, with E.O.
        Griffiths: completely new the-
        atre on site
  1979 Unknown: backstage area and
        dressing rooms improved

  1980 TACP: stage and orchestra pit
        extended
  1998 Ellis Williams: major improve-
        ments and extension
Listed   Grade II
Current use Theatre
Capacity   2348

The Milburn theatre was built on the site of an earlier Empire as a variety house. This is, in national terms, one of the most striking regional theatres of the inter-war years and an outstandingly important element in the theatre resources of Liverpool and the region. It is also one of the best surviving works of W. and T.R. Milburn, who are gaining recognition as being amongst the most competent theatre architects in a period when consensus over the design of such buildings had all but collapsed. It is a Liverpool landmark, in a group of buildings which includes St George's Hall and the Walker Art Gallery.

The Classical facade, with its order of coupled Ionic columns in antis above a tall ashlar base, is modest in comparison with the powerful facing elevation of St George's Hall, but the large auditorium is impressive.

The Milburns were not natural heirs to the design traditions of the late Victorian theatre building boom. By this time, at least, they were looking to North America for exemplars. The auditorium of the Empire is a great space with a curving and nodding frame to the proscenium arch.This has an ante-proscenium which embraces the boxes and is flanked by pendentives in the form of fan vaults supporting the ceiling. The ceiling itself is divided by beams into variously shaped areas, with an oval dome at the centre. The seating slopes up at the row ends, so that the stalls form a shallow saucer, improving sight lines and maintaining audience contact in what might otherwise have been cold, nearly straight rows. The space is considerably wider than it is deep. There are interesting 'standing-room boxes' enclosed by balustrades on either side of the stalls. A simple flat-fronted balcony with curving ends, rakes down towards the proscenium.

Extensive improvements were carried out in 1998.   *JE/SM*

Garston Empire ★
James Street, Garston
Original architect
  1915 Unknown: after earlier plans
        by Thomas George Carroll
        (1913)

Lincoln, Theatre Royal (Ian Grundy)

Liverpool, Empire (Ian Grundy)

Later works
1918 Unknown: converted to cinema
1962 Unknown: converted to bingo
Current use **Bingo**
Capacity **c.1000**

The Empire had only three working years as a theatre, followed by 40 as a cinema and (to date) 30 as a bingo house. It has a single-storey, rendered entrance block on the corner of James Street and Church Road, behind which the main body of the theatre rises to three storeys, irregular in plan and massing. The elevation treatment has a slightly industrial flavour. A single tall corner bay is in red brick faced with channelled quoins and a stone-cornice parapet. The other elevations are in machine-made brick relieved by red brick arch and cill bands and a red brick parapet.

The auditorium is approached down a short flight of steps from a plain foyer. A marble staircase leads to the single balcony, which retains theatre seating. The curved balcony front terminates in a box on either side of the high arched proscenium. The boxes have curved fronts and are dressed with drapes and chandeliers.

Painted outlines on the balcony and box fronts suggest that the plasterwork here was once ornate. The stalls area is converted for bingo and the rear stalls for sales. The front of the orchestra-pit enclosure has been removed at centre to allow access to what is now a bar, below the stage. SM

Neptune ★★
85 Hanover Street
Other names
1911 Crane Hall
1913 Crane Theatre
Original architect
1911 Unknown
Later works
1968 Unknown: removable apron constructed; repainted and refurbished
1969 Unknown: safety curtain motorised; backstage refurbished
Listed **Grade II**
Current use **Theatre**
Capacity **445**

Crane Building, built for the Crane Brothers to accommodate their music shop and offices is a five-storey stone and brick building, six bays with canted wall to Hanover Street, and five bays to School Lane. Mezzanine and attic. The Mezzanine has small-paned casements between flat pilasters and entablature; the three upper storeys have flat pilasters with some carving. The Concert Hall is above the music shop (the latter now modernised) and the fly tower is within a mansard roof. The hall was conceived as a showcase for instrumental recitals, but took the form of a theatre and was used as such, though it continued to be referred to as the Crane Hall until 1938.

The auditorium is reached from a corner entrance by a wide curving staircase with dark polished wood dado, which sets the style of the interior, created with mahogany and plaster splendour reminiscent of the luxury liners. Through a rectangular foyer with booking office and access to the theatre bar, the theatre is reached through pairs of mahogany doors. The interior, almost square, has a flat panelled ceiling, with centre cluster of lights, walls with fluted Ionic pilasters, modillioned cornices and busts of famous composers in wreaths. There is a

Liverpool, Olympia (Ted Bottle)

small balcony with panelled front; urn decorations above the doors are echoed in the square proscenium decoration at the sides. The lower parts of the walls are panelled with polished mahogany with a Greek frieze; the plasterwork is decorated ivory on a deep green. Although the architect has not yet been identified, the stylistic references are very reminiscent of S.D. Adshead's Liverpool Playhouse interior of 1912.

No longer associated with the Crane Brothers, the theatre was saved by the Corporation taking a lease in 1968. It was renamed after Neptune who figures in the City Coat of Arms. It is an unusual, extremely pleasing and intimate house, suitable for plays and chamber music. *SM*

Olympia ★★★
West Derby Road, Everton
Other names
New Olympia
Olympia Cinema
Original architect
1905   Frank Matcham
Listed   **Grade II***
Current use **Live venue**
Capacity   **est. 2300**

Rare surviving example of a circus-variety theatre (cf Brighton Hippodrome). Despite conversion to a cinema in 1925 and, later, to bingo and then a discotheque, it is basically intact, apart from the raising of the stalls floor to stage level and the insertion of staircases from the ends of the first balcony down to the stalls. The auditorium is vast, fanning outwards from the 14.6m (48ft)

proscenium to three very wide balconies at the rear. The 1st balcony is of 12 rows, with ten boxes underneath at the back of the stalls. Above is a 2nd (benched) balcony of six rows with a further six rows behind a parapet and, higher still, a gallery with unpadded concrete steps and serious accessibility problems. The balcony fronts, which are intricately decorated with oriental motifs, are set out on a shallow curve to meet the side walls. These are enriched by three bays of oriental panelling divided by pilasters topped by large plaster elephants' heads. The rectangular proscenium which has open scrollwork in the corners and interlaced blind arches above, is flanked by two large boxes on each side, at 1st balcony level. One of these is facing away from the stage and is sur-

mounted by an opulent onion-domed canopy. It can only have been of use for circus performances. The ceiling, which is canted upwards from the proscenium towards the gallery, is divided into rectangular panels, but is otherwise strangely plain.

The stage is 12.5m (41ft) deep and the grid 20.7m (68ft) high. Originally there was a traditional arena of 12.8m (42ft) diameter projecting halfway into the auditorium and capable of being hydraulically sunk and flooded with water for aquatic performances. Although the pit below still remains, the elaborate machinery has gone. Apart from a small foyer with a deeply coved ceiling, the front-of-house spaces are very cramped for so large a theatre.

The facade is of enormous width, reflecting the rear wall of the auditorium. The entrance is though a central pavilion with a columned loggia at second-floor level, and surmounted by a steep, pyramid roof above a lunette window. The side wings are canted away from the centre and terminate in two-bay pavilions.

The theatre could be fairly readily restored to use, although located outside the City Centre in an area which for some years was largely cleared of other buildings. Renovation works have recently taken place and the venue is currently being used for pop music shows, boxing matches and is also hired out for receptions, etc. However, it may be some time before this becomes a place with a recognisable identity again. Notwithstanding all its physical and environmental problems, the Olympia must rate as a 'sleeping beauty' of national significance. *JE/CB*

Liverpool, Playhouse (Ted Bottle)

Philharmonic Hall
Hope Street

Original architect
1849   John Cunningham

Later works
1939   Herbert Rowse: rebuilt on
         same site
1995   Peter Carmichael: major refur-
         bishment and alterations

Listed   Grade II*

Current use Concert hall

Capacity   1700

The first Philharmonic Hall, a fine stone-faced Italianate building, was destroyed by fire in 1933. Its replacement, which opened just before outbreak of the Second World War is a large building of warm grey-pink brick with a facade in the Dutch Dudok style. Mainly of three-storey height it has a symmetrical front flanked by semi-circular stair turrets. Above the canopied entrance are seven large vertical windows separated by piers topped by abstract emblems. Detached piers contain poster panels with rounded mounts.

The auditorium contains a continuous rising plane of seats broken at one level by a line of horseshoe boxes panelled in light wood, six each side ten at rear, and is backed by an end wall of sound-absorbent material. Above the balcony the suspended ceiling curves like a lobster back, narrowing to meet the resonant wall at the platform end.

The large concert stage, rounded in front, has the provision of a disappearing proscenium and screen for projection driven by an electric motor (revolutionary in 1939 and still uncommon). The organ console, on a revolving base, rises by the same means between the conductor's rostrum and the curves of seats for the choir. *SM*

Playhouse ★★★
Williamson Square

Other names
1866   Star Music Hall
1895   Star Theatre of Varieties
         Star Theatre
1911   Liverpool Repertory Theatre

Original architect
1866   Edward Davies

Later works
1898   Harry Percival: auditorium
         reconstructed; foyer area
         improved; electricity installed
1911   Stanley D. Adshead: auditori-
         um redesigned; bar
         converted from beer cellar
1960   Unknown: adjoining café at
         left of frontage demolished

and single-storey extension built for paintframe/workshop
1961   Unknown: stage lighting con-
         trol system installed at rear of
         auditorium (first in country)
1966   Colin Wilson: stage enlarged;
         dressing rooms, rehearsal
         rooms and workshops added
1968   Hall, O'Donaghue and Wilson,
         with Ken Martin: new glass
         tower constructed with new
         main entrance and booking
         office, restaurants, etc., all
         linked to main house

Listed   Grade II*

Current use Theatre

Capacity   758

Built in 1866 on the site of the Star Concert Hall, which had been purchased by David Lazarus with the intention of building a new music hall, and today the only surviving working theatre in Merseyside from the Victorian era.

The excellent, stuccoed exterior of the old Star Music Hall survives largely unaltered. Seven bays wide and two main storeys with an attic.First floor articulated by Corinthian pilasters, with a straight entablature over. The attic storey, again with pilasters, has oval windows in the two flanking bays and circular windows in the three central bays which are further emphasised by a broken triangular pediment. Small cupolas over the corners.

Intimate auditorium with two slightly curved balconies of six rows each, supported by iron columns with foliated capitals. The balconies probably date from the 1898 reconstruction. The deli-

cate trellis work decoration on their fronts, together with the single, pedimented side boxes and Greek Revival style pilastered panels above, date from 1911. Plain, flat ceiling.

In 1968 a new glass tower containing entrance with booking office, restaurants and bars was added to the left of the facade, with workshops, etc., behind, higher than the main building. Views on the juxtaposition of this dominantly projecting addition are divided. The theatre is the home of one of Britain's senior repertory companies, founded in 1911. *CB/SM*

Royal Court ★★
Roe Street

Original architect
1938   James B. Hutchins

Later works
1972   Unknown: projection box built
         and films introduced
1997   Unknown: major refurbishment

Listed   Grade II

Current use Music venue

Capacity   c.1600

Built in 1938, designed in the modernistic style of the period after a fire destroyed an earlier building in 1933. On a corner site, the elevations are red brick with dressings of Aberdeen granite. Of four storeys with attic, the facade has a rectilinear pattern with horizontal banding in brick and fluted stone, and vertical brick ribs with grouped pairs of windows on all levels. A plain canopy is carried round above the ground floor. At attic level there is a fluted-stone parapet. Rounded corner containing the main

Liverpool, Royal Court (Ian Grundy)

entrance and stairways.

The entrance lobby with box office is paved with San Stefano marble bordered with green and black Issorie marble; the walls are panelled in walnut. Below is the basement lounge and bar - said to be a replica of the main lounge on the Queen Mary. A nautical theme runs through the design, in keeping with the traditions of the city. The curved staircase has a dado of panelled ash and a decorative balustrade. Originally all areas were lit by concealed lighting.

The auditorium comprises stalls, grand circle and balcony and is well decorated. The proscenium is gilded with delicate plaster ornament; coffered sounding board over a splayed ante-proscenium, containing a box at first-floor level each side with its front extended to the circle by a curved bay. Shallow curved circle fronts. The ceiling is in a series of arches with concealed lighting.

The stage with original revolve and flies remains. Used since c.1981 as a venue for pop concerts. In the mid 1990s there was a limited return to live theatre use, with touring productions by, e.g., RSC. However, the Court is once again in use, almost exclusively as a music venue.   *SM*

Theatre Royal, Breck Road

Breck Road, Anfield

Other names
   1891 Theatre Royal Palace of
           Varieties
   1920 Super Royal Cinema

Original architect
   1888 W. Redman

Later works
   1920 Unknown: converted to cinema
   n.d.   Unknown: auditorium
           enlarged
   c.1965 Unknown: converted to bingo

Current use **Carpet warehouse**

Capacity c.500

The theatre was built with pit, dress circle, balcony and boxes, with fibrous plasterwork to the circle, box fronts and other areas. It has a proscenium stage and six dressing rooms. A drama theatre, presenting variety for some years before returning to drama. Various extensions were added, together with modernisations over its forty years as a cinema before conversion to bingo.

The building today in its disused state retains some older fabric.Architecturally modest. The facade seems to be mainly of the cinema era. A brick flank wall with terracotta dressings may be earlier. The

auditorium was extended and re-roofed for bingo. Little of the theatre interior remains.   *SM*

LLANDRINDOD WELLS
Powys

Plaza Playhouse

Middleton Street

Other names
   New Victoria

Original architect
   c.1893 Unknown

Current use **Furniture shop**

Capacity   **(was)** c.275

Red brick with some moulded brick dressings. Good facade to the street, now with a shopfront. Clocktower on left, with semi-circular window in gable. Date stone (1893) on rear building, but plaques on front seem to celebrate 1897 Jubilee.

The theatre (a flat-floored multi-purpose space) is on the first floor, approached by an iron staircase. Small stage with well-modelled cartouche over square proscenium arch with enriched architrave. End balcony and one separate side balcony. Full of furniture but otherwise not much altered.   *TR/JE*

LLANDUDNO
Conwy

Grand ★★★

Mostyn Broadway

Other names
   Revivals Disco
   Broadway Boulevard

Original architect
   1901 George Humphries of the
           Mostyn Estate, with Edwin
           Sachs (consultant)

Listed   **Grade II***

Current use **Discotheque**

Capacity **est. 1000**

A large, free-standing building, sited just outside the town centre near the south end of the promenade. Gaunt, red brick facade surmounted by low, semi-octagonal towers. Very fine, intimate auditorium which, before conversion to disco, had 1000 seats. Two well-curved balconies of eight rows each, terminating in two boxes either side at 1st balcony level and one above. The boxes are divided by slender colonnettes with enriched shafts. Spanning the auditorium above the boxes is a segmental arch with lattice decoration, which has richly decorated panelled reveals. Saucer-domed ceiling with a plaster sunburst round a central rose.

The plasterwork generally on balcony fronts, boxes, proscenium and ceiling is of excellent quality with delicately modelled foliated scrolls, festoons, putti, musical instruments, etc.

The exterior has been well maintained. Internally, the auditorium and stage form one discotheque space, with the stage carpeted and furnished as a sitting-out area, complete with upstage bar. The original auditorium plasterwork together with the proscenium arch are said to remain in situ and the garish modern disco fittings and decorations have been superimposed upon them. The house tabs have been taken down and folded away and the iron is still in place and in working order.

During freak storms in the early 1990s the theatre was flooded both by rising water and a cascade through the roof. It remains to be seen how the concealed plasterwork has been affected.The substage area was flooded to a considerable depth, but the important original wooden machinery all appears to be in place and potentially in working order. The old wind machine is present but no sign can now be seen of the star-trap fitting.

This is potentially the best traditional theatre in North Wales. It is sad that such a fine building is not playing a major role in the revival of Llandudno as a regional performance arts centre.   *TR*

Palladium ★

Gloddaeth Street

Other names
   Palace

Original architect
   1920 A. Hewitt

Listed   **Grade II**

Current use **Dark**

Capacity c.1030

Built 1920 but probably designed prior to 1914. Originally with two balconies and boxes, the interior was subdivided but not completely gutted to create a cinema and bingo. As a result decorated box fronts and part of the proscenium remain in the bingo hall. A splendidly robust Edwardian Baroque stuccoed facade. The central bay, above the entrance, has giant Ionic demicolumns supporting a triangular rusticated arch and a large oriel window. Symmetrical square flanking towers, with angle pilasters carrying segmental pediments, and surmounted by octagonal domes.

The building closed in 1999 and, at the time of writing, J.D. Wetherspoon's

Llandudno, Grand (Terence Rees)

had submitted plans for conversion to a pub.   *TR*

Prince's
74 Mostyn Street
Other names
    1893   St George's Hall
    1958   Prince's Kinema
Original architect
    1881?   Humphrey and Bradley
Current use **Supermarket**

Only the vaguely Gothic facade survives above an altered ground floor. A slightly recessed centre with four tall segment-headed windows is flanked by end bays with coupled windows under a segmental arch. Above is an attic storey with a series of small closely spaced windows under a steeply pitched roof. This is an interesting, if not particularly distinguished, facade and makes a distinctive contribution to the streetscape.   *CB/TR*

LLANFAIR TALHAEARN
Conwy

The Playhouse
Garthewin
Other names
    Y Theatr Garthewin
Original architect
    1722   Joseph Turner: as a barn
Later works
    1937   Clough Williams Ellis (also attrib. T.S. Tate): converted to theatre

Current use **Dark**
Capacity   **176**

The Playhouse was created by the conversion of a barn (built in 1722). The walls are of stone and a slate roof is carried on two substantial brick arches, one of which is now the proscenium arch. The stage and associated works were undertaken in 1937-38. The building stands in close association with the country house Garthewin. The whole estate was sold in 1995.   *TR*

LOCHGELLY
Fife

Opera House
Main Street
Other names
    1908   Reid's Hall
    1910   Opera House
Original architect
    1908   Unknown
Current use **Bingo**
Capacity   **originally 1500**

Dull three-storey frontage of five bays in red brick and roughcast. Pediment over central bay and shop units flanking entrance. Auditorium in brick box to rear. Undistinguished interior with barrel-vaulted ceiling, pilastered side walls and one balcony with truncated slips. Now obscured by suspended ceiling and used for bingo.   *BP*

LOFTUS
Redcar and Cleveland

Empire
Deepdale Terrace and Cowscote Terrace
Other names
    Regent Bingo Hall
Original architect
    c.1914–1918   Unknown
Current use **Disused**
Capacity   **(was) c.800**

The Empire Theatre, Loftus, of uncertain date (probably about the First World War), is situated on a back street corner on the edge of this small mining town. It is built on a steeply sloping site giving the auditorium far greater height than appears from the street. There is a small stage area with a very slightly raised tower. It ceased to be used as a cinema in 1964, became a bingo house and is now used for storage. Extremely plain design externally with a corrugated asbestos roof and brick walls. Rectangular auditorium with triangular foyer tapering away at stage end. Seating was in two areas, the raked front stalls and steeply stepped rear stalls (the better seats) - a fairly basic stadium plan separated by a barrier and aisle. The better positioned 818-seat Regal Cinema in Loftus also had a stage but the auditorium was demolished many years ago and the long derelict foyer was finally cleared in 1996.   *IG*

LONDON

Academy ★★★
211 Stockwell Road
Lambeth
Other names
    Astoria
Original architect
  1929 Edward A. Stone (with
        Somerford and Barr)
Listed   Grade II
Current use Concert venue
Capacity c.2100 (or 4000+ standing)

Built in 1929 as the Astoria Cinema, the Academy, like many super cinemas, is fully equipped for live performance. It has a huge stage with extensive counterweight system, easy get-in, and generous front and backstage accommodation.

This was one of the most impressive of Britain's few 'atmospherics', designed in the manner of John Eberson, the originator of the style, and reminiscent of that architect's Spanish Garden and Italian atmospherics (for example, Chicago Capitol, 1925). Auditoria for big cinemas make design demands which are difficult to reconcile with live theatre needs. The way in which earlier theatres wrapped the audience round the auditorium with stacks of boxes completing the framing of the proscenium, was quite impractical for film viewing. The long, nearly straight rows of seating suitable for watching a film in darkness are inclined to remove all sense of community and leave intimidating expanses of unrelieved side wall. The best super cinemas turned the walls, the ceiling and the proscenium into an architectural playground. Fantastically varied forms intensified the escapist atmosphere of cinema while creating a sense of enclosure, in some cases (as here) of 'dream landscape' character and scale.

The exterior of the Academy, with its semi-domed entrance porch, is not particularly memorable and it certainly provides no preparation for the amazing interiors. The entrance lobby is circular. Its dome is painted to represent a night sky with stars and planets. The foyer, which is big enough to serve on occasion as a performance space in its own right, is freely classical with staircases on either side rising to circle level, where a ring of columns defines an open well which looks down on the stalls bar. The auditorium is of impressive breadth with a single balcony and a continuously curved ceiling, approximately 36.6m

(120ft) x 44.2m (145ft), which originally had twinkling stars and 'atmospheric' effects.

The proscenium is framed by octagonal towers linked by an arcade bridge with a central broken-pedimented bay. On either side the architectural treatment extends along the side walls with deep modelling suggesting a Mediterranean townscape of clustered buildings with tiled and domed roofs, balconies, statues in niches, balustraded loggias, Baroque doorways and garden walls, above which rise naturalistically modelled trees.

In its present use as a space for pop concerts, bands play as often from auditorium rostra as from the stage. The stalls seating has been removed and the atmospheric lighting is absent, but the redecoration and recarpeting of the foyer by Simon Parkes (lessee from 1973 to 1997) gives some impression of what a totally restored theatre would look like. His publicity literature stated that he was 'dedicated to restoring the historic building to its original condition'. His successors, the McKenzie Group, have already (April 2000) committed themselves to restoration of the auditorium, with financial support from Lambeth Council and English Heritage. *JE*

Adelphi ★★
The Strand
City of Westminster
Other names
  1806 Sans Pareil
  1858 Theatre Royal (New) Adelphi
  1901 Century Theatre
  1902-40 Royal Adelphi
Original architect
  1806 Unknown
Later works
  1814 Unknown: redecorated and
        new front constructed
  1838 Unknown: auditorium raised
  1840 Samuel Beazley: new facade
        constructed
  1848 M. Digby Wyatt: partially
        reconstructed with new audi-
        torium
  1858 T.H. Wyatt and Stephen Salter:
        completely rebuilt
  1869 Joseph Lavender: altered; new
        Royal entrance constructed
  1882 probably John Clemence: back-
        stage rebuilt
  1887 Spencer Chadwick: enlarged,
        with new facade
  1891-3 W.B. Pinhay: altered
  1901 Ernest Runtz and Ford: again
        largely reconstructed with
        extended facade

Adelphi (David Crosswaite)

  1930 Ernest Schaufelberg:
        extensively rebuilt
  1937 T.P. Bennett: facade altered
  1993 Jaques Muir and Partners:
        restored and improved
Listed   Grade II
Current use Theatre
Capacity 1486

The Adelphi is an extraordinary complex of many periods. Although most of what is observed by the public dates from 1930 or later, the building incorporates the rear elevation, flank walls and roof construction of much earlier theatres. Nothing now remains of the Sans Pareil of 1806, the Beazley facade of 1840 or the auditoria of 1848 (M.D. Wyatt), 1858 (T.H. Wyatt) or 1901 (Runtz and Ford). The Royal entrance in Maiden Lane is probably of 1868-9, a surviving alteration by Joseph Lavender to the 1858 theatre. The remainder of this frontage is of 1882, by Spencer Chadwick. Part of Chadwick's classical facade of 1887 (once the Adelphi Restaurant) can be seen in the Strand alongside the theatre, but no longer forming part of it, where it makes an interesting contrast with Schaufelberg's geometric 1930 front.

Given the Adelphi's record of successive reincarnations, the many-windowed, somewhat domestic Maiden Lane elevation is a remarkable survival, as is the elderly roof over the auditorium. The Royal entrance, close to the door where William Terriss was murdered in 1897, adjoined the site of the notorious Cyder Cellars concert room, a proto-music hall rebuilt in the 1840s, later used as a rehearsal room by Diaghilev. The

Strand facade, interfered with by Bennett in 1937 and later obliterated by signage, has been restored by Jaques Muir and Partners (1993) to a form closer to Schaufelberg's 1930 design. Described in their time as 'bizarre and opulent', the Schaufelberg interiors are now perceived to be of considerable interest as good, if low-key, examples of a new design philosophy (presently lumped with much contemporary work as 'Art Deco'). The sensitive 1993 restorations were accompanied by quite extensive new works which successfully picked up the Schaufelberg decorative vocabulary with its ordered geometrical black, mirror glass and chromium plate forms and the warm veneered surfaces in the auditorium. The incorporation of modern equipment has been achieved without damaging the original design concept. Within the stage house and the orchestra pit, radical reconstruction was necessary in 1993 to accommodate a technically highly complex production. The last fragments of the 1930s' revolve were removed at this time. JE

Albery: motif above proscenium arch (London Metropolitan Archives)

Albery ★★★
St Martin's Lane
City of Westminster
Other names
   1903 New Theatre
Original architect
   1903 W.G.R. Sprague
Listed   Grade II
Current use Theatre
Capacity 877

Built by Sir Charles Wyndham on land he had to acquire before building Wyndham's Theatre, with which it stands back to back, separated only by St Martin's Court and with a modern linking bridge. Stone free classical facade to St Martin's Lane, in three major bays, the centre slightly advanced and pedimented over an Ionic pilastered order. Flank and rear elevations in yellow and glazed brick.

The interior has suffered little alteration of any consequence. Its planning provides a striking example of the tendency, during the commercial building boom at the turn of the century, to impose the largest practicable auditorium on the smallest practicable site. Like a watchmaker, Sprague packed all the working parts into an impossibly confined volume. The way in which he met increasingly stringent safety regulations, while providing public spaces which, even if less than generous, were not mean, is instructive.

The auditorium, in restrained French style, (described as 'of the period of Louis XIV') is typical of Sprague, but Claude Ponsonby is credited with the decorative details. Three variously curving balconies set back, one behind the other, the lowest (dress circle) being lyre-shaped and the upper two extending forward into narrow slips. All have bombé fronts. The proscenium wall makes a tangent to the circular ceiling. There are three tiers of boxes on either side of a square proscenium opening which is completely framed on all four sides by a moulded architrave. Full-relief figures, Peace and Music, in panel over. Brass orchestra rail now set back to line of proscenium. The usual clutter of front-of-house lights includes a particularly ugly fairing on the 2nd balcony front. The decorations now look tired and feeble except where (presumably original) paintings survive on balcony fronts. The hangings are also rather too sparse for such an opulent interior. JE

Aldwych ★★★
Aldwych
City of Westminster
Original architect
   1905 W.G.R. Sprague
Later works
   1963 Unknown: boxes altered (since reinstated)
Listed   Grade II
Current use Theatre
Capacity 1074

Built as a twin to the Strand Theatre in symmetrical relationship at either end of Marshall Mackenzie's slightly later Waldorf Hotel, all forming part of the Aldwych/Kingsway improvement and perhaps, except for Bush House, the only part to measure up fully to the monumental conception of the great curved highway.

The Aldwych is a fine stone-faced classical building in its own right. Like the Strand Theatre, it is a corner building, in three major bays, each of four storeys plus a sheer attic over the main entablature. The two outer bays, facing Aldwych and Drury Lane respectively, display a giant order of engaged columns through second and third floors, carrying pediments with enriched tympana pierced by lunettes at attic level. The centre bay is recessed and turns the corner as a bold pilastered bow.

The auditorium underwent a series of alterations from the 1960s to 1980s, during the Royal Shakespeare Company's tenancy, almost entirely to its architectural detriment. In accordance with the then fashionable idea that drama was harmed by the distracting presence of architecture, the auditorium was ruthlessly 'painted out'. It has since been handsomely restored and can now be seen as an excellent Sprague design.

It was described when first opened as being 'Georgian' in style. It has two balconies, the gallery being the rearward extension of the upper circle. The boxes are framed by Ionic piers on tall pedestals, carrying entablature blocks

Aldwych (Mark Douet)

Understage machinery at Alexandra Palace Theatre (London Metropolitan Archives)

and semi-circular arches. The proscenium is square with a deep panelled frieze, central cartouche and coved sounding board. *JE*

Alexandra Palace Theatre ★

The Alexandra Palace, Muswell Hill
Haringey
Original architect
  1875   J. Johnson
Later works
  1922   Unknown: altered
Listed   **Grade II**
Current use **Disused**
Capacity   **est. 1500**

Johnson's partner, Alfred Meeson, designed the first Palace which burnt down in 1873, soon after it was built. It was immediately replaced by the present building. Although the theatre is large, it forms a relatively small part of the entire Palace complex, whose history is not traced in this entry. It is not known whether Johnson had assistance with the design of the theatre, but the evidence of the building itself suggests that it was the work of someone with little previous experience of theatre design. Its history has been depressing. It was an abject commercial failure in the decades when theatre business generally was at its most profitable. The theatre, last used as a television scene store, now looks abandoned. It is completely embedded in the Palace complex. Although it has one external wall, its separate identity is not discernible in the long north elevation of the Palace. The auditorium is extraordinary - more like a big music hall or con-cert hall than a theatre; a great rectangular room with raked floor, the long sides now occupied by low enclosed corridors (presumably inserted to improve means of escape) which give the impression of side slips. There is a single balcony, facing and far distant from the stage and there was originally a 2nd, upper balcony, now removed. The present appearance of the room probably owes more to Macqueen Pope, who ordered the 1922 alterations, than to Johnson. Coarse plaster ornament of two periods, the bolder work on the ceiling not unpleasing. Figure sculpture, probably original, in niches either side of the proscenium. The existing, faded 'toy theatre' colour scheme, although not original, is highly evocative.

The most interesting survival is the stage, designed for elaborate transformations. It has a fine complex of wooden machinery both below stage and in the fly tower, all in restorable condition. A primitive set of scene grooves from this theatre is now in the possession of the Museum of London .The auditorium is one of the oldest now surviving in London; archaeologically of rare interest but intractable as a theatre. It would make a splendid concert room or large cabaret restaurant, if there was ever call for such an enterprise in N22. The future, if it has one, must lie with music and variety, rather than drama. Alternatively, the auditorium might be reconstructed in a more intimate and usable form and the stage restored as a spectacular working exhibit for public enjoyment. *JE*

Ambassadors ★★★

West Street
Camden
Original architect
  1913   W.G.R. Sprague
Listed   **Grade II**
Current use **Theatre**
Capacity   **425**

A small theatre on an impossibly small site, it is a planning tour de force by Sprague, probably his most striking feat of compression, front and back of house. Next door to the St Martin's Theatre. Low, three-storey ashlar-faced elevation, curving into Tower Court. Restrained classical style with channelled pilasters carrying segmental pediments. Crowning parapet and balustrade with ball ornaments.

Elegant auditorium, described in contemporary reports as being in Louis XVI style with ambassadorial crests and a colour scheme of Parma violet, ivory and gold. Apart from redecoration, the auditorium has remained virtually intact. Circular ceiling with central chandelier, panelled border and deep cove penetrated by arches springing from fluted Ionic pilasters. Richly framed and festooned roundels with armorial decorations in arches. Flat basket-arched proscenium flanked by single tall boxes. Horseshoe-curved single balcony with raised tier at rear. An architecturally pleasing auditorium with an intimate atmosphere. *JE*

Apollo ★★★

Shaftesbury Avenue
City of Westminster
Original architect
  1901   Lewen Sharp, with H. van Hooydonk
Later works
  1932   Ernest Shaufelberg: altered internally
  1991   Paul Jenkins (Stoll Moss house architect): old box office removed; minor alterations within entrance
Listed: **Grade II**
Current use **Theatre**
Capacity   **756**

This was Sharp's only complete theatre (he made major alterations to Camberwell Palace in 1908) and it is externally quite unlike any other theatre of its time in London. It would look perfectly at home in Paris.

Together with the Lyric, the Gielgud and the Queens, all grouped on the north side of Shaftesbury Avenue, the

Ambassadors (London Metropolitan Archives)

Apollo contributes to one of London's most important theatre streetscapes. The main facade is in a free Renaissance style with a distinct Art Nouveau flavour; stone, in three main storeys with a tall attic above the cornice; three major bays, the outer two treated as pavilions with flat canted fronts round which the main cornice breaks. Prettily framed oeil-de-boeuf windows to the attic. The pavilion attics are treated as short, flat-domed towers with striking figure sculpture (pairs of winged female figures with flowing drapery) by T. Simpson. Well-restored iron and glass canopy over entrance. Flank and rear facades in red brick.

Lively auditorium with splendid plaster enrichment in what was described as Louis XIV manner, somewhat interfered with by Shaufelberg in 1932. Three cantilever balconies (arguably one too many, producing sight line problems at several levels) terminating in elaborately modelled serpentine-fronted boxes. The angle of view from the upper balcony is said to be the steepest in London. Proscenium arch with bold architrave moulding, lyre-buckled at intervals. Relief in tympanum over proscenium. Finely enriched oval ceiling on pendentives. Good foyer and anteroom to Royal Box. Modern stalls bar. *JE*

Apollo Victoria ★★★

17 Wilton Road
City of Westminster
Other names
   New Victoria
Original architect
   1930   **E. Wamsley Lewis and W.E. Trent**

Later works
   1980   Michael Sassoon: front of house redecorated; foyer chandeliers; new dressing rooms
Listed   **Grade II***
Current use **Theatre**
Capacity   **1524 (in current configuration)**

The New Victoria was the first cinema to adopt the Germanic expressionist style, an equivalent of the Savoy but on a more prominent site. The Europhile critic, P. Morton Shand, captioned the 'stop press' frontispiece of his *Modern Theatres and Cinemas*, calling it 'a symbol of hope' for the future.

The site was a tight wedge between two major streets. Hence the parallel and almost equal facades, ribbed like a radio set and originally with long, low canopies to shelter the queues as well as the present high ones over the once elaborately lacquered doors. The use of colour was, like the mouldings, carefully controlled; even the neon light co-ordinated with the overall streamlining. Stone reliefs of cinemagoers by Newberry A. Trent on the facade entertained the waiting queues. The whole design was a carefully conceived plan, which wrought a maximum of space by extending the stalls area under the pavement and putting the lavatories and foyers in a mezzanine between the stalls and rear circle. Only the stage was cramped. Intended as a ciné-variety hall, large stage shows were dropped within a month of opening but live acts and big bands played here throughout the 1930s.

The novelty of the plan came out of architect E. Wamsley Lewis's training in the United States. It is clear from the drawings that the design is entirely his, with W.E. Trent acting as the executant who produced the finished drawings to satisfy the London County Council's committees. What is more extraordinary than the planning or even the sophisticated facades is the interior. A strong Wrightian sympathy, with bright rubber floors and rich mouldings, continues through the large entrance lobby and small circle foyer. A rather skeletal mermaid by N.A. Trent hovers over the stairs, and the auditorium is an oceanic outburst of suspended scallops round a giant dome, originally all painted in marine blues, greens and silvers. Lewis is said to have conceived the underwater theme on a whim to satisfy PCT's Managing Director's love of boats.

Apollo Victoria (© Crown copyright. NMR)

The New Victoria's vast size and slight off-West End location made it an early target for adaptation, once cinema audiences began to decline in the 1950s. Its stage was its salvation. In 1958, the installation and dressing rooms were overhauled and live shows and ballet supplemented the film fare. Since 1980 the building has been leased by Apollo Leisure, who first upgraded the shows and then in 1984 brought in *Starlight Express*. The Lloyd-Webber extravaganza has kept the venue financially solvent, but the physical price for the interior has been high. Contracts have been signed to ensure the building's restoration when *Starlight* eventually closes, but in the meantime uplighters are in store, the lower walls are painted black and a roller-skating track weaves round the lower stalls and balcony front. Disco lights obscure the remaining architectural splendour above. Nevertheless this is one cinema that seems to have found a successful second life in theatrical use, in appreciative hands.   *EH*

Arts ★

6-7 Great Newport Street
City of Westminster
Other names
1962-64   **New Arts**
   1967   **Unicorn**
Original architect
   1927   **P. Morley Horder: internal conversion of existing building**
Later works
   1934   **Basil Ionides: altered and redecorated**
   1951   **Unknown: reconstructed after fire**

Current use **Dark**
Capacity **340**

The Arts makes no grand architectural statement, but it is remarkable in other ways, as one of the first theatres in the heart of the West End to which the term 'fringe' might reasonably be applied and also, in one of its manifestations, as the only building-based children's theatre in such a location (the Unicorn).

The Arts Theatre Club, founded in 1927, built the basement theatre in a building leased from the Salisbury Estate, to the designs of P. Morley Horder, at a cost of £18,500. Altered and redecorated by Basil Ionides in 1934, its auditorium and stage boxes were severely damaged by fire in 1951 but immediately reconstructed.

There have been proposals to rebuild the whole, pleasantly varied block of property in which the theatre stands and there has been concern that the Arts might go down with the building or be moved permanently to a less amenable site. It is arguable that the continuance of theatre activity in this 'off Charing Cross Road' location is more important than the survival of the bricks and mortar.

The facade is older than the theatre; red brick with a plain rendered ground floor, giant pilasters uniting second and third floors, framing a shallow central recess containing a canted bay. The auditorium is rectangular, with an end balcony and side slips and is architecturally undemonstrative. *JE*

Banqueting House
Whitehall
City of Westminster
Other names
    for a time the United Services
    Museum
Original architect
1618-22   Inigo Jones
Later works
    1699   Sir Christopher Wren: convert-
           ed for use as Chapel Royal
    1798   James Wyatt: North bay set-
           back and staircase added
    1809   James Wyatt: second, lower
           gallery added for use as a mili-
           tary chapel
 1829-37   Sir John Soane: roof renewed;
           redecorated; facade totally
           refaced in Portland
           stone in exact reproduction of
           Jones's design
    1895   Aston Webb and Ingress Bell:
           building added at South end
    1907   H.M. Office of Works: ceiling

paintings removed, restored
and refixed
    1963   Ministry of Public Building and
           Works: interior fully restored
Listed **Grade I**
Current use **Rooms for State
           occasions/exhibitions**

A key building in the history of art and architecture in Britain and revered as one of our most precious monuments. Notwithstanding later additions and a total renewal of the facade stonework in 1830 (faithfully reproducing the original design), it can be seen as one of Inigo Jones's few complete and perfect works. It is not, strictly, a theatre but it was purpose-designed for regular theatrical fit-ups and its importance in theatrical history makes it impossible to omit.

It was built to replace Smythson's Banqueting House of 1609, which had been destroyed by fire in 1619. Jones had been designing prosceniums, stage machines, etc., for court masques by Jonson and others since the early years of the C17 and the new building contin-ued to be used for this purpose until 1635 when the masques moved to a wood building nearby. Jones's design for the Banqueting House provided for the requirements of such entertainments in, for example, its avoidance of internal columns. His most sophisticated machines and single-point perspectives were devised for this noble room. In 1649 the Banqueting House had a win-dow temporarily removed so that it could serve as the ante-room to the exe-cution scaffold of Charles I. The interior has been magnificently restored. The Banqueting House has been well docu-mented and many published works deal with its architectural, historical and the-atrical significance. *JE*

Bob Hope
Wythfield Road, Eltham
Greenwich
Other names
1946-81   Eltham Little Theatre
Original architect
    n.d.   Unknown
Current use **Theatre**
Capacity **202**

The Eltham Little Theatre (amateur) company leased the parish hall, which became their permanent home, from 1946. Bob Hope, who was born in Eltham, became the theatre's benefac-tor, enabling the company to purchase the hall in 1981 and carry out major improvements in the early 1990s.

Externally it still has much of the char-acter of a village hall, but internally it has been completely redesigned. The old hall had a proscenium arch which has been blocked to enlarge the backstage accommodation. The new stage occu-pies the full width of the building, a false proscenium being inserted as required. There is no fly tower. The old balcony has been removed and the auditorium is now a single rake with manually operat-ed retractable seating. A large bar has been created to the side of the foyer and this also serves as a small performance space for music, readings, storytelling groups, etc. *KW*

Borough (Rex)
Stratford Broadway
Newham
Original architect
    1896   Frank Matcham
Later works
    1906   H. Pike: altered
    1910   J.M.H. Gladwell: projection
           facilities installed
    1933   George Coles: completely
           reconstructed internally as a
           cinema; created rounded cor-
           ner sweep in 1930s' style
    1958   Unknown: stage removed
    1969   Unknown: converted to bingo
    1997   Barry Reynolds Associates:
           Coles's 1933 interior restored;
           balcony reseated (for cinema
           use); fly tower dismantled;
           stage modified
Current use **Live music venue with cine-
           matograph licence**
Capacity **c.1800**

Brick and stone facade to the Broadway in Jacobean style with tower. Shops on Broadway front. Name of theatre in large letters at high level. The corner entrance composition was massively altered in the cinema conversion and now presents an almost plain rendered face. Deprived of its main architectural emphasis, what is left of Matcham's external design seems lacking in coher-ence. Nothing of his remains internally where the building must be judged as a creation of 1933.

Its present form results from its pur-chase by Sokoloff and Pearl of Essell Cinemas, when George Coles was com-missioned to transform it into a super-cinema. The auditorium was reconstructed in 1933 in his characteris-tic Art Deco style, to provide a two-tier auditorium with projection box and two cafés, with full stage facilities left behind a larger proscenium. An organ was

Borough (Rex)

installed. Opened as the Rex with a policy of ciné-variety. Installation of Cinemascope in 1958, however, covered the orchestra pit and removed the stage.

Years of closure from 1975 and a fire that year led to increasing fears that the building would never reopen. However, supported by the London Borough of Newham and Stratford City Challenge, the exterior has been restored in its curious mixture of styles. The auditorium has been lavishly restored. The fly tower and stage were demolished, and a new high-tech stage built to serve the huge dance floor which now covers the stalls area. Reopened in 1997 as a live music venue, the balcony has been reseated to modern standards to accommodate use as a cinema. 'Fun' bars have been created in different styles.

The building still seems to have some limited theatre potential.   *SM/JE*

Bow ★

adjoining Poplar Town Hall, Fairfield Road/Bow Road
Tower Hamlets
Other names
    Poplar Civic Theatre
    Poplar Town Hall Theatre
Original architect
    1937   Clifford Culpin (Ewart Culpin and Son)
Current use Disused
Capacity 1250

The theatre is part of a 1937 Town Hall building of historic interest in its own right as having been commissioned by the poorest of the Metropolitan Boroughs. The theatre is of pleasant, if somewhat spartan, Moderne appear-

ance. Most of the original fixtures and fittings are still present in the foyers as well as the auditorium. It has a variety, rather than scenic, stage with a low grid, a metal cyclorama and very large and deep orchestra pit. There are ample dressing rooms.

As a municipal theatre of its date (a time not generally productive of good theatres) it is of surprising quality. Part raked auditorium. The stage itself is shallow, about 5.5m (18ft), but wide, with a proscenium opening of about 10.7m (35ft).

Permission was given in 1989 for a development which would involve its demolition, but this has not so far been implemented.   *JE*

Bromley Little

North Street
Bromley
Original architect
    c.1938 Unknown: conversion of former bakery
Current use Theatre
Capacity 112

An amateur theatre presenting one play a month. The building was formerly a bakery approached through a yard and has the modest appearance of a cluster of outbuildings with no architectural pretension whatever. Road widenings have made it clearly visible from Tweedy Road and Bromley North Station and could now well be given just a little more in the way of architectural presence.

Only an amateur theatre with dedicated support could have been successful for so long with the difficulties this one labours under. Roof, brickwork and

floors are all in need of repair or replacement. The public entrance and the stage door are both at first-floor level, approached by steep staircases, the auditorium has strained sight lines, the crossover has extremely low headroom, the lighting operator has an oblique view of the stage and the sound operator cannot see it at all! The company receives no grant of any kind but the extent of the refurbishment now needed will only be achieved with a substantial capital subvention.

Proposals were put forward in 1998 aimed at providing significant improvements whilst maintaining an informal character. The Little Theatre provides a useful, simple playhouse, to complement the larger, more sophisticated professional Churchill Theatre.   *KW*

Byfeld Hall

117 Church Road, Barnes
Richmond upon Thames
Other names
    1925   Barnes Theatre
    1952   Vandyke Cinema
            Olympic Studio
Original architect
    1906   probably J. Harrison (also attributed to Arthur Osborne)
Later works
    1910   Unknown: projection room added
    1951-52 Unknown: reinstated following small fire
    c.1966 Unknown: cupola on tower at SE corner removed
    1989   Christopher Watts: interior gutted and redesigned as suite of sound studios
Current use Recording studios
Capacity (was) c.500

Built in 1906 as a public hall, the Byfeld was licensed for both stage plays and music and dancing 'with a proper stage'.The floor was suitable for dancing. The bioscope was an item in the opening programme. A permanent projection room was added in 1910 when the Byfeld obtained its first cinematograph licence. From this time on it operated mostly as a cinema under a variety of managements, but it became the Barnes Theatre in 1925 under Philip Ridgeway's management. Ridgeway employed Komisarjevsky to direct and design five Russian plays and, although the operation was tightly constrained for cost, this short tenure was of significance in theatre history.

After Ridgeway the theatre reverted to cinema use with several changes of name and management, until it became a film studio in 1960 and a sound studio in 1966. It is now known as the Olympic (Sound) Studios. The exterior is of red brick and stone in a mildly flamboyant Dutch baroque style, now lacking some ornamental features (e.g. the cupola on the south-east corner tower). At ground-floor level the facade is divided into two main elements, the entrance and three separate shopfronts. The originally three-doored entrance to the hall is given rather grand treatment with heavy stone arches, above which is a stone panel with the date 1906. At first-floor level is a bay (now blocked) which must have served a public room. On the side elevation, above an arched window, is the name Byfeld Hall.

The hall was on the first floor. In its life as the Ranelagh Cinema (1932-41) it had what was described as a pretty auditorium with floral murals and ceiling decorated in an attractive trellis pattern. In 1989, the exterior was refurbished but the interior was virtually gutted to form the present studios. The shops have now been absorbed into studio use, with opaque-glazed doorless fronts. The original entrance has been altered. GC

Cambridge ★

Earlham Street, Seven Dials
Camden

Original architect
   1930 Wimperis, Simpson and
           Guthrie, with Serge
           Chermayeff

Later works
   1950 Unknown: redecorated inter-
           nally; new light fittings
           installed
   1988 Carl Toms: redecorated and
           interior partially restored;
           stage enlarged
Listed   Grade II
Current use Theatre
Capacity 1230

The Cambridge is one of the theatres of the high point of the 'little boom' in West End theatre building, which started with the Fortune, 1924, and went on for just over a decade. The design is credited to Wimperis, Simpson and Guthrie, but the interior treatment was by Serge Chermayeff and it is possible that his influence went more than skin deep.

The theatre occupies a corner site on Seven Dials. The main elevations are faced with Portland stone, the rear parts with brick. The corner entrance front and return elevations are flat ashlar,

Camden Theatre, Camden Town.

Camden

almost devoid of relief, with semi-circular openings at ground-floor level and windows in regular ranks of varying sizes above. At first-floor level there is a surprising touch of ornament, alternate windows having classical moulded surrounds with cornice hoods. Plain parapet, minimally articulated corner tower with open three-sided loggia round the set-back top storey, which rises just a little above the main facade.

The interior was given a ghastly salmon-red paint-out and a jumble of unsuitable light fittings in 1950, but has since been redecorated by Carl Toms in a style more consonant with the original intention. The auditorium is spanned by a series of bold 'acoustic' arches with concealed lighting. There is a single, curving balcony front with geometric ornament, flowing into single wall-hung boxes with flat pelmets decorated with symbolic designs. JE

Camden ★★

Camden High Street and Crowndale Road
Camden

Other names
  Camden Hippodrome
  Royal Camden
  Music Machine
  Camden Palace

Original architect
   1901 W.G.R. Sprague

Later works
   1981 Michael Gibson Assocs: con-
           verted to discotheque
   1994 Maddocks Chadwick: refur-
           bished and reconstructed
           internally

Listed   **Grade II**
Current use **Discotheque**
Capacity **est. 1400**

Symmetrical stone facade in free classical manner. Large copper dome, now lacking its open lantern. Still an imposing corner building, viewed across a busy road junction.

Radical internal alterations were carried out when the theatre was converted to disco use. Despite this, and the usual proliferation of lights, it remains a beautiful auditorium with two partly cantilevered balconies (gallery now levelled through to front of building to form new public room). Modelled plasterwork by Waring and Gillow. Marble proscenium arch with segmental pediment and, on either side, marble columns rising from caryatids, defining four bays, containing boxes at three levels. Shallow domed ceiling. The alterations included the laying of a dance floor covering a large part of the stalls area and penetrating the deeply cutaway stage, unfortunately all in determinedly permanent construction. Balconies have been formed over the stage. The floor level at the front of the dress circle has been raised, necessitating a guard rail above the original circle front.

Small, elaborate foyer (bronze plaque of Ellen Terry), above which was originally a 'promenade and winter garden'. Proscenium 9.75m (32ft) wide.

Despite the extensive conversion works, the theatre would be perfectly capable of restoration to theatrical use. Sadly, the expense of such a reconversion has been unnecessarily increased by the nature of the 1981 alterations. JE

Foyer at the Carlton, c.1972 (London Metropolitan Archives)

Carlton
62-65 Haymarket
City of Westminster
Other names
   1979 Classic
   1985 Cannon
   later MGM, Virgin, ABC
Original architect
   1928 Verity and Beverley
Later works
   1977 Unknown: stage house demol-
           ished to make way for office
           block
   1979 Unknown: converted to triple
           cinema
   1985 Unknown: refurbished follow-
           ing fire
Current use **Cinema**
Capacity c.1150 (prior to subdivision)

The Carlton opened in 1927 to act as a sister to the Plaza, Lower Regent Street. Both were designed by Verity and Beverley, both largely funded by Paramount, and both opened with live shows. The theatre was built on Anglesea Yard (which was the subject of the safety curtain painting). The Carlton was only the second completely new theatre to be built in London after the First World War (see Fortune). It was equipped with complete stage facilities – the stage was 18.25m (60ft) wide, 13.7m (45ft) deep, with orchestra pit and fourteen dressing rooms.

Both exterior and interior are in Italian Renaissance style, except for the Adam-style foyer. The three-storey symmetrical exterior, of Portland stone, is little altered, though hidden by modern advertising boards.

Plain, rounded proscenium, and finely modelled friezes. Two Venetian-window style boxes, with drapes, were at either side of the proscenium (unhappily these were lost in the tripling). A dado of panelled mahogany surrounded the stalls levels. The house was lit with crystal chandeliers.

The Carlton prospered until the 1970s, when it became dilapidated. In 1977, the large stage house was sold off to form an office block, ending stage use, and the theatre closed. In 1979 it was tripled, though leaving much of the original decorations and the foyer visible. In 1985 a major fire almost destroyed the foyer and damaged the auditorium, but this was restored.

Theatre use is not likely to return, following the loss of the stage house. *SM*

Castle Hotel Theatre and Assembly Rooms
Whittaker Avenue
Richmond upon Thames
Other names
   1890 New Richmond Theatre
   1910 Castle Electric Theatre
Original architect
   1889 Unknown
Later works
   1890 Unknown: part of hotel rebuilt
           as a theatre
Current use **Fragment**

Following the demolition of part of the C19 Castle Hotel, for the construction of Whittaker Avenue, another part (the large asembly room) was converted to a theatre by F.C. Mouflet in 1890. Mouflet later employed Matcham to build the Richmond Theatre on another site (1899).

It had a stage with proscenium, and a balcony and music gallery, but all has been much altered and the remains are now fragmentary. *SM*

Clapham Granada ★
St John's Hill
Wandsworth
Original architect
   1937 Leslie C. Norton and H.B.
           Horner, with Cecil Masey and
           Theodore Komisarjevsky
Later works
   1973 Unknown: tripled
   1980 Unknown: converted to bingo
           (full volume of auditorium
           restored)
Listed   **Grade II***
Current use **Disused**
Capacity   **c.2475**

The Granada was built at the top of St John's Hill on the site of Battersea County School, the stage house dominating the bridge over Clapham Junction Station. It is said to be the finest of the Granada exteriors, in restrained Moderne design with rounded corner entrance and fin tower at stage end. Faience base with neon and undercanopy lighting.

The auditorium was approached through a grand foyer lined with mirrors, overlooked, in Komisarjevsky style, by the balcony foyer, with café on circular corner. The interior, in free Italian Renaissance style, was remarkable for its lavishness. The colour scheme was a warm stone with ornament in gold, blue, green and red. There were full stage facilities with a counterweight system.

The Granada was tripled in 1973, but detripled in 1980, when it was converted for bingo, which use protected it until closure in 1997. Although listed in 1998, the building is under threat, and remains closed. Its survival depends on persuading developers to include the building in their plans. *SM*

Clapham Grand ★★★
St John's Hill, Clapham Junction
Wandsworth
Other names
   1900 New Grand Theatre of
           Varieties
           Grand Palace of Varieties
   c.1930 Essoldo Cinema
   1972 Grand (Mecca) Bingo
Original architect
   1900 E.A.E. Woodrow
Later works
   1908/9 Frank Matcham: vestibule,
           stalls and back balcony
           altered
   1927 Unknown: new haystack
   1927 Walter Gibbings: new bio box
   1931 Clifford Aish: back projection
           room added
   1935/6 Unknown: full front projection
           installed

Clapham Grand, c.1905

1972   Unknown: converted to bingo
1991   Sean Madigan: partially
       restored and altered for live
       music use
Listed   Grade II
Current use Discotheque
Capacity   c.1000

The only completely surviving theatre by Woodrow and a testimonial to the competence and flair of this little-known theatre designer. It was designed for a consortium headed by Dan Leno and Herbert Campbell, who had already built the Granville, Walham Green (demolished) and the Camberwell Palace (demolished). They took over Munts's Hall, a flat-floored concert room, nearby, to 'test the water' before commissioning Woodrow to build the Grand. By 1910, Leno and Campbell had been elbowed out of the market by the syndicates, so this was their last venture.

The exterior is unusual, if not unique. Massive and confident, in red brick with pink Mansfield stone dressings, it relies on crisp geometry, rather than opulence, almost anticipating architectural movements to come. In so far as a stylistic label can be attached, it should probably be 'Colonial Indian'. The two ogee-domed and arcaded towers certainly have an Indian flavour, although the sparse mouldings and other details are classical.

The interior is also unique amongst British theatres (at least until the rise of the super cinemas), being in the Chinese taste, with a lavish display of plaster ornament, shallow-domed ceiling (originally decorated as a willow-pattern plate), festive pagoda canopies to the boxes, dragon's heads with gleaming electric eyes, etc. Two balconies, with a serpentine curved front to the lower one. The original lavish decorations by Campbell Smith, the painted act drop and the rich box hangings have all gone, but the Grand remains a most remarkable theatre, fully capable of being returned to its designed use. The alterations made for concert use are all readily reversible. Its location, opposite Clapham Junction Station and close to Central London, would give it a wide catchment. Capacity would depend on whether or not the gallery was brought into use. Sight lines are excellent from every level. *JE*

Collins' Music Hall

10-11 Islington Green
Islington
Other names
    Red Lion
    c.1850   Lansdown Arms

Collins' Music Hall, c.1908

Lansdown Arms Music Hall
Sam Collins' Music Hall
    1897   Collins' Theatre of Varieties
briefly 1908 and First World War
    Islington Hippodrome
Original architect
    1862   Unknown
Later works
    1885   Edward Clarke: adjoining
           house taken to provide new
           entrance and hall largely
           rebuilt
    1897   E.A.E. Woodrow: new audi-
           torium and other improve-
           ments
    1908   Unknown: repaired and
           altered after fire; six circle
           boxes removed
    1911   Lovegrove and Papworth: bal-
           cony reseated and other reno-
           vation works
    1931   Wingfield, Bowler and Clay:
           new heating and ventilation
           installed
Current use Facade only (bookshop
behind)

The music hall active at the rear of the pub since 1863 and associated until its destruction 95 years later with the name of Sam Collins was actually only licensed to him for the two and a half years before his death in 1865. The site backed onto a former burial ground (New Bunhill Fields) which restricted development so that no major improvement was possible after the 1897 reconstruction. Following a destructive fire in 1958, the hall itself was demolished. The pub facade in its late C19 form survives, somewhat modified, but the rooms behind have been radically altered to

form a bookshop. The space formerly occupied by the theatre itself served for many years as a timber yard and is now a car park. The side walls and some traces of escape staircases serve to identify it but (contrary to popular belief) there is nothing else left to be seen of the music hall. The facade carries a blue commemorative plaque. There has been continuing discussion of the possibility of building a new theatre on the site of the hall and this might very well be successful in the 'Little Theatreland' between Sadler's Wells and Highbury Corner. *JE*

Comedy ★★

Panton Street
City of Westminster
Other names
    Alexandra (proposed name, not used)
    Lyric (proposed name, not used)
    1881-84
       Royal Comedy
Original architect
    1881   Thomas Verity
Later work
    1911   Whiting and Peto: vestibule
           and bars reconstructed
    1933   Unknown: altered and 'drasti-
           cally redecorated'
    1955   Cecil Masey and A.
           Macdonald: alterations to
           dressing rooms, gallery
           entrances
           and stage door
    1980   Sir John Burnet-Tait and
           Partners: new entrance canopy
Listed   Grade II
Current use Theatre
Capacity   798

The Comedy is one of only three substantially complete pre-1890 theatres in the West End (the others are the Royal Opera House and the Criterion – all other early West End theatres having undergone complete rebuilding of their auditoria). It is a particularly beautiful example of a small 1880s' theatre which, if fully restored, would be recognised as an architectural work of outstanding quality. Despite its small stage, the Comedy was originally intended for comic opera. Its external appearance (apart from a rather mean modern entrance canopy) has changed very little.The stone classical facade to Panton Street has a 3-storey, 3-bay pedimented centre with a draped female figure carrying a torch in the central blind window recess at first-floor level. A simply detailed elevation returns into Oxendon Street.

Internally, Verity's design has suffered alterations, some of which now seem regrettable, but it could be readily restored. The auditorium has three balconies with pretty plaster ornament. The 1955 works changed the line of the lower fronts but the top tier, unaltered, follows the curve of the elegantly ornamented circular ceiling, which has a fretted centre, originally accommodating a gas sunburner. The slips boxes have been blocked off in a rather off-hand way. The square proscenium is closely flanked by stage boxes, each of which is set in a dominant, round-arched frame. The boxes were originally in three tiers but the fronts have been taken out to form single tall openings which are now packed with an over-obvious collection of lanterns. Accommodating front-of-house lighting positions will be a major problem for anyone attempting a sympathetic restoration.

The dressing rooms are now in an adjoining modern office building behind the back wall of the stage in Oxendon Street/Orange Street.

There appears to be no authoritative architectural account of the Comedy. It merits the kind of detailed study accorded by the *Survey of London* to Verity's Criterion. The account in *Survey of London* vol. XX is not in any way adequate.   *JE*

Coronation Picture Palace
High Street North, Manor Park
Newham
Original architect
 1911   Sydney Burwood
Later works
 1921   Clifford A. Aish: extended
Listed   Grade II
Current use Snooker Club (lower floor only)
Capacity   originally 1900

The Coronation opened in 1911 and was extended in 1921. The auditorium lies parallel to High Street North with entrance approached by steps on the right side. Plain, rendered elevation to street with the name CORONATION on upper level at each end. The interior has a barrel-vault ceiling with ornate plasterwork, echoed on the balcony front. Until 1938, it had a fully equipped stage, getin and dressing-room facilities and operated a ciné-variety policy. In 1932, a Morgan and Smith two-manual organ was installed. During the 1960s, it became a Mecca Bingo Club; this lasted until 1985 when the building was converted to a snooker club, with a false ceiling extending from under the

Coronet, c.1909 (John Earl Collection)

balcony area, which is now disused. *SM*

Coronet ★★
Notting Hill Gate
Kensington and Chelsea
Other names
 1950   Gaumont
Original architect
 1898   W.G.R. Sprague
Listed   Grade II
Current use Cinema
Capacity   c.800

Exterior in painted stone and, despite some architectural losses, important to the local townscape. Classical with giant pilasters above the ground floor; alternate major bays emphasised by pediments breaking the crowning balustrade. Over the corner, a short, round tower is crowned by a dome.

The auditorium, as might be expected, is in slightly lower key than Sprague's contemporary West End theatres but it is remarkable complete and cries out for restoration. Plaster ornament in Louis XVI manner. Two elliptically curved balconies. Square, enriched architrave to proscenium, flanked by blank bays where the boxes should be – but it would be easy to reinstate their missing fronts. The box bays are framed by attenuated Corinthian columns with enriched lower shafts, set on lofty pedestals and carrying an entablature with segmental broken pediments. A flat arched ceiling spans between the boxes. There is a domed ceiling over the auditorium. Consent was given in 1993

for the insertion of a small cinema auditorium on the stage, but designed so that the stage remained intact and the new works could be easily removable.

Although the Coronet had a comparatively short life (18 years) before cinema began to intrude, the architectural and theatrical quality of Sprague's design makes it fair to regard this as one of London's most important theatre buildings no longer in its designed use. In such a location, with many theatregoers in the local population, an outstanding fringe theatre (the Gate) nearby and very easy access from the West End, a live theatre of this size might be expected to succeed today.   *JE*

Criterion ★★★
Piccadilly Circus
City of Westminster
Original architect
 1874   Thomas Verity
Later works
 1878   Thomas Verity: extension to east
 1884   Thomas Verity: partially reconstructed
 1903   Unknown: renovated
 1992   RHWL: backstage and bars altered (in connection with complete redevelopment of adjoining buildings)
Listed   Grade II*
Current use Theatre
Capacity   600

Originally planned as a square concert hall to form part of a large development with restaurants and public rooms for

Messrs Spiers and Pond, on the site of the old White Bear coaching inn, at nos 219–221 Piccadilly and at 8 and 9 Jermyn Street. The decision was taken to provide a theatre instead while the building was in carcase. The theatre and restaurant building has a fine classical stone facade to the Circus in Second Empire manner which, 'despite alterations and disfigurements . . . may still be regarded as the best surviving work of Thomas Verity' (*Survey of London* vol XXIX).

This was the first completely subterranean theatre in London, the auditorium volume being entirely below the level of the Circus. In safety terms this was regarded as beneficial, a rush up a staircase being less prone to mishap than a rush down, but the change of design intention during building produced safety deficiencies which led to closure by the Metropolitan Board of Works in 1883. After alterations to improve fire separation and ventilation the theatre reopened in 1884. At this time electric light was installed. Relatively minor alterations since then have left the auditorium close to its 1884 form, itself a modification, rather than a reincarnation, of the 1873 design. It is, thus, one of the best preserved of the West End's few pre-1890 theatres, most others having been built, rebuilt or much altered after the London County Council came into existence in 1889.

It has two balconies supported on slender iron columns. The dress circle is serpentine-fronted, terminating at the curved box fronts, which are at a slightly higher level; the upper circle is in a continuous lyre-shape, meeting the proscenium wall and incorporating boxes. Flat circular ceiling. The recent redecoration, with rich and generous hangings in the boxes, has restored the elegance and warm embrace of this delightful auditorium. There are splendid coloured Minton tile and mirror decorations to vestibule, stairs, etc., marred only by a heavy 'Chippendales' style retouching of figure painting on the entrance hall ceiling. The decoration system has been extended into the new bars, using old tiles (figure designs by A.S. Coke and possibly W.S. Coleman) and coloured glass together with new, exactly matched material. The restaurant suites and Long Bar (all now independent of the Theatre) have also been well restored and adapted, the latter with its striking 'glistering' ceiling.

The underground location imposes severe limitations on the stage in overall dimensions, height (there is a minimal

grid over, with no flying space) and get-in arrangements (formerly through the hinged front of a stage left box, with a ramped gangplank down to stage level). Backstage planning, dressing rooms, etc., have been improved in the rebuilding of the surrounding property but get-in conditions remain tortured and the opportunity was missed to gain a convenient crossover passage.

This is one of the most important surviving mid-Victorian theatres in Britain, rivalled only by the Old Vic, Royal Opera House, Margate Theatre Royal and Tyne Theatre and Opera House   *JE*

Dalston Theatre ★
12 Dalston Lane
Hackney
Other names
  1886 North London Colosseum
  National Hippodrome
  Dalston Theatre of Varieties
  (and variations on these names)
  1920 Dalston Picture House
  1951 Gaumont
Original architect
  1886 Alfred Brandreth
Later works
  1898 Wylson and Long: major
  alterations
  1921 Robert Cromie: reconstruct-
  ed as Dalston Picture House
  1960 Unknown: converted to
  warehouse
Current use **Nightclub**
Capacity   **2260 (following 1921 recon-**
  struction)

Opened as a circus but quickly became a variety theatre, converted to cinema in 1920, closed 1960 and became a car auction room c.1964. Modest exterior but interesting as a theatrical survival in a changing inner suburb. Narrow single-bay entrance front with Corinthian pilasters; single storey on line of shops in Dalston Lane and taller, to align with older terrace, behind. This entrance, containing the old front offices was new in 1898. Flank elevation to Roseberry Place has low relief stucco arcading. The roof covering was stripped in the 1990s.

The auditorium was an astonishing sight in the 1960s with up to 80 cars parked on the raked floor and auctioneer's offices and rostrum on the stage. As now seen, it dates from the adaptation to cinema use in 1920-7. Luxury abounded with the main colour scheme being black and gold. Unusually the stage facilities were not retained in the reconstruction.

A striking auditorium, near-rectangular, with sharply raked wood-boarded concrete floor. Very wide and deep, fully cantilevered balcony with serpentine front between long side slips, broken on either side by a big pedimented box and terminating with a false stage box turned to face obliquely into the auditorium. The balcony is of concrete construction at the front. The rear, wood part is probably older. A formerly existing (pre-cinema) upper balcony has been removed. Ceiling stripped but the framing retains the original forms. It had a flat-domed centre within a broad flat band containing small domes at intervals. Wide proscenium.

Still surprisingly complete, the building now houses a number of nightclub/music venues. It is remarkable, considering the rough usage the theatre had in the 1960s that it has survived at all. It might be possible, with some ingenuity, to restore it and bring it back into theatre use but it is difficult to see a demand arising for such a large house in this location. Club and similar uses probably represent the best chance of retaining such architectural and local historical interest as it now has. The entire site has been under threat of redevelopment since 1996.   *JE/SM*

Dominion ★★
Tottenham Court Road
Camden
Original architect
  1928-9 W. and T.R. Milburn (William
  Milburn Junior)
Later works
  1930 W.R. Glen: stalls bar, circle
  cloakroom, gallery bar and
  chorus room removed
  1933 W.E. Trent: cinema organ
  installed
  1945/8 W.E. Trent: converted old café,
  carpenters' store, etc., to
  offices; dressing rooms on
  third floor converted to offices
  1958 Unknown: installation of Todd
  AO screen and new projection
  box; upper circle closed
  1972 Apollo Leisure Property
  Services Division: stage rebuilt;
  dressing rooms added
  1992/3 Unknown: front of house
  refurbished
Listed   **Grade II**
Current use **Theatre**
Capacity: **2007**

The Dominion was built on the site of the Meux Brewery and the tiny Court Cinema (opened in 1911). Proposals for

Dominion, c.1933 (John Earl Collection)

a theatre there were first made in 1923, but it was only in 1928 that Moss Empires became interested in development. The result is typical of the work of the younger William Milburn. The Dominion is vast, yet distances from the stage are never great (save in the upper circle) and the sight lines are excellent. The foyer and circle circulation areas are also remarkably generous for a London theatre, and there was originally also a café over the entrance. The style, howeverer was the rather frigid neo-Renaissance of the 1920s' Milburn houses; despite its original pink lampshades, the auditorium must always have been a cold, impersonal place best suited to large-scale extravaganzas. Its recent redecoration in dark colours suits it well.

It was not one of Moss Empires' successful ventures. A musical based on golf opened the theatre but, within a year, it was being rented to film distributors. From September 1930, it became a permanent cinema, with W.R. Glen employed to strip out the cloakrooms and bars to expand the 'crush' areas to cinematic requirements. In January 1933, the building was sold to Gaumont British. Further alterations were made after the Second World War, when shortage of office space forced Gaumont, from 1940 part of the Rank empire, to convert the old café, carpenter's shop and the upper floors of dressing rooms into offices. Then in 1958, a vast Todd AO cinema screen was installed, along with a new projection box, and the

upper circle was closed.

The decommissioning of these important seating areas leaves the Dominion still one of London's largest theatres, and one with remarkable potential. This was not, however, recognised until recently.

From November 1981 the Dominion became primarily a venue for one-off live shows; then, in 1986, it was painted black and hung with a velarium for *Time*. A legal dispute ensured the theatre was not subsequently restored, and Rank took the opportunity to seek the site's redevelopment. Only in 1990 was demolition for a hotel averted, when the building was acquired by Apollo Leisure.

No other London theatre has an empty upper circle stepped to modern standards, nor so much potential front-of-house space awaiting readoption. Restored, the Dominion could again house close to its original capacity of 2835 seats. *EH*

Drury Lane Theatre Royal ★★★
Catherine Street
City of Westminster
Other names
1663   **Theatre Royal on Brydges Street**
1674   **Theatre Royal**
1783   **Theatre Royal Drury Lane**
Summary of architectural history
1635   **Unknown: a temporary play-house**
1663   **Wren or Webb or possibly Richard Ryder: first**

permanent building following grant of Royal Patent
1672   **Sir Christopher Wren: completely new theatre**
1775   **Robert Adam: auditorium reconstructed**
1794   **Henry Holland: entirely rebuilt**
1812   **Benjamin Dean Wyatt: entirely rebuilt following fire**
1814   **Unknown: proscenium altered; major redecoration of interior**
c.1818 **Unknown: saloon altered**
1820   **James Spiller (also attributed to Sir John Soane): portico added**
1822   **Samuel Beazley: auditorium remodelled; backstage improved**
1831   **Samuel Beazley: colonnade added on Russell St front**
1837   **Crace: interior decorated**
1841, 1847 and 1851
       Beazley and others: various minor alterations
1870   **Marsh Nelson and Harvey: interior altered**
1901   **Philip Pilditch: auditorium reconstructed**
1922   **Emblin Walker, Jones and Cromie: auditorium entirely rebuilt**
Listed   **Grade I**
Current use **Theatre**
Capacity   **2237**

Architecturally and historically this is one of the most important theatres in the world. No other site in Britain has a longer history of continuous theatre use. The right of the Lane to present dramatic entertainments dates from the Royal Patent (still in the possession of the theatre) granted by Charles II to Killigrew in 1662.

Drury Lane shares with Haymarket Theatre Royal the distinction of being entirely pre-Victorian in external appearance (the Lyceum has a pre-Victorian portico). As now seen, the main theatrical shell, the staircase, rotunda, saloon, etc., of 1811–12, are by B.D.Wyatt and comprise the only substantial Georgian theatre fabric in London.The entrance facade is the earliest now surviving in London on a working theatre. It is a pity that the portico of 1820 is so obviously an addition to Wyatt's restrained but elegant neo-classical design, but Beazley's side colonnade of 1831 is a worthy later adornment and a fine townscape feature, especially when viewed from Covent Garden Market.

The great staircase, rotunda and saloon are important late Georgian mon-

Drury Lane Theatre Royal (Ian Grundy)

uments in their own right and unparalleled in any British theatre for their splendour and sense of theatrical occasion. Inevitably, after the architectural promise of these public spaces, the comparatively modern (1922) auditorium disappoints, but only by contrast. It is of considerable quality and, from a theatrical viewpoint, remarkably successful and intimate. This is surprising when it is remembered that, in the 1920s, theatre architecture had no clear direction.

This is the last London auditorium to be designed in the rich fin-de-siècle manner established by Matcham, Sprague and Crewe (the Fortune is only two years later and belongs to a totally different era). It has some points of kinship with Manchester Opera House (1912) and, more so, Manchester Palace (1913). The style is Empire with a rectangular proscenium and a modelled elliptical tympanum over. The proscenium is separated from three tiers of curving balcony fronts by deep canted side walls containing three bays of boxes at three levels, framed by pilasters and columns of imitation lapis lazuli. They have gilt capitals carrying an entablature from which a flared and coffered elliptical-arched ceiling springs across to form a deep sounding board.

The stage is raked at the front, flat at the back, with an extensive counterweight system. Elaborate metal stage machinery with six bridges (two tilting), described in the *Stage Year Book* for 1910, survived the 1922 works but is not regularly used.

Drury Lane is, unlike almost every other West End theatre, generously planned, with a 39.6m (130ft) frontage

and a depth of well over 92m (300ft). Within this area, the auditorium, stage and additional backstage areas are contained in a succession of approx. 24.4m (80ft) cubes. The vast backstage presents valuable opportunities for future improvements but could also constitute a temptation for non-theatrical development if the theatre ever fell into the hands of less well-disposed owners.

The antiquity of the theatre and its complex building history makes it important that all future works, especially at lower levels should be monitored for recordable evidence of earlier phases. *JE*

Duchess ★★
Catherine Street
City of Westminster
Original architect
   1929   **Ewen S. Barr, with Marc Henri and Laverdet**
Current use **Theatre**
Capacity   **470**

Ewen Barr was not a great theatre architect but, on this site, to his great credit, he pulled off a planning trick with which Matcham might have been pleased. The irregular trapezoidal site, enclosed on three sides, appeared to be undevelopable on account of ancient lights rights. Barr succeeded in creating the required theatre by setting back the upper storeys, making the circle noticeably narrower than the wholly subterranean stalls and reducing the stage depth above ground level. Foyers and box office are tucked under the single steeply raked balcony, the Royal Box backs onto the street and the dressing rooms are stacked onto the auditorium.

The stone facade with three canted bays is in a curious, busily ornamented style described variously as 'vaguely Elizabethan' (*Survey of London*) and 'modern Tudor Gothic'. The interiors must owe more of their architectural character to Henri and Laverdet than to Barr. The auditorium is fan-shaped with a rectangular proscenium opening set in an elliptically arched recess with curved jambs and a deeply coved head forming a sounding board. There are unseated ornamental loggias on the flank walls above the balcony and a recessed domed ceiling. Marc Henri and Laverdet's interiors throughout made extensive use of concealed lighting, silver plaster and coloured glass. The stage is small with especially restricted wing space on stage left. The grid embraces only the front 5.8m (19ft), the rear extension of the stage being below ground level and only about 4m (13ft) in clear height.   *JE*

Duke of York's ★★
St Martin's Lane
City of Westminster
Other names
   1892-94
      Trafalgar Square Theatre
   1894-95
      Trafalgar
Original architect
   1892   Walter Emden
Later works
   1950   Cecil Beaton with W. Wylton Todd: altered and redecorated
   1979   RHWL: altered internally
Listed   **Grade II**
Current use **Theatre**
Capacity   **640**

Painted brick and stone elevation, four storeys in height in three major bays, the centre one being three windows wide on the top two storeys, with a pretty open loggia at first-floor level, guarded by a balustrade between Ionic columns. The facade at present lacks its original crowning balustrade above the main cornice. Ornamental iron and glass canopy over the entrances.

The Duke of York's is detached, with narrow passageways to the left and right, each with wrought iron gate, overthrow and lantern. The dressing rooms are in a separate building at the rear which is barely separated from the flank of the Garrick Theatre. The theatre has a narrow auditorium with the proscenium opening spanning the whole of the end wall, the boxes alone forming the frame. There are three balconies with single boxes at each level and double boxes

Duke of York's

flanking at dress and upper-circle levels. Good plaster ornament. Emden's original design did not overcome the difficult sighting problems of such a long and narrow theatre. Under the unusually deep balconies, which were of early concrete construction, he placed a forest of columns, making many seats almost unusable. The cut-off at higher levels was also severe. In 1979 many of these columns were removed and the number of usable seats was thereby increased. The loss of the columns, which, in this case, had practically no architectural value, was not as damaging as it would be in some other theatres, but the price paid for the improvement was the introduction of a very deep beam over the gallery which, as a result, is permanently out of use. It is a pity that, due to enforced economies, this beam (necessary only for the suspension of the upper balconies after removal of the columns) was not placed above the roof as was originally intended.

The box office, removed from the foyer at the same time, was a 1950 addition by Cecil Beaton. It is now in the Theatre Museum entrance.   *JE*

Dutch House

148 High Street, Tottenham
Haringey
Other names
    Markfield Hotel
Original architect
    1893   Unknown: as part of a
        pub/hotel complex
Current use Auction room

Apparently built as a multi-purpose concert room forming part of an hotel, which by the 1890s usually meant a big pub with hotel rooms. A late, stylistically rather backward-looking, and unusually large example of its kind. It was probably originally meant to seat about 1000, but under modern conditions its capacity might be no more than half that. Surprisingly, the hall has no balcony.

The internal architectural treatment is derived from Gothic, but with some personal, even wilful features. The stage is small and obviously intended primarily for concert performance, but there is a pair of get-in doors at the back, opening onto an easily accessible yard. The stage has a cellar below and a simple, low wooden soffit above.

There is a lower hall which has had its columns removed and deep beams inserted, spanning the whole width of the building. It is difficult to see what gain justified the expense of doing this work.

An uncommon and interesting survival.   *JE*

Embassy

Eton Avenue
Camden
Other names
    Eton Avenue Hall
    Hampstead Conservatoire
Original architect
    c.1890   Unknown: as a concert hall
        (successor to a smaller hall)
Later works
    1928   Andrew Mather: converted to
        theatre
    1945   Unknown: repaired and
        reopened after war damage
after 1956
        Unknown: rear of auditorium
        partitioned off
    1989   Cullum and Nightingale: work-
        shops added
Current use Theatre
Capacity   266

The theatre was adapted in 1928 by Andrew Mather from the Hampstead Conservatoire of Music, previously the Eton Avenue Hall. The mixture of architectural styles reflects the history of the building, now part of the adjoining Central School of Speech and Drama, which is itself a warren of interconnecting old buildings. The complex has grown from a double-fronted stucco Italianate Victorian villa, much altered and extended over many years. The theatre, at the rear of the original house is approached by way of an entrance foyer

with box office and corridor.

It is a simple high-ceilinged hall with pilastered walls and an end balcony. The Embassy became a famous repertory theatre from the 1920s, and this continues today with school productions open to the public.

The school complex is undergoing major improvements, including extensive rebuilding by Cullum and Nightingale. The theatre, on completion, will have a full fly tower and an auditorium in a single rake.   *SM*

Empire

Leicester Square
City of Westminster
Other names
    1887   Empire Theatre of Varieties
    1898   Empire Theatre
    1928   Empire (Cinema)
Original architect
    1884   Thomas Verity (succeeded by J.
        and A.E.Bull)
Later works
    1887   Romaine Walker and Tanner:
        redecorated
    1899   Frank Verity: new foyer and
        secondary entrance
    1904   Frank Verity: major reconstruc-
        tion
    1928   Thomas W. Lamb with Frank
        Matcham Co (F.G.M.
        Chancellor): rebuilt as a cine-
        ma
    1962   George Coles: completely
        reconstructed as cinema and
        ballroom
Current use Cinema
Capacity   1330

The history of the site and the buildings which have occupied or been planned for it is extremely complex. The *Survey of London* vol.XXXIV account is full and authoritative. Saville House, formerly Aylesbury House of 1684, which stood here, was used for various exhibitions and entertainments from the first years of the C19. The *SOL* volume notes that between 1846 and 1865 various parts of the house were given 14 different names. After the house was burnt down in 1865, plans for theatres on the site included the Denmark Theatre and Winter Garden, and the Alcazar Grand Theatre of Varieties. What was eventually built was the Royal London Panorama. Thomas Verity prepared plans for the conversion of the panorama into a theatre but the work was delayed and completed by another architect. Names proposed for the new theatre were Plaza, Phoenix, Pandora and Queen's, but it opened in 1884 as the Empire Theatre.

The subsequent, eventful history of this building is well recorded in histories of music hall and English ballet. After a brilliant career it closed in 1927, was almost entirely rebuilt and reopened as a cinema. Since the 1962 reconstruction its theatrical interest is slight and there is nothing left to recall the extraordinary history of the first Empire and its notorious promenade. Parts of the external structure are remnants of the Frank Verity works (notably on the west side). The Empire of 1928 was the only cinema in Britain constructed to designs by the American specialist Thomas Lamb. The elevation is closely based on his Albee Theatre in Cincinnati, built a year earlier. The deep portico is the only surviving element of his work. The auditorium was the biggest ever seen in the West End, and the most opulent constructed in the inter-war period. Its programming matched this pre-eminence, and not just by showing the latest films. In 1949, in a bid to combat changes in filmgoing and licensing, alterations were made so that elaborate shows could be staged in accompaniment to the feature film. The Empire Girls, Empire Ballet and Empire Concert Orchestra, together with well-known variety acts, had a brief but spectacular life until March 1952. After a further major reconstruction, the Empire reopened in 1962 with a ballroom in the old stalls area and a new stadium cinema in the former circle and foyer. The Ritz cinema next door became a subsidiary auditorium reached by a common entrance. *JE/EH*

Evans's Music and Supper Room

43 King Street, Covent Garden
City of Westminster
Other names
    Evans's Song and Supper Room
Original architect
 c.1835   Unknown: conversion of coffee
            room
Later works
            The house went through many
            changes in the C18 and C19.
            The following refer to parts
            used for live entertainment
            only:
 1844   Unknown: Supper Room
            improved
 1855   William Finch Hill: new large
            music hall
 1871   J.H. Rowley: hall enlarged;
            boxes formed all round
 1877–80
            Unknown: doorway from

            Piazza given present form
 1911–12
            Mewes and Davis: further
            alterations for National
            Sporting Club
 1930   E.A. Shaw Partners: altered to
            serve as fruit warehouse
 c.1977   Fitzroy Robinson: altered to
            form offices, last traces of
            music hall eliminated
Current use **Fragment only**

No. 43 King Street is an early C18 house attributed to Thomas Archer. It was converted to an hotel which, by the 1830s, had a thriving supper room. The original song and supper entertainment was held from the mid-1830s in a basement coffee room. It was very popular by the 1840s. Under John Green a large new music hall (to which the old room formed a vestibule and picture gallery) was built to cover almost the whole of the rear garden. This fine hall, by William Finch Hill, is usually dated to 1856 but actually opened in December 1855. With the Canterbury Hall (1854) and Weston's Music Hall (1857) the new Evans's set the style and standard for the first generation of giant supper-room music halls in London. It was a rectangular, flat-floored room with an open stage, backed by a triumphal arch.

The hall was enlarged and improved by J.H. Rowley in 1871. Although licensed to 1881, it effectively ceased to operate in 1880, but remained as a recognisable room well into the C20. Doubt has been expressed as to whether the Mewes and Davis alterations planned in 1911/12 for the National Sporting Club (in occupation from the 1890s) were ever carried out, but the evidence of a Phil May sketch published in 1932 suggests that they were. The altered Archer house front still dominates a corner of the Covent Garden Piazza and provides telling evidence of disregard for those aspects of architectural history which, until recently, were given scant scholarly attention. In course of an imperfect 1970s' reinstatement of the facade, the iron arched entrance to the early room was destroyed (the bits were salvaged by the Museum of London). Nothing is now recognisable of the room itself, a key stage in the history of music hall. *JE*

Fortune ★★

Russell Street, Covent Garden
City of Westminster
Original architect
 1924   Ernest Schaufelberg

Listed   **Grade II**
Current use **Theatre**
Capacity   **440**

Evaluation of C20 theatres has been greatly hampered over the years by the kind of determinism which leads historians to judge buildings by how well they accord with a received view of what 'good' architects should have been doing at the time. Having regard to the generally dismal showing of mainstream architects in designing workable theatres, judgements need to be made on a rather more informed basis. The Fortune is not one of the great theatres of the century but it is, in a number of ways, notable. It was the first completely new theatre to be built in the West End after the First World War (immediately before a surge in the building of big cinemas) and it represents, at least in London, a sudden and radical departure from the style set by the turn-of-the-century 'boom' theatres of the Matcham school. The contrast with Sprague's St Martin's of 1916, or Emblin Walker, Jones and Cromie's new Drury Lane auditorium of 1922, could not be more striking. Externally and internally it breaks completely with established theatre design norms.

Although it is one of the West End's smallest houses, the three-dimensional design ingenuity required to fit such a theatre, meeting all the safety requirements, on such a site was considerable. In this respect (but no other) it invites comparison with the neighbouring Duchess. The Fortune, however, is more innovatory, making extensive use of reinforced concrete construction and presenting frankly cubist forms (curiously described as 'mediaeval' by a contemporary commentator) to the outside world. The original appearance of hard textured walls, minimally relieved by ornamental lead strips, has been blurred by overpainting, but the entrance front and doors are almost intact. The gilt nude female figure of Fortune (wrongly identified as Terpsichore) is a striking feature, high up on the facade. Internally, the marble and copper ornament in the foyer is original. The two-balconied auditorium, the first in London to make a merit of abandoning stage boxes and curving balcony fronts, has had its original mural decorations painted out. The balcony rows are, inevitably, rather tightly set, but more difficult space problems had to be met backstage. The stage itself, 7.9m (26ft) deep, is extremely restricted. *JE*

Forum

Uxbridge Road
Ealing
Other names
  1961 ABC
  later Cannon, ABC (again), Virgin
Original architect
  1934 J. Stanley Beard and A.
      Douglas Clare
Later works
  1975 Unknown: tripled
Current use Triple cinema
Capacity 1133

Built for Herbert Yapp, together with the Forum, Fulham Road, and the Forum, Kentish Town (to name but two), all by J. Stanley Beard.
  The building is in Classical Roman style. The facade has central bay of six giant Doric columns in antis, rising above entrance canopy to attic above the entablature. Outer bays are plain, topped with squat square turrets; single-storey exit blocks at side extremities. The classical style is continued inside where much of the original detail remains. Full stage facilities and fly tower. Proscenium, also with Doric columns, much obscured by present large screen mounted in front. Restoration of former café/restaurant at first-floor level is under consideration. *SM*

Garrick ★★★

Charing Cross Road
City of Westminster
Original architect
  1889 Walter Emden, with C.J. Phipps
Later works
  1997 Jaques Muir and Partners:
      entrance canopy reinstated to
      original design

Listed **Grade II***
Current use **Theatre**
Capacity **700**

It now seems clear (Hugh Maguire, *Theatre Notebook* 1988) that the design of the theatre is essentially Emden's. The contribution made by Phipps, who was still under a cloud as a result of the fatal fire at his Exeter Theatre Royal, was a matter of argument at the time and the relationship between the two architects seems to have been an uneasy one. The long facade occupies a key position at the curved southern end of Charing Cross Road, where it widens into an approximately triangular space marked on the south side by the classical stone flank elevation of the National Portrait Gallery. The eastern side is formed by the Portland and Bath stone facade of the theatre. This is divided into three related but independent elements. On the left, the main entrance is classical with colonnaded loggia at first-floor level. On the right, two less elaborately articulated compositions relieve the long flank of the auditorium. The entrance canopy was hideously altered in post-war years, but reinstated to its original design in 1997.
  Excellent three-balconied auditorium in a free, but not excitable, Italianate manner. The U-shaped balcony fronts are stacked one vertically above the other, differentiated only by their plaster-relief ornaments. Like its neighbour the Duke of York's, which it almost touches at the rear boundary, there is no proscenium frame as such, the stage opening being defined by flat box fronts whose flanking coupled columns and pilasters carry arched supports to the proscenium wall and twin caryatids at the gallery abutment. The present decoration scheme, in pale veined marbling, is by Carl Toms. The gallery has been disused for some time and still has the character of a late Victorian top tier, but the sight lines from the centre are good and plans have been discussed for bringing it back into use. The Northern Line of the Underground, which passes under the auditorium, can occasionally be heard in the theatre. As is commonly the case in West End Theatres of pre-1914 date, the front-of-house accommodation is tightly constrained and past alterations have led to the waste of some of the better spaces as rooms denied to the public. *JE*

Gaumont State ★★

Kilburn High Road and Willesden Lane
Brent
Original architect
  1937 George Coles
Later works
  1960 Unknown: area beneath bal-
      cony subdivided for ballroom
  1975 Unknown: former restaurant
      converted to cinema
  1980 Unknown: division beneath
      balcony removed; whole audi-
      torium converted to bingo
Current use **Bingo**
Capacity (was) c.4000

Opened at the end of 1937, the Gaumont State, Kilburn, was George Coles's crowning achievement, and a concept of grand and impressive size. It was built for the Hyams Brothers and took over two years to complete, but was sold to Gaumont Super Cinemas before opening. It is said that the name 'State' came from the 36.56m (120ft) tower, reminiscent of the Empire State building in New York. The cream faience tower originally housed the theatre's broadcasting studio in its base. It is flanked by two shorter towers, a little higher than the surrounding buildings, and the entrance is covered by a large canopy. The body of the auditorium lies behind rows of (older) shops on the main high street. The upper parts of these were given a similar faience treatment. There is a large car park and access for loading at the rear of the stage end. On the corner, on Willesden Lane, was an imposing second entrance with restaurant and dance floor above.
  The foyer is in what was called at the time 'Italian Renaissance style', with pillars, marble, elaborate plaster cornices, chandeliers and huge mirrors. Grand stairways lead to the vast auditorium.

Garrick (Tina Walkling)

This seated 4004 on two levels, making it today the largest surviving conventional auditorium in the country. It is in Classical style, with a fully equipped stage, workshops and dressing rooms. The orchestra pit had at one time a separate lift for the organ console; the organ is now positioned permanently to one side of the front stalls area.

The State closed at the outbreak of war, reopened for weekends in 1940 and resumed normal opening in 1944. In the 1960s, the rear stalls area was separated by a dividing wall to form a ballroom, and this was later converted to a bingo club. A smaller cinema was made from the restaurant area. In 1980, the building was listed and the dividing wall removed, the whole auditorium converting to bingo. The small cinema closed in 1990 and remains boarded up. Apart from adaptations for bingo, the original atmosphere of the building is easily experienced. *SM*

George Inn
Borough High Street, Southwark
Southwark
Original architect
   n.d.   Unknown
Listed   Grade I
Current use Courtyard performances
   (mainly amateur)

Not a purpose-built theatre but has occasional performances in the yard. The George Inn, Southwark, stands on the site of a much older inn of the same name. It is now London's only remaining galleried inn. Inn yards were fitted up before the first public theatres were built

Gielgud, c.1990 (Bob Williamson)

and this is one of the best-known examples, close to the Elizabethan Bankside theatreland. Until the 1880s it was enclosed on three sides of the yard. Only the south wing is left standing, and it is against the heavy balustrades that performances of Elizabethan plays take place, annually.

Now a National Trust property, the George stands back from the High Street, and the part-cobbled courtyard is entered through an archway of wrought iron. A plaque on the High Street entrance records the fact that Dickens used the Inn as a background in his novel *Little Dorrit*. *SM*

Gielgud ★★★
Shaftesbury Avenue
City of Westminster
Other names
   1906-09   Hicks Theatre
   1909-94   Globe Theatre
Original architect
   1906   W.G.R. Sprague
Later works
   1914   J. Emblin Walker: inserted
             boxes at back of dress circle
             (since removed)
Listed   Grade II
Current use Theatre
Capacity   889

Forms part of an important group of theatres on the north side of Shaftesbury Avenue, all built as speculations on land released by the opening of this street in 1886. Designed with the Queen's (1908) as part of a single architectural treatment embracing a whole block. The symmetry has since been lost by the reconstruction of the Queen's frontage. The facade is of Portland Stone in a robust Edwardian Baroque manner. Two bays to Shaftesbury Avenue, three to slightly recessed corner quadrant and three to Rupert Street. Four storeys, with an iron canopy on ornamental brackets over the entrances. Above this, cornice hoods to the windows, oeil-de-boeuf at third floor and crowning cornice and balustrade. The corner is more grandly treated, with a giant Ionic order of attached columns rising through second and third floors. Short buttressed corner tower with a stone dome.

The auditorium is in characteristically restrained Sprague manner, in Louis XVI style. Two balconies, the upper one describing two thirds of a circle, following the line of the circular ceiling, which is shallow-domed with an outer band divided into panels with musical trophies. The lower balcony (dress circle)

is elliptical on plan. The side walls are concave, but not struck from the same centre as the ceiling. The walls at each upper level are enriched with pairs of Ionic columns, carrying an entablature with crowning urns. The entablature continues over the square-headed proscenium opening, which is framed by boxes in two tiers, set between Corinthian pilasters. Allegorical cartouche over centre of proscenium. The Grand Saloon with balconied bar repeats the paired Ionic columned treatment of the auditorium. A most impressive interior, but Sprague's tasteful designs are easily undermined by lifeless decoration (unlike Matcham's architectural fireworks, which can survive all kinds of indignities). The Gielgud is also as instructive an example as can be seen anywhere of the effects of uncontrolled front-of-house lighting installations. It would be more than an act of piety to remove all the junk and restore Sprague's original decorative scheme. Some original substage wooden machinery, including grave and four-post traps. *JE*

Golder's Green Hippodrome ★★
North End Road
Barnet
Original architect
   1913   Bertie Crewe
Later works
   1969   Unknown: converted to TV
             studio
   1972   Unknown: converted to radio
             concert hall
Listed   Grade II
Current use BBC Concert Hall
Capacity   700

The theatre stands on a prominent site alongside Golders Green Underground station and viewable across a large open forecourt. The principal facade is symmetrical, in stucco or reconstructed stone, with a three-storey centre in seven bays divided by piers with Ionic capitals, carrying a full entablature with urns above the cornice. On either side, channelled and quoined pavilions rise as short pedimented towers, between which the back wall of the house is set back as a plain attic with a prominent pitched roof and central cupola. Return one elevation is plainer. The main entrance is in a curved corner bay. Even allowing for the fact that this entrance served only the best seats, front-of-house accommodation was clearly always cramped and there is little scope for gaining space. No

Golder's Green Hippodrome

bars were shown in the first design and those eventually provided were barely adequate for such a large house.

Alterations made for the BBC Concert Orchestra have partly obscured, but not irreparably damaged, Crewe's interior. Those parts of the original architectural treatment which are visible are well maintained. The auditorium design aimed at decadent Roman splendour but, as with some other theatres of the immediate pre-First World War period, it missed the mark. This is, nevertheless, a notable interior. It has a square proscenium opening, with its lintel supported on console brackets. Above this, a huge and bare sounding board (which an old-fashioned allegorical painting would have relieved) shelters flanking pavilions which contain two levels of boxes with an extra, impractical box facing directly toward the audience at the upper level. The boxes are framed by 'correct' Roman Doric columns which, on one side, rise from uncomfortable pendant corners. They support a full entablature, which continues over the proscenium. Over the boxes are lion-drawn chariots, reminiscent of Matcham's London Coliseum, but somewhat too small to astonish. The Doric theme is continued in a triglyph frieze on the upper of two balcony fronts.

The upper part of the fly tower and the stage wings have been colonised since 1970 by a big rehearsal room, offices, band room, plant, etc. The greater part of the auditorium floor has been levelled as an orchestra stage (the raked floor survives beneath) and a big sound control room and storage space have been inserted at the rear. A suspended structure obstructs the view of the ceiling centre. Audiences for broadcasts and recordings now occupy part of the orchestra floor and the 1st balcony. The 2nd has been blocked off but still has its original thinly upholstered and backed bench seats.

Reconversion to live theatre would not be impossible, but it is difficult to imagine a better use for such a building in such a location than the one it now fulfils *JE*

Grand Palais

133 Commercial Road, Stepney
Tower Hamlets
Other names
c.1911   **New King's Hall and Queen's Hall**
c.1914   **Cohen Moses Cinematograph Hall**
Original architect
c.1911   **Unknown**
Current use **Wholesale clothing depot, storage and offices**

Although not much now remains to be seen, this building played its part in East End social life and deserves more attention than it has had.

It opened about 1911 as two multi-purpose halls, the King's Hall at ground-floor level and the Queen's Hall below. The King's was probably designed with future cinema use in view and it became the Cohen Moses Cinematograph Hall from 1914/15. The Queen's Hall was mainly used for dances.

About 1926 the cinema became a Yiddish theatre, the Grand Palais, remaining in this principal use until 1961 with occasional benefit performances after this date. A music and dancing licence was retained until at least 1963. It was described as 'public hall' in official records,

even during its period as an active theatre. By the 1970s it had become a thriving little Indian cinema; then, following a period of neglect, it became a wholesale clothing store in 1981–82.

The Grand Palais is easily missed, embedded as it is in the middle of a uniform early C20 row of shops with a facade in machine-made bricks with stone dressings. The entrance doorway to the Grand Palais is still distinguished by an ornamental pedimented hood but the iron and glass canopy bearing the name, present in 1980, has gone (it is said to have been rescued from a skip by a resident of the Isle of Dogs) and a pedimental hump in the cornice crowning the facade has been removed with the rebuilding of the parapet in plain brickwork. The interior is now a perfectly plain space, all plaster ornament having been stripped, but the end balcony is still discernible in offices above the ground floor.

The Grand Palais needs to be distinguished from the Palaseum, specifically built as a Yiddish Theatre in 1912. This stood on the opposite side of the road at no. 226 and was demolished in 1995 to make way for a car park. *JE*

Greenwich ★

Stockwell Street
Greenwich
Other names
    Rose and Crown Music Hall
    Parthenon
    Crowder's Music Hall and Picture Gallery
    Parthenon Palace of Varieties
    Greenwich Hippodrome
    Barnard's
    Green's – and many variants of all the above
Original architect
1855   **Unknown**
Later works
1871   **W.R. Hough: reconstructed**
1885   **J.G. Buckle: reconstructed**
1895   **Unknown: rebuilt 'for Mr Hancock'**
1969   **B. Meeking: reconstructed internally**
Current use **Theatre**
Capacity   **423**

The first building of any consequence on this site was probably the 1871 Crowder's Music Hall, previous rooms having been modest appendages to, or rooms within, the old Rose and Crown Public House. Rebuilt or remodelled in 1895 as the Hippodrome, it became a cinema in 1924 and closed altogether in

1949. A long campaign to reopen as a theatre and arts centre was headed by Ewan Hooper to avert a threat of demolition in 1962. Music Hall entertainments held in the large concert room at the Green Man in Blackheath (dem.) attracted a great deal of attention and reopening was achieved in 1969.

The narrow entrance facade to Croom's Hill is modern, by Meeking. The flank wall to Nevada Street is probably a relic of Crowder's in a modification of its 1885 dress. A stucco panel on this side will still, in some lights, reveal the legend 'Parthenon Palace of Varieties'. The Rose and Crown Public House on the corner of Nevada Street is on the site of the parent pub but was rebuilt in 1888, possibly by Frank Matcham. It is now separate from the theatre.

Although contained within an old shell, the interior is, for all practical purposes, a new building by Meeking. The auditorium, now above street level, is in a single rake with open thrust stage. JE

Hackney Empire ★★★

Mare Street
Hackney
Original architect
    1901   Frank Matcham
Later works
        Alterations to date have been mainly of a minor scale
Listed   **Grade II***
Current use   **Theatre**
Capacity   **1000 (excluding gallery)**

A magnificent example of a turn-of-the-century variety palace showing Matcham at his most imaginative, the Hackney Empire is the fourth and only theatrically active surviving example of his big suburban variety houses in Greater London. Built for Oswald Stoll, it opened in December 1901 with a 'two shows a night' policy. Equipped from the outset with a small ciné-projection box.

Excellent site next to the Town Hall with street frontages on three sides. Great townscape value. Splendidly exuberant terracotta facade to Mare Street, described at the time as being 'carried out in Victorian design'. Three bays, the wide centre one having a curiously framed and arched first-floor opening, the narrow outer bays treated as short towers, very slightly advanced. Topped by finely modelled domes with a pediment and figure of Euterpe between, removed 1979 and subsequently reinstated; all very eclectic and uninhibited.

Grand vestibule and double staircase with marbled finishes. Opulent auditorium, again highly mannered and eclectic in its details, with three balconies. Dress circle with boxes at back. Square, deeply coved and ornamented ceiling, with sliding centre. Marble proscenium, the opening flanked by splayed buttresses with elaborate niches (originally containing electric number panels) and crowned by Indian domes. The arch itself and its pierced tympanum form a serpentine pediment.

This is one of the most perfect examples of Matcham's work in London. During the period of occupation by Mecca Bingo, however, the auditorium was painted in their too-recognisable house style. This removed practically all trace of the old painting and gilding which had survived, soiled but pleasing, until early 1978. Now only the marble and alabaster surfaces and most of the allegorical paintings, richly framed in rococo plasterwork, remain untouched.

One interesting result of bingo use was the levelling of the back of the stalls to form a promenade bar, strangely reminiscent of the music halls of the immediately 'pre-Boom' era. The Empire was, even so, one of the last variety halls with a bar overlooking the stage (glazed panels behind stalls promenade on stage left).

The return of this theatre to variety use has been one of the most impressive and unlikely examples of theatre revival in recent years. The owning Trust still needs to raise a large sum to complete the architectural restoration and technical upgrading of the theatre, but the spin-off social and environmental benefits have already demonstrated the good sense of investing public money in such ventures. JE

Hackney Empire (Martin Charles)

Hammersmith (London) Apollo ★

Queen Caroline Street, Hammersmith
Hammersmith and Fulham
Other names
   1932   Gaumont Palace
   1962   Odeon
   1992   Labatt's Apollo
Original architect
   1932   Robert Cromie
Listed   Grade II
Current use Theatre and concerts
Capacity   3579

Hammersmith (London) Apollo (John R. Rifkin)

The Gaumont Palace, Hammersmith, which assumed its present name in 1999, opened in 1932. It was originally commissioned for the Davis Company, which explains why the architect was Robert Cromie, who had designed their massive Davis Cinema in Croydon (1928). However, the scheme was taken over by Gaumont in 1930, before construction began. The cinema's preservation as a single auditorium, complete with full stalls seating, has been due to its use as a live venue for pop concerts since the 1960s, and this has evolved under Apollo's management into its refurbishment as a full-time theatre. The organ has been in store since 1996 and the stage has been extended over the orchestra pit. A bar has been inserted into the curved tearoom that ran over the entrance to the building, blocking the first-floor windows, and some light fittings were taken in about 1980 to the State Cinema in Grays, Thurrock, but the building is otherwise completely intact.

The exterior has always been noted for its tremendous width of 57.9m (190ft), served by nine pairs of double doors. This width is the secret to its very logical plan, excellent sight lines and ease of circulation. Foyers run on two levels along the full width of this front, with staircases at either end, and give directly onto the auditorium. The tremendous width of the circle is also the cause of the massive capacity. It is 51.8m (170ft) wide at the rear, and achieves its high capacity without overhanging the stalls by more than a dozen rows. The largest steel girder across the balcony front weighs 56 tons, yet the building was noted for its economical use of steel by combining steel framing with load-bearing brick. Apollo report that its great structural strength has enabled exceptionally heavy sets and gantries to be installed successfully. The stage has a 19.21m (63ft) proscenium and a depth of 9.41m 31ft).

The art-deco mouldings of the shal-low aedicules on the walls are typical of Cromie's work, and are repeated at his Regal Cinema, Kingston; but other elements of the design are typical of the Gaumont circuit, especially the use of deep ceiling coves and the murals by Newbury A. Trent in the entrance hall. There are some good light fittings in the auditorium and on the staircases. Other unusual features are the way in which the projection box is concealed behind the deep elliptical skylight above the circle, 12.2m (40ft) in advance of the back of the auditorium (another Gaumont conceit), and the positioning of the organ chamber above the stage. Organ chambers were sometimes placed below the stage in Britain, but their positioning above it is very rare, and allows no space for an elaborate proscenium arch. Instead the effect of a decorative proscenium was given by curtains (long gone), which repeated the aediculed motifs of the surrounding walls. The curved upper foyer, reached by an imperial staircase to each side, is a particularly strong architectural space, with a line of columns that formerly separated it from the tearoom to one side and a central lightwell that corresponds with a deeply coved ceiling above.

Robert Cromie worked for Bertie Crewe between 1910 and 1914 and so had an excellent training in theatre planning. The demolition of the Davis in 1959 has left the Apollo as his finest surviving work. In a special issue of *Architectural Design and Construction*, published in March 1938, Cromie wrote that cinemas had a special place in society because they were 'very human milestones in our domestic history - temples to the passing hour – to Peace, not merely to prosperity.

'Of all buildings none are more fasci-nating to design, more difficult to construct nor more satisfying when built. The architect's job is so much of a struggle to squeeze a quart into a pint, a week into a day, to make a hundred pounds produce a lot. But there is no reason why cinema building should not present in plan and form something of the comfortable elegance and repose of our best domestic work.'

The Apollo starred as the exterior of the Grand, Sloughborough, in the film *The Smallest Show on Earth* (1956), starring Virginia McKenna, Bill Travers and Margaret Rutherford. More theatrical success came with *Riverdance*, which enjoyed a two-year uninterrupted run in 1995–97, and was followed in 1999 by *Doctor Doolittle*. It seems destined to continue a mix of energetic musical theatre and live shows.   EH

Hampton Court Palace Great Hall

Hampton Court Palace
Richmond upon Thames
Original architect
   1532–34 James Nedeham, master car-
             penter/surveyor of King's
             Works, re-using parts of earlier
             Great Hall
Listed   Grade I
Current use Great Hall (part of a Royal
             palace and a public monu-
             ment)

Most great halls in palaces, substantial houses, Inns of Court, etc., were fitted up from time to time for masques or other theatrical entertainments but some had such long and notable theatre use that they need to be included in this gazetteer (cf London, Whitehall Banqueting House and the Middle Temple Hall). Hampton Court Great Hall, built by Henry VIII to replace the more modest hall of Wolsey's palace, was so used regularly from the reign of Elizabeth I.

A stage was erected beneath the Minstrels' gallery in 1572; a chamber adjoining served as a dressing room and the Great Watching Chamber was used for rehearsals. By the reign of George I the theatrical fit-up had become semi-permanent. In 1718 performances were open to the public with, for example, *Henry VIII* performed in its actual setting. The final performance in the Great Hall was on 18 October 1731 but the stage was not finally cleared away until 1798. Fit-ups have continued to be made at long intervals on special occasions.

The hall, as now seen, is less colourful than it once was, the decorative painting having been removed from the roof trusses in the 1920s. The great hammer-beam roof is enriched in every part with mouldings, tracery and carving, incorporating amidst carved foliage, the Royal coat of arms of Henry and sometimes those of Anne Boleyn and Jane Seymour. The elaborate lantern pendants on the trusses show the influence of Italian art. At the entry end an oak screen supports the minstrels' gallery.

It is sometimes said that Hampton Court Great Hall is the only example of a regularly used roofed Elizabethan theatre now to be seen. Given that no purpose-built theatres have survived, this room must certainly claim the attention of theatre historians.   *JE/SM*

Haymarket Theatre Royal ★★★
Haymarket
City of Westminster
Other names
    Haymarket or Hay-Market Theatre
Original architect
    1821   John Nash
Later works
1837–53   Unknown: various alterations, including widening of proscenium opening
1843   Unknown: forestage cut back and proscenium doors abolished
1853   G. Somers Clarke: various improvements, front and back
1871   G. Somers Clarke: redecorated in Pompeian style
1880   C.J. Phipps: auditorium rebuilt
1905   C.Stanley Peach with S.D. Adshead: interior rebuilt
1939–41   John Murray: bars and cloakrooms improved
1994   John Rowe-Parr: interior restored; stage improved

Listed   **Grade I**
Current use **Theatre**
Capacity   **905**

The Haymarket is of great importance in theatre history. The first theatre to defy the monopoly of the patent houses, the 'Little Theatre in the Hay' (adjoining the present site) was built in 1720. It gained a limited Royal Patent in 1766–77 and was afterwards granted a special licence. The theatre was rebuilt on the present site by John Nash in 1821, closing the view from St James's Square.

This is a much studied theatre, the subject of many books and papers but, so far, no detailed and authoritative architectural account has been published. *The Survey of London* (vol. XX) is, for once, quite inadequate (compare the *Survey*'s outstandingly full account of Her Majesty's Theatre, opposite). The building is, nevertheless, of exceptional interest in its own right and of great townscape value. It is one of the few pre-1880 theatre buildings in London and shares with Drury Lane Theatre Royal and the Lyceum the distinction of presenting a pre-Victorian external appearance.

The present stucco porticoed classical facade, rear elevation and much of the structural envelope are by Nash. The rear Suffolk Street elevation is designed as a stuccoed house front, domestic in conception apart from its tall scene door.

The auditorium is by Adshead (for Peach), 1905, completely replacing the Phipps auditorium of 1879–80 (Phipps had provided Bancroft with the first four-sided picture frame stage). Subsequent internal alterations to bars, etc., mainly by John Murray and sympathetic in character. The 1994 works to the auditorium constituted a careful restoration of Peach's and Murray's works.

The 1904 drawings show that the Peach works were limited to the public interiors with only minor improvements backstage. Beyond this, little seems to be later than mid-C19 in date .

The auditorium has two balconies, the upper one extending back into a gallery of great interest and limited comfort, with padded benches. Architecturally and decoratively this is one of the most distinguished and brilliantly preserved interiors in London.

There are some traces of old stage machinery. The main roof space and stage house roof are still lit by dormers, but the property rooms and scene painting room have long been removed.   *JE*

Her Majesty's ★★★
Haymarket
City of Westminster
Other names
    1705–14   Queen's Theatre
    1714–1837 King's Theatre
    1837–1901 Her Majesty's

Haymarket Theatre Royal (John Rowe-Parr Architects)

(also) 1837–1847
    Italian Opera House
1901-1952 His Majesty's
Original architect
  1704–5 Sir John Vanbrugh
Later works
    1778 Robert Adam: interior remod-
         elled
    1782 Michael Novosielski: remod-
         elled
  1790–91 Michael Novosielski: complete-
         ly rebuilt after fire, on an
         enlarged site
    1793 Michael Novosielski: concert
         room added
    1796 Marinari: altered
  1816–18 John Nash and George
         Repton: new facade built;
         Royal Opera Arcade added
1842, 1846 and 1850
     John Johnston: renovated and
     redecorated
  1860–63 Unknown: auditorium altered;
         proscenium boxes removed
  1868–9 Charles Lee: rebuilt within
         existing shell after fire
    1897 C.J. Phipps with Romaine
         Walker: entirely rebuilt (with
         exception of Royal Opera
         Arcade)
    1961 Unknown: redecorated
    1993 H.L.M. and C.G. Twelves: roof
         and dome reclad in copper;
         new air conditioning; toilets
         improved
Listed   Grade II*
Current use Theatre
Capacity   1210

Her Majesty's stands second only to Drury Lane and Sadler's Wells for the extraordinary longevity of theatrical entertainment on one site.

Founded as a new theatre for Betterton's company, then at Lincoln's Inn Fields, it was built as a personal speculation by Vanbrugh, the architect and playwright, with the support of thirty subscribers. It was designed by Vanbrugh himself, possibly with some assistance from Hawksmoor. Alongside the theatre it had a long room for assemblies and masquerades.

The Queen's Theatre, as it was originally called, opened in 1705 with the Queen's authority, under the management of William Congreve. For the greater part of its life until 1896, this theatre and its successors, operated principally as the home of the Italian opera, and hence, in the mid-C19, also as a centre for the Romantic ballet. Operas by Handel and also his first oratorio were performed here.

Despite its distinguished beginnings, Vanbrugh's massive theatre was inadequately planned, lacking necessary backstage spaces; lack of modelling (ornament was largely trompe l'oeil painting except round the proscenium) may have contributed to the theatre's notorious acoustic shortcomings. With various remodellings, it lasted 85 years until, after a fire, it was completely rebuilt in 1791 by Michael Novosielski. A series of further remodellings and a rebuild in 1869, after another fire, were followed by C.J. Phipps's total rebuilding for Beerbohm Tree in 1897. All that Phipps left of the old building was the Royal Opera Arcade added by Nash in 1818.

The Phipps theatre is a magnificent pile in French Renaissance style, robbed of its originally more impressive symmetry by the demolition of its companion building, the Carlton Hotel (by Phipps, completed after his death by Isaacs and Florence), conceived as part of the same architecturally unified scheme but replaced in 1957 by the unsympathetic bulk of New Zealand House. The theatre alone nevertheless makes a considerable impact in the street scene with its open loggia and imposing dome. It makes an instructive contrast with Nash's Haymarket, nearly opposite. Nash's Royal Opera Arcade (at the rear) is an important work in its own right and of great townscape value.

The auditorium of this, 'one of the best planned theatres in London' (*Survey of London*), is opulent. Although it is recognisably a Phipps theatre in its geometry, the main features of its design and all of its decoration are by Romaine Walker. Architecturally it is a two-balcony design (the gallery being a backward extension of the upper tier) with details freely adapted from Gabriel's Opéra at Versailles. Scagliola proscenium frame with three tiers of boxes on either side framed by Corinthian columns with rich entablature, carrying deep, elliptical, coffered arch. Blind-arcaded side walls; deep enriched cove carrying ceiling and saucer dome. Paintings in C18 manner.

It has what is reputedly the first flat stage to have been built in Britain. Very important and complete complex of wooden stage machinery in excellent state of preservation, including four sub-stage bridges, sloats, grave trap, four post traps, cellar drums, etc. The sub-stage machinery is archaeologically a most important survival of its kind recorded in London and it appears to be restorable. The modern machinery required for the effects in *The Phantom of*

Her Majesty's (Ian Newman)

the *Opera* were cunningly interlaced into the forest of old timbers and those parts of the wood machinery, which had then to be removed, were recorded and will be reinstated.

It is impossible to give a short account of this outstandingly important theatre without significant omissions. *Survey of London* vol. XXIX contains a comprehensive (28-page) account of its buildings but adds that 'the history of the theatre has still to be satisfactorily elucidated.' Handel, Haydn, Sheridan and Jenny Lind were all associated with earlier buildings. Beerbohm Tree had a suite and his 'acting academy' in the dome over the present structure and substantial traces of these rooms remain.
JE

Hippodrome ★

Hippodrome Corner, Cranbourn Street
City of Westminster
Other names
    Hippodrome Theatre
  1958-83 Talk of the Town
Original architect
    1900 Frank Matcham
Later works
    1909 Frank Matcham: converted to
         variety theatre
    1958 Unknown: converted to
         cabaret restaurant
Listed   Grade II
Current use Discotheque
Capacity   c.1300 (as variety theatre)

Originally built for Edward Moss as a Hippodrome for circuses, it had a vast tank for water spectacles. The sight lines were adjusted to suit both circus arena and proscenium action. The 1909 works enlarged the stage and advanced the

London Hippodrome: Matcham's auditorium sadly ravished in 1958 (London Metropolitan Archives)

proscenium to suit the theatre for variety rather than circus and, from 1912, revue. The Hippodrome occupies an island site with principal elevations to Charing Cross Road and Cranbourn Street, and contains, in addition to the theatre, ground-floor shops on the main frontages, with Cranbourn Mansions in the upper storeys. Elevations in red sandstone, red brick and terracotta in a free classical style, the bays divided by giant Ionic pilasters supported on elongated brackets which occupy the full height of the first floor, the pilasters rising through the second and third floors to carry a weakly accented fourth-floor attic storey and a crowning balustrade. There were formerly giant figures of Roman soldiers above. Most bays have canted windows rising from terms and linked by a

balustrade at second-floor level. The corner bay is framed by giant Ionic engaged columns carrying entablature blocks and an open pediment, above which rises a short but floridly detailed tower with a skeletal iron dome crowned by a lively sculptured group of a chariot with rearing horses. Giant letters with the name of the theatre on the Little Newport Street front. In 1959, the old iron and glass entrance canopy was replaced by one of no distinction.

Matcham's gorgeous auditorium was utterly ravished in the 1958 conversion works but some traces of its original character could still be seen in the upper reaches above the suspended ceiling. Cabaret use (as 'The Talk of the Town') seemed preferable to total loss in the 1950s, but it is a great pity that consent

was ever given to the present use, in which live music and acting (other than miming to a sound track) are not significant elements.

This may even now be regarded as a recoverable theatre. Not quite as big as it looks, but a theatre potentially suitable for grand musical productions in this position, at the very heart of Theatreland, is an obvious candidate for reawakening. *JE*

Hoxton Hall ★★★

128a Hoxton Street
Hackney
Other names
  1863 Mortimer's Hall
  1863 Hoxton Hall Dancing Academy
1866-72 McDonald's Music Hall
       May Scott's (unofficial name in
       1960s)
Original architect
  1863 James Mortimer
Later works
  1867 Unknown: hall raised in
       height; existing balcony
       extended along sides; upper
       balcony inserted
1879-80 Cooper and Goulding: altered
       and extended for Blue Ribbon
       Army
  1909 Bertie Crewe: altered
1909-11 Lovegrove and Papworth: hall
       altered; basement excavated
       under hall
1976-82 Lidbetter, Betham and
       Farrance (later Richard
       Betham and Associates):
       improvements; hall partially
       reconstructed; Wilks Place
       facade partially restored
  1982 Adrian Betham: adjacent property incorporated
Listed   Grade II*
Current use Arts centre and community
       theatre
Capacity   120

This building is unique in Greater London and one of the most important early music hall buildings now to be seen anywhere (cf only Wilton's, the (Royal) Clarence, Glasgow Britannia, Cardiff Philharmonic, and Nottingham Malt Cross which survive as relatively complete supper-room style relics). Hoxton Hall, which was fully active only from 1864 to 1871 is an unusually early survival from an insufficiently investigated phase in music-hall evolution. An historical study of the building by Victor Belcher, with Alan Fagan's related survey drawings and reconstructions, undertaken in 1996–97 prior to the formulation of restoration and improvement plans, make Hoxton the best documented of all the early halls in terms of its physical character.

The hall is remarkable (though not originally unique, even in Hoxton) for being a purpose-built music hall which did not have its origins in a pre-existing pub. It was built by James Mortimer, who brought the attitudes of 'five per cent philanthropy' to a venture which he saw as offering social improvement to Hoxton. It was, perhaps, too high-minded and failed. The next licensee, James McDonald, had a music hall background. He carried out improvements and ran the hall with moderate success from 1866 until he lost his licence in 1871. The room as it is seen today, with all its subsequent alterations, is essentially McDonald's.

It was purchased by the Blue Ribbon Temperance Mission in 1879 and then, in 1893 by the Bedford Institute (Quaker) who incorporated it into a complex of new buildings in 1910. Use for entertainments, although sporadic under the Bedford Institute, never ceased, and was intensified as part of a highly active neighbourhood centre under warden May Scott, in the 1960s. The British Music Hall Society held its inaugural exhibition and entertainments there in 1963 and 1964. It is now a thriving arts centre in regular theatrical and community use.

There was never an elevation to Hoxton Street, only a narrow passageway. The present entrance resulted from the acquisition of property in 1982. There is a simple, pedimented, classical stucco facade to a side street, Wilks Place, originally one storey lower, bearing the legend HOXTON HALL in bold letters. Keystones bear Mortimer's monogram and the date 1863. It is not clear whether this was ever the main entrance for which its position, behind the stage, was not ideal.

The auditorium is a remarkable room of outstanding archaeological, as well as historic, importance. It was originally a pilastered hall with fireplaces on either side, and an end balcony carried on two wooden columns, facing an open platform stage. This first form is still clearly discernible, despite the fact that McDonald raised the room height substantially, extended the original balcony along the sides and added an upper balcony, the two levels being supported on slender iron columns and having non-matching ornamented cast-iron bombé fronts.

Hoxton Hall (John Earl Collection)

The stage has been altered more than once but the total effect is still that of a pre-1880s' music hall with a very high platform, the original height of which is seen in a vestigial section at the back, with a lower and later extension in front. The original architectural treatment of the stage end wall is not known. The balconies, which had been partly cut away over the stage, were extended to the end wall in 1976 when the present ceiling was created, a replacement for a temporary post-war damage job, but now lacking its original rooflight.

Very small two-balconied halls (this one measures only 4.9m (16ft) between the balcony fronts) were probably always rare. Any major intervention must necessarily be approached with the utmost care, but the opportunity should not be missed to reinstate those elements which can be restored with confidence. Also every piece of physical evidence brought to light during building works will need to be meticulously recorded. Fortunately the hall is in the

hands of an organisation which has a remarkable record of care. *JE*

Intimate

Green Lane, Palmers Green
Enfield
Other names
    1931 and again 1990s
        St Monica's Hall
Original architect
    1931   Gallagher
Later works
    1989   Unknown stalls seating and orchestra pit removed; movable seating installed (downstairs only)
Current use **Amateur theatre and hall**
Capacity   **435**

The Intimate Theatre was built by Father Gallagher, a priest of St Monica's and a builder who had taken the cloth late in life. It was called St Monica's Hall, the name by which it is known today. Built in 1931, it opened as a theatre in 1934, and in 1937 became a full-time repertory theatre. Professional theatre continued until 1987, when use became amateur. The exterior is that of a red brick Church Hall with stone facings, and a high roof. This is fronted by a theatre entrance with a canopy, three leaded lights over and a cartouche 'Deus per Omnia'. On either side are ante-rooms, with double-leaded windows at ground level. Steps up to double mahogany doors lead to a spacious foyer and stairs to the balcony. The balcony front is panelled wood, probably maple. Downstairs the seats are now movable to provide a floor space for alternative use. At the side of the auditorium at the stage end is the entrance to the bar, decorated with a curious mix of memorabilia of church events and posters from professional repertory days.

The stage has a delightfully ornamental proscenium. Sunbursts at either corner are complemented by plaster urns, each with a lamp, on either side at stage level, and English roses at intervals form an interesting frame with a curtained crest at the centre. The safety curtain from 1935 bears the masks of Comedy and Tragedy and figures from classical drama. Flying is very limited, and cloths are rolled; get-in is through the main entrance. Four dressing rooms, the old band room, now a dressing room, and chorus room to the rear and above the bar area complete the surprise of a charming theatre in ecclesiastical surroundings. *SM*

Inverness Court Hotel (London Metropolitan Archives)

Inverness Court Hotel ★

Inverness Terrace, Bayswater
City of Westminster
Original architect
  c.1905 Mewes and Davis
Listed   **Grade II**
Current use **Hotel bar**

The original house on the site probably dated from the late 1850s but it later underwent radical alteration and enrichment, amounting almost to rebuilding. Mr Louis Spitzel, a merchant banker, took a 99-year lease in 1905 and the theatre was probably made for him. He died the following year. The house became a hotel in 1966 and was reopened after refurbishment in 1972.

The house front is of stone in an elaborate Franco-Flemish style which must have made it stand out in an area whose older buildings are predominantly stucco Italianate. The interiors at ground and first-floor levels are panelled and painted in opulent taste, equal to the most elaborate contemporary work in Mayfair. The private theatre in the ground-floor rear room is a spectacular plaything, con-

trasting with Normansfield Hospital Theatre which was intended to work for its living. It now serves as a bar but appears to be practically complete and, in this use, it can be seen by hotel residents every day.

It consists of two rooms, the front circular and domed, the second rectangular with a proscenium arch between them. Both rooms have much Rococo plaster ornament and the domed room (probably the auditorium) is mirror-lined with a movable bombé-fronted balustrade, presumably to enclose the seating area. The rooms are flat-floored with no trace of a raised stage and it is likely that the performance and audience areas were always level. There is nothing in the way of stage equipment since this type of private theatre was normally fitted up when required. The wall paintings in the rectangular room appear to be relatively modern but are not discordant.

There is a persistent tradition that the theatre was created for Lillie Langtry by her Royal patron. Their affair was notorious twenty years earlier when he was Prince of Wales but by 1905 he was king. No evidence has been found to support the story but without positive disproof it is likely to go on running. *JE*

King's Cross Theatre

Birkenhead Street
Camden
Other names
  Royal Panormonium (and
    variants)
  Royal King's Cross

1832	Royal Clarence
1838	New Lyceum
1840	Regent
1854	Cabinet
	Century

Original architect
  c.1820 **Stephen Geary: not as a**
        theatre
Later works
  1830 **Unknown converted to theatre**
Current use **Facade only (offices behind)**

The Survey of London vol XXIV states that a stuccoed facade on the west side of Birkenhead Street, just south of Euston Road, is that of the former Royal Clarence Theatre, active from c.1830 to 1879. The present facade has clearly been much altered, but is certainly that of the theatre. The internal structure, however, shows no trace of its theatrical origin. *JE*

Kings Road Theatre

279 Kings Road
Kensington and Chelsea
Other names
  1910 Palasseum
  1911 Kings
  1943 Ritz
  1949 Essoldo
  1972 Curzon
  1980 Classic
  1984 The Arts
  1986 Cannon, MGM, ABC
Original architect
  1910 A.W. Hudson
Later works
  1949 C. Edmund Wilford: remod-
        elled

Current use Four-screen cinema
Capacity   960 (prior to subdivision)

Opened as ciné-variety in 1910 as Palasseum, renamed Kings in 1911, later becoming a cinema. No description of interior found. Exterior square three-storey building on corner site, now with modern entrance canopy, readograph, etc. The interior was remodelled in modern style in 1949.

In 1973, the theatre reopened as the Kings Road Theatre, presenting the popular *Rocky Horror* show. It closed in 1979, at the end of the run. In 1980, the auditorium was subdivided and it reopened as a four-screen cinema.

Kingston Empire
Clarence Street
Kingston upon Thames
Other names
    1910   New Empire
Original architect
    1910   Bertie Crewe, with C.J. Bourne
Later works
    1930   Unknown: completely refurbished; pit and stalls merged; neon introduced to light tower
    1956   Unknown: gutted internally for supermarket and offices
Current use Pub and offices
Capacity   originally c.2000

After a false start in 1907 the theatre was built to the designs of Bertie Crewe and opened in October 1910. The theatre had a fine interior. The exterior was in modern English Renaissance style in terracotta and red brick. There was an ornamental wrought-iron and coloured glass verandah, and a turret at the south-east elevation which was lit at night and could be seen from many parts of the town. In 1930, the theatre was bought by Kingshott Theatres and was refurbished. Neon lighting was introduced to light the dome, the second theatre in the country to do this (the first being the London Coliseum). The theatre continued the policy of twice-nightly variety into the 1950s when business declined so much with the popularity of TV, that it finally closed in 1955. It was auctioned but failed to meet the reserve price, and was later bought by an investment company. The interior was gutted and a supermarket opened in 1956. Today, it is easily recognisable as a theatre. The upper storeys are well preserved, and used as offices. The shell of the building is unchanged, save for the street level and the tower. The word EMPIRE is picked out in brick, and many exits at

the side and rear are preserved, though some are bricked up.   *SM*

Lewisham Theatre and Studio
Rushey Green
Lewisham
Other names
    Catford Public Halls
    Broadway Studio
Original architect
    1932   Bradshaw, Gass and Hope
Listed   Grade II
Current use Civic Centre
Capacity   845

Despite its name, the Lewisham Theatre is in the heart of Catford. Built as an adjunct to the Town Hall (a much extended and finally completely replaced building of 1875-1901) the public halls of 1932 were always multi-purpose rooms, the main hall becoming a recognised local centre for concerts, etc. With the wanton destruction of Matcham's magnificent Lewisham Hippodrome, within sight of the Town Hall, Catford gained a much-praised, but now rather dated, office block and lost one of the best theatres in south-east London. The Lewisham Theatre with its 102-seat studio then assumed greater importance, the new name reflecting the fact that this is now the only working theatre in the borough apart from the Albany in Deptford. Architecturally, it has a little more presence in the town than many later civic-centre theatres, but none of the landmark quality and none of the theatrical magic of the old Hippodrome. *JE*

London Coliseum: at opening in 1904, with the Royal Box in its original central position

London Coliseum ★★★
St Martin's Lane
City of Westminster
Other names
    1931-68   Coliseum Theatre
Original architect
    1904   Frank Matcham
Later works 1968 Martin Carr: partially restored and improved
Listed   Grade II*
Current use Opera House
Capacity   2358

This theatre is of outstanding architectural and theatrical significance, demanding a much more detailed account than can be given here.

It was Matcham's masterwork and Oswald Stoll's flagship, conceived as a magnificent and elaborately equipped variety theatre with splendidly appointed public rooms, designed for a new West End audience, enticing people in who might never have set foot in an ordinary variety house.

The Coliseum tower dominates the southern end of St. Martin's Lane. Its bold silhouette is important in the view from Trafalgar Square, where it is seen behind and beyond St Martin-in-the-Fields and also from the opposite direction, where the two baroque towers, separated by nearly two centuries, are seen in close company. Terracotta facade now painted. Original convex glazed roofs on either side of the tower no longer exist. Facade in free Italian Renaissance style, channelled, with lavish ornament. Pedimented and balconied windows set in a loggia at second-floor level. Entrance bay, off centre and slightly advanced, forms the base of a channelled square tower. Iron-stayed entrance canopy set in a giant two-storey archway, then a balconied Venetian window at second-floor level, above which the tower rises high over the facade, and is crowned by an elaborate cornice and a finely modelled Borrominesque spire derived from Wren's west towers of St Paul's but incorporating four lions (since removed) and terminating in a great glass globe, originally rotating but now fixed. Flank wall to May's Court with name of theatre in gigantic Art Nouveau letters.

Vast auditorium, of Roman grandeur, whose capacity exceeds those of both Drury Lane Theatre Royal and the Royal Opera House. A superbly modelled room, seducing the eye in every view. At the back of the stalls there is a ring of stalls boxes which originally had at its centre Britain's only permanent central Royal Box. The Grand Circle rises over and behind these boxes, there being no overhang at all. Over the Grand Circle there are two further 'cantilever' balconies with pairs of two-tier boxes on either side; between these and the proscenium, elaborate niches. These were originally for an auditorium choir, but were subsequently converted to stage boxes (that on stage left, now the Royal Box) on two levels. Fine domed ceiling, which originally had an openable 'hit or miss' centre for instant air change between performances (no longer operating).

Very large stage. The pioneering triple revolve was removed in 1976-77.

The theatre is the home of English National Opera. Works planned for 2000 and succeeding years should lead to architectural restoration internally and externally (including the reinstatement of the glazed roof flanking the tower) and major improvements both front and back of house. *JE*

London Palladium (London Metropolitan Archives)

London Palladium ★★★

Argyll Street
City of Westminster
Other names
     Corinthian Bazaar
     1871   Hengler's Grand Cirque
     1884   National Skating Palace
     1910   Palladium Theatre
Original architect
     1868   Owen Lewis: as Corinthian
             Bazaar
Later works
     1871   J.T. Robinson: converted to circus building

     1884   C.J. Phipps: circus enlarged and reconstructed
     1886   ? C.J. Phipps: circus again altered
     1896   Phipps and Hancock: converted to ice skating rink
     1902   Alexander Forrester: converted to panorama
     1907   W. Hancock: boxes added to circus tiers
     1910   Frank Matcham: demolished most of old building, retaining facade, and built a variety theatre; Great Marlborough Street frontage properties and no.8 Argyll Street later absorbed
     1996-8 RHWL: main entrance and bars restored and refurbished; other alterations
Listed   Grade II*
Current use Theatre
Capacity   2298

On the site of the C18 Argyll House, the London Palladium is the successor to the Corinthian Bazaar of 1868 and Hengler's Circus of 1871. It was built for Walter Gibbons in 1910 as a palatial variety theatre to rival the London Coliseum, the Hippodrome, the Palace Music Hall and the Lyceum (during that theatre's short music hall life). The facade, modified and with lively sculpture added by Matcham, is a striking relic of the old Corinthian Bazaar, a painted stone classical temple front with Corinthian columns on tall pedestals.

The booking hall, which has its own separate entrance (formerly a passageway through to Haig's wine merchants building, now incorporated in the Palladium complex), is as big as a branch post office. Also now linked to the theatre is the adjoining, altered Georgian house, no.8 Argyll Street.

Foyers and bars are generous with most of the original ornament intact. The grand staircase and Cinderella Bar, in particular, have recently been magnificently restored to Matcham's original detailed designs. Big, but remarkably intimate auditorium, wider than it is deep, a late and magnificent creation of the variety palace boom. Elaborate ceiling with laterally elongated dome. Two balconies spanning the auditorium with no intermediate support. Boxes at three levels in paired arched niches. Fine proscenium arch. The style was described as 'French Rococo' but the ornaments are variously derived and freely juxtaposed in a piece of bold Matcham mannerism.

Some basic fabric to the left of and behind the main facade and also backstage was incorporated from earlier buildings, a typical theatre-builder's procedure for time-saving rather than cost reduction.

Of the select company of giant variety houses built in the West End in the decade before the First World War, the Palladium has the most complex building history. The way in which Matcham adopted earlier fabric, turning Owen Lewis's front into one of the most remarkable theatre facades of its time, demonstrates architectural skill of a high order. The Palladium is one of the finest surviving examples of his later work.

The *Survey of London* account is full and authoritative. *JE*

London Pavilion
Piccadilly Circus
City of Westminster
Other names
   Black Horse Inn
   Salle Robin
Original architect
   1885   Saunders and Worley
Later works
   1900   Wylson and Long: interior
           reconstructed; auditorium
           floor raked
   1918   Unknown: interior altered
   1934   Matcham and Co. (F.G.M.
           Chancellor with Cecil Masey):
           gutted and converted to
           cinema
   1986   Chapman Taylor: gutted for
           shops and tourist fun-trap;
           roof storey and sculpture
           above parapet added
Listed   Grade II
Current use Facade only (shops and wax-
           works)

The building history of the London Pavilion is complex, involving two sites. The first entertainment room was attached to the Black Horse Inn in Tichborne Street (what is effectively now Great Windmill Street). In 1859 Loibl and Sonnhammer roofed in the irregularly shaped inn yard and created the first London Pavilion music hall. It did not amount to much as a building but it was successful as an entertainment house. A

gallery was added on the north and east sides in 1862, and further improvements followed in 1876. Progress was then halted by land transactions for the cutting of the new highway to be called Shaftesbury Avenue. The site, by now in the hands of R.E. Villiers was acquired by the Metropolitan Board of Works and the hall closed in 1885. In the same year, Villiers built a new London Pavilion on a triangular site created by the roadworks. It was the first building completed in the new Shaftesbury Avenue.

The new London Pavilion, by James Ebenezer Saunders, with elevations by R.J. Worley was the most lavishly appointed variety hall yet seen in London. It was remodelled in 1900 and again in 1918 for C.B. Cochran. It ceased to be a variety house in 1934 and was converted to a cinema, although it continued to be licensed for stage plays and music. It has since been gutted and contains shops and an outstation of Madame Tussaud's.

Despite all these changes, the exterior below roof level remains essentially that of the 1885 London Pavilion and it should, perhaps, be regarded as the key building in the Piccadilly Circus group. The most recent conversion works removed all internal trace of former theatre use, but provided a compensating benefit by removing the clutter of illuminated signs which had disfigured its Circus facade.

The *Survey of London* (vols XXXI and XXXII) account of the building is full and authoritative. *JE*

Lyceum ★★★
Wellington Street, Strand
City of Westminster
Other names
   Theatre Royal
   Lyceum
   Theatre Royal, English Opera House
   English Opera House
   Royal Lyceum Theatre
Original architect
   1834   Samuel Beazley
Later works
   1882   C.J. Phipps: partially recon-
           structed and improved
   1884   C.J. Phipps: circle fronts redec-
           orated and altered
   1904   Bertie Crewe: rebuilt behind
           Beazley's facade and portico
   1919   Edward Jones: minor alter-
           ations
   1951   Matthews and Sons: converted
           to Mecca Ballroom
   1996   Holohan Architects: recon-
           verted to theatre; total
           rebuilding of stage house;
           auditorium restored and
           redecorated; adjoining build-
           ing incorporated
Listed   Grade II*
Current use Theatre
Capacity   2000

The Lyceum is a building of outstanding national importance, architecturally and theatrically. Its history is complex. A public building of this name stood on an adjoining site (now covered by Wellington Street) in 1772, then a theatre from 1794 until Wellington Street was formed, when a new theatre was built on the present site. This opened in

Lyceum: Crewe's 1904 interior

1834. It was for a long time managed by Sir Henry Irving and was famous for its association with him and Ellen Terry (their last performance in 1902). The Crewe interior is post-Irving and was intended to be a variety house to compete with the Palace and the London Coliseum but it was not a success in this mode and soon reverted to drama. It was purchased by the LCC in 1939 for demolition in connection with a road improvement, later abandoned.

Leased to Mecca, it became a ballroom. The abolition of the GLC in 1986 led to a period of darkness and uncertainty, during which the London Residuary Body sold a 125-year lease to Brent Walker before transferring the freehold to The Theatres Trust. They eventually negotiated a transfer of Brent Walker's unexpired term to Apollo Leisure, who set about works of restoration and improvement. The theatre reopened in 1996 as a home for large-scale musicals.

Despite the fact that the symmetrical neo-classical composition was altered at upper level by 1904 and the domed attic lost, Samuel Beazley's 1834 facade and portico remain today as rare and valuable pre-Victorian survivals. The portico stands over the public footway (cf Haymarket) and is a striking incident in the view up Wellington Street from the Strand.

The Crewe theatre occupied a wider plot than the earlier building and the portico and entrance staircase are, as a consequence, offset from the axis of the auditorium. The splendid foyer and staircase lead now to Crewe's richly ornamented variety house interior. The rococo-ornamented panel over the proscenium is, perhaps, rather too deep for complete comfort, but the auditorium must, nevertheless, be rated as one of the most flamboyant in Britain.

The most striking alteration in the 1996 works was the total rebuilding of the stage house to give flying height for the most demanding modern productions. The old stage house was the result of a patchwork of alterations and additions to the Beazley/Phipps stage with further enlargement by Crewe. The new fly tower is, as it must be for a major musical house, a landmark. The orchestra pit has been enlarged to a size suitable for Grand Opera.

Apollo's initial auditorium decorations were criticised by some and the renewed ceiling paintings are, undoubtedly, a touch raw and startling, but this remains one of the most impressive reawaken-

ings of recent years and one which would have seemed highly unlikely as recently as the mid 1980s. It is time that this building was fully researched and an authoritative architectural account published. *JE*

Lyric ★★★

Shaftesbury Avenue
City of Westminster
Original architect
   1888 C.J. Phipps
Later works
   1904 A. Blomfield Jackson (successor to Phipps): Great Windmill Street front altered
   1932 Michael Rosenauer: crush rooms and bars reconstructed; completely redecorated (except for Grand Hall and upper circle)
   1997 RHWL: refurbished and redecorated internally
Listed   **Grade II**
Current use **Theatre**
Capacity: **967**

Built on an irregular site acquired from the Metropolitan Board of Works on completion of the newly cut Shaftesbury Avenue, it was the third theatre (after the London Pavilion and the original Shaftesbury) built in this thoroughfare. Intended for musical comedy but, after mid 1920s, used mainly as a playhouse.

 The exterior, like that of many of C.J. Phipps's theatres, is in unmonumental, almost domestic manner (compare the Vaudeville) of brick and stone with weakly accented bays, variously treated with somewhat hesitant Franco-Flemish

Renaissance details, gables and dormers. The left-hand gable, with the name of the theatre, has below it a tall arched doorway with broken scrolly pediment, looking like a main entrance but actually an exit. The entrances are at the right-hand end, under an iron canopy.

Considered in isolation, the exterior lacks excitement, but it forms the westernmost element in an outstandingly valuable group comprising the Lyric, the Apollo, the Gielgud and the Queen's, at the midst of one of the worlds's greatest concentrations of working theatres.

The facade to Great Windmill Street is of unusual historic interest, being the remaining part of a house (no.16) built in 1776 by Dr William Hunter, anatomist, as his home, anatomical theatre and museum. The rear of the house was demolished to make way for the Lyric's stage and the three-storey front portion (effectively one-room's depth) was remodelled internally to form a four-storey stack of dressing rooms. Despite all this and further alterations made in 1904, together with the painting over of the brickwork, it is still recognisable for what it once was and bears a commemorative blue plaque, erected by London County Council in 1952.

The design of the theatre included shop premises on the Shaftesbury Avenue front. These were neither architecturally nor structurally separate, but were nevertheless sold off by the London Residuary Body after the abolition of the GLC and before the theatre itself was handed over to the Theatres Trust. The transfer to the Trust also excluded the stage which, by historical accident, was

Lyric, c.1994 (Tina Walkling)

not owned by the GLC. The LRB's administrative vandalism will forever compound the problems of a theatre whose planning was already uncomfortably tight and which has now been denied the one opportunity which might have existed for future improvement – a warning against leaving accountants in charge of matters of architectural and social consequence.

The auditorium, a sort of preliminary smaller-scale essay for Her Majesty's of 1897 is, after recent redecoration, one of the most pleasing in London and rich in theatrical atmosphere. It has three balconies partly cantilevered from set-back columns. The straight sides of the dress circle are divided into three boxes. Above this the balconies are of circular plan and all three terminate against the superimposed boxes on either side of the stage. The top balcony front continues as a notional entablature to the pedestalled giant Corinthian columns which frame the boxes and carry the deep elliptical arch over the proscenium. The circular ceiling centre follows the line of the upper balcony. Pretty plasterwork, alabaster and later wood panelled finishes.

The alterations and extensive redecoration by Michael Rosenauer in 1932 mainly affected the entrance vestibule, crush room and stalls bar. His work was in a rather plain, inoffensive manner, with walnut panelling and mirrors. It is a matter of great good fortune that Phipps's auditorium, although altered, was not at that time completely devastated in the name of passing fashion. The RHWL refurbishment has nicely reconciled the Phipps and Rosenauer works. JE

Lyric Theatre, Hammersmith ★★

King Street, Hammersmith
Hammersmith and Fulham
Original architect
 1979 **Hammersmith and Fulham Borough architect (following the original design by Frank Matcham)**
Current use **Theatre**
Capacity **537**

Matcham's original Lyric Theatre was designed and built in 1895. Following a public inquiry in 1969, the theatre was demolished but key parts of the plasterwork were recorded, removed and stored. The auditorium was, after a long delay, reconstructed by the Borough Council in 1979 within a modern building.

Lyric, Hammersmith

The new building is a typical town centre block of the 1970s, unexceptional inside and out. The discovery of a late Victorian Rococo theatre embedded within it, two storeys above ground, is one of the most bizarre architectural suprises that London has to offer. The new auditorium is still essentially Matcham's beautiful 1895 design, modified in dimensions but adhering so closely to the original architectural vocabulary that only the keenest observer would be aware of the changes.

The widening of the proscenium by about 1.2m (4ft) necessitated an increase in the height as well as the span of the semi-circular arch, and this, in turn, led to changes in the height of the auditorium and the overall dimensions of the ceiling. The problems have been cleverly overcome by stretching Matcham's design without obviously interfering with the proportions of the parts or introducing any new ornamental elements. Lighting positions and ventilation inlets above the ceiling have been accommodated by introducing mesh in place of the flat plaster ceiling bed, the paintings on which had been lost in the 1920s.

This is a splendid interior with a wealth of lively Rococo ornament (one of the very few for which an original Matcham sketch exists). It has two balconies. The proscenium has a round arch enriched with leaf scrolls in the architrave and a fantastic openwork valence made of repeating scrolly elements. The ceiling is boldly coved. There is now a forestage elevator with three positions

(forestage, orchestra pit or additional seating) carefully planned into the old plasterwork details.

The most disappointing aspect of this fine theatre is that, apart from its name in large letters, there is nothing externally to announce its presence in what can only be seen today as a dull and uninviting block. This should be rectified. A theatre should be a cultural landmark, recognisable by architectural signals (a distinct and notable frontage, an ornamental canopy, etc.) as well as by daytime and evening signage. The original theatre was listed. The difficulty of listing part only of a modern, clearly unlistable, building is obvious, but in this case it seems absurd not to recognise and protect what is, in all material respects, a Frank Matcham design. JE

Marlborough Hall

307 Regent Street (University of Westminster)
City of Westminster
Other names
 Great Hall
 Polytechnic Theatre
 Cameo News Theatre
 Cameo-Polytechnic
 Classic Poly
 Regent Poly
 Cameo Victoria
 Regent
 Regent Theatre
Original architect
 c.1834 **Unknown**
Later works
 1848 **Unknown: enlarged**
 1881 **Unknown: rebuilt and enlarged after fire**
 1912 **Frank Verity and George A. Mitchell: front block rebuilt**
 1923 **Unknown: remodelled as cinema theatre with stalls and balcony**
 1927 **F.J. Wills: reconstructed**
Current use **Lecture hall**

The Marlborough Hall is on the ground floor of the former Regent Street Polytechnic (now part of the University of Westminster). The Polytechnic started life as a 'gallery of sciences' in either 1834 or 1838, as an early example of its kind. By 1839 The Royal Polytechnic Institution, as it had become, had a Great Hall housing a canal with an iron diving bell, model boats and scientific wheels. After an accident when the gallery staircase collapsed and a child was killed, there were so many injury claims that the Institution began to lose money. In 1882 it was bought by the founder of the Polytechnic in its modern form, Quintin Hogg. Although the building expanded, the basic structure (not the internal appearance) of the Great Hall, or Marlborough Hall, remains basically unchanged. The Marlborough Hall was the site of the first demonstration in Britain of motion pictures, presented on 20 February 1896 by Félicien Trewey, a French music hall entertainer, engaged by the Lumière brothers.

The Hall had galleries on three sides and a balcony at the Regent Street end. A section of this Victorian gallery survives at the back of the stage (from 1937 it held an organ chamber). In 1910, the front of the building was reconstructed by George A. Mitchell with a facade by Frank Verity. In 1927, the Marlborough Hall was redecorated, the circle extended and the proscenium created. It became a full-time cinema, except during the latter part of the Second World War when it had live use. In 1974 it closed as a cinema to become a live theatre called the Regent, which lasted until 1979. It reverted to cinema use until the following year, when it was subdivided for use as lecture rooms. SM

Middle Temple Hall
Fountain Court, Middle Temple
City of Westminster
Original architect
    1570   Unknown
Listed   Scheduled Ancient Monument
Current use Benchers' dining hall

The halls of the Inns of Court have all been fitted-up as playhouses by professional companies and by the benchers for their own private entertainments throughout their history. However, the Middle Temple Hall is outstanding in this connection in that it hosted the earliest recorded performance of *Twelfth Night* in 1602, almost certainly performed by Shakespeare's company. Unlike, for example, the Inner Temple and Gray's Inn halls, it is seen almost perfectly complete, as it was at that time.

The hall was completed in 1570, severely damaged in the Second World War, but carefully restored. It is a brick building with stone dressings, in five bays with a roof louvre, bay windows on either side at the west (dais) end and a porch at the north-east corner entrance, which leads into the screens passage. It has a double hammerbeam roof. The hall screen is magnificent, Elizabethan, in oak with rich carving. Some alteration was made to the screen in the later C17 but without damage to the total effect. *JE*

Myddelton Hall
Almeida Street, Islington
Islington
Other names
    related to Wellington Hall
Original architect
    ? before 1890: Unknown
Later works
    ?1891 Unknown: possibly enlarged
        and altered
Current use Joinery shop and offices
Capacity c.600 (in 1892)

The relationship between the Myddelton and Wellington Halls (the latter in use by the Barnsbury Debating Society in the 1850s) and the sequence of changes which produced the present building still need to be fully researched. Wellington Hall was probably on a neighbouring site. The Myddelton Hall may have been a replacement serving the same purpose, but it stands, curiously, almost face-to-face with the Islington Literary Institute of 1837, a handsome neo-classical building, now converted to the Almeida Theatre. The Myddelton carries the date 1891, but this could be the date of improvements. Its status had clearly changed by 1892 when it is recorded as being licensed for music with a capacity of 600. It remained licensed until at least 1912 (when the hall is noted as being in use for 'theatrical performances, concerts and dances') and probably until 1916. Some well-known music hall artists, including Charles Coborn are said to have appeared here.

The street elevation is in gault brick with stone or stucco ornament, the single-storey body of the hall being in five, probably originally blind, recessed bays with segmental arches over. The parapet has lost its cornice. To the right, a two-storey entrance section is divided into three bays by brick pilasters. It has a segmental central pediment and the name of the hall and the date 1891 in the frieze.

The fact that a generous, more or less contemporary staircase rises from the present entrance to what was the rear of the stage, rather than to the auditorium, suggests the building may have been altered early in its life. The hall was certainly divided horizontally in post-War years with a shopfitting joinery works and showroom on the ground floor and offices above. This left the lower part of the proscenium, framed by fluted columns, visible in the workshop, and the upper part of an arched opening on the floor above.

At the time of writing the building was undergoing a radical domestic conversion. *JE*

New Rainbow/ Finsbury Park Astoria ★★
232–238 Seven Sisters Road
Islington
Other names
    1931   Paramount Astoria
    c.1950 Odeon Astoria
    1971   Odeon
    1971   Rainbow
Original architect
    1930   E.A. Stone with Tommy
            Somerford and Ewen Barr, job
            architects
Later works
    1998   Nicholas Rule, of Farrington
            Dennys Fisher: auditorium
            restored (for church use)
Listed   Grade II*
Current use Church
Capacity c.2300

Four cinemas, all named 'Astoria', were built for a limited company, the Picture House Trust, founded by A. Segal with Edward A. Stone as its chairman and principal architect. How much was the work of Stone and how much was in fact designed by the job architects, such as Thomas Somerford and Ewen Barr is a matter for serious speculation; nevertheless there is a consistency of external treatment in the team's work, whether cinemas or theatres, while the interiors of the Astorias – and Brixton and Finsbury Park in particular – are exceptional in any oeuvre. They are indeed the finest constructed in Britain in the 'atmospheric' style, championed in the United States by John Eberson, an Austrian emigré with a specialisation in mechanical engineering who used elaborate lighting effects and stageset 'flats' to achieve remarkable scenic effects at relatively modest cost. Audiences were made to think they were seated in Italian Gardens or a Spanish courtyard by virtue of the surroundings, and of twinkling stars and cloud effects produced by complex lighting circuits and smoke machines. The illusion of being outdoors on a warm Mediterranean or sub-tropical night is an essential part of the architecture. In Britain only the Astorias at Brixton and Finsbury Park attempted this wholeheartedly, and Finsbury Park is the only one to feature twinkling star lights, produced using a complex electric circuit whose contacts expand and contract to complete or cut out the current intermittently. While Brixton is consistently in the popular Renaissance style, Finsbury Park veers from its ostensible representation of a Moorish hillside village set on either side of the proscenium towards more eclectic effects, a merger of Indian Moghul motifs and popular Art Deco swirls and zigzags in the spectacular foyer being particularly hard to define. The centrepiece of this is a fountain in a star-shaped pool that mirrors the octagonal form of the double-height and balconied space around it (a similar fountain at Brixton was removed as too many cinemagoers fell in it). At Finsbury Park, however, the elaborate foyer and complex geometry are an essential mask to a complex site, where the auditorium is well to the rear of the corner entrance, reached via a corridor at 60° angle to the outer vestibule.

The Astoria, Finsbury Park, opened on 29 September 1930, the same day as Stone's Whitehall Theatre .Through most of the 1930s the programming combined film with live entertainment, including the Astoria Orchestra, conducted by 'Anton' and the Astoria Girls; indeed the opening gala evening featured no film at all, but a *Spectacle of Empire* with music and dance. The spectacular cinemas built by the Picture House Trust were made possible because of money from the American Paramount Corporation and, from 1931, they became known as the Paramount Astorias. The chain was acquired by Odeon in 1939 and after the war Finsbury Park became known as the Odeon Astoria, predominantly showing films but with occasional interludes from the Wurlitzer organ. In the 1960s it began to be used for concerts, including Frank Sinatra, Miles Davies, the Beatles and Cliff Richard, because the best available films went to the Odeon in Holloway Road. In September 1971 it closed, reopening in November as a full-time rock concert venue with a show by The Who. Chipperfield's Circus followed with a Christmas season. Rock concerts were held regularly between June 1972 and January 1982, run by Biffo and Strutworth who in turn fell foul of Greater London Council safety regulations and its demands that maintenance be carried out to what became a listed building in January 1984. It lay derelict from 1982, with a brief use in the early 1990s as an Elim Pentecostal Church, until in 1996 its freehold was acquired from Rank by the Universal Church, a Brazilian foundation. Served with a repairs notice to carry out an extensive backlog of minor repairs, the Universal Church employed Nicholas Rule of Farrington Dennys Fisher to supervise the restoration of the building. The auditorium is being restored first, the aim

Normansfield Hospital Theatre

being to bring it into use for worship before restoring the foyer and exterior.

The interior decoration of the auditorium is remarkable, placing it in the top flight of cinemas in Britain. The stage is extensive, but appears, from the limited inspection made, to be simple in form. The backstage is not large, but is complex, with a wealth of passages and stairs, including a hazardous route through the modelled 'village' over the proscenium. The use of the theatre for many of the most innovative rock concerts in the 1970s gives it a special place in the hearts of a whole generation.   *EH*

Normansfield Hospital (Entertainment Hall) Theatre ★★★

Normansfield Hospital, Kingston Road, Teddington
Richmond upon Thames

Original architect
    1879   **Rowland Plumbe**
Listed   **Grade II***
Current use **Disused**
Capacity   **est. 300**

Not a public theatre, but included, like a number of other private theatres (e.g. Abercrave, Adelina Patti), because of its extreme rarity and vulnerability. A complete and virtually unaltered survival of the

1870s and of outstanding architectural, historic and archaeological importance.

Normansfield was founded in 1868, as an institution for people with congenital mental conditions (in modern parlance, with learning disabilities) by John Haydon Langdon-Down, who gave his name to Down's Syndrome. The patients were (unusually for the time) given training and encouraged in remedial activities. This, together with Dr and Mrs Langdon-Down's great love of the theatre, led to the building of the Entertainment Hall, so called. This was, in fact, a private theatre, intensively used by staff and patients apparently for both therapeutic and recreational purposes, Langdon-Down having observed that drama and mimicry provided great stimulation to the intelligence. There was also a very active amateur theatre group. Mrs Langdon-Down was acting manager.

Externally it is unimpressive: like a large chapel, attached to one wing of the much extended original house. It makes no architectural impact from any public viewpoint. The auditorium, situated above what was originally the 'Kindersaal' or rinking room (a playroom/skating rink) is, by contrast, spectacular.

Flat floor with open pine-trussed roof, fair-faced brick walls and tall windows, like an assembly hall. Iron-fronted balcony across the end and a complete, well-preserved sunburner in the roof. Richly modelled, coloured and gilded proscenium with pairs of doors (one practical, one dummy) on either side, giving on to a shallow forestage and steps with iron balustrades. The whole of the original decoration to the proscenium, including figure-paintings (as yet unattributed), seems to have survived intact.

The stage is particularly interesting as a miniature version of a regular theatre of the period. It has a simple groove system, still workable, with very old wings and borders and painted cloths. There are about ninety pieces, made for this stage, the finest collection of old stock scenery in the country. There is also a scenepainter's model. Six painted panels from the original Savoy production of *Ruddigore* have been removed for safe storage.

Understage, a basement and cellar level, but these are simple rooms and there is no evidence of machinery.

The theatre building is at present in good condition, but the future of the institution itself had been insecure for some years and is now closed and has been sold for redevelopment. The scenery, in particular, is vulnerable, since it cannot be fully protected by listing. The Theatres Trust was, at the time of writing, leading the efforts to secure the future of this nationally important theatre and its contents. *JE*

Odeon Leicester Square

23-27 Leicester Square
City of Westminster
Original architect
    1937 Harry Weedon with Andrew Mather and Eric Lyon (job architects Horace Ward and Thomas Braddock)
Later works
    1940 Unknown: repaired after bomb damage
    1953 Unknown: wide screen facility installed
    1967 Unknown: altered internally and externally; auditorium mutilated
    1975 Unknown: auditorium again altered
    1987 Unknown: facade and advertising panel altered; auditorium reseated; decorative lighting installed
    1998 Unknown: auditorium refurbished; foyer remodelled; exterior balcony constructed
Listed   **Grade II**
Current use **Cinema**
Capacity   **1943**

The site has played a crucial part in the history of public entertainment in London, having been occupied in turn by the Royal Panopticon and the Alhambra (a conversion of the Panopticon) in a series of guises, as the Alhambra Circus, Alhambra Palace Music Hall, etc., rivalling the Empire as (inter alia) a variety palace and, for a time, a home for the otherwise neglected art of the ballet.

The Odeon which replaced the Alhambra in 1937, does not at once spring to mind as a live theatre, but it was, in fact, built with a big stage. In some ways, its history has been an architectural tragedy. The striking black granite exterior with its 36.5m (120ft) high cubist tower has had some minor alteration, but the original interior was all but destroyed in 1967.

The story might serve as a horrible warning to all who believe that anything old needs to be brought 'into the present day'. The Odeon auditorium had one of the finest interiors of its time, using coved light, rippled surfaces and figure relief by Briton Rivière to outstanding effect. The modernisers, following the latest five-minute fashion, bashed it all into a state of insensibility. Later works have been directed to retrieving the situation and, in particular, Rivière's elegant 'flying ladies' have been recreated, but a truly civilised society would restore this key monument to a perfect state. *JE*

Odeon West End

40 Leicester Square
City of Westminster
Other names
    1930 Leicester Square Theatre
    1931 RKO Theatre Leicester Square
    1932 Olympic
    1932 Leicester Square Theatre (again)
Original architect
    1930 Andrew Mather
Later works
    1931 Edward Carrick: interior redesigned; revolving stage installed
    1932 Alister MacDonald: entrance redesigned
    1955 Unknown: new canopy erected; entrance remodelled
    1968 Arnold Dick Assocs with Cassidy Farrington and Dennys: major refurbishment, new auditorium, gallery closed, facade altered
    1991 Northern Architects: twinned
Current use **Twin-screen cinema**
Capacity   **c.1400** (prior to subdivision)

Opened 1930 as Leicester Square Theatre. Essentially a cinema, but with some recognisable theatrical attributes surviving from the original design. Good front and flank elevations in faience, front now obscured in part by signage which cuts across the classical detail. The fly tower is externally complete with haystack lantern. There is an original 'temporary' enclosure on the east side where an extension over the adjoining, still vacant, site was never built.

Internally the architectural treatment is minimal. Two nearly identical and featureless cinemas (whatever happened to cinema style?), one above the other, occupy the original volume of Mather's auditorium. There are some 'archaeological' remains of his designs. Above the false ceiling of the upper screen, for example, fairly extensive areas of boldly modelled plasterwork can be found. The grid is still in situ but there is no stage. The dressing rooms have been converted to offices. *JE*

Old Vic ★★★

The Cut, Lambeth
Lambeth
Other names
    Royal Coburg Theatre
    Royal Victoria Theatre
    Victoria Theatre
    New Victoria Palace
    Royal Victoria Hall Coffee Tavern
    Royal Victoria Coffee Music Hall
Original architect
    1818 Rudolphe Cabanel
Later works
    (Note many minor works omitted from this list)
    1821 Unknown: looking-glass curtain installed
    1836 Unknown: gas light installed
    1871 J.T. Robinson: interior entirely reconstructed
    1879 Elijah Hoole: altered
    1927/8 Matcham and Co (F.G.M. Chancellor): new facade and other alterations
    1930 Wells Coates: proscenium altered
    1950 Douglas Rowntree, with Pierre Sonrel: proscenium remodelled
    1960 Unknown: proscenium again altered
    1963 Sean Kenny: proscenium again totally remodelled
    1983 RHWL: auditorium restored; front of house remodelled; other works
Listed   **Grade II***
Current use **Theatre**
Capacity   **1067**

Old Vic

was subsequently converted by the Coffee Palace Association and reopened as the Royal Victoria Coffee Music Hall under Emma Cons in 1880. It became world famous under Cons and Lilian Baylis. The management of the Vic and the history of its productions have formed the subject of innumerable books and papers, but there has never been a completely authoritative architectural study. *The Survey of London* vol. XXIII offers little more than a sketch. Like the Haymarket, the Vic deserves meticulous research, close physical investigation and interpretive recording. *JE*

Open-Air Theatre ★
Inner Circle, Regent's Park
City of Westminster
Original architect
    1932   Office of Works(?)
Later works
    1966   Ministry of Public Building and
           Works: stage reconstructed,
           other improvements
  1972-5 Howell, Killick and Partridge:
           major reconstruction
    1983   Unknown: dressing rooms
           rebuilt after fire
    1999   Haworth Tompkins: further
           major improvements
Current use Seasonal theatre (May to
           September)
Capacity 1187

The Old Vic occupies a prominent site at the crossing of Waterloo Road and The Cut/Baylis Road. The present facade is a recreation by RHWL, based on early C19 views, with some discreet amendments and simplified moulding profiles. It is stuccoed in five bays, three storeys high, crowned by a broken pediment with a coat of arms at the centre. Simple entrance canopy with iron columns. The roof and the exterior brick shell are otherwise largely of the first period of building, as is the massive internal timber construction of the roof. The brick flank walls, relieved by a blind arcaded treatment of tall round-arched recesses are as seen in the earliest views of the theatre. The north flank has been less interfered with than the south.

From the 1930s to the 1960s the 1871 Robinson auditorium suffered a series of radical attacks in the name of production fashion. By the 1980s the proscenium architecture together with the adjoining boxes had been obliterated. The RHWL works of 1983 for Ed Mirvish, however, restored the Robinson auditorium faithfully, being amended only to meet modern seating and lighting requirements, the latter being handled with particular sensitivity.

This is an auditorium of lyric beauty. The ceiling still has some suggestion of Cabanel's earlier design. The two vertically stacked lyre-shaped balconies are supported on slender cast-iron columns, the top tier having musical trophies in cartouches. The restored boxes are in three tiers of two on either side of a basket-arched proscenium framed by two rope-twist mouldings. The arch is slightly uncomfortable at the springing, the drapes look a mite thin and the safety curtain is dull, but the proscenium coat of arms, decked with venerably dusty flags puts the seal on a wonderfully satisfying whole. RHWL also remodelled the front-of-house spaces in characteristic manner, with a single staircase to give access to all levels.

Historically, as well as architecturally, the Vic is one of London's most precious theatrical possessions. Built as a 'minor' for melodrama and pantomime, it was important in the history and development of popular theatre. An attempt to convert it to a music hall in 1870 (architect: J.H .Rowley) was abortive, but it

The Open-Air Theatre is, as befits a building in such a setting, architecturally reticent, with raked graded seats occupying just over a quadrant of a circle, in two bands, the lower of nine rows, the upper of ten. Two entrances and the bars, café, etc., are accommodated under the top rake .The whole complex is set among and largely concealed by trees, which also form a dense background to the stage, a feature exploited by designers and directors over the years.

Ben Greet's Woodland Players performed in Regent's Park as early as 1900 but the history of the theatre proper begins with Sydney Carroll's four performances of Robert Atkins's *Twelfth Night* in 1932. The theatre was formally opened in June 1933. After the reconstruction of the stage and improvements to the dressing rooms, David Conville took over in 1962. A major reconstruction took place in 1972–75, when present permanent seating took the place of the former deck chairs. Further major improvements were completed in 1999, including new screen wall round the auditorium and provision of lighting gallery, rehearsal room, etc. *JE*

Palace

Palace ★★★

Shaftesbury Avenue
City of Westminster
Other names
    Royal English Opera House
    Palace Theatre of Varieties
Original architect
    1891 T.E. Colcutt, G.H. Holloway
           and J.G. Buckle
Later works
    1892 Walter Emden: converted to
           variety theatre
    1908 F. Emblin-Walker: amphithe-
           atre reconstructed
    1989 Jaques Muir and Partners:
           facades restored: minor inter-
           nal alterations
    1997 Jaques Muir and Partners,
           minor alterations (wheelchair
           spaces, etc.)
Listed   Grade II*
Current use Theatre
Capacity   1404

An outstandingly important late Victorian monument, built for Richard D'Oyly Carte as a home for English grand opera. Having failed in this role it became a highly successful variety theatre and in more recent years, a home for major musicals. It is extraordinary to think that a building of this quality was ever seen, as it was in post-war years, as little more than an opportunity for profitable redevelopment. It was hideously defaced externally in the 1950s, by the shaving away of a great deal of the terracotta ornament and, about the same time, the interior was painted over, smothering the marble and other fine finishes, with a job lot of plum red paint. Much of this damage was, however,

made good in 1969 when the exterior was spectacularly restored. Only the continued success of the long-running *Les Misérables* appears to prevent full restoration of the interior.

The authorship of the building was a matter of interest and discussion in 1891/2. It was said not to have had an architect in the regular sense, being credited to D'Oyly Carte himself, but a team was involved, over which he, no doubt, exercised autocratic control. G.H. Holloway provided the initial drawings, afterwards acting in the role of general contractor. J.G. Buckle was what would now be called the theatre consultant, ensuring that the sight lines worked and the means of escape satisfied the official controllers. The distinguished architect T.E. Colcutt was appointed after the plan and principal lines of design had been determined, to dress the exterior of the auditorium and other public spaces. This design by committee should have resulted in a mess but, in the end, it created a fine theatre and a major London landmark.

As well as having the rare advantage of being on an island site, the Palace is architecturally unlike any other London theatre (although the early designs for the Clapham Grand could be seen as a homage to Colcutt's Palace treatment). The elevations are in Colcutt's free early northern Renaissance manner, with octagonal shafts dividing the red brick and terracotta banded facade into bays, with many small arched windows, linked vertically and horizontally into varied groupings, all with terracotta balconettes and floridly ornamental friezes. The shafts and octagonal corner towers rise

above the parapet and are crowned by domes. A broad, banded gable rises behind the main facade facing the circus.

Vestibule with marble and alabaster staircase. Opulent auditorium with three balconies; marble and onyx linings. Reputedly the first in Europe to be 'cantilevered', i.e. with no columns supporting the balconies.

The relics of Walter Dando's hugely elaborate opera machinery, above and below the stage, are unique in London and of considerable archaeological significance. The wood and iron installation, occupying a deep cellar and mezzanine, has had all its moving parts taken away, but what remains is a forest of framed timber with traps, chariot slots, etc. Restoration could only be achieved at prodigious cost and would provide little practical advantage, but expert recording is called for if removal is contemplated. *JE*

Pavilion

Shepherd's Bush Green
Hammersmith and Fulham
Other names
    1955 **Gaumont**
    1962 **Odeon**
           Odeon 1/Top Rank Club
           Mecca Bingo
Original architect
    1923 **Frank Verity**
Later works
    1955 **S. Beverly: reconstructed after
           1944 bomb damage; auditori-
           um and proscenium
           redesigned for Cinemascope**
    1969 **Unknown: subdivided for
           bingo**
Current use **Bingo at lower level, disused
           cinema above**
Capacity **c.2000 (prior to subdivision)**

With the Shepherd's Bush Empire, this large red brick building in restrained classical style dominates the green. The auditorium lies parallel to the road. A huge square tower with bold cornice rises at the south end. Here a large round-headed window is supported by pillars which enclose the entrance. There are two pedimented windows at either side. Large entrance foyer, originally decorated with Roman theme, dominated by a bust of the Emperor Caracalla.

The entrance to stalls lies to the right. Stairs lead to first-floor level, originally with a tea lounge/dance hall, and to the original circle level. The style of the auditorium was, again, originally Roman. The Pavilion had full stage facilities, orchestra pit and a large organ. From

1927, the building was under Gaumont ownership.

A flying bomb severely damaged the stage and stalls areas in 1944; the organ was removed and the building was unused until 1955. Redesigned by Samuel Beverly, the proscenium was rebuilt for Cinemascope and the auditorium reduced in size by curving the walls towards the proscenium. The Pavilion was subdivided for bingo and cinema in 1969. The cinema closed in 1983 and remains unused. Bingo operates in the stalls area. *SM*

Phoenix ★★

110 Charing Cross Road
Camden
Original architect
    1930   Sir Giles Gilbert Scott, Bertie
            Crewe and Cecil Masey
Listed   Grade II
Current use Theatre
Capacity 1012

Phoenix (Ian Grundy)

One of the London theatres built in the curiously productive theatre-building year of 1930. The unique co-operation between Giles Gilbert Scott, Bertie Crewe, Cecil Masey and Theodor Komisarjevsky produced an unusual theatre. The site has frontages to Charing Cross Road and Phoenix Street, making architectural statements and both seeming to compete for the status of the principal entrance front. The Charing Cross Road facade, on a curved corner, has a loggia with four giant columns above the canopy and is topped by an attic with square windows. The main entrance is in Phoenix Street, with a more freely treated two-storey, three-bay arcade with twisted columns.

Lively and colourful auditorium with figure-painted panels in attic over boxes, but the Komisarjevsky decorations are now in need of revival. Particularly sad is the present dull appearance of Polunin's splendid safety curtain, based on an Italian Renaissance painting of the *Triumph of Love*. It is an important work of theatrical art in its own right. *JE*

Piccadilly ★

Denman Street
City of Westminster
Original architect
    1928   Bertie Crewe with Edward
            Stone
Later works
    1968   Unknown: improvements,
            including modular stage
Current use Theatre
Capacity 1232

A theatre on one of the West End's less prominent sites. Facade in eleven bays with right-hand end curving at the junction of Sherwood and Denman Streets. Looking like stone but actually in white cement, the ground floor takes the form of a rusticated arcade under a projecting canopy. Above this, two channelled storeys are united by giant pilasters carrying an entablature with a sheer attic storey above.

Entrance foyer walnut-panelled. Auditorium with two balconies and square architrave-framed proscenium. Early Vitaphone sound movies were shown at the Piccadilly in the year of its opening. It has had a slightly chequered history but in recent years has remained a mainstream theatre. A big stage suitable for musicals. *JE*

Playhouse ★★★

Northumberland Avenue
City of Westminster
Other names
    1882–1933
            Royal Avenue Theatre, or
            Avenue Theatre
Original architect
    1882   F.H. Fowler and Hill
Later works
    1890   F.H. Fowler and Hill: redecorated
    1905   Detmar Blow and Fernand
            Billerey: interior remodelled
            (not completed)
    1907   Detmar Blow and Fernand
            Billerey: rebuilt internally after
            a wall of Charing Cross Station
            collapsed on the building
    1987   Graham Berry: restored to
            theatre use, additional storeys
            built; entrance canopy rein-
            stated; redecorated
Listed   Grade II
Current use Theatre
Capacity 786

Initiated in 1882 by Sefton Parry, a speculative theatre builder, who bought the site hoping it would have to be purchased from him by the South Eastern and Chatham Railway Company, whose Charing Cross terminus was alongside. He usually claimed to design his own theatres but, in this case, his architects were Fowler and Hill. Fowler's pompous, Central European-looking Opera House on the Embankment at Westminster Bridge was never built. The Playhouse was in a decided lower key, but a pleasing enough architectural event, on a site at the bottom of Northumberland Avenue/Craven Street and visible from the Embankment.

The Playhouse served as a BBC radio studio from 1951 to 1976. In 1986, a move to bring it back into live theatre use was encouraged by allowing upward extension in the form of a sheer attic and a roof storey, available for commercial letting. This 'sweetener' was, sadly, not legally tied up so as to provide the theatre with a continuing endowment.

The external elevation in Portland stone, curving round the corner from Craven Street to Hungerford Lane, are those of 1882, raised in proper classical manner by the additional storey. The long absent figure sculpture above the crowning balustrade of Fowler's building has not been reinstated.

The theatre had already been substantially altered after 1905 when, during a remodelling of the interior, a mass of masonry from the side of Charing Cross Station fell onto the theatre, resulting in six fatalities. The compensation, however, made it possible to reconstruct the interior completely in fashionable French taste, to the designs of Detmar, Blow and Billerey (essentially Fernand Billerey).

Excellent foyers, etc., lead to a magnificently uninhibited auditorium in Franco-Venetian taste, a design of flowing curves with fine plasterwork and painting. Deep proscenium whose splayed architectural frame embraces two tiers of boxes with spirited female terms carrying the upper tier. The proscenium jambs sweep into a depressed basket arch. The curving walls of the auditorium similarly sweep up into pendentives carrying a dome. The dome, pendentive-roundels and large ellipticalheaded wall panels are filled with art decoration, the walls paintings being in a dream-like Watteau-inspired manner. Serpentine balcony fronts in two tiers with iron balustrades, the upper balcony terminating abruptly against the wall paintings. The 1987 decorations did not attempt to reproduce the original Billerey scheme, which was in warm orange and chocolate tones. As a result, the paintings now look too dark for their present bright settings. The painting of the safety curtain at that time in the style of the original act drop was commendable.

Extensive basement accommodation with good headroom below auditorium (this is the result of raising the 1905/7 auditorium by about 1.5m (4ft 11in) above the level of that of the 1882).

There is a splendidly preserved complex of substage machinery, second

in importance in London only to Her Majesty's, with grave, bridges, thunderrun, etc. *JE*

Plaza Cinema
Lower Regent Street
City of Westminster
Other names
    1968–72
        Plaza/Paramount
    1972–75
        Paramount/Universal
Original architect
    1926   Frank Verity
Later works
    1967–68   Verity and Beverley: reconstructed as twin cinema
    1977   Unknown: further subdivision
Current use Cinema
Capacity   originally 1896

The Plaza was one of the first truly elaborate large cinemas built in the West End with American money. It featured a supporting stage act supplied by the Plaza Tiller Girls, who performed a new routine appropriate to each new feature and who were noted for their precision. Of perhaps greater interest was the plan of the cinema, which survives vestigially. Paramount were the only company to build cinemas in Britain with small, prestigious mezzanines (here variously called the 'Royal Circle' or 'Foyer Loge') between the stalls (or parterre) and the circle. The conversion to twin cinemas in 1967–68 was the most expensive job undertaken. Sadly, this means that an exceptionally thorough job was done. Whilst the position of the old stage is evident, there remain only fragments of the old decoration at the very top of the building. *EH*

Prince Edward ★★★
Old Compton Street
City of Westminster
Other names
    1936–39 and 1946–54
        London Casino
    1942–46
        Queensberry All Services Club
    1954–78
        Casino Cinerama Theatre
Original architect
    1930   Edward A. Stone
Later works
    1935   Edward Stone: converted to Casino (dinner/dance hall) new stage kitchens and loges
    1942   Thomas Braddock: stage altered for All Services Club
    1946   T. and P. Braddock: restored as theatre

    1954   T. and P. Braddock: converted to Cinerama
    1974   Unknown: altered
    1978   RHWL: restored as theatre
    1992–93   RHWL (N. Thompson, D. Wright and C. Ferraby): new boxes, loges, seating, lowered ante proscenium; auditorium walls and interior decorations altered; new entrance canopy
Current use Theatre
Capacity   1622

Externally, the Prince Edward Theatre bears a close resemblance to at least one of Edward A. Stone's cinemas, the former Streatham Astoria. Indeed, the two buildings were designed in the same year, 1929, but the interiors were very different. The Prince Edward was intended for musicals and revues, and had a high auditorium with balconies and seven conventional side-wall boxes. The designers of the interior, Marc Henri and Laverdet, chose rectilinear patterns for the walls, and René Lalique ambro glass to frame the proscenium arch which has now gone.

The first musical, opening on 3 April 1930, was *Rio Rita*. It was not a success, and neither were the shows that followed. After the 1935 pantomime, *Aladdin*, the theatre was converted to the London Casino, reopening in Spring 1936 as a cabaret restaurant with a spectacular stage show. Stone was brought back to make the alterations. They included the installation of a velarium over the upper balcony, and a new apron stage for dancing linked by stairs to the balconies – where new stepped loges added at the sides at that time have subsequently become the principal novelty of the interior. A kitchen was installed under the old stage, the stalls lounge became a cocktail bar and the upper foyers served as waiters' rest rooms. With the outbreak of war in 1939 it closed, to be revamped again in 1942 as the Queensberry All Services Club by Thomas Braddock; he gave it on-stage seating round a boxing ring and a new velarium that re-exposed the upper circle.

In 1946 the Casino was restored to theatrical use by Thomas and Peter Braddock, and reopened in December with *Mother Goose*. For a time Ivor Novello's *Dancing Years* and three editions of Robert Nesbitt's revue *Latin Quarter* kept it going, but in 1954 it became a full-time cinema, with the installation by the Braddocks of a deeply curved 19.5m (64ft) wide screen, stereophonic sound, and three synchronised

Playhouse (Ian Newman)

Prince Edward (David Crosswaite)

projection boxes. The Casino was to mark a revolution in moving picture technology - Cinerama. For as long as films were available in this complicated tripartite format all was well, but the technique was not sustained. In 1974 the vast screen was removed, and in 1978 full-time theatrical use and the original name were restored, accompanied by the hit musical *Evita. Chess* and *Anything Goes* continued the success. A more thorough-going restoration and revitalisation followed in 1992/93, which has left the Prince Edward looking more impressive than ever. Adaptation by RHWL for Cameron Mackintosh has left one uncertain as to what is original and what new, for by the successful adoption of Stone's vocabulary, the auditorium is now more 1930s in style than it was before. New boxes and extra loges at the sides and the lowering of the ante-proscenium arch have reduced the old impression of high, cold side walls, and openings have been made in the side of the stalls to allow continental-style seating without a central aisle. Restored lay-lights, new balcony lighting and a sympathetic colour scheme have made the auditorium glow. The circular entrance and basement bar have always been impressive spaces, and these have been restored and enhanced. *EH*

Prince of Wales ★
31 Coventry Street
City of Westminster
Other names
    1884 Prince's Theatre
Original architect
    1937 Robert Cromie
Later works
    1963 Unknown: proscenium, orchestra and stage remodelled
Listed   **Grade II**
Current use **Theatre**
Capacity **1133**

The first theatre on the site, by C.J. Phipps, 1884, formed part of a speculation by actor-manager Edgar Bruce, which included a hotel and restaurant. Contemporary engravings show that the site did not allow Phipps to adopt his favoured and instantly recognisable theatre form with a circular ceiling and deep cove. It was a narrow room with a sloping ceiling, three end balconies, straight rows of boxes and a square proscenium.

Little or nothing of Phipps's fabric was left after Robert Cromie's root-and-branch rebuild in 1937. Cromie succeeded in producing a considerably roomier auditorium with a 50% larger capacity and a much better stage. Following the 1963 alterations, his Art Deco treatment is incomplete. The site

still imposes severe limitations in that the bars and foyers are all ranged along one side, extending to the rear.

The exterior, with the entrance on the corner of Coventry Street and a long flank facing Oxenden Street, is not, perhaps, an outstanding work of architecture but it is something of a little landmark, very much of its time, spare and angular. The principal excitements are a tall display frame on the corner and a short, rectangular tower with a rectangular opening on each face. The elevations are in artificial stone, but the tower appears to be rendered. *JE*

Queen's ★★
Shaftesbury Avenue
City of Westminster
Other names
    Wardour Street Theatre (name adopted but changed to Queen's before opening)
Original architect
    1908 W.G.R. Sprague
Later works
    1958-9 Westwood, Sons and Partners (B. Westwood) with Hugh Casson: front of house rebuilt; auditorium restored and modified
Listed   **Grade II**
Current use **Theatre**
Capacity **979**

Designed with the Gielgud (formerly Globe) as part of a balanced composition with closely similar architectural treatment to the two corners of the block, but now, since partial rebuilding of the Queen's after war damage, presenting a stark contrast. No doubt in 1957 the restoration of the facade to its original appearance seemed impractical if not undesirable. The glass curtain wall, revealing the foyers and bars to the street and described, in 1982, as 'outdated, untheatre-like, even heartless', has, with the passage of time, become an interesting 1950s' antiquity in its own right. It is, nevertheless, an architectural gatecrasher, wearing the wrong suit to the party. The flank and rear elevations are original, in red brick with repetitive stone dressings. Westwood's/Casson's rebuild at least gave the Queen's a foyer and bars with a greater feeling of spaciousness than one would have thought achievable on so restricted a site. The modern detailing is here low-key, making no particularly memorable statement. The rehabilitation of the auditorium was handled with sensitivity. The box fronts were altered and, regrettably, the loggia boxes which gave a little in the way of opulence to a restrained design, were removed. The total effect, however, is still that of a typically controlled Sprague interior, with elegant Italian Renaissance plaster details, exhibiting none of the architectural abandon of his master, Matcham.

As always, with Sprague, the auditorium is an architecturally unified room, designed to be satisfying in all views. It has two curving cantilever balconies linked to three-tiered boxes flanking a rectangular proscenium frame. The upper boxes are set between square Corinthian columns supporting an entablature and an arch. A coved, panelled sounding board links the two arches.

The ceiling has an oval saucer dome containing four semi-circular lunettes, each guarded by pairs of full-length relief figures of muses. The modern 'floating moulding' lighting ring is not wholly successful and rather confuses the view of the dome. The 1950s' adaptations included discreet front-of-house lighting positions in ports formed in the upper balcony front but these have proved insufficient for the voracious lighting demands of modern productions. Later bars and gantries have introduced a deal of clutter into Sprague, Westwood and Casson's pretty interior.
JE

Richmond Odeon
Hill Street
Richmond upon Thames
Other names
  1930 Richmond Kinema
  1940 Premier
Original architect
  1930 Julian Leathart and W.F. Granger
Later works
  1973 Unknown: tripled
Listed **Grade II**
Current use **Triple cinema**
Capacity **originally 3200**

The Odeon was built as a ciné-variety house in atmospheric style. It opened with variety.

The auditorium was intended to evoke a C17 Spanish nobleman's courtyard house. The coffering and weathered oak beams over the balcony formed a loggia from which the audience looked out over an open courtyard with steep pitched, terracotta-tiled roofs and side loggias surrounded by olive trees. Foliage tumbled over the balconies and peeped over the roofs, and banners were draped over the balcony rails, like car-

pets airing in the sun. Much of the decoration survives, though a wide screen obscures the proscenium arch and the original Holophane 'sunrise to sunset' effect of the ceiling lights has been removed. The wide stage and the dressing rooms are intact, and have, since opening, seen large shows and hosted the local symphony orchestra.

The facade is in the restrained, Art Deco influenced Classical tradition of the 1920s, with neo-Egyptian touches, and green pantiled roofs over the flats and shops that lie in front of the auditorium block in Hill Street. *SM*

Richmond Theatre ★★★
The Green
Richmond upon Thames
Other names
  1899 Richmond Theatre and Opera House
  1902 Prince of Wales
  1909 Richmond Hippodrome
         Theatre Royal, Richmond
         'The Theatre on the Green' (popular name)
Original architect
  1899 Frank Matcham
Later works
  1915 Unknown: theatre refurbished
  1960s Unknown: entrance canopy added
  1975 Unknown: foyer restored; gallery reseated as upper circle
  1990 Donald Armstrong: entrance canopy removed; complete restoration internally of original features and gilding; major improvements to facilities for disabled, bars, toilets and dressing rooms; creation of corporate entertainment suite; improved technical facilities

Listed **Grade II***
Current use **Theatre**
Capacity **840**

Of outstanding importance as one of the most completely preserved Matcham theatres in Greater London and one of his most satisfying interiors. Symmetrical with red brick and terracotta facade; twin towers with cupolas; Baroque centre piece with arched entrance below a scrolled pediment. The central terracotta figure of Euterpe is identical with the one on the otherwise completely different facade of Hackney Empire. Comparison between the two theatres is, in fact, quite instructive. Hackney, a variety palace, built for Stoll, is architecturally extremely eclectic and highly assertive, inside and out. Richmond, built for a local theatre proprietor and aimed at a different kind of audience, is entertaining, but in a more restrained, almost respectable mood.

Mahogany main doors open into a small vestibule and then into a large foyer, both panelled in mahogany, with a painted ceiling in the latter. In the main entrance there is a plaster roundel of Edmund Kean, commemorating his association with an earlier Richmond Theatre.

Magnificent auditorium with rich plasterwork in 'Elizabethan' style; two balconies; marble proscenium arch with massive key panel; proscenium flanked by truncated columns covered with linenfold to produce an elaborately draped effect and carrying figures of Tragedy and Comedy; fine domed ceiling with relief plaster ornament of scenes from Shakespeare plays. At the back of the dress circle is a spacious promenade.

Richmond Theatre, c.1905

The 1990 renovations made major improvements front and back of house, all the visible new works being sympathetic and subordinate to Matcham's own. The auditorium redecoration scheme (by Carl Toms) was not a restoration of Matcham's but is harmonious and pleasing. *JE/SM*

Royal Brunswick Theatre
Ensign Street
Tower Hamlets
Other names
    Brunswick Theatre
    New Brunswick
    Royalty (earlier building)
    East London (earlier building)
Original architect
    1828   Stedman Whitwell
Current use **Fragment**

One of the smallest and most easily overlooked of Metropolitan fragments, but of sufficient antiquity and interest to merit inclusion here. The area to the north and east of the Tower of London had been a little East London Theatreland since Odell opened his Goodman's Fields (Alie Street) Theatre in 1729 and John Palmer the Royalty in 1787. The Brunswick, built on the same site as the Royalty in 1827-28, was of an unusual neo-classic design by a somewhat eccentric architect, Stedman Whitwell. Three weeks after completion the theatre fell down during a rehearsal. Religious fanatic opponents of the stage moralised over the ruins while the bodies of the victims were still warm. The cause seems to have been overloading by the iron roof (intended to be fireproof) before the walls were properly set.
    A row of cast-iron bollards, each bearing the monogram 'RBT' defines the precise position of the theatre front on the pavement edge in Ensign Street (near Wellclose Square and Wilton's Music Hall). Their simple survival, which could never have occurred on a busier highway or alongside a commercially valuable central London site, is quite remarkable. *JE*

Royal Clarence Music Hall ★
College Approach
Greenwich
Other names
    Clarence Music Hall
Original architect
    c.1839   probably Joseph Kay
Later works
    1875   Unknown: major refurbishment

?1970s Unknown: converted to film and television studio
1998 Russell Associates: converted to bar/restaurant and art gallery
Listed   **Grade II**
Current use **Bar and restaurant**
Capacity   **(was) c.175**

An extremely rare survival of an 1830s'/40s' purpose-built public house concert room. This is a large room built at first-floor level over the colonnaded (originally low built and pedimented) entrance to Greenwich Market, which is itself a quadrangle enclosed by terraced frontages in College Approach, Nelson Road, Greenwich Church Street and King William Street.
    Correspondence in a local newspaper had pointed to a need for a multi-purpose concert room in Greenwich before its erection in c.1839. Although the room is approached by staircases from its own street entrances, it was originally linked by a doorway to the Admiral Hardy pub, adjoining to the east. It underwent some later improvements, notably in 1875. By 1888 it was 'principally used for dancing but occasionally as a music hall'. Finally closed in 1890 as a result of the 1878 Metropolis Management Act and the access from the pub was then blocked. It is a flat-floored rectangular room with a shallow tunnel-vaulted ceiling, balcony across the end and, originally, a small platform stage. A report of 1878 refers to a 'new stage . . . proscenium . . . balcony and private boxes'.
    It appears that the boxes (possibly added about that time) were under the balcony. A blocked doorway on the first floor, linking the hall with the pub, was still visible as late as 1996. In later years the ceiling, balcony front and other features were much obscured by acoustic and other linings.
    After some years of disuse, prior to which it had been a film studio and, before that, a dance hall, permission was granted in the 1980s to convert the building to a video cinema to present the history of Greenwich to tourists. This scheme was never implemented, perhaps because the capacity was too low and the trade too seasonal. In 1997 a further permission was given to convert to bar and restaurant and work commenced the following year. This involved radical alterations to the staircases but permitted uncovering of the shallow, elegantly curved ceiling. The bombé balcony front has, however, been moved

forward substantially and the boxes (evidence of which was found to be still present) were removed. It is a matter for great regret that the planning authority failed to exercise its powers of control to better effect. *JE*

Royal Court ★★★
Sloane Square
Kensington and Chelsea
Other names
    Court Theatre
Original architect
    1888   Walter Emden (and Bertie Crewe, who withdrew before contract started)
Later works
    1897   J. Kingwell Cole: minor changes to gallery; redecorated
    1904   C.E. Lancaster Parkinson: addition of third floor as rehearsal room (for Harley Granville Barker)
    1920   Burdwood and Dunt: forestage added; both circles altered to present shape with swagged fruit and flowers (removed 2000) and back-lit glass panels at side to give Elizabethan effect
    1955   Apron stage restored
    1964   Jocelyn Herbert: redecorated
    1969   Roderick Ham: Theatre Upstairs added in old rehearsal room/nightclub
    1990   Roderick Ham: new rehearsal room added
    2000   Haworth Tompkins: major reconstruction, extended to rear and under Sloane Square
Listed   **Grade II**
Current use **Theatre**
Capacity   **c.400 proposed (main house)**

Built to replace the earlier Court Theatre on another site, the Royal Court had been through a succession of changes, including use as a cinema from 1934, until it suffered bomb damage in 1940. It stood derelict until reopening as a theatre in 1952. Since then, as the home of the English Stage Company, it has become a world-famous centre of innovative writing and productions. Alterations and additions have continued to take place, particularly from 1964 onward, including the creation of the experimental Theatre Upstairs in 1971.
    A brief account cannot do justice to this historically important theatre. Perhaps the most remarkable thing about it, in architectural terms, is that, through repeated campaigns of alteration,

Royal Court Theatre (Andy Chopping)

addition and reconstruction (including the removal in 1934 of Emden's balcony-supporting columns), it has retained much of the character of a Victorian theatre. Even more remarkably, the English Stage Company were determined to maintain its basic form in the immense programme of works (which included extension under the road into Sloane Square itself) undertaken 1998–2000. 'The . . . auditorium has been an important factor in the success of the English Stage Company for over 40 years.' (1995 Feasibility Study)

The philosophical approach adopted in the recent project was an interesting one. Despite the radical nature of the works, the extensive subterranean additions and the frankly modern treatment of the new flank (where valuable backstage accommodation had been gained) the general impression is that interference with the old fabric has been limited to what was essential. Plain, rather than luxurious finishes have been adopted and historically interesting variations of internal construction (e.g. riveted iron members supporting balconies, traces of old staircases, etc.) have been left clearly visible. This is a sound approach from a conservation viewpoint, but has also added materially to the visual interest of the building.

Externally, the fine red brick, moulded brick and stone facade to Sloane Square is still, in its essentials (and depite alterations to the entrances and above parapet level), as designed by Emden.

The auditorium, which had undergone a series of alterations, achieving its present form in 1920, has now been further amended (re-raked stalls, simplification of plaster ornament, etc.) but in such a way that its familiar character

appears untouched. It is a pleasing intimate room with two parallel-sided horseshoe balconies and a flat-domed ceiling.

The approach to the theatre from the open space of Sloane Square and the restaurant beneath the road provide a satisfying build-up to the revelation of the main auditorium.

The (Jerwood) Theatre Upstairs is considerably improved from its old form. The only significant loss of old fabric occurred with the removal of a complex of wood stage machinery to permit the major improvements to the main stage. The machinery was recorded by David Wilmore. The traps are now installed and in working order in Harrogate Royal Hall. *JE*

Royal Opera House, Covent Garden ★★★

Covent Garden
City of Westminster
Other names
   1732   **Theatre Royal (in) Covent Garden**
   1847   **Royal Italian Opera**
   1892   **Royal Opera**
   1939   **Royal Opera House . . . and many other variants**
Original architect
   First building on site,
   1732   **Edward Shepherd (occupied only part of present site)**
Later works
   The building history is far too complex to set down in detail.
   The main events were:
   1782   **John Inigo Richards: auditorium of Shepherd building remodelled**
   1792   **Henry Holland: extensively reconstructed**

   1809   Sir Robert Smirke: entirely new theatre built
1815–17   Unknown: gas light introduced
1837–38   Unknown: limelight introduced
   1847   Benedict Albano: auditorium rebuilt
   1858   Edward M. Barry: new theatre built after fire
   1883   Unknown: rear curving stair to stalls removed; pit and stalls combined, etc.
   1892   Unknown: electric light introduced
1899–1902 E.O. Sachs: stage entirely reconstructed including removal of apron and minor alterations to auditorium and foyers
   1933   Unknown: offices and dressing rooms built in Mart Street
   1955   Unknown: exit stairs from stalls moved out of orchestra pit
   1960   Dennis Lennon: box partitions cut back and angled
   1964   Peter Moro: amphitheatre altered; gallery removed; single rake and vomitories created
   1982   Gollins, Melvin and Ward: major additions (rehearsal and dressing rooms)
   1992   BDP: stalls reconfigured
   1999   Dixon Jones BDP: auditorium refurbished, new stage house constructed; extensive new buildings
Listed: Grade I
Current use Opera House with resident ballet and opera companies
Capacity   2268

The present building is essentially that designed by Edward M. Barry in 1857 and opened in 1858 but with some sculptural work salvaged from Smirke's theatre. (Barry designed the adjoining Floral Hall at the same time, which opened in 1860.) The Opera House is an imposing monument in E.M. Barry's Roman Renaissance manner. Although it has always been seen in the main from narrow streets in foreshortened views, its impact is considerable. On the Bow Street front a tall hexastyle Corinthian portico is raised on a rusticated base, formed by the enclosure of the original porte cochère. The facade incorporates two magnificent bas reliefs designed by Flaxman and carved by Rossi and one statue each by Flaxman (the Comic muse) and Rossi (the Tragic muse) from the 1809 theatre. The upper level of the portico contains a glazed conservatory, extending the crush bar.

On the departure of Covent Garden fruit and vegetable market to Nine Elms in the 1970s, the entire island site occupied by the Opera House and surrounding properties, including property on the opposite side of Floral Street, was acquired. The first phase, an elongation of Barry's building toward James Street, was completed in 1982, partially replacing the dressing rooms, etc., built in 1933.

As seen now, following the 1999 reopening, Barry's Opera House appears as one element in a unified (but not architecturally uniform) development bounded by Bow Street, Russell Street, the Piazzas, James Street and Floral Street and incorporating the Floral Hall, a second auditorium, chorus and orchestra rehearsal space, offices, workshops, side stages, ballet rehearsal rooms and ground-floor shops. The new elevations to the left of the old facade in Bow Street and round the corner in Russell Street are frankly modern and relatively low-key (apart from the iron and glass end of the Floral Hall) but, facing the Market, a colonnaded ground floor provides an historical echo of the Inigo Jones arcades which are now represented only by Clutton's Victorian reinterpretation on the north-west side of the market. Turning into James Street, the facade of the 1981 extension is in a Barryish Italianate style returning to Floral Street and linking with the flank of Barry's theatre. The raised fly tower, seen over the loggia promenade crowning the Piazza elevation, is a considerable landmark.

The Floral Hall, restored and raised in height, now roofs a majestic public space with escalators and viewing balconies. The loss of the facade toward the Market, which was a witty iron paraphrase of the Inigo Jones facade originally surrounding the Covent Garden piazza may be regretted, but it is difficult to see how it might have been incorporated into such a comprehensive redevelopment project.

The interior of the old Opera House is superb. 'Few would dissent from the view that (it has) the most beautiful auditorium in Great Britain.' (Survey of London, 1970) It has been improved and refined in a number of ways, including the re-raking of the stalls (by virtue of the rebuilding of the stage house) raising the previously oppressive pelmet to give greater working height to the stage, which is now multi-zoned and equipped to the highest modern standards. Only the keenest observer in the audience

Royal Opera House (Rob Moore)

would be aware, however, of the changes which have been made.

The auditorium was designed (as were many earlier theatres) to be readily convertible to ballroom, assembly room and exhibition hall use. The design is a compromise between the European style of box-tiered opera house and a deep-tiered playhouse. The well of the auditorium (originally pit and stalls) is enclosed by the lowest box tier, above which there are three horseshoe tiers of balconies cantilevered forward from their supporting iron columns, plus an amphitheatre-gallery. By the 1930s most of the old box-divisions, with their twisted gilt shafts, had been removed and the benched amphitheatre slips and gallery were rearranged (1964) as a single, spaciously seated tier extending back from the top balcony and again rearranged in the 1999 work. The horseshoe curve of the main balcony fronts is governed by a semi-circle of the same radius as the saucer-domed ceiling, which is supported on four elliptical arches and pendentives, the arch on the west side enclosing a parabolic sounding board above the stage, which formerly had an apron of the same depth as the recess so formed.

The plaster ornament is rich and robust. The proscenium has a coved frame with gilt twisted shafts on either side, which were originally designed to move (and now do again) thereby widening the scenic opening. The sounding board carries a modelled relief of the head of the young Queen Victoria and symbolic figures by Monti. The tier fronts, also by Monti (and not to Barry's taste) are of bombé section, enriched with trellis and foliage and divided into bays by winged female terms representing three stages of life (7, 14 and 21 years of age) and with foliage developing in symbolic stages from leaves to buds to flowers. The saucer dome has a wide margin band and panelled sectors with a central oculus.

Barry's splendid grand staircase and entrance hall, crush bar and Royal Suite are somewhat altered, but, as with the auditorium, the original design has not been damaged and the auditorium decorations, in cream, crimson and gold, are still much as Barry wished them to be. The 1858 theatre completely abandoned the old scene groove system, all back scenes being flown. The stage was completely reconstructed between 1899 and 1902 by Edwin O. Sachs with a flat stage surface and elaborate metal machinery, now replaced after detailed recording. It was the most extensive system of substage machinery of the kind existing in London.

No brief summary can do justice to this building. Covent Garden occupies a key position in the history of the theatre, opera and ballet in England. The theatre shares with Drury Lane the distinction of never having been subject to either Lord Chamberlain's or local authority formal licensing control. Its right to present theatrical entertainment derives from the Royal Patent conferred by Charles II on Davenant in 1662, which after many vicissitudes, came to rest on the present site. The document itself is in the Philip H. and A.S.W. Rosenbach Foundation Museum, Philadelphia, having been sold after the fire of 1856, but the fact that Gye reopened his opera house in 1858 without a licence is evidence that the Lord Chamberlain accepted that the patent was still effective and its authority attached to this site and no other. The exterior is later in date than Drury Lane, the Haymarket, the Lyceum and the main shell of the Old Vic, but the Royal Opera House is the oldest theatre building executed to a single design now standing more or less intact in London. Its architectural importance cannot be overrated. *JE*

Sadler's Wells
Rosebery Avenue
Islington
Other names
    Sadler's Wells Musick House
    1699   Miles's Musick House
Original architect
    1683   Unknown: as wooden music house
Later works
    1765   Thomas Rosoman (builder): first theatre on site
    after 1772 Unknown: interior remodelled
    1802   Rudolphe Cabanel: completely reconstructed auditorium
    1838   Unknown: major alterations
    1879   C.J. Phipps: interior remodelled
    1901   Bertie Crewe: partly remodelled
    1931   Matcham and Co (F.G.M. Chancellor): rebuilt
    1938   Stanley Hall, Easton and Robertson: extended and improved after aquisition of additional land
    1959   Martin Card and Hope Bagenal: proscenium altered

    1960   Unknown: wardrobe accommodation improved; other works
    1988   Chamberlin, Powell, Bonn and Woods, with Wolff Olins Hamilton: Lilian Baylis Theatre added
    1998   RHWL, with Nicholas Hare: radical reconstruction and improvements
Listed   **Grade II**
Current use **Theatre and Opera House**
Capacity   **1550**

In all essentials, a completely new theatre and strictly, therefore, the Wells falls outside the scope of this survey. However, some parts of earlier theatres have survived and, as a location, the record of almost continuous occupation by an entertainment house on a single site is exceeded only by that of Drury Lane. On this basis it cannot be ignored.

A wooden 'musick house' was erected on the site in 1683, after discovery of medicinal wells in the grounds of Thomas Sadler. Successor theatres presented popular work of outstanding elaboration and quality, but it was not until the breaking of the Patent Theatres monopoly in 1843 that it became a mainstream theatre under Phelps. It became a music hall in 1893, then a cinema. In 1906 it fell into dereliction. Acquired by a charity initiated by Lilian Baylis, it was completely rebuilt and opened in 1931 in harness with the Old Vic and with the same policy of bringing quality theatre to the people. From 1934 it was dedicated to opera and ballet. The rather cheerless 1934 theatre was one of the first in London to be protected by

inclusion in the Statutory List, an honour which must have been bestowed more in recognition of the historic 'holy ground' reputation of the site (and its wells) than for reasons of architectural quality.

A fully researched architectural history of the various Wells theatres is long overdue, including, as it would, Cabanel's historically important 1802 reconstruction and its subsequent evolution. Where will we find a Leacroft or a Southern to do it? *JE*

St Martin's ★★★
West Street
Borough of Camden
Other names
    Irving Theatre (proposed name, not used)
Original architect
    1916   W.G.R. Sprague
Later works
    1998   Unknown: replica of original 1916 canopy constructed
Listed   **Grade II**
Current use **Theatre**
Capacity   **546**

The St Martin's Theatre was planned at the same time and should have been completed with the Ambassador's but was delayed by the outbreak of the First World War. The two theatres were separate ventures but they were designed as companion buildings and stand on either side of Tower Court. Further research is needed to establish whether the executed design was modified in any way during the three years' delay in building. St Martin's has a rather more imposing facade than the Ambassador's;

St. Martin's (Karl Davey)

ashlar-faced in five bays with giant attached Ionic columns through the upper three storeys, supporting an entablature and parapet. A coat of arms above the parapet was blown down in the Second World War. Plain modern canopy over the entrance. Good foyer.

The prettiness of the Ambassador's auditorium gives no warning of the classical sobriety to come at the St Martin's. Sprague's St Martin's auditorium abandons completely the exuberant displays of fibrous plasterwork which typified theatre design (including Sprague's own designs) in previous decades. The style was described as 'Georgian'. Much polished hardwood. Flat side walls with imposing fluted Doric columns and piers, rising from pedestals at 1st balcony level to carry a correct entablature with triglyphs and mutules, continuing over the rectangular, cavetto-moulded proscenium. Two serpentine balconies, their fronts differently curved, both with turned hardwood balustrades. The lower one runs into single boxes on either side of the proscenium. One box is real, the other a dummy, but fully draped. Boxes also at rear of circle. The auditorium was splendidly redecorated in 1996.

At the time of the 1973 GLC survey, the substage had a fine set of wooden stage machinery, almost complete but marred by the insertion of a control room, eliminating paddle levers and slides. *JE*

Saville

Shaftesbury Avenue
Camden
Other names
  1961 Gaiety (name proposed but
          not adopted)
  1970 ABC
  1986 Cannon
  1992 MGM
  1995 ABC
Original architect
  1931 T.P. Bennett and Son
Later works
  1955 Unknown: interior redecorated
          and new mural in stalls bar
  1970 William Ryder and Associates:
          converted to twin cinema;
          stage house altered
Listed   Grade II
*Current use:*Twin cinema
Capacity 1250 (prior to subdivision)

The Saville Theatre opened in 1931. It was steel-framed with mainly brick cladding, generally rectilinear in character, but with a striking facade to Shaftesbury

Savoy (Matthew Weinreb)

Avenue. This has a channelled artificial stone base, above which is a lively sculptural relief frieze, nearly 40m (130ft) long, by Gilbert Bayes, representing 'Drama through the Ages'. Above this is a moulded band and a blind, parapeted upper storey in channelled brickwork. The entrance is set in a giant arched opening (its original bronze glazed screen now gone), flanked at high level by ornamental plaques by the same artist. The Bayes work has been described recently (1998) as 'perhaps the most significant sculpture of the 1930s on a prominent building'. The interior was originally three-tier. The large stalls bar and a lounge had mural paintings by A.R. Thompson, added to in 1995 by John Collins.

It is ironic that the Saville, possibly the most suitable of all the West End theatres for film exhibition, remained strictly for live performance until 1970. However, in that year it was acquired by EMI as a West End flagship for ABC, and was subdivided for twin cinemas in such a way as to make reversal difficult. The stage area was modified for offices and ancillary accommodation at the same time. Internally, a luxury lounge style was created. Nothing of the original architectural character and decoration can now be seen. *SM*

Savoy ★★★

Savoy Place, Strand
City of Westminster
Other names
  Beaufort (proposed before building
      but not used)
Original architect
  1881 C.J. Phipps
Later works
  1903 A.B. Jackson: altered to give
          entrance alongside hotel
  1929 Frank A. Tugwell, with Basil

          Ionides: totally reconstructed
          internally
  1929 Easton and Robertson: Savoy
          Court elevation altered; new
          canopy to theatre and hotel
  1993 Whitfield Partners: restored
          and improved after fire
Listed   Grade II*
Current use Theatre
Capacity 1158

When the Savoy Theatre was totally gutted by fire in February 1990 it seemed to many that it was unlikely ever to be restored and reopened in its old form, but this was magnificently achieved in summer 1993. When account is taken of the extent of the devastation and the fact that most original records had been destroyed (not by fire but by the D'Oyly Cartes), the restoration is a triumphant example of what can be achieved by a meticulous examination of fragmentary remains, coupled with research and deductive skill. Uppark (National Trust property in Sussex) is the most famous example of 'post-fire archaeology' and reconstruction, but, amongst theatres in Britain, the Savoy is the only one to have had this kind of care lavished on it. The fire did little damage backstage and here the alterations are not obvious, although the stage itself has been completely modernised and re-equipped. Substantial parts of the structural shell of the 1881 theatre, built by Phipps for Richard D'Oyly Carte to house Gilbert and Sullivan operas, still survive. The interiors, however, as recreated, are entirely those designed by Ionides or (in places where provision for modern demands made it necessary) by Whitfield Partners in the Ionides manner.

Whitfields raised an additional storey above the theatre to contain plant and a health club (linked to the hotel) with a

Shaftesbury, c.1972 (London Metropolitan Archives)

two panels are alike. There is one recessed box with an iron balustrade in the panelled wall on stage left.

The rear half of the auditorium has boldly fluted all-over wall decoration. The main ceiling is painted as a sky with clouds, now penetrated by a neatly inserted lighting position. The fourth wall is completed by richly coloured and roped house tabs. Apart from the painted ceiling and the painted elongated geometrical panels on the balcony soffits, the ornamented surfaces on all sides are aluminium-leafed, as they were by Ionides, and over-lacquered in subtly varied transparent tints. The seat covers, reproduced from a discovered fragment, are variously coloured, with commendably clear numbers on the fore edges.

The total effect is striking. It would be a great pity if this fine theatrical interior were to be marred by the casual additions and subtractions of those (thankfully few) directors and lighting designers who still undervalue the contribution which architecture plays in the experience of theatregoing.   *JE*

Shaftesbury ★★
Shaftesbury Avenue
Camden
Other names
　　1911　New Prince's
　　1914-63　Prince's
Original architect
　　1911　Bertie Crewe
Later works
　　1980　Dowton and Hurst: roof altered to accommodate counterweight system
　　1988-93　Dowton and Hurst: minor internal alterations
　　1997　Dowton and Hurst: orchestra pit enlarged; other minor alterations
Listed　　Grade II
Current use Theatre
Capacity　1305

swimming pool above the stage house. This top hamper is carried on cunningly concealed stanchions and massive beams. Although it was the profits from the theatre that originally paid for the building of the hotel, the latter has become visually dominant, so that it is the theatre that now looks like the later addition. Externally, the only recognisable surviving part of the Phipps theatre is the former main entrance on the curved Carting Lane/former Somerset Street corner, a remnant dressed in a rusticated Italianate style. On the formerly plain front facing the now little frequented Carting Lane, Whitfields have created a unified elevation with two boldly projecting pavilions concealing, inter alia, part of the structure supporting the added storey. Their design picks up the architectural vocabulary of the 1881 relic, but makes a rather more vigorous statement than the average Phipps facade.

The Savoy Court elevation is the restored 1903 entrance, as modified by Easton and Robertson in 1929, with a row of heavy glazed metal doors under a forward extension of the pedimented stainless steel-faced canopy of the hotel. The doors open into a small booking hall and staircase leading down to foyers, bars and auditorium, all in a full-blooded Art Deco manner which owes little to Tugwell and everything to Ionides.

The auditorium is one of the truly outstanding examples of geometrical Deco invention. There are two balconies with tongue-fluted faces, the upper one set back, with thin slips. From the slips forward to the proscenium, the side walls are canted and carry a deep sounding board, all divided into panels in an illusionistic perspective pattern. The glazed sounding board panels conceal house lighting. The 82 side wall panels are decorated in low relief with Chinese motifs, mainly derived from a great lacquer screen of the Ming Qing dynasties in the Victoria and Albert Museum. No

The Shaftesbury (ex Princes) was the northernmost and, in point of time, the last of the eight pre-First World War theatres built in Shaftesbury Avenue. The theatre occupies a prominent corner site and is viewed across a wide road junction. The elevations, however, are in a quite subdued Baroque manner, the corner tower making a punctuation of spirited but unmonumental character.

Good foyers. Spacious auditorium with two cantilevered balconies (the upper circle is the front section of the former gallery), the fronts varied in both form and treatment. Uninhibited plaster decoration, robust rather than elegant, but producing a splendidly theatrical atmosphere. Rectangular ceiling with enriched cove and cornice and circular flat-domed centre. Segmental proscenium arch with figure reliefs in spandrels over. Bow-fronted boxes, paired in two tiers and magnificently framed by elegant Ionic columns, rise from heavy console brackets and carry an entablature. The whole of this composition is crowned by a semi-circular arch. In the arch tympanum a sculptural group is set over each upper box. The auditorium was designed with a sliding roof to give an instant air change when required.

Designed as a melodrama house this theatre has had a varied history and was dogged by misfortune for some years. After the run of *Hair* (1968–1973) its survival appeared to be in doubt. A ceiling fall in the auditorium in 1973 necessitated closure and seemed likely to lead to the demolition of the theatre. It was then, however, added to the statutory list and the ceiling was eventually restored and the theatre reopened.

The Shaftesbury was an early battle honour for the Save London Theatres Campaign. It has recently served the Royal Opera in exile.   *JE*

Shepherd's Bush Empire ★★
Shepherd's Bush Green
Hammersmith and Fulham
Original architect
    1903   **Frank Matcham**
Later works
    1953   **Unknown: converted to television studio**
    1995   **Torres Design Associates: converted to live music venue; part architectural restoration**

Strand: Putti above boxes (London Metropolitan Archives)

Listed   **Grade II**
Current use **Concert venue**
Capacity: **c.1000**

An unusual Matcham design; an interesting example of the Arts and Crafts spirit leaking into his later work. Roughcast with terracotta dressings. Asymmetrical front, the centre with four-bay arched entrance; to the right, a taller bay with segmental gable and, beyond that, a broad, splayed return; to the left, a stocky round tower with little windows and a lively Baroque top stage, lantern and cupola, now lacking some ornament.

Side additions were made and the interior was radically altered to adapt it for use as a BBC TV studio (1953-91) when substantial parts of the ornament were removed or obscured. The auditorium was of some magnificence, only two years later than the Hackney Empire

but quite different in architectural treatment. The ornament has been extensively restored for its present use but a full restoration would require a complete ensemble of Matcham-style decorations. Nevertheless, it is more complete than would have seemed feasible 15 years ago.   *JE*

Strand ★★★
Aldwych
City of Westminster
Other names
    1905   **Waldorf**
    1909   **Strand**
    1911   **Whitney**
Original architect
    1905   **W.G.R. Sprague**
Later works
    1930   **Unknown: dress circle altered; redecorated**
    1963   **Unknown: balcony reseated**
Listed   **Grade II**
Current use **Theatre**
Capacity   **927**

Built as part of the Aldwych/Kingsway development and designed as a pair with the contemporary Aldwych Theatre, with elevations closely similar but not identical to its twin. In Portland stone with a boldly bowed corner, it is a landmark in views from the Waterloo Bridge end of Aldwych. The interior, described in contemporary accounts as being in Louis XIV style, must be rated as one of the finest surviving works of W.G.R. Sprague, here assisted by the shadowy, but important, decorator van Hooydonk. Tightly planned but elegantly detailed foyer, staircase and bars. The auditorium has three balconies, stepping back to a top level which follows the line

Shepherds Bush Empire (John Earl Collection)

of the circular ceiling, to which the proscenium wall is tangential. The proscenium opening is square with fleur de pêche marble gilt-enriched architrave. On either side, two tiers of full-bosomed boxes (not level with the balconies) are set between marble Ionic pilasters carried on massive console brackets and supporting a rich entablature crowned by full-relief groups of putti. The entablature continues over the proscenium opening, above which is an arched tympanum containing a painted relief of Apollo driving his chariot out of the sun, with winged attendants. Pendentives carry the circular ceiling, which has a fruit-enriched perimeter beam and bracketed cove round a flat field with allegorical painting and a central chandelier. The C17 French taste and the Ionic theme continue with painted marble pilasters and elaborately framed mirrors with musical trophies at each level on the curving side walls. All the marble was 'painted out' in 1930 or later, but has been revealed and refreshed recently. Boxes formerly at the back of the dress circle were removed in 1930.

The painting on the safety curtain is modern but in amusing C19 Parisian style, à la Chéret. The only disappointment is that all four boxes are habitually used as lighting positions, robbing them of their designed function, and concealing the hangings which should 'read' with the architecture. *JE*

Stratford East Theatre Royal ★★★

Gerry Raffles Square
Newham
Other names
   (1897 only) Theatre Royal and Palace
   of Varieties
Original architect
   1884 J.G. Buckle
Later works
   1887 and 1891
   J.G. Buckle: additions
   1902 Frank Matcham: minor alter-
         ations; entrance corridor
         improved; drapes and carpets
         renewed; reseated and
         redecorated
   1981–84 Unknown: improved and
         redecorated
Listed   Grade II*
Current use Theatre
Capacity   471

The modern setting of the building for long provided depressing evidence that it had been only grudgingly excluded

from the massive clearances which preceded the Stratford town centre developments, but it has now become an object of civic pride and the pivot for the creation of a Stratford cultural oasis. In metropolitan terms it is a rare and precious survival and it is an excellent working theatre.

The Royal is the only London suburban theatre with a complete pre-cantilever (hence iron-columned) auditorium. Designed by J.G. Buckle, the author of *Theatre Construction and Maintenance* published in 1888, Stratford Theatre Royal seems to be his only surviving work. Although designed as a suburban theatre, with a distinctly provincial character, it achieved national significance as the home of 'Theatre Workshop' from 1953 and was the birthplace of many Littlewood/Workshop 'originals'. It maintains to the present time its reputation of being a theatre which serves the people of the neighbourhood but does work of national significance.

The external architectural treatment is offhand in the extreme, with an oriel (perhaps a touch of Matcham?) as one of the few notes of relief on an otherwise plain brick facade.

The auditorium, by contrast, is pleasing and efficient, with good sighting from all parts of the house. Shallow in depth. Two balconies supported on cast-iron columns; delicate plaster ornament to balcony fronts and ceiling. Box fronts have arched heads with pendant centres. Enriched architrave to proscenium with scrolly cartouche and festooned frieze over.

The plan of the building reflects the 'paste on' manner in which the site was assembled and additions were made. The main vestibule extends along one side of the auditorium and leads to a long bar projecting to the right, alongside the stage - a mystifying but happy arrangement, which means that one's first view of the auditorium is across its width.

The stage provides further evidence of the development of the theatre to its present form. It has been extended backwards in such a way that it has the character of two rooms of different dimensions and with their grids at different levels, an odd arrangement which designers have learned to exploit.

A major improvement project, including a new theatre of contrasting character alongside as part of a wider development, was in progress in 1999/2000. *JE*

Streatham Hill ★★

Streatham Hill
Lambeth
Original architect
   1929 W.G.R. Sprague and W.H.
         Barton
Later works
   1950 Unknown: reconstructed after
         bomb damage
Listed   Grade II
Current use Bingo
Capacity   originally c.3000

The last theatre designed by Sprague, possibly his largest and, at the time, one of the largest and best-equipped in London, outside the West End. The theatre has an imposing facade from Streatham Hill in faience by Doulton. It is in three bays, the centre with five main double entrance doors, above which a shallow promenade balcony with cast-iron balustrade behind a colonnade of four Doric columns in antis which rise majestically to attic level, with the legend STREATHAM HILL THEATRE above. The outer bays: each has rows of four windows at each level and a pedimental gable containing a wreath.

The foyer is spacious, with tall gilded Ionic columns and arches, terrazzo floor and two round kiosks each side of the grand central stairway. This sweeps up to dress circle and balcony levels, parting at the centre into two flights with iron balustrading. The auditorium is lavish. There are six bow-fronted boxes in two stacks on either side. A panelled ceiling dome with a glazed centre, originally backlit, dominates the three tiers, below which there is a tier of arches, continuing over the square proscenium. Coupled, attenuated Ionic columns divide the side walls and the boxes. The foyers, auditorium and public areas were described as being 'in the Adam manner' but are quite eclectic, with friezes of sphinxes, angels and garlands in abundance. The bar at first-floor level is mahogany and has murals of scenes of old London.

For many years the theatre was run by Clavering, in conjunction with the Golders Green Hippodrome, until it received a direct hit in 1944. In 1950, the theatre was reconstructed on the original designs. It was slightly modified for bingo in 1962, but remains almost in original state, with the tip-up theatre seats remaining in situ in the two circles. It is believed that the original stage machinery is in situ. It is now in private ownership as a bingo club. *SM*

Tooting Granada ★★★

58 Mitcham Road
Wandsworth
Other names
  Granada Theatre
  Granada Bingo
  Gala Bingo
Original architect
  1931 **Cecil Masey and Reginald Uren**
         with Theodore Komisarjevsky
Later works
  1991 **Unknown: restored; new**
         canopy and entrance doors
Listed   **Grade II***
Current use **Bingo**
Capacity   **originally 3750**

The Granada, Tooting, was built in 1931 by Sidney Bernstein (his third Granada). The architect Cecil Masey designed a square-towered street facade in Italianate style, covered in faience, with four slim columns topped by the neon Granada sign. A vertical fin sign repeated the name and the whole frontage could be floodlit from the long, wide canopy.

The interior design was entrusted to Komisarjevsky, who created an interior in Venetian Gothic style that has been described as his masterpiece. The outer foyer contains two payboxes set into richly decorated mirrored walls. Through a further set of doors the grand foyer is designed as a huge Medieval Baronial hall with carved panelling and a heavily beamed ceiling. A stone staircase leads to a minstrels' gallery which formed the entrance to the tearoom above the outer foyer. The inner stalls foyer, set with large mirrors framed by marble columns in Italian Renaissance style, has a wide curved twin staircase leading to the balcony lobby. There is a great hall of mirrors, 45.7m (150ft) long, lined with 70 cusped arches backed with mirrors and decorative light fittings. Oak and gilded-stone tables and chairs by Komisarjevsky, some of which can still be seen, adorned all the waiting areas.

The auditorium is a brilliant essay in eclectic style, based on Venetian Gothic but drawing architectural inspiration and detailed treatment from all parts of Europe. The beautifully coffered ceiling above the balcony is lit by chandeliers. Side walls, rich in detail with painted figure murals by Vladimir Polunin and Leslie Le Bond are crowned by an open Gothic framework of arches lit from behind (some of this lighting needs restoration). The ceiling above the front stalls is part coffered, part painted sky and the proscenium arch is a series of cusped Gothic pendants. The front stalls

exits are surmounted by giant Gothic arches and the side proscenium walls are filled with Gothic stained-glass windows, which, like the proscenium, are back-lit. The under-balcony ceiling is richly detailed and lit by small ornate chandeliers. The original colour scheme was polychromatic with a deep tone of gold.

The stage was fully equipped for variety shows which continued to be part of the programme for many years. The large orchestra pit also housed a Wurlitzer organ. Dressing-room accommodation remains, on two levels.

The building survives under sympathetic ownership, with minor modifications for bingo. These include the covering of the orchestra pit, though the organ is played regularly. *SM*

Tottenham Palace ★★

Tottenham High Road North
Haringey
Other names
  Mecca Bingo
  Jasmine Bingo
Original architect
  1908 **Wylson and Long**
Later works
  1926 **Unknown: converted to cinema**
  1969 **Unknown: converted to bingo**
Listed   **Grade II**
Current use **Dark**
Capacity   **c.1500**

A large, relatively late variety theatre (but perhaps never the capacity of 3000, including standing, quoted in the *Stage Year Book* 1912). Restrained symmetrical entrance facade in red brick and stone; a well-considered composition with Ionic pilasters and pediments. The Ionic theme is carried consistently through the foyer and auditorium.

Auditorium with two balconies; good plaster decoration; impressive three-bay

loggia on either side at dress-circle level, containing two boxes, the centre bay with a broken segmental pediment, the boxes now looking rather naked without their drapes. Gilded figures of Muses in niches flanking the proscenium. The building has been cared for and the conversion to bingo (principally the introduction of a stepped-level floor in the stalls) was achieved with no significant architectural loss. In 1997, conversion to a church was proposed.

Now the only complete example in London of a theatre by the architects who rebuilt the Oxford Music Hall in 1893 (demolished), built the Bath Palace of Varieties 1895, reconstructed the Blackpool Winter Gardens auditorium 1897, designed the first Brixton Empress of 1898 (demolished) and reconstructed the interior of the London Pavilion 1900 (gutted). One of the few surviving big suburban variety palaces (cf Hackney Empire) and, given a fair wind, a perfectly recoverable theatre. *JE*

Troxy ★

Commercial Road
Tower Hamlets
Other names
  1963 **The London Opera Centre**
  1992 **Top Rank Bingo**
Original architect
  1933 **George Coles (actual design**
         by Arthur Roberts)
Later works
  1954 **Unknown: Cinemascope**
         installed
  1963 **George Coles and Company:**
         reopened as the London Opera
         Centre; stage transformed to
         replicate that of Covent
         Garden, removing orchestra
         pit; rear stalls converted to
         scenery painting studio; lecture
         theatre erected in rear circle

Tottenham Palace

1992 Metcalfe Roundhill Design:
       converted to bingo
Listed   **Grade II**
Current use **Bingo**
Capacity (was) 3250

Erected on the site of a former brewery, The Troxy (opened September 1933) was one of the largest and most palatial cinemas in the area, seating 3250. The dignified facade of faience, with terracotta ornament at roof level, offered a good frontage to the main road. Over the wide central entrance were three large windows in a stone-faced surround. The main vestibule was exceptionally lofty and spacious, with a marble floor in bands of red corona, campan verde and golden travertine, richly veined. The skirtings to the walls were in black marble. A gold onyx staircase with large ornamental mirrors and coved lighting led up to the stalls and balcony entrances. The auditorium featured ornamental grille-work on the side walls and three-colour cove lighting on either side of the large proscenium. A central ornamental plaque in the ceiling delivered the air-conditioning, and the balcony front contained floodlights, controlled by the stage switchboard. The stage contained four revolving stages, an orchestra pit which could be raised or lowered, and the most modern stage lighting.

The Troxy operated a policy of ciné-variety, as well as ballet, stage and big-band shows, circus and pantomime. It escaped damage in the blitz, and today remains virtually unaltered. Surviving as a cinema until 1960 the decline of local residential population, and the popularity of television, forced closure. It was given a new lease of life in 1963 when it reopened as the London Opera Centre, a training school for Opera singers. The interior was altered to provide a full-size replica of Covent Garden's stage, the rear stalls were converted to a scenery painting studio, and a lecture theatre was erected in the rear circle, with a rehearsal room, and several other studios. There remained 500 seats in the circle for occasional performances. In 1992, the Royal Opera House relinquished the option on their lease, and Rank refurbished the interior, removing the 1963 alterations, to reopen as Top Rank Bingo, reinstating the huge auditorium. The interior colours are an astonishing array of pinks, mauves, blues, grey and white, and the proscenium is outlined in matching neon. Live artists have since appeared, but whether 'staged' is unclear. *SM*

Twentieth Century Theatre

Twentieth Century
291 Westbourne Grove, Notting Hill
Kensington and Chelsea
Other names
    1863 Victoria Hall
    1866 Bijou Theatre
       Century Theatre
       Rudolf Steiner Hall
    1937 Twentieth Century Theatre
       Twentieth Century Playhouse
Original architect
    1863 Unknown
Later works **1893 Unknown: altered**
Listed   **Grade II**
Current use **Arts and antiques showroom**
Capacity (was) c.300

A rare survival of its date and kind in London, originally with frontages to Westbourne Grove (formerly, at this point, Archer Street) and Portobello Road, backing onto Stanley Gardens Mews.

A flat-floored multi-purpose room with a long, if patchy, record of theatre use, embedded in a larger mid-Victorian residential and shop development. It is at first-floor level, approached by a wide staircase. Between 1911 and 1918 it was being used for cinema shows but remained licensed for stage plays, music and dancing. From 1925 it was occupied by the Lena Ashwell Players and from 1937 by the Rudolf Steiner Association, who changed the name to Twentieth Century Theatre.

Pedimented entrance in a stucco-fronted terrace. Foyers, etc., altered. Auditorium a rectangular room with pilastered walls and brackets supporting ribs to tunnel-vaulted ceiling with roof light. Balcony at end. Good plasterwork. Basket-arched proscenium flanked by fluted Corinthian pilasters. It appears to have real theatre potential, but a return to such use would depend on ensuring that rear access is available and that it is

not deprived of space for backstage improvements.

It is at present a venue for antique and art exhibitions and is available for hire for private receptions. The current owners are seeking a theatre licence and hope to have a limited return to live use. *JE*

Vaudeville ★
Strand
City of Westminster
Original architect
    1870 C.J. Phipps
Later works
    1887 C.J. Phipps: altered
    1891 C.J. Phipps: front rebuilt; auditorium altered
    1897 Unknown: pedimented canopy added to Strand front
    1926 Robert Atkinson: substantially, but not completely, rebuilt; extended at rear
    1927 Unknown: Strand canopy replaced by a new one
Listed   **Grade II**
Current use **Theatre**
Capacity **690**

The Vaudeville, like many of London's earlier West End theatres, suffers from a constricted site which allows for little in the way of improvements unless additional property is acquired (a move which may be highly unlikely at today's West End land prices). In 1882, Captain Shaw estimated that the safe capacity was 792, at a time when the management was claiming nearly double that. The modern figure of 690, in a slightly

Vaudeville

larger auditorium, gives some indication of the trend over the last 100 years for theatres to become more comfortably (and safely) seated.

The second front supplied by Phipps in 1891, as an alteration to his 1870 theatre, remains with little obvious change, apart from the canopy, which dates from shortly after Robert Atkinson's 1926 reconstruction. This Strand facade is in stone, four storeys in height, five windows wide, with a balustraded front to an arcaded first-floor loggia (now glazed) and rather domestic-looking windows with thin Italianate detail above. Parapet originally had central panelled blocking crowned by pediment. Atkinson carried out major alterations behind; he gave the rear elevation to Maiden Lane an elegant facade in an Adamesque manner, built in yellowbrick and stone with a fan lunette, all contained under a brick arch.

The auditorium is rectangular, two balconies with neo-Adam ornament. The rear stalls have some cut-off, as a reminder of the existence of a benched pit in Phipps's theatre. Although largely Atkinson's work (1926), the cove and ceiling date from Phipps's 1891 building.

Some wooden machinery still existed in 1972 above and below stage, including a thunder run stored on OP fly floor.

For a full account of building history of the site see *Survey of London*, vol. XXXVI pp 243–5. *JE*

Victoria Palace ★★★
Victoria Street
City of Westminster
Original architect
   1911   **Frank Matcham**
Later works
   1993   **Christopher Stedman: altered internally and extended**
   2000   **Christopher Stedman: further additions to front of house**
Listed   **Grade II**
Current use **Theatre**
Capacity **1517**

From 1892, when the Royal English Opera House reopened as the Palace Theatre of Varieties (see Palace), companies headed by Augustus Harris (Palace), Edward Moss (London Hippodrome, 1900), Oswald Stoll (London Coliseum, 1904) and Walter Gibbons (London Palladium, 1910) busied themselves ratcheting up the competition for new family audiences to fill their new and palatial West End music halls. Alfred Butt joined the fray in 1911 by acquiring and demolishing the old

Victoria Palace (London Metropolitan Archives)

Royal Standard Music Hall in Pimlico (a hall licensed since at least 1848) and employing Frank Matcham to build the Victoria Palace on the same site. It has been used for variety and musical productions for practically all of its life since then (briefly as a playhouse, 1934–35).

A distinctive building with a main entrance block faced with white patent stone. Symmetrical classical facade; the lower three storeys channelled with a modern canopy over the entrances and a central giant arch; above this is an open loggia with Ionic columns, flanked by festooned oval windows. The elevation is crowned by an entablature with a central pediment behind which rises a baroque tower with pedestalled Ionic columns and a dome, originally crowned by a figure of Pavlova.

The auditorium is splendid. Two balconies with heavily enriched cartouches and consoles and two tiers of three boxes on either side (the lower tier stepped). Architraved proscenium. Domed ceiling. The manner in which the junction is formed between the upper-box front and the top balcony demonstrates that any architectural problem can be solved with Matcham's confidence and a riot of fibrous plaster. Fine foyers. *JE*

Westminster
Palace Street
City of Westminster
Other names
   St James's Picture Theatre
Original architect
   1923   **J. Stanley Beard: remodelled as theatre**
Later works
   1931   **Arnold Dunbar-Smith**
   1966   **John and Sylvia Reid: remodelled internally and externally**
   1972   **Unknown: two additional floors erected over auditorium**

Current use **Occasional theatre**
Capacity   **585 (main house)**

A theatre with an extraordinary evolutionary history. There was a chapel of 1766 (the Charlotte Chapel) on the site, which fell into disuse in 1921 and was refronted and altered to open in 1924 as a cinema. Major alterations were made in 1931 before reopening as a theatre. Further remodellings and additions took place in 1966 and 1972. Since 1960 it has been controlled by Moral Rearmament and run as a theatre until it fell dark in 1990, after which the owners sought a purchaser. Its future has seemed uncertain since then.

The Westminster has always seemed well off the edge of West End Theatreland, but there is no reason why a fringe theatre should not succeed in this position, particularly given the complex of rooms surrounding it, including a second 105-seat flat-floored theatre and separable (and lettable) office or studio space.

The internal architectural treatment is not memorable. The theatre stands at an interesting kink in Palace Street, comfortably placed next door to a pub. The refronting with simple geometrical forms and with what looks a grey rock face, no longer seems quite as fashionable as it once did, but what has been done can be undone. Next time it may be made to look more like a theatre. *JE*

Westminster School
Dean's Yard
City of Westminster
Listed   **Grade I**
Current use **School**

Westminster School does not have a permanent theatre, but its theatrical tradition, continuous from at least the mid-C16, is rare in European terms and claims attention in this book. The Abbey and its dependencies held dramatic presentations from at least 1413. Latin plays were introduced at the school by Alexander Nowell between 1543 and 1555 and became an annual event from 1560. English plays were also performed and Nowell's successor, Nicholas Udall, was the author of what is generally regarded as the first true English Comedy, *Ralph Roister Doister*, written while he was headmaster at Eton.

From 1722 the Latin play was performed in 'College', then the single-floor dormitory building designed by Lord Burlington. It was elaborately adapted for each performance in a manner remi-

niscent of C17 Court masque fit-ups, a procedure which continued unaltered until 1938. The Burlington building was bombed in 1941 and rebuilt in 1949 with an inserted floor, ending its theatrical use. The Latin play was, however, revived in 1954 in outdoor performance, with the projecting wings of Ashburnham House (part of the School) serving as framing 'mansions'. It has since been discontinued.

The use until recent times on Westminster School's fit-up stages of the scenic device of 'Howses', represented an extraordinary survival of pre-Renaissance stage practice, which appears to have had no modern parallel. Mansions, houses or towers, were three-dimensional constructions of painted canvas and wood, set on either side of the stage. They were a hangover from mediaeval drama in the open air, in which the action and the audience moved from one mansion to another, each representing a particular location in the narrative. The first documentary references to 'towers' and 'painting as much canvasse as covered an house' occur in Westminster accounts in 1565-69. By the end of the C17, practically all indoor theatres had adopted scenic flat settings, but at Westminster it would appear that the houses were regularly renewed until, in the mid-C19, they appeared as modern (i.e. typical early Victorian) two-storey house fronts with practical doors and windows.

At least one of these houses survived the Blitz, to be described by Richard Southern in 1949, but it had disappeared a few years later. Once again, probably in the later 1950s, replacements were made, but this time as sim-

ple, single-storey structures with tented roofs. They seem to have been discarded finally in the 1970s.

The School can, however, still claim two fine pieces of old scenery which must be regarded as extremely rare in a British context. They are the backdrops designed by C.R. Cockerell, 'at once the most fastidious and least pedantic of neo-classical architects' (H.M. Colvin). They were painted by Frederick Fenton of Sadlers Wells in 1858, to replace an earlier backdrop depicting Covent Garden. Expertly conserved and transferred from rollers to stretchers, they now hang in the School hall. One is an idealised view of Athens, the other a representation of an unidentified classical theatre. *See* Abercrave Adelina Patti Theatre and London Normansfield Theatre for other scenic rarities. *JE*

Whitehall ★★
Whitehall
City of Westminster
Original architect
    1930   Edward A. Stone
Later works
    1955   Unknown: restored
Listed   **Grade II**
Current use **Theatre (occasional other uses)**
Capacity   **648**

The Whitehall opened in the peak year, 1930, of the West End's little inter-war boom in theatre building. Opening as a playhouse it became, from 1942, a home for the revues of Phyllis Dixey, the stripper. A series of memorable farces followed, from 1945 to 1969. In 1971 Paul Raymond took over, producing a nude musical. In the later 1970s he turned it

Whitehall (Ian Grundy)

into a 'Theatre of War' (actually a tourist-trap war museum), a use which was unauthorised, and which led to enforcement action by Westminster City Council, followed by an important public inquiry in which Westminster were supported by the newly-formed Theatres Trust and the Save London's Theatres Campaign. The decision, which went against Raymond, set a crucial precedent in the defence of theatre use in London's West End (later reinforced by the strengthening of the Use Classes Order).

The Maybox Group, in which Ian Albery was the guiding spirit, acquired the Whitehall from Raymond, set about restoring it from its gloomily 'painted-out' state and reopened it as a live theatre. Its position on the very edge of Theatreland, a little too close to the stiffness and pomp of Government offices, has given the Whitehall a patchy subsequent career and exposed it to regular pressures for relaxation of strict theatre use, but it has nevertheless continued to have successes. Its unusual achitectural character should be 'sold' as one of its attractions.

Externally, the Whitehall, which has Portland stone public elevations, front and back, set a style which was copied elsewhere, occasionally with a sort of 'chapter and verse' homage (as at Bournemouth Playhouse). The plain geometric Whitehall facade was praised by modernists and, notably, by Professor C.H. Riley, as 'so clean and simple . . . that it makes the Government offices, banks and public houses . . . look as if they need a shave'.

Early programmes (perhaps using the architect's words) described it as 'modern without being outré . . . the 'Boulevarde' theatre of one's dreams.' The interior, 'a dream in black and silver', was the work of Edward Stone's collaborators on other theatres, Marc Henri and Laverdet (see, e.g. the Prince Edward). The single-balconied auditorium relied on crisp geometry, sharp Art Deco forms and concealed lighting for its dramatic effect. Black, tinted silver, green and rose were used in a manner reminiscent of Ionides's Savoy of the previous year but, in this small space, so highly concentrated that the few multicoloured panels of flat decoration have a quite remarkable impact.

The thoughtful restorations ordered by Albery in 1985 were more faithful than it was reasonable to expect for a then unlisted building. The blotted-out colours and decorative motifs were care-

Wilton's Music Hall (London Metropolitan Archives)

fully copied from a few remaining untouched fragments. Alterations to front of house were made using the established architectural vocabulary. The long-lost glass-beaded house tabs, with Art Deco patterns illuminated by the (also lost) concealed lights in the proscenium cove have not been restored, but an owner following the example of 1985 might, perhaps, be persuaded to make this further contribution to the enrichment of this fine theatre.

The auditorium is as intimate and pleasing as any architect succeeded in designing in the uncertain 1930s (Stone did not actually train as an architect) and it is remarkable that it remained without the protection of listing until 1997.

The stage is extremely constricted in both wing space and depth and, with a road at front and back, no improvement is to be looked for. This defect has not prevented skilful designers from creating space on its stage. *JE*

Wilton's Music Hall ★★★
Grace's Alley, Wellclose Square
Tower Hamlets
Other names
Prince of Denmark Public House
Mahogany Bar (by c.1839)
Albion Saloon (by 1843)
1874   **Frederick's Royal Palace of**
         Varieties
1888   **Beulah Gospel Mission**
         London Wesleyan Mission
         Old Mahogany Bar Mission
Original architect
1859   **Jacob Maggs**

Later works
1878   Probably J. Buckley Wilson of
         Wilson, Willcox and Wilson of
         Swansea: reconstructed after
         fire, introduction of raked
         auditorium floor
1888   Unknown: converted to
         mission hall
1979-89 Peter Newson: a number of
         major repairs including the
         strengthening of the north
         wall
Listed   **Grade II***
Current use **Theatre**
Capacity   **c.400**

This is the most important surviving early music hall to be seen anywhere and (although altered) is now the only representative of the 'new generation' giant pub halls of 1850s London, modelled on the success of the second Canterbury Hall (1854), Evan's New (Supper Room) Music Hall (1856) and Weston's (1857), all long demolished. It is of outstanding architectural and archaeological significance.

The Prince of Denmark tavern was reputedly the first in London to have mahogany counters and fittings, hence its alternative name, which stuck to it for well over a century, of Old Mahogany Bar. A concert room existed before 1843, as a purpose-built room behind the pub, at right angles to the axis of the present hall. Matthew Eltham obtained a licence for it as the Albion Saloon in 1845, but it soon reverted to proto-music hall form. John Wilton rebuilt it as his first music hall in 1853. He then acquired adjoining properties (the pub front still exhibits the original party lines and varying levels) in order to obtain the rear land, over which he built a vastly enlarged grand music hall, opening in 1859 (inscribed foundation stone still present between pub and hall). The hall was very seriously damaged and unroofed by fire in 1877. Engravings of the first hall show that the rebuilding was on closely similar lines to the original building, but with a proscenium stage in place of the former apsidal platform and a gently raked floor instead of the flat supper-room floor.

Typically of its kind and period, the hall was originally completely landlocked by the surrounding property and it therefore had no external elevations apart from that of its parent pub, through which it must still be entered. The face brickwork, where it is visible, shows signs of hurried execution and the staircase in the entrance lobby (to take one obvious element) is of extraordinary makeshift construction. The hall, nevertheless, fully merits the contemporary epithet, 'handsome'.

Entered through the paved lobby, it is an astonishing survival. A big, rectangular room with an apse at the back and a high stage. Single balcony on three sides with bombé carton pierre front, supported on unusual helical-twist ('barley sugar') cast-iron columns, whose bases are progressively overtaken by the rake of the floor. Side walls with paired arched recesses above the balcony, the arches supported on alternating piers and ornamental brackets. Elliptical vaulted ceiling with ornamental fretted ribs, originally with a lantern skylight and gas chandeliers. The former presence of a hot sunburner flue has left charring on some of the roof timbers.

Wilton's became a mission hall in 1888 and spent a longer life in this form than it had as a music hall. By 1963 it was a rag-sorting depot and warehouse. It was acquired by the Greater London Council in 1966 and subsequently transferred to a Trust. Broomhill Opera have a long lease and the building was returned to active theatre life in 1999.

In its post-fire 1878 state, it still exhibits the essential attributes of a first-generation classic grand music hall, with space for supper tables, benched area and encircling promenade. A bar previously opened from the pub into the hall at stage left. An unelaborate but profoundly evocative room.   JE

Wimbledon Theatre

Wimbledon Theatre ★★

Wimbledon Broadway
Merton
Original architect
   1910 Cecil Masey and Roy Young
Later works
   1968 Unknown: partially refurbished and redecorated
   1991 Borough architect: altered internally, including re-tiering gallery; shopfronts altered; statue over dome reinstated
   1992 RHWL: interior redecorated
   1998 Christodolou Marshall (CMA): major improvements
Listed   Grade II
Current use Theatre
Capacity 1670

The Masey and Young theatre may possibly have been developed from a 1908 design by Frank H. Jones. On a prominent corner site and a real landmark in Wimbledon. Brick and stone facade, the outer bays differently treated but both with open pediments over lunettes. Recessed concave corner containing a projecting entrance, above which an octagonal Baroque tower with dome and prominent lantern topped by a globe and winged figure (the figure itself reinstated in early 1992 after wartime loss).

Good entrance foyer with Corinthian columns. The impressive and well-decorated three-balconied auditorium with iron balustraded fronts is of a type most unusual in Britain (cf in London only the Playhouse) but common in Spain and Portugal. Two tiers of bow-fronted boxes framed by giant marble Corinthian columns supporting entablature blocks and Baroque segmental broken pediments. Segmental proscenium arch set in a deep recess spanned by an arched sounding board. Boldly modelled reclining figures in the spandrel panels over. Shallow, semi-domed ceiling with painted allegorical panels.

Ill-advised alterations to the gallery tiering in 1991 resulted in massively over-prominent guard rails and terrible sight lines. These errors were corrected in the 1998 works which also involved the complete rebuilding of the dressing-room block, major improvements to the stage, installation of a orchestra lift and other improvements.

There is a 115-seat arena studio adjoining the main house.   JE/KW

Windmill

17–19 Great Windmill Street
City of Westminster
Other names
  c.1909 Palais de Luxe
  1974 Raymond Revue Bar
  1984 La Vie en Rose
  1986 Paramount City
Later works
  1931 F. Edward Jones: converted to theatre
  1964 Anthony Wylson and Murray Waterston: converted to cinema and casino
Current use Table dancing club

Capacity   (was) 320 (following 1964 conversion)

The theatre was a conversion of an Edwardian cinema, the Palais de Luxe, dating from c.1909. The exterior is five storeys high, with cornice bands at each storey. Domed twin turrets were added when it was converted to a theatre in 1931, supposedly to suggest windmill towers, perhaps an architectural allusion to Parisian prototypes.

The theatre was tiny, the capacity having been reduced to allow for enlargement of the stage. Quite plain, single-tier interior. Famous as a comedy and striptease house, it was the training ground for three decades of variety artists and comedians, for the most part under the direction of the legendary Sheila Van Damm. During the Second World War it was one of very few theatres to remain open without interruption (apart from the few days' closure forced by Government direction).

In 1976, it became a theatre restaurant, under Paul Raymond, and in 1986, a live entertainment and recording studio. It is currently in use as a lap-dancing club.   *SM/JE*

Woolwich Granada (Ian Grundy)

Wood Green Empire

Wood Green High Road
Haringey
Original architect
    1912   Frank Matcham
Current use **Bank and shop on ground
        floor**

The theatre was built for Oswald Stoll in 1912. For a period in the 1950s and 1960s it was leased to the BBC for use for variety shows. Largely demolished in 1970, but the redevelopment left the entrance block together with three-storey shop terraces on either side, which seem to have been designed to form a uniform composition with the theatre.

The remaining front consists of three bays, the centre with a tall hipped roof and dormer, now lacking its crowning turret and cupola. The three-storey outer wings, in brick with stone dressings, are each crowned by a stubby tower with ogee roof and finial. Still a welcome landmark in the street, it is a pity that the ground-floor shopfronts blur the effect. A little more thought in their design might have maintained the architectural emphasis.   *JE*

Wood Green
Gaumont Palace ★★

Wood Green High Street
Haringey
Other names
    c.1937   Gaumont
    1962   Odeon
        Top Rank Bingo
Original architect
    1934   W.E. Trent and Ernest F. Tully
Later works
    1973   Unknown: two cinemas
        formed under balcony
    1984   Unknown: returned to original
        volume for bingo
Listed   **Grade II**
Current use **Disused**
Capacity   originally c.2160

Narrow front to High Street, a rectangular four-storey facade standing above the adjoining three-storey terraces; thin brick facings on either side of a stone or artificial stone-faced centre with geometric ornament embracing triplet windows through first and second-floor levels. The name 'Gaumont Palace' in relief letters (reinstated 1993) stands in for a crowning cornice. Vestigial entrance canopy.

The auditorium lies behind the shops, parallel to the High Street. It is plainly faced with fletton bricks and has a prominent fly tower with get-in which, even after surrounding redevelopment, is still reasonably accessible.

The interior is a most impressive survival, an almost unspoilt example of its kind and time, in an unusual manner, much more dependent on pure geometry than most of the lavishly decorated 'supers'. Allen Eyles calls it 'a spectacular achievement' and suggests that the auditorium is partly indebted to the 1926-7 Titania Palast, Berlin. It is a big, rectangular room with the side walls decorated with thin parallel bands interrupted by niches and flowing into the proscenium wall. The proscenium arch (now partly concealed) is semi-circular with a nodding ante-proscenium, echoed by nodding arches to the deep, grilled niches on either side.

The ceiling has a stepped, geometrically ornamented and pierced cornice and a long centre with domelets for light fittings.

Like the Tottenham Palace, the Gaumont Palace is well sited and tragically wasted.

Woolwich Granada ★★★

Powis Street
Greenwich
Original architect
    1937   Cecil Masey, and Slater and
        Uren with Theodore
        Komisarjevsky
Listed   **Grade II**
Current use **Bingo**
Capacity   originally c.3000

The exterior, by Cecil Masey and Reginald Uren, is of brick, dramatically modern, with large streamlined windows in Dudok style above which is an

Wyndham's (Ian Grundy)

Wyndham's ★★★

Charing Cross Road
City of Westminster
Original architect
   1899   W.G.R. Sprague
Listed   **Grade II***
Current use **Theatre**
Capacity   **759**

Built on Salisbury Estate lands, which until Charles Wyndham's approach, had firmly resisted theatre building. Backs on to the later Albery Theatre. Principal elevation, stone in free classical style with (as commonly with Sprague) a distinctly French flavour. Three major bays; the wide centre bay with oeil-de-boeuf windows at the first floor and arched balconied windows with shell tympana at the second floor, set between pilasters carrying a rich pediment contained in a sheer attic with crowning balustrade; the outer bays narrower, subdivided by piers carrying sculptured terms at attic level.

The auditorium is one of Sprague's most delightful and best-preserved inventions. Extravagantly decorated in Louis XVI style. Two curving cantilever balconies with prettily painted panels. The gallery is the rearward extension of the upper tier. Boxes with bowed fronts in three storeys (the lowest at dress-circle level) paired, with semi-circular arches at the two upper levels and set between pilasters carried on massive brackets. The proscenium was designed as a complete picture frame of the kind originated by Squire Bancroft at the Haymarket nearly 20 years earlier. It has an elegantly enriched architrave, above which is a composition of allegorical winged figures in the round, carrying festoons and supporting framed portraits. The elaborate festooned house curtain was replaced in the late 1960s by the Alberys, the last in the long family succession at this theatre, with a new curtain which faithfully reproduced the original design, a rare and costly gesture. Magnificent circular ceiling painted in the manner of Boucher, restored with other paintings about the same time. The saloon and public foyers, etc., are in complementary style.

The site is contained by Charing Cross Road and three pedestrian ways, so that (as with many West End theatres of this period) improvements can be attempted only within the containing walls. There is now a bridge link to the Albery Theatre at rear. Despite the tight planning, this has to be regarded as one of London's finest theatres.   *JE*

attic which carried the name GRANADA in neon. Thin brick tower with open look-out top.

The interior, like that of the Tooting Granada, is the work of Komisarjevsky and, although smaller, is spectacular. From the foyer a handsome double staircase with ornamental wrought-iron balustrade leads to the upper foyer, a 'hall of mirrors' with the same Moorish cloister appearance of the Walthamstow Granada. The auditorium is a Venetian Gothic fantasy, reminiscent of Tooting, with high-arched panels and pilasters, elaborate ceiling and chandeliers;

proscenium with cusped pendants above and panelled decoration. There is a theatrical stage, fly tower and orchestra pit, though these areas, together with parts of the auditorium, have been modified for bingo.

Komisarjevsky's brilliant heraldic colours have been dulled by nicotine deposits, but this magnificent auditorium would, if restored, be one of the most impressive interiors of its time in south-east London.   *SM*

LONG EATON
Derbyshire

St James Theatre
Derby Road
Other names
   1910   Vint's Picturedrome
   1916   Coliseum
   1923   Scala
Original architect
   1907   C.D. Ross
Later works
   1935   Dawson H. Hardwick
           (Nottingham): reconstructed
           after fire
Current use Derelict
Capacity c.1500

Externally the building has a long narrow appearance with a slightly raised fly tower at one end. This minor ciné-variety house was substantially rebuilt after a fire in 1934. Because additional land is available to the rear of the building, it would be possible to initiate changes which would make this a facility of greater significance. It remains disused, although there is evidence that the roof has recently been repaired.   *TB*

LOUGHBOROUGH
Leicestershire

Sparrow Hill Theatre
Sparrow Hill
Original architect
   1823   Unknown
Later works
   1855   Unknown: converted to church
   1856   Unknown: converted to lecture
           hall/music salon
Current use Shop

Important as a relic of an early theatre of which only the brick shell is (largely) original, together with certain features in the cellar. The building presents a gabled front to the street. The two first-floor windows, however, are now bricked up and below there is a conventional shopfront with a central entrance in place of the original two arched doorways. There is a central coat of arms above the windows. The fretted bargeboards would seem to be of mid-C19 date. Internally, there are no surviving traces of a theatre connection although beneath the ground floor(inserted, apparently, in 1855), there are many indications of the original pit and stage layout. These suggest, in the opinion of Richard Leacroft, a marked similarity with the theatre at Richmond, Yorkshire.
TB/JL

LOWESTOFT
Suffolk

Hollywood Cinema
41 London Road South
Other names
   1926   New Playhouse
   1927   Playhouse Theatre
   1948   New Playhouse Theatre
   1953   Arcadia Theatre
   1960   Theatre Royal
   1962   Royal Casino
Original architect
   1926   Unknown
Later works
   1948   Unknown: rebuilt following
           fire
   1962   Unknown: converted to night-
           club
   1989   Unknown: converted to
           cinema
Current use Triple cinema
Capacity c.700

Built on or near the site of the Bridge Hall Pavilion, originally as a theatre. Gutted by fire in 1946, it was rebuilt and enlarged, with a fly tower added. It was then used as a repertory theatre but later became a nightclub and bingo house. It is now a three-screen cinema.
   The frontage is utilitarian. Screen One was originally the stalls. The safety curtain and the flies remain. The original wooden floor of the stage is still in place but the stage now has a false ceiling. The proscenium arch is rectangular. Some of the original ceiling mouldings can be seen.   *KW*

Marina
London Road North
Other names
   1878   Rink Theatre
   1963–75   ABC Cinema
Original architect
   1878   R.F. Brett
Later works
   1901   E. Runtz & Co: rebuilt as a
           theatre
   1930   Unknown: converted to
           cinema
   1988   Borough Architect: recon-
           structed as theatre
Current use Theatre
Capacity 781

The theatre stands on the site of an earlier (1878) building of the same name, which had, itself, started life as a roller-skating rink (the original name was the Rink Theatre). The present building is one of Runtz's few theatres still standing, but what is seen today is the result of the

1980s' works to a building which was, in essentials, a 1930s' cinema. The original cinema conversion works dealt harshly with the Runtz theatre. Further architectural damage occurred when the ABC house style was imposed on the exterior in 1963, the elegant full-width glass and cast-iron canopy being removed and the walls covered to first-floor level with blue-grey tiling. It closed finally at the end of 1984. Fierce political controversy resulted in the Council purchasing the building in time to prevent demolition and they then set about a major refurbishment. The dressing-room block was demolished and rebuilt, new toilets were built and the exhibition/crush area was formed. The exterior tiling was removed, revealing original features.
   The theatre reopened in 1988 with a programme of live one-night stands and films. The present lighting was acquired when the Sparrows' Nest Theatre was demolished. There are eight dressing rooms accommodating a total of 64. The fly tower has 12 sets of hemp rigging lines and six counterweights. The cyclorama is new.   *KW*

LYME REGIS
Dorset

Marine
Bridge Street
Original architect
   1740   Unknown
Later works
   1805   Unknown: bath house built
   1920s   Unknown: converted to
           cinema
   1930s   Unknown: converted to
           theatre
Current use Theatre
Capacity 180

The theatre is approached through what could have been the coach entrance to an old house, bearing a large notice THEATRE. At the end of a small courtyard, the facade is that of a small 1930s' cinema, white rendered brick with the merest suggestion of Art Deco. An iron staircase leads up to offices and the bar area, which is housed in the old balcony. The left wall of the theatre seems to be hewn from the cliff. The body is that of a Victorian hall, built off a former bath house. The rear has a makeshift air, with prefabricated-style dressing-room area. The auditorium roof has wooden trusses and the stage is slightly raked. The proscenium has the minimal rounded form of a 1930s' cinema.   *SM*

MALTON
North Yorkshire

Palace
Yorkersgate
Other names
   Exchange Cinema
Original architect
   n.d.   Unknown: as Corn Exchange
Later works
   1914   Unknown: converted to cine-
          ma
   1934   Bordie (Audsey, Leeds): incor-
          porating C19 building
   1987   Unknown: stalls and stage
          converted to shopping mall;
          former circle converted to
          cinema
Current use Disused
Capacity c.850 (following 1934 works)

Built in the C19 as the Corn Exchange, the building was converted to a cinema in 1914. It was subsequently rebuilt, retaining the facade, in 1934 and reopened as the Palace Theatre – a ciné-variety house. Unusual design – the entrance foyer is on the street, then comes the stage (with full fly tower on which is emblazoned PALACE THEATRE) with the auditorium at the rear. The auditorium had a wide aisle at both stalls and circle level for access – the circle therefore had a U-shape with one of the legs missing as there was not a corresponding exit on the other side. The aisle in the stalls was also used for getting scenery to the stage as the high get-in doors were at the rear stalls! This is due to poor access in Yorkersgate and good quiet access at the rear. The mystery is why was the stage placed in the middle and not, more conventionally, at the rear of the building? Substantial remains in the cinema (circle area) and above shopping mall which can be seen from the still functional exit to the front of the Palace. A new cinema entrance and foyer have been constructed at the rear – the original foyer at the front is little altered and has three fine stained-glass windows of 1934 at first-floor level.

   The mall and cinema closed mid 1998. Whilst there has apparently been some interest expressed in the site from a number of independent cinema operators, the building remains unused.   *IG*

MALVERN
Worcestershire

Malvern Theatres★
Grange Road
Other names
   1885   Assembly Rooms
   c.1929   Festival Theatre
Original architect
   1885   J. Johnson (London)
Later works
   1928   A.V. Rowe (Worcester):
          Assembly Rooms rebuilt to
          become Malvern Theatre
   1949   Unknown: extensive renova-
          tion, addition of new dressing
          rooms and workshop/scene
          dock
   1986   Unknown: formation of bar
          and lounge leading off foyer
   1998   RHWL extensive alterations
          and improvements
Listed   Grade II
Current use Theatre
Capacity   840

This is now a two-theatre venue with a cinema. The first step towards the creation of an entertainment centre for Malvern was taken in 1883 when the Promenade Pleasure Gardens were purchased by a newly formed company. A new Great Hall and Assembly Rooms with a glazed promenade were built in 1885. Alterations and additions were made over succeeding years. The most important of these were the building of a picture house in 1923 and a new hall replacing the promenade and conservatory in 1928. A three-storey building was erected in 1949 to provide dressing rooms.

   However, the £6.5 million reconstruction which took place in 1997/98 transformed the whole complex. A new fly tower was built with 36 counterweight lines, the auditorium was altered, new foyers and a new theatre space (The Forum) were created, the latter within the existing hall.

   The main auditorium now houses 840 on two levels. The old stage boxes have been removed and the slips have been extended creating a spacious feel to the auditorium. The circle and box fronts have been decorated with a geometric pattern which reflects that of the frieze. The proscenium arch is framed by ornamental moulding and the whole redecoration has followed the colour scheme of 1885. It is said that part of the 1885 ceiling remains above the newly suspended ceiling at circle level. There is also an interesting archaeological rem-

nant in the administration corridor which runs behind the circle and where the 1997 building programme exposed part of the orginal external wall – this has been retained as a feature.

   Public space is of an exceptional quality – light attractive, airy and abundant, it furnishes the theatre with an exciting modern entrance, which can also be used for performance as the wood floor is sprung.

   The Forum Theatre (formerly the Elgar Hall) is a flat-floored space, transformed into a theatre by retractable tiered seats and a balcony. The cinema is also used for conferences.   *TB/MS*

MANCHESTER

Alhambra
Old Ashton Road, Upper Openshaw
Original architect
   1908   H.A. Turner
Current use Restaurant

Opened as a music hall, but was soon operating as a picture palace. The theatre entrance was through a central pavilion originally surmounted by a square dome. Flanking shops with straight gables and mullioned windows.

   There was a fan-shaped auditorium with a balcony of fourteen rows and one box at each side with pilasters and canopy over, sharply angled away from the proscenium. The dressing-room block and fly tower have disappeared during conversion to its present use, that of a restaurant. The auditorium has been gutted, leaving only the facade.   *CB/SM*

Apollo
Ardwick Green
Other names
   1962   ABC
Original architect
   1938   Peter Cummings and Alex
          Irvine
Listed   Grade II
Current use Live music venue
Capacity 2634 (c.3500 standing)

The Apollo was formerly a cinema built in 1938 and is now a concert hall. It has a rectangular form with rounded front corners – brick in Flemish red. The faience facade is in modernistic style with rectangular centre and large rectangular tripartite openings on both floors, flanked by vertical panels with Art Deco ornament.

   Extensive modernisation in the 1970s permitted expansion of the range of stage performances, moving the Apollo into the mainstream, presenting pantomime and variety with film presentations. The interior is substantially intact save for the outer foyer which has been split to allow for separate fire escapes. The plasterwork round the columns in the former café is intact (this is now a bar).

The splendid Art Deco auditorium has a sweeping cove-lit ante-proscenium. The seats in this area are removed for concerts. The horseshoe gallery terminates in four overlapping tiers of slip boxes. From above the balcony the side walls stretch forward in a bold graceful curve, plunging in a V-shaped band to the front of the stage, enhancing the scale of the vast auditorium. Now painted in deep red, puce and gold, it is well maintained. *SM*

Grand ★

Peter Street

Other names

  Grand Theatre of Varieties
  Grand Pavilion
  1916 Palladium
  Futurist

Original architect

  1883 Unknown (for Edward Garcia)

Later works

after 1883 Unknown: converted from
       circus to theatre
  1916 Unknown: reconstructed
       internally as a cinema, with
       different balcony arrange-
       ments, reducing auditorium
  1924 Unknown: modified for use as
       a church; foyer areas/back of
       house adapted for business
       use; balcony areas divided
  1970s Unknown: new facade
  2000 Design LSM: converted to
       restaurant

Current use Restaurant

Capacity c.900 (following 1924 conver-
       sion)

Recently converted for restaurant use, the remains of the Grand Theatre lie behind a modern facade in Peter Street. Built by Edward Garcia and opened in 1883, the theatre is said to have been hastily constructed. It underwent various improvements and some restructuring under several owners, seemingly the least successful of Manchester's variety theatres before closing as a theatre in 1916. It was then remodelled as a cinema with new balconies, the size of the auditorium being reduced. Known as the Palladium and then the Futurist, the cinema seated c.900 and closed in 1924, when it was acquired by the Fourth

Church of Christ Scientist. The front became a car showroom, with alterations to the facade. In the 1970s the facade was found to be unsafe and was replaced by the present brick frontage.

Despite the alterations, it is still possible to see aspects of the cinema conversion of 1916 and a few from the theatre, including the open-lattice balcony fronts and part of the proscenium. *SM*

Hulme Hippodrome ★★★

Preston Street, Hulme

Other names

  1901 Grand Junction Theatre and
       Floral Hall
  Also known as Second Manchester
       Repertory Theatre

Original architect

  1901 J.J. Alley

Later works

  1950 Unknown: refurbished and
       redecorated; gallery reopened
  1962 Unknown: converted for casi-
       no/bingo
  1987 Keith Davidson and Partners:
       foyer divided horizontally

Listed Grade II

Current use Disused

Capacity c.2000

A splendid music hall, built in 1901, which has survived intact, built alongside the Hulme Playhouse (1902) by the same architect; the two were connected by an arcade which was flanked by the Broadhead Circuit offices. In 1950, together with the Playhouse, it was purchased by the James Brennan circuit and extensively renovated and redecorated throughout.

The sequence of changes of name of the two adjoining theatres can cause

confusion. This building opened as the Grand Junction Theatre and Floral Hall, originally seating 3000 and concentrating on melodrama, whilst the adjacent building, itself originally called the Hulme Hippodrome, later the Playhouse, presented music hall. In 1905, the name Hippodrome was transferred to this building, the larger of the two theatres. Nothing is now visible of the original exterior which is concealed behind a C20 rendered ground floor with metal cladding above.

Splendid foyer with balcony on four sides originally had the character of a mid-Victorian concert room. The magnificent auditorium, which has two galleries and a proscenium arch in original state, is a riot of gilded Rococo plasterwork. The basic design is very like that of the Playhouse next door, but apart from this and other, now demolished, theatres designed by J.J. Alley for the Broadhead Circuit, the concept is quite unlike any contemporary theatre or music hall. The upper of the two balconies is of eight straight rows spanning directly between the side walls; the lower one is of nine straight rows in the centre, with side arms of four straight rows parallel with the side walls, diminishing to two. The ends are divided off to form a stage box on either side of the proscenium. Above each box is a further box, reached by a little staircase at the side of the balcony. The box and balcony fronts are decorated with delicate Rococo plasterwork. The balconies are supported by iron columns with foliated capitals (some of them Gothic!). At the sides the columns are carried up from the balcony fronts to support the main ceiling which is decorated with festoons at the sides and pan-

Manchester, Hulme Hippodrome (Mike Sell)

elled at the centre. The proscenium is surprisingly formal, being flanked by giant fluted Ionic columns with an enriched straight entablature over, and a large central cartouche supported by putti.

Used for bingo from the mid 1970s until its closure in 1986, the theatre has since stood empty, and is now somewhat obscured by the housing development of the 'regenerated' (now, again, regenerating) area. A fine and important theatre crying out for a new use. *CB/SM*

Hulme Playhouse ★★
Warwick Street
Other names
    1902   Hippodrome
    1905   Grand Junction Theatre
    1929   Junction Picture Theatre
    1951   Playhouse
    1956   BBC Playhouse
    1991   Nia Centre
Original architect
    1902   J.J. Alley
Later works
    1950   Unknown: refurbished and
            redecorated
    1990   Mills Beaumont Leavy:
            converted to Nia Centre
Listed   **Grade II**
Current use **Disused**
Capacity   **c.700**

Opened as the Hippodrome. Renamed Junction Theatre c.1905 and Playhouse in 1951. In 1950, it was extensively renovated and redecorated throughout when, together with the Hippodrome, it was acquired by the James Brennan

Manchester, Hulme Playhouse
(Ted Bottle)

circuit. From 1956-1987 it was used by the BBC as a recording studio for radio and television.

Paired with the Hulme Hippodrome and, although smaller, the design of the auditorium is very similar, with two straight balconies, the front upper balcony set well back from the one below. As at the Hippodrome the 1st balcony (there are six rows in the centre) returns to the sides with four rows diminishing to two. Unlike the Hippodrome, however, the upper balcony also has slips (of one row) which run along the side walls directly to the proscenium. Again, the balconies and their slips are supported by iron columns, although here, despite the fact that the rest of the plasterwork is Baroque, the capitals are all of stiff-leaf Gothic foliage with polygonal tops – there is even a Gothic frieze and cornice on the inner face of the underside of the second balcony! The ceiling is again divided by beams on the lines of the columns: each section decorated by a lozenge-shaped panel.

The proscenium is framed by giant fluted Ionic demi-columns supporting a straight entablature with a trophy of arms above. The plasterwork, although rich, lacks some of the vibrancy of the Hippodrome. The balcony fronts are decorated with large shell motifs between trophies of musical instruments.

In 1990 the theatre was converted into the Nia Centre, a middle-scale touring venue for promotion and production of culturally diverse programmes of drama, music and dance: Nia is Kiswahili for 'purpose'.

The many demands made on space by this multiple use led to some unfortunate alterations (e.g. loss of stage depth and unsatisfactory sight lines from parts of the house). The larger theatre, the Hippodrome, would have been more suitable. The new use, in fact, failed and the theatre is now dark. *CB/SM*

Library ★
Central Library, St Peter's Square
Original architect
    1933   **E. Vincent Harris: as lecture**
            theatre
Current use **Theatre**
Capacity   **308**

E. Vincent Harris was appointed architect of the central library building in 1928 as the result of an architectural competition. The site has important frontages to St Peter's Square, Peter Street and Mount Street and a circular form was

adopted for the whole building.

The library design is classical, faced with Portland stone to a height of 27.4m (90ft). The main entrance is marked by a Corinthian portico facing St Peter's Square.

A lecture theatre seating 300 was built in the basement. Entrance was from stairs leading down from the Shakespeare Hall, behind the great portico, to the crush hall. Tiered, it had a fan-shaped auditorium, with apron stage, three dressing rooms and projection box. The Manchester Corporation Act of 1946 empowered the Libraries Committee to utilise the theatre fully for 'lectures, concerts, displays and the performance of stage plays...' It was managed initially under the direction of Manchester Intimate Theatre Group. In 1952, the Libraries Committee took control.

Today, the cloakroom has been replaced by the Library theatre cafeteria and a small ante-foyer, curved round the two entrances. The auditorium has been painted black, with seats furnished in scarlet. Minor modifications have taken place to the technical areas. *SM*

Odeon (Paramount)
Oxford Street
Original architect
    1930   F. Verity and S. Beverley
Later works
    1974   **Odeon house architect: auditorium subdivided**
Current use **Multi-screen cinema**
Capacity   **originally 3000**

The theatre was built in 1930 by the Paramount Film Company of America. The architects Verity and Beverley, who had spent two years studying theatre design in America, were commissioned to build the Plaza in London as part of the Lower Regent Street redevelopment. The company decided to build a magnificent theatre in the North of England and, having previously leased the Theatre Royal, built the theatre in Manchester.

The stone-faced facade of four bays offered a dignified street frontage, with canopy the full width. Built on three levels, one a mezzanine. The internal decoration of the foyers and auditorium was a free treatment of the Baroque, with a huge rounded proscenium, and an almost 'atmospheric' effect of an open sky on the ceiling. The stage productions were Francis A. Mangan creations, already famous at the Plaza in London and the Paramount in Paris, accompanied by a full orchestra. It has the finest Wurlitzer theatre organ in Europe. Full-size orchestra pit and stage facilities. The theatre, acquired in 1941 by Rank, passed to Odeon, and was subdivided in 1974. However, the stage, proscenium, ceiling and foyer areas were left intact, though some parts are now obscured. It continues to operate as a multi-screen cinema, but could be restored to its original form, as long as no further works make this impossible. *SM*

Opera House ★★
Quay Street
Other names
   1912   New Theatre
   1915   New Queen's Theatre
Original architect
   1912   Farquharson, Richardson and Gill
Later works
   1979   Unknown: converted to bingo
   1984   Smith and Way: returned to theatre use
Listed   Grade II
Current use Theatre
Capacity   1920

Manchester, Opera House (Ian Grundy)

Originally named the New Theatre and renamed New Queen's Theatre in 1915, it became the Opera House in 1920. For some years before its closure in 1979 it was Manchester's principal touring theatre. It spent the next five years as a bingo house but was sold to the Palace Trust in 1984 and returned to live theatre use. The Trust had previously refurbished the Manchester Palace Theatre. In 1990 the two theatres were acquired by Apollo Leisure. The Opera House has become the home of large-scale musicals.

The stuccoed facade is an impressive essay in the neo-Classical manner of C.R. Cockerell (via the nearby Theatre Royal). The whole facade is channel-rusticated. Above the ground floor there is a broad frontispiece of 3 + 5 + 3 bays, the centre with an order of Ionic engaged columns, the outer pairs of columns advanced, with the cornice breaking forward. In the outer bays, the order is expressed with pilasters. Above the three middle bays is a large relief of a horse-drawn chariot, framed within a semi-circular arch. This rises into a very broad pedimental gable with a bracketed crowning cornice.

The large auditorium has two very deep, slightly curved cantilevered balconies of approximately 500 seats each, which overhang to an excessive degree, evidence, perhaps, of the architect's unfamiliarity with theatre design, producing poor sight lines at the rear and a

feeling of oppressiveness.

The space between the balcony fronts and the stage is architecturally impressive. It displays an assured handling of Neo-Classical motifs. Flanking each side is a stack of superimposed boxes between pairs of giant fluted Corinthian columns. The upper boxes are a later insertion, following the removal of heavily draped canopies over the dress-circle boxes. The balcony and box fronts are formed of enriched iron balustrading. Spanning between the entablatures over the giant columns is a deep, coffered segmental arch which forms the tympanum above the high rectangular proscenium, filled by a large circular medallion flanked by winged gryphons. The immensely high main ceiling, covering the full width and depth of the auditorium, is in the form of a coffered segmental tunnel vault.

The theatre is ingeniously planned to take maximum advantage of the site, with the stalls below street level and the main entrance foyer formed within the void of the 1st balcony – the rear wall of the auditorium thus forming the wall of the street facade. *CB/JE/KW*

Palace ★★★
Oxford Street
Other names
   1891-1913 Manchester Palace of Varieties
Original architect
   1891   Alfred Darbyshire and F.B. Smith
Later works
   1896   Frank Matcham: altered struc-

turally; redecorated
   1913   Bertie Crewe: auditorium reconstructed
   1953   Unknown: altered; exterior refaced
   1979-80 Smith and Way (job architect Derek Boulton): whole stage house and orchestra pit enlarged; theatre refurbished
Listed   Grade II
Current use Theatre
Capacity   2000

Darbyshire's splendidly opulent facade was obliterated by unprepossessing faience tiles in 1953. In his reconstruction of the theatre in 1913 Bertie Crewe retained the stage and basic outside shell of the 1891 building. Although the stalls of Darbyshire's theatre were already below street level it does nevertheless appear that Crewe may have been influenced by Richardson's Opera House, Manchester, in the design of his auditorium. Again there are two very large, slightly curved balconies of sixteen rows each, with the entrance foyer partly formed within the void of the first balcony. It also appears that Crewe may have been influenced by the Graeco-Roman style of the Opera House. His London Opera House (demolished) and Shaftesbury Theatre of 1911 were both in an extremely opulent version of the French Renaissance style whereas the Palace and also his Golders Green Hippodrome, both of which opened in December 1913, are distinctly Graeco-Roman. But Crewe was no academic, as were Richardson and his partners. He was, however, a well practised theatre architect and a comparison between the design of the Palace and the Opera House will clearly show this. Partly as a result of a more robust interpretation of the Neo-Classical repertoire, but also due to the more satisfactory overall proportions of the auditorium, the Palace is vastly superior theatrically. A major contributory factor is the way the wide, though not too deep, auditorium relates to the wide proscenium. The side walls are impressively articulated by ranges of boxes under curved and draped canopies, separated by giant fluted Ionic columns. The high ceiling has a central, coffered saucer-dome.

Following threats of closure to both the Palace and the Opera House, the Palace was chosen in early 1979 as Manchester's large touring theatre for the future. The initiative was taken by Mr Raymond Slater who purchased the building from Moss Empires. The Manchester Palace Theatre Trust was formed and a major restoration scheme put in hand. This included the acquisition of land and office buildings at the rear, allowing the stage to be extended by 20 feet. The fly tower was extended by 12 feet. Dressing-room facilities were considerably enlarged and improved, and the orchestra pit was enlarged to accommodate 110 musicians. The first computerised box office system in Europe was installed.   *CB/SM*

Theatre Royal ★★
Peter Street
Other names
   Royal Cinema
   Royal Bingo
   Royale
Original architect
   1845   John Gould Irwin and Francis Chester
Later works
   1875   Edward Salomons: interior reconstructed
   1921   Unknown: interior reconstructed as cinema
   1963   Unknown: converted for Cinerama
   1972   Unknown: converted to bingo
   1990s G.N. Design: converted to nightclub
Listed   Grade II
Current use Nightclub
Capacity   c.1075

The Theatre Royal is Manchester's oldest surviving theatre, though now in use as a nightclub. Built in 1845 on an island site, it is an impressive building in Classical style; the giant recessed portico with fluted Corinthian columns in antis seems to dominate Peter Street even today. The monumental facade is one of the finest examples of theatre architecture to have survived in Britain from the first half of the C19. It is symmetrical, stuccoed, in three unequal bays with three storeys and an attic. The modillioned cornice is treated as a parapet and gabled in the centre. The portico contains three steps to three altered doorways, with a pedimented aedicule in the

centre with a Carrara marble statue of Shakespeare leaning on a pedestal. The entablature bears a frieze inscribed 'Theatre Royal Erected 1845'. The facade of the Theatre Royal, as well as that of Cockerell's banks, was clearly a source of inspiration for Richardson and his partners when designing the front of the Royal Opera House.

A massive water tank was incorporated into the roof, in case of fire. Originally with three balconies and designed for drama and opera, in 1921 the auditorium was remodelled as a cinema, with the stage removed. From this time it had two balconies, connected to an elaborate proscenium arch by balcony slips. The ornate ceiling, now not easily visible, has deeply coved sides and basketwork enrichment reminiscent of Covent Garden.

In 1972, the building took on a new lease of life as a bingo hall and, following conversion to a discotheque, various lighting bridges and gantries, etc. have been added. The 1845 facade is virtually intact and the building retains the balcony from 1875. The internal conversion for its present use seems to have obscured rather than destroyed the theatre interior, which appears to be restorable.   *CB/SM/JE*

MANSFIELD
Nottinghamshire

Grand
Leeming Street
Other names
   Royal Opera House (name proposed but not adopted on opening)
Original architect
   1906   T.V. Woodhouse (Nottingham)
Later works
   1907   Excell: sight lines altered; stage enlarged
   1923   Unknown: facade redesigned and rebuilt
   1928   J.H. Tomlinson: rebuilt internally
Current use Snooker hall
Capacity   1400 (following 1928 rebuild)

The Grand might have been a better choice than the Palace for a civic theatre, but it now seems unlikely to return to live use.

Built as a touring house in 1906, it was rebuilt internally in 1928 when a three-storey dressing-room wing was added. It became a cinema soon after this and has since been tripled. Its undistinguished exterior is largely original but the facade has had metal cladding

Manchester, Palace (Ian Grundy)

Mansfield, Grand (Ian Grundy)

applied in a dreary 'modern' style. The interior has been divided horizontally by a permanent floor separating stalls from circle. The 1928 proscenium arch is visible behind the cinema screen. Stage house about 12.2m (40ft) deep and 18.25m (60ft) high externally.

Cinema use ceased in 1997 with the opening of the new ABC multiplex in the town and it is currently in use as a snooker hall. *TB*

Palace
Leeming Street
Other names
    Electric Palace Theatre
    1956 Civic Theatre
Original architect
    1910 F.P.Cook and Lane
Later works
    1937 Unknown: new facade constructed
    1956 Unknown: renovated; stalls rake increased
    1970 Unknown: small extension at rear of stage
    1994 Graham, Brown Partnership: circle enlarged; dance studio added
    later Unknown: new stage house and fly tower
Current use Theatre
Capacity 582

Built as a ciné-variety house in 1910, originally with an ornate street front. Present facade of two storeys, probably of 1937, but now with the brickwork rendered over; plain canopy, big windows above and coat of arms to right, all appropriately dull, to suit its dreary name, recently changed, of Civic Theatre (which it had been since 1956).

One end balcony with panelled front. Square proscenium flanked by splayed walls with ornamental grilles. Ceiling divided by beams supported on massive ornamental brackets. Small stage with low grid. Twelve dressing rooms.

Quite pleasing of its kind and still capable of some technical improvement, but nothing can be done to increase seating capacity, which severely limits the quality and size of shows that can be booked. There can be little doubt that the Grand would have been a better choice for a municipal theatre, having been originally designed to house professional touring drama. *TB*

MARGATE
Kent

Dreamland
Marine Terrace/Hall by the Sea Road
Other names
    1867 The Hall by the Sea
    1919 Palais de Danse
    1919 Dreamland Hall
    1923 Dreamland Super Variety Theatre
Original architect
    c.1860 Unknown: as railway terminus
Later works
    1867 Spiers and Pond: converted to The Hall by the Sea
    1935 Julian Rudolf Leathart and W.F. Granger: new frontage and auditorium
Listed   Grade II
Current use Cinema/bingo
Capacity   2050 (following 1935 reconstruction)

A terminus built by the London, Chatham and Dover Railway Company was never used for its designed purpose and was converted into an entertainment hall by Spiers and Pond, known as The Hall by the Sea. In 1874 the building with surrounding land was purchased by Lord George Sanger as a headquarters

for his circus empire. The main hall was let for variety, concerts and dancing and the adjacent land was used for his menagerie, exhibitions and waxworks. In 1893, a skating rink was added which was soon converted to a ballroom. By 1905, the menagerie had disappeared and the space became an amusement park; when Sanger retired, the hall was used for concert parties and variety together with cinematograph presentations.

A catastrophic fire in 1930 destroyed the whole amusement park except for the hall and the ballroom. Leathart and Granger designed a spectacular frontage, modelled on new designs appearing in Germany, but the first of its kind to be seen in this country. A huge fin tower, edged in neon with the legend DREAMLAND dominated the seafront end, taking in the site of the demolished hall. It had a large café area on the first floor over ground-floor shops.

The corner entrance, under a domed rotunda, led to the auditorium, the ballroom (retained from 1893), and stairs to the circle bar and foyer. The auditorium (1935) was of plainer design, with a deep recessed ceiling and a square proscenium with sea nymph reliefs by Eric Aumonier either side. The house was designed with full stage facilities, which still remain.

The café area became a music hall from 1955 to 1968, before conversion to bingo. The 1935 auditorium was subdivided in the balcony area for twin cinemas, whilst the stalls area became live theatre in 1973. By 1975 the theatre was converted to bingo.

There are regular concerts on an early Compton organ. *SM*

Theatre Royal ★★★
Addington Street
Other names
    1912 Theatre Royal and Opera House
    1933 Kinema Royal
Original architect
    1787 Unknown
Later works
    1874 J.T. Robinson: auditorium and stage reconstructed and enlarged; frontage on Addington Street extended
    1988 Jaques, Muir and Partners: remedial and improvement works
    1994 Jaques, Muir and Partners: new scene dock constructed; stage basement extended
Listed   Grade II*

Margate, Theatre Royal (Ralph Holt)

Current use Theatre

Capacity 360 (but potentially 550)

Margate Theatre Royal was used as a live theatre from 1787 to 1963, with a period of chapel use during the 1840s and cinema between the wars. In 1988 it returned to live theatre following essential works for licensing but operated only falteringly until closure again in 1991. From 1992 to 1994 it had occasional use only, and from 1995 operated on a theatre club basis. In 1998 it reopened licensed for limited-capacity public performances.

This remarkable theatre is located on a promontory site at the junction of Addington Street, Princes Street and the south-east corner of Hawley Square. When the Theatre Royal first opened in 1787 the overall site area was largely that occupied at present. The auditorium and stage housing were contained within a simple rectangular brick building, with pitched and slated timber roof of 24m (78ft) depth by 14.5m (47ft) width. Flanking this on the south side was the original, so-called 'Royal House' (manager's house). The paybox and entrance foyer formed a single-storey adjunct to the Addington Street frontage.

The structure of the 1787 building partly remains, but Robinson drastically remodelled the theatre by removing the old auditorium and stage, increasing the width by demolishing one side wall, and doing very odd things with the old roof trusses in order to extend their span. In so doing the depth of the Royal House was effectively halved and reduced to lit-

tle more than a facade, of which there now remains almost nothing to suggest its original form.

Robinson also rebuilt the front-of-house areas and frontage. This is in stucco, very restrained – of two storeys and four bays, defined by fluted pilaster strips topped by a cornice and parapet. The two bays to the right curve round into the side street, with the entrance in the corner bay. Robinson's auditorium is delightful, like a smaller version of his earlier London Old Vic auditorium of 1871 – two horseshoe balconies supported by slender iron columns along the line of their fronts, which are of pulvinated section and decorated by swags. The balconies curve round the sides to meet the elliptically arched proscenium which rises directly to the underside of the saucer-dome ceiling. Stage left boxes were blocked in the 1940s to form an escape staircase.

Of even more particular note is its comparison with a contemporary etching of his Alexandra Theatre, Camden (1872) of which it is a scaled-down version but clearly employing identical decorative detailing from the proscenium arch to the balcony fronts and ceiling.

The recent addition of the scene dock at the rear of the stage revealed the footings to the 1787 rear wall well above the present and suggesting that the first theatre had no significant stage basement.

The theatre, which is of major significance, is returning to active live theatre use and is well supported by its local community, but its serious lack of both FOH and backstage facilities and accommodation will arrest this progress and limit the scale and quality of its productions until its much deserved restoration and development are carried out. *CB/JM*

Winter Gardens and Queen's Hall ★

Fort Crescent

Original architect

1911   E. Borg, borough engineer and surveyor

Later works

1935-36   Unknown: part of amphitheatre converted to sun lounge; café created

1946   Unknown: repairs after war damage

1963   Unknown: amphitheatre roofed over to form Queen's Hall

Current use Theatre and concert halls

Capacity Winter Gardens 1400/Queen's Hall 550

The Winter Gardens opened in 1911 on the site of an old fort. Low built and D-shaped on plan, with a typical seaside dance/concert hall in front of an open, semi-circular colonnaded amphitheatre. In 1935, part of the amphitheatre was converted to a sun lounge, then, in 1963, the whole of the area was roofed over to form the Queen's Hall.

The old, flat-floored, main Winter Gardens hall has a proscenium stage on the long side and balconies across the short ends. Bleacher seats and sprung dance floor. The Queen's Hall has a smaller proscenium stage and a small balcony with kitchens under. Neither hall was designed with an orchestra pit. Both have their own dressing rooms. *KW/JE*

MARKET DRAYTON
Shropshire

Theatre
Stafford Street/Cross Street
Original architect
   1792 Unknown
Current use **Retail**

Only the front wall facing Stafford Street and the left-hand wall (i.e. stage right) facing Cross Street, can be readily inspected. The remaining external walls are obscured by other properties.

It is over 150 years since the theatre was used for live entertainment and much alteration has occurred since. It is likely that all the windows on the Cross Street wall are later insertions. There are also a bricked-up entrance which may or may not be original and the faint out-lines of two bricked-up windows nearer Stafford Street.

The frontage appears part of a ter-raced line of properties and has not the appearance of those Georgian theatres which stood in isolation. One suspects that two small windows at the very top of the front may be original. A plaque fixed by the Market Drayton Civic Society on the left-hand side of the front wall reads: 'Market Drayton Theatre. 1792. Built under the patronage of Sir Corbet Corbet. In 1811 it was licensed for an annual season of sixty days. About 1840 a boy actor was killed when a gun went off after it was dropped on the stage. In 1843 it was still in partial use.'

The building is at present divided lengthwise into two shops, one current-ly vacant and the other used by a firm of plumbers. The most interesting feature is to be found in a passageway approxi-mately 17 feet from the rear stage wall.

This affords ingress to the buildings and properties on the other side but is unlike-ly to be original as one would expect such access to have been available at the rear of the theatre. The visible timbers in the ceiling in this passageway may offer clues to the internal construction. It was not possible to enter the building, but such dimensions as could be checked or surmised appear not dissimilar to those found at Richmond, Yorkshire.

The substantial remains of this theatre could reward detailed survey and expert interpretation. *TB*

MARYPORT
Cumbria

Empire Palace
Senhouse Street
Original architect
   1911 Unknown
Current use **Carpet warehouse/retail**
Capacity   (was) c.850

A ciné-variety house. Facade of banded brick with central segmental pediment. Interior almost completely stripped. Bare remains of proscenium arch; fly floors marooned. Two ornamental arches in foyer. Auditorium floor levelled and con-creted. Small segment of ceiling above circle area (circle removed) shows plain barrel vault with very slight Art Deco motif with ornamental ventilation ducts. Balcony was flat-fronted, there were no boxes, and approximately six to seven rows of seats. Very fine iron and glass canopy with EMPIRE ELECTRIC THEATRE now absent and lower half of facade obscured by projecting shopfront and glazed addition. Facade and fly tower, nevertheless, seem to be intact. Walls were replastered on outer shell – ceiling mainly demolished showing timber roof. No sign of dressing rooms (possibly under stage). *IG*

MATLOCK BATH
Derbyshire

Pavilion
South Parade
Original architect
   1884 John Nuttall (Matlock)
Current use **Disco and occasional shows**
Capacity: c.500

Opened in 1883, with a central hall with lantern roof and promenades. The 'orchestra' was described as being 'adapted for the requirements of drama'. The Pavilion is part of a large complex, the theatre itself being on first-floor level

over a permanent Peak Mines Historical Society exhibition (former pump room). It is flat floored, about 23.5m (77ft) long and 13.5m (44ft) wide. The lower parts of iron arches are still visible but modern tile linings now conceal the upper parts of the original curved ceiling. The proscenium wall is covered with black metal cladding.

The main external elevation is in modest classical style in two storeys, the centre with a melon dome ('Unimaginative and not too costly spa architecture', says Pevsner, dismissively).

The Pavilion is now used for discos and occasional shows. With all its pre-sent weaknesses and low-key uses, it is the only venue for live entertainment within a wide area and could fulfil a gen-uine need. *TB*

MERTHYR TYDFIL

Theatre Royal
Pantmorlais, Penydarren Road
Other names
   Theatre Royal and Thespian House
Original architect
   1891 T.C. Wakeling (Merthyr)
Later works
   1982 Unknown: converted to bingo
Listed   **Grade II**
Current use **Bingo (occasional)**
Capacity   c.1200

Massive rendered brick frontage set into the slope opposite Penydarren Park. Lower block attached on right.

Two storeys and attic, five-bay classi-cal front with modified parapets over centre (pediment removed); lean-to flanking parapets. Centre three-bay cor-nice over small vents, THEATRE ROYAL panel below. First-floor sash windows; central oculus over broken segmental pediment with urn finial and scrolled brackets. Modern canopied entrance (replacing arched openings) to left. At rear, corrugated-iron fly tower above wide slate roof.

Fine auditorium completely rebuilt in late 1920s with a large balcony inserted. Splendid sunburst ceiling rose (1890s?) over stalls; Art Deco borders, rosettes, etc. Art Deco proscenium with ramped and stepped surround, Royal Arms to centre, splayed crestings. Side walls with linked low-relief panels with stepped detailing, acanthus and anthemion cor-nices over. Organ pipes to niches flank-ing stage. Recessed coffering over gallery with convex, cantilevered front, Art Deco embellishments. Polygonal, pendant light-fittings. The possibility of

Merthyr Tydfil, Theatre Royal (Terence Rees)

return to live theatre use should not be dismissed.   TR

METHIL
Fife

Gaiety
Wellesley Road
Other names
1930s Western Cinema
from 1970s various names as nightclub, currently Rick's
Original architect
1907 J.D. Swanston
Current use Nightclub

Small variety theatre in former mining town, located behind existing rough-cast-clad two-storey terrace with entrance denoted by a bay window to first floor and pediment above. The auditorium block is still obviously a former theatre with a prominent fly tower. The interior has, however, been gutted. BP

MIDDLESBROUGH

Empire ★★★
Corporation Street
Original architect
1899 Ernest Runtz
Current use Themed pub
Capacity est. 1100

Like Tunbridge Wells Opera House, this was a bingo house at the time of the first *Curtains* survey and is now a themed pub. Like the Tunbridge Wells theatre it is an excellent 'Sleeping Beauty' which, if the ground had been better laid, could,

by now have returned to theatre life. The first *Curtains* assessment said that it was 'likely that the day (would) soon come when the Empire, with its fine auditorium . . . will be better able to stage touring opera, ballet and drama, which cannot visit Teesside at present because of the limited size of the (nearby) Billingham Forum'. Teesside is still, sadly, without a first-rate classic proscenium theatre, for reasons similar to those which bedevilled the Tunbridge Wells Opera House. Fortunately the conversion works have done little harm to theatre potential and much of the tawdry bingo overlays have been removed and

more appropriate decoration restored.

Architecturally, the two theatres are quite different, but the Empire, faced in terracotta, makes a significant contribution to the townscape of central Middlesborough, as does the Opera House in Tunbridge Wells. Built on an open island site alongside the splendid Town Hall (whose impressive great hall houses many concerts and theatrical events it is ill-designed for) the Empire originally had square towers on the four corners, each surmounted by a crested parapet and octagonal dome. Between the towers, in the upper storeys of the front and the two side elevations, are a series of closely-set arched windows divided by slender columns. The style was described in the opening souvenir brochure as being 'Spanish Renaissance'.

The stage was bombed during the Second World War and the rebuilding omitted two flanking towers. Fine and intimate auditorium with two curved balconies of six rows each, terminating in superimposed stage boxes, with each box framed within an arch and flanked by colonnettes with enriched shafts. Rectangular proscenium and circular ceiling incorporating six circular panels. The plasterwork on the balcony fronts, proscenium, etc., is in a rich and delicate Renaissance style.

The Empire is important as being the best of the only three surviving theatres designed by Runtz, the others being the New Theatre, Cardiff, and the Hippodrome, Hastings (where only the

Middlesbrough, Empire (Ian Grundy)

exterior now survives). The present owner seems to be proud of the building, so regret must, in this case, be tinged with relief.   *CB/JE*

Hippodrome
Wilson Street
Original architect
   1906   G.F. Ward
Later works
   1930s and 1954
      Unknown: auditorium altered
   n.d.   Unknown: converted to nightclub
Current use Nightclub and bars
Capacity est. 1600

Exterior intact with a few extra entrance doors inserted in the rear wall of the stage. Faced in red brick and terracotta, the main entrance at the rear auditorium end is flanked by two stocky towers with pyramidal roofs. Two-storey, broad arched entrance with a large demi-lune fanlight. Above this, a three-bay top storey with bowed balustrades to each bay, the centre bay framed by coupled Ionic columns carrying a segmental pediment. Each of the two towers contains a window with features echoing the central window.

At the stage end is a three-storey dressing-room block. There is no raised fly tower. The rear stage wall is completely plain and the lower half is metal clad.

The auditorium was drastically streamlined in the 1930s and again in 1954. The two balcony fronts had all decoration stripped from them and the boxes were removed. The stage remained intact. More recently the auditorium has been further altered on conversion to nightclub/bars.

The Hippodrome has much in common with the Palace, Warrington, and the Civic (formerly Hippodrome), Darlington, and is unmistakably by the same architect. The effect of the splendid facade has been marred by a flyover passing within yards of the building. *IG*

Pavilion (North Ormesby)
Gibson Street, North Ormesby
Original architect
   c.1906   Unknown
Current use Children's play centre
Capacity (was) c.800

A surprising survival of a small local variety theatre of c.1906/8, used as a cinema for most of its life, now as a children's play centre. When it became a

cinema in 1916, a rolled screen permitted continued use of stage.

Externally extremely plain, with one flank wall in red brick, the others rendered. Small central entrance in gabled facade. Stage access doors are now blocked. Internally there is one flat-fronted balcony which may originally have returned to the proscenium wall. The balcony area is now partitioned off and the rear stalls area is used as offices and stores. A new entrance was constructed in 1992 on the side of the building.

Closed in the mid 1950s, it became a bingo hall then, after a period of dereliction, converted to its present use, for which the stalls floor has been levelled and the stage subdivided. The top of the simple proscenium arch is concealed by a false ceiling.   *IG*

MIDSOMER NORTON
Bath and North East Somerset

Palladium
High Street
Other names
   1913   Empire
Original architect
   c.1850   Unknown (as vat house to brewery)
Later works
   1913   Unknown: converted to cinévariety
   1934   Unknown: stage end remodelled and improved; balcony introduced; refurbished
   1955   Unknown: proscenium adapted for Cinemascope
Current use Disused

The history of the Palladium is linked with the Welton Old Brewery Company. The building, which housed the brewery vats, was converted into a ciné-variety house with stage, dressing rooms and raked auditorium. At some point a billiards room was also incorporated. In 1934, the auditorium was enlarged and improved using all the available space, reversing the stage end and introducing the 'balconette' together with Art Deco niches, concealed lighting and moderne decoration throughout. The exterior was outlined in neon.

The Palladium has been disused since about 1990. The present building retains the original outline of the brewery building, with entrance extension, all rendered local stone. The name 'Palladium' is inserted into a small tympanum. *SM*

MILFORD-ON-SEA
Hampshire

Hurst Castle Garrison Theatre
Keyhaven
Original architect
   1860   Unknown (as casemates)
Later works
   1938   Unknown, converted for use as theatre fit-up
Current use Part of heritage exhibition
Capacity c.200

Hurst Castle is situated at the seaward end of a shingle spit extending a mile-and-a-half from Milford-on-Sea, The end is three-quarters of a mile from the Isle of Wight, and so the location was perfect for defending the western approach to the Solent. The castle was built by Henry VIII in 1544 as one of a chain of coastal forts. In the 1860s two enormous armoured wings were constructed, and in the Second World War Hurst was manned with gun batteries, etc. For the provision of entertainment for the troops stationed at Hurst, a garrison theatre was formed in the west Victorian wing by knocking two casemates together. A wooden proscenium was constructed, the back wall painted with a figure design, and a rostrum to one side carried a piano (all these still in situ), with possibly a small ensemble on occasions. A passageway at rear stage left to another casemate provided the stage entrance from a dressing area. On military benches, it would probably have seated 200.

The theatre was not used after the War until about 1995 when a local society began staging small shows to mark various events. The theatre is preserved, and may be seen by visitors to the castle. *SM*

MINEHEAD
Somerset

Queen's Hall
Strand
Original architect
   1914   W.J. Tamlyn (Minehead)
Later works
   n.d.   Unknown: converted to indoor market
Current use Indoor market
Capacity originally 726

Opened in 1914 with stage productions alternating with films. The building is of local brick from the owner's works (he was also the contractor), with Bath stone dressings. Three bays; the central bay with entrance has a large arched window at first-floor level. Facade is elegantly decorated at attic level with part-balustraded parapet topped with four urns and ornamental gable carrying a motif with QUEEN'S HALL. An iron and glass canopy covered the entrance until 1996, when it was destroyed by storms (the hall also suffered flood damage).

Seen today as an indoor market, it is a plain hall without foyer, with only glimpses of original features through a mesh suspended ceiling. Above this, at balcony level, the original character of the room can be clearly seen. Teak doors originally led to a marble vestibule with paybox and cloakroom and stairs to the balcony. Both stalls and balcony were well raked; there were two private boxes (since removed), one at either side of the proscenium. The auditorium still has its barrel-vaulted ceiling and elliptical proscenium arch with ornamental cartouche. There is an ornamental frieze band with brackets carrying the ceiling ribs. The stage with dressing rooms, storage space, backstage crossover is thought to be intact.

Restoration, even for present use, would be desirable. Returning the building to theatre use would be even more so. *SM*

MONMOUTH
Monmouthshire

Magic Lantern ★
18 Church Street
Other names
  c.1832 **Flannel Exchange and Assembly Rooms**
  c.1842 **Oddfellows' Hall**
    1849 **Bell Assembly Rooms**
    1851 **New Theatre or Theatre Royal**
    1865 **Corn Exchange**
    1909 **The Bell (rink)**
    1910 **Rinkeries Living Picture Palace**
    1914 **Palace**
    1920 **Scala Cinema**
    1927 **New Picture House**
Original architect
  c.1832 **Unknown: as Flannel Exchange and Assembly Rooms**
Later works
1849–51 **Unknown: converted to Assembly Rooms and New Theatre**
    1875 **Unknown: converted to skating rink**
    1910 **Unknown: converted to cinema**
    1917 **Unknown: redecorated and entrance moved to Church Street**

    1927 **Unknown: completely rebuilt as ciné-variety**
    1987 **Unknown: refurbished and reopened as Magic Lantern Theatre**
Listed   **Grade II**
Current use **Dark**
Capacity **c.180**

The site has had a splendidly varied history. The Flannel Exchange and Assembly Rooms were built at the old Bell Inn in the 1830s (a granary still standing at the rear bears the date 1751). J.F. Rogers opened the New Theatre in this building in 1851, by which time it had become known as the Bell Assembly Rooms. The Assembly Rooms were converted into a skating rink in 1875. In 1910, the much altered building was converted to a picture house. It served briefly as a place of worship in 1911, then, after various changes of cinema ownership, it was totally rebuilt as a ciné-variety house in 1927 by Albany Ward.

The 1927 building is still entered through an altered late Georgian three-storey three-bay building which has a plain rendered facade with a shopfront to the left of the cinema entrance. It is a fine and complete example of a richly detailed cine-variety house with a single balcony. Segmental vaulted ceiling with enriched ribs and grilles. Plaster-panelled walls with garlanded figure medallions. Stage is 5.4m (18ft) deep. Flying height is limited and cloths need to be rolled or tumbled. A few items of old scenery are stacked in a corner of the stage. The orchestra pit would probably accommodate twelve musicians. *TR*

Monk Street Theatre
Monk Street
Original architect
  1838 or earlier Unknown
Later works
    1846 **G.V. Maddox: converted to Masonic Hall**
Current use **Masonic Hall**

The theatre was taken over by the Freemasons in 1846 and given an entirely new facade, though the interior was allowed to retain much of its theatrical identity. The compiler was told that the foyer, gallery and dressing rooms are still extant, but permission to inspect was refused. *TR*

St Mary's Street Theatre
St Mary's Street
Original architect
  late C18 Unknown
Current use **Disused**

Stucco facade, lined out as stonework; three storeys, the right-hand section domestic in appearance, one window wide with shopfront on ground floor. Left-hand bay is higher with carriage entrance and two storeys of loading doors above. Barn-shaped building at rear (a fit-up?) now divided into three storeys. It is presently vacant and up for sale. As part of its recent history it has been a furniture warehouse and part of it an antique shop. The compiler was unable to gain admission but was told that there was 'a balcony still inside'. Roger Kemble brought his company here in 1775. *TR*

MORECAMBE
Lancashire

Alhambra ★
Marine Road West
Other names
    1930 **Astoria Super Cinema**
Original architect
    1901 **H. Howarth**
Later works
    1930 **Unknown: converted to cinema**
Current use **Cabaret bar and discotheque**
Capacity **originally 1000**

A sad sight. One would need to be a determined optimist to believe that the Alhambra could be returned to theatre use, but it has been a remarkable building and enough remains to sharpen one's regrets about what has happened to it.

It is a large, free-standing stone building on the seafront, originally with elaborate Dutch gable and a loggia at second-floor level. The music hall, which was on the first floor, over shops, was a single-balconied rectangular room with an arched ceiling spanning from side to side, rather like a smaller version of the Morecombe Winter Gardens (Victoria Pavilion). Pavilion-like boxes were set closely on either side of the proscenium at balcony level. The proscenium had a splendid cartouche over, with winged full-relief figures as supporters. The ceiling was divided into lively painted panels (one with a sunburner) by arching enriched beams and there was a magnificently painted act drop.

In 1970 a fire gutted the interior and destroyed the roof. The reconstruction as a disco omitted the fanciful gable, depriving the exterior of much of its character. The fly tower is still present but the stage was bricked off.   *CB/JE*

Victoria Pavilion ★★★
Marine Road Central

Other names
  Winter Gardens Music Hall
  Victoria Pavillion (sic)
  King's Pavilion
  People's Palace and Aquarium
Original architect
  1897   Mangnall and Littlewood
Later works
  1910-11   Unknown (possibly Frank
      Matcham): additions and alter-
      ations; balcony added to
      facade
  c.1934 Unknown: alterations and
      extensions; stage house possi-
      bly rebuilt
  1997   Lancaster City Council
      Architects' Department:
      restoration of exterior; other
      repairs
Listed   **Grade II***
Current use **Dark, undergoing restoration**
Capacity   **probably c.1200**

Morecambe, Victoria Pavilion (Ian Grundy)

The spelling 'Pavillion' which has been adopted recently, derives from what appears to be a foreign paviour's error in working the name into a mosaic paving. We will not be seduced into perpetuating this historical blunder. The building, previously called the Winter Gardens, is too important to be misspelt.

This is a music hall of a rare type, probably now unique of its kind (following the loss of the Islington Palace, London, formerly Mohawks' Hall of c.1869, demolished 1982) – i.e. a big concert party or minstrels' hall. It was built in 1897 alongside the earlier glass-roofed Winter Gardens and Empress Ballroom (Waugh and Issott, 1878), to the designs of Mangnall and Littlewood, with Frank Matcham as consultant. Prominently sited on the seafront, the main elevation is an ornate, symmetrical composition in brick and terracotta. A big central gable with an elaborately scrolled outline expresses the rear wall of the auditorium and is flanked by projecting square towers with shaped gables. At ground level, the entrance is set between shopfronts.

Internally, a flavour of Matcham is detectable in a building quite unlike any of his surviving works. The general form must be Mangnall and Littlewood's although the design of the balconies and some other details may have been mod-

ified as a result of Matcham's involvement. The foyer is richly appointed, with mosaic, coloured and modelled faience tiling, plaster decorations and a pair of remarkably preserved bow-fronted ticket kiosks. The stair hall is equally elaborate, with marble, coloured tiles and fine joinery. This leads to curving promenades at two levels with glazed screens looking into the hall.

The hall itself is impressive, very wide and covered by a vast segmental tunnel-vaulted ceiling which soars over the whole space, including the area over the tops of the boxes and is divided into richly decorated panels. The curve of the ceiling embraces a huge tympanum above the proscenium and boxes, decorated at the sides with painted muses, etc. (all now badly discoloured). The proscenium is framed by coupled columns with garlanded shafts supporting an enriched entablature and an elaborately modelled, scrolled and panelled gable-like attic ornament. On either side are two tiers of paired boxes set in splayed pavilions against which the balconies terminate. A deep serpentine-fronted balcony returns along the side walls with five rows of seats. The upper (gallery) tier is set back and has shallow slips above the side promenades of the lower tier.

The fly tower is plain rendered with dressing rooms on either side, providing a quite mean stage for such an auditorium. For some conventional stage productions this great space has too large a capacity and too small a stage. The narrow proscenium also makes the sight lines from the side slips particularly uncomfortable and this limits usable

capacity for stage shows. However, the large floor area would permit the staging of some kinds of events within the auditorium with temporary seating, making the side balcony seats saleable. The future treatment of the theatre needs to provide for use in different formats and also to open up the possibility of occasional profitable non-theatre uses to underpin financial viability.

When the original glass-roofed Winter Gardens was allowed to be demolished after 1978 it was replaced by a particularly depressing amusement arcade development. It was understood that one reason for permitting this development was that the music hall would be restored and reopened but, in the event, it fell into a seriously dilapidated state, standing uncared for, for most of the following decade. The prospects for repair and reopening under different ownership seemed reasonably good in 1997 and the exterior has already been well restored, but care must now be taken not to destroy the long-term theatre potential of this remarkable building for short-term advantage. The stage area and fly tower, in particular, need to be carefully considered in any future proposals.

The Victoria Pavilion is a highly visible, architecturally striking building in the heart of Morecambe and its fate could well be a major factor in determining whether the town experiences an exciting revival or goes into terminal decline. In this respect it illustrates a phenomenon observed in other places, that the neglect of a theatre has a deadening effect on a town, but its reopening can power an urban revival. *JE*

NELSON
Lancashire

Grand
Market Street
Original architect
   1888   T. Bell
Later works
   1923   Unknown: galleries removed,
        single balcony built
Current use Fragment (fire May 2000)

Closed and near derelict (last used as a cinema). Imposing and unusual facade, mixed Gothic and classical. Stone-faced, of three storeys and seven bays, divided by pilaster strips, all under one big pedimented gable. Closely spaced mullioned and transomed first-floor windows with cusped heads and a continuous series of small rectangular windows below the pediment. In 1923 the galleries of the old auditorium were removed and replaced by one large balcony.   *CB/IG*

Palace Hippodrome ★★
Landless
Original architect
   1909   Unknown
Current use Bingo
Capacity   est. 2000

A once fine theatre reduced to near dereliction by a road 'improvement' which took no account of its existence, simply slicing off the front and its corner tower and leaving a blank wall exhibiting only one low window and a ventilation grille. Entrance is now through a former side exit door.
   The interior, which as recently as

1980 had two balconies and single boxes framed by columns on either side of the enriched proscenium frame, has now lost all its plasterwork on one side and has severe visible cracking in its walls. The building remains in use after a fashion but, if nothing is spent on repairing it soon, is not likely to survive.   *CB/IG*

NEW BRIGHTON
Wirral

Floral Pavilion
Virginia Road
Original architect
   1913   Unknown: as open-air theatre
Later works
   1925   Unknown: theatre enclosed in
        glass structure; stage raised
   1965-66   Unknown: glass roof
        replaced by metal
Current use Theatre
Capacity   950

Part of the New Victoria Gardens, built on the site of the old Ham and Egg Parade, opened in 1913. It took the form of an open-air summer theatre. In 1925 the theatre was covered by an iron and glass roof; the stage was raised and tip-up seats were installed. From 1933, shows were broadcast from the Pavilion. In 1965/1967 the theatre was partly rebuilt, with most of the glass roof panels replaced by metal. In the auditorium are the wrought-iron pillars supporting the roof which evoke the atmosphere of the seaside Pavilion. The iron porch is the only 1913 survivor.   *SM*

NEW MILLS
Derbyshire

Art
Jodrell Street/Wood Street
Other names
   1911   Empire and Hippodrome
Original architect
   1911   John Fraser and J.B. Fraser of
        Chapel-en-le-Frith
Later works
   1921   Albert Winstanley: major
        reconstruction
Current use Amateur theatre
Capacity   511

The theatre opened in 1911 as a ciné-variety house, became a cinema in 1939 and returned to live theatre use in 1948. Cinema use ceased completely in 1959 when the present company took over.
   The main building is rectangular with no fly tower. A building of irregular plan form fronts Jodrell Street; pebble-dashed with slate roof. The interior is pleasing, with a single circle, 10m (33ft) deep, curving round to two projecting flat-roofed boxes on each side, one lower than the other, linked by a dummy balcony front. The boxes adjoining the proscenium arch are not used by the public. The arch itself is framed by a rib-boned, reeded moulding. The ceiling has all-over low relief ornament. The balcony fronts have pretty wreaths and garlands.   *TB*

NEWARK
Nottinghamshire

Palace ★★
Appleton Gate
Original architect
   1920   Blagg (as ciné-variety)
Later works
   1974   Gordon Benoy and Partners:
        offices inserted beneath circle;
        outside canopy renewed
   1988   John Perkins (Borough archi-
        tect): stalls floor altered and
        dummy stage boxes formed;
        width of stalls reduced
Current use Theatre
Capacity   647

The Palace opened in 1920 as a cinema with facilities for stage shows, but after a period in use as a cinema and bingo hall it reverted to full-time theatre in 1974. The 1988 face-lift cost £200,000.
   The main entrance facade follows the angle of the road junction, being divided into two bays by shafts with pinnacles rising several feet above the parapet. The

Nelson, Palace (Ian Grundy)

New Mills, Art (Ted Bottle)

stage tower has a mansard roof. Ample foyer and refreshment room.

The auditorium has a curiously archaic appearance, like an early music hall, with balconies on three sides. The ceiling is flat, made up of eight panels each bordered with delicate plaster mouldings. The proscenium has a flattened arch with a width of 8.5m (28ft) and a height of 6.7m (22ft). The orchestra pit has been rebuilt and is capable of being covered over to provide an apron. Originally the stalls floor was only slightly raked. Since the alterations in 1988, the front eight rows of the stalls retain a slight rake but have been raised, so reducing the apparent height of the stage. Beyond a crossover gangway the remaining seven rows are double tiered to the underside of the circle front. The shallow side balconies have been converted to ten boxes, five each side. The rear circle is deep, rising to a headroom of only 9 feet.

Full use of the deep flat stage is curtailed by the peculiar nature of the mansard roof which makes it impossible to fly wide cloths or anything at all in the rear 12 to 15 feet from the back wall. The scenery is still hemp worked. There are six dressing rooms.

The fortunes of this delightful house would appear to be in the ascendant, with a varied menu of popular artists visiting the town. *TB*

Robin Hood Theatre ★

Church Lane, Averham
Other names
1913   Robin Hood Opera House
Original architect
1913   Rev. Joseph Cyril Walker: as a private theatre
Later works
1974   Gordon Kermode: supper room added
1967   Unknown: rear of auditorium raked; courtyard between auditorium and bar covered
Current use Amateur theatre
Capacity 150

A timber-built private theatre of 1913 set in the grounds of the former Rectory; outbuildings which were once stables are now used for storing scenery, properties and costumes. One such outhouse contains two small dormitories which can accommodate drama students on their occasional visits to the theatre.

The auditorium is on one level, the rear half raked, arranged as fifteen straight rows each containing ten seats.

This is a most interesting and much-loved little playhouse. The backstage arrangements are quaint, compact and different. *TB*

NEWCASTLE UPON TYNE

Balmbra's

6 Cloth Market
Other names
1859   Royal Music Saloon
1864   Wheatsheaf Music Hall
1865   Oxford Music Hall
1891   Oxford Restaurant and Music Hall
Balmbra's Music Hall
Original architect
?1862   Unknown: first purpose-built hall
Later works
1883   Lamb and Armstrong: gallery floor converted to showroom
1885   Lamb and Armstrong: music hall and bar altered
1891   J.E. Stout: converted to restaurant and pub
1901   Arthur Stockwell: rebuilt as hotel
Listed Grade II
Current use Facade only

Opened in 1848 as a first-floor room in the Wheatsheaf pub. Advertisements refer to the Royal Music Saloon in 1859 and the Wheatsheaf Music Hall in 1864, which may confirm a rebuilding as a purpose-designed hall c.1862, which is the

Newark, Palace (Ian Grundy)

date given for the present facade in the *Curtains !!!* (1982) account. It was the Oxford Music Hall, 'late Balmbra's' by 1865. Advertisements ceased to appear in 1879. A later plan shows a stage only 5 feet deep. The gallery was removed about 1883 but the music hall continued to be listed in directories until 1895.

The building, which had become the Oxford Restaurant and Public Hall in 1891, was largely destroyed by fire in 1899, by which time the former music hall was a billiards room. The new building, the Carlton Hotel, opened in 1901 and this, too, included a billiards room which was converted into 'Balmbra's', a pastiche music hall with a balcony at one end, in 1962, but this was quite different from the old hall in dimensions and nothing, in fact, survives from the famous mid-Victorian Balmbra's.   *DW*

Gaiety
Nelson Street
Other names
    1838   Music Hall
    1879   New Tyne Concert Hall
    1884   Gaiety
    Grainger Theatre
Original architect
    1838   John Dobson
Listed   Grade II
Current use Facade only (at rear of W.H. Smith store)

Opened as The Music Hall – a small concert hall at first-floor level above a lecture room. Auditorium reconstructed at various times. All that now remains is the fine, classical, ashlar facade, articulated by pilasters at first-floor level.   *CB/DW*

Majestic
Condercum Street, Benwell
Original architect
    1927   Dixon and Bell
Current use Disused
Capacity   c.1100

Designed by Dixon and Bell, this was opened with a long repertory season by the Denville Players. The auditorium was on two levels, the circle being extended down the side walls to an onion-domed box on either side of the proscenium arch. The balcony front was decorated with panels of acanthus leaf wreaths on a basketwork background. This design was repeated in the proscenium arch which had a Roman column at each side. In front of the stage was a full orchestra pit. The ceiling was a shallow barrel vault divided into three panels over the stalls with a raised flat section

over the balcony. There were demi -lune windows in the balcony for natural ventilation.

The entrance doors (two only; the pit and front stalls had a separate entrance) were unusual being of sheet metal with theatre masks (both comedy) and lion heads (now missing).

The stage was large and had scenery get-in at the rear. There was a full-height mansard fly tower, slated, as was the main roof.

Stage use declined after Union Cinemas took over the building. The stage house was, at some time, reduced in height. The theatre closed in 1961 and became a bingo hall. This too closed and the building, in an important road in the middle of one of Newcastle's problem areas was for some time in poor condition and boarded up. Purchased by a property company in 1999 who said they wished to restore the building for a purpose unstated.

Worth an internal inspection. The doors should certainly be rescued.   *IG*

Odeon (Paramount)
Pilgrim Street
Original architect
    1931   Frank Verity and Samuel Beverley
Later works
    1975   Unknown: converted to three-screen cinema
    1980   Unknown: fourth screen added
Current use Multi-screen cinema
Capacity   originally c.2600

Brick facade with stone dressings. Divided into five bays, each containing windows at first-floor level, the three central bays also having small balconies at first-floor level and smaller windows at second floor. The brick bays are surmounted by a plain frieze and cornice capped by a parapet. At street level a canopy extends the full width of the front elevation. Originally the interior was lavishly decorated in Art-Deco style designed by Charles M. Fox.

Live performances ceased in 1936 giving way completely to cinema presentations. In 1975 it reopened with three screens and in 1980 a fourth screen was added in the space originally occupied by the stage.   *DW*

Plaza
Westgate Road and Gowland Avenue
Original architect
    1928   S.J. Stephenson
Current use Disused
Capacity   est. 1200

Built as a cinema with a stage, six dressing rooms, orchestra pit and music room, but no fly tower. Used by amateurs and professional variety artists. Foyer block projects from the rectangular main body; all elevations in brick with sparse dressings. The design included two shops. Closed 1960 and derelict until reopened as a bingo hall in 1964. Closed again in 1990s and now boarded up. Externally appears to be in good condition and located at a busy crossroads, but not a promising location for a theatre.

At the time of writing there were plans to convert the building to a public house.   *IG*

St Nicholas Hospital Theatre ★
Salter's Road
Other names
    Jubilee Theatre
Original architect
    c.1897   John W Dyson
Listed   Grade II
Current use Multi-purpose amateur theatre
Capacity   400

Vestibule entrance leading to a flat-floored auditorium, flanked on each side by six bays of windows, with narrow balcony at rear of the room. The main feature of the auditorium is the signed Royal Doulton proscenium arch by W.J. Neatby, a striking composition, depicting two pre-Raphaelite female figures playing musical instruments and seated amidst swirling branches with flowers festooned round a tree trunk. The central cartouche of the proscenium arch is a female mask. Dyson, the architect, and Neatby were also both associated with the new Victoria Royal Infirmary in Newcastle, which has a fine collection of Doulton tile pictures.

Neatby's other theatrical work included a set of 28 panels with paintings of women in pre-Raphaelite costumes for the Winter Gardens in Blackpool; a set of medallions illustrating the history of costume for the Theatre Royal, Birmingham; the modelling of the plaster pendentives in the dome of the Gaiety Theatre, London (1903); and the mermaid panels at the Palace Theatre, Plymouth. He also designed the tiled interior of Harrods Food Hall in London.

The stage of St Nicholas Hospital Theatre is fully equipped with timber fly floors and grid. There is no substage machinery, and no evidence of scenic grooves as at the Stanley Royd, Wakefield. Backstage there is a small suite of purpose-built dressing rooms.   *DW*

Theatre Royal ★★★

Grey Street

Original architect
1837   John and Benjamin Green
Later works
1867   C.J. Phipps: interior
1895   Walter Emden and W. Lister
       Newcombe: auditorium and
       front of house reconstructed
       in concrete and iron
1901   Frank Matcham: interior
       rebuilt and theatre enlarged
       by incorporation of shops
       (after a fire)
1986-88 RHWL: interior refurbished;
       rehearsal rooms and new
       dressing rooms added
Listed   Grade I
Current use Theatre
Capacity   1294

Outstandingly fine classical exterior of 1837, unusually monumental for an English theatre and playing a crucial part in the splendid sweep of Grey Street. A free-standing building in ashlar sandstone. The symmetrical facade is dominated by a portico of giant Corinthian columns projecting over the pavement. Flanking bays with giant pilasters at the angles repeated round each corner. Restrained three-storeyed side elevations with an attic above the cornice. Following a fire in 1899, the auditorium was completely reconstructed in 1901 by Frank Matcham and is remarkably intimate for its capacity.

The alterations to the Theatre Royal, with auditoria in succession by Benjamin Green, Walter Emden and finally Frank Matcham, have created an interesting relationship between the external elevations and the present interior. It is interesting to compare Green's longitudinal section with that of Benjamin Wyatt's Drury Lane. The similarities are immediately apparent, particularly with reference to the foyer rotunda. The Walter Emden auditorium was inserted in the shell of Green's theatre and retained the original rotunda. However, the sight lines and apparently the acoustics were far from ideal, and it may have been considered fortunate when less than a year after its construction it was gutted by fire. Frank Matcham was engaged to design a new interior within Green's exterior which remained largely undamaged. The Matcham auditorium remains, along with front-of-house alterations and improvements carried out by RHWL, in 1986–1988. The Matcham auditorium is curiously restrained. The overall effect, coupled with a pale pastel

Newcastle upon Tyne, Theatre Royal (Ian Grundy)

colour scheme creates an elegant but understated effect quite unlike many of Matcham's other masterpieces.

The auditorium consists of relatively open tiers, split into stalls and cantilevered dress circle, upper circle and amphitheatre/gallery. The boxes are configured with two per side at upper-circle and dress-circle level, and one stalls box for use when an enlarged orchestra pit is not required. Rectangular proscenium framed in alabaster and fibrous plaster. Over the proscenium a bust of Shakespeare (in the year the Theatre Royal reopened a plaque was placed over the Tyne Theatre proscenium containing the word 'Shakespeare' – surely a tongue-in-cheek comment!) The

ceiling is flat, but elaborately panelled and punctuated with ventilation grille-work for natural convection. Strangely absent from the auditorium are the usual murals or art decorations common in Matcham's other work. This may be due to loss, though there are few areas within the auditorium which would offer such opportunities. The overall effect might be summarised as intimate but restrained.

The foyers have been completely remodelled, though retaining Matcham's original staircase to the Dress Circle. The ceiling murals in the foyer have been restored, and the new section of the foyer has been adorned with modern-style murals which seem less than appropriate for the atmosphere of a traditional theatre. As with other RHWL schemes the tiers are all linked with one large staircase which provides ease of access to bars, toilets and restaurant facilities alike.   *CB/DW*

Tyne Theatre and Opera House ★★★
Westgate Road
Other names
1919–74   Stoll Picture House
Original architect
   1867   William B. Parnell
Later works
   1893   Oliver and Leeson: Grand
          Saloon extended
   1901   Unknown: balcony fronts
          altered
   1919   Unknown: projection box
          installed by the Frank
          Matcham office
   1986   David Wilmore: Theatresearch,
          stage house restored after fire
Listed   **Grade I**
Current use **Theatre**
Capacity   **1000**

Interesting Italianate brick and stone facade of 1867. Three storeys and five bays with round-arched Venetian Renaissance traceried windows in the upper storey. Bracketed cornice, with a pediment over the three central bays. Magnificent auditorium of 1867. Three horseshoe balconies sweeping splendidly round to superimposed boxes which flank the imposing, richly framed, elliptically arched proscenium, 8.53m (28ft). Extraordinary and beautiful circular panelled ceiling, tilting upwards from the proscenium towards the gallery. Excellent plasterwork.

This auditorium, undoubtedly one of the finest of its date in Britain, remains

Newcastle upon Tyne, Tyne Theatre (Ian Grundy)

structurally the same as when originally built. There have, however, been modifications worthy of note. The original gallery boxes have been blocked in by semi-circular panels inserted into the framing and embellished with stencilwork and low-relief decoration. The plasterwork to the dress and upper circle tier fronts was further embellished with cartouches in 1901. These bear the names of dramatists and composers of the day. At the same time a large central cartouche was added above the proscenium, bearing the name of Shakespeare. This may have been a tongue-in-cheek gesture to the Theatre Royal, Newcastle, which in the same year (1901) was reconstructed internally by Frank Matcham - the proscenium being centrally surmounted by a bust of Shakespeare. The box fronts were also modified with cartouches at this time and flanked at dress-circle level with Corinthian columns (identical to those of the Victoria Theatre, Salford), and at upper-circle level by caryatids. This decoration was superimposed upon the rather simpler, slender columnar decoration of the 1860s. In 1919 when the theatre became a cinema, a projection box was inserted into the upper circle, being designed for Oswald Stoll, the new owner, by the Frank Matcham office. This remained until after the fire of 1985; at this point the front wall of the box was moved backwards, and the box became the technical control room. The stalls box fronts were removed many years ago – possibly pre-1900.

Externally the theatre facade remains almost unaltered from 1867. One addition was the insertion of a leaded coloured-glass window in 1919 bearing the words 'Stoll Picture House'. In 1893 Oliver and Leeson added the red brick building to the right of the frontage, at the same time as the Grand Saloon was built. This was a large retiring/refreshment room serving the front stalls and dress circle. Prior to this, part of this site had been occupied by a scene dock for the theatre, and there had also been for a very short period another theatre on the site known as The Westgate Music Hall.

When cinema use ceased, the stage retained all its original machinery without alteration, and this was restored to working order after 1980. On Christmas Day 1985, however, a fire broke out backstage which completely gutted the fly tower. Remarkably the stage house was completely rebuilt to the original specification, using salvaged ironwork where possible. The machinery was

again reconstructed and remains in full working order, an achievement without parallel in the whole country. The stage represents perhaps the most complete working example of the English wood stage - possessing four bridges, eight cuts, one carpet cut, two corner traps, two staircase traps, three object traps and one grave trap. Overhead there is a series of drum and shaft mechanisms to operate synchronised scene-changes, and a hemp fly floor stage left with drum and shaft for the act drop. A single purchase counterweight system has since been installed on the stage right wall. Further building work has recently been carried out in neighbouring buildings and land acquired by the theatre, to provide teaching facilities for the College of Arts and Technology. This work included the provision of a small studio theatre.   *CB/DW*

NEWMARKET
Suffolk

The Doric
High Street
Other names
   Celebrities Cabaret Club
Original architect
   c.1928   **Unknown**
Current use **Nightclub and bar**
Capacity   c.1100 (prior to subdivision)

The Doric was built about 1928 as a ciné-variety. It has an unusual neo-Georgian front; brick with stucco dressings, parapet with a deep, simply moulded cornice. Semi-circular arched windows on first floor. A boldly projecting semi-circular bay is set well off-centre, containing the entrance in a recessed colonnade with coupled Doric columns. Other elevations are plain brick. Low fly tower.

Internally, an inserted floor divides the Cabaret Club on the ground floor from the nightclub above. The stage, originally about 9.14m (30ft) deep with a 9.14m (30ft) proscenium, has also been subdivided horizontally. It seems to have been used for variety and pantomimes but was a cinema exclusively by the 1950s.   *KW*

Theatre
High Street
Other names
   by 1863   **Public Hall**
   by 1907   **Town Hall**
Original architect
   c.1825   **Unknown**
Current use **Shop**

The Fisher Circuit made use of a cockpit in Newmarket in 1823. Having acquired the land, they built a theatre on the site soon after. The earliest documentary references to the new building appear to be of 1825 and 1829. Theatre use ceased in 1848. The theatre had become a public hall by 1863, and was later known as the Town Hall. Whether this change involved works of total reconstruction or major elaboration is not known, but the hall remained in use for a variety of public events. In 1907, while in use by Gaumont for a film show, the unenclosed projector was accidentally upset. The lime light ignited the celluloid film, leading to panic in which 300 people were injured and three died of burns. This was one of the several tragedies which led to the passing of the Cinematograph Act of 1909.

As seen now, the building is stucco-faced (originally brick with stucco or stone quoins and dressings). The facade to the street takes the form of a broad canted bay extending across the whole front. Semi-circular arched windows at first floor above a modern shopfront. An upper floor has been inserted, supported by a spiral staircase. There is no external or internal evidence of theatre use. *KW*

NEWRY
Newry and Mourne

Town Hall Theatre ★
Bank Parade
Original architect
    1893   Unknown
Later works
    1913   Unknown: small extension
           added to Mall side
    1992   Smith and P.G. Faye: refur-
           bished; stage equipment
           upgraded
Listed   Grade B
Current use Theatre and concert hall
      (multi-purpose)
Capacity   500

The theatre is a most picturesque sight standing astride a three-arched bridge over the Clanrye River in the centre of the town. Its front five-bay facade of brick with local granite embellishments is vaguely Lombardic-classical in style. There are brick pilasters and a Venetian window to the three centre bays which break forward and rise up to terminate in balustrading and a small pedimented pavilion where a clock is the centrepiece.

The original entrance (still in use) leads into a small domed rotunda with robust plaster embellishments. On either side there are wide staircases up to the first-floor auditorium where the main features are a horseshoe shaped balcony and the painted proscenium. In front of the stage a concealed hoist moves chairs from the auditorium to the Minor Hall at the back of the permanent cyclorama. The stage is raked.

The new (1992) decor in the auditorium where walls and ceilings are painted out in a vibrant middle blue (with gold stars on the ceiling) and the Corinthian pilasters between the semi-circular headed windows all create a strong theatrical night-time atmosphere; but it is the painted proscenium with its marbled panels above the elliptical opening and smaller side arches (erected about 1910) which adds the necessary sparkle. Unfortunately the centre portion of the ornamental cast-iron balcony front has been obliterated by crude sound-absorbent panels.

Large gold letters at the base of the balcony front read: 'We are the music-makers and we are the dreamers of dreams yet we are the movers and shakers of the world it seems' (Arthur O'Shaughnessy). A fitting motto.

The fine Edwardian Council Chamber on the ground floor of the Town Hall is still used by Councillors – all other Council offices have moved. *RMcK*

NEWTON ABBOT
Devon

Alexandra
Market Place
Other names
    Corn Exchange
Original architect
    1871   Unknown
Later works
before 1920 Unknown: fitted with stage
           and dressing rooms
    1930   Unknown: interior remodelled
    1970   Unknown: refurbished and
           reseated
    1996   Unknown: cinema twinned
           (retaining stage use)
Listed   Grade II
Current use Cinema and theatre
Capacity   c.200 (theatre)

The Alexandra opened in 1871 as the Corn Exchange, with entertainment and lecture facilities. Later it was popular as a skating rink. The building is a long two-storey market hall in Devonian limestone (recently cleaned), with a dominating tower at the market end, marking the entrance. Later rendered additions either side of tower. Pre-1920, the interior was remodelled to accommodate stage and dressing rooms. It was used for films from 1920, when the windows were filled in. In the 1930s, the entrance was remodelled as a box-office/foyer. In the auditorium the balcony front has plaster garlands. The otherwise stark interior has been cleverly draped with soft furnishings and warmly lit. Run as a cinema for much of the year, the stage has been used regularly for pantomimes and shows.

In 1996, the balcony area was converted to a second cinema, leaving the stage facilities and proscenium untouched, but with a smaller seating capacity.   *SM*

NORTHAMPTON
Northamptonshire

ABC
Abbington Street
Other names
    1936   Savoy
           Cannon
Original architect
    1936   W.R. Glen
Later works
    1974   Unknown: tripled
Listed   Grade II
Current use Dark
Capacity   c.1700 (prior to subdivision)

The ABC Northampton is a special example of a complete 1930s' interior, a notable survivor of the work of W.R. Glen. It is also (at the time of writing) the only Glen cinema listed Grade II.

Opened as the Savoy in 1936, it was dominantly sited at the corner of Abbington Street and Lower Mounts, with the main entrance on the corner flanked by lower wings for four shops. The facade had four vertical fins, outlined by neon after dusk, placed between two outside fins against a plain background of terrazzo. Today these fins are truncated, and lower flanking projecting curved corners above the entrance canopy have disappeared. The canopy has been replaced and decorative metal work in the doors has also gone.

Entrance through five pairs of double doors led to a spacious entrance hall, with terrazzo and marble floor, and with wide staircases down to the stalls, and up to balcony level. The auditorium, with one curving balcony, originally furnished in autumnal colours, was lit by an oblong ceiling centre panel with concealed lighting. Proscenium set in deep double-arched recess, flanked by decorative grilles of abstract design. For its time, the design was regarded as progressive; most of the ornamental detail remains.

In 1993 it was described by Eyles as one of the least altered of the remaining ABCs, still lit in the original way and still with its organ.

Closed following the opening of a new multiplex, prospects looked bleak. A Public Inquiry in November 1998 required the retention of the balcony and prevented it from being turned into a theme pub, although at the time of writing plans had been submitted for conversion to restaurant. It seems more likely, however, that the building will become a place of worship for a Jesus Army group.

Royal ★★★
Guildhall Road

Other names
1946   Repertory Theatre
Original architect
1884   C.J. Phipps
Later works
1887   C J Phipps: restored after fire
1889   Unknown: proscenium widened, new system of floats
1960   Osborne Robinson: restored and redecorated
1983-7 RHWL: extensive backstage improvements
Listed   Grade II
Current use Theatre
Capacity   583

One of the smallest of Phipps's theatres – comparable in scale internally with the Royal Hippodrome in Eastbourne.

The entrance front, in painted Ancaster stone, is of extremely modest proportions – just wide enough for three closely spaced bays defined by pilasters, with three arched doorways on the ground floor and three plain rectangular first-floor windows. Pedimented attic with lunette above central bay, linked to ball finials above the end pilasters. The legend 'Royal Theatre and Opera House' appears in the frieze above the entrance canopy.

Delightfully intimate auditorium. Two horseshoe-shaped balconies supported on six columns, with rich and delicate plasterwork on their fronts. Single boxes on each side at 1st balcony level, between pairs of Corinthian columns. The entablature above the columns supports a deep elliptical arch in front of the enriched frame of the narrow but high proscenium. Phipps was not afraid of repeating himself and the theme of deep

Northampton, Royal (Ted Bottle)

panelled coves above the gallery slips, rising to a circular ceiling, may be seen in many of his theatres. (Eastbourne, Wolverhampton, Glasgow Theatre Royal, Edinburgh Lyceum, etc.) At Northampton the plain surface surrounding the Rococo plasterwork in the centre of the ceiling was repainted in the form of stylised clouds in 1960 by Osborne Robinson who added other murals elsewhere at the same time. The theatre possesses a rare painted act-drop of c.1897 by Ernest Howard with an oval Venetian scene surrounded by elaborate draperies. This is now in storage due to its fragile condition. There is also another, smaller act drop, painted for an earli-

er theatre. Very few other old painted act-drops survive in use (cf the Grand Theatre, Wolverhampton, the Gaiety Theatre, Douglas, the Adelina Patti Theatre, Abercrave, and the Normansfield Theatre, London).

An unusual feature of the theatre is that, because of the constricted site, the scenery store and paint frame, etc., had to be located on the other side of a narrow street to the rear, linked to the stage, which is below street level, by an underground passage. The theatre has been used as a repertory playhouse since 1927 and was purchased by the local authority in 1960. In mid 1980 a multipurpose concert hall/theatre (the

Derngate) with a seating capacity of approximately 1500 was built to the rear of the Royal. At the same time, the Royal's backstage was extended.

The long overdue refurbishment of the theatre, front and back stage, is planned to take place during 2000. CB/TB

NORTH SHIELDS
North Tyneside

New Prince's
Russell Street
Other names
   Princes
   Crown
   Gaumont
   Classic
Original architect
   1929   **George Bell of Dixon and Bell**
Current use **Bingo**
Capacity **originally c.1450**

A ciné-variety of 1929. Flank wall, red brick with stone dressings, faces Russell Street; original main entrance at one end set behind a pair of Doric columns and surmounted by a semi-circular arch and parapet with central tablet. Bay to right of entrance rises an additional storey and has arched, balustraded balcony, off-centre at first floor. Stage house and large fly tower.

Interior not seen but said to have false ceiling at 1st balcony level, stage and stalls levelled, but proscenium arch untouched. Bingo entrance has been moved to the other flank of the building, by the railway station.   *IG*

NORWICH

Maddermarket ★
St John's Alley
Original architect
   1794   **Unknown: as a chapel**
Later works
   1921   **Noel Paul with W.F. Town and**
          Walter Nugent Monck: con-
          verted to theatre
   1953   **J. Owen Bond: auditorium**
          extended
   1966   **Lambert Scott and Innes, of**
          Norwich: thrust stage created;
          other modifications
Listed **Grade II**
Current use **Theatre**
Capacity **c.310**

Before 1921, the original building had served at various times as a Roman Catholic chapel, a warehouse, Salvation Army hall and general store. Its conver-sion for Nugent Monck and the Norwich Players was designed for the perfor-mance of pre-Restoration drama, for which Monck believed that 'modern' (i.e. proscenium) theatres were unsuit-able. As it is seen today, the theatre may be considered in two parts, first the ex-chapel, now the auditorium, standing to the right of the theatre complex and, second, the later 1960s' extensions.

The Maddermarket was claimed to be the first attempt in this country to recre-ate an Elizabethan stage, but the con-straints of the building prevented the scholarship of the time being fully realised and an end-stage, incorporating two pillars and an apron was created, rather than a thrust. The auditorium was fitted out in the appropriate period style and the entrance off St John's Alley was similarly treated. The rear of the audito-rium was extended in 1953 to provide 100 additional seats and other ancillary accommodation. In 1966 the stage was extended into a thrust format and mod-ifications were made to the gallery. Both stalls and gallery are raked, the latter rather steeply. The acoustics are good, largely due to the retained barrel-vaulted ceiling of the original chapel.

The 1966 extensions were made in a contrasting style with white rendered walls, generous glazing, black timber panels and mono-pitch roofs. An enlarged bar, entrance foyer and exhibi-tion space were provided plus backstage accommodation, including a rehearsal room and enlarged wardrobe area. These are arranged to form an entrance courtyard and service yard, both off St John's Alley.   *JL*

Regent
Prince of Wales Road
Other names
   Cannon
Original architect
   1923   **George Fitt with J. Owen Bond**
Current use **Cinema**
Capacity **c.1800 (prior to subdivision)**

Constructed behind Alexandra Mansions, using former shops as an entrance, the Regent was built as a ciné-variety but, curiously, the projection rooms seem to have been added as an afterthought in a space originally intend-ed for circulation.

It had a raked stage and fly tower. The auditorium had a plaster barrel-vaulted ceiling and box fronts on either side of an elliptically arched proscenium. Live shows ceased in 1927. It was tripled as an ABC in the 1960s, but it is likely that the original interior has been con-cealed rather than destroyed.

Theatre Royal ★★
Theatre Street
Other names
   1758–68   **New Theatre**
   1903– 4   **Norwich Hippodrome**
   1915–16   **Empire and Theatre Royal**
   1956–67   **Essoldo**
Original architect
   1758   **Thomas Ivory (on adjacent**
          site)
Later works
   1800 and later
          William Wilkins Senior: front
          colonnade added; auditorium
          and stage improved
   1826   **William Wilkins the Younger:**
          new theatre built on present
          site
   1913   **Unknown: substantially**
          enlarged; new stage built
   1935   **W.H. Barton: completely new**
          theatre built following fire
   1970   **Unknown: modernised**
   1992   **Norwich City Architects Dept:**
          modernised
Current use **Theatre**
Capacity **1312**

There has been a theatre on or adjoining this site since 1758. After a fire in 1935, the present theatre was built to the designs of W.H. Barton. The street or north elevation is brick, modern and very plain, with its five bays marked by three-quarter height pilasters. The ground floor is clad in white PVC-coated sheet steel in a manner imitative of channelled stucco. There is a similarly clad canopy running full width. The top storey of the building is of open timber framing, masking mechanical roof plant. To the right is a narrow, two-storey, steel-clad service bay. To the left is the two-storey entrance wing. The entrance doors are covered by a canopy set at the same height as that to the auditorium block. The new stage house is clad in coated steel and has a segmental metal roof.

The entrance foyer and associated public spaces are part restorations of the original 1935 decor and part later work inspired by that style. The Art-Deco audi-torium is proportionally quite wide; there is a deep, moulded plaster cornice which supports a circular ceiling panel. The four original boxes are unused: the fronts of those nearer the dress circle retain their fronts but are curtained-off and those nearer the stage are treated as blind, Art-Deco ornaments.

A remarkable continuity of dramatic use on this site is due, not least, to the City Council's decision in 1967 – in the years of nationwide theatre destruction – to purchase. The radical works of 1992 provided a new stage house and back-stage provisions, enlarged the stage left wing space and impressively refurbished the front-of-house area. The restored 1935 auditorium, while showing the influence of contemporary cinema design, remains essentially a space intended for drama.   JL

NOTTINGHAM
Nottinghamshire

Malt Cross ★★
16 St James Street
Other names
   The Potters House
Original architect
   1877   Edwin Hill: as a music hall
Later works
   1998   Helmore Bewers, majors works
           of restoration and improve-
           ment
Listed   Grade II
Current use Entertainment with catering
Capacity   c.200

A mid-Victorian pub music hall set behind a three-storey frontage building. It was built for a plumber named Weldon and was originally intended to contain a skating rink below a hall, but both the design and the proposed uses went through several changes before the work was completed. What can be said with confidence is that it has no precise counterpart in any other surviving or known pub music hall design.

The only access, as was commonly the case, was via the front bar. The music hall itself is at ground level, flat floored, about 13.71m (45ft) long, 9.14m (30ft) wide and 7.62m (25ft) high to the springing of the timber arches support-ing the semi-circular glazed roof. An iron balustraded balcony round three sides is supported on slender cast-iron columns with elaborate dolphin caps. There is a simple, bow-fronted, high platform stage (modern, but reflecting the proba-ble original form). Dressing booths on either side at balcony level have been removed. Immediately below the music hall was a lower hall also originally bal-conied but now horizontally divided. This room is now used as a restaurant (as it was in 1877). This was lighted by a central balustraded well in the music hall floor, an arrangement which meant that the centre of the hall floor had to be

Nottingham, Malt Cross Music Hall
(Music Hall Trust)

clear, with banquette seats at the sides, rather than the more usual café table and chairs layout. Under the lower hall was a vaulted cellar. The music hall roof is structurally of some interest. Designed to have cast-iron arched beams, it was actually constructed with laminated wood arches.

The Malt Cross had closed as a music hall by 1914. It is now owned and occu-pied by a trust, a 'community-based car-ing operation' who carried out a major restoration in 1998.

This is an extraordinary building look-ing like a cross between an early supper room music hall and a draper's shop (which, it once was). Although well researched in documentary terms, it has probably not yet yielded up all the his-torical facts one would wish to have con-cerning its physical peculiarities and the processes by which it achieved its pre-sent form. Its present employment is about as close as one might get today to its original use.   TB/JL

Nottingham Playhouse
Goldsmith Street
Other names
   1910   Pringles Picture Palace
   1913   Picture House (known locally
           as Goldsmith Street Picture
           House)
   1942   New Repertory Theatre
   1943   Little Theatre
Original architect
   1910   Unknown
Current use Pub
Capacity   c.460 (as repertory theatre)

Opened in 1910 as Pringles Picture Palace with a small ciné-variety stage. Exterior stucco faced with a dome. Served as a repertory theatre from the mid-1940s and became Nottingham Playhouse in 1948, remaining in opera-tion until the new Playhouse (too late in date to appear in this book) opened. One of the principal regional repertory houses in its time, despite the limitations of an impossibly small stage. Following a number of uses the building is now a public house.

Theatre Royal ★★★
Theatre Square
Original architect
   1865   C.J. Phipps
Later works
   1884 and 1890 C.J. Phipps: altered to
           increase accommodation: new
           pit entrance in Sherwood
           Street; two omnibus boxes
           added below first tier boxes;
           new large crush room at
           entrance
   1897   Frank Matcham: auditorium
           reconstructed
   1978   RHWL: new front of house and
           stage; altered internally
Listed   Grade II
Current use Theatre
Capacity   1186

Nottingham was Phipps's second theatre commission and his splendid colonnade of giant Corinthian columns survives to terminate the vista up the steep gradient of Market Street. In 1897 Frank Matcham removed the three balconies and the boxes of Phipps's auditorium and replaced them by three new can-tilevered balconies with improved sight lines and a new stack of boxes flanking the proscenium; the whole richly deco-rated with lively Rococo plasterwork. The result was an auditorium of remark-able intimacy and vibrantly theatrical atmosphere. It now seems certain that the proscenium, as it existed prior to the reconstruction of 1978, was the result of redesign by Phipps in 1884 that had been left intact by Matcham. It was cer-tainly not Phipps's 1865 proscenium and was quite untypical of Matcham. It did, however, have much in common with prosceniums designed by Phipps later in his career. Further evidence of a return visit by him were the small bulbous-based columns re-used by Matcham at the sides of the auditorium, again char-acteristically late Phipps and to be seen at his Royal Lyceum Theatre, Edinburgh, of 1883. It is a pity that the old prosce-

Nottingham, Theatre Royal (Ian Grundy)

nium was demolished in 1977 and replaced by the present arrangement of giant Corinthian columns awkwardly surmounted by the curiously shaped arch springing directly off the capitals. Matcham's distinctive 2nd balcony-level boxes and their plasterwork canopies were also at that time removed in favour of the present upper boxes, which are poorly related to the new proscenium and expose areas of blank wall.

These are the less favourable points in what was otherwise a magnificent revitalisation of the old theatre. In the auditorium the part-pastiche colonnade encircling the stalls seating, the arcaded boxes at the rear of the dress circle (inspired by the arcade at the rear of the dress circle of the Phipps's Edinburgh Royal Lyceum), the reseating of the old gallery and the green and gold colour scheme are all a success. Equally welcome are the spacious new foyers and bars replacing the cramped wedge between the facade and the curved wall of the auditorium. Backstage everything is transformed, with a heightened grid, side stage, scene dock, new dressing rooms, offices, etc. Phipps's facade is improved by new return-bays, setting it off from the receding curves of the new building on each side, and by the restoration of balustrades and urns.

The project was courageously financed by Nottingham Corporation at a time of economic austerity. A new 2500-seat concert hall was built in 1980 to the rear of the Royal and connected to it both backstage and through the

stalls bar to the right of the auditorium. This involved the loss of the adjoining Empire Theatre.   *CB/TB*

NUNEATON
Warwickshire

Empire
Leicester Road
Other names
>   1909   **Empire Hall and Roller Skating Rink**
>   1912   **Vint's Picturedrome**
Original architect
>   1909   **G.F. Ward**
Current use **Nightclub**
Capacity   **originally 4000 (reduced to 2000 on conversion to Vint's Picturedrome)**

This building opened as a skating rink but was designed so that it could be readily converted into a variety theatre, which it became in 1910. Accommodation included stalls, end balcony, circle and boxes. It is thought to have closed c.1917. By 1948 it was in use as a factory.

The premises, although owned by one person, are now operated on two separate and distinct levels; the ground floor being a snooker hall and the upper a nightclub.

There is little within the shell of the theatre to suggest its former use although it is likely that the offices and access stairway at the front of the building are original. The stage side of the proscenium wall now houses three substantial mezzanine floors the middle one

being a lounge to the nightclub. Above this is a storage level from which the brick arch in the proscenium wall is visible. The proscenium pillars remain either side.

As now seen, the building has an undistinguished brick and terracotta facade of three storeys with a triangular central pediment enclosing a subsidiary serpentine pediment. It has undergone many changes since it closed as a venue for entertainment. The present squat fly tower, which extends approximately 8 feet above the main roof, would suggest that full flying of scenery was not possible. There is nothing in the present stage roof to suggest the existence of a grid. The roof lights probably date from the days when it operated as a factory.   *TB*

Scala
122 Abbey Street
Other names
>   **Grand Theatre**
Original architect
>   **1915   H. Mayo and Son of Nuneaton**
Current use **Amusement hall**
Capacity   **c.900**

A ciné-variety house. The building is long and narrow with a fly tower at the rear with a pitched roof. Except for the frontage the walls are of unadorned red brick. The facade to Abbey Street is of red brick with faience or artificial stone dressings. On the first floor, the centre bay has an arched window with a bowed balustrade, bearing the inscription SCALA THEATRE.

The second floor has narrower sash windows set between pilasters, above

Nuneaton, Scala (Ted Bottle)

which is a frieze and a modillion cornice. The facade is crowned by a pediment, in the tympanum of which is a roundel with the date 1914, although the building did not, in fact, open until the following year. Auditorium with one balcony and panelled side walls. Shallow stage. *TB*

OLDHAM

Coliseum ★★
Fairbottom Street
Other names
1885–1939 Colosseum
Original architect
1887 Thomas Whittaker: relocated an existing building to present address
Later works
1931 Unknown: projection box introduced and modifications to facade: stage house demolished
1939 Mr Armitage and James Fazakerly: circus auditorium divided; stage area reinstated; dressing rooms built from former circus stables; facade altered and simplified
1964/6 Tom Hayes and Son: old timbers replaced by masonry; safety curtain installed; bar and coffee lounge built; projection box removed
1974 Unknown: fly tower added and stage house enlarged
Current use Theatre
Capacity 580

Originally called the Colosseum, the wooden circus was built for Mr Myers, proprietor of Myers' Grand American Hippodrome Circus. Myers, however, was unable to pay for the building on completion and, after a court judgement, Thomas Whittaker, the designer and builder, became the theatre owner. Sited on Henshaw Street, it opened with a Chinese Fair. After an equestrian season Whittaker converted the circus to a music hall and, soon after, stage plays were presented. The site in Henshaw Street then became untenable, with plans for the building of the Market Hall imminent, so the theatre was dismantled in 1887 and moved to the site of the disused Holebottom Colliery in Fairbottom Street, adjacent to the Theatre Royal (now demolished). It was about this time that the name was changed to Coliseum.

Various adaptations have since taken place: all the timber was protected against fire, means of escape were greatly improved (capacity was over 3000), gas and coloured limelight illumination was introduced, as was a paint-frame. The auditorium floor could be raised for use as a ballroom or exhibition centre. An efficient ventilation system was also installed. An attempt to convert to a cinema in 1931 failed to obtain a licence. After further alterations, it was reopened as a theatre club in 1939.

The remaining original timber construction was replaced by masonry in the 1960s. The stage house and fly tower were added in 1974, with other backstage improvements.

The auditorium seen today follows the original music hall form with balcony and gallery supported by pillars. The lower balcony front has gilded decorative roundels against deep red. It continues to the (1963) proscenium which is 9m (29ft 6in) wide. This is plain, but until recently was dressed with circus-style swagged curtains as a reminder of the theatre's origins. Although replaced in 1963, the exterior retains its 1930s' character, belying the charming auditorium with its traditional character and atmosphere. *SM*

Grand
King Street/Union Street
Other names
Grand Theatre and Opera House
1937 Gaumont
1962 Astoria
Original architect
1908 Thomas Taylor, with 'a leading London architect'
Later works
1937 Unknown: converted to cinema
1962 Unknown: converted to bowling alley
1973 Unknown: converted to nightclub
Current use Disused
Capacity 1842 (following conversion to cinema)

A large theatre, with brick and terracotta facade now much altered and corner entrance rebuilt in 1936 with tower and clock. Originally 'an elaborate interior' and the most prestigious theatre in Oldham. The building was internally altered at the same time for a 1930s' cinema. No further description found.

Converted to a bowling alley and then a nightclub, the building is currently disused and under threat of demolition. *CB/SM*

Hippodrome
Union Street
Other names
1875 New Adelphi Music Hall
1878 New Adelphi Temperance Theatre of Varieties
1878 Adelphi
1880 Princes Theatre
1881 Gaiety Theatre of Varieties also Gaiety
1906 Hippodrome
1920 Victory Cinema
1962 Continental
Original architect
1875 T. Crossley
Later works
1880 R. Owen: new proscenium installed

Oldham, Coliseum (Ian Grundy)

1920   Roberts and Taylor: converted to cinema
1970   Unknown: converted to bingo
1978   Unknown: foyer converted to amusement arcade
Current use Amusements

Opened on the site of its predecessor (the Adelphi Music Hall) in August 1875 as a variety building of some grandeur: private boxes, centre boxes, pit, side balcony and upper balcony. In 1880 it had a short-lived run as a drama theatre, but it reverted to variety. It ran with popularity under a succession of owners, as its many names reflect, until 1919. It was then converted to the Victory Cinema.

The rendered facade, altered at ground-floor level, stands intact in Union Street. The foyer now houses an amusement arcade; the cinema is not used as a public area. *SM*

OSWESTRY
Shropshire

New
Willow Street
Original architect
    1819   Unknown
Later works
post 1852 Unknown: converted to malthouse
Listed   Grade II
Current use Disused

Built 1819 for Charles Stanton's Company of Comedians. Converted to a malthouse after 1852. Red brick with uncoursed limestone rubble to left side and regularly coursed limestone to rear

gable; slate roof with pedimented gable facing street. Three levels. Stone band with widely spaced plain modillions to front gable and brick eaves cornices to left and right. Three bays, the centre slightly projecting, segmental-headed fixed-light windows with door to lower right; infilled roundel to gable. Mid to late C19 two-storey gabled range to rear may have been dressing rooms, etc. Interior now has the character of a malthouse, with an inserted first floor. *TB*

OXFORD
Oxfordshire

Apollo ★★
George Street
Other names
1933–77   New Theatre
Original architect
    1933   W. and T.R. Milburn, with T.P. Bennett
Current use Theatre
Capacity   1826

Built on a site previously occupied by the New Theatre of 1868, which was demolished by fire and replaced by Drinkwater's New Theatre of 1886. This was, in turn, remodelled by W.G.R. Sprague in 1908 and, by all appearances, internally remodelled in modern style rather than rebuilt by W. and T.R. Milburn in 1933. The theatre was in the ownership of three generations of the Dorrill family until 1972.

The present theatre has a stone facade, probably in the main that of 1908, with little in the way of architectural relief apart from a lonely-looking

aedicule on the long flank. Plain attic above a squashed modillion cornice. Entrance on chamfered corner.

The auditorium is in Art-Deco style. High, arched proscenium with pelmet set within deep banded ante-proscenium. No boxes. Two balconies, the lower one divided by a barrier into dress and upper circle, decorated with 'Roman' stud decoration and terminating at the ante-proscenium. At stalls level, two gilded murals depict Antique scenes. In the foyer, the mirrors and staircase decoration are in similar style. Difficult get-in, the stage being more than 2m (6ft 8in) below street level. The theatre is now a major touring house. *SM/KW*

Holywell Music Room
The Music Faculty, Holywell Street
Original architect
    1748   Dr Thomas Caplin
Listed   Grade II*
Current use Concert room with occasional plays
Capacity   200

An open-platform, flat-floored concert room, used mainly for music and occasionally for plays and other entertainments which require no scenery. It nevertheless demands a mention here as the oldest surviving purpose-built concert hall in Europe.

Externally a chapel-like brick box with a stone pedimented three-bay facade and later advanced single-storey extension containing the entrance. Slate roof. Quite plain internally. An apsed room with curving steps on either side of a platform. At the rear, behind the performance area, is a 1790 John Donaldson organ. *KW/JE*

Playhouse ★★
Beaumont Street
Original architect
    1938   Sir Edward Maufe
Later works
    1964   Martin Card (Fred Rowntree and Son): auditorium remodelled
    1996   Michael Reardon and Associates: new entrance canopy; box office and other internal improvements; auditorium reseated and remodelled
Listed   Grade II*
Current use Theatre
Capacity   650

Edward Maufe was not known as a theatre architect and his two essays in this field, both in University towns, were

Oxford, Playhouse

severely constrained. At the Cambridge Festival, he did little more than carry out Terence Gray's explicit wishes. In Oxford, he felt the need to conform to the Georgian discipline of the adjoining terraces. Would that all architects took such notice of their surroundings! – but it might be argued that Maufe was a little too careful. Total reticence was reasonable in earlier times when the sole theatre in a town had no competition. Today there is a great deal on offer and theatres must be visible, even in Oxford.

Maufe's seven-bay stone facade is almost self-effacing, picking up the cornice line and fenestration pattern of the terrace to the right with so little variation that, from a short distance and but for the absence of party divisions and chimney stacks, it could be mistaken for a row of houses. The canopy is thin and the name of the theatre elegantly and almost invisibly lettered on the facade.

The single-balconied auditorium was also quite undemonstrative but was remodelled in 1964 with dark wood linings. These were removed in a further remodelling in 1996 which returned to a form rather closer to the original design. Work done since 1991 has greatly improved the visibility and attractiveness of this theatre. Two adjoining houses are united with front of house as offices.   *JE*

PAIGNTON
Torbay

Palace Avenue
Palace Avenue
Other names
   Paignton Public Hall
   1940-44   Garrison Theatre
   1946   Palace Avenue Hall
Original architect
   1889   W.R. Fletcher and George
      Soudon Bridgeman
Later works
   1936   Unknown: new proscenium
      arch
   1948   Unknown: internal and exter-
      nal improvements including
      new stage floor and new
      lighting
   1974   Unknown: refurbished and
      redecorated
Current use Theatre
Capacity   399

Opened in 1889 as a Public Hall and Assembly Rooms, it cost £3000, including the land. The stage had a mahogany and gilt proscenium which came from the Royal Bijou Theatre when that was

dismantled; in 1936 a new proscenium was installed and the former became a false pros. The basement space below the main hall was used mainly for storage, although it was also used for roller skating, and for gun training by the local Naval Reserve Force, evidence of which remains in the form of a mounting for an A.A. gun. During the Second World War, it was used as a Garrison Theatre, when improvements were made. In recent times the theatre use has diminished, except for amateur theatricals, and community activities.

As now seen, there is no flying height, so cloths are rolled; there is no iron. The hall ceiling is divided by seven trusses. The stage has an unusual get-in created by taking out a window and making it into a door. There are two dressing rooms.   *SM*

Rotunda
Oldway, Preston
Original architect
   1873   George Soudon Bridgeman
Later works
   c.1946   Unknown: building subdivided
      into offices
Current use Offices

About 1871, Isaac Merritt Singer (founder of the Singer Sewing Machine Co.) purchased land and various properties including a villa 'Little Oldway' and commissioned a local architect, Bridgeman, to design a mansion (Oldway) and a separate building as a 'Riding and Exercising Pavilion' – now known as The Rotunda. The circular building was the first completed. Inside, the walls were of cream-coloured brick with Portland stone dressings. It was used for stabling and teaching children to ride, and had a movable wooden floor which covered a swimming pool. There was a balcony for spectators and the central area was used for entertainment of all kinds. On one occasion a circus was hired to perform there.

There was also a theatre, later removed, in the mansion. In 1946, Oldway was acquired by Paignton Council and, until 1988, leased for offices. Externally the Rotunda is unaltered; access is not possible, but it is thought that internal alterations are superficial. There were plans (1994) for various leisure uses, but restoration to original form has also been discussed.   *SM*

PENARTH
Vale of Glamorgan

Paget Rooms ★
Victoria Road
Original architect
   1906   John Contes Carter of Penarth
Listed   Grade II
Current use Theatre
Capacity   398

Built on land donated by the Earl of Plymouth, the building is roughcast rendered and painted over a brown glazed-brick plinth. The upper storey has a row of seven small-pane casement windows, with a small round window to left and a parapet above. The central main entrance is set in a low round arch flanked by Ionic columns with exaggerated capitals. The entrance arch is flanked by two taller arches. The vestibule has panelled side walls with oval mirrors, leading to the entrance hall which has been modernised. The auditorium has a broad coved ceiling that has two central ventilators with moulded architraves. Each side has four round-arched bays; the theatre boxes have bulbous balcony fronts.   *TR*

Pier Pavilion
The Esplanade
Other names
   New (Pier) Pavilion
Original architect
   1929   Unknown
Later works
   1931   Unknown: rebuilt after partial
      destruction by fire
Listed   Grade II
Capacity   c.600

Following the construction of a series of buildings on H.F. Edwards' pier of 1895, the Pier Pavilion was added at the landward end in 1929. It faces Bridgeman Road. Reinforced concrete, in Indian style, main block with tapering corner towers, capped by Moghul style roofs with deeply overhanging bracketed eaves and windows with diaper grilles. West (landward) end at ground level flanked by concave wings, containing shops, kiosks, etc., in classical style with Roman Doric columns. Pierced parapet between towers. First-floor convex bay with large glazed openings onto terrace. Flanks have four tall lucerne windows set in a curved roof. Adamesque interior decorations.

The auditorium housed in more recent years a penny arcade and a snooker club. Afterwards it was, for some time, disused until repair and restoration works to the pier totalling over £2 million were carried out in 1994 and 1996. *TR*

PENRITH
Cumbria

Alhambra
Middlegate
Original architect
   1906   Unknown
Later works
   1930s Unknown: internal alterations
   1984   Unknown: circle converted to cinema, with bingo remaining in stalls
Current use Cinema and bingo
Capacity c.800 (prior to subdivision)

Squared and coursed rubble-stone facade with red stone dressings; twin Dutch gables at the end of a uniform gabled three-storey row. As built, with a 5.2m (17ft) deep stage with rear get-in, it was a simple single-balconied room of little architectural pretension. It closed as a cinema in 1971, in favour of the Regent, and was converted to bingo. In 1984, when the Regent closed, the circle was converted to a cinema.

The original auditorium has been divided horizontally. The upper (cinema) space, does not occupy the full length, but consists of 5 rows of a raked balcony plus three added at the front, facing a wide false proscenium. The ground-floor bingo room occupies the whole of the old stalls area, with the lower part of the original proscenium and stage visible. A false ceiling had been inserted above the remaining slips.

Foyer is not original (from 1930s) but the original plasterwork exists approx 1.8m (c.6ft) above. Exterior condition is good. A second cinema screen is to be added. *IG*

PENZANCE
Cornwall

Grand Casino (Pavilion)
Promenade
Other names
   1919   Pavilion and Winter Gardens
Original architect
   1912   F.G. Drewitt
Current use Amusement arcade
Capacity c.1000

A typical seaside theatre of its date. Small rectangular auditorium with segmental tunnel-vaulted ceiling, lunette windows, panelled side walls and flat

floor. Segmentally arched proscenium with Baroque plasterwork enrichment. Shallow stage without fly tower. The circle is now divided off and serves as a restaurant. By 1974 the whole building was in a poor condition and there have been many alterations to interior and exterior which have resulted in the loss of some of the original plasterwork.

The long, low facade to the Promenade is in Cornish granite. A five-bay Tuscan colonnade between two squat, square towers, each with an oeil-de-boeuf window in the upper stage. The towers were originally capped with copper cupolas but these were replaced by slate in the 1970s. Large doorways with open segmented pediments carried by Atlantes. The interior is an amusement arcade, a large area consisting of the original auditorium plus foyer extending the width of the building to a depth of 8.2m (27ft) and taking in a room, stage right, 12.8m (42ft) long and 3.7m (12ft) wide. The restaurant area 'stage left' contains some original doors. Balustrades and glasswork have been partly restored.

There is also a series of architects' drawings of the original 1912 building on display. *MS*

Theatre *
Union Hotel, Chapel Street
Other names
   Georgian Theatre
Original architect
   1787   Unknown
Listed   Grade II
Current use Store and garage
Capacity   originally c.500

Situated at the rear of the Union Hotel, but a separate structure, constructed of rubble with a slated pitched roof and gabled ends. Overall external dimensions 18.58m x 9.44m (61ft x 31ft). The ground level slopes steeply away along one side and the space under the theatre was used as part of the hotel stables. It now houses cars rather than horses and wide openings have been formed in the side wall. The theatre was entered through a gabled elevation facing a narrow alley. Simply framed double doors in the centre and a single door to the right. Although much altered and subdivided internally, there are still vestiges of the original use, e.g. remains of a gallery now encased and possibly a refixed proscenium door. Closed as a theatre in 1831 and dismantled in 1839. Further investigation is necessary to uncover every scrap of evidence to discover suffi-

cient evidence for a complete restoration of this Georgian playhouse, an increasingly rare type of theatre following the regrettable demolitions at Dorchester and Newbury. A study was made in 1989 but no action followed. *CB*

PERTH
Perth and Kinross

Perth Theatre and Opera House ★★
High Street
Other names
   Royal Theatre
Original architect
   1900   William Alexander
Later works
   1924   Unknown: renovated following fire damage
   1981   Gordon and Dry Partnership: renovated
Listed   Grade B
Current use Theatre
Capacity   490

A discreet entrance arch with glazed canopy set into four-storey ashlar tenement block leads to a spacious conservatory-style inner foyer with a glazed ceiling in the back court. The brick-clad block to the rear contains a delightfully intimate auditorium of two tiers (including the disused top balcony). Noteworthy Rococo plaster ornamentation – the 1st balcony is decorated with foliated scrolls and consoles and the upper balcony has delicately modelled festoons. The slips of both tiers curve round to meet slim stacks of superimposed boxes, framed by pilasters with enriched shafts. The ceiling is a plain saucer dome, reputedly a simple replacement for the fire-damaged original and dating from repairs in 1924. The auditorium has been narrowed at circle level by the insertion of side fire escape routes. Housing a well-established and successful repertory company and hosting touring productions, the theatre is bustling with activity. It is well cared for and a joy to visit. *BP*

Theatre Royal
Atholl Street
Original architect
   1820   Unknown
Listed   Grade B
Current use Restaurant

The theatre has long-since been gutted for various industrial uses and now only the restrained three-storey ashlar facade at the junction of Atholl and Kinnoull

Streets remains, containing a restaurant. Three bays to Atholl Street with arches to the ground floor and windows above. BP

PETERBOROUGH

Embassy
Broadway
Other names
  ABC
  Cannon
  Academy
Original architect
  1937   David Evelyn Nye
Later works
  1981   Unknown: tripled
  1996   Mason Richards Partnership: converted to pub
Current use Theme pub
Capacity originally c.1500

The only theatre built by this noted cinema architect. Two of Nye's cinemas, in Berkhamsted and Esher, are listed buildings. A difficult site required that the stage occupied the most externally visible part of the building with a wide fan-shaped auditorium behind, and with the main entrance in the rear corner of the site. The narrow stage end has been altered with a canopy now wrapped around the corner. Originally the horizontal band extended only to the limits of the vertical fins and below this was the stage door and, in the centre, the high scene dock door. Inside the wide auditorium there was one steep circle and stalls. The front of the circle was close to the stage and the sight lines excellent. Restrained Art Deco decoration and lighting resulted in a pleasing, if cinemaish, theatre. Dressing rooms, six

Peterborough, former Embassy
(Ian Grundy)

floors of them (14 in total) were at the apex of the building above the scene-dock door. The cinema was tripled in 1984, closed in 1989 and, after a long dark period, was converted to a pub in 1996. Entrance now via what was the rear, with bars situated in the former stage area. IG

PLYMOUTH

Globe ★★
Stonehouse Royal Marine Barracks, Durnford Street
Original architect
  1788   Unknown: as racquets court
Later works
  1831   Unknown: converted to theatre
  1864   Unknown: Bijou Theatre built
  1887   Unknown: altered and enlarged
  1928   Unknown: reseated; cinema equipment installed; modernised
  1971   Unknown: restored close to 1887 state
Listed   Grade II
Current use Amateur theatre
Capacity   c.250

A former racquets court of 1788, which was permanently converted into a theatre in 1831 and enlarged in 1887. The part covered by the present stage was once a hay loft. The auditorium is Neo-Classical in character suggesting late Regency rather than the mid-Victorian period. There is a single horseshoe gallery supported on slender iron columns which continue up to the ceiling. On each side of the well-proportioned rectangular proscenium arch are false proscenium doors, set between engaged square Tuscan columns, reminiscent of the theatres of William Wilkins (e.g. Bury St Edmunds). In 1928 new exits were introduced which reduced the seating capacity to 250. (In the 1880s it had been 600-700). The building was overhauled and redecorated in 1971. It is now used by Marines and local amateur groups, as well as for cinema. The famous 'thunder run' is still in situ. The theatre is of particular significance as a rare example of its kind and period. CB/SM

Palace ★★
121-123 Union Street
Other names
  1898   Palace of Varieties
Original architect
  1898   Wimperis and Arber

Later works
  1906   Unknown: improved; sliding roof installed
  1954   Unknown: improved
Listed   Grade II*
Current use Disused
Capacity: c.1400

Built for the Livermore Brothers, the Palace opened in 1898, as a music hall, forming part of a development which included the adjoining Grand Western Hotel. Elaborate Flemish Renaissance style facade in terracotta – three main bays and three storeys with steeply pitched tiled roofs. Wide central entrance bay surmounted by a big Flemish gable with two statues of Spanish soldiers standing against the front face on protecting brackets. Small, closely spaced, arched windows in the upper storey. Three large arched windows between Ionic demi-columns in the piano nobile, flanked in the end bays by semi-circular panels of coloured tiles depicting scenes of the Spanish Armada. The ground floor has seven bays of Tuscan columns supporting a continuous entablature. The elevational treatment of the front is continued for one main bay round the corner and the angle is surmounted by an octagonal turret with cupola and projecting balcony; probably intended to resemble the top of a lighthouse. Much Art Nouveau decorative detail, e.g. on the frieze above the first-floor windows and in the panels below the windows. The facade is at present marred by a crude modern canopy projecting from halfway up the height of the columns. A wide, balustraded staircase leads from the entrance foyer to an unusually spacious saloon lit by the three large first-floor windows.

The elaboration of the exterior is not, unfortunately, fully matched in the auditorium - it was originally, but a serious fire occurred eight months after the opening and presumably funds were not available for a complete restoration. The fronts of the two deep balconies are, however, decorated with plasterwork incorporating military motifs, and the large boxes flanking each side of the proscenium at dress-circle level have canopies with two projecting ship's lanterns. Plain, domed ceiling. Unusually a tunnel crosses beneath the stalls. After a period of use for bingo, the theatre was courageously reopened as a private commercial venture in 1978, despite the proposal of the Local Authority to build the new Theatre Royal (which opened in

1982). The building, however, reverted to bingo use and then became a nightclub. After a period empty and vandalised, there had appeared to be some prospect of a return to use, but there has, disappointingly, been no movement for some time.   *CB/SM*

PORTADOWN
Craigavon

Town Hall Theatre ★
15/17 Edward St
Original architect
   1890   T. and R. Roe
Later works
   1990   James McCormick and Co: hall
          remodelled and interior refur-
          bished; fly tower built
Current use **Theatre**
Capacity   **320**

Portsmouth, Southsea King's (Ted Bottle)

The five-bay entrance facade faces Edward Street. Its red brickwork and rich terracotta ornamentation is in the Dutch-Jacobean style. On each side of the central entrance door (with its canopy-balcony) there is a tall gabled block. Brick pilasters flank the entrance and extend upwards to parapet height where a curvilinear centre piece carries the words TOWN HALL. Apart from a small Citizens' Advice Bureau and a Tourist Information Bureau in a new flat-roofed extension at one end of the building the original facade remains undisturbed.

Inside there is a double-height entrance hall with a T-plan stairway serving the auditorium on the first floor and also the Minor Hall. Decoration is generally low-key and domestic in feeling with Arts and Crafts overdoors copied from the one that still survived.

The original plain hall and stage have been cleverly reshaped so that a system of removable raked seating rises up to the level of the original decorative cast-iron balcony front which has been retained along with the stepped balcony. There is a large scissors-operated forestage or orchestra pit, and the proscenium opening, made up of curtains, is demountable. A subtle refinement is the front-of-house stage lighting concealed behind a rise-and-fall panel. Colours in the auditorium are pink and white with claret curtains and seating.

Craigavon Council's move to the new Civic Centre has meant that the theatrical element, always present in the Old Town Hall, now reigns supreme. The theatre has its own identity, is particularly well equipped and serves the people

of Portadown and the county around with competence.   *RMcK*

PORTHCURNO
Cornwall

Minack ★★
Original architect
   1933   Rowena Cade
Current use **Seasonal open-air theatre**
Capacity   **750**

The creation in every sense of Rowena Cade. Hewn out of granite cliffs on one of the farthest rocky tips of Cornwall, a wildly romantic theatre where the backdrop to the circular stage is the moody Atlantic. Work began in 1932 on what is probably one of the finest and most skilfully adapted open-air playhouses. Visited by companies from all over the country, productions are from June to September, and range from Shakespeare and Restoration comedy to Ayckbourn.   *SM*

PORTSMOUTH
Hampshire

King's ★★★
Albert Road, Southsea
Original architect
   1907   Frank Matcham
Later works
   1987   City Architect: roof and audi-
          torium ceiling repaired
Listed   **Grade II***
Current use **Theatre**
Capacity   **1450**

Sited between two converging roads

with the entrance at the apex, dominated by a hexagonal tower with a steeply pitched roof surmounted by a cupola. The auditorium has three well-curved balconies and is intimate for its large capacity. The 1st and 2nd balconies abut two superimposed stage boxes on each side. The lower boxes have arched canopies which also form the fronts of the boxes above. These are framed by squat Ionic columns and are backed by shell-hooded niches. The gallery front curves directly into the walls and is separated from the stage boxes on each side by a further large shell-hooded niche (a favourite Matcham decorative motif). The ceiling is in two sections – a flat lower part spanning between the stage boxes and a large oval saucer-dome at a higher level, decorated with six painted panels. The proscenium is segmentally arched with an enriched plaster outer frame and an inner frame of alabaster. That the King's is 'late Matcham' is apparent in the heavy modelling of the Baroque plasterwork when compared with, for example, his Grand, Blackpool (1894), or Gaiety, Douglas (rebuilt 1900), and also in a relative coarseness in the handling of some of the forms, e.g. the composition of the boxes and the heavily emphasised proscenium frame. When considered in an overall context, however, the King's is an important and complete example of Edwardian theatre architecture.

There were undeveloped proposals c.1994 for upgrading the technical facilities, improvements to the front of house, retiering of gallery and new orchestra pit.   *CB/SM*

Palace

Commercial Road
Original architect
   1921   A.E. Cogswell
Current use **Club**

In an unusually spirited Indian Islamic style with five domes and minarets, this seems to be the only surviving cinema by the local architect A.E. Cogswell. It escaped demolition in 1975, following a public inquiry into a Compulsory Purchase Order. The screen was originally at the entrance end. It is now a club, with live entertainment. The facade is perfectly preserved.   *SM*

Savoy

335 Commercial Road / Fitzherbert Street
Other names
   1961   ABC
   1985   Cannon
Original architect
   1937   W.R. Glen
Later works
   after 1944 Unknown: reinstated after war
         damage
   1960s Unknown: stucco frontage
         covered with mosaic tiles;
         refurbished in luxury lounge
         style
   1967   Unknown: proscenium
         modified for Todd-AO (70mm)
         screen
   1982   Unknown: tripled
Current use **Dark**
Capacity c.1000 (prior to subdivision)

William Glen designed the theatre in his characteristic style: the frontage featured flowing lines and a round tower. On the upper levels, the small flat roofs were arranged to give a stepped 'ocean liner' effect. A feature of the interior, which was in the same flowing style as the exterior, with the decorative metal grilles to the windows and doors, and the metal handrails. The main foyer had a terrazzo floor. Dressing rooms were provided backstage. There was a Compton Organ. It is thought that live entertainment could not be accommodated after the 1967 modifications to the proscenium and stage for the installation of Todd-AO. Now sits on a traffic roundabout.

   The cinema closed at the end of 1999 and the building is threatened with demolition.   *SM*

Portsmouth, New Theatre Royal

Theatre Royal ★★★

Guildhall Walk/White Swan Road
Other names
   1884 and 1980 New Theatre Royal
Original architect
   1856   Unknown: Landport Hall
         converted to theatre
Later works
   1882   C.J. Phipps: theatre rebuilt
   1900   Frank Matcham: auditorium
         enlarged
   1994   Roderick Ham: renovated and
         part reconstructed
Listed   **Grade II***
Current use Theatre and arts centre
Capacity currently limited to 320

In the 1840s a building called the Landport Hall was converted from a racquets court attached to the Swan Tavern. In 1854, Henry Rutley, a circus proprietor, took over the tavern and applied for a licence to convert the hall into a theatre, which opened in Sept 1856. Rutley died in 1874, and Boughton, who acquired the theatre in 1882, purchased adjoining land, commissioning C.J. Phipps to build a larger theatre. This had three balconies, and three boxes, one at each level, on either side, as well as two boxes at the rear of the first tier. Continuing to buy up land, Boughton decided to enlarge the auditorium and improve the stage facilities, engaging Frank Matcham, with whom he had worked at the Prince's Theatre (demolished).

   Phipps's restrained but handsome pedimented classical facade of 1884 survived this reconstruction. Matcham did, however, make an addition which completely transformed the appearance of the theatre – a projecting enclosed balcony of enriched iron and glass, supported by an arcade of slender coupled colonnettes

Matcham built a new stage 19.8m (65ft) deep and enlarged Phipps' auditorium by absorbing part of the old stage 10.66m (35ft) deep within it, and building a range of four bow-fronted boxes on each side between the the ends of the balconies and the new proscenium, which was 9.14m (30ft) wide. He also partly reconstructed the balconies themselves, although making use of Phipps's supporting iron columns.

The lyre-shaped first balcony of six rows is pure Matcham and is cantilevered out from a line of columns which rise up to support the fronts of the two Phippsian horseshoe balconies above. The sides of the upper balconies were altered to improve sight lines. The overall decorations (by de Jong) are of an incredible richness. The boxes are framed by giant polygonal columns and each upper box has an arched canopy which bellies forward with a scrolled top above an oval panel. Linking the capitals of the columns on each side is a wide semi-circular arch, originally framing a bust. The proscenium is flanked by niches, originally with statues. Surmounting the opening is a large flared panel with trumpeting Tritons in plasterwork at its base.

The whole is held together by a scheme of extremely detailed plasterwork with a predominantly nautical theme. The first-tier panels are decorated with naval symbols – mermaids, dolphins, anchors and shells. The second tier honours the army; laurel wreathed lions spouting forth electric globes, while between are draped guidons and colours. The third has continuous deeply moulded Rococo acanthus motifs which gently emphasise its earlier form. Most of the panel painting was lost in a thoroughly insensitive 1948 redecoration, although there does survive the excellent large panel over the proscenium showing Thespis and boys at play.

In 1959 the theatre became a bingo hall. In 1971 an application for listed building consent to demolish was refused. The stage was destroyed by fire in 1972 (children playing with fireworks; fortunately the fire brigade lowered the iron curtain) and the building was closed. Further serious vandalism of the interior followed.

Following this, members of the Theatre Royal Society worked at weekends to protect the building from decay and vandalism. The New Theatre Royal Trustees (Portsmouth) Ltd was formed and in 1980 sufficient funds were raised to buy the freehold.

Despite the Trust's worthy efforts, the recovery of this superb theatre has been proceeding at an agonisingly slow pace. A phased scheme by Rod Ham has led to the restoration of the facade, improvements to front-of-house spaces, major repairs in the auditorium and the laying of the foundations for a completely new dressing-room and administration wing, but the rebuilding of the stage house is still awaited.

The sight lines from the balconies are very good and allow a forestage to be built forward of the proscenium which enables the splendid auditorium to function as a most exciting setting for drama. The comparatively large volume, which does not detract at all from the intimacy of the theatre, and the unusual sloping angle of the ceiling, suggests a superb acoustic for opera and musical theatre, as well as for speech.

Even in its incomplete form, the fact that the public face of the theatre is in excellent condition and that the building is used for occasional performances (and regularly as a shoppers' café rendezvous) has brought confidence to a part of the City which had formerly seemed doomed to decay. With a potential capacity of 600, the reopening of this fine theatre, with programming to complement that of the King's, will be celebrated far beyond the City and the region.   *CB/IM/SM*

PORT SUNLIGHT
Wirral

Gladstone Theatre
Greendale Road
Other names
   Gladstone Hall
Original architect
   1891   William Owen
Current use Amateur theatre
Capacity   500

Situated in the Garden Village founded in 1888 by William Hesketh Lever to house his soap factory workers, the Gladstone Hall was originally an assembly and recreation hall, with a platform stage for entertainments.Half-timbered over a red brick ground floor with tiled roofs and tile-hanging. Fine Art Nouveau panel over doors, commemorating opening of the room by W.E. Gladstone.

The auditorium, slightly raked at the rear, has a curved barrel ceiling divided by series of arched, bolted trusses with tie rods. The proscenium stage seen today was introduced in the 1920s. This curves slightly at the top with simple gilded plaster ornaments above and on each side, these being picked out in gold in an otherwise black-painted interior. *SM*

PRESTON
Lancashire

Longridge Palace
Market Place, Longridge
Other names
   Music Hall/Kinema House
Original architect
   C19   Unknown: as a workshop

Port Sunlight, Gladstone Theatre (Ian Grundy)

Later works
    c.1905 Joseph Fletcher: converted to music hall
    1976 Unknown: converted to cinema
Current use **Cinema**
Capacity c.500

The Palace opened as the Music Hall, adapted by local builder and entrepreneur Joseph Fletcher from a workshop. Two-storey building in local stone with facings and attic. The stage had flies, and there were dressing rooms built below stage. This area remains today, as do the original emergency gaslight fittings. Nothing otherwise remains of the original interior. With short intervals as both a skating rink and as a bingo hall, the Palace survived until 1976 when, under new management, it was run successfully as full-time cinema. *SM*

RAMSGATE
Kent

Granville
Victoria Parade
Original architect
    1947 Unknown
Current use **Theatre**
Capacity **587**

Built 1947, a typical seaside seasonal theatre of the time, with an adequate stage. Narrow balconies on three sides (three rows facing stage). Auditorium has been reduced in size, the rear portion being a cinema. The Channel Theatre Company is based here. *KW*

Royal Victoria Pavilion
Harbour Parade
Other names
    Pavilion Theatre
    1976-96 Club Tiberius
    since c.1996 Grosvenor Casino
Original architect
    1904 S.D. Adshead
Later works
    1976 Unknown: converted to club
Current use **Casino**
Capacity originally c.2000

An unusual work for an architect better known in other fields (although he designed the present auditoria at London Haymarket and Liverpool Playhouse).
    The exterior is comparatively little altered, a long, low building with a distinctly French seaside flavour. Single-storey base, open as a colonnade with iron columns toward the sea, enclosed at

the ends with Greek Doric columns engaged to the piers of (now blind) arcade. On the town side the entrances have been altered but domes flanked by reclining figures are still present. The platform above the ground storey is enclosed on all sides by an ornamental iron balustrade. The main block is set back, rising above the platform with a boldly curved, metal-clad roof with a robust crowning moulding.
    The interior had been altered at various times before it was finally gutted in 1976 to house a club. *KW/JE*

READING

Everyman
London Street
Other names
    Theatre Royal
    New Hall
Original architect
    n.d. Unknown
Listed **Grade II**
Current use **Business centre**

The New Hall in London Street was given a new proscenium and opened in 1853 as the Theatre Royal, New Hall. In 1843 Charles Dickens had given a solo reading of *A Christmas Carol*.
    In 1860s audiences dwindled and 1866 the hall was sold to the Primitive Methodists. In 1949, the Everyman Theatre Co. was formed and, a year later, persuaded the Borough Council to buy the then disused chapel. Renamed the Everyman Theatre it opened on Easter Monday 1952. In 1957 the Company fell into financial difficulties. The administration was taken over by the Borough Council and December saw the demise. The Theatre was in occasional use by various amateur groups, until April 1960, when it was sold to the Reading Newspaper Co.
    The original foyer and plasterwork can still be seen, and the spiral staircase from the lower foyer remains intact. Offices now occupy the shell of the building. There is no evidence of a fly tower. *SM*

REDDITCH
Worcestershire

Palace ★
Alcester Street/Grove Street
Original architect
    1913 Bertie Crewe
Later works
    c.1930 Unknown: additional exits created; capacity reduced

    1971 B. Bunch (?): new three-storey frontage added in Grove Street
    1976 Ian Coley: derelict factory at rear of building converted to new suite of dressing rooms
    1979 Nigel Lomas: new scene dock and workshop added
Listed **Grade II**
Current use **Theatre**
Capacity **399**

A small theatre, indeed diminutive when compared with other jobs which Crewe was handling at about the same time (e.g. Manchester Palace Theatre). Stuccoed facade alongside the auditorium/stage in a rather coarse Neo-Classical manner – three storeys and nine bays; the five middle bays with a rusticated ground floor supporting panelled Ionic pilasters in the upper storeys. Straight entablature and parapet. Intimate and quite pleasing auditorium with restrained Neo-Classical plasterwork. One eight-row balcony on a shallow curve, linked to one large box on either side, framed by Ionic pilasters with pediment over. Rectangular proscenium with reed-moulded frame. Flat ceiling with central circular rose. No safety curtain. Green room and seven dressing rooms. After a period of use for bingo the theatre was purchased by the Local Authority in 1971, refurbished and a three-storeyed extension built to the right of the original front, with a new entrance round the corner. It is mainly used by amateurs with occasional professional tours. Various plans have been proposed in recent years for improvements and incorporation into a new development. *TB*

RETFORD
Nottinghamshire

Majestic ★
Coronation Street
Original architect
    1927 Alfred Thraves (Nottingham)
Later works
    1981 Unknown: converted to twin cinema
    1994 Unknown: reconverted
Listed **Grade II**
Current use **Theatre**
Capacity **650**

The main axis of the building is parallel with Coronation Street with the main entrance on the left-hand side and the stage, with get-in doors, on the right. There is an unfortunate lack of space front of house. The ground floor is at present subdivided into two areas by a vertical wall following the curve of the front circle. The space beneath the circle was converted into a small cinema.

Between the ends of the circle and the proscenium are two boxes each side, the fronts of which are adorned with simple moulding. The proscenium arch is almost square and bordered by several bands of plaster mouldings. The richly decorated ceiling is divided into panels supported by four tall mermaid figures.

Six dressing rooms are available on three floors to stage right. The interior is a good example of its kind, and it is to be hoped that the theatre use will become permanent. *TB*

RHOSLLANERCHRUGOG
Wrexham

Miners' Institute ★
Plas Mwynwyr
Other names
'The Stiwt' (popular name)
1929–75 Palace Cinema
Original architect
  1927 John Owen (Wrexham) and
    F.A. Roberts (Mold)
Later works
  1996 TACP: major refurbishment
Current use Theatre and cultural centre
Capacity c.1800

The Miners' Institute had live entertainment periodically from the start. Built above street level with a railed forecourt and steps up. In an attractive Baroque manner, red brick with ample stone dressings. Front in three major bays (1+3+1) the outer with entrances and segmental crowning pediments. Advanced portico divided by coupled Doric columns supporting an entablature and balustrade. Steep pyramidal slate roof crowned by a timber clock-cupola with Ionic half-columns. Reinforced concrete internal construction. Galleried auditorium with stylised classical detailing; shallow segmental vault with guilloche bands carried on corbel-pilasters in Art Deco style, reflected in door surrounds. Sinuous gallery front. Rectangular proscenium with foliate surround. A major refurbishment scheme (£2 million plus) to improve stage facilities, dressing rooms and ancillary accommodation and to turn the Institute into an important cultural centre, was completed in 1996. *TR*

Rhosllanerchrugog, Miners' Institute (Ted Bottle)

RHYL
Denbighshire

Coliseum
West Promenade
Other names
  1962 New Coliseum
Original architect
  1921 Unknown: as open-air theatre
Later works
  1960 Unknown: amphitheatre
    roofed over
Current use Theatre
Capacity 630

A low-lying, unattractive building on the promenade within a few yards of the beach, its form determined by the need to enclose what was originally an open-air amphitheatre and give protection from the weather. The auditorium is still circular on plan. *TR*

Lyric Hall
Glanglasfor, off Market Street
Other names
  Operetta House
  Central Hall
  1906 Cheetham's Cinema (or) the
    Silvograph
  1923 The New Palladium
Original architect
  1890 Unknown
Current use Store
Capacity (was) c.500

The Lyric Hall opened in May 1890 and closed within two weeks. It reopened in June 1890 and remained active (mainly

as a cinema) until March 1931. It is on the upper floor of a plain red brick building, the long axis of which runs along Market Street, but whose main facade stands in Glanglasfor. When the Hall was built, provision was made for a gallery holding 200 persons but, in the event, this was never constructed. The facade along Market Street has been whitewashed and the ground floor given over to shops. The building is in good condition but the Hall has long since been cleared of all theatrical and cinematic fittings, and it is now used as a warehouse for a nearby furniture store. *TR*

Queen's
Other names
  Queen's Palace Theatre
  1908 Queen's Skating Rink
Original architect
  1902 C.J. Richardson
Later works
  1907 Unknown: rebuilt following
    fire
  1926 Unknown: auditorium recon-
    structed
Current use Discotheque?
Capacity c.1500 (following 1907 recon-
    struction)

Long two-storey range with large domed central pavilion destroyed by fire in 1907 and rebuilt, without the pavilion, in a similar manner to the adjacent hotel. Brick with oriel bay-windows and a tiled pitched roof. Auditorium reconstructed in 1926. *CB/TR*

Richmond, Georgian

RICHMOND
North Yorkshire

Georgian Theatre ★★★
Victoria Road/Friar's Wynd
Original architect
   1788   Unknown
Later works
   1963   Richard Southern and Richard
          Leacroft: restored
Listed   Grade I
Current use Theatre with museum
Capacity   220

From the outside, this tall almost windowless building, which measures only 7.9m (26ft) by 18.6m (61ft) in plan, looks like any stone barn of the Yorkshire Dales. All exterior indications that it is a theatre (e.g. the discreetly detailed present entrance) date from the restoration of the 1960s, but inside almost everything from paybox to proscenium doors is authentically Georgian. Nowhere else in England is the earthy immediacy of

the C18 playhouse evoked so strongly. The proscenium is tiny but well proportioned. This sense of scale within so small a building allows at once for big acting as well as a remarkably intimate actor-audience relationship.

The auditorium itself is on three levels: square benched pit reached by pit passages running underneath the side boxes; an enfolding level of eleven boxes, four on each side and three facing the stage with a playwright's name over each box (the lettering over the centre box, SHAKESPEARE, is original as is the Richmond Borough coat of arms on the front of the stage box on the actors' left); and, above, the rectangular gallery supported by eleven Tuscan columns which are not taken up to the ceiling. The auditorium was redecorated in 1963 in a range of recreated Georgian greens relieved by red trompe l'oeil swagged curtains on canvas at the back of the boxes. The attempt to create a period lighting effect was only half

successful – the miniature bulbs on the simulated candelabra providing too steady a light, while there was no attempt to provide the oil 'rings' over the stage.

Late C19 gilt ballroom chairs are often substituted for the correct backless benches in the boxes but elsewhere the seating is original or a faithful copy of the 'knife edge' benches, not quite so closely spaced as they once were. The capacity is now 220 while records show that the theatre held approximately 450 during its first life from 1788 to 1841. Then it closed and became first an auction room and later a wine store.

Moves to restore the theatre started in 1943 and were not completed until 1963, under the supervision of Dr Richard Southern and Richard Leacroft. The chief problem was that at some time in the late C19 brick-built vaults had been inserted into the length of the building immediately below stage level. Thus the dressing rooms and trap room under the stage, like the pit and orchestra pit, are reconstructions.

On the stage itself, which is 8.5m (28ft) wide and 7.3m (24ft) deep, no trace of the original grooves or any C19 suspension system has survived. The stage joists show evidence of three trap doors, two corner traps and a grave trap. The substage cellar floor was reconstructed in 1963 and the level is conjectural. The float mechanism installed then is based on a drawing in the Eyre manuscript.

The museum has been redesigned since 1963. It is situated on the ground floor, immediately behind the stage, with public access from Friars Wynd. The early C19 woodland scene in the museum did not originate from this theatre but it is an important and, possibly, earliest known surviving complete example of theatre scenery in Britain (see R. Southern, *Changeable Scenery*, 1952).

At the time of writing, a redevelopment programme, which will embrace further restoration works, was under consideration.   *IM/DW*

RIPLEY
Derbyshire

Oxford Hippodrome and New Hippodrome
High Street
Original architect
   1913   G.W. Bird
Later works
   1921   Unknown: interior dismantled
Current use Nightclub

Built in 1913, the Oxford Hippodrome was of brick with Matlock stone dressings. It had a single balcony and no fly tower. In 1920 the New Hippodrome (a ciné-variety house) was built at 90 degrees to and at the rear of the Oxford. Shortly after, the interior of the Oxford was dismantled, with the shell becoming the entrance to the New.

The New was later subdivided horizontally and became a two-screen cinema. The lower space subsequently became a bingo hall and is now a nightclub. The remains of the Oxford are still in use as the entrance to the rear auditorium and, although much altered from its original internal form, the space below the stage (now a storage area) is still traceable. *TB*

RIPON
North Yorkshire

Georgian Theatre
Blossomgate and Park Street
Other names
    Drill Hall and Bus Depot (!)
Original architect
    probably 1790s Unknown (but 'built by' George Hassell, Esq.)
Current use **Disused**

Erected toward the end of the C18 by a Recorder of Ripon, George Hassell. The first performance was by Mr Butler's company in August 1792. Butler is recorded as having played in a Ripon theatre, possibly an earlier building, in 1790.

The theatre was later acquired by the Marquess of Ripon and became a military riding school. It was used as the drill hall of the Ripon Rifle Volunteers but when they moved to a new-built hall the adjacent house and yard were converted to a bus depot. The bus company probably used the theatre premises as offices. It had vacated by the late 1990s. As now seen, the theatre is abutted by a modern garage building.

It stands on the corner of Blossomgate and Park Street, the front facade now rendered with cement, the roof of Welsh slate. The facade shows clear evidence of windows at ground-floor level flanking a central doorway. There is evidence at first-floor level of three central windows surmounted by a semi-circular panel. All the windows and the central door have been blinded. A late Victorian shop abuts to the left of the facade. There was probably an earlier entrance down this side of the theatre. It has not been possible to inspect

the interior, but it is known to be much subdivided. *DW*

Victoria Opera House
Water Skellgate
Other names
    Victoria Hall
Original architect
    1885 Unknown
Current use **Antique shop**

The theatre was gutted by fire in April 1976, whilst being used as a furniture factory by Croft Upholstery Ltd. Built as the Victoria Hall, a flat-floored room at first-floor level, of modest dimensions, with a proscenium and 6.1m (20ft) deep stage at one end and a single balcony.

Externally, the front elevation formed the side of the theatre. Plain brick construction with Welsh slate roof. The auditorium portion contained at first floor five large sash windows set at regular intervals. At ground floor there was an entrance, set centrally about the auditorium section of the elevation, flanked to the left by an arched doorway and a single sash window which was subsequently bricked up.

The stage portion of the elevation contained a small attic upper first-floor sash window, below which was another sash window. At ground-floor level modifications were undertaken by the upholstery company. As now seen, the ground floor has been remodelled to contain large shop windows. *DW*

ROCHDALE

ABC
The Butts
Other names
    1938 Regal
    1962 ABC
    1985 Cannon
Original architect
    1937 W.R. Glen, with Leslie C. Norton
Later works
    1978 Unknown: tripled
    1992 Unknown: auditorium restored and returned to full volume
    1997 Unknown: converted to pub
Current use **Pub**
Capacity **c.1700 (prior to pub conversion)**

In its original state, a splendid cinema theatre design by W.R. Glen, with Leslie C. Norton.

In 1997, it was converted to a pub by Wetherspoons. The exterior has been restored, the front canopy retained. However, internally the stage house and proscenium have been removed to pro-

vide a wide entrance and a fascia, with outside patio, at the rear. The foyer entrance, ceiling and lay light below the balcony appear to be the original, but in the public area, there is nothing further to see of the building's past use. The balcony area is unused, and it is from here that the ceiling and other decorative features may be seen, restored in 1992 when the auditorium was detripled for bingo. *SM*

Empire Music Hall
Town Hall Square and Packer Street
Other names
    Empire Hall
    Pringle's Picture Palace
Original architect
    1904 Unknown
Later works
    1930 Unknown: horseshoe balcony removed and replaced by a curved balcony; proscenium taken back and enlarged
    late 1950s Unknown: converted to bingo
    1995 Amicable Estates (Wigan): converted to pub
Current use **Café-bar**
Capacity **originally c.1150**

The date of opening would appear to be 1904. If this is correct, the facade of the building was designed to reflect the Gothic architectural style of the Town Hall (1864, by W.H. Crossland of Leeds). The Empire stands in Town Hall Square and a curiosity is a speakers' balcony above the entrance, with access from an arched opening with French windows. Five bays, the outer ones with a pinnacle roof; the central bay, the highest, with a pediment carrying the legend 'EMPIRE HALL'.

Rochdale, Empire (Sally McGrath)

The auditorium dates from 1904; it has a barrel-vault ceiling, banded with geometrical plaster ornamentation. The original horseshoe-shaped balcony was removed in 1930 and a curved balcony, more suitable for cinema, installed. The proscenium was also taken back and enlarged. Some stained-glass windows were inserted at this time. Stairs to balcony and foyer areas have a wooden dado, probably the original.

After years as a cinema, the Empire was converted to bingo in the 1950s. The building is now a café-bar, which occupies only the stalls and stage areas. The balcony is divided off, out of public use, by a drop wall from the ceiling to the balcony front edge. Boxes, two each side, may have been added recently to enhance the theatrical theme and to provide platforms for lighting, etc.   SM

ROCHESTER
Medway

Theatre Royal
Star Hill

Other names
   1863   Lyceum Theatre
Original architect
   1791   Unknown
Later works
   1846   Unknown: new ceiling; refurbished
   c.1851   Unknown: possible internal reconstruction
Listed   **Grade II**
Current use **Incorporated into Conservative Club**

Built in 1791 by Mrs Baker (who died in 1815) for her Company, the theatre was altered in 1842, in 1846 (when it was acquired by Henry Thornton) and again, apparently, in 1851 (after his death in that year). It continued as a theatre, finally under the name of The Lyceum, until 1894.

The theatre originally had a plain five-bay facade with simple cornice and parapet and a classical porch extending over the full depth of the public footway. What is seen today is the red brick and stone, late C19 facade of the Conservative Club, flanked by Georgian houses. The club lost part of the depth of its own porch in the widening of Star Hill.

Behind the facade there is an altered fabric, whose joinery details suggest that substantial parts of a dwelling house attached to the theatre may still remain.

The rectangular brick extension at the rear looks, in external views, very like the shell of an C18 theatre, but there is

nothing visible internally of a date earlier than the late C19 and many alterations clearly date from the 1980s. There is a small auditorium with stage, but it has more of the character of a church hall than a theatre. A modern suspended ceiling conceals the roof construction. *JL/JE*

ROTHERHAM
South Yorkshire

Empire
Westgate (High Street Corner)

Other names
   Essoldo
   Classic
   Cannon
Original architect
   1913   Chadwick and Watson
Later works
   1921   Unknown: extensively altered to cinema
   1974   Unknown: circle and balcony closed off
   1978   Unknown: converted to cinema
Current use **Nightclub/warehouse**

The theatre occupies a large corner site. The foyer block, largely separate from the auditorium, is in a free Classical style, faced in white faience which is in remarkably good condition. Prominent stage house. The tall auditorium was altered for a cinema in 1921 but retained three levels. In 1974, the circle and balcony were closed off with just the stalls in use, again as a cinema. In 1978, the stage area was partitioned and sublet, the stalls cinema reduced in size and the balcony (top level) reopened, walled off,

as a 314-seat cinema. Both closed in 1990. No trace of the Empire remains in the nightclub or bar, but remains may possibly survive in the upper levels.   *IG*

ROTHESAY
Argyll and Bute

Palace
East Princess Street
Other names
   Rothesay Public Hall
Original architect
   1879   J.R. Thomson
Current use **Facade only**

The auditorium, which was destroyed by a landslide, c.1977, was conceived as a concert hall, but resembled contemporary variety theatres. Now, only the imposing four-storey ashlar tenement block of seven bays, topped by mansard roofs in Louis XV-style, survives of this once grand venue. The entrance was between shop units with a full length iron-and-glass canopy on columns, now removed.   *BP*

Pavilion ★
Argyll Street
Original architect
   1936   James Carrick
Listed   **Grade B**
Current use **Multi-purpose venue**
Capacity   **1250**

Clearly influenced by Mendelsohn and Chermayeff's De La Warr Pavilion at Bexhill, this competition-winning design by James Carrick is the best of its kind in Scotland. A rectangular auditorium, clad

Rotherham, Empire (Ian Grundy)

in stone, forms the main bulk of the building, with a massive glazed semi-circular café projecting forward of the first floor like the bow of an ocean liner. Above is a roof terrace with a sweeping canopy. Within, there is a grand staircase. Such advanced architecture offered the pre-war Glasgow holidaymaker an experience at the forefront of the 'moderne' style. Regrettably, the building was, for some time, unappreciated and the interior especially could be much improved by sensitive restoration. *BP*

Winter Gardens
Esplanade Gardens
Original architect
  c.1895 **Alex Stevens and design staff of Walter Macfarlane, iron-founder**
Later works
  1924 **Macfarlane's design staff: enclosure created**
Listed **Grade B**
Current use **Concert hall, cinema and restaurant**
Capacity **c.1100**

Standing proudly in the middle of Rothesay's immaculately maintained waterfront lawns, the Winter Gardens started life as an open-air bandstand, and, indeed, the stage area dates from this time. Later, in 1924, Walter Macfarlane's Saracen Foundry produced the attractive circular hall in cast iron which enclosed the seating area. The building has a more angular sister at Ryde on the Isle of Wight. It is an elegant design with Art Nouveau details, corner towers and a wide, curving expanse of windows overlooking the bay. Its broad, gently domed roof is supported by an ingenious system of exposed, curving iron beams which are functional, yet elegant. The original paybox is preserved inside and the building has been successfully rescued after years of dereliction to act as the focus for Rothesay's consequently improved waterfront. *BP*

RUGBY
Warwickshire

Granada
North Street/Newbold Road
Other names
  Plaza
Original architect
  1933 **Julian R. and W.F. Granger**
Current use **Bingo**
Capacity **c.1700**

A red brick building at the junction of North Street and Newbold Road. Pitched roof and fly tower. Quite plain auditorium with barrel-vaulted ceiling. Shallow curved circle front. Workable depth of stage (stripped of counterweights) only 6.4m (21ft). Used for pop concerts until 1970s. Although used for bingo, restoration to theatre use would be possible but for the vast, impersonal and cold auditorium which is not to its advantage. *TB*

Palace
Railway Terrace/ Market Street
Other names
  1912 **Vint's Hippodrome**
  1922 **Prince of Wales**
  1931 **Regal**
Original architect
  1910 **Franklin and Newman (London)**
Later works
  1931 **Unknown: converted to cinema**
Current use **Furniture shop**
Capacity **originally c.1000**

Stuccoed facade in free classical style. Wide central bay of two storeys with a large lunette window. Flanking pavilions of $2\frac{1}{2}$ storeys, their parapets and urns now missing. Auditorium had two balconies with single boxes either side of the proscenium. Restrained plasterwork. Major alterations occurred in 1931 when converted to Regal Cinema, and again for change to current use. Little now remains internally apart from a small paybox for the pit entrance, the dress-circle staircase and circle foyer. *TB*

Rugby Theatre
Henry Street
Other names
  1913 **Empire Theatre**
  1917 **Empire Palace**
  1923 **Scala**
Original architect
  1913 **Eames and Jackson**
Later works
  1949 **Unknown: circle re-raked**
Current use **Amateur theatre**
Capacity **315**

Opened in 1913 as ciné-variety. Became a cinema and subsequently reopened as a theatre in 1949. Slightly concave gabled and rendered facade. Now has a functional interior. Fragments of the Empire proscenium arch remain. Slightly raked auditorium with balcony. Well equipped to fulfil local needs. *TB*

RUNCORN
Halton (Cheshire)

Palace
High Street
Other names
  Scala Ballroom
  La Scala Bingo
Original architect
  1897 **W.S. Snell**
Later works
  1957 **W. Owen: converted to ballroom**
  1970 **Unknown: converted for bingo**
Current use **Bingo**
Capacity **c.800**

Originally a theatre, the Palace became a cinema in the 1930s and is now a bingo hall. It has a sprung floor from a period of use as a ballroom.

It would appear that present entrance foyer and single-storey shops were added to the original front, which had a cupola, now visible only from the side. The original stage door and dock doors can still be seen. There is a box-office, still in use. The ladies' powder room from ballroom days is preserved and original cinema frames advertise the various bingo sessions. There is no balcony. The stage has a false ceiling. An ornamental iron spiral staircase leads to the former projection room. All in all, an interesting survival. *SM*

RUSHDEN
Northamptonshire

Ritz ★
College Street
Original architect
  1936 **Paul J.J. Panter of Talbot, Brown and Fisher (Wellingborough)**
Current use **Bingo (occasional live performance)**
Capacity **c.1190**

The theatre opened in 1936, with the idea of replacing the Palace. In 1976 it became a bingo house. Three-bay facade in brick and artificial stone, the centre bay advanced with a big mullioned window above the entrance canopy, all topped by a recessed frieze and overhanging coping, giving a slightly Egyptian flavour. Blind windows with balcony panels to the outer bays. Fly tower and easily accessible get-in.

The balconied auditorium is almost unaltered, quite plain with decorative grilles flanking the proscenium arch. The stage is the largest for many miles

Ryde, Esplanade Pavilion (Sally McGrath)

around, with a 11.9m (39ft) proscenium and 10.6m (35ft) depth.

The Ritz could easily return to live theatre use but local enthusiasm for such a move has been subdued. The big stage and large capacity have deterred the local operatic societies, who have used it in the past, from joining any campaign for its revival.   *TB*

RYDE
Isle of Wight

Esplanade Pavilion

Esplanade

Original architect

   1926   Walter Macfarlane, iron-founder (Glasgow)

Listed   **Grade II**

Current use **Entrance to bowling alley**

The Pavilion is an ornate cast-iron seaside building on the Eastern Esplanade, built in the Chinese manner. It was the work of Walter Macfarlane of Glasgow, from the same mould as its twin, the Pavilion in Rothesay, Isle of Bute, built two years earlier. It entertained concert parties and a variety of summer and winter entertainment for many years. After the fire at the Theatre Royal (1961), it was the town's only theatre. It was on one level with a platform stage. A proscenium was installed later. There was no fly tower.

In 1991, a bitter local battle developed when it was proposed to demolish the Pavilion. The shell was saved when a bowling alley was built on the seaward side to which the Pavilion itself was coupled, forming an entrance and

refreshment area. This development subsidised the restoration of the pleasing exterior. The Ryde Theatre now serves the town, but the Pavilion could have been restored and used for summer entertainment; a possibility which, perhaps, should still be kept in view.   *SM*

ST HELENS

Hippodrome

Corporation Street

Other names

   1903   Empire Palace of Varieties

Original architect

   1903   J.A. Barron (St Helens)

Later works

   1930s   Unknown: auditorium remodelled

1956   Unknown: proscenium widened to accommodate Cinemascope

1968   Cormall and Wainwright (St Helens): converted to bingo

Current use **Bingo**

Capacity   **originally c. 2300**

Opened 1903 as Empire Palace of Varieties, on site of the earlier People's Palace of 1893.

Symmetrical, largely unaltered, in eclectic and rather uncertain style, with ornamental surrounds to windows in terracotta. All that is known of the original building is that it had two balconies and boxes and great attention was paid in the design to fire precautions and exits for speedy evacuation in the event of fire.

In 1930s the auditorium was remodelled for cinema use with one deep balcony; the boxes were removed. The splendid ceiling dome, originally for the sunburner, decorated in fibrous plaster with garlands and musical instruments, however, remains as a reminder of the once lavish interior. The wide proscenium dates from 1956.

The stage with fly tower remains. Current plans are to extend the stage area into the defunct dressing-room area, perhaps extending the back wall, to give extra space for bingo, and possibly to insert a 2nd balcony for additional accommodation.   *SM*

Theatre Royal

Corporation Street

Other names

   1889   Theatre Royal and Opera House

   1964   Pilkington Theatre

St Helens, Hippodrome (Ian Grundy)

Original architect
1889 Frank Matcham
Later works
1901 Frank Matcham: reconstructed after fire to different design
1964 B. and N. Westwood, Piet and Partners: completely reconstructed
Current use Theatre
Capacity 704

Built by Matcham, the original facade was a free version of the classical style with three bays of giant pilasters with an elaborate gable at the centre. The auditorium had two balconies, supported by iron columns and single, canopied boxes either side of the proscenium. There was a large centrepiece in the ceiling to support the sunburner.

Severely damaged by fire in 1901, it was reconstructed by Matcham with a Baroque facade, a variation only of the 1889 facade. The interior, also in Baroque style, was designed this time with cantilevered balconies and flamboyant plasterwork.

All that survives of Matcham's building today are the outside walls and stage. Owned for some years by Pilkington Bros Ltd and used by many local societies, the Pilkington Players in particular, in 1964 the theatre was gutted and rebuilt with a glass facade. The entrance incorporates a lofty foyer; the auditorium has a single balcony. The auditorium walls are panelled in pine-colour wood, and the house is warmer than the plain glass exterior might lead one to expect – but a sad fate for a Matcham theatre.

The original stage area is large enough today to accommodate many touring shows, and the new management seeks to provide a range of live-theatre product. *SM*

Theatre Royal/Citadel

Milk Street/Waterloo Street
Original architect
1862 E. Beattie
Later works
1889 J.W. Dunford: converted to Salvation Army citadel; boxes removed
1904 Oswald Archer: altered further
1987 Unknown: converted to arts centre
Current use Arts Centre
Capacity 200

Although the building was extensively altered when the Salvation Army took up occupation, it retains much of the char-

St Helens, Theatre Royal/Citadel (Ian Grundy)

acter of an 1860s' theatre and should be rated as an uncommon survival, worthy of further detailed research and physical investigation.

There was an Apollo Concert Room and Assembly Room on the Waterloo Street site, opened in 1858 by a Mr R. Davies, in connection with his beer shop. The Apollo was succeeded by the Colosseum (whether or not a total rebuild is unclear) but this failed within two seasons and was purchased, with adjoining land in Milk Street, by Thomas Haddock, a solicitor. He commissioned a local architect, E. Beattie, to build a new, larger theatre.

What is seen today appears to be an altered, but still surprisingly recognisable state, of Beattie's theatre. A three-storey corner building, it is stuccoed on three faces, one flank only having some exposed brickwork. It comprises an entrance element, one bay deep, and a five-bay main body, which has a curious double-ridge roof, possibly, given that the two halves are not exactly symmetrical, the result of extending a pre-existing building. A close examination of the roof and ceiling construction might solve some of the building's puzzles.

The elevations were elaborated by the Salvation Army, probably in 1904. The front and flank are channelled up to first-floor level, the bay divisions on the flank being defined by plain pilasters rising from piers, with arched doors and windows between. The main front is framed by coupled, half-fluted pilasters and has a broad, plain gable. Some of the stucco facade ornament above ground-floor level has gone, but the entrance doorway itself, is nicely detailed in mid-C19

'pub classical' style, rather closer to the design of the original entrance than to the one shown on the Salvation Army drawings of 1904. It is set in a semi-circular two-storey arched recess (a feature of the 1862 design) with a window at first-floor level and a blind window above. To the left is a two-storey dwelling (reputedly built as the manager's house), stuccoed in typical mid-C19 manner, with a modern sliding door replacing the ground-floor window.

The interior, despite the major alterations made by the Salvation Army, still retains two horseshoe balconies and a strong sense of its former use. The alterations themselves now form part of an interesting record of historical change.

Plans are in hand to carry out improvements for the present use as an arts centre. The facade would be very attractive if restored to either its 1889 or 1904 design. *SM/JL*

ST HELIER
Jersey

Opera House ★

Gloucester Road/ Newgate Street
Other names
Royal Amphitheatre
Theatre Royal
Original architect
1900 Adolf Curry
Later works
1921 Jesty and Baker: reconstructed after fire
1943 Unknown: converted to cinema
1958 Unknown: reconverted for theatre use; 6 boxes added
1978 Unknown: proscenium enlarged; backstage improved

1993 Unknown: major improvements to bar and foyer areas; facade restored
1999/2000 MEBP: major improvements
Current use Under reconstruction
Capacity 650

Built on the site of Henry Cornwall's Royal Amphitheatre and Circus of 1865, the Opera House has an impressive stucco facade (a charming provincial interpretation of a Parisian commercial theatre of the 1880s) and this is, in fact, the only architectural feature now surviving of Curry's 1900 building. The interior was completely rebuilt in 1921 after a fire, and is in the ciné-variety manner of the day: two simple balconies, surmounted by a fine panelled ceiling radiating out from a semi-circular dome. The slips of the dress circle dip down towards the proscenium, while the gallery is nearly straight-fronted. Both have somewhat sparse gilded plaster festoons. In c.1960, when the building returned to theatrical use after post-war years as a cinema, six badly-designed boxes were added to the side walls. If reshaped and redecorated, these boxes would be a definite gain to the bleakness which must have prevailed earlier. The simple proscenium frame, topped by a curious stepping-up to the ceiling, has a 1930s' flavour, but was in fact built when the opening was widened to 8.2m (27ft) in 1976. For a building of the period there are quite spacious foyers and bars at various levels, and these were improved in 1993 when the facade was also restored.
VG/SM

SALFORD

Victoria ★★★
Great Clowes Street, Broughton
Original architect
  1899 Bertie Crewe
Later works
  1919 Mr Watson: refurbished
  1923 Unknown: operating box built
  1973 Unknown: converted to bingo
  c.1990 Unknown: partially restored
Listed Grade II
Current use Bingo
Capacity c.775

The theatre has a terracotta facade - two storeys and five main bays with Ionic pilasters separating pairs of tall first-floor windows. The pedimented central bay was originally surmounted by a small tower with a square dome but this has been removed together with the straight-sided pavilion roofs over the end bays and the parapet ornaments across the whole facade. The interior alone, however, justifies listing.

The intimate auditorium has two balconies. The first has a raised rear section behind a balustraded parapet (a most unusual arrangement). There are two superimposed stage boxes at each side. The lower boxes are flanked by squat Corinthian columns, and upper boxes by draped figures which support arches framing richly scrolled plasterwork. The balcony and box fronts are divided into panels which contain gilded plasterwork. Spanning the auditorium between the tops of the boxes is a deep elliptical arch which frames a tympanum above the rectangular proscenium.

The theatre was opened in 1899 by Sir Henry Irving. Pictures were shown as early as November 1901 and, in 1913, the theatre was granted a cinema licence. In 1917, the Victoria became a theatre again until 1919, and then reverted to predominantly cinema use until July 1958 when it closed and was used as a furniture store for some time. Repertory was tried in 1963 but bingo took over in 1973. However, this, too, failed. After standing for some time in a disused state during the 1980s, the theatre was purchased by independent owners and reopened for bingo. The auditorium has been sympathetically repainted.

There are substantial remains of wood substage machinery with paddle levers and the construction for corner traps and four bridges. The grave trap is complete with its platform. The theatre has been used as a 'live' theatre location for TV and film.

Salford provides a telling example of what can happen when the presence of a theatre (even a listed theatre) has been totally ignored in the post-war redevelopment of a city area. Improvements to its present forlorn surroundings are imperative if this fine Crewe building is to be seen in appropriate context. It is,

Salford, Victoria (Sally McGrath)

on the other hand, also a fine example of the beneficial effects of bingo in providing life and continued care to a theatre which would otherwise certainly have been demolished in the 1970s.

The Victoria could readily return to live use as an excellent middle-scale venue. It would complement the facilities at the new Lowry Centre, and together they could provide the City of Salford (and Manchester beyond) with a superb resource of performance spaces. *SM/JE*

SALISBURY
Wiltshire

City Hall
Fisherton Street/ Malthouse Lane
Other names
   1937   **New Picture House/Picture House**
         House
   Odeon
Original architect
   1937   **W.E. Trent, W.S. Trent and R.C.H. Golding**
Later works
   1961   **Unknown: converted to City Hall**
   1985   **Unknown: refurbished**
Current use **Theatre/multi-purpose**
Capacity   **953**

The last cinema in Salisbury to be built and the first to close; opened in 1937 by Gaumont British (which later became Odeon) it was bought by the City Council in 1961 and converted into the City Hall, a multi-purpose civic centre, in memory of the servicemen of Salisbury who gave their lives in the Second World War. It was originally built to fulfil the need for cinema when the Picture House next door became a Drill Hall (and then the Arts Theatre and subsequently the Playhouse), and was very smart. A long spacious vestibule led to a roomy foyer. The striking auditorium was of the stadium type, with seats behind the stalls entrances rising in a steep rake, rather than having the conventional balcony.

Slender silver columns framed the stage with its curtains of cream and peach trimmed with gold and green. When the building was purchased from Odeon, with the understanding that films would not be shown, the basic stadium design remained but with part retractable raked and part flat floor seating. The spacious vestibules and foyers became areas for banquets and conferences. It is used now for professional and amateur stage productions and as a

multi-purpose hall.

The facade to Fisherton Street had a pair of cylindrical towers flanking an entrance with a curved canopy and the name PICTURE HOUSE above, all set between curved brick jaws with ornamental shafts at outer edges. One of the jaws, the canopy, the lettering and the necked caps to the towers have been removed and a shopfront formed. Despite these rather unsympathetic alterations the City Hall has in some ways more atmosphere than the Playhouse, although its long auditorium is not ideal for intimate productions and plays. Together with the Playhouse, it forms Salisbury's 'Entertainment Centre'. *SM*

SANDOWN
Isle of Wight

Pavilion
Sandown Pier, Esplanade
Original architect
   1934   **Ernest Latham**
Later works
   1989/90   **Unknown: backstage and dressing rooms rebuilt after fire; refurbished and improved**
Current use **Amusements**
Capacity   **est. 750**

The Pavilion Theatre was built at the landward end of the pier, designed with walkways either side on the pier itself, so it could function independently.

The 1934 theatre was a steel-framed structure, reminiscent of a 1930s' cinema. Externally the distinctive feature was the colour and texture obtained by the use of patent cement paints with an ivory white decorative finish. The entrance foyer is entered from the Esplanade. Two wide staircases lead to the balcony foyer, former tearoom balcony.

The original interior decor was intended to suggest sea and sunshine. The auditorium had simple direct lines, with horizontal bands and concealed lighting. It had a single raked balcony.

In 1989 the seaward side of the Pavilion was destroyed by fire: the stage and auditorium survived but suffered extensive smoke and heat damage. The theatre was completely refurbished and redecorated and rebuilt backstage, with improved and enlarged dressing-room accommodation. It is now given over to amusement machines and has been recently granted permission for conversion to 'mini-golf'. *SM*

Town Hall
Grafton Street
Original architect
   1869   **Unknown**
Current use **Multi-purpose hall**
Capacity   **c.430**

The earliest theatre building in Sandown, it was built with a main hall and adjoining offices. Two storeys with attic; tripartite windows; the attached office block, in plainer style, has a separate entrance. The facade is in local stone in classical style with six engaged attenuated columns and pediment over, with embossed Sandown Crest, date 1869, and a ribbon inscribed 'Town Hall'. The column capitals and part of the main entablature seem to have undergone some later simplification. Handsome iron canopy supported by cast-iron pillars covers entrance steps from street.

The main hall is multi-purpose but was used for 100 years for stage entertainment, particularly repertory and operatics, both by professional and local companies. For over a decade live use has been replaced by community events and the interior has deteriorated.

With the loss of Sandown Pier Pavilion to amusements in 1998, it is not inconceivable that the Town Hall Theatre could revert to stage entertainment use. *SM*

SANDWICH
Kent

Empire
15 Delf Street

Original architect
   1937   **Albert and Vincent Burr**
Later works
   1971   **Unknown: converted to bingo**
   1987   **Unknown: divided horizontally to form two snooker halls**
   1993   **Unknown: former circle converted to cinema**
   1996   **Unknown: stalls area converted to function room (retaining stage)**
Current use **Function room**
Capacity   **Originally c.600**

Designed on the same lines and by the same architects as the Friars (now Marlowe), Canterbury. The building replaced an earlier theatre in the same street. Three-storey, steel frame and brick, rendered, originally outlined in neon. Central entrance with metal and glass canopy. Tripartite windows at ground and first-floor level. Plain attic, stepped above entrance.

Auditorium in modern style with stage facilities, retained today in spite of 1987 subdivision. Remains in independent ownership. *SM*

SCARBOROUGH
North Yorkshire

Alexandra Music Hall
Aberdeen Walk
Other names
   St George's Hall
   Old Spa Music Hall
Original architect
   1858   Unknown
Listed   **Grade II**
Current use **Disused**

Built as a music hall adjoining the Old Spa Vaults. It has one of the more interesting facades in Aberdeen Walk consisting of five tall arched windows, grouped 1-3-1 at first and second-floor level. Above this is a low attic storey with five square windows, now blocked up. The ground floor has been heavily altered with modern shopfronts inserted. The entrance 'a wide and ornate staircase' was originally on the left of the front but this has now been converted into a shop.

The auditorium is at first and second-floor levels, flat-floored with a horseshoe balcony supported on six to eight cast-iron columns. The balcony front is formed from delicate open cast-iron panels. The balcony consists of eight rows at the rear and three rows down each side. The ceiling, now badly damaged, contains a small but deep central saucer dome and two stained-glass lay lights. A deep cornice runs down all four sides of the room. The stage was no more than a raised platform - no trace of it remains. There are plain decorative arches down each side - the whole space has a feel of Wilton's Music Hall of the same period. A false ceiling has been inserted at balcony level.

After an application for demolition early in 1998 the building was spot listed Grade II and a further application in September resulted in consent to demolish being granted apart from the facade which will be incorporated into new shops. A sadly lost opportunity. *IG*

Capitol ★
Albemarle Crescent/Westborough
Original architect
   1929   E.S. Gray (Gray and Evans)

Scarborough, Open-Air *(Ian Grundy)*

Current use **Bingo**
Capacity   **est. 2100**

This is a large ciné-variety theatre opened just before the advent of sound films with a fully equipped stage, fly tower, dressing rooms and orchestra pit. Despite these facilities the Capitol was used as a cinema with only rare live performances on its stage.

The white faience facade is in three major bays, the outer two lower than the centre, which has a slightly advanced frontispiece containing a trio of tall, semi-circular arched windows rising to an enriched cavetto cornice. The arch tympana contain well-modelled Greek masks with musical trophies and, at the centre, profile comedy and tragedy masks as supporters. On either side of the frontispiece are single doors with windows above. The outer bays, again, have single doors and tall, pedimented blind windows. The facade is completed with a blind attic with cartouche and the name CAPITOL in elegant sunk letters.

A secondary entrance was provided on Westborough again in faience (now painted) and with a repeat of the cartouche. On the opposite side, in a back access road, are the stage get-in, stage door, dressing rooms, etc.

The single-balconied auditorium is lavish, with a blind arcade to the side walls terminating in splayed pavilions containing ornamental organ gilles on either side of the proscenium arch. Above the arch is a classical frieze with a central medallion containing the letter C. The ceiling is a plainer shallow barrel vault.

The stalls foyer is small but at circle level the former café now gives a spacious foyer in the circle void lit by three large windows. *IG*

Open-Air Theatre ★
North Stead Manor Gardens
Original architect
   1932   Scarborough Corporation
Current use **Disused and part derelict**

The largest open-air theatre in Europe (since Antiquity) was built by Scarborough Corporation and opened by the Lord Mayor of London in 1932. A striking landscape feature with the action staged on an island and viewed across a lake. The first production was *Merrie England*. There was fixed seating in five blocks for 5876 with the balance made up of deckchairs. The house record, set in August 1952 was an audience of 8983, but an official 11,000 was claimed for a free recording of *It's a Knockout* in the 1960s.

The theatre was built on land known as Hodgson's Slack, taking advantage of ground contours which created a natural amphitheatre. In its heyday, it was an important theatrical venue of national repute mounting lavish musicals with casts (largely amateur) of up to 200. During the season of three months two performances were held each week.

Musicals ceased in 1968 after *West Side Story* (apart from a YMCA production in 1982). For eleven years *It's a Knockout* games were staged to ever-increasing losses, yet concerts with the likes of James Last were able to fill the theatre in 1983 and 1986. In 1997 the dressing rooms and stage building on the island were demolished and the seating removed.

Many attempts to start a restoration have been made, but the theatre is likely to be demolished in a major redevelopment of the area. Only very short leases have recently been available. *IG*

Royal Opera House ★★★
St Thomas Street
Other names
  1876 Charles Adnam's Grand Circus
  1877 Hengler's Grand Cirque
  1878 Prince of Wales Circus
  1900 Zalvas Hippodrome
  1908 New Hippodrome
  1910 Opera House
  1914 Grand Opera House
Original architect
  1877 John Petch
Later works
  1908 Frank Tugwell: almost completely rebuilt
  1976 Dennis Hitch: refurbished; re-roofed; bar added at rear
Listed   **Grade II**
Current use **Derelict**
Capacity **c.970**

The building had a short-lived predecessor, as Charles Adnam's Grand Circus, a wooden building which opened in 1876. It was rebuilt the following year as a brick structure designed by John Petch. This building lasted as a circus and music hall until February 1908 when it was demolished apart from the outer walls and a series of cast-iron columns. Local architect Frank Tugwell (architect of the town's Futurist Theatre) designed the present theatre which opened in 1908. The foyer block is separate from the auditorium and possibly of a different date and may have originally been a terrace of three houses. The left-hand one forms the foyer which links through to the auditorium. Above are flats.

The auditorium is on three levels. The layout of the three boxes either side of the proscenium is most unusual with two at dress-circle level and the major one suspended above the stalls. The circle is high above the stalls giving unusually good sight lines from the rear. There are twenty-one rows of seats in the stalls, seven in the dress circle and three in the balcony which has been reduced in size.

The circle has a horseshoe form with a restrained scroll and tasseled decoration. The balcony is serpentine in shape

Scarborough, Royal Opera House

with straight slips returned to the proscenium wall. The proscenium is segmentally arched and richly decorated with scrolls, groups of cherubs and a central cartouche containing horses' heads, recalling the early circus use and Hippodrome name. The circles are partly cantilevered with one supporting pillar at stalls and circle levels. Sight lines are excellent throughout. The ceiling is plain and simply panelled.

This must now be one of the most important 'sleeping beauties' in the country and is crying out for restoration and reopening, especially with the likely demise of the Futurist. However, the auditorium is now flooded, the foyer block ruined after a series of arson attacks and action is urgently needed to halt the rot. *IG*

Spa Theatre and Grand Hall ★
South Bay
Original architect
  1880 Verity and Hunt
Later works
  c.1900 Unknown: stage depth increased
Listed   **Grade II* (theatre)**
Current use **Theatre and concert hall**
Capacity **630/1800**

At first-floor level on the right-hand side of the imposing entrance to the Spa Complex is the Spa Theatre. This area was originally intended to be a floral lounge but was adapted before the opening of the Spa (which almost totally replaced the 1839 Gothic Saloon, by

Henry Wyatt, which had been radically altered by Sir Joseph Paxton in 1857/8 and gutted by fire in 1876).

Very unusual auditorium with a large stalls floor, raked at the rear, a side balcony at right angles to the stage, accessed from the stalls, not the circle, and a flat-fronted balcony of ten rows. The side balconies are divided by a central square pillar whilst there are three cast-iron pillars supporting the balcony and two in the balcony supporting the roof. The ceiling is plain, rectangular and rises above a range of clerestory windows. The entire complex was restored in 1980/1 reinstating the shallow niches originally existing either side and frieze above the proscenium. When it was first improved and fitted out as a theatre around 1900, the proscenium was moved forward and the stage depth effectively doubled, but there is still only minimal flying height, the wings are cramped and dressing rooms poor. Getting in is difficult.

The tiny stage has, nevertheless, been trodden by some of the greatest names in the theatre, from Henry Irving to Judi Dench. For several years it has been the base for the annual National Student Drama festival. It housed a successful series of variety shows from the 1920s to the 1970s. However, the venue is now under almost constant threat of closure.

To the left of the main foyer, with its wide marble staircase, is the 1800-seat Spa Grand Hall which is also used occasionally for theatrical presentations. It is, despite its severely limited stage facilities, a magnificent concert hall on two

Scarborough, Spa Grand Hall (Ian Grundy)

levels with monumental iron arches supporting the three-sided balcony and ceiling. Also in the complex is a Music Room, restaurant, two ballrooms and an open-air sun court for daytime concerts and dancing. *IG*

SCUNTHORPE
North Lincolnshire

Palace
Cole Street
Other names
   1912 Palace Theatre
   1938 Savoy
   1954 Essoldo
   1972 Classic
Original architect
   1912 King
Later works
   1938 Unknown: auditorium rebuilt as cinema
   1954 Unknown: Cinemascope installed
   1978 Unknown: converted to retail
Current use **Disused**

Opened in 1912 with amateur operatic production. It had a varied career as a theatre and cinema until it was gutted in 1978.

The interior has been completely altered to form supermarket premises. The stalls and stage areas were levelled to form one continuous floor. The upper part of the volume is disused. *TB*

SEACOMBE
Wirral

King's
Borough Road
Other names
   1899 Irving Theatre
   1912 La Scala
   1918 Hippodrome, Embassy
Original architect
   1899 Unknown (possibly A. Shennan)
Later works
   1908 Owen and Ward: reconstructed after fire, enlarged with new balcony
   1936 Unknown: auditorium altered to cinema
Current use **Bingo**
Capacity   c.2500 (following 1908 reconstruction)

Opened by Sir Henry Irving and said to be the only theatre with which he allowed his name to be associated, for so long as the theatre produced drama (hence the name changes when music, opera and ciné-variety were introduced).

An interesting 3-bay facade, the outer bays two windows wide with pyramidal tower roofs (since removed), the centre three windows wide with crowning framed medallion, originally with a relief portrait head of Irving, now absent, all otherwise intact above altered ground floor. Continuous frieze of festoons and scrolls in terracotta at second-floor level. An interesting front, which makes a significant contribution to the streetscape.

The original auditorium comprised stalls, a steep horseshoe-shaped balcony supported by six pillars, with boxes in

two tiers at either side of the proscenium, the upper ones arched up to a decorative plaster frieze with garlands and medallions at ceiling level. The stage was well equipped and with fly tower. Reconstruction following a serious fire in 1908 enlarged the auditorium, thought to be three-tier.

In 1936 the auditorium was remodelled as a luxury cinema. Later, a false ceiling was introduced with a new interior and the proscenium styled to bingo. However, the fly tower, complete with hemps in situ, remains, with further hints of the building's theatrical past.   *SM/CB*

SEAHAM HARBOUR
Durham

Empire
South Terrace
Other names
   Empire Vaudeville Theatre and Picture Palace
Original architect
   1912 W. and T.R. Milburn (attributed)
Current use **Derelict**
Capacity   c.950 (prior to removal of balcony)

Built as a ciné-variety with a good-sized stage but no fly tower. Became exclusively cinema c.1944 and later bingo. Single balcony was probably removed after a fire in 1977. Now vacant and derelict.

Externally downright ugly. A brick shed with cement-rendered panels and slated roof. Tall, featureless entrance frontispiece. Scar on end wall shows former position of projection room. *DW/IG*

SHANKLIN
Isle of Wight

Shanklin Theatre
Prospect Road
Other names
   1879–1933 The Institute
   1934 New Town Hall Theatre
Original architect
   1878 E.G. Cooper: as the Institute
Later works
   1933 Cooper and Corbett: reconstructed as theatre
Current use **Theatre**
Capacity   670

The first building on the site opened in 1878 as The Institute, designed by E.G. Cooper, in classical style with a pedimented Corinthian portico. As the Institute, the building incorporated the

Town Hall, as well as having an entertainments hall, and various reading and meeting rooms. After a serious fire it was rebuilt as the Shanklin Theatre and opened in 1934. It is not clear precisely how much of the original fabric was retained, but the right-hand return elevation is identifiable part of the 1878 design and the main body of the building is probably of the same date. The present facade, however, bears little resemblance to that of the old Town Hall, being taller by one storey.

The entrance front of the building is three-storeyed, classical, finished in stucco, taking the form of a five-bay mansion in French style set upon an advanced ground-floor podium. This floor consists of two channelled pavilions with modillion cornice and blocking, each having a central semi-circular headed window with a keystone, modillion cornice and blocking. Between the pavilions, slightly set back and approached by a wide flight of steps are glazed metal doors beneath a canopy. The 'mansion' has a three-bay centre with giant Ionic columns supporting an entablature and pediment. On either side, single bays are defined by broad pilasters with carved cartouches at their heads.

The auditorium, which is probably an adaptation of the original hall, with an added balcony decorated with plain plaster panels, is striking. Seating is traditional, but the stalls seating can be moved for dances, etc. A fly tower was added in 1934. The theatre is an all-year touring house and also serves local amateur dramatic companies. Set away from the beach, on the hill at the top of town, it is slightly off the beaten track. The old Town Hall serves as the theatre bar. *SM/JL*

Summer Theatre
Esplanade
Original architect
  1921 Messrs Simmonds: existing building relocated
Later works
  1938 Unknown: converted to store
  n.d. Unknown: converted to amusement arcade
Current use Amusement arcade

In 1919, the wooden stage and tented pavilion used by Powis Pinder at Millers Green were destroyed by fire. Messrs Simmonds brought a seaplane hangar from Bembridge and reconstructed it on a site on the Esplanade (about the same

time as the Bognor Pavilion, now demolished, was created from a similar hangar). It opened in 1921 as The Summer Theatre. The interior was fitted out as a concert pavilion with platform stage and proscenium. It was the big success in the 1920s and 1930s on the Island.

During the Second World War, it was requisitioned for storage in connection with PLUTO (Pipe Line Under the Ocean). It was also badly damaged. It later reopened as an amusement arcade and survives in that form. *SM*

SHEERNESS
Kent

Criterion Music Hall
Criterion Alley, Blue Town
Other names
  Royal Oxford Music Hall
  New Music Hall
  c.1904 Reymond's New Palace Theatre of Varieties
  Criterion Palace of Varieties
Original architect
  c. 1851 Unknown: room within tavern
Later works
  before 1877 Unknown: music hall built
  probably early C20 Unknown: rebuilt as variety theatre
  early 1920s Unknown: converted to cinema
Current use Fragment

Little is known about this building. A pub named the New Inn probably had a singing room from about 1851. By 1877 it was active as a music hall, built behind the pub and approached from Criterion Passage. By 1904/5 it was being referred to as Reymond's New Palace Theatre of Varieties and had probably been rebuilt, but still as a gabled shed-like structure behind the pub. It is thought to have been altered in the early 1920s to become the Criterion Cinema, which was gutted in 1951 and afterwards used as a store and workshop.The shell of this building can still be seen, but the interior has gone. Curiously, this little music hall is as well remembered locally as the Hippodrome (demolished 1970). *JE*

SHEFFIELD

Abbeydale Picture House
Abbeydale Road
Original architect
  1920 Unknown
Current use Showroom/snooker hall

Built 1920. Ciné-variety from 1928. In 1930 it changed to talkies. Closed in 1975, it became an office furniture showroom and warehouse. Despite these changes it has been described as 'still one of the best preserved cinema buildings in Sheffield'.

The auditorium is divided horizontally but its floor is still steeply raked, and there is a balcony whose front bows out into boxes on either side of the proscenium. The walls have plaster decoration of the 1920s. The rear part of the balcony has been partitioned off and levelled. The stage deck has been lowered but the stage house, 35m (88ft) wide and 9m (30ft) deep with its grid extending only half the depth, is largely intact. Rumoured to be a possible candidate for conversion to a mosque. *TB/KW*

Library
Tudor Place
Original architect
  1930s Unknown
Later works
  1961 Colin Windle (City Architects Dept): stage enlarged; auditorium redesigned; lighting gallery installed
Current use Theatre
Capacity 260

Within an existing 1930s' building, adjoining the Lyceum theatre. Originally designed as a lecture hall on a flat floor, the subterranean hall was used for drama within months. However, legal difficulties precluded payment for tickets and the experiment soon folded. During the war, it was used as an air-raid shelter and, by 1947, the legal situation having been rectified, dressing rooms were added and the Library Theatre began its career. It had inherent problems with poor sight lines and a small stage and, in 1961, the theatre was redesigned. A plain but rather attractive proscenium with a Corinthian column each side was replaced by a utilitarian proscenium arch typical of the 1960s. A foyer was constructed at the rear, the seating was put on a permanent stepped rake and the stage enlarged. This resulted in the loss of 140 seats. A technical gallery was also introduced above the foyer. The theatre has been little altered since and is now in need of further updating.

The auditorium contains 17 rows of seats, with good sight lines in a fairly low-ceilinged rectangular hall. The decor is Art Deco in style, sparse, but quite attractive. Carpeting, new seats and an

Sheffield, Lyceum

imaginative decoration scheme would transform the theatre at relatively low cost. The backstage area is cramped and the grid too low. *IG*

Lyceum ★★★
Tudor Street
Original architect
    1893   **Walter Emden (with E. Holmes)**
    1897   **W.G.R. Sprague: new theatre on site**
Later works
    1990   **RHWL: theatre restored with major additions**
Listed   **Grade II***
Current use **Theatre**
Capacity   **1099**

The Lyceum is one of the most spectacularly reawakened of the *Curtains* (1982) 'sleeping beauties'. It is also the only completely surviving Sprague theatre in the regions. Sprague was responsible for some of the most beautiful theatres in London (e.g. Wyndhams, the Albery, the Globe, the Strand) and the Lyceum is worthy to be set beside any of these.

Built in 1897 on the site of the City Theatre (1893), this is a free-standing building with an emphasised corner-block topped by a domed tower, originally containing the main entrance, a feature in common with some of the architect's London theatres.

The auditorium is very fine, with superb Rococo plasterwork. Two slightly curved cantilever balconies; unusual treatment of the side walls, which are articulated by broad pilasters at each level, forming bays containing bow-fronted boxes. All the surfaces are enlivened by delicate plasterwork and at dress-circle level the pilasters have attached coupled columns. The proscenium has a rectangular moulded frame which encloses a riotous Rococo open-work plaster valance along the top, in the corners and spreading halfway down the sides. Coved and panelled ceiling with fine plasterwork.

The Lyceum closed in 1968 and became a bingo house. Bingo failed in 1972. An application to demolish was then made by the owners but was refused on appeal. The building was subsequently offered for sale without result. Proposals in 1981 for a popular music venue and discotheque were granted planning permission but did not proceed. A Lyceum Theatre Trust had been formed in 1975 but progress was slow, due in part to the ambivalence of the City Council, which had built the immediately adjoining Crucible (RHWL's first theatre) in 1971. In the late 1980s, the Lyceum was still dark and (thanks to precautionary action taken to arrest rapid deterioration) smelling of dry-rot fluid.

The climate changed in 1990 when the World Student Games were allocated to Sheffield. An ambitious programme of restoration and improvement was set in action which embraced not only the theatre but an adjoining cleared space, to be known as Theatre Square, defined by the two theatres and neighbouring properties. Work was completed and the theatre reopened in December 1990.

The upgrading of the theatre, which is now run jointly with the Crucible, was impressive. The main entrance was moved from the front corner tower to the long elevation facing the new square and major additions were made at side and rear containing a new stage house and rehearsal space, improved dressing rooms (for 108), education department, passenger lifts, etc. The auditorium was magnificently restored with a colour scheme appropriate to Sprague's manner (more architecturally disciplined than Matcham's but far from solemn) and with a finely painted safety curtain to shame those theatres which still tolerate a grubby grey screen being lowered in the interval. The new internal public spaces were decorated in a pleasing Deco-inspired manner, contrasting but chiming well with Sprague's busier ornament.

Sheffield now has a traditional proscenium theatre worthy of its status as the country's sixth largest city and a wholly satisfying complement to its modern thrust-stage Crucible. *JE/CB*

SHIREBROOK
Derbyshire

Empire
Station Road/Market Street
Original architect
    1910   **Frederick Hopkinson of Worksop and Chesterfield**
Current use **Bingo**
Capacity   **c.600**

A ciné-variety with better than average provision for live performance.

The exterior is of plain red brick with sparse stone dressings, divided into two two-storey and four single-storey bays by brick piers surmounted by ball finials. A stone cornice breaks forward at each pier. The entrance is in the long flank.

Sheffield, Lyceum

Shrewsbury, Music Hall (Ted Bottle)

Hardly any foyer space. The auditorium is on one level, heavily raked with spare decoration. The stage provides a good working area and, together with a generous provision of dressing-room accommodation, would make this a suitable venue for amateur groups. Its small capacity has economic limitations for a professional revival.   *TB*

SHREWSBURY
Shropshire

Granada
Castle Gates
Original architect
  1934 **Cecil Masey, with interior by Komisarjevsky**
Later works
  1973 **Unknown: converted to bingo**
Current use **Bingo**
Capacity **c.1490 (prior to 1973 conversion)**

The building occupies an irregular sloping piece of land with the facade angled at approximately 45° between Castle Gates and Meadow Place. The facade is narrow and tall. Above the entrance are four Corinthian columns supporting a deep architrave. The entrance and vestibule are on the same level as the front circle.

The stalls is now divided into three sections, of which the front retains the original rake and the rear two are terraced. The proscenium is framed by fluted Ionic columns. In the side wing walls are similar columns at the end of a long balustrade behind which rise three tall arched metallic grills which give a symbolic appearance of boxes at slightly

below dress-circle level. Frieze and cornice over, continuing along the top of the proscenium with classical figures. Single deep balcony with plain side walls.   *TB*

Music Hall
The Square
Original architect
  1840 **Edward Haycock the Elder**
Later works
  1981 **Unknown: new entrance constructed**
  1984 **Unknown: old balcony demolished; stage relocated; pilasters repaired and new added**
  1986 **Unknown: various alterations**
Listed   **Grade II**
Current use **Theatre**
Capacity **398**

Classical front and rear elevations: that facing the Square is stone-faced with entrance in the centre. On either side are windows fronting a restaurant and Tourist Information Office. Above is a giant pedimented portico with attached Ionic columns. The rear wall, in College Hill, once held the main entrance: the ground floor here corresponds to first floor at the opposite end owing to the difference in ground levels. There are two doorways on this front leading to the stage and a third which is bricked up. A giant order of six pilasters with a moulded wreath in each intervening space unites the upper floors. Only two long windows appear on this side. On the ground floor is a small cinema seating 100.

The Music Hall is a long, flat-floored room with pilastered walls. The prosce-

nium is curtained. Entrances are alongside a retractable bleacher seating unit. Three rows of seats are placed on the flat floor, 15 on the bleacher unit, and the remaining five on a fixed balcony.

Behind the stage is a crossover. The forestage is 2.4m (8ft) deep, within which are covers which can be lifted to reveal an orchestra pit.

The Music Hall is not the most suitable venue for the presentation of professional theatre, as the seating capacity is small and the stage and orchestra facilities are inadequate. Some of the internal alterations made in the last thirty years have lacked architectural distinction.   *TB*

Repertory
Swan Hill
Other names
  1863 **Working Men's Hall (Sometimes referred to as Wightman Hall and Temperance Hall)**
Original architect
  1863 **John L. Randal (Shrewsbury)**
Current use **Antique shop**

Converted from an assembly hall and used as a theatre in the 1940s and 1950s. Now an antique shop. The present facade is incorporated with the adjacent shop and is therefore indistinguishable from it. The interior is lined with red and yellow bricks with several windows down both sides and a large doorway in the centre of stage right auditorium wall. The ceiling is divided into square wooden panels, those nearest the four sides sloping downwards to meet the tops of the walls. Most panels have small ventilation holes inserted. The main floor is flat and was so during its period as a repertory theatre. The stage has been removed but the position of the proscenium top can be seen. One of the windows on 'stage right' had been converted into a get-in. There was no balcony. The interior has a sparse, bare and cold feel to it. Tradition states that it was an icy and draughty place to sit in. *TB*

Royal County
18 Shoplatch
Other names
   Chalton Hall
   Theatre
   Theatre Royal
   1912 Picture House
Original architect
   1791 Unknown (theatre con-
          structed within medieval
          building)
Later works
   1834 Unknown: new theatre on
          site
   1887 J.L. Randal: alterations
   1898 John P. Briggs: new theatre
          incorporating some old fabric
   1912 Unknown: converted to the
          Picture House
   1945 Unknown: gutted and con-
          verted to shop
Current use Retail store

The site has been occupied by a theatre since about 1791. The 1898 theatre incorporated some fabric from the second 1834 New Theatre on the same site. The axis of that theatre lay parallel to Shoplatch. The stage was to the left. The facade, which was incorporated by Briggs, originally had three statues in niches, but was altered after a fire in 1945. It is 30.5m (100ft) long, ren-dered, with tall windows. Even in its altered state, it is recognisable as deriv-ing from the original 1834 design. The two end and opposite long walls are of red sandstone blocks with red brick at the upper levels suggesting that during the rebuild of 1898 all the walls were raised and a fly tower added. Remains of a winch system for hoisting scenery to the first-floor stage level can be seen on the 'stage right' outer wall.

The theatre never reopened after the 1945 fire but was gutted and became a shop. Floors have been inserted internal-ly corresponding more or less to the orig-inal stalls, circle and gallery levels. The lower two are used as a shop, the upper for storage. The proscenium opening is visible on floors one and two. On the top floor, part of the auditorium ceiling can be seen, at the centre of which is the outer ring of the former dome.

The building is not rectangular. The stage was considerably narrower than the rear width of the auditorium. The gallery was probably around 11m (36ft) wide, whereas the rear stage wall is only 7.4m (24ft 3in) wide. The stage grid, fly galleries and safety-curtain guides can still be seen. It is difficult to envisage how this much altered building could ever be returned to theatre use. *TB*

SIDMOUTH
Devon

Manor Pavilion
Manor Road
Other names
   1891 Manor Concert Hall
   Manor House Theatre
Original architect
   1891 Major Balfour
Later works
   1953 Unknown: modernised;
          stage probably improved;
          canopy added
Current use Theatre and Arts Centre
Capacity 282

The Manor Pavilion comprises two main elements, built by Major Balfour and his father. The earlier part, the former Georgian Pavilion of 1860, which now houses the Arts Centre, is of two storeys, built on a gradient, red brick and gabled in low-key Queen Anne style. The single-storey theatre, originally the Manor Hall (a concert hall), was at higher level at the rear. It was built in 1891 and was later attached to the 1860 building. It has a modern, plain brick entrance addition. The complex as a whole has been known since the 1950s as the Manor Pavilion.

There is no fly tower. Get-in is diffi-cult, and facilities, except for the addi-tion of a workshop, new stage, proscenium and extra dressing-room space, remain almost as in concert hall days. The auditorium has been raked and sight lines are good. A small foyer and bar complete the public areas. There is no box office; tickets are sold from a kiosk on the Esplanade. *SM*

SKEGNESS
Lincolnshire

Embassy Centre
Grand Parade
Original architect
   c.1926 Unknown
Later works
   1982-93 RHWL: various alterations
   1999 Franklin Ellis: proposed
          extensions

Current use Theatre and restaurant
Capacity 1158

The Embassy opened in 1926 on sand dunes. It had a ballroom at street level, with a restaurant below. The ballroom was also used for variety and concert party performances.

The external appearance of the Embassy is a mixture of an older frontage with a modern, metal-clad octagonal structure at the rear. The older frontage, believed to date from around 1926, consists of three bays each having two storeys, the central one being slight-ly taller, with a pseudo-pediment sur-mounting the parapet. The canopied main entrance is in the central bay. The foyer is of an elongated octagon shape.

The present auditorium is an addition to the original building and was con-structed partially on the site of a former seawater bathing pool. The auditorium shell is octagonal, flat floored with seat-ing on two levels. The circle occupies five sides of the octagon.

There is no fly tower. The roller safety curtain is set behind a deep apron. There is no orchestra pit. Dressing rooms are situated in the front-of-house basement section. This necessitates artists crossing the public corridor in order to get to and from the stage.

The building is used exclusively for stage shows during the season. There were proposals in 1999 for major alter-ations and extensions. *TB*

SLEAFORD
Lincolnshire

Theatre
Westgate/Playhouse Yard
Original architect
   1825 Unknown
Later works
   1855 Messrs Kirk and Parry: con-
          verted to school room
Listed   Grade II
Current use Disused

This building, isolated on three sides, with its main front in Westgate, is con-structed from small limestone blocks (Ancaster?). There are windows at ground and first-floor levels in both side walls and the facade, all of which date from after 1856. A small oeil de boeuf which appears to be original, exists at the top of the facade beneath the gut-tering. The present main entrance door is on the right-hand side of the front with a decorated lintel. Along the left-hand side wall is a narrow passage lead-

Smethwick, Empire (Ted Bottle)

ing to a door at the rear. There is no obvious bricked-up aperture along the wall fronting Playhouse Yard. The lower part of the rear stage wall is not visible owing to the presence of single-storey wooden garages. The interior from the Westgate end for a distance of 13.7m (45ft) is open to the ceiling which is constructed of plain wooden boards supported by posts and braces from the side walls. No cellars have been discovered so far, however it would seem unlikely that a theatre of this period was ever constructed without a cellar for dressing-room accommodation. The auditorium had a pit, gallery and boxes.

At the time of compilation it is understood there are plans to re-establish theatre use. *TB*

SMETHWICK
Sandwell (West Midlands)

Empire
St Paul's Road/St Albans Road
Original architect
1910 G Bowden and Son
(Smethwick)
Later works
1919 G. Bowden: stage enlarged;
dressing rooms extended
Current use Temple

Facade, brick and stone, now all painted. Symmetrical in five unequal bays, the centre and outer bays framed by rusticated piers on the ground floor, rising to simplified Ionic pilasters on the second floor, above which a sheer attic is crowned on the outer bays by segmental pediments. The centre bay has a lower, steeply raked pediment. Two arched

doorways at centre, approached by steps.

The plan is rhomboidal rather than rectangular. In the 1930s, the auditorium was completely remodelled and the gallery was probably removed at this time, leaving a single balcony. The stage house has been completely absorbed into the rest of the building which is used as a temple. *TB*

SOUTHAMPTON

Mayflower ★★★
Commercial Road

Other names
1928 Empire
1941 Gaumont
Original architect
1928 W. and T.R. Milburn
Later works
1987 Brian Andrews: major refurbishment
1991 Weguelin Yearley: new box office
Listed   Grade II
Current use Theatre
Capacity   2299

Built in 1928 as the Empire, the last to be built for the Moss Empire circuit, it operated as a theatre for more than fifteen years. Became a Gaumont cinema in 1941. A change of use to bingo was refused on appeal and the theatre was sold in 1985 to the City Council.

The facade to Commercial Road is undemonstrative, almost severe, with spare neo-Grec ornament. Stone and red brick flat-fronted between demi-octagonal stone towers only slightly forward of and taller than the main face. Five storeys in five bays, with stone pilasters rising above the first-floor windows to a modillion cornice. Cinema-style entrance canopy.

The interiors are typical of the period; foyer with marble-lined lower walls; 'luxury liner' staircases on either side rising the full height of the building. The auditorium is strongly related to other

Southampton, Mayflower

Milburn theatres of the time, notably the London Dominion and Edinburgh Empire (Festival). Two balconies, the upper one set back, both with slender columns, again set well back. Ceiling divided into square and rectangular panels with a dome at the centre. Tall, curving proscenium arch penetrates a deep sounding board and is flanked by decorative canted bays and paired boxes, stepped up on either side and set under a semi-circular arch with richly modelled tympanum. The 22 mahogany 'standing boxes' are rare survivals. Backstage and stage facilities are excellent, and the venue is capable of large productions of opera, ballet and musicals.

Apart from the restoration of the auditorium, enlargement of the bar areas and modernisation of the box office, a new lighting, sound and communication system and closed-circuit TV were introduced in 1985. On stage there was a new floor with traps, a completely refurbished counterweight system, new house curtains and an enlarged scene dock with improved access for get-in. The dressing rooms were modernised. The theatre was reopened in 1987 as The Mayflower 'because the pilgrimage to Southampton will be well worth it'.

It is run by an independent trust as a national touring house. *SM/JE*

SOUTHBOROUGH
Kent

Royal Victoria Hall ★
High Street
Original architect
  **1900 William Harmer (Council
          Surveyor) with Sir David
          Salomons**
Later works
  **1977–79 Unknown: altered
            internally and facade mod-
            ernised**
Current use **Multi-purpose hall**
Capacity **450**

The gift of Sir David Lionel Salomons, to provide theatrical and other rational amusements to people who could not afford to go to theatres in the adjoining towns. It was supported by Southborough Urban District Council whose surveyor designed it, but it was said that 'the plans were really Sir David's own'. A national journal described it at the time as 'the only municipal theatre in England' and it is particularly interesting as probably the first of its kind.

A red brick, rectangular building with a low fly tower and, originally, a chapel-

Southborough, Salomon's (Broomhill Trust/Simon Annand)

like facade set back from the road. It now has a later, bland forward extension, with a curved gable bearing a resited date stone reading 1897 and the inscription, ROYAL VICTORIA HALL.

A pretty cast-iron porch was removed a few years ago (purchased by a Councillor who thought its removal regrettable) and replaced by a lumpish 'modern' canopy more suitable for a filling station. The auditorium was designed with a scenic stage, permanent seating in a straight-across end balcony and a flat floor with removable raked seating to part (but now no longer on the original stepped platforms).

The regrettable alterations to the entrance, the provision of a new box office and the insertion of a bar running the full length of the hall, occurred in 1977–1979. Although a multi-purpose hall, run by the local authority, it was licensed for stage plays and authorised to use the Royal coat of arms from the beginning. Used by both professionals and amateurs.

Salomon's Centre ★★
David Salomon's Estate, Broomhill Road
Other names
  **Broomhill Theatre
  Scientific Theatre**
Original architect
  1896 Sir David Lionel Salomons
Later works
  **1902/3 Sir David Lionel
          Salomons: extended and
          improved**
Listed **Grade II**

Current use **Private theatre**
Capacity **c.250**

Sir David Salomons (1797–1873), a financier and a central figure in Anglo-Jewish emancipation, purchased a small villa in 1829 and had it enlarged into a substantial country house. Extensive later additions have completely embedded the original Decimus Burton design. Sir David's nephew and heir, Sir David Lionel Salomons (1851–1925) added a water tower and stables of lavish proportions and, in 1896, a 'scientific theatre'. He employed an architect (W. Barnsley Hughes) for the stables, but the water tower and the theatre were built to his own designs.

The younger Salomons was a scientist, electrician, engineer, photographer and expert on motor design and mechanics. He invented burglar alarms, automatic railway signals and installed electric generating and lighting equipment in his own house. By the time the theatre was complete, the house contained 25 machines and 60,000 tools. Electricity was used for cooking and butter-making.

The scientific theatre, said at the time to be the largest private theatre in the country, was designed to serve Sir David's interests as a scientist and music lover. It was a flat-floored room, originally benched, with a gallery supported on columns on three sides. Rectangular-arched proscenium and ante-proscenium, both higher than wide. For the demonstration of scientific effects and theatrical illusions, it had projectors, painted scenery and electrical apparatus for producing the effects of thunder and lightning. From 1913 it also had a 2400-pipe automatic Welte Philharmonic organ and echo organ. The stage had flying space, fly galleries, a prompter's box and traps.

The house, theatre and gardens were given to the people of Kent in 1937 to be used as a technical institute and museum, but the house became a convalescent home in the Second World War and later passed to the National Health Service, who relinquished it in 1971. A proposal in 1978 to turn the theatre into a National Musical Museum, based on the Frank Holland Collection, failed to make progress.

In 1991 Broomhill Opera was founded and, with the support of the Arts Council, the theatre became a community opera house. Dressing rooms were provided under the stage and an orchestra pit was formed, retractable raked seating installed and means of escape improved, but the room was not ideal for the purpose and the venture failed to attract audiences in sufficient numbers. Since 1999 Broomhill Opera has occupied Wilton's Music Hall in London.

The auditorium is now used infrequently for concerts. In recent years some of Salomons' scientific items kept in the theatre seem to have been lost and some have been removed to store, but the scientific theatre is still, in large part, complete and restorable.

The importance (still not sufficiently recognised) of Sir David Lionel Salomons to the history of modern science and engineering is such that his theatre should be regarded as a working exhibit of not less than national importance. *KW/JE*

SOUTHEND-ON-SEA

Empire
22 Alexandra Street
Other names
   1920 **Rivoli**
   1962 **ABC**
   later **Cannon , ABC (again)**
Original architect
   1896 **Unknown**
Later works
   1920 **Adams and George Coles: converted to cinema**
   1962 **ABC house architect: modernised**
   1980 **Unknown: twinned**
Current use **Amateur theatre**
Capacity   **c.1200 (prior to subdivision)**

The Empire was built in 1896 on the site of a former Public Hall, which had become the Alexandra Theatre. No description of the 1896 building has been found.

In 1920, it was converted to the Rivoli cinema. This was two-tier with boxes, but made no use of the excavated area formerly used for understage, orchestra pit, stalls, etc. Further modernisation and twinning in 1962.

The only parts of the original building, apart from external walls and exits, are stairs to stalls and pit stalls and original signs, and possibly some other areas at the lowest level, under the 1920 cinema, now a basement.

In 1998 the cinema closed and stood empty. At the end of the year, it was acquired for use by local groups and is now used by two different theatre groups for amateur theatre, one in the former stalls area and one in the balcony area. *SM*

Kursaal
South Church Avenue/Marine Parade
Other names
   Kursaal Palace
   Luna Park
Original architect
   1901 **George Sherrin and John Clarke**
Listed   **Grade II**
Current use **Leisure centre**

In 1875, the brewery firm Meux developed 26 acres of farmland into a marine park. The first plans of the Kursaal site were drawn up in 1898 to include a tower, circus, theatre, arcade, etc. The architects George Sherrin and John Clarke designed a large, domed tower in Baroque style to mark the main entrance of the Kursaal site. The Kursaal Palace of 1901 was a large, flat-floored single-balcony music hall and ballroom in the centre of the complex. Pictures show a barrel-vaulted ceiling, with ornate balcony on three sides, supported by pillars from balcony level, as well as the balcony from floor level. The coffered proscenium framed a shell-shaped decorative rear wall; the stage was built at two levels, one apron, one almost thrust. There were dressing rooms and a band room. A local guide-book of 1904 described it, inaccurately, but no doubt reflecting the company's ambitions, as a replica of Blackpool's Winter Gardens.

American-born Clifton Jay Morehouse reopened the site as an amusement park in 1913, with many ideas taken from New York's equivalent Coney Island. It was later called Luna Park. The Morehouse family owned the Kursaal site until 1985, but the Kursaal Palace was used for the last time in the mid 1970s. After it was sold, the new company were unable to fulfil plans to restore the Palace and the stage was removed. Finally the local council intervened in the 1990s when the building was becoming increasingly unsafe and, save for the dome, its supporting walls and the facade, it has now been virtually demolished and rebuilt as a leisure complex which includes a bowling alley. *SM*

Victoria Hall
Alexandra Street
Original architect
   before 1904 Unknown
Current use **Snooker club**
Capacity   **est. 500**

Thought to have been built as an entertainments hall which, by 1904, was presenting variety; by 1908, bioscope had been introduced between theatre seasons. Live entertainment ceased as cinemas were built. Subsequently used for social functions and is now a snooker club. *SM*

SOUTHPORT
Sefton (Merseyside)

Floral Hall
Promenade
Original architect
   1930 Archer and Gooch
Later works
   1973 B.R. Andrews: theatre added
Current use **Multi-purpose hall**
Capacity   **1200**

A flat-roofed building on Classical lines, presenting a rendered frontage with pairs of columns to the promenade. The rear of the building which faces the sea/estuary is in Art Deco style and is at a lower level. The multi-purpose hall is flat-floored with a large stage, band room and dressing rooms. The proscenium and the doors throughout are in Art Deco style.

From the main entrance and box office, stairs lead down to the front part of the hall. This area was extended to make a larger foyer/catering area during the construction of the adjacent Southport Theatre (built in 1973 and too late for inclusion here). *SM*

Southport, Garrick (Ian Grundy)

Garrick ★★
Lord Street
Other names
  Essoldo
  Lucky 7
  Top Rank
  Mecca
Original architect
  1932 George E. Tonge
Current use **Bingo**
Capacity est. **1200**

Built on the site of the previous Opera House and said to be George Tonge's finest design. A massive building in red brick with stone dressings in what was described, loosely, as Italian Renaissance style, but actually a spendid Art Deco invention. Frontages to Lord Street and Kingsway are linked by a curved corner with skyscraper-like ornamental pilasters. Many tall windows with shouldered heads. The Lord Street entrance was originally surmounted by a high canopy with an open colonnade above at first floor which served as a promenade.

The now modified foyer had a domed ceiling and niches in Egyptian style. Spectacular Art Deco auditorium has a rounded proscenium with a vast splayed anti-proscenium almost engulfing the four boxes on either side. Curved ceiling follows the contours, previously lit by trough lighting; walls are splayed and panelled, with, at stalls level, panels with recessed lighting. The ceiling has a decorated centrepiece which surrounded the chandelier. The original colours were yellows and golds, with green and black.

Although converted to cinema use in the 1930s, the exterior is largely

unchanged. The interior remains intact, save for modifications for bingo and alterations to the foyer. The stage is about 12m (c.40ft) deep with a 12m proscenium opening. Grid still in situ.
SM

Little
Houghton Street
Original architect
  1937 Albert Schofield
Later works
  1966 Unknown: adjoining property acquired and rehearsal studio built
  1984 Unknown: refurbished following fire
Current use **Amateur theatre**
Capacity **430**

Southport Dramatic Club, formed in 1920, performed in various venues including the Garrick Theatre. When that became a cinema, the club raised funds to build their own theatre in 1937. The theatre is situated behind Victoria House, Houghton Street, and is approached through a passageway which opens into a quadrangle. The theatre is plain, brick built. The foyer houses a box office and stairs lead up to the rear of the well-raked single-tier auditorium. This has decorated treatment on walls which curve slightly towards the proscenium which is plain but relieved with white columns on either side with concealed lighting. The ceiling is plain with three plaster troughs, also containing concealed lighting.

Stage with fly tower, two traps. Paint frame and workshop space at rear.   *SM*

SOUTH SHIELDS
South Tyneside

Empire Palace
King Street
Other names
  Empire Theatre of Varieties
  Black's Regal Cinema
  Odeon
Original architect
  1897 Frank Matcham and William and T.R. Milburn
Later works
  1898 Frank Matcham: arcade entrance
  1899 William and T.R. Milburn: additions to entrance from King Street and arcade
  1920 Milburn: additional dressing rooms in converted house adjacent
  1929 Milburn: internal walls in auditorium removed; store room converted to bars and toilets
  1934 Edwin M. Lawson: converted to cinema
  1936 Lawson: extended
Listed   **Grade II**
Current use **Fragment**

The theatre was built on the site of Thornton's Theatre of Varieties. The layout of the building was most unusual, with the entrance foyer on King Street separated from the auditorium and stage block by a narrow street with the stalls reached by a tunnel and the first-floor balcony by a bridge. The gallery had direct access by means of a staircase from the rear street. The auditorium and stage were completely remodelled as a cinema in the 1930s with only parts of the external wall retained. The auditorium was demolished in the 1970s, however. Matcham's narrow, stone-faced entrance front on King Street survives largely intact, however, apart from an altered ground floor. It is one wide bay with a large semi-circular arched window occupying the full width at first-floor level. Above this are two small arched windows separated by a shallow niche which rises up into a tall gable consisting of five stages linked by scrolls.
DW

Theatre Royal
14 King Street
Original architect
  1866 C.J. Phipps with T.M. Clemence (South Shields)
Later works
  1891 J.H. Morton (South Shields):

circle and gallery fronts altered

1893   J.H. Morton: pit entrance altered

1899   J.H. Morton: cast-iron canopy over main entrance

1934   Jones and Rigby: converted to shop

Current use **Facade only**

The Phipps/Clemence partnership was the result of the promoters establishing a competition to build the new theatre. Only the 1866 facade by Clemence remains, less columns and pediment, following conversion to shops in 1934. Three bays defined by giant Corinthian pilasters. An unusually ambitious theatrical landmark for its time and place. Situated immediately alongside the Empire. *DW*

STAFFORD

Sandonia

248 Sandon Road

Original architect

1920   **Unknown**

Later works

1921   **Unknown: annexe (for refreshments) created at rear of circle**

n.d   **Unknown: subdivided horizontally**

Current use **Snooker hall**

Capacity   **c.1100 (prior to subdivision)**

The building, which was a theatre until 1923, when it became a cinema, is long and narrow. White stone facade to Sandon Road, with central entrances flanked by one small shop each side. Above is a semi-circular arch and a circular window surrounded by garland and a central figure decoration. Fly tower with a long lantern on the roof. The three-storey dressing-room block is behind the stage, rectangular except for a cut into one side, due to the presence of an adjacent brook which necessitates a permanent pump in the cellar. There are eight dressing rooms.

The lower part of the auditorium is used as a snooker hall. The stalls rake has been split into two terraces providing room for thirteen full-sized tables and the stage has a false floor over the original rake, providing for four more tables. A false ceiling divides the snooker hall from the circle - at present left without seats. The auditorium before its horizontal division was tunnel-like. Long barrel-vaulted roof with parallel ribs can be seen above the false ceiling. The back of

the circle is just short of 30.5m (100ft) from the proscenium opening. Staffordshire knot ornament within wreaths on circle front. The decoration is otherwise quite plain. The proscenium arch has a large plaster motif consisting of two female figures. The fly tower is cut off from the stage by two false ceilings. The safety curtain remains in situ. *TB*

STALYBRIDGE
Tameside

Hippodrome
Trinity Street/Corporation Street

Other names

1890   **Grand Theatre**

1920s   **Grand Theatre and Hippodrome**

Original architect

1890   **Unknown**

Current use **Shops/offices (behind facade)**

Opened in 1890 as the Grand Theatre. Accommodation was private boxes, orchestra stalls, 2nd circle and upper circle. No other details of decoration or design found. The Grand was devoted to variety until the early 1920s when films were introduced, sometimes as part of the bill, and sometimes on alternate evenings. Leased by the H.D. Moorhouse circuit, it became a full-time cinema until 1954, when it closed mid-performance as it was discovered that the lease had expired!

After lying empty for a few years, the auditorium and stage were demolished to form a car park and public lavatories. The facade is left, flanked by shops, as when it first opened; behind are offices and shops. The letters HDMC, visible over the front door, are a reminder of the Harry D. Moorhouse Circuit days. *SM*

STAMFORD
Lincolnshire

Stamford Theatre
(Arts Centre and Theatre) ★
St Mary's Street

Other names

1768   **Theatre**

Original architect

1768   **Unknown**

Later works

1848   **Unknown: extensive alterations**

1853   **Unknown: auditorium altered (possibly as a concert hall)**

1871   **Unknown: converted to gentlemen's club**

1978   **Unknown: converted to arts centre**

1992   **Borough Architects Dept: foyer altered and provision made for film projection**

Listed   **Grade II**

Current use **Theatre/Arts Centre**

Capacity   **165**

Now part of an Arts complex of which the theatre is the right-hand element. Built in 1768, only the original shell and ashlar facade remain, the interior having been stripped out in 1871 with a further remodelling in 1978 to provide the present interior.

The facade is a rare and valuable surviving example of the front of a Georgian playhouse. It is of two storeys and five bays under a continuous bracketed cornice and straight parapet. There is a large pedimented central doorway with an arched window over and two small side doorways. The 1978 works provided a theatre for amateur use and occasional professional tours. Repeated pleas for an authentic reconstruction were rejected on the assumption that insufficient evidence remained. The present interior bears no resemblance whatsoever to a Georgian playhouse. However, the evidence still extant in the 1970s and the lesson learned at Richmond, Yorkshire, and King's Lynn would have made restoration possible.

A description of the theatre as it existed before 1978 may be found in the RCHME volume for the *Town of Stamford, 1977. TB*

STANFORD ON SOAR
Nottinghamshire

Stanford Hall Theatre ★★

Original architect

1938   **Cecil Aubrey Masey**

Listed   **Grade II***

Current use **Theatre**

Capacity   **352**

A small well-equipped private theatre which has been used by professional companies. Stanford Hall theatre is a little Glyndebourne in that it is a purpose-built, fully equipped playhouse in the Midlands countryside. Stanford Hall itself was built between 1711 and 1714. In 1938, Sir Julian Cahn, then owner of the Hall, responsible for a successful furnishing empire and, as it happened, an expert conjuror, built a private theatre to the east of the hall for the purpose of staging his own shows of magic.

The exterior wall is of unrelieved red brick, except for a series of square windows just below the roof level. The original entrance to the auditorium was via a large and sumptuously decorated foyer (now converted into a dining room) from the Hall. The public entrance, consisting of double doors, stands to the right of the facade whilst at the extreme left is the stage-door entrance with dock doors above at the first-floor level. The auditorium and stage run along the same axis as the Hall.

The foyer is small. Two ascending stairways, one on either side of the foyer, with a small box office to the extreme right, lead to the auditorium. The right-hand staircase enters the single-floor auditorium at the rear whilst that on the left enters at front stalls level. Sight lines are excellent. Above the rear of the auditorium is a projection box capable of showing films - now an infrequent event.

The Art Deco interior is in its original condition except for the addition of speakers and spotlights. House lighting is entirely concealed in the vertical and horizontal covings of the walls and ceiling. Most of these lights point towards the stage except for those surrounding two ornamental plaster vases.

The lower parts of the walls are panelled in mahogany veneer topped with a wide band of ebony. The entrance doors are also mahogany veneered. The large mural and ceiling panels are by Beatrice MacDermott. MacDermott also decorated a series of screens, in similar style, which slotted across the proscenium opening so as to complete the decorative effect. Two of these survive, one situated on each side of the stage.

There is an orchestra pit, the centre of which is taken up with the console of a Wurlitzer organ which was built for the New Theatre Madeleine, Paris, in 1926 and from which it was brought for the opening of the Theatre in 1938. The front of the stage is bowed and conceals a curved row of three circuit functioning footlights.

Deep beneath the auditorium Cahn built a substantial 'bomb proof' shelter. Below the stage is a large green room and six small dressing rooms, toilets and bathroom.

The framework of the counterweight flying gear of 30 lines remains - a novelty for 1938 and especially in a private theatre.

Sir Julian died in 1944 and the whole estate was purchased by the Co-operative Society in 1945. Shortly afterwards the

theatre was used by The Midland Theatre Company before their move to Coventry Belgrade and then by the Lincoln Theatre Royal Repertory Company on their touring schedule for a number of years but all professional productions ceased around the 1960s. It is now used by a number of dramatic and operatic societies from a wide area, each putting on two or three productions in the year. They are well supported, and the theatre is properly managed and well maintained. *TB*

STIRLING

Alhambra Music Hall
Shopping Arcade
Other names
   1882 Arcade
Original architect
   1882 John McLean
Current use **Derelict**

Opened in 1882 as the Arcade Theatre, closed in 1939 and partially converted for retail use. It is now abandoned, but fragments of the theatre are still present under later fittings. The form of the auditorium is still evident and an ornate twisting staircase in the entrance, together with fragments of plaster decoration, remain. *BP*

STOCKPORT

Plaza ★★
Mersey Square
Original architect
   1932 W. Thornley

Later works
   1967 Unknown: converted to bingo
Listed   **Grade II**
Current use **Disused**
Capacity   **originally c.1875**

The Plaza was built in 1932, by W. Thornley, who designed a number of super cinemas in the Greater Manchester area (it bore a great similarity to the Regal, Altrincham, designed by him). The rear of the site had to be excavated, in some places by up to 12.8m (42ft) to accommodate the building, and allowed little space for a deep stage or a dressing-room block. Nevertheless, a grand super cinema was created, facing onto Mersey Square, which survives with many original features and as a single auditorium, thanks to many years in use as a bingo hall.

The facade, above the entrance, is faced in pearly faience tiles, with tripartite windows at three levels, between slim ornamental grilles; the tall, central bay bears the name PLAZA at attic level. The interior is Egyptian-themed and is said to have been inspired by the Paris Exhibition of 1925, with gold ceilings and bas-relief murals of nymphs. The auditorium, in lavish style, with ornamental grilles and decorative lights is topped by a large dome. There is a square, decorative proscenium.

In 1967, the Plaza was converted to bingo, the stalls and the stage area (the organ remaining in a central position) being adapted for that purpose. The

Stockport, Plaza

Stockton-on-Tees, Theatre (Ian Grundy)

building was listed prior to closure in 1998, and the design is such an important surviving example of Art Deco that it has been considered for acquisition by the National Trust.

STOCKTON-ON-TEES

Theatre
Green Dragon Yard
Other names
   Theatre Royal
   Stockton Theatre
   Oxford Music Hall
   Oxford Theatre of Varieties
   Royal Concert Hall
   Georgian Theatre
Original architect
   probably C17
      Unknown: as a tithe barn
Later works
   1766 Unknown: converted to a
        theatre
   1818 Unknown: repaired and 12
        boxes added
   1874 Unknown: converted to
        Salvation Army citadel
Listed   **Grade II**
Current use **Theatre**
Capacity **c.100**

Built as Stockton's tithe barn, the theatre conversion of 1766 was quite radical, raising the original sandstone walls in brickwork (a fact recorded by Winston in *The Theatric Tourist*, 1805). From 1874–93 it was used by the Salvation Army and afterwards became a confectionery factory. Gabled with pantiled roof, approached at the south end from the cobbled passage called Green

Dragon Yard. A lean-to structure at the southern end is relatively modern. Adjoining is a cottage, the upper floor of which was used as a dressing room, actors entering the theatre through a door at the stage end of the east wall. Internally, an uninterrupted volume with an open timber roof and no architectural features of note. The evidence of the Georgian theatre is now of an archaeological nature (Richard Southern found traces of a former balcony). It has been fitted up as a theatre for special occasions since 1980. *DW*

STOKE-ON-TRENT

Regent ★★★
Piccadilly, Hanley
Listed
   1929 Regent
   1950 Gaumont
   later Odeon
Original architect
   1929 W.E. Trent
Later works
   1972 Unknown: converted to
        triple cinema
   1999 Levitt Bernstein Assocs:
        reconstructed as a major
        touring theatre
Listed   **Grade II***
Current use **Theatre**
Capacity **1615**

Before the recent alterations, this was still essentially Trent's impressive 1929 cinema with full stage facilities, occupying an area between Pall Mall, Piccadilly and Cheapside. Excluding the Theatre Royal, the Regent now represents the only purpose-built proscenium theatre in the Potteries after the regrettable loss of the Longton Empire. The side fronting Cheapside originally housed the main exits from the rear of the stalls and circle. It was a three-storey building with channelled ground floor, red brick above, divided into three unequal bays by pilasters; the name REGENT in a central panel; stone cornice and parapet. The rear side facing Pall Mall was of three storeys to the right. It had a monumental fly tower to the left, red brick with white faience dressings; the name

Stoke-on-Trent, Regent (Levitt Bernstein)

REGENT again in a central panel. The main entrance in Piccadilly was and is in white faience with a large window above an altered canopy. Mask ornaments.

The auditorium was a striking work of its time in ciné-Deco style (described at the time as 'modern French'). Square coved proscenium flanked by organ panels. Boxes stepped down from circle front. Ornamental dome with lantern in ceiling. Conversion to triple cinema in 1972 did not irreversibly destroy theatre potential or architectural treatment.

The 1999 works, by Levitt Bernstein (Axel Burrough), constituted one of the most radical reconstructions of a theatre to be undertaken in recent decades (compare Edinburgh Festival Theatre). The stage house and the back-of-house elevation to Pall Mall have been totally reconstructed, the stage and proscenium advanced into the auditorium and the front-of-house accommodation considerably improved, adopting throughout, internally, the Art Deco architectural vocabulary of the Trent cinema. Large orchestra pit. *TB*

Repertory
College Road/Beresford Street
Original architect
1879 Unknown: as a church
Later works
1932 Unknown: converted to theatre
Current use **Disused**
Capacity **c.200**

The amateur Stoke-on-Trent Repertory Theatre used the former Church of St Simon and St Jude as its venue. The exterior is typical of a small late Victorian church with neither tower nor steeple. There is a south aisle but a series of gables on the north side, in place of the usual aisle,where the scene dock is situated. At the rear is an annexe (original) which was formerly the church school and later used as the theatre workshop until around 1990.

There was virtually no foyer, the entrance doorway leading almost directly into the rear of the auditorium. Seating (part raked) was confined within the line of wooden pillars supporting the roof. There was no orchestra pit, any musicians having to be accommodated on the same level as the front seats. Flat stage. The building was in deteriorating condition and was too small for the company by the 1990s. The new Repertory Theatre opened in 1998 on a site in Leek Road. The company had been trying to purchase the Longton Empire as their new

home and were within two days of signing when that theatre went up in flames on the last day of 1992. *TB*

Theatre Royal ★
Pall Mall, Hanley
Listed
1850 The People's Hall
1852 Royal Pottery Theatre
Original architect
1850 or 1852 Unknown: converted from a Methodist Chapel
Later works
1857 T.C. Shaw: interior reconstructed as three-tier theatre
1871 R. Twemlow or T. Hinde: reconstructed and modernised
1887 C.J. Phipps and Frank Matcham: reconstructed with new auditorium, old theatre becoming the stage area
1894 Frank Matcham: remodelled and extended; electricity introduced
1934 Unknown: partial rebuild after fire; cinema projection box installed
1951 Forshaw and Greaves: rebuilt after another fire
Current use **Theatre**
Capacity **c.1400**

Tradition suggests that the first theatre opened as a People's Hall, converted from a Methodist Chapel which may, in turn, have had a previous existence as a colliery winding house.

Following the 1949 fire, only the rear wall of the 1894 theatre was left. The plain three-storey facade to Pall Mall (with four sets of double doors) and the dressing-room block facing Brunswick Street may possibly belong to the 1871 rebuild. The rest was rebuilt in 1951 (at a time of stringent building restrictions), not in the fashionable post-war idiom of that time but in the manner of a 1930s ciné-theatre. It would seem, therefore, to predate what is usually documented as 'the first new theatre to be built in this country since the war'- Middlesbrough Little Theatre (1957), the Vanbrugh (1954) at RADA being discounted as a drama school theatre.

Stalls with seventeen straight rows. Dress circle has a flat U-shaped front. Three boxes forming slips at gallery level. Flat stage with very little wing space on stage left.

Ensuring that all the Art Deco recessed illumination and light panels in the auditorium are in full working order

is no small matter as some 360 individual bulbs are involved. Additional light was originally supplied by six Waterford Crystal chandeliers formerly in the German Embassy in London. Four of these are still in situ. A fifth is now hung in the foyer. The proscenium arch, which had been altered, has been returned to its original 1951 state - complete with two illuminated number frames on each side, possibly the only extant working examples. The facade has been completely re-covered with maroon tiles replacing the former yellow ones. A television 'challenge' operation to get the theatre up and running again was mounted in 1993.

It cannot be said that the Royal is an outstanding design and it has undoubted defects, including imperfect sighting from upper levels, which would be difficult to remedy. A recent study of theatre and concert venues in Stoke, commissioned by the City Council from Arts Business Ltd, concluded that the Royal had 'cramped facilities' making it impossible to host large-scale modern touring musicals. This report favoured the neighbouring Regent as a touring house, making the prospects for the Royal seem bleak. However, it is a working theatre which still provides a service.

Victoria
Hartshill Road
Original architect
1914 Unknown
Later works
1931? Unknown: orchestra pit removed and stage depth reduced to increase accommodation
late 1960 Unknown: converted to nightclub
1962 Unknown: former auditorium converted to theatre-in-the-round
Current use **Shops/car park**

A former ciné-variety. Opened in 1962 as a pioneering theatre-in-the-round by Stephen Joseph. Seating arranged in one tier – no balcony. The flat stage had a shallow grave trap. There was no orchestra pit. Two dressing rooms at stage level. Closed in 1984. Replaced by New Victoria Theatre on another site.

The old building is still standing with part of the auditorium in use as a car park and part in use as shops. *TB*

see also **TUNSTALL**

The original Shakespeare Memorial Theatre, c.1920s

STRATFORD-UPON-AVON
Warwickshire

Royal Shakespeare and Swan Theatres ★
Waterside

Other names
1879–1960 Shakespeare Memorial Theatre

Original architect
1879 Dodgshun and Unsworth (William Frederick Unsworth): Shakespeare Memorial Theatre

Later works
1889 A.S. Flower: scene dock added
1898-9 Unknown: dress-circle escape staircase added (also groove system removed)
1913 Unknown: proscenium arch altered; orchestra pit lowered
1932 Elisabeth Scott (Scott, Chesterton and Shepherd): Royal Shakespeare Theatre built, after fire destroyed Memorial Theatre
1933 Scott, Chesterton and Shepherd: old Memorial Theatre converted to conference and rehearsal room
1936 Scott,Shepherd and Breakwell: gallery seating of new theatre extended and refreshment room created on river front
1938 Scott, Shepherd and Breakwell: tearoom built on ground floor with restaurant above
1940-49 Unknown: rolling stages dismantled; orchestra pit covered; forestage extended;

stage machinery overhauled; musicians' balconies built either side of proscenium
1951 Brian O'Rorke: auditorium altered; dress circle extended forward; stalls re-raked and polished wood wall linings removed; forestage widened
1958-59 Robert Harvey (Yorke, Harper and Harvey): glazed outer foyer built; box office enlarged
1960-91 Various: a continuous series of alterations to Scott building, including building of hexagonal forestage and false proscenium; installation of revolving stage; hydraulic lifts installed (and later removed); side bal-

conies created on flank walls at gallery level; paint frame removed; some restoration of 1930s' detail
1986 Michael Reardon Associates: former Memorial Theatre converted to Swan Theatre and Ashcroft Room; new tower built on site of former (Unsworth) tower

Listed   **Grade II***
Current use Theatres
Capacity   **RST 1412/ Swan 464**

The building of a Shakespeare Memorial Theatre was a delayed consequence of the Tercentenary Festival which took place in Stratford in 1864. The original Garrick Jubilee in 1769, marking the bicentenary (five years late) of Shakespeare's birth produced no permanent memorial. A Stratford theatre was built in 1824 and was used for a Shakespeare festival in 1830, but it was demolished in 1872.

For the 1864 celebration a huge wooden pavilion, like a temporary circus building, but lavishly furnished and decorated, was erected to the designs of local architects Thompson and Colbourne. The stage had a 9.4m (31ft) proscenium and a depth of 17m (56ft). Opposite the stage was a second platform or 'orchestra' for up to 530 musicians and singers. The architects had never designed a theatre before and the whole thing, from design to completion, was executed in five months but it was, by common consent, a functionally effective and acoustically excellent design. It was, nevertheless, dismantled and the parts sold at near-scrap prices when the Festival ended in debt.

Stratford-upon-Avon, Royal Shakespeare Theatre (Val Earl)

In 1875, a Shakespeare Memorial Association was founded to raise money for a new, permanent theatre, library and art gallery to be built on a riverside site donated by Charles Edward Flower. Following a competition, Dodgshun and Unsworth were commissioned. Unsworth was probably the principal author. The Shakespeare Memorial Theatre opened on 23 April 1879.

The original idea of the building being a recreation of a Shakespearean playhouse (or what such a playhouse was then thought to have been like) was clearly modified as soon as lines were put on paper, but what emerged was a quite unlike any other contemporary theatre in Britain, a delightful and fantastic blend of Mediaevalism, somewhat in the manner of William Burges, combined with Elizabethan or 'Old English' elements. The auditorium sight lines were imperfect, but Unsworth's theatre, taken as whole, was certainly an interesting (and perhaps always underrated) invention of its time. The associated museum wing was completed in 1881 and the scene dock in 1887.

This building was destroyed by fire in 1926, leaving only a shell. The museum wing, which was linked to the theatre by a galleried bridge, was undamaged. Once again, an architectural competition was held, which was won by Elisabeth Scott, in consultation with Alison Sleigh. The new theatre opened in 1932. The results have generated argument ever since. The RIBA-approved judges were determined to have an innovative design and ignored (the case is not unique) the views of those whose expertise was in making theatres work. Writing long after the event, the architect and historian Goodhart-Rendel said (1953) that the theatre was a 'monument of some importance.... a notable work of architecture, well befitting its purpose... a people's theatre in which the play is the thing'. Iain Mackintosh, by contrast, says (in 1995) that the 'farce' of the competition 'set back the cause of Shakespeare and the creation of a national theatre for a generation,' producing a design which 'was almost universally praised by architects and almost universally condemned by the theatre'.

Following the normal pattern of appreciation of C20 buildings, the design which excited the architectural world in 1932, became a serious embarrassment to the modern movers by the 1950s, but a precious and rare object to architectural historians of the 1970s. In the context of this study we should

judge Scott's design without paying too much attention to opposing theological arguments, but it is impossible to ignore the extraordinary sequence of modifications (and modifications of modifications) the place went through in successive, varyingly successful, attempts to remedy its inbuilt theatrical defects.

Unlike some contemporary and later buildings, the exterior has improved with age and the modifications made on the river front by Scott herself have been to its advantage. It is a striking work of its time, its plain brick forms, originally conceived as concrete, relieved by a minimum of geometric ornament. The entrance front is curved with cut brick sculptural reliefs by Eric Kennington. Most of the public interiors are delightful, until one reaches the auditorium, which is and always was a grave disappointment.

By the 1930s, those parts of the 1879 building which survived could be dismissed by architectural critics as 'excrescences' and it is remarkable that they were incorporated by Scott rather than demolished. She failed, regrettably, to recreate Unsworth's highly picturesque jettied storey over the Memorial Theatre, but her work may be seen as sensitive for its time. The shell of the old theatre was first converted by Scott into a conference centre and later became a rehearsal room. In 1986 it was splendidly restored to full theatrical life as the Swan Theatre by Michael Reardon. This has an interior, admired alike by architects, performers and audiences. It has embracing wood-balustraded galleries and a narrow thrust stage. The audience is on three sides.

Major refurbishment of the complex, including partial rebuilding, was proposed in 1999. *JE/TB*

SUNDERLAND

Avenue
Gillbridge Avenue
Other names
Avenue Theatre and Opera House
Original architect
1882 Charles Dunn (Sunderland) and Richard Thornton
Later works
1890 William and T.R. Milburn: new scene dock
1891 Milburn: proscenium front moved forwards
1899 Milburn: new frontage with portico extended; new circle lounge and bar above entrance

1901 Milburn: new scene dock with workshop/store below
Current use **Bottling hall**

A rather industrial-looking building, rendered with crow-stepped gable and low stage house. Flank divided into windowed bays, rising to a brick modillioned eaves and slated roof. Interior not seen. Was exclusively cinema from 1932. *DW*

Empire ★★
High West Street
Other names
Civic Theatre
Original architect
1907 William and T.R. Milburn
Later works
1989 Tyne Theatre Construction (Jack Dixon): construction work during reopening of gallery
Listed **Grade II***
Current use **Theatre**
Capacity **1850**

Built as a large variety theatre and in excellent condition inside and out. The style of the auditorium is typical of the Milburns' earlier work, and an important comparison can be made between this theatre and their West Hartlepool Empire Theatre (now demolished) built two years later in 1909. There, the auditorium layout was highly reminiscent of Sunderland, which now seems to be the only example of this phase of their work. Wide auditorium with two deep, slightly curved balconies, two very big, almost overbearing, boxes with elaborately tiered cupolas facing the audience at upper-balcony levels, and dress-circle slips which rake steeply down the side of the auditorium wall.

At each side of the 1st balcony is a little six-bay arcade with four of the bays made into boxes. Rectangular proscenium with a large, flat tablet above the centre. The ceiling has very high coves over the proscenium and at the sides, divided into panels by strips of moulding. Heavily modelled and sparsely applied Baroque plasterwork.

The exterior is mostly hidden behind the frontages of the main street, but above the corner entrance is a big, circular, domed tower with a boldly projecting cornice and oeil-de-boeuf dormers. Beyond the tower, along the side, is an unexpectedly charming series of Arts and Crafts bow windows in the upper floor.

The Empire was purchased by the

Sunderland, Empire (Ian Grundy)

Sunderland Corporation in 1960 - one of the first local authorities to take the initiative of giving a new lease of life to an ailing commercial touring theatre. At the time of writing (1998) the theatre has already undergone a number of enlargements including new dressing rooms, and a study on its further enlargement and full restoration has been undertaken.

For the Milburns' quite different later work, see the Empires in Edinburgh (now the Festival Theatre), Southampton (now the Mayflower), Liverpool and, in London, the Dominion.   *CB/DW*

SUNNINGHILL
Windsor and Maidenhead

Novello
2 High Street
Other names
   The Sunninghill Mission Hall
Original architect
   **1900 or later Unknown: converted
   from mission hall**
Later works
   **c.1918 Unknown: cinema installed
   1960s Unknown: converted to theatre; dressing-room block
   added at rear; modern
   canopy added**
Current use **Theatre**
Capacity **158**

When the Sunninghill Mission Hall came on the market at the turn of the century, it was purchased by the Hon. Ashley Ponsonby and Mr F.J. Patton, and reconstructed internally with a well-equipped stage and a gallery. They handed over the management of the hall to the Ascot

District Liberal Association, but it was used more by the local Conservative Association.

Sir Charles Wyndham was the most notable enthusiast professionally, producing, acting with his leading lady, Mary Moore, and donating scenery and curtains. Although not grand, the theatre was fashionable. Later, in the First World War, it became the local cinema, and was later fitted with sound, continuing to serve Ascot and Sunninghill both as theatre and cinema.

In 1966, it was purchased by Miss Rose, Principal of the Redroofs Theatre School in Maidenhead, for productions mounted by the School, and at other times available for hire. At this time a dressing-room block was built, the stage facilities modernised and a modern entrance canopy added. The theatre has a proscenium stage with three traps, but no flying facilities. There are two dressing rooms and a scene dock. Get-in is at street level.   *SM*

SUTTON COLDFIELD
Birmingham

Highbury Little Theatre
41 Sheffield Street, Boldmere
Original architect
   **1942 John English: mission hall
   converted to theatre**
Later works
   **1960 John English: adjacent build-
   ing incorporated into the
   front of house as a coffee
   bar**
   **1982-86 John English: new brick
   auditorium; stage widened**

and deepened; new studio
theatre added
Current use **Amateur theatre**
Capacity **135**

A mission hut was converted into a theatre in 1942 by the addition of a fly tower, stage and dressing rooms. In 1960 an adjoining shop was incorporated into the front of house as a coffee bar and, in 1982, the auditorium was rebuilt in brick and other improvements made, including the addition of a studio theatre and workshops. This piecemeal process, extending over half a century has produced a small community theatre.   *TB*

SWANSEA

Grand ★★★
Singleton Street
Other names
   1933-47 The Swansea Cinema
Original architect
   1897 William Hope
Later works
   **1982 City Architect: extensively
   rebuilt and altered**
Listed   **Grade II**
Current use **Theatre**
Capacity **1019**

The completion of an extensive programme of rebuilding, alterations and additions (1982-87) has meant significant changes to the exterior of the building described in *Curtains!!!* 1982. Everything behind the proscenium has been demolished and a vast new stage and fly tower built, together with a generous provision of dressing and rehearsal rooms and other facilities.

The excellent auditorium has two well-curved balconies and two superimposed bow-fronted boxes on each side, framed by pilasters. The proscenium is flanked by fluted colonnettes standing on extremely elongated pedestals. The head of the proscenium originally reached the ceiling but a lighting bridge has been installed together with a new ceiling of decorative fibrous plaster some three metres higher. There is rich and lively plasterwork on balcony and box fronts and proscenium. The balconies are supported by iron columns with remarkable Art Nouveau capitals.

An orchestra pit has been constructed on two lifts so that, when not in use, stalls seating can be extended down to the stage; for performances of opera, the pit can be opened to a size suitable for a Mozart orchestra or for a Richard Strauss orchestra of 90. In the latter case there is

Swansea, Grand (Graham P. Matthews)

a loss of 35 stalls seats. From the new stage house two entirely new additions extend along the sides of the theatre (as east and west wings) and it is these which allow ante-rooms to be added to the side boxes of the auditorium. Their facades have pediments broken into by Venetian windows. These forward projections are connected across the original front facade by a rusticated colonnade with a glass conservatory over, the forward extension of the theatre facade resulting in a narrowing of Singleton Street.

This rebuild has created a lively and intimate theatre of great charm. It is the only remaining complete (though altered) theatre by William Hope. *CB/TR*

Palace ★★

High Street
Other names
1888   **Pavilion Theatre of Varieties**
1892   **Empire**
1901   **Palace Theatre of Varieties**
by 1912 **Swansea Popular Picture Hall**
1923   **Palace Theatre of Varieties (again)**
Original architect
1888   **Bucknall and Jennings**
Later works
1889   **Bucknall and Jennings: two boxes added**
1953   **Unknown: restored following fire**

1961   **Unknown: converted to bingo**
Listed   **Grade II**
Current use **Nightclub**
Capacity   **est. 450**

Opened in 1888 as a music hall, the Pavilion Theatre of Varieties. Dramatic exterior on triangular site, in brick with ample stone dressings. Circular tower at the apex (stage end) originally domed, and a square tower at each of the other two corners with curved pavilion roofs. The base of the triangle (rear wall of the auditorium) faces a narrow street and is in plain brickwork. The other two facades, however, flank major streets, and on approaching the theatre from the High Street both fronts can be seen simultaneously as they splay outwards from the corner. The elevational treatment of the two fronts is similar - ground floor with banded rustication and a series of semi-circular arched doorways and windows, and the two upper floors embraced by giant Tuscan pilasters. These form an interesting rhythm of bays – alternately blank and with windows; vertically linked by panels containing busts and pedimented in the upper storey. Above the pilasters is a deep entablature, carried continuously round both fronts.

The auditorium is at first-floor level, in order to provide space below for the necessary ancillary accommodation on the tight site. It is very intimate with two steeply raked balconies which curve

round to the proscenium, now without boxes. The balconies have iron open balustrades which have been juggled around to suit altered stepping at the lower level. The upper balcony has its original gallery seating. The stalls floor has been flattened for dancing. As the stage is at the narrow end of the site, it is small and wedge-shaped, but adequate for variety turns not requiring elaborate sets.

The exterior has looked sad and neglected for some years with windows boarded up, but club use has done no irreparable harm and there are encouraging signs that the restoration and reopening of this charming theatre might prove feasible.   *CB/TR*

Patti Pavilion

Victoria Park, Brynmill
Original architect
c.1891   **Bucknall and Jennings (Alfred Bucknall) at Craig-y-Nos**
Later works
1920   **Unknown: reassembled in Swansea and adapted for public entertainment**
Listed   **Grade II**
Current use **Multi-purpose**
Capacity   **490**

A glass and iron structure with roof of Tudor arch profile. This is the Winter Garden of Craig-y-Nos, Abercrave (qv), dismantled and brought to Swansea as the gift of Adelina Patti in 1919. It was reassembled in Victoria Park in 1920 and opened to the public in 1922. In order to make it more suitable as an entertainment venue, the glass roof and upper side walls were covered in sheet iron and a stage was installed along one side of what became the new auditorium. There was no balcony, and the flat auditorium floor had no permanent seating. Single-storey red brick annexes were added to either side to house cloakrooms and other public facilities. By the early 1990s the Council-owned building was in rapidly declining condition and it seemed likely that it would be permanently closed and (but for its listed status) demolished. In summer 1994 a crash programme of repair and re-equipment costing £750,000, undertaken as part of a television 'challenge', was completed in less than three days. The roof was re-covered, the walls re-glazed, dressing rooms and bars updated, modern lighting and sound equipment installed and the building redecorated inside and out. The stage was moved to a position facing the entrance. The results of this refurbishment have been criticised in architectural conservation terms but, for the time being, it broke a cycle of neglect and inaction. *TR*

SWINDON

Mechanics Institute ★
Emlyn Square, Railway Village
Other names
  1930 Playhouse Theatre
        Civic Playhouse
Original architect
  1853-55 Edward Roberts (London)
Later works
  1893 Brightwen Binyon: market
        hall removed; building
        greatly enlarged
  1930 Unknown: partly rebuilt after
        fire in former first floor hall
Listed   Grade II★
Current use Disused
Capacity   c.600 (following 1930
        rebuild)

The Mechanics Institute is perhaps one of the finest surviving examples of its kind. Designed in Tudor Gothic style of Swindon limestone rubble with Bath ashlar dressings, externally it gives the appearance of a great hall with buttressed sides of eight bays. It was built by GWR as a social and community centre for railway staff, opening in 1855, with a library, coffee room, reading room, etc. It had a lecture/concert hall with a stage. There was originally an octagonal market hall at the south end.

A proposal to erect a full-scale theatre at the rear in 1878 never came to fruition. In 1892 the market hall was demolished and the Institute greatly enlarged. These and most later additions and alterations were carried out in matching style.

In 1930 the centre of the building was badly damaged by fire. The first-floor hall was rebuilt as a theatre, the Playhouse, later known as the Civic Playhouse, with an enlarged stage. It had pit, stalls and dress circle, a pretty theatre with an elaborate proscenium and (unusually for its kind) a fly tower. The Playhouse took the place of the Empire, when that turned to cinema, and also served local amateur companies who were later accommodated at the Wyvern. The theatre closed in 1986 and has since been disused and in some disrepair. In 1990 planning permission was granted (on appeal) for conversion to an hotel, but this had not been implemented by 1999. *SM*

TAUNTON
Somerset

Gaumont Palace ★
Corporation Street
Other names
  Odeon
Original architect
  1932 W.T. Benslyn
Later works
  1981 Unknown: converted to bingo
        and refurbished
Listed   Grade II
Current use Bingo
Capacity   c.1275 (prior to 1981 conver-
        sion)

A large brick building in Art Deco style; three entrance doors under a canopy, three first-floor windows to a balcony, centrally arranged within a picture-frame-like facade, the whole flanked by lower, quadrant wings, each with an entrance door. Fly tower at rear.

The main entrance to the theatre is in Corporation Street. Staircases at each end give access to small circle foyers which originally led to the café. The decorative treatment of the coffered ceiling and marble enrichments, together with the warm-toned Ruboleum floor, combine to create a pleasing atmosphere.

The auditorium has a spacious circle, the rear of which extends over the entrance hall. The ceiling is centred on an impressive shell-like formation, with lighting concealed. There is a perimeter band. The proscenium arch, emphasised by a ribbed lighting cove on which changes of colour could originally be made from concealed cornices, is striking. On the flank splayed walls are two great flower-like features, which run almost from floor to ceiling. The stage is 6.4m (21 ft) deep and 22.5m (74 ft) wide and would need to be improved to make it suitable for medium-scale tours. Eleven dressing rooms. Well decorated and maintained for its present bingo use. *SM*

TEIGNMOUTH
Devon

Riviera
Den Crescent
Other names
  Assembly Rooms
  Riviera Cinema
Original architect
  1826 William Patey
Later works
  1924 Unknown: converted to hotel
        and restaurant with ballroom

  1933 Unknown: cinema constructed
        in shell
  1970 Unknown: converted to cine-
        ma/theatre with amusement
        arcade below
Listed   Grade II
Current use Cinema with regular live the-
        atre use
Capacity   417

The Riviera was built in 1826 as Public Assembly Rooms, later becoming the headquarters of the Teignmouth and East Devon Club. It has an imposing 7-bay facade with a giant Ionic order of columns and a crowning pediment above a ground-floor Doric colonnade.

In 1912, films were shown. In 1924, it was in use as a hotel and restaurant, live entertainment and films continuing in the hotel ballroom. In 1933 the interior was demolished and a 900-seat cinema was constructed in the shell. This was converted to its present form in 1970 - a theatre/cinema above an amusement arcade.

The auditorium retains features of its 1930s' moulded plasterwork, cove lighting and panelled ceiling. It has raked seating with excellent sight lines. There are no flying facilities. The foyer upstairs is spacious and enjoys views over the bay. As well as the amusement arcade, retail outlets have been introduced at street level and an owner's flat was added, somewhat incongruously, in the 1960s, in the form of a penthouse. *SM*

TENBY
Pembrokeshire

Royal Playhouse
White Lion Street
Other names
  Royal Gate House Assembly Rooms
  Royal Playhouse Cinema
Original architect
  1865 Unknown
Later works
  n.d. Unknown: stage house
        demolished
Current use Cinema
Capacity   479

Built as assembly rooms in 1865, equipped for theatrical use. Became a cinema by 1912 but retained stage plays and music and dancing licence. Now exclusively a cinema. Stuccoed, parapeted facade, in three major bays, the centre advanced and pedimented. Entrances and blind first-floor openings in tall arched recesses, framed by plain pilasters. Interior has single balcony.

Tidworth, Garrison (Sally McGrath)

The entire stage house has been demolished to permit the building of squash courts for the adjacent Royal Gate House Hotel. The back wall is now situated just behind the proscenium arch and the cinema screen is flown in front of it with a consequent loss of the front four rows of seats. *TR*

THETFORD
Norfolk

Theatre
White Hart Street
Original architect
  c.1812   Unknown
Listed   Grade II
Current use Offices

A two-storey building, originally faced in flint with an attic under a slated roof with hiplet towards the street. The facade, intended to give a four-square appearance, three windows wide and three storeys high; the cornice slightly raised in the centre and the outer attic windows blind; now roughcast finish with smooth quoins and lintels, entrance door on left beside ex-shop window both under a bracketed hood. The cornice reputedly carried six or eight classical busts in the time of the Fisher circuit. A plaque commemorating the theatrical past of the building is on the facade at eye level. Flank wall flint with brick chimney.

It would seem that the facade was added about 1812 when the Fisher circuit became the theatre's sole users until its closure in 1833. Subsequently, for many years a residential property but recently offices. *JL*

TIDWORTH
Wiltshire

Garrison Theatre ★
Lowa Road, Tidworth Garrison
Original architect
  1909   Unknown
Current use Garrison theatre
Capacity c.800

Tidworth (originally an old estate called Tedworth) has a rare survivor in its purpose-built garrison theatre. It has staged every kind of entertainment for the recreation of troops stationed there, from pantomime and concerts to full-scale variety shows, as well as being used for military briefings from Montgomery and Eisenhower.

Typical of a military building, a flat-floored hall, originally gaslit, functional and unadorned; much survives in original condition, from roof trusses to radiators. In latter years, an elliptical barrel-vault suspended ceiling has been inserted, masking the varnished wood sloping roof lining, except for the stage area where it is still visible. The proscenium arch, which follows the curve of the ceiling probably dates from the same time. There is an extension one side, to give extra room for a bar, foyer space and management offices. The auditorium has a small balcony with fixed seating. It has always been a multi-purpose space and retained its original Canadian pitch-pine floor until very recently when it had to be replaced from the wear of soldiers' boots for nearly ninety years. The stage has a small grid, but flying room is limited, requiring the use of rolled cloths.

The broad gabled facade expresses the theatre's very basic form, but the entrance is emphasised by an advanced central open-pedimented porch with unfluted columns. Above this, a blind Venetian window. *SM*

TODMORDEN
Calderdale (West Yorkshire)

Hippodrome ★
Halifax Road
Other names
    New Todmorden Hippodrome
  1914   Hippodrome Theatre and
          Electric Palace
  1980s Empire?
Original architect
  1908   Unknown
Later works
  1993   Cooper and Jackson: new roof;
          stage house altered
  1994   Abbey Hanson and Rowe:
          facade improved
Current use Amateur theatre
Capacity 495

Opened as a theatre in 1908 with *Two Lancashire Lasses in London*, the Hippodrome introduced film interludes as part of the variety programme from 1911 and by 1917 films had all but taken over.

The Hippodrome is a plain red brick building whose main street front is the flank of the auditorium. The original single-storey foyer with ornamental terracotta segmental pediment is now divided off and sub-let as a retail outlet. The auditorium block at first-floor level is divided by pilasters into six bays. Stone decoration in the form of draped pelmets between the pilasters was added in 1994. 'Hippodrome Theatre' in large letters above and also in a new shallow slate canopy above the entrance. Three sets of doors were formerly labelled Circle, Stalls and Pit - the last of these now forming the main entrance. Plain gabled stage house.

Former pit now converted to a large bar/rehearsal room resulting in a small stalls capacity almost entirely in front of the circle. Plain segmented barrel-vaulted ceiling. Circle slips extend to square proscenium arch with decorative tablet above. Three plaster panels on each side of slips, possibly originally boxes, with a single deep circle. Baroque plaster decoration to balcony front. Apart from the subdivision of the pit, the auditorium is almost certainly very little altered from 1908. Some upgrading of interior is required but essentially in good condition. Eight dressing rooms, mainly under stage. Limited flying.

Todmorden, Hippodrome (Ian Grundy)

Now owned by Todmorden Players and Todmorden Operatic Society, the theatre is regularly used by them and is available to outside hirers, both amateur and professional.   *IG*

TOLLARD ROYAL, CRANBORNE CHASE
Wiltshire

Singing Theatre ★★
Larmer Tree Gardens, Rushmore Estate

Original architect
1886   Pitt-Rivers

Later works
1994   Michael Pitt-Rivers: gardens restored, together with theatre and other buildings

Listed   **Grade II**
Current use **Open-air theatre**

The Larmer Tree Gardens are in Tollard Royal, in the heart of Cranborne Chase. They were laid out in 1880 by the distinguished archaeologist General Pitt-Rivers for the recreation of the population of the neighbouring towns, to offer opportunities to acquaint people with aspects of unfamiliar culture. It was the first privately owned park to be open to the public. The gardens take their name from the Larmer tree, a wych elm which existed in the C10, and which later constituted a landmark indicating Parish and County boundaries. The spectacular chalk uplands which lie between the valleys of the Stour and Avon were known as Cranborne Chase before the Norman conquest, patronised by Royalty for hunting by the middle of William the Conqueror's reign. From King John, Tollard derived its name of Royal.

Ownership of the rights of the Chase passed through a number of families, and ultimately to the Pitt family. Peacocks, ornamental pheasants and free-flying macaws are permanent residents, descendants of the the original birds introduced in the 1880s.

The gardens feature Indian structures said to have been acquired from a London Colonial Exhibition, Nepalese buildings with carved wood elevations, a Roman temple, sculptures and the Singing Theatre, an open-air stage famous for operatic and dramatic presentations.

A band was formed in 1866 from farmworkers on the Rushmore estate to perform at the bandstand and to play the prelude and entr'actes to productions on the open stage.

The Singing Theatre itself is of a type rare in Britain, in the style of a plein-air café chantant. Of wooden construction, the raised stage is contained within a semi-circular arch flanked by Roman Corinthian pilasters supporting a full entablature. The pilasters continue in simplified form to the sides and rear. The stage itself is of exedra form, semi-domed and painted at the back with Classical landscape. The design is attributed to Pitt-Rivers, together with other outside buildings, inspired by similar designs seen on travels or at the Exhibition. It was built by estate carpenters and the original scene was painted by Douglas, the fifth son of Pitt-Rivers.

The attractions in the gardens were closed to the public in the early years of the C20, and gradually became overgrown. In 1995 they were reopened. Each year more restoration is undertaken and in 1997 featured the 'Days of the Raj' pavilion tearoom with bedouin-tented ceiling. Concerts and performances are held at the Singing Theatre throughout the summer months.   *SM*

Tollard Royal, Singing Theatre (Copyright Antony Pitt-Rivers)

TONYPANDY
Rhondda Cynon Taff

Hippodrome
Dunraven Street
Other names
   Alexander's Circus
   New Hippodrome
Original architect
   1901   Unknown
Later works
   1912   Unknown: reconstructed as
          ciné-theatre
Current use Bingo ?
Capacity c.900

Built as a circus in Pandy Field, with an arena, boxes, stalls and promenade. Became a music hall, then from 1912, a ciné-variety theatre. Simple auditorium with one balcony. Shallow stage c. 6m (20ft) with low fly tower. Entrance is through a terrace of shops with flats over. Brick built, with a series of first-floor bay windows. The ground rises steeply behind, with the utilitarian auditorium/stage block at a higher level.   *TR*

TORQUAY
Torbay

Pavilion
Vaughan Road
Original architect
   1896   Edward Rogers (revised in
          1903 with H.C. Goss)
Listed   Grade II
Current use Shopping arcade

Henry Augustus Garrett, Borough Engineer of Torbay, laid out the Princess Gardens, the Terrace Walk, Pier Pavilion and Torquay Pavilion: the work lasted from 1890–1930. The Pavilion was built on a site formed partly of land reclaimed from the sea, on a concrete raft on which a framework of steel stanchions and girders was erected. The architect was Edward Rogers, winner of a competion in 1896 who, with H.C.Goss, drew up the final plans, which were passed in 1903. Because of Rogers's death, construction started only in 1911, the work having been taken over by Garrett. The facing tiles, in Doulton's Carrara enamelled stoneware made the Pavilion appear like a white Palace. The impressive central copper-covered dome was topped with a life-size figure of Britannia. Two smaller domes on each side of the entrance were surmounted by copper figures of Mercury. Fine cast-ironwork in Art Nouveau style edged the steps to the promenade deck and the

octagonal bandstands or summerhouses. Other exterior decorations were of flowers, urns topped with pineapples, scrolls, etc.

Opened in 1912, there were a foyer and auditorium with lounges and café, all oak-panelled and elegantly plastered. There were a curved balcony, stained glass and potted palms, with open-air promenade and tea garden. A Municipal Orchestra was founded. In the 1970s, demolition was proposed but the building was listed in 1973. It closed in 1976, when it was leased to Rank and the interior was destroyed in adaptations for various types of amusements including, later, skating. Today it is a shopping arcade, but the exterior is well preserved.   *SM*

Royal Theatre and Opera House
Abbey Road
Other names
   1870   Opera House
   1933   Royal
   1936   Odeon
   2000   Merlin
Original architect
   1878   Unknown
Later works
   1880   C.J. Phipps: extended as a
          theatre and royal box built
   1888   C.J. Phipps: altered
   1933   Unknown: converted to cinema
   1960s Unknown: twinned
Current use Cinema
Capacity   c.1200 (prior to conversion
              to cinema)

Opened in 1878 as Winter Gardens, it was extended in 1880 and opened in April of that year as the Royal Theatre and Opera House. It bankrupted the lessee and closed after six and a half months, before reopening under new management.

Interior completely rebuilt as cinema and, more recently, as two smaller cinemas. Only the basic structural shell with slated pitched roof survives from 1888. The entrance front is on Abbey Road, parallel to the axis of the auditorium. The ground floor with three arched doorways under a modern canopy is largely original. Above this, however, the facade was altered in 1933 with a three-bay, columned loggia. Behind Abbey Road front the ground level falls away steeply so that, from the entrance, one descended to the stalls. The tall rear elevation, fronting a narrow street, shows the original stone-rubble walling, patched up with later brickwork, and a

serpentine cornice to a lower entrance of c.1920.

It closed as the Odeon in November 1999 but reopened, following redecoration, as the Merlin some three months later. Further improvements are planned.   *CB/SM*

Scala
Torwood Street
Original architect
   1909   Richardson, Gill and More
Listed   Grade II
Current use Shopping mall

A Bath stone building of magnificent classical elevations in three storeys, with a giant Roman Ionic order rising above a lower order of Doric columns and piers. The splayed corner entrance has a tetrastyle pedimented temple front with fine figurative carving and trophies in the tympanum. The long parapeted frontage to Torwood Street has recessed end pavilions with rusticated quoins and large round-headed two-storey windows. The pavilion parapets are raised to form pedestals for sculptural groups. At the rear is a statue and the carved name of Garrick. The shopfronts are nearly all later insertions. Owing to the interruption of the First World War, the interior was never completed. It eventually opened as a skating rink and occasional concert hall. Later it became a garage and is now a shopping mall. Although it never opened as a theatre, it is included here as one of the most ambitious examples in Britain of a monumental theatre design.   *CB/SM*

TOTNES
Devon

'Theatre'
28 High Street
Listed   Grade II*
Current use Store

An entry is needed for the building, which was included in the 1982 *Curtains*, simply to establish that it was not in fact a theatre. Despite strong local tradition and the presence of grotesque masks ('folkloric' rather than dramatic) on the window keystones, the room at the rear, described as 'hall' by 1962, seems never to have had a theatrical use. It may possibly have served at some time as a cinema attached to an C18 house and shop premises.

The Totnes Playhouse, which is known to have been active by 1806, was in fact at the rear of the present no.6 The

occurred at intervals have been removed. The proscenium arch is a depressed curve, supporting a baroque foliated shield at its highest point, and is attractively decorated over its entire length with plasterwork representing fruit and flowers.

The stage was originally very shallow and the demands of varying theatrical functions have led to the construction of a semi-permanent apron. There is no orchestra pit. Behind the back wall of the stage, and built as a lean-to structure, is a corridor giving crossover access between the wings. There is no substage machinery.

A scheme by Roderick Ham was put forward as long ago as 1989 for the upgrading of the main auditorium to the standard needed to receive first-class opera productions but this has never been implemented.   *TR*

Treorchy, Parc and Dare (Terence Rees)

Truro, Theatre Royal (Mike Sell)

Plains. It closed in 1836 and was burnt down in 1860. Another one opened at the rear of the Royal Seven Stars Hotel and was active in the 1850s. Some evidence of this room survives. The Lion Inn which had a theatre c.1863-85 was at the other end of town.   *JE*

TREORCHY
Rhondda Cynon Taff

Parc and Dare Theatre ★★
Station Road
Original architect
   1913   **Unknown**
Current use **Theatre and cinema**
Capacity   **c.800**

The external style of the building was very much influenced by the contemporary architecture of Welsh chapels. The front facade, rising to four floors, is divided into three bays, the centre one pedimented. Carved on the lower, horizontal stone course of the pediment is the name of the building, PARC & DARE WORKMEN'S HALL. To the right of the hall and running along the side of it is the former Parc and Dare Institute. This is now connected at various levels to the hall and provides the rehearsal rooms, offices and public areas, spaces which are not plentiful in the main building.

The facade conceals an unexpectedly ambitious auditorium which, as with most of its kind in Wales, is at first-floor level. It is a fine hall with two curved galleries, the slips of each extending to and meeting the proscenium wall. Each gallery front retains its original decorative plasterwork, but the gas brackets which

TRURO
Cornwall

Theatre Royal
High Cross
Original architect
   1772   **Charles Ebden**
Listed   **Grade II***
Current use **Offices**

Only the exceptionally fine ashlar facade remains, situated close to the towering west front of the cathedral. Two storeys and three bays, surmounted by a pediment. Wide, arched doorway with fanlight in the centre of the ground floor, flanked by single arched doorways with straight-headed surrounds. Three tall sash windows at first-floor level, each with a finely carved relief above: two gryphons supporting a tripod within a rectangular frame over the central window, flanked by profile busts of Shakespeare and Garrick in circular frames. The tympanum of the pediment contains a circular plaque with a draped female figure holding a mask and a mirror. Used as a seasonal theatre and assembly room until 1869, when replaced by new Public Rooms.

Although the interior survived for some time afterwards, it has since been completely rebuilt behind the facade. A thorough restoration of the facade, which received a European Architectural Heritage Year Award, was carried out in 1975.   *CB*

TUNBRIDGE WELLS
Kent

Assembly Hall
Crescent Road
Original architect
   1939   **Unknown**
Current use **Multi-purpose civic theatre**
Capacity   **940**

It is there, it works and it is the only theatre in the Wells apart from the Trinity Theatre and Arts Centre (a church conversion of 1982). So much can be said in its favour. In every other way it pales into insignificance compared to the splendid Opera House which has been cruelly wasted by conversion to a pub.

The Assembly Hall, adjoining the Council offices, is a brick building, externally a good representative of the civic architecture of its time. Odeonesque entrance canopy with streamlined terminals at either end. Above this, three tall recessed windows with spikey-patterned glazing bars, carved stone lintels and thin hoods over. The interior is not memorable.   *JE*

Opera House ★★★
Mount Pleasant Road
Original architect
   1902   **John Briggs**
Later works
   1996   **Unknown: converted to**
               Wetherspoon's pub
Listed   **Grade II***
Current use **Pub**

This is one of Britain's finest 'Sleeping Beauties' and one which, in 1995-7

Tunbridge Wells, Opera House (Lawrence Tring Architects)

developed at the same time. Its entrance is, in fact, only the centrepiece of a 23-bay symmetrically composed composition housing shops with two storeys of offices above. It is in the form of a single, wide bay, flanked by coupled pilasters above the ground floor carrying a broken pediment and framing a deep niche with a projecting balcony. Set back above the pediment and dominating the facade is a big Baroque dome. Flanking this centrepiece, on either side, are three plain bays with ground-floor shopfronts, and then giant coupled pilasters surmounted by steep pediments. Beyond these, on either side, are two further groups of three plain bays, defined by rusticated pilasters, before the curved ends of the facade which are emphasized by subsidiary domes.

After all this bombast it comes as a surprise to enter the small foyer and intimate auditorium which suffered very little damage from its previous bingo use. The auditorium has two slightly curved balconies of six and eight rows each with straight slips running to ranges of superimposed boxes - four on each side. The upper boxes have gryphons at the head of each subdividing pilaster. The proscenium is rectangular with elaborately scrolled brackets in the corners and a curved pedimental tablet above the centre. The main ceiling is in the form of a panelled saucer dome set within a richly moulded rectangular frame. Over the stage (now a bar) the grid and fly floors remain visible.

The theatre could have made an excellent home for a repertory company with occasional touring opera, ballet, etc.   *JE/CB*

Theatre
The Pantiles
Original architect
   1802   Unknown
Later works
   n.d.   Unknown: converted to corn exchange
   1989   Unknown: extensive internal reconstruction
Current use **Facade only (small shopping centre behind)**

Only the Greek Doric porch and three-bay, three-storey stucco facade of Sarah Baker's second theatre on this site are said to have been retained when it was replaced by the Corn Exchange. The interior space, now a covered courtyard shopping centre, is pleasant and retains some of the Corn Exchange character. Despite evocative decorations, it is not a

showed every promise of being awakened to active theatrical life. The fact that it is now a pub (albeit a splendid one, restored and furnished with unusual care) contains an object lesson about a major weakness in the protective measures applied to theatres, and also a warning that noisy conflict is not always the best way to get results. There is no space in this place to tell the whole story but one point needs to be heavily underlined: a vital aid to theatre preservation is the fact that theatres in use as such are in none of the defined planning use classes and, therefore, any change of use needs planning permission. When, however, as in this case, a non-theatre use is already well established, then further changes may be difficult to resist. Changes within the established use class do not require permission at all. The listed building consent processes provide an additional defence for listed theatres, but if the proposed works preserve the

special interest and do no permanent harm to future theatre potential, consent is likely to be granted. The fact that a different applicant with different ideas might be preferred is not, without other cogent supporting reasons, a watertight reason for refusal. This (and a number of serious tactical errors) have resulted in a theatre which was ripe for recovery, of the right size and in the right place, being lost in favour of a use which could have found a perfectly acceptable home elsewhere.

The grandiose design of the exterior (which is a real event in the townscape) is quite misleading as it gives the impression of being the front of a major theatre with 2000 rather than only approximately 750 seats (to present seating standards). The style is a mixture of Edwardian Baroque and Neo-Georgian carried out in brick with ample stone dressings. The theatre is in the centre of an island block, most of which was relic of the Baker theatre. A curious fact about this theatre was that at one time its auditorium was in Kent and its stage in Sussex.

TUNSTALL
Stoke-on-Trent

Theatre Royal and Opera House
Ladywell Road/Harewood Street
Other names
   1865   Royal Prince of Wales Theatre
   1871   Prince Albert Concert Hall
Original architect
   1865   Ward and Ford (Hanley and
          Burslem)
Later works
   c.1882   Unknown: major internal
          remodelling as Salvation Army
          citadel
Current use **Disused**
Capacity   **originally c.1500**

Closed and heavily remodelled in 1880s to become a Salvation Army citadel. A small, pitched roof building in brick with a rendered three-bay gabled facade with tall arched windows. The auditorium originally had two balconies. It now has a single U-shaped balcony supported on six columns. The ceiling, which has two additional timber supporting columns, is not original. *TB*

ULVERSTON
Cumbria

Coronation Hall
County Square
Original architect
   1914   Unknown
Current use **Theatre/multi-purpose hall**
Capacity   **636**

A multi-purpose hall with theatrical atmosphere. Riotous plasterwork of good quality and in excellent condition. Very ornate barrel-vault ceiling. Range of windows down each side. Curved circle front not returned to proscenium wall. Permanent tiered theatre seats in circle. Removable linked chairs in stalls. Rectangular proscenium arch with Britannia and maidens frieze above in somewhat Arts and Crafts style. Rendered 'council office' facade with bay window and portico above main entrance. Symmetrical slightly projecting wings with three lower, and two first-floor rectangular windows surmounted by one circular window at second floor. Stage house in rubble stonework. *IG*

Roxy
Brogden Street
Original architect
   1937   Unknown
Later works
   1975   Unknown: auditorium and
          foyer subdivided
Current use **Bingo/cinema**
Capacity   **c.300**

Old stuccoed facade with thinly rusticated quoins. Worth further investigation; stage seems deep and with full fly tower, plus a selection of posters/programmes in foyer indicating good live use. Five dressing rooms. *IG*

VENTNOR
Isle of Wight

Grand Pavilion
Esplanade
Other names
   The Gaiety
   Summer Theatre
   Casino and Hippodrome
   Gaiety Amusement Arcade
Original architect
   1896   Unknown
Current use **Amusement arcade**

The Pavilion was constructed in the late C19 for concert parties and seaside entertainment. It is a square building with ornate dome covered with tiles like silver fish scales; the top part of the dome was removed in 1986. The original entrance was between towers on the seaward side, each with a dome. The entrance facade today is a glitzy announcement of the amusements inside. The interior is on one level, with a platform stage, and was used for a variety of entertainment including skating. During the First World War it was used to assemble aircraft parts, and afterwards never fulfilled its potential as a theatre again. Used variously for dodgems and amusements over the years. *SM*

Ventnor Theatre
Albert Street
Other names
   Town Hall Theatre
Original architect
   1877   T.R. Saunders
Later works
   c.1990   Unknown: converted to flats
Listed   **Grade II**
Current use **Flats (shell and facade remain)**

Three-bay, two-storey classical stucco frontispiece, arched pilastered windows. Outer bays with paired pilasters above

ground-floor piers and deep parapet over cornice. Pedimented centre with coupled Ionic columns on ground floor, Corinthian above. Large keyed arched portal.
   The facade remains intact. The building served as the theatre and later as the Town Hall. It reverted to theatre use and in 1978 became a dance hall, then a nightclub. In 1990 it was gutted and subdivided into flats. The theatre is remembered with affection by residents - its use declined when both railway stations at Ventnor closed. *SM*

Winter Gardens
Pier Street
Original architect
   1937   A.D. Clare
Current use **Theatre and multi-purpose**
Capacity   **400**

Replaced early C20 Winter Gardens which were demolished in 1935. Completed in 1937, the new Winter Gardens command the cliff site adjacent to the cascade: a striking white building with a glass-fronted tower 'inspired by Bexhill - a brave attempt' (Pevsner). When it opened, there was a sun terrace on the roof. Offices are now built over the terrace. The ground floor is occupied by a large theatre/concert hall with small foyer, which looks as though it had Art Deco features originally. In the winter the theatre used to be converted into a ballroom; now it has varied leisure uses. Theatre is very plain, with an almost bland proscenium, the only feature being a large lay light. Flat-floored, no balcony, temporary stackable seating. Get-in is through the front door into the auditorium. At rear is dressing-room accommodation. The front part houses a café and bar, looking out to sea. The stairs are encased in the glass-fronted tower. It is a touring house for shows and concerts. *SM*

WAKEFIELD

Playhouse
Westgate/Prospect Yard
Other names
   Picture House
   Classic
Original architect
   1913   Albert Winstanley
Current use **Club**

Built for Sidney Tolfree as a cinema by Albert Winstanley in 1913, the building had an orchestra pit, stage and a trap. The following year dressing rooms were added, and it was in use for live entertainment.

Auditorium, two-tier of simple design, the balcony slips extending two-thirds down the sides. Curved ceiling with circular ventilation grille. Rounded proscenium, with large deep squared quasi-boxes to ceiling level, with rounded fenestration and ornamental banding.

The exterior is easily recognisable today, making a handsome presence on Westgate, with its close neighbour the Opera House. Two-storey stone facade of five bays, the central entrance surmounted by a terracotta leaded window and pediment with ornamental stone garland. The outer bays, narrow but similar in design, house exits. The upper storey has three narrow windows either side; two shops with arched entrances are incorporated at street level. The name PICTURE HOUSE appears between the levels.

Acquired by Classic, it was run as a full-time cinema before being sold, probably when Cannon acquired ABC. It was then used as a skateboard centre and later a club. Today only the balcony and original ceiling remain, though these are concealed. The interior is stripped of all other features and the present stage for live acts is situated at the side of the former auditorium. *SM*

Stanley Royd Hospital Theatre ★

Aberford Road
Original architect
   1861   **Watson and Pritchett of York**
Later works
   1893   **Bernard Hartley (County Surveyor): stage house rebuilt**
Listed   **Grade II**
Current use **Disused**

The Recreation Hall, as it was originally known, was a multi-purpose room. It was built in 1859 primarily as a male patients' dining room and first used, in incomplete state, for a Christmas party in 1859. It was finished in 1861. In jokey playbills for occasional entertainments it was called the 'Theatre Royal' but in the 1860s it probably had only an end platform, fitted up as required for theatricals. In 1893 the end bay of the room was demolished and the present, traditionally equipped theatre stage added. Interestingly, this reincorporated the 1859 foundation stone.

Large halls, adaptable for dining, meetings, dances, theatricals and concerts were not uncommon in enclosed institutions, but the scale and quality of

theatrical provision seen here is unusual and, as lunatic asylums throughout the country are abandoned, will become rarer.

As seen now, the theatre is a small element in a huge complex of asylum buildings dating from 1818 onwards. The room is flat-floored, more than 27.5m (90ft) long and nearly 15.25m (50ft) wide, in nine bays divided by piers and ceiling beams, each bay containing a window with an Italianate surround, alternate windows being pedimented. There were no fewer than six fireplaces, all in use, before central heating was installed. There is an end balcony. The capacity was said to be 700 and, even today, it might hold more than 400.

The proscenium, flanked by pass doors, has a three-centred arch and an enriched frame. There is a well constructed fly tower, providing all the facil-

ities that might be expected in a small professional theatre of the period. Fly floors are provided at each side of the stage and there is a timber grid with full flying height for hemp sets.

Attached to the underside of the fly floors are original timber upper grooves, being important survivors of this now virtually extinct system of scenic handling (*see* London, Normansfield). The grooves are divided into four bays on either side, each providing accommodation for three scenic flats. Only a few old flats survive, and these are not of significant importance or quality. Lower grooves are also present (possibly unique in Britain), forming guides, with no raised 'beds', the flats running on the stage floor itself. The proscenium is fitted with a later rolled safety curtain.

There is no evidence of any substage machinery having ever been in place.

Wakefield, Stanley Royd

The area is allocated to dressing-room space, as was often the practice in this type of theatre.

Like most great asylums this one faced an extremely uncertain future at the time of writing. *JE/DW*

Theatre Royal and Opera House ★★★
Drury Lane/Westgate
Other names
   Wakefield Opera House
   1955   Essoldo
Original architect
   1894   Frank Matcham
Later works
   1955   Unknown: converted to cinema
   1966   Unknown: converted to bingo
   1986   Joe Parker, TACP: restored internally and externally; backstage facilities improved; internal link with corner shop created; dressing room block at rear added
   1996   Joe Parker: theatre redecorated; technical improvements made
Listed   Grade II*
Current use Theatre
Capacity   508

The Theatre Royal and Opera House was built on the site of the C18 Theatre Royal, and is the smallest of Matcham's surviving theatres, perhaps his smallest ever. The facade, as restored in 1986, is of red brick and cast stone of five bays and two storeys. The upper level has five circular windows with arched surrounds, each pair separated by a projecting bust of a composer in a circular frame with a scrolled top. The keystones of the window arches continue up, in the form of pilaster strips to a broad gable containing the name OPERA HOUSE. A canopy, reflecting the style of the original, was reinstated in 1986, extending along the frontage, which now incorporates the corner shop as a restaurant/bar, 'Matcham's'. This is lower, with a small copper dome above the curved corner. An inscription stone from 1994, marking the centenary of the building, unveiled by Brian Matcham, has replaced the original, removed to the interior for safekeeping.

The entrance vestibule with box office has richly decorated ceiling. A wide stone staircase to one side leads to the upper levels, and double doors to one side of the stalls. The theatre has a delightful auditorium typical of Matcham's earlier style and similar in scale to his original design for the Lyric, Hammersmith. The balcony fronts have

Wakefield, Theatre Royal (Ian Grundy)

frothy Rococo plasterwork. They are separated from the proscenium by elaborate plasterwork panels. Flat circular ceiling with oval panels recently repainted, each with Muses surrounded by Rococo plasterwork. Original sunburner in situ. The painted panels on the lower balcony front have also been reinstated. Segmentally arched proscenium with richly banded frame and central grotesque mask. Boxes each side behind seating in the 1st balcony.

After use as a cinema and then bingo, the Opera House was restored in 1986 for use as a modern theatre. A dressing-room block was added at the rear, and a full counterweight system installed. The stage was reinstated and an orchestra pit excavated. Many original features, such as stained-glass panels and windows remained and other features were restored. The corner site was annexed internally to enhance refreshment facilities, the stalls and 1st circle floors were re-raked, and the projection box removed. *CB/SM*

WALLSEND
North Tyneside

Borough ★★
High Street East
Other names
   Gaumont
   Borough Theatre and Hippodrome
Original architect
   1909   J. Fleming Davidson and C.D. James
Later works
   1911   J.F. Davidson: operating box at rear of circle installed
   1935   James L. Ross: operating box altered
   1949   Percy L. Browne and Harding: theatre renovated and altered
Current use Bingo
Capacity   est. 1100

Wallsend, Borough (Ian Grundy)

Good auditorium, completely intact but at present with a suspended ceiling cutting off the upper balcony. The two balconies, of about eight rows each and slightly curved, come well forward toward the stage and end in a single semi-circular box on each side. The lower boxes have plaster canopies supported by slender Ionic columns. Between the boxes and the stage, on either side, are two levels of niches holding female figures, all contained within a giant enriched Ionic order standing on pedestals at stalls level. The lower balcony front is decorated with heavy, paired consoles forming panels filled with cartouches. Oval ceiling with central gas burner. Apart from alterations to the entrance the exterior is also intact but of little merit. The main front is slightly concave with brick walls and plain, painted stone pilasters with crudely detailed tops. Stage 9.14m (30ft) deep. The building is in good condition and could be restored to use relatively easily.   *DW*

WALSALL

Imperial
Darwall Street
Other names
   1869   **Agricultural Hall**
   1871   **Theatre Royal and Agricultural Hall (also Theatre Royal)**
   1886   **St George's Hall and Theatre**
Original architect
   1869   **G.B. Nichols (West Bromwich)**
Later works
   1883   **Unknown: altered**
   1899   **Unknown: reburbished**
  c.1915   **Unknown: converted to cinema**
Current use **Pub**

Opened as the Agricultural Hall but used for theatrical performances from the beginning. From 1899 it was known as the Imperial Theatre. It became a cinema from 1908, latterly a bingo house and, from 1997, a pub.

The simple three-bay facade with broad entrance arch and a little pedimental gable at the centre appears to be, in its essentials, that of the 1869 Agricultural Hall. The interior is that of a cinema, presumably dating from conversion about 1915. It is a rectangular room with a raked floor and a slightly curved end balcony. The side walls are panelled between piers, from which spring shallow arched beams. Square proscenium, behind which an earlier proscenium arch can still be traced. Small foyer. No fly tower.   *TB*

WALTON-ON-THE-NAZE
Essex

King's
off Mill Lane
Original architect
  c.1900   **Unknown**
Current use **Disused**
Capacity   **originally c.700**

A long disused theatre or variety hall of which little is known. It is free-standing on land behind the frontage buildings on the corner of High Street and Mill Lane. It existed before 1912 and probably became a cinema. It had ceased to be recorded as either cinema or theatre by 1947.

The building is in poor condition and not readily accessible, but a restricted view obtained of the interior shows that it still has a proscenium arch and some stencilled and figurative painting of unknown date on the walls. Much subdivided internally. There was probably a courtyard entrance from Mill Lane, but this has been blocked by the subsequent building of public lavatories and a temporary structure used as a shop.

This appears to be Walton's only purpose-built theatre, but it cannot be regarded as a promising candidate for revival.   *KW*

WALTON-ON-THAMES
Surrey

Playhouse
Bridge Street
Original architect
   1920   **George Carvill: as a power house**
Later works
   1924   **George Carvill: converted to theatre**
Current use **Amateur theatre**
Capacity   **220**

The building which has survived as The Playhouse for seventy years, was built by Cecil Hepworth, Head of Hepworth Film Studios (among the first indoor studios), as the power house to provide the necessary artificial light. When the studios closed in 1924, the equipment was sold. The building was bought by George Carvill, the architect who had designed it and an enthusiast of amateur theatre.

He designed a raked stage, wings, dressing rooms, orchestra pit, lounge and bar so that Walton would have a local theatre. Today it is used as a community theatre allowing the auditorium hall use for ballet, etc. The building is quite low, with

no balcony, the lounge and bar accommodation being upstairs. There is a Venetian window at the front, set in white painted brickwork. Inside, the minimal foyer with small round box office leads into the auditorium where the brickwork is painted dark red, with some gold designs over the plain proscenium. In 1991 the building was under threat of demolition, but such was the public outcry that the Elmbridge Arts Council relented and its use continues.   *SM*

WARMINSTER
Wiltshire

Athenaeum
High Street
Other names
   1912   **Electric Picture Palace**
 1912–66   **Palace**
            Athenaeum Theatre/West Wiltshire Arts Centre
Original architect
   1858   **W.J. Stent: as Athenaeum Literary Institution**
Later works
   1879   **T.H. Wyatt: rebuilt behind facade**
   1912   **Unknown: converted to cinema**
   1969   **Eric G. Stevens: converted to arts centre**
   1993   **Chris Walker (District Council): modified to provide exhibition room etc.; redecorated**
Listed   **Grade II**
Current use **Theatre/Arts Centre**
Capacity   **230**

The Athenaeum, a literary institution, was built in 1858 to designs by local architect W.J. Stent. It included a large lecture room, a reading room, classrooms and a librarian's residence. In 1879 it was largely rebuilt behind a slightly modified facade. The architect for these works was T.H. Wyatt.

In 1895 the building was handed over to the Urban District Council. In 1912 Albany Ward took on the lease of the lecture room (the Bleeck Hall) and fitted it with the latest lighting and cinematograph equipment, refurbishing the seating and reopening it as the Picture Palace. As well as films, the Palace also presented plays, pantomimes, opera and music, and productions of the Warminster Operatic Society. Further improvements were made in 1935.

In 1969 the Warminster and District Arts and Civic Society refurbished the building at a cost of £10,000. It is now the West Wiltshire Arts Centre, serving the local community with theatre, film,

music, dance, art and lectures.
The attractive gabled stone front has been well preserved with its iron entrance canopy. The proscenium is plain but attractive, and the auditorium well maintained. The balcony is iron-fronted and supported on two iron pillars.   *SM*

WARRINGTON

Palace ★
Friars Green
Other names
   1907 New Palace Theatre and
          Hippodrome
Original architect
   1907 George F. Ward
Current use **Disused**
Capacity **est. 1100**

Opened as the New Palace Theatre and Hippodrome. It became a cinema in the 1930s and a bingo hall in 1967. The auditorium, never particularly attractive, was mutilated by the removal of boxes and of the plasterwork from the fronts of the two balconies. It is otherwise intact, however, and could be restored without too much difficulty. The balconies (the upper one now blanked off by a false ceiling) have eight rows each and curve round slightly to meet the splayed walls where the boxes originally were. There was one box on either side with pilasters and a pediment similar to the arrangement at the Civic Theatre, Darlington, by the same architect. The panelled ceiling and rectangular proscenium, where visible, retain their Baroque plasterwork but the upper part of the proscenium is now concealed.

The exterior is little altered, apart from the ground floor and entrance canopy. The main front, in brick with stone dressings, is an asymmetrical composition in an odd mixture of Edwardian Baroque and Arts and Crafts. To the left, on the corner, is a four-storeyed square tower with rusticated base and quoins and a pyramidal roof crowned by a cupola. To the right is a three-storeyed, stubby tower with a low dome. The entrance, in the middle, is marked by two narrow, slightly projecting turrets with little domes, flanking a wide central bay with curved parapet and a broad elliptically arched window at first-floor level. Plain brick side elevation, relieved only by blank arcading.

Bingo from 1977; this ceased in 1997 and the future for the theatre looks bleak.   *CB/KW*

Watford, Palace

WATFORD
Hertfordshire

Palace ★★
Clarendon Road
Other names
   Watford Palace of Varieties
Original architect
   1908 H.M. Theobold
Later works
   1910 Unknown: facade completely
          reconstructed; gallery inserted
          above circle level; circle bars
          installed
   Later Unknown: orchestra pit intro-
          duced
   1981 Clare Ferraby: redecorated
   1984 Unknown: new wing with
          Green room,bar/café and
          administration offices
Listed   **Grade II**
Current use **Theatre**
Capacity **643**

For some years a marquee had been used in a meadow forming part of the grounds of the Lime Tree Hotel. Despite oppostion from the residents of Clarendon Road, the foundations were laid and the theatre building was com-

pleted in 1908. It had a plain, gabled front.

It was later decided to extend and improve the facade which gave it its present appearance: a red brick building flanked by two squat towers with lead cupolas; this was completed in 1910. It was essentially a music hall, called the Watford Palace of Varieties. At this time a skating rink which later became a cinema (now demolished) was built on the corner of the remainder of the meadow, and run by a subsidiary company.

In 1911 the front was rebuilt, and a cantilevered gallery placed above the circle (it was previously behind). The boxes were enlarged and the proscenium, boxes and circle decorated with fibrous plaster. The auditorium is intimate with excellent sight lines. The small foyer with paybox is directly under the circle, with stairs leading upwards at either side. It was redecorated in 1981 and is (since 1996) used as a repertory theatre.

A planning agreement with the developers of the former cinema site provided the theatre with improved offices. Backstage facilities remain cramped, but improvements are proposed.   *SM*

WELLINGBOROUGH
Northamptonshire

Palace
Gloucester Place
Original architect
  1911   Unknown
Later works
1969/70   Unknown: new entrance; seat-
         ing capacity reduced; other
         improvements
  1979   Unknown: converted to triple
         cinema
  1990   Unknown: stalls converted to
         twin cinemas and former circle
         to snooker halls
Current use Snooker hall
Capacity   690 (prior to 1979 subdivision)

Built as a ciné-variety theatre on the site
of the Empire Music Hall, which was a
wooden building, erected in 1910 and
burnt down in 1911. The building is of
red brick with a corner entrance and
shop units along the two streets. There is
a small squat fly tower.
   The building was divided in 1979 and
further converted in 1990 to form two
snooker halls, one on top of the other, in
the stage area. Remains of the ornate
plaster balcony front can be seen but
both boxes at circle level have been partially dismantled.   *TB*

WELLS
Somerset

Regal
Priory Road
Original architect
  1935   Ernest S. Roberts
Listed   Grade II
Current use Bingo
Capacity   c.590

A rectilinear brick building with the
south-east corner chamfered to form a
grand entrance. The brick facades facing
the roads to the south and east are articulated with bands of locally quarried
stone. An unusual survival is a free-standing street advertisement, comprising an
open lattice steel frame surmounted by a
four-sided vertical sign with the name
REGAL. The building is thought to be the
best work of its architect Ernest Roberts.
It was built to double as a theatre, with
generous stage, and four dressing
rooms. Certainly, it is a remarkable survival of a cinema theatre of the 1930s,
retaining original Art-Deco features
throughout.   *SM*

WESTCLIFF-ON-SEA
Essex

Palace Theatre Centre
London Road
Other names
     Raymond's New Palace
     Palace Theatre
     New Palace of Varieties
Original architect
  1912   Unknown
Later works
  1960s   Unknown: major front-of-
         house alterations
  1982   Unknown: extended with
         studio theatre
  1986   Unknown: auditorium refur-
         bished
Current use Theatre
Capacity   600 (Dixon Studio 100)

Jolly facade characteristic of its date, in
red brick and stucco. Broad centrepiece,
with a high-level panel, originally bearing the name of the theatre in bold lettering (now removed), topped by a
curved moulding enclosing an oeil-de-
boeuf window. Above is a straight,
balustraded parapet linked by scrolls to
symmetrical flanking towers with curly
parapets and two stages of closely
spaced pilasters. Entrances at the base of
each tower (formerly leading to pit or
gallery) have bold semi-circular pediments enclosing cartouches supported
by mermaids. The towers were originally
capped by small domes but these have
unfortunately been removed. A pretty
iron entrance canopy has also been lost.
   In the 1960s the main entrance doors
and windows were completely altered.
The design of the auditorium is an interesting example of the tail-end of the
Victorian/Edwardian tradition; clearly
showing the influence of the ciné-variety
type. Although the present seating
capacity is only 600 (including gallery
with benched seating) the impression is
of a much bigger auditorium. This is
largely due to height and depth rather
than width - which is only 13.1m (43ft).
The 1st balcony has 10 rows then a
gangway, but beyond this is a narrower
rear section with a further 6 rows, the
last of which is 22.85m (75ft) from the
stage - a considerable distance. Both balconies directly abut the side walls but are
linked decoratively by concave plasterwork panels to the most impressive features of the auditorium - pairs of boxes
on either side of the proscenium at 1st
balcony level, surmounted by rather
splendid, onion-domed, plasterwork
canopies. The proscenium is rectangular,

7.92m (26ft), and has a curved sounding-board above it. Set in front of this,
on a line midway between the domes of
the boxes, is an unusual feature - a flattened, pointed arch which spans the full
width of the auditorium. Above this is
the main ceiling which is flat and geometrically subdivided by fruit and flower
mouldings. The auditorium still has its
original brass light fittings. On either
side of the proscenium are decoratively
framed panels which were used to indicate the programme number of variety
acts - few such panels now survive. The
fly tower is very shallow and to supple-
ment this a permanent apron stage was
put in at an early date
   In 1982 the theatre was extended to
the right with a plain brick facade, deep
projecting band at roof level and
entrances under a plain canopy. This
extension contains the Dixon Studio
Theatre.   *CB*

WESTON-SUPER-MARE
North Somerset

Knightstone Pavilion
and Opera House ★
Knightstone
Original architect
  1902   J.S. Stewart (London)
Later works
  1958   Unknown: auditorium
         modernised; verandah extend-
         ed; dressing rooms rebuilt and
         stage relaid
  1978   Unknown: converted to leisure
         centre
Current use Disused
Capacity   est. 950

The Knightstone was a 'barren outcrop'
of an island, bought by Dr Edward Fox,
a spa doctor from Brislington. He established a practice in a large house with
medicinal baths, establishing the town
as a health resort. The island was purchased by the council on his death, and
a portion of Glentworthy Bay enclosed
by a retaining wall, linking the island to
the mainland and making sufficient
room to build a theatre. It opened in
1902.
   A good example of a typical seaside
all-purpose hall/theatre jutting out to
sea. A long, low pitch-roofed hall, partly
stone and partly rendered. On the
entrance side the gable of the hall is
flanked by square Italianate towers with
low pyramid roofs. Projecting forward
from each of these is a two-storeyed
gable-ended wing with a low entrance
foyer fitted between, now altered. At the

Weston-super-Mare, Knightstone Pavilion (Sally McGrath)

stage end of the hall roof (there is no fly tower) are smaller square towers with depressed domes. Stretching between these and the bigger towers at the front are low colonnades of coupled Tuscan columns with balustraded parapets. These form open promenades at the sides of the auditorium, reached by means of wide, segmentally arched windows.

The auditorium is a long rectangular hall with a segmental barrel-vaulted ceiling. The main floor was originally flat but a rake was provided in 1958. At the rear is a straight balcony which continues along the sides where it is supported at the front edge by square piers in five bays. These rise above the level of the balcony and are linked by segmental arches below the ceiling. Very restrained plasterwork.

Closed at the beginning of the Second World War, when it served as a battledress factory, it reopened in 1942. In 1978, the seating was removed for leisure centre use. There may have been other alterations.   *SM*

Pier Pavilion
Birnbeck Pier
Original architect
    1898   J.S. Stewart
Current use Disused

The Birnbeck Pier was designed by Eugenius Birch and is unusual in that it runs from the shore to a stoney outcrop (Birnbeck Island, which is similar to the Knightstone nearby). A Pier Pavilion was built in 1898, replacing an earlier one of 1884, which was destroyed by fire. It takes the form of a concert pavilion typ-

ical of the period. It has been disused for some years and the Pier is in a state of some neglect.   *SM*

Winter Gardens Pavilion
Royal Parade
Original architect
    1924   Harold Brown (Town Surveyor)
Later works
    1963   Unknown: Starlight Room added
    1970   Unknown: open colonnade to left of ballroom glassed in and canopy added
    1979   Unknown: colonnade to right of ballroom glassed in and equipped as the Terrace Room
    1992/3   Unknown: completely restored and modernised; Prince Consort Hall added
Listed   Grade II
Current use Multi-purpose hall
Capacity   600

An impressive pavilion in Bath stone, classical style. The domed convex facade of the main pavilion, with round-headed windows set between attached, unfluted Doric columns is flanked on either side by Doric colonnaded wings with gardens behind. The Starlight Room was added in 1963. The colonnades were glassed in in 1970 and 1979, and in 1992/3 an extensive £5.5 million renovation and modernisation programme was carried out to give the Winter Gardens full conference facilities, which included the addition of the Prince Consort Hall with a concert stage. The facade has been carefully restored, as have the interior features of the ballroom, and the Italian Gardens.   *SM*

WEYMOUTH
Dorset

Pavilion
Pier
Other names
    Pavilion and Palm Court
    1950s The Ritz
Original architect
    1908   Mangnall and Littlewood
Later works
    1960   Verity and Beverley: new building on site of old
Current use Multi-purpose theatre
Capacity   Theatre 1000
          Ocean Room 720

The original building was a fine example of an Edwardian multi-purpose concert hall of wrought iron and wood with lavishly decorated interior. There was a single promenade balcony, with three boxes each side and delicate plasterwork on boxes, proscenium arch and ceiling. The Pavilion also had elegant tearooms and a skating rink. This building closed about 1938 and throughout the Second World War. Reopened subsequently but destroyed by fire in 1954.

The new complex, built in 1960, is typical of its date. It comprises theatre, Ocean Room, meeting rooms and bars. The theatre itself is occasionally used for exhibitions, etc.   *SM*

WHITBY
North Yorkshire

Spa
West Cliff
Other names
    Pavilion
    West Cliff Saloon
Original architect
    1879   Julius Oscar Mayhew (Westminster),
          Edward Henry Smales (Whitby)
Current use Theatre
Capacity   513

A plain Victorian building of domestic appearance externally having a flat-floored hall with a balcony of nine rows and slips divided into three unequal bow-fronted segments supported on plain pillars. Plain barrel-vaulted ceiling over stalls with a raised steeper pitch section above the circle. Very much the feeling of a pier theatre on dry land!

The stage is shallow and has no flying facilities. It has been used for repertory seasons but is currently a seasonally operated variety venue. A new conference/exhibition suite was added in the mid 1990s (known as the Northern Lights Suite) but the theatre does not seem to have benefited from conference use. It is currently under threat of closure. *IG*

WHITLEY BAY
North Tyneside

Empire
Whitley Street
Original architect
    1913   Unknown
Later works
    1920s Unknown: converted to cinema
    n.d.   Unknown: interior gutted and converted to ballroom
Current use **Ballroom**

Largely rebuilt in the 1920s as a cinema (Gaumont), only part of the basic structure being retained. The present neo-Adam stuccoed facade dates from the rebuilding. Interior completely gutted on conversion to ballroom. The building is currently in use as a nightclub. *JD-N/CB*

Playhouse
Park Road
Other names
    Kursaal
    Essoldo
Original architect
    1911   Unknown
Later works
    1920s Unknown: reconstructed after fire
Current use **Multi-purpose**
Capacity   **746**

Built by Donald Gilbert as the Jesmond Playhouse, stage facilities were retained when it became a cinema. Opened as the Kursaal. Burnt out in the 1920s and largely rebuilt as a ciné-variety theatre with a shallow stage and fly tower. Completely plain exterior. Plain, remodelled interior with seats on one level. Owned by the local authority and used for theatre, cinema, concerts, etc. *JD-N/CB/DW*

Spanish City
Promenade
Other names
    Empress Ballroom
Original architect
    1910   Cackett, Burns Dick (Newcastle)
Listed   **Grade II**
Current use **Bingo**

Part of leisure complex comprising theatre, entertainment hall, shops, cafés,

roof gardens, promenades, funfair and pleasure ground. Facade of three major bays set between skinny towers. Big central arched entrance flanked by shops. Open loggia with Doric piers at first-floor level. Internally the construction is innovatory (for 1910) in its use of Hennebique reinforced concrete. Coffered barrel vault divided into bays by arched beams. Segmental arch to proscenium, following the same curve, set in heavily moulded and splayed recess. Deep balcony with mildly Roman plaster ornament.

WHITSTABLE
Kent

Assembly Rooms
Horsebridge Road
Other names
    1868 **Music Hall**
    1882 **Theatre and Assembly Rooms**
Original architect
    1868   J.G. Browning
Later works
    c.1920 Unknown: subdivided
Current use **Community support centre**

Built by J.G. Browning, who had built the house next door, the theatre opened as the Music Hall. It became the Whitstable Institute for Promotion of Literature, Science and Art, a multi-purpose room, inscribed as THEATRE AND ASSEMBLY ROOMS on the facade. Two-storey building with arched roof; single bay with entrance at one side and two round-headed mullioned windows at first floor and oeil-de-boeuf window above in semi-circular gable. It had a balcony, but no further interior description has been found. It was later enlarged by taking in the site of Mr Browning's house and a property by other side, and was used as offices by the Whitstable UDC when it was formed in 1894. About 1909 films were shown briefly. In c.1920, the interior was subdivided, converting the first floor to a dance hall, leaving the hall underneath to a variety of uses (as a club during the Second World War). It suffered bomb damage in 1940. Pop concerts were held from 1950–60. From 1960 the lower level was used as a supermarket for a decade, moving the entertainment to the hall above. Since 1987 the building has been in use as a community support centre.

    Today, the facade is plain-faced and parapeted in three bays, retaining the original arched first-floor windows and with additional outer bays in the same

style, obscuring the rounded roof from the front. *SM*

Hippodrome
Harbour Street/Victoria Street
Other names
    Palais de Luxe
Original architect
    n.d.   Unknown: as two shops
Later works
    c.1910 W.G.R. Sprague: converted to ciné-variety (from designs by A.A. Kemp)
Current use **Retail units**

The Hippodrome was a conversion of two shops to a ciné-variety house by Sprague. Between 1914 and 1918 use was solely as cinema. From the 1920s the theatre became the home of The Landswingers Concert Party. It returned to retail use in 1931.

    Seen today, the building is two-storey, shops at street level, plain facade at first-floor level. The only clues to the building's theatrical past are the hall behind with exit doors and dock door, and the evidence of supports for a balcony within the 'arcade' of shops (so-called, in reality a few shops sharing a common entrance). The first floor is now converted to flats. *SM*

WIGAN

ABC
Station Road
Other names
    Ritz
Original architect
    1938   John Fairweather and Son
Current use **Cinema/bingo**
Capacity   **originally c.2500**

Substantial remains of this once magnificent ciné-variety lie largely concealed from view. The bingo hall in the stalls area (used to seat 1676) leaves nothing remotely recognisable of the theatre, but under the stage are dressing and band rooms and the entrance (now blocked) to the orchestra pit. In the cinemas (Screens 1 and 2 in former circle, Screen 3 in restaurant) the restaurant ceiling has survived but is painted black. In each of Screens 1 and 2 are three enormous Corinthian fluted columns supporting a richly embellished architrave. Ceilings hidden. But the real surprise is forward of the extended circle where (torch required) access is possible to one of the two vast boxes. Since access is so difficult they were probably ornamental rather than functional. Two more

Wigan, Royal Court (Ian Grundy)

Corinthian columns visible either side, together with about one third of a huge saucer dome set in a plainish ceiling. More columns frame the wide stage. This theatre is smaller but very similar in appearance to Green's Playhouse, Dundee (demolished), with the same owner and architect/designer. *IG*

Royal Court ★
King Street
Original architect
    1886   **R.T. Johnson**
Later works
    1899   **J.P. Briggs: remodelled**
    1930   **Unknown: converted to cinema**
Listed   **Grade II**
Current use **Dark**
Capacity   **c.1000**

Externally the theatre is little altered. Internally, however, the auditorium was rebuilt as a cinema in 1930 when the boxes were removed and some of the stage area was incorporated within its volume. The interesting red brick and terracotta facade is of two dates. The upper storey, of round-arched windows and surmounting gable, with the name 'Royal Court Theatre' dates from 1886. The two-storeyed lower part, projecting forward from the original building, dates from 1899. At first-floor level, above a canopy of 1930, are five bays divided by fluted Ionic pilasters, the four outer, large windows with elliptical arches, the centre one small, with a broken pediment and oeil-de-boeuf over.

The auditorium as remodelled on conversion to cinema still has two curving balconies, but the upper now concealed by a false ceiling. Thin, Adam-style plasterwork. Small foyer, impressive with marble and brass fittings.

Following its closure as a cinema, the Court was for many years used for bingo. However, this has also now ceased and the building is currently dark. It seems to be a prime candidate for conversion to a pub. *CB/IG*

WIMBORNE MINSTER
Dorset

Tivoli ★
West Borough
Original architect
    1936   **E. de Wilde Holding**
Later works
    1992   **Unknown: theatre restored**
Listed   **Grade II**
Current use **Theatre**
Capacity   **500**

The entrance and foyers are part of the Georgian Borough House, the Tivoli having been built at the rear to the design of E. de Wilde Holding, a well-known architect who lived and worked in Bournemouth. He enjoyed a business arrangement with local builder A.S. Prince, in building cinemas, etc., and running them speculatively until a buyer could be found. Weeks after opening, Prince sold out to Portsmouth Town Cinemas, who ran the Tivoli until 1968. It closed in 1981, not from lack of support, but because the Dorset County Council had plans for a new road and compulsorily purchased the site. In 1991, The Friends of the Tivoli group was formed and a petition raised to persuade the council to donate the building to the town for the arts and entertainment. Eventually the building was handed over to Project Tivoli, as it became called.

The Tivoli was built as a cinema/theatre, designed with a large stage and orchestra pit; the lack of dressing rooms is thought to have been a last-minute cost-cutting measure. Local societies are consequently required to provide temporary accommodation when theatrical productions are staged.

The theatre is rectangular with a single balcony and a shallow, arched roof, divided into segments by plain rounded pilaster strips which continue across the ceiling arch ending either side of a lighting transom running the length of the auditorium. The simple proscenium is in the same style, but with curved fluted jambs. A shallow fluted frieze runs round the hall. Above is a frieze of stencilled decoration of leaves hanging from stems, a rare survivor of the style of decoration. There is a single balcony. With hidden bulbs in lighting troughs used with metallic paint on the ceilings and upper walls, it was originally possible to take a sea of light slowly through the colours of the spectrum.

There are two shops on the street front, used as a box office and for promotional displays. *SM*

WINCHESTER
Hampshire

Theatre Royal ★★
Jewry Street
Other names
   New Theatre Royal
Original architect
   1850 Owen Browne Carter: as a
       hotel
Later works
   1913 F.G.M. Chancellor: theatre
       added
   1981 Unknown: renovated; circle
       bar formed; theatre pub refur-
       bished
   1985 Ware, MacGregor: major
       restoration works
Listed   Grade II
Current use Closed, undergoing improve-
      ments
Capacity c.400

An excellent example of a small ciné-variety theatre which has survived in remarkably complete condition. The building evolved in an interesting way. In 1850, the Market Hotel was built in Jewry Street, to serve the adjacent market and corn exchange. The hotel closed and was acquired in 1913 by John and James Simpkins (who ran the local Palace Theatre). An auditorium and stage were constructed in the yard behind the hotel, retaining the two main wings of the hotel in Tower Street and Jewry Street, of which the main elevations survive today in altered condition.

The Theatre opened as a ciné-variety in 1914 and, in 1916, had become a 'Revue Theatre'. In 1922, live shows ended and life as a cinema began. Sound was installed in 1928.

The auditorium was designed by F.G.M. Chancellor with a typical segmental barrel-vault ceiling over the full width, and a slightly curved balcony. In this case however, something rather more positive than usual was retained in the earlier theatre/music hall tradition, in that the balcony has side arms which become bow-fronted boxes at each end, flanking the proscenium. Florid Baroque plasterwork on balcony and box fronts. Typically shallow stage and fly tower.

Pleasing stuccoed facade which incorporates earlier work and ties in well with the adjoining terrace. The first floor has four wide bays defined by coupled Ionic pilasters. Each bay has a single rectangular window with an ornamented surround and three festoons above. Straight bracketed cornice and a low attic storey above the centre.

The Rank Organisation bought the theatre in 1939. In 1974, it was closed and planning permission sought to demolish it and build a supermarket. This was rejected and the Winchester Theatre Fund was formed to acquire the building, which it did in 1977. Major works of improvement and restoration have since been carried out to front of house and backstage, including the enlargement of the fly tower and the provision of an orchestra pit. The suspended steel lighting grid is somewhat intrusive. Further extensive improvements are now under way. *SM/MS*

WINDSOR
Windsor and Maidenhead

Theatre Royal ★★
Thames Street
Original architect
   1815 Unknown
Later works
   1902 Sir William Shipley: new the-
       atre on site of old
   1912 F.T. Verity: interior reconstruct-
       ed
   1985/6 Unknown: circle bar built;
       theatre redecorated and
       improved
   1990 Verity and Beverley: scenic
       design/painting/carpentry
       shops enlarged
   1994 Unknown: theatre re-roofed
       and structural repairs under-
       taken; hospitality suite estab-
       lished
Listed   Grade II
Current use Theatre
Capacity 633

The original playhouse on this site, described as a 'beautiful and elegant theatre', was built in 1815. When it was finally destroyed by fire it had a capacity of 500 and was on three levels with an iron balcony. The replacement, on the site of the old theatre and adjoining pub, opened in 1902. It was designed by William Shipley, who was also the owner.

Situated in the shadow of Windsor Castle, it has a tall, narrow, stone facade with big mullioned and transomed window. Frank Verity's 1912 auditorium has one deep balcony and boxes on either side linking it to the proscenium which is flanked by engaged columns. The rear part of the stalls (the former pit) is raised up behind a curved parapet and has a good rake. French Neo-Classical style plasterwork on ceiling, proscenium, etc. In 1965, Verity's open ironwork

Windsor, Theatre Royal

balustrades to the balcony and boxes were replaced by solid fronts, ornamented with plasterwork in a style sympathetic with the remainder but perhaps to be regretted. Ironwork balustrades are rare generally in theatre architecture in Britain but a few appeared around this period: Verity's own London Scala Theatre, 1905 (demolished), Wimbledon Theatre, 1910, and the Opera House, Manchester, 1912. *CB/SM*

Waterloo Chamber
Windsor Castle
Original architect
   1824-37 Sir Jeffry Wyatville
Current use Private theatre

Prior to 1830, the Waterloo Chamber was an interior courtyard. It was then floored and roofed to form a gallery in which to display portraits. It was never converted to a theatre in such a thoroughgoing way as Hampton Court Great Hall, but has been regularly fitted up since 1891 when the chamber saw the Savoy production of *The Gondoliers*. In later years, the Royal audience was seated on a railed dais and the orchestra played from the side on their left. The tradition continues and the chamber is still occasionally open to the public for theatre performance. *SM*

WISBECH
Cambridgeshire

Angles ★
Alexandra Road
Original architect
   1793 Unknown

Later works
1897   Unknown: converted to school
1976   Unknown: reconverted to theatre
Listed   **Grade II**
Current use **Theatre**
Capacity   **112 (plus studio, 80)**

A country town theatre, first on Lincoln and later (from 1847) on the Norwich circuit. In 1897 it became part of a school and was considerably altered internally. In 1977, however, Richard Leacroft made a careful survey of the building and discovered sufficient evidence to enable him to produce an account of its internal arrangement (*Theatre Notebook* vol. XXXII (2)).

The basic structural shell survives - a plain brown brick rectangle, measuring 18.28m x 7.92m (60ft x 26ft) inside the walls, with a pitched roof. Internally it now consists of a hall with a timber roof and a room partitioned off at one end, and a basement below.

Under the floor Leacroft discovered a beam which had formerly supported the front edge of the stage and also beams which had supported the front edges of the side boxes and front boxes. These beams revealed a rectangular arrangement of boxes similar to Richmond Theatre, Yorkshire (qv). He also found, part-way up the height of the partition dividing the hall from the smaller rooms, beams which had supported the gallery, and two cast-iron columns which rose from the basement to support these beams. The line of the auditorium ceiling is also original - flat over the pit area and sloping upward over the gallery area. Thanks to this careful research it has been possible to add considerably to our knowledge of the design of a typical Georgian country playhouse. In 1978 an amateur theatre/cinema was opened in the building, which was renamed the Angles Theatre.

The present theatre does not reflect the precise original extent and form which, nevertheless, remains recoverable. A fire in 1991 caused no irreparable loss. CB/JL

Empire★
Blackfriars Road
Original architect
1932   **Ward and Woolnough**
Listed   **Grade II**
Current use **Bingo/Cinema**
Capacity   **722**

A virtually mint ciné-variety built in 1932. The foyers and auditorium are

Wisbech, Empire: original 1930s Art Deco doors (Jim Lee)

remarkably complete with an impressive array of Arts Deco plaster decoration and joinery. The proscenium arch is angular with reeded and prismatic ornaments, flanked by clustered organ pipes and recessed boxes. The balcony front is adorned with Aztec plaques. Main elevation in three bays, the centre higher with tall canted bay window and Art Deco pinnacle. Geometrical glazing bars to steel windows. A jewel of its time. Bingo and films in recent years. JL

WOLVERHAMPTON
Civic Halls
North Street
Original architect
1938   **Lyons and Israel**
Later works
1998   **Penoyre and Prasad: major
improvements, additions and
restoration (planned)**
Listed   **Grade II**
Current use **Multi-purpose civic halls**
Capacity   **Proposed: 2632 (+ 700)**

Traditional theatre to modern standards is well provided for in Wolverhampton by the Grand. The Civic Halls require inclusion only insofar as they are used from time to time for some kinds of dramatic productions.

The building contains two halls, the larger being the Civic and the smaller the Wulfrun. The Lyons and Israel design has a tightly disciplined geometry with deceptively simple massing of plain blocks with sparse external ornament, apart from a portico in antis with atten-

uated proto-Ionic columns. The capitals are wonderfully mannered, looking like buffalo horns. The original internal detailing of the two halls and their foyers and main corridors has been surprisingly little eroded over the last sixty years.

Hope Bagenal was consultant acoustician for the two halls which were regarded as having fine natural acoustics. The larger was designed mainly for choral and orchestral concerts, the smaller (which has a proscenium stage) for chamber music with some theatrical presentations and film shows. Demands have changed in recent years, with a greater emphasis on popular music and a need for amplification. Major concerts also call for a greater capacity than can be provided by the Civic Hall.

Current proposals (1997–8) envisage extensive improvements, including an added upper balcony in the Civic Hall, adjustments to both halls to solve changed acoustic requirements, additions to accommodate improved foyer and bar spaces and internal restoration of architectural detail.

The proposed alterations and additions are ingeniously designed to be absorbed by the existing internal and external architecture. The most noticeable change, the long glazed addition at upper level on the flank, is handled with sensitivity. JE

Grand ★★★
Lichfield Street
Original architect
1894   **C.J. Phipps**
Later works
1898   **Messrs A.R. Dean: renovated**
1969   **Unknown: auditorium and
front of house altered**
1983   **Tarmac Refurb Ltd: refurbished**
1987   **Unknown: new canopy**
1998   **RHWL: major refurbishment,
extensive improvements**
Listed   **Grade II★**
Current use **Theatre**
Capacity   **1200**

This is amongst the most important of Phipps's remaining theatres and he himself regarded it as one of his most successful designs. The auditorium has a remarkable degree of intimacy for its size. This is achieved largely by two means. First: the width is greater than the maximum depth. Second: the rows of the balconies, especially the first one, are very fully curved and come round close to the stage, to the detriment, it must be admitted, of sight lines at the extreme sides. This drawback, however,

Wolverhampton, Grand (Ian Grundy)

is a small price to pay for the superbly vibrant atmosphere which this auditorium possesses.

The balconies are partly cantilevered and partly supported on iron columns and have plasterwork of early Renaissance character. The ends of the balconies are separated from the stage by a single box on each side at dress-circle level. These are framed by fluted Corinthian columns which carry curly broken pediments. The design of the beautiful ceiling follows a pattern frequently used by Phipps - a flat, circular centre, divided into richly decorated radiating panels supported at the sides, above the upper balcony slips, by high, panelled coves. The proscenium is well related in width, 10.4m (34ft), to the scale of the auditorium. The design of its reticent rectangular frame, decorated with filigree plasterwork and surmounted by a pedimental tablet, has much in common with the proscenium which existed at Nottingham Theatre Royal prior to its removal in 1978. There was a splendid contemporary painted act-drop which is still on site but recent inspection suggests it was heavily repainted between the Wars (cf Gaiety Theatre, Douglas, for example, where the original drop is still in use). It depicted a classical landscape with dancing nymphs, hung about with elaborately swagged and tasselled draperies (the present drop is a 1997 copy of the original). The facade to Lichfield Street is of considerable width, more than 30.5m (100ft). It is in brick with painted stone dressings and the design is very French in character. In the centre is a tall, arcad-

ed loggia, set in front of the first and second-floor saloons. This is flanked at the end of the facade by two-bay pavilions with steep dormered mansard roofs.

Following a threat of closure in 1969, the theatre was promptly acquired by Wolverhampton Corporation. At that time some unfortunate alterations were made (e.g. in auditorium and dress-circle saloon) and the delicate arabesques on the auditorium cove were painted out, but in 1997–8 major improvements were carried out. The auditorium was restored and redecorated, additional bar and foyer spaces were created, air conditioning installed, the fly tower raised and the stage re-engineered. *CB/TB*

Tettenhall College Theatre

Wood Road, Tettenhall
Original architect
after 1860 Unknown (for Col. Thorneycroft)
Later works
after 1880 Unknown: room altered and permanent proscenium stage built
1948 Unknown: height of room reduced and upper balcony removed
Listed **Grade II***
Current use **College assembly hall and theatre**
Capacity **250**

A school theatre, but included here because of its unusual architectural and historic interest.

The theatre now forms part of a col-

lege. It is used daily for assemblies and occasionally licensed for public performances. It was designed originally as the Great Music Room of Tettenhall Towers, the house of Col. Thomas Thorneycroft, scientist, engineer, ironmaster and public-spirited capitalist.

The house at Tettenhall was built about 1770, altered probably in the 1820s and added to extensively by Thorneycroft from 1860, incorporating innovatory heating and ventilating systems. His large room was built 'for concerts, penny readings, theatricals, lectures and public meetings' because the village had been unable to provide itself with a hall.

In its earliest form it was a wide rectangular room panelled in the Old English manner, with a deep recess at what is now the stage end. There were two balconies of unequal depth, the upper one set forward with a balustraded front. There was an elaborate carved alcove containing a chimney piece under the end balcony and an understated proscenium division at the recess end. The floor (laid on rubber springs for dancing) was level throughout. In this form it would have served well for concerts and a published plan shows that, for more ambitious theatricals, a 'fit-up' scenic stage was built.

Some time after 1880 the room was altered and turned into a permanently equipped theatre. In 1948 a floor was inserted at upper-balcony level, reducing the height of the room and producing the single-balconied ground-floor theatre seen today.

There is now a raised stage and permanent wood and plaster proscenium, with curving jaws linking it to the old structural division. This proscenium probably dates from 1880–1890 but shows signs of later alteration. The stage itself is unusually generous in size for a house theatre, about 6.1m (20ft) deep with a proscenium opening of about 6.4m (21ft). Col. Thorneycroft was interested in lighting effects and described the way in which coloured lights in the 'pleasure grounds', seen through the end window, could 'make the (old fit-up) stage look about 200ft long' (i.e. 61m). The lower balcony, continuing through the present stage, serves as a fly gallery. The balustrades here may be relics of the earlier treatment of the room.

A fragile survival of this kind deserves detailed study and further documentary research. Any modernisation or fire safety works required will need to be undertaken with considerable skill and understanding. *JE*

WOODBRIDGE
Suffolk

Riverside
Quayside
Other names
    Electric House
    Woodbridge Cinema
Original architect
    1915 Unknown
Later works
    1985 Unknown: extensively renovated
Current use **Cinema plus some live shows**
Capacity **288**

Built as a ciné-variety, almost on the water's edge, the Riverside continues to be used mainly as a cinema, with occasional live shows (about 10% of the time) by both professional and amateur groups. Major works in 1985 improved stage conditions.

Externally, a broad gabled rectagular building with sparse ornament. Internally, raked auditorium with shallow end balcony (not used for seating). Barrel-vaulted ceiling, like many of its kind and date.

The original ciné-variety stage was trapped. The present stage has a 4.87m (16ft) revolve owned by an amateur company. *KW*

Theatre
Theatre Street
Original architect
    1814 Unknown
Later works
    1860 Unknown: converted to a school
Current use **Auction room**

A single-storey building set into the hill behind and below Theatre Street from which it is gained by a long, sloping, enclosed passage. The further, downhill side is pierced by a series of tall windows dating, in all probability, from its days as a school. Although it is not inspected internally, it is unlikely that any theatrical features survive. *JL*

WORCESTER
Worcestershire

Prince of Wales
Lowesmoor Wharf
Other names
    1869 Worcester Concert Hall
    1874 Prince of Wales Concert Hall
    1875 Prince of Wales Palace of Varieties
    1879 Winwood Varieties

Workington, Opera House (Ian Grundy)

    1881 Salvation Army citadel
    1988 Vesta Tilley Centre
Original architect
    1869 A. Bell and Co (Worcester)
Later works
    1877 Unknown: alterations and improvements
    1906 Unknown: gallery altered
Current use **Disused (offices at upper level)**

In 1869 a foundation stone was laid on the site of the Navigation Inn for what was going to be the Canterbury Concert Hall – within a stone's throw of the Alhambra (demolished). Opened with stalls, and front and side galleries, chairman and orchestra. Had a 'commodious oriental lounge'. A stage plays licence was obtained in 1870, but the place was run in the main as a variety hall.

The frontage to Lowesmoor Wharf disguises an unusual triangular plan. The wall facing the street is not straight, the half nearest the town angling inwards to a position where the rear wall joins it at a point.

The building as now seen does not look theatrical and its appearance seems to result mainly from its former Salvation Army occupation. The Salvation Army balcony remains, made up of three straight sections supported by iron pillars. It is not possible to say whether this balcony is a modification of that previously existing since details of the alterations have not survived in the Salvation Army Archives. *TB*

WORKINGTON
Cumbria

Opera House
Pow Street
Other names
    Queen's Jubilee Hall
Original architect
    1888 Unknown
Later works
    1897 Unknown: reconstructed after explosion
    1927 Unknown: reconstructed after fire
    1963 Unknown: facade rebuilt
Current use **Bingo**
Capacity **c.1200**

Originally opened as the Queen's Jubilee Hall and Opera House - a small theatre with two balconies. Gutted by fire in 1927 and rebuilt completely as a ciné-theatre except for part of the structural walls on one side. The narrow street front has been rebuilt in aluminium and glass.

Fine, wide auditorium with one balcony intact from 1927 rebuild. Ornamental ceiling with sunburst and mask. Stage has false ceiling. Understage used as bar with entry through orchestra pit and band doors. Modernised foyer now sold/let as retail outlet with no access to theatre. Apart from the ceiling and a frieze running the full width of the proscenium wall there is little in the way of plaster decoration. It is too large for the town but in the right location the building could be a more than functional theatre with its good sight lines and large stage. *CB/IG*

Workington, Theatre Royal (Ian Grundy)

Theatre Royal
Washington Street
Original architect
   1866   Unknown
Later works
1879/88   Unknown: altered
   1912   Unknown: reconstructed as
            cinema
   1976   Unknown: dressing rooms and
            workshops added
Current use Amateur theatre
Capacity   249

Of the original building all that now remains is the basic structural shell and the stage. The 1866 auditorium had a horseshoe balcony with arms to the proscenium and a gallery above. In 1912 the balconies and side arms were removed and a single balcony constructed with ten straight rows. Completely plain side walls and ceiling. In overall form the auditorium is long and narrow.

The rear seats of the balcony appear particularly remote from the stage, although the actual distance is not great. The proscenium was also redesigned in 1912 as a rectangular moulded frame with a central cartouche. The condition is mostly good but some damp patches appear on the right-hand wall and there is need for a new roof. The colour scheme is dark green, white and gold.

The narrow stuccoed facade forms part of the general street frontage and in overall appearance and detail dates from 1912 – three storeys of unequally disposed windows under a steep pedimented gable.

Closed as a cinema in 1932, as it never converted to sound; it has been an amateur theatre since 1935. A restrictive covenant (originally to protect the Opera House) prevents the theatre from being hired out. *CB/IG*

WORKSOP
Nottinghamshire

Gaiety
Bridge Street
Other names
   1875?–1908   Criterion Hall
   1911   Gaiety Theatre Picturedrome
Original architect
   1875   Unknown
Later works
   1908   Unknown: converted to
            theatre, stage added with fly
            tower; gutted to side walls;
            old balcony demolished
   1994   Unknown: facade remodelled
            for retail use
Current use Retail

Information on the physical nature of the building is scant. No details given in local paper for any of the major openings or events. In 1908 there was seating on two levels. By April 1911, it was mainly in cinema use. In 1962 it became a bingo hall and fell vacant in 1979. In 1994 the front of the building was completely remodelled.

The conversion into a shop has left some evidence of the theatre but reconversion would be expensive and is unlikely even to be proposed. Although it had a deeper stage than the Regal the facilities at the latter are better.   *TB*

Regal Arts Centre
Carlton Road
Other names
   1926   Miners' Welfare Hall
   1929   Pavilion
   1933   Regal Cinema
Original architect
   1926   Richardson and Lloyd
Later works
   1931   Unknown: fly tower added
   1933   Unknown: converted to cinema
   1972   Unknown: tripled
   1980   Unknown: Studios 1 and 2
            reconverted to a single unit
Current use Theatre (cinema above)
Capacity   326

Opened in 1926 as a multi-purpose Miners' Welfare Hall. Became the Pavilion Theatre in 1929, with variety and revue, and had a fly tower added in 1931. Used solely as a cinema from 1933 and later tripled but Screens 1 and 2 reconverted to a single unit in 1980. The theatre (professional and amateur) is now on the ground floor. The original asymmetrical facade still exists, with an adjacent building acquired for offices, etc.

The theatre has one level of seating with twelve straight rows. The former circle front (the cinema is in the circle) is now boxed in. The auditorium, which is wider than it is long, is relatively plain. No orchestra pit; raked shallow stage, with a forestage. Three dressing rooms. The low seating capacity and small stage are considerable drawbacks, but the theatre seems, at present, to satisfy local need. *TB*

WORTHING
West Sussex

Connaught Theatre and Ritz ★
Union Place
Other names
   Picturedome
   New Connaught Theatre
Original architect
   1914   Peter Stoneham: as
           Picturedome
Later works
   1916   Unknown: Connaught Hall
           built adjacent (later Ritz)
   1933   A.T. Goldsmith: stage, dressing
           rooms and fly tower added;
           auditorium extended
   1935   A.T. Goldsmith: new facade
           with entrance foyer and bar
           above
   1986   Borough Architect: refurbished
Current use Connaught: theatre with
           cinema use Ritz: studio
           theatre and cinema (under-
           going restoration)
Capacity   Connaught 514/Ritz 225

Two buildings now jointly operated. The Connaught Theatre was built as the Picturedrome in 1914 on the site of Stanmore Lodge, which had been acquired by the newly formed Picturedrome (Worthing) Ltd. Seating capacity was 850 in a single tier, with four boxes at rear. The main entrance from Chapel Road had a canopy crowned with a dome and led to a crush lobby, whilst that from Union Street led directly into the auditorium. Plans show a steel framework and an elegant rounded auditorium, richly panelled, with an octagonal ceiling feature. In 1933, a new stage and proscenium were constructed, together with dressing rooms and a scene dock, by taking in land at the rear, at the same time the interior was modernised and most of the original plasterwork obscured. Two years later the Union Place front was rebuilt in Moderne style, two rendered storeys, parapeted, in three bays; the centre bay slightly taller and slightly advanced

with the name of the theatre in relief sans serif letters; curved end bay set back to the right. Strip windows continue round the corners; entrance canopy projects from storey band at first-floor level.

Until recently, the safety curtain was that of 1895 from the Theatre Royal (demolished), brought to the venue by Seebold, who had acquired the theatre in 1904 and was responsible for much of the town's entertainment history. A new one was installed c.1990.

The Ritz (also known at various times as the Ritz Ballroom and, briefly, as Vaudeville and Garrison Theatre) was built in 1916 by Connaught Buildings Syndicate Ltd, and opened as the Connaught Hall, above a newly built parade of shops in Chapel Road. An entrance between the shops then served the Picturedrome. The exterior was neo-Georgian in style; the auditorium was built for dances and concerts, and is typical of an early cinema with elegant plaster mouldings of fruit and roses, surrounds with cross-ribbon detail, heavy shields on the walls and a rounded proscenium.

The Hall became a repertory theatre, which proved so popular that it had to be moved next door to the larger theatre. During the war the Hall was used by the Home Guard and, later, after acquisition by the Connaught Theatre, for painting scenery and for private hire. *SM*

Pavilion ★
Marine Parade
Other names
   Concert Pavilion
   Pavilion Theatre
Original architect
   1926   Adshead and Ramsey (on Pier
           of 1862)
Later works
   1970   Unknown: projecting canopies
           added
   1980-81 Borough architect?: altered
           and refurbished
Listed   Grade II
Current use Multi-purpose
Capacity   850

The 292.6m (960ft) long pier was completed in 1862. Its head was widened in 1889 to accommodate a 'recreational' pavilion. The Concert Pavilion, at the landward end of the pier, was built in 1926, following the purchase (in 1920) of the pier company by Worthing Corporation. The pier and its buildings have suffered some damage and rebuilding over the years. Today, the pierhead

pavilion (rebuilt 1935) and the (Concert) Pavilion are listed with the pier itself and with the Lido, a close neighbour, also by Adshead and Ramsey.

The single-storey (Concert) Pavilion, constructed half on the shore and half on the pier, is in continental Kursaal style, stucco-faced with curved, metal-clad roofs with oculus dormers. It comprises a central polygonal block with a long, low crowning lantern and pavilions of varied shapes on each side. The oval, domed entrance block has engaged columns with vases above the entablature. Neo-Grec interior. The auditorium was built as a concert Hall and was home to the municipal orchestra. Plays were also presented before the local company moved to the Connaught. The pier was closed during the war but the Pavilion reopened as a garrison theatre in 1942. Entrance canopies of heavy and unsympathetic design were added in 1970 and the auditorium was refurbished and modernised in 1981. It is now a multipurpose hall. *SM*

WREXHAM

Hippodrome
Henblas Street
Other names
   1873   Public Hall
   1909   New Opera House and Public
           Hall
   1911   Wrexham Public Hall
           Hippodrome
Original architect
   1909   Messrs Davies and Sons (of
           Chester)
Later works
   n.d.   Unknown: subdivided
Current use Dark
Capacity   originally 800

Built on the site of a public hall which was destroyed by fire, the building has a plain, two-storeyed brick front. Before the subdivision it had an interesting lozenge-shaped interior with one curved balcony with Baroque plaster ornament. No boxes. Tiny triangular stage in one corner of the lozenge. This interior was divided into two small cinemas, but is now closed. *TR*

YORK

Grand Opera House ★★
Cumberland Street
Other names
   Empire
   Grand Opera House and Empire
   S.S. Empire (ballroom)

York, Grand Opera House (Ian Grundy)

Original architect
   1868   Unknown: as a Corn Exchange
Later works 1902 J.P. Briggs: converted to
         theatre
   1916   Frank Tugwell: dress circle and
          gallery altered increasing
          capacity
   1950s Unknown: converted to ball-
          room
   1989   Theatre Developments
          (Michael Holden): restored
Listed   Grade II
Current use Theatre
Capacity   1032

Originally a Corn Exchange and ware-house of 1868, reconstructed as a the-atre in 1902 and opened as The Grand Opera House. Renamed the Grand Opera House and Empire in 1903. The elevation to King Street, which is the rear wall of the auditorium, is basically that of the warehouse, with four storeys of nar-row, segmentally arched windows. The rear wall of the stage on Cumberland Street still has the semi-circular arched windows of the corn exchange hall, and it is possible to make out the shape of the original gable in the brickwork - later heightened for the fly tower. The theatre does not have a show-front of its own, the main entrance being through a side arch in the ground floor of a three-storeyed row of shops with offices over, also part of a corn exchange develop-ment. The style is vaguely Italian Gothic with closely spaced arched windows at first-floor level, separated by stone shafts. The entrance foyer is long and narrow with a good plaster ceiling.

The original auditorium design was modified before construction and lost some of its architectural coherence, but it is still pleasing and intimate. There are two balconies, the 1st having a serpen-tine front decorated with an unusual repeated arched panel motif. The sight line to the stage in the vertical plane from the rear of this balcony is severely cut by the extremely low overhang of the upper balcony. The upper balcony, however, has unusually good sight lines in the vertical plane, its front being set well below the edge of the main ceiling. There are two bow-fronted boxes at the level of each balcony on either side, tied together as a composition of giant Corinthian columns linked at the top by arches. The main ceiling is in the form of a saucer dome, decorated by a plaster sunburst radiating from the centre. Rectangular, moulded proscenium frame with cartouche.

Reopened 1989 after restoration and improvement.   CB/JE

Joseph Rowntree

Nestlé Rowntree, Haxby Road
Original architect
   1935   Barry Parker
Current use Theatre
Capacity   420

A free-standing building set back from the road in gardens on a corner of the Rowntree (now Nestlé) factory site a couple of miles from York city centre. It opened in 1935 principally for the facto-ry workers - 'The aim has been to build a hall which may be a fitting centre of those recreational and educational activ-ities which make for a full and happy life' (from the opening programme). There was no bar - still isn't - and amazingly no confectionery was available until around twenty years ago.

A simple, dignified 1930s' facade in three blocks is symmetrically pierced by small steel windows. The two lower, pro-jecting blocks are the circle stairs. Three second-floor windows in the centre illu-minate the former projection suite. Behind the plain brick auditorium block with its pitched tiled roof rises the tall fly tower. The building is gloriously and unmistakably a theatre.

The stalls (seventeen rows) are unusu-ally steeply raked giving outstanding sight lines. There is a high dado panelled in light wood. The severely elegant lines are almost unaltered, the only addition being two rather ugly lighting platforms high on the walls above the front stalls. The ceiling slopes down, with deep plas-ter ribs originally containing concealed lighting, until the final one before the proscenium which is considerably higher than the preceding level to allow for more stage lighting positions. The circle front is covered by a curtain which parts to reveal more stage lighting positions. Sight lines from the circle are excellent. The stage is generous with a sunken orchestra pit which can be covered over to form a forestage.

The building is in excellent condition. A more vibrant colour scheme would transform the interior.   IG

Theatre Royal ★★★

St Leonard's Place
Original architect
   1765   Unknown
Later works
   1822   Unknown: reconstructed
   1835   John Harper: Gothic arcade
          added
   1880   George Styan (City Surveyor):
          new facade
   1902   Frank Tugwell: new auditorium
          and stage
   1967   Patrick Gwynne: new foyer
          alongside
   1994   Allen Tod (Leeds): altered and
          reseated
Listed   Grade II*
Current use Theatre
Capacity   863

A theatre was first built on the present site in 1765, and a Royal patent was granted in 1769. The building was often reconstructed but never at any time totally demolished, so that it is now an extraordinary complex of many periods. At the rear there is Georgian fabric, including a complete three-storey, three windows wide, house front with hipped roof and eaves cornice. The present main facade dates from 1880, and the present auditorium and stage from a major rebuilding of 1902. The stone facade is in a gutsy Victorian Gothic style – three storeys under a wide gable flanked by corbelled turrets, and crowned by a crocketed niche containing a statue. A big oriel window projects from the centre of the first floor and at ground level there is an open arcade of five pointed arches. In 1967 the stonework was cleaned, ugly accretions removed and the arcade opened up.

The auditorium is superbly intimate, yet also has a feeling of noble spaciousness. This is partly due to the overall dimensions and partly to the sweeping curves of the closely spaced shallow balconies (six rows each). Sight lines are excellent, even from the sides of the steeply raked upper balcony. Flanking the stage are ranges of superimposed, bow-fronted boxes - two on either side at the levels of the 1st and 2nd balconies and a single, wide box at the top. The boxes are framed by tall, panelled pilasters, linked just below the ceiling by a wide elliptical arch. The proscenium has a segmentally arched top and a deep curving sounding board. Although some of the plasterwork is conventional Baroque, e.g. the balusters on the fronts of the lower boxes, the majority is in an imaginative and fluid version of the Art Nouveau - possibly the only example of the full-blooded use of this style in British theatre design.

In 1967 the stalls were reseated with continuous rows and the rear part partitioned off to form a new cloakroom and exhibition space. The seating capacity was reduced from 1300 to 950 - unfortunately at the same time reducing the theatre's viability for touring opera and ballet, etc. Also in 1967, a new entrance foyer, restaurant and bars were added to the left of the theatre. These were housed in an elegant glass-walled pavilion by Patrick Gwynne. Slender concrete columns sprout into hexagonal mushroom heads which link and spread to form the flat roof. The lightness of the new work forms a pleasing contrast with the Gothic solidity of the old. It is infi-

York, Theatre Royal (Bob Williamson)

nitely more successful than the similarly briefed, and near contemporary addition, at Liverpool Playhouse. Access to all levels is now gained by a single, sinuous staircase set alongside the exposed stonework of the flanking elevation of the old building. As part of the same project, the dressing rooms, offices, workshops, etc., were modernised and partly rebuilt. The auditorium was also redecorated in a rather dull scheme using twelve shades of green. Fortunately in 1979 this was changed to a warmer, more attractive scheme using brown, cream and gold. In 1993 problems with the glazing of the 1967 addition had to be dealt with and the joints are now a little more visible than Gwynne intended.

The theatre is owned by the City Council. A producing theatre with some touring productions. *CB/JE*

YSTRADGYNLAIS
Powys

Miners' Welfare Hall
Brecon Road
Other names
   The New Theatre
   Workmen's Hall
Original architect
   ?c.1930   Unknown
Later works
   **1991   Borough Architects
           Department: refurbished as
           arts centre**

Current use **Multi-purpose venue**
Capacity **367**

A simple rectangular building of rendered brick with auditorium occupying the centre area and rising a full floor above the surrounding offices and lobbies.

The auditorium has a flat floor with removable seating, and at the rear is a raised flat area just a few steps above the main floor. There is no balcony. The orchestra pit can be covered to allow extension of the seating. There is no stage tower and no sub-stage machinery. The original Art Deco box office survives in the lobby; it is now a telephone kiosk. *TR*

PART TWO ~ APPENDICES

Buxton Opera House

Appendix 1 • Demolitions

This list was compiled by Jean Sedley with assistance from the editors and the various compilers. Note that demolished theatres listed as Early Theatres in Appendix 2 are omitted from this list. A number of demolished theatres are excluded because of absence of reliable information.

It should be noted that in some instances little or no information has been found, beyond the mere fact that a theatre is known to have existed in a town.

Information provided in the list of demolished theatres is arranged in the following manner:
• the town/city followed by the administrative area
• the theatre name, including all known other names
• in brackets, the period of use as a theatre (fl = flourished)
• the remaining information gives dates of construction, alterations, changes of use and ultimately the date of demolition (**D**)

ABERAFAN (PORT TALBOT) Neath Port Talbot
Grand (–):1972 **D**
New (1912–):1912 Unknown; 1938 fragmental remains, after fire
Palace (1911–1922): 1911 Unknown; n.d. **D**
Prince of Wales (–): n.d. **D**
Vint's Electric Palace/The Palace (1911–1972): 1911 Unknown; 1972 **D**

ABERDARE Rhondda Cynon Taff
Empire/Empire Pictorium (–): n.d. **D**
Grand (1903–30): 1903 Unknown; n.d. **D**
New (–): n.d. **D**
Star (fl 1870s): n.d. **D**

ABERDEEN
Theatre Royal (1789–1877): 1877 **D**

ABERDYFI Gwynedd
Pavilion (1920–1957): 1920 Unknown; 1957 **D**

ABERGAVENNY Monmouthshire
Theatre Royal (–): n.d. **D**

ABERSYCHAN Torfaen
Empire (c.1908–): c.1908 Unknown; n.d. **D**
Grand (–): n.d. **D**

ABERTILLERY Blaenau Gwent
Pavilion (1900–c.1927): 1900 Unknown; c.1927 **D**

ABERYSTWYTH Ceredigion
King's Hall (1932–): 1932 L.G. Mouchel and Partners; 1989 **D**
Little (1946–1961): 1946 Unknown: 1975 **D**
Playhouse (1831–1845): 1831 Unknown; c.1857 **D**
Phillip's Hall (1891–1902): 1891 Unknown; 1902 **D** (fire)
Rink (Bijou) (188?–1900): n.d. **D**

ACCRINGTON Lancashire
Grand/Prince's (1882–1964): 1882 Turner; 1964 **D** (fire)
Hippodrome (1903–1908): 1903 Unknown; 1908 fire
New Hippodrome/Hippodrome (1908–1955): 1908 Crewe; 1955 **D**

ALDERSHOT Hampshire
Alexandra Music Hall (c.1870–c.1914): c.1870 Unknown; n.d. **D**
Apollo/Victory Music Hall (1859–1889): 1859 Unknown; 1889 **D**
Canterbury Music Hall (1880s–): 1880s Unknown; n.d. **D**
Cavalry (Garrison) Theatre (c.1890–1960): c.1890 Unknown; 1960 **D**
Country Theatre (1891–1953): 1891 Unknown; 1960 **D**
Hippodrome (1913–1952): 1913 Crewe; 1962 **D**
Marlborough Lines Theatre (1880s?–): 1880s Unknown; n.d. **D**
Pavilion (1926–1956): 1926 Henry G. Baker; after 1956 **D**
Red White and Blue Music Hall (c.1854–): c.1845 Unknown; n.d. **D**
Royal Arms Music Hall (1880s–): 1880s Unknown; n.d. **D**
Royal Engineers' Theatre (1890–1960s): 1890 Unknown; n.d. **D**
Theatre Royal and Opera House (1891–1955): 1891 Unknown: 1955 fire; 1959 **D**
Theatre Royal/South Camp (1856–): 1856 Unknown; n.d. **D**

ALFRETON Derbyshire
Empire (1922–1930): 1922 Unknown; 1986 **D**

ALTRINCHAM Trafford
Central/Shakespeare (1906–1964): 1906 Unknown; n.d. **D**
Hippodrome (1912–1950s): 1912 Butterworth & Duncan; 1987 **D**

AMESBURY Wiltshire
Plaza (1934–c.1990): 1934 E. de Wilde Holding; 1990 **D**

AMMANFORD Carmarthenshire
(New) Palace (1914–): 1914 Unknown (possibly Henry Herbert); after 1960 **D**

ANNFIELD PLAIN Durham
King's Pavilion (pre 1912–early 1960s): c.1988 **D**

ARNOLD Nottinghamshire
Bonnington (–): 1963 **D**

ASHFORD Kent
Corn Exchange Theatre (1862–1966): 1966 **D**
Garrison (–): n.d. **D**

ASHTON-UNDER-LYNE Tameside
Star (–   ): 1879 Unknown; 1909 converted to cinema use; 1947 closed; 1960s **D**
Theatre Royal (1891–1953): 1891 Matcham; 1931 Unknown: converted to cinema; 1937 Unknown: returned to theatre use; 1957 closed; 1972 **D**

AYLESBURY Buckinghamshire
Market (1911–c.1980): 1911 Unknown; 1924 Taylor and White: rebuilt after fire; c.1980 **D**

BANBURY Oxfordshire
Bear Garden (–   ): n.d. **D**
Palace (1857–1916): 1857 Unknown; 1979 fragmental remains

BARNSLEY
Alhambra (1915–1960): 1915 Hinchcliffe; 1982 **D**
New Empire Palace (1909–1955): 1909 Unknown; 1955 **D** (fire)

BARNSTAPLE Devon
Forester's Hall (–   ): n.d. fragmental remains
Theatre Royal (1843–1930): 1895 Petter; 1930 **D**

BARROW-IN-FURNESS Cumbria

Carlisle Palace (1873–1903): 1873 Unknown; n.d. **D**
Coliseum (1907–1964): 1907 Winstanley; 1978 **D**
Her Majesty's/Theatre Royal (1869–1967): 1973 **D**
Palace/New Amphitheatre (1912–1915): 1873 Unknown: as Salvation Army citadel; 1912 G. Walker: reconstructed as theatre; 1915 Unknown: converted to cinema; 2000 **D**
Royal Theatre (1872–1937): 1894 Mackintosh; 1937 **D**
Theatre Royal (–   ): n.d. **D**
Tivoli/Regal (1868–1931): 1868 Unknown; n.d. **D**

BARROWFORD Lancashire
Empire (1914–1930): 1914 Unknown; 1977 **D**

BARRY Vale of Glamorgan
American Pavilion (1894–   ): 1894 Unknown; n.d. **D**
Empire Music Hall (1895–   ): 1895 Unknown; n.d. **D**
Princess (1889–1891): 1889 Unknown; 1891 **D**
Theatre of Varieties (1892–   ): 1892 Unknown; n.d. **D**

BATLEY Kirklees (West Yorkshire)
Theatre Royal (1896–1921): 1896 Unknown; 1961 **D**

BEDFORD
Empire (c.1912–1930s): c.1912 Unknown; 1977 **D**
Granada (1934–1960s): 1934 Benslyn, Morrison and Furneaux with T. Komisarjevski; 1991 **D**

BEDLINGTON Northumberland
Palace (c.1896–c.1927): c.1896 Unknown; n.d. **D**
Prince of Wales (c.1890–c.1918): c.1890 Unknown; n.d. **D**

BELFAST
Alhambra (1873–1907): 1873 Stevenson; 1859 **D** (fire)
Coliseum/Alexandra/Palladium (1909–   ): 1875 Unknown: as Alexandra Music Hall; 1909 Swanston and Syme: rebuilt; 1959 fragment as part of garage

Empire/Theatre of Varieties (1894–1965): 1894 Farrell; 1965 **D**
Royal Hippodrome/New Vic (1907–1960s): 1907 Bertie Crewe; 1996 **D**

BEVERLEY East Riding of Yorkshire
Thespian Theatre (1904–   ): 1904 Unknown; n.d. **D**

BEXHILL-ON-SEA East Sussex
Bijou/New Palace (1910–pre 1931): 1912 Unknown: modernised; c.1980s **D**
Egerton Park/Pergola (1906–c.1935): 1906 Unknown; after 1935 **D**
Gaiety/York Hall (1895–1944): 1895 Randolf Richard; 1944 bombed
Pavilion Theatre/Kursaal (1896–c.1935): 1896 G.H. Grey; 1936 **D**

BIDEFORD Devon
Palace (1869–1961): 1869 Unknown; 1879 Gould and Sons; c.1971 **D**

BILSTON Wolverhampton
Hippodrome/Royal (1880–1957): 1874 Unknown; 1880 Unknown: rebuilt; 1902 James Tomkinson: rebuilt; 1957 **D**
Waterloo Music Hall (fl 1870s/90s): after 1894 **D**

BIRKENHEAD Wirral
Argyle (1868–1940): 1868 Unknown; 1940 bombed
Gaiety (1888–1905): 1888 Unknown; n.d. **D**
Hippodrome (1888–1932): 1888 Hesketh; 1932 converted to cinema; 1940 bombed
King's (1908–   ): 1908 W. Ward; n.d. **D**
Music Hall/Claughton Music Hall (1862–1911): 1862 Unknown; 1912 converted for films; 1957 converted for bingo; 1982 **D**
Theatre Royal/Scala (1864–1921): 1864 Lewis Hornblower; 1905 Unknown; 1921 James Stoneman Branwell; 1937 **D** (replaced by cinema)

BIRMINGHAM
Adelphi (1857–1864): 1857 Unknown: as circus; n.d. **D**
Aston Hippodrome (1908–1939): 1908 Lister Lea; 1912 Unknown: alterations; after 1980 **D**
Blackheath Hippodrome (c.1907–c.1916): c.1907 Unknown; n.d. **D**
Bordesley Palace/Imperial (1899–1928): 1899 Owen and Ward; 1929 converted to cinema; 1959 **D**
Coliseum/Carlton (1900–1941): 1900 T.Guest; 1921 converted to cinema; 1941 **D**
Elite (1913–1942): 1913 Darlaston and Walker; 1942 bombed and **D**
Empire Palace/Day's Crystal Palace (1862–1940): 1862 Thomas Nelson; 1894 Matcham, rebuilt; 1911–13 W. and T.R. Milburn; 1940 bombed
Futurist (1922–   ): 1922 Unknown; n.d. **D**
Gaiety Music Hall/Rodney Inn Concert Rooms/Grand Concert Hall/ Coliseum (1846–1920): 1846 Unknown; 1938 **D**
Grand/Theatre of Varieties (1883–1933): 1883 Ward; 1901 Ward Markham and Nicol and Goodman; 1907 F. Matcham, with Essex, Nicol and Gordon; 1963 **D**
King's Hall (1897–1932): 1897 Unknown; c.1963 **D**

Ladywood Palace/Steam Clock (1883–1914): 1883 Unknown; n.d. **D**
Lyric/Queen's Hall (1909–1935): 1909 E. Harper: conversion from church; 1911 Darlastan and Robinson: alterations; 1935 **D**
Metropole/Imperial/Queen's/New Star (1885–1941): 1885 Unknown: as a hall; 1886 Oliver Essex: rebuilt internally; 1911 Unknown: converted to cinema; 1941 bombed, **D**
New Palace (1911–1939): 1911 W. and T.R. Milburn; 1940 **D**
Newtown Palace (1914–   ): 1914 W. and T.R. Milburn; 1990 **D**
Oldbury Palace (1899–c.1927): 1899 Ramsell; 1978 **D**
Palace of Delight (1895–1897): 1895 Unknown; n.d. **D**
Prince of Wales/Royal Music Hall (1856–1941): 1856 Cranston; 1892 Matcham and Tugwell; 1941 bombed;1986 **D**; New Birmingham Symphony Hall on site
Robin Hood (1927–1970): 1927 Henry Farmer; 1970 **D**
Theatre Royal/Astoria (Aston Road) (1893–1925): 1893 G.H. Ward; 1912 Unknown: reconstructed; 1927 Unknown: converted to cinema; 1955 Unknown: converted to television studios; 1970 **D**

BIRTLEY Sunderland
Theatre Royal/Bolams (1910–1958): 1867 Unknown: as chapel; 1910 converted to theatre; 1968 **D**

BISHOP AUCKLAND Durham
Eden (1865–1966): 1865 Unknown; 1871 W.V. Thompson; 1892 Frank Matcham; 1901–3 F.H. Livesey; 1975 **D**

BLACKBURN Lancashire
Grand (1880–1956): 1880 Trevenson; n.d. Rodney and Keeley: rebuilt; 1958 **D**
Lyceum Music Hall (1880–1902): 1880 Culshaw; c.1902 **D**
New Theatre (1899–1936): 1899 Livermore; 1936 Unknown: converted to cinema; after 1977 **D**
Palace (1899–   ?): 1899 Wimperis and Arbour; 1988 **D**
Theatre Royal (1886–1931): 1886 Matcham; 1909 Crewe; 1967 **D**

BLACKPOOL Lancashire
Alhambra (1899–1961): 1899 Wylson and Long; 1961 **D**
Central Pier Pavilion (1874–1956): 1874 R.K. Freeman ; after 1956 **D**
Empire (–   ): n.d. **D**
Queen's Theatre/Feldman's (1877–1971): 1877 Unknown; 1928 Derham, MacKeith: rebuilt; 1972 **D**
South Pier Pavilion/Rainbow/Victoria Pier (1892–1965): 1893 J.D. Harker; 1965 McKeith Dickenson: reconstruction after fire; 1998 **D**

BLAENAVON Torfaen
Palace (–   ): after 1912 **D**

BLAINA Blaenau Gwent
Empire Theatre (–   ): before 1994 **D**

BLANDFORD FORUM Dorset
Palace/Ritz (c.1918–1934): 1918 Unknown; 1927 Unknown: modernised; 1940s reopened as cinema; 1957 **D**

BLAYDON Gateshead
Empire (1910–1930): 1910 Gibson and Steinlet: converted from shop; 1912 Gibson and Steinlet: extended; 1960? **D**
New Theatre Royal (–   ): n.d. **D**

BLYTH Northumberland
Gaiety Music Hall/ Gaiety Theatre of Varieties (1906–   ): 1906 Unknown; n.d. **D**
Hippodrome (1902–1920): 1902 Unknown; c.1927 **D**
Theatre Royal (i) (1870–1888): 1870 Unknown; 1888 **D** (fire)
Theatre Royal (ii) (1890–   ): 1890 Hope and Maxwell; c.1982 **D**

BOGNOR REGIS West Sussex
Esplanade Theatre (1946–1980): 1901 bandstand; 1946 Unknown: roof built; 1950 Unknown: alterations and additions; 1951 Unknown: proscenium arch constructed; 1980 **D**
Pavilion (–   ): after 1948 **D** (fire)
Theatre Royal/ Kursaal (1911–1939): 1911 W.T. Barlow; 1976 **D**
Victoria Hall Theatre (1897–1903): 1897 Unknown: conversion from chapel; c. 1967 **D**

BOLTON
Grand/Continental (1894–1963): 1894 Matcham; 1960 Unknown: conversion to bingo; 1963 **D**
Hippodrome (1908–1961): 1908 Unknown; 1961 **D**
Temple Opera House (1877–1882): 1877 Unknown; 1882 **D** (fire)
Theatre Royal/Star/ Museum (1832–1928): 1832 Unknown; 1852 Unknown: rebuilt; 1862 Unknown: improvements; 1888 Matcham: complete renovation; 1928 reconstructed as cinema; 1963 **D** (fire)

BOOTLE Sefton
Royal Muncaster (1890–   ): 1890 Pennington; n.d. **D**

BOSTON Lincolnshire
New/Palace/New Electric (1862–1960): 1855 Bellamy and Hardy: as corn exchange; 1862 Unknown: converted to theatre; 1909 Unknown: fly tower built; 1926 P. Brown and Son: rebuilt; 1933 Unknown: additional access ; 1961 **D**

BOURNEMOUTH
Pier Theatre (i) (1885–1959): 1885 Unknown; 1859 **D**
Westover Palace (1910–1937): 1910 Unknown; 1937 **D**
Winter Gardens (i) (1877–1935): 1877 Fletcher Lowndes and Co.; 1935 **D**

BRADFORD
Alhambra Music Hall/ Birrell's Diarama/Jollity Vaudeville (1873–1897): 1873 Unknown; 1897 **D**
Elite (1925–1968): 1913 Unknown: cinema; 1925 Unknown: stage added; 1988 **D**
Empire (1899–1918): 1899 Unknown; 1952 **D** (fire)
Essoldo (1919–   and 1947–1965): 1919 Unknown; 1976 **D** (fire)
Mechanics' Institute (1947–1965): 1947 Unknown; 1974 **D**
Palace/Star (1875–1938): 1875 Jackson and Langley; 1938 **D**
Prince's (1876–1959): 1876 Unknown; 1900 Jackson and Longley; after 1975 **D**
Theatre Royal/Royal Alexandra (1864–1921): 1864 Andrews and Peffer; c.1989 **D**

BRIDGEND
Pavilion (fl 1873): n.d. **D**

BRIDGNORTH Shropshire
Bijou (–   ): n.d. fragmental remains

BRIDLINGTON East Riding of Yorkshire
Floral Hall (1919–1923): 1919 Unknown; 1923 **D** (fire)
Grand Pavilion (1906–1936): 1906 Unknown; 1936 **D** (replaced by 3B'S)
New Spa Theatre (1899–1906): 1899 Mangnall and Littlewood; 1906 **D** (fire)
Opera House (1907–1932): 1907 Unknown; 1932 **D** (fire)
People's Palace (1896–1942): 1896 Unknown; 1942 bombed
Royal Victoria Theatre (–1933): 1933 **D** (fire)

BRIGHTON Brighton and Hove
Alhambra/Palladium (1888–1914): 1888 Matcham; 1956 **D**
Gaiety/Royal Hippodrome (1876–1910): 1876 Unknown; 1910 fragment
Grand/Eden (1887–1955): 1887 Matcham; 1955 **D** (fire)
Oxford/Empire/Coliseum/Court/Dolphin/Her Majesty's (1863–1955): 1863 Unknown; 1892 Unknown: rebuilt; 1967 **D**
Palace Pier Theatre (1901–1973): 1901 R. St John Moore; 1986/7 **D**
Regent (1921–   ): 1921 Robert Atkinson; 1970s **D**

BRISTOL
Alhambra/Forester's Music Hall (1870–1900): 1870 Unknown; 1874 destroyed by fire and rebuilt; c.1900 **D**
Bedminster Hippodrome (1911–1914): ?1911 Crewe; 1914 bombed; 1915 converted to cinema
Canterbury Music Hall/Western Counties Music Hall (1855–1867?): 1855 Unknown; 1860 Unknown: rebuilt after fire; 1863 converted to dining room; n.d. **D**
Empire (1893–1954): 1893 Wylson and Long; 1963 **D**
Glen (1923–   ): 1923 Unknown; after 1983 **D**
Park Street Music Hall (1840s–1860s): 1840s Unknown; n.d. **D**
Post Office Tavern (1848–1866): 1848 Unknown; 1866 **D**
Prince's (1867–1940): 1867 Phipps; 1889 Matcham; 1902 Matcham; 1940 bombed
Ship and Castle/ Williams's (1857–1880): 1857 Unknown; 1880 **D**
Tivoli (1870–1901): 1870 Unknown; 1879 Unknown: rebuilt after fire; 1895 Hancock; n.d. **D**

BROADSTAIRS Kent
Bohemia Theatre (1895–1962): 1895 Unknown; 1912? **D** apart from box office (fire)

BROMSGROVE Worcestershire
Assembly Rooms/ Empress (1907–c.1923/4): 1907 Unknown; n.d. fragmental remains

BURNLEY Lancashire
Gaiety (1880–1916): 1880 Unknown; 1916 **D**
Palace Hippodrome (1907–1974): 1907 Horsfall and Sons; 1974 **D**
Princess Alexandra Music Hall (1870–1978): 1870 Unknown; 1978 **D**
Victoria Theatre and Opera House (1886–1955): 1886 G.B. Rawcliffe; 1955 **D**

BURTON UPON TRENT Staffordshire
Alhambra Music Hall/New (1856–c.1889): 1856 Unknown; 1867 Unknown: enlarged; 1869 Unknown: renovation; c.1889 **D**
Queen's (1932–1939): 1932 Unknown; 1941 converted to Salvation Army Hall; 1988 **D**
Theatre of Varieties/Star (fl 1878): after 1899 **D** (possibly a temporary building)

BURY
Hippodrome/Phillips Hall/Barbary Club/Palace Theatre Club (1875–1956): 1875 Unknown, assembly hall; 1904 converted to music hall; 1966 **D** (fire)
Theatre Royal (1889–1933): 1889 Matcham; 1919 Longbottom: alterations; 1937 converted to cinema; 1983 **D**

BURY ST EDMUNDS Suffolk
Playhouse (1925–1959): n.d. fragmental remains

BUXTON Derbyshire
Royal (1871): n.d. **D**

CADOXTON Vale of Glamorgan
Theatre Royal (1891–1910): 1891 Richards and Gethin; 1964 **D**

CAERPHILLY
Palace Music Hall (1910–c.1921): c.1904 Unknown: skating rink; c.1910 converted to music hall; 1976 **D**

CAMBRIDGE
Theatre Royal/New (1896–1956): 1896 Runtz ; 1961 **D**

CANNOCK Staffordshire
Forum/Hippodrome (1912–1955 and 1962–1984): 1912 Unknown; 1925 converted to palais de danse; 1962 converted back to theatre; 1985 **D**

CANTERBURY Kent
Empire/Theatre Royal (1861–1926): 1861 Unknown; 1926 **D**
Garrison Theatre (fl late C19): n.d. **D**

CARDIFF
Capitol (1921–1978): 1921 R.S. Phillips; 1983 **D**
Empire/Levino's Hall/Empire Palace/Gaumont (1887–1961): 1886 Unknown; 1896 Matcham; 1900 Matcham: reconstruction after fire; 1915 W. and T.R. Milburn: total rebuild; 1933 converted to ciné-theatre; 1962 **D**
Pavilion (–   ): n.d. **D**

CARLISLE Cumbria
Bijou (1853–1874): 1853 Unknown; 1924 **D**
Her Majesty's/ Victoria Hall (1874–1963): 1874 Unknown; 1905 Beadle and Hope: rebuilt after fire; 1980 **D**
Palace (1906–   ): 1906 Owen and Ward; 1975 fire (fragmental remains)
Royal (1851–   ): 1851 Unknown; 1990s **D**

CARMARTHEN Carmarthenshire
Theatre (fl mid C19): before 1995 **D**

CASTLEFORD Wakefield
Queen's (1909–1921): 1899 R. McDowell: as a hall; 1909 Albert Winstanley: conversion to theatre; c.1990 **D**

Theatre Royal (1873–1958): 1911 Matcham; 1964 **D**

CHATHAM Medway
Alhambra/Simpson's (fl 1864–): n.d. **D**
Barnard's Palace (1850–1934): 1850 Barnard: as fit-up; 1886 Unknown (possibly Bond): rebuilt; 1934 **D** (fire)
Empire/Gaiety (1890–1960): 1890 George Friend; 1912 Matcham; 1962 **D**
Garrison Theatre (1861 or 1872–): n.d. **D**
Globe Theatre (1879–1971): 1879 Bernays; 1971 **D**
Opera House (c.1850–1902): c.1850 Whitehead and Vennell; n.d. **D**
Royal Marines Theatre (c.1870–): c.1870 Unknown; n.d. **D**

CHELMSFORD Essex
New Empire/Hippodrome (1912–1940?): 1912 Unknown; 1961 **D**

CHELTENHAM Gloucestershire
Theatre of Varieties (1886–1914): 1886 Unknown; n.d. **D**
Theatre Royal/Old Wells (Royal Pump Room) (1854–1890): c.1850 Unknown: as Pump Room; 1854 S. Onley: rebuilt to include theatre; 1890 **D**
Winter Gardens Theatre (1878–1940): 1878 Robson; 1942 **D**

CHESTERFIELD Derbyshire
Palace (1910–1920s): 1910 Unknown; n.d. **D**
Royal/Hippodrome (1896–1955): 1896 Rollinson and Sons; 1961 **D**

CHESTER-LE-STREET Durham
Empire (1911–1971): 1911 Unknown; 1971 **D**
Hippodrome (1911–1917): 1911 Unknown; n.d. fragmental remains?

CHOPWELL Gateshead
Kings(i) (1911–1920): 1911 Marshall and Tweedy; n.d. **D**

CHORLEY Lancashire
Grand (1912–1914): 1912 Unknown; 1914 **D** (fire)
Theatre Royal (1911–1952): 1911 Unknown; c.1952 converted to cinema; 1960 **D**

CHORLTON–CUM–HARDY Manchester
Theatre Royal (1911–1925): 1911 Unknown; 1960 **D**

CLACTON–ON–SEA Essex
Palace/Palace of Varieties (1912–): 1912 Unknown; n.d. **D**
Queen's Hall Theatre (–): n.d. **D**

CLAY CROSS Derbyshire
Hippodrome (1925–1940): 1925 Unknown; 1940 **D** (fire)

CLAYTON–LE–MOORS Lancashire
Empire (fl 1914): n.d. **D**

CLEETHORPES North East Lincolnshire
Theatre Royal (1921–1963): 1921 Unknown; n.d. **D**

CLEVELEYS Lancashire
Beanland's/Pavilion (c.1919–c.1935): c.1919 Unknown; c.1960 **D**
Queen's (c.1930–1961): c.1930 Unknown; c.1987 **D**

CLYDEBANK West Dunbartonshire
Gaiety (1904–1929): 1904 Unknown; c.1960 **D**

COATBRIDGE North Lanarkshire
Adelphi (1909–1960): 1909 Robertson and Dobbie; 1960 **D**
Theatre Royal (c.1880–1958): c.1880 Unknown; 1962 **D**

COLCHESTER Essex
Vaudeville Electric/Vaudeville (1911–c.1920): 1911 Unknown; 1971 **D**

COLNE Lancashire
King's Theatre/Free Trade Hall (1893–1935): 1881 as Free Trade Hall; 1893 Lindley Bell: rebuilt as theatre; 1944 **D**

COLWYN BAY Conwy
Arcadia/Wedgwood (1924–1981): 1924 Sidney Colwyn Foulkes; 1981 **D**
Bijou (–): 1993 **D**

COVENTRY
Britannia Music Hall/Gaiety (1873–1891): 1873 Unknown; 1892 **D**
Empire (1880s–1931): 1856 Unknown: as Corn Exchange; 1885 Unknown: new proscenium; 1906 Harrison and Hatrell: ceiling and proscenium altered; 1933 Unknown: rebuilt as cinema; 1973 **D**
Grand/Royal Opera House (1889–1940): 1889 Essex and Nicol with Phipps; 1898 Sprague: rebuilt; 1961 **D**
Hippodrome (1903–1906): 1903 Unknown: wooden building; 1906 **D**
Sydenham Palace of Varieties (1891–1894): 1881 Unknown: concert hall; 1891 converted to music hall; after 1895 **D**

COWES Isle of Wight
Pavilion/Victoria Pier Pavilion (1902–1951): 1902 Unknown; 1910 R.E. Cooper; 1951 **D**

CRADLEY HEATH Worcestershire
Empire Palace of Varieties/Theatre Royal (1893–1938): 1893 Morton; 1916 Joseph Pritchard: alterations; after 1938 **D**
New Alexandra (1890–c.1893): 1890 Unknown: a wooden theatre; 1894 **D** (parts sold)
Palace of Varieties/Worton's Music Hall (c.1881–1913): c.1881 Unknown; c.1990 **D**

CREWE Cheshire
Coliseum (1911–c.1920s): 1909? Unknown: skating rink; 1911 Unknown: converted for entertainment; n.d. fragmental remains
Grand (1922?–): 1922 Unknown; c.1983 **D**

CROOK Durham
Theatre Royal (1894–1895 and 1902–1957): 1893 Unknown; n.d. **D**

DALMUIR West Dunbartonshire
Empire (1915–): 1916 Unknown; c.1975 **D**

DARLINGTON
Barn Theatre (1858–1865): 1858 Unknown; 1881 **D**
Gaiety Music Hall (1890–1907): 1890 Unknown; 1946 **D**
Theatre Royal (i) (1864–1874): 1864 Unknown; after 1874 **D**

(New) Theatre Royal (ii) (1881–1936): 1881 William Hodgson; 1887 Phipps; 1937 **D**

DARWEN Blackburn with Darwen
Theatre Royal (1877–1960): 1960 **D**

DEAL Kent
Pier Pavilion (–   ): n.d. **D**

DERBY
Empire (–   ): n.d. **D**
Palace/Corn Exchange (1892–1921): c.1861 B. Lisbon: as Corn Exchange; 1890s converted to theatre; after 1987 converted to offices, fragmental remains

DERRY
Opera House (1877–   ): n.d. **D**

DEVONPORT Plymouth
Alhambra/Metropole (1895–1941): 1895 Unknown; 1941 bombed
Empire (1890–1941): 1890 Phipps; 1941 bombed
Hippodrome/Odeon (1908–1941): 1908 Crewe; 1929 Marshall and Tweedie: enlarged; 1941 bombed
Public Hall (1850–1910): 1850 Unknown; 1941 bombed

DEWSBURY Kirklees (West Yorkshire)
Empire (1909–1955): 1909 Chadwick and Watson; 1960 **D**
Hippodrome (i) (1880–1896): 1880 Unknown; 1896 **D** (fire)
Hippodrome (ii) (1896–1919): 1896 Chadwick and Watson; 1950 **D**
Theatre Royal (1865–1931): 1865 Unknown; 1965 **D**

DONCASTER
Palace (1911–): 1911 Ward and Ball; 1952 **D**

DORCHESTER Dorset
Palace (1930s–1980s): 1930s Unknown; 1991 **D**

DOUGLAS Isle of Man
Crescent Pavilion (1923–1962): 1923 Unknown; 1962 **D**
Derby Castle (1895 –   ): 1895 Alfred Darbyshire; 1962 **D** (fire)
Grand (–   ): 1984 **D**
Henglers Cirque (1896 –   ): 1896 A. Hengler; n.d. **D**
Hippodrome (–   ): n.d. **D**
Onchan Head Pavilion (–   ): n.d **D**
Palace Coliseum and Ballroom (1913–): 1913 G. Kay and Sons; 1924 Matcham and Co.: new entrance; c.1966 **D**
Prince of Wales (1847–1853): 1847 Unknown; n.d. **D**
Theatre Royal (1858–   ): 1858 Unknown; n.d. **D**; fragment remains
Wellington Street Concert Room (1900–   ): 1900 Edward Forrest; n.d. **D**

DOVER Kent
Empire Palace (c.1880–1927): c.1880 Unknown; 1944 **D** (shelled)
Pier Pavilion (1899–1926): 1899 Adcock; n.d. **D**
Royal Hippodrome (1858–1944): 1897 Phipps; 1957 **D**

DOVERCOURT Essex
Empire (1913–1940): 1913 Unknown; 1962 **D**

DOWLAIS Merthyr Tydfil
Victoria (fl 1880s): n.d. **D**

DROITWICH Worcestershire
Salters Hall (1881–c.1930): 1881 Unknown; 1907 Unknown: alterations; c.1930 **D**
DUDLEY
Colosseum (1889–1899): 1889 Walter Bagshaw: Lloyds circus conversion; 1899 **D**
Empire Palace (1903–1912): 1903 A.D. Gammage; 1975 **D**
Opera House/Hippodrome (1899–1936) 1899 A. Ramsell; 1936 **D** (fire)

DUDLEY PORT (TIPTON) Sandwell
Alhambra/Colosseum/Palace of Varieties (1902–1933): 1902 converted from Salvation Army barracks; 1933 **D**

DUMFRIES Dumfries and Galloway
Lyceum (1912–1936): 1912 Boswell; 1930 Alistair MacDonald; n.d **D**

DUNDEE
Empire (1904–1911): 1904 Unknown; 1962 **D**
Gaiety/Victoria (1903–   ): 1903 McCulloch and Fairley; 1910 Alexander; c.1991 **D**
Her Majesty's/Majestic (1885–1919): 1885 Alexander; 1960 **D** (fire); cinema on site
Palace/Royal (1893–1972): 1893 Unknown; 1977 **D** (fire)

DUNFERMLINE Fife
Hippodrome and Opera House (1900–1921): 1900 Roy Jackson; 1921 Swanston: reconstructed; 1982 moved to USA
La Scala Music Hall (1852–1924): 1852 Clerk; n.d. **D**

DUNOON Argyll and Bute
Pavilion (1905–1949): 1905 Unknown; n.d. **D**

DURHAM
Albany (1891–c.1930): 1891 Unknown; after 1930 **D**
Palace Music Hall (1909–1964): 1909 Unknown; 1964 **D**

EARLESTOWN St Helens
Empire (c.1900–1912): c.1900 Unknown; c.1912 **D**
Hippodrome (–   ): c.1921 **D**

EASINGTON Durham
Hippodrome (–   ): n.d. **D**

EASTBOURNE East Sussex
Theatre (1832–1900): 1832 Unknown; 1900 **D**

EAST GRINSTEAD West Sussex
Whitehall Theatre (1910–1936): 1910 Unknown; 1936 fire; 1943 bombed

EASTLEIGH Hampshire
Institute (1891–1983): 1891 Jonas Nichols; 1983 **D**
Variety/Regal (1910–   ): 1910 Unknown; c.1960s **D**

EBBW VALE Blaenau Gwent
Palace of Varieties (c.1908–   ): c.1908 Unknown; after 1914 **D**

EDINBURGH
Alhambra (Leith Walk) (1914–1958): 1914 Unknown; 1974 **D**
Edinburgh Theatre (1875–1977): 1875 Sir James Gowans; 1965 **D**
Garrick/Prince of Wales/New Pavilion (1897–1921): 1897 Unknown; 1921 **D** (fire); facade remains
Grand/Tivoli (1900–1960): 1900 Unknown; n.d. **D**
Operetta House/Gaiety/Moss's Theatre of Varieties (1875–1939): 1875 Unknown; c.1950 **D**
Palladium (1886–1968): 1886 Unknown; 1984 **D**
Pier Theatre (Portobello) (1871–1917): 1871 Unknown; 1917 **D**
Princess's (1862–1912): 1862 Unknown; 1912 **D**; replaced by cinema
Queen's/Caledonian/Adelphi/Theatre Royal (1820s –1946): c.1820s Unknown; 1855 D. Bryce: rebuilt; 1863 Unknown: rebuilt after fire; 1876 C.J. Phipps: rebuilt; 1884 C.J. Phipps: rebuilt after fire; 1960 **D**

EGREMONT Cumbria
Lyceum (?   –1920) n.d. **D**

ELLESMERE PORT Cheshire
Hippodrome (i) (1890s–1931): 1890s Unknown; 1931 **D**
Hippodrome (ii) (1933–1963): 1933 Unknown; 1963 **D** (fire)

EPSOM Surrey
Capitol/Granada (1929–1960): 1929 R. Cromie; 1947 Unknown: modernised; 1955 G.H. Dickinson: improvements; 1961 **D**
Odeon (1937–1971): 1937 Whinney and Austen Hall; 1971 **D**
Pavilion Theatre/Cinematographic Hall (1910–1929): 1910 Harry Smallman; 1916 converted to theatre; 1953 **D**
Public Hall/Picture Palladium (1883–1934) 1883 J. Hatchard Smith; 1934 **D**

EXETER Devon
Hippodrome (1908–1942): 1820 public rooms; 1908 Kendall: conversion to theatre; 1931 Lucas and Langford: conversion to cinema; 1942 bombed
Queen's Hall/Palladium (1912–1921): 1912 Unknown; after 1921 **D**
Savoy (1936–1972): 1936 W.R. Glen; 1987 **D**
Theatre Royal (ii) (1886–1887): 1885 Phipps; 1887 **D** (fire)
Theatre Royal (iii) (1889–1962): 1889 Darbyshire; 1962 **D**
Victoria Hall (1885–1919): 1873 Unknown: a public hall; 1885 converted to circus; 1910 converted to ciné–variety; 1919 **D** (fire)

EXMOUTH Devon
Coffee Palace Hall/Little (1850s–1920s?): 1850s Unknown; n.d. **D**
Harry Wright's Theatre (1870s –   ): 1870s Unknown; n.d. **D**
Pier Pavilion (c.1890–1940?): c.1890 Unknown; c.1940s **D**
Public Hall/Savoy (c.1890–c.1960): c.1890 Unknown; n.d. **D**

FALKIRK
Grand/Opera House (1903–1929): 1903 Cullen; 1932 **D**; fragment remains in cinema
Hippodrome (1909–   ): 1909 Robertson and Dobbie; n.d. **D**

FALMOUTH Cornwall
Grand (1928–1968 and 1970–1988): 1928 C.R. Corfield;1968

Exeter, Theatre Royal (iii)

Unknown: converted to bingo; 1970 Unknown: returned to theatre use; 1988 **D**; facade remains

FAREHAM Hampshire
Alexandra (1906–c.1920): 1906 Unknown; 1928 reconstructed; after 1933 **D**
Savoy (1934–c.1960): 1934 Unknown; after 1960 **D**

FARNWORTH Bolton
Queen's/Ritz (1899–1922): 1899 Bradshaw and Gass; 1922 Unknown: converted to cinema; c.1988 **D**

FELIXSTOWE Suffolk
Pier Pavilion (1911–1970): 1911 Rogers; after 1980 **D**
Playhouse (1914–1920): 1914 Hooper (attributed); 1970 **D**
Ranelagh (c.1901–1955): c.1901 Unknown; 1987 **D**

FELLING Gateshead
Imperial (1901–1929?) 1901 Unknown; n.d. **D**

FILEY North Yorkshire
Gaiety (–   ): n.d. **D**

FLEETWOOD Lancashire
Empire (1909–1915): 1909 Winstanley; 1960 **D**
Queen's Theatre/Palace (1909–1937): 1909 Unknown; 1970 or 1976 **D**
Victoria Pier Theatre (1911–1953): 1910 G.J. Lumb; 1953 **D** (fire)

FOLKESTONE Kent
Pleasure Gardens Theatre (1888–1914): 1888 Gardiner?; 1964 **D**
Victoria Pier Pavilion (1887–1945): 1887 Ridley and Chatterton; 1945 **D** (fire)

FROME Somerset
Palace (c.1900–1939): c.1900 Unknown; after 1939 **D**
Vaudeville (1922–1922): n.d. **D**

GAINSBOROUGH Lincolnshire
Empire and Hippodrome (1908–   ): 1871 Unknown: built as temperance hall; 1908 Unknown: reopened as theatre; n.d. **D**
Grand (1910–1911): 1821 Unknown: built as chapel; 1910 W. Eyre: converted to theatre; 1911 Unknown: converted to cinema; 1955 **D**

GATESHEAD
Alexandra Theatre and Music Hall (1870–1879): 1870 Unknown; 1954 **D**
Empire (1905–1950): 1905 S.M. Mold; 1968 **D**
King's Theatre of Varieties (–   ): n.d. **D**
Metropole/Scala (1896–1919): 1895 Hope; 1919 converted to cinema; 1960 **D**
People's Music Hall (–   ): 1924 **D**
Queen's/New Hippodrome (1882–1922): 1882 Unknown; 1922 **D** (fire)
Webb's Theatre (1896–1906): 1896 Unknown; 1968 **D**

GERRARDS CROSS Buckinghamshire
Playhouse (1925–   ): 1925 Unknown; n.d. fragmental remains

GILLINGHAM, Medway
Gem Music Hall/Victoria Hall (1912–c.1928): 1910 Unknown: converted to ciné-variety house; c.1992 **D**
Grand (1911–1959): 1911 Unknown; 1960 **D**
Lyceum (1912–1912): 1912 **D** (fire)

GLASGOW
Alexandra (1898–1899): 1898 Unknown; n.d. **D**
Alhambra (1912–1969): 1912 Burnet; 1970 **D**
Bridgeton Olympia (1910–1930s): 1910 G. Arthur and Sons; c.1984 **D**
Cambridge Music Hall (1909–   ): 1909 Robertson and Dobbie; n.d. **D**
Casino (1911–   ): 1911 Unknown; n.d. **D**
Empire Palace (1897–1963): 1897 Matcham; 1963 **D**
Folly (–   ): n.d. **D**
Gaiety Music Hall (1896–1960s): 1896 Unknown; 1960s **D**
Grand Theatre (1867–1915): 1903 Spence, Donaldson; 1918 **D** (fire)
Hippodrome (1902–   ): 1902 Crewe; 1978 **D**
Lyceum (1898–1940s): 1898 Barclay; after 1940 **D**
Metropole/Scotia/West End/Playhouse/Empress (1862–1961): 1862 Unknown; 1874 Sellars; 1898 Hope and Maxwell; 1910 W.B. Whitie; 1961 fire; after 1981 **D**
Oxford (1911–   ): 1911 Unknown; n.d. **D**
Palace (1870–1919): 1870 Unknown; 1904 Crewe; 1972 **D**
Queen's/Star/Shakespeare (Watson Street) (1878–1952): 1870 Unknown; n.d. **D**
Royal Coliseum (1836–   ): 1836 Unknown; n.d. **D**
Royalty (c.1870–1953): c.1870 Thompson; 1879 Matcham and Eadie; 1960 **D**
Savoy (1912–   ): 1912 Miller; 1973 **D**

GLOSSOP Derbyshire
Palace (1911–1930s): 1911 Unknown; 1959 **D**
Theatre Royal (c.1896–1920): 1896 Unknown; 1905 rebuilt; after 1920 **D**

GLOUCESTER Gloucestershire
Hippodrome (–   ): n.d. **D**
King's/Alhambra (1860–1907): 1860 Unknown: hall converted to music hall; 1884 Unknown: converted to theatre; 1907 Poole: converted to cinema; 1957 **D**

GOLDTHORPE Doncaster
Hippodrome (–1914) 1914 **D** (fire)

GOOLE East Riding of Yorkshire
Coliseum/Tower (1912–1964): 1912 Unknown; 1938

Unknown: modernised; 1964 converted to bingo; 1995 **D** (fire)
Palace of Varieties (1909–1916): 1909 Unknown; n.d. **D**

GORSEINON Swansea
New Palace (–   ): n.d. **D**

GOSPORT Hampshire
Olympia (1916–1935): 1916 Unknown; 1942 bombed

GRANGE VILLA Durham
Coronation Pavilion (1911–1959): 1911 Unknown; n.d. **D**

GRANTHAM Lincolnshire
Empire/Royal (1875–1952): 1875 Unknown; 1889 Cogan: rebuilt; 1954 **D**
Granada (1937–1963): 1937 J. Owen Bond; 1988 **D**

GRAVESEND Kent
Grand Theatre (1894–1932): 1894 Unknown; 1955 **D**
Palace/Empire/Super Cinema (1915–1919 and 1930–1932): 1915 Unknown; after 1990 **D**
Pavilion (Wrotham Road) (1879–1895): 1879 Unknown; 1895 whole building moved to Milton Road; 1970s **D**
Rosherville Gardens (1837–c.1912) containing:
   Baronial Hall (1840-late 1850s): 1940 Unknown; c.1926 **D**
   Drawing Room Theatre (1857-1866): c.1857 Unknown; n.d. **D**
   Bijou Theatre (1866–c.1900): 1866 Unknown; 1903 converted to restaurant; c.1926 **D**
   Café Chantant/Open Air Theatre/Orchestra (1857-c.1912): 1857 stage only; 1874 Unknown: converted to Café Chantant; c.1912 **D**

GREAT HARWOOD Lancashire
Grand Theatre (–   ): n.d **D**

GREAT HUCKLOW Derbyshire
Playhouse (1928–1972): 1928 Unknown; n.d. **D**

GREENOCK Inverclyde
Alexandra (1905–1928): 1905 Boston, Menzies, Morton and Cullen; 1973 **D**
Empire (c.1906–c.1970): c.1906 Unknown; c.1970 **D**
Hippodrome/Theatre Royal (1858–c.1930) 1858 Unknown; c.1930 **D**

GRIMSBY North East Lincolnshire
Empire Theatre (1893–1906): 1893 Unknown; n.d. **D**
Hippodrome (1895–1905): 1895 Unknown; 1922 **D** (fire)
Palace (1904–1931 and 1943–1955): 1904 Owen and Ward; 1979 **D**
Prince of Wales (1886–1936): 1886 Farebrother; 1936 **D**
Theatre Royal (1865–1904): 1865 Unknown; after 1964 **D**
Theatre of Varieties (1883–   ): 1883 Unknown; n.d. **D**
Tivoli (1905–1909 and 1914–1943): 1905 Unknown; 1943 bombed; 1955 **D**

HADFIELD Derbyshire
Woolley Bridge Palace (1911–1929): 1911 Unknown; 1930 **D** (fire)

HALIFAX Calderdale (West Yorkshire)
Gaiety (?   –c.1888): 1888 **D** for site of Grand

Grand (1889–1924): 1889 Matcham; 1958 **D**
Palace (1903–1958): 1903 Runtz and Ford; 1906 Horsfall and Sims; 1958 **D**
People's Palace (1900–1959): 1900 Unknown; 1963 **D**

HAMILTON South Lanarkshire
Hippodrome (1907–1946): 1907 Unknown; 1947 **D** (fire)
Playhouse (1882–1947): 1882 Downie; before 1976 **D**
Victoria Music Hall (1881–   ): 1881 Unknown; n.d. **D**

HARROGATE North Yorkshire
St James's (1882–1959): 1882 Unknown; n.d. **D**
Swan Hotel Theatre (–   ): n.d. **D**
Town Hall Theatre (–   ): n.d. **D**

HARTLEPOOL
Alexandra Music Hall/People's Music Hall (1866–1871?): 1866 W. Harrison; n.d. **D**
Alhambra Palace of Varieties/Alhambra Theatre and Opera House (1890–1926): 1890 Knill-Freeman and Robins; 1896 Milburn: alterations; 1899 Hope and Maxwell: alterations; n.d. **D**
Empire/Empire Variety (1909–1956): 1909 Milburn; 1956 converted to cinema; 1958 **D**
New Theatre Royal (1868–1957): 1867 William Harrison; 1871 Unknown: converted to music hall; 1904 Unknown: refurbished; 1913 F.W. Turner: alterations to circle; 1968 **D**
Theatre Royal (i) (1854–c.1922): 1854 Unknown; 1899 W. McDonald: alterations; 1910 R.C. Stansfield: alterations; 1921 Kitching, Lee and Aitchinson: alterations; 1969 **D**
Victoria Music Hall (c.1859–1900): c.1859 Unknown; 1863 T. Moore and Sons: alterations; c.1900 **D**

HARWICH Essex
Alexandra (1946–   ): 1946 Unknown; n.d. **D**
Cliff Pavilion (c.1910–1973): c.1910 Unknown; 1973 **D**

HASTINGS East Sussex
Pier Pavilion (1881–1939): 1881 Unknown; 1951 **D**
Royal Opera House (St Leonards) (1897–1921): 1897 Briggs; 1942 bombed

HEANOR Derbyshire
Empire Palace (1911–1983): 1911 Unknown; 1989 **D**

HEBBURN ON TYNE South Tyneside
Grand Theatre (1897–1913): 1897 Simpson; 1950 **D** (fire)

HEDNESFORD Staffordshire
Empire (1911–1914): 1911 Unknown; c.1963 **D**

HEREFORD Herefordshire
Alhambra (fl 1860s): 1936 **D**
Garrick/Athenaeum (1880–1939): 1880 opened as Forrester's Hall; 1890 Unknown: converted from drill hall; 1895 reopened as Athenaeum; 1939 became ARP HQ; 1978 **D**
Kemble (1911–1939): 1861 W. Stanton: as Corn Exchange; 1911 Groome and Betterton: conversion to theatre; 1927 W.W. Robinson: new roof; 1963 **D**

HERNE BAY Kent
Pier Pavilion (1910–1978): 1910 Unknown; 1928 **D** (fire)
Town Hall Theatre (1859–1925): 1859 Welby; 1925 **D** (fire)

HIGH WYCOMBE Buckinghamshire
Grand (1913–1962): 1913 T. Thurlow; 1962 fragmental remains in retail store
Intimate (1947–1957): 1947 converted from skating rink; 1957 closed; 1984 fragmental remains in offices
Majestic/Odeon (1930–1969): 1930 S.B. Pritlove; 1944 Odeon; 1969 **D**
Palace (i) (1909–1912): 1909 Unknown: conversion; 1912 fire; after 1912 **D**
Palace (ii) (1922–1983): 1922 Gilbert Booth; 1985 **D**

HINCKLEY Leicestershire
Royal (1896–1898): 1896 Unknown; 1898 **D** (temporary building)

HORSHAM (West Sussex)
Capitol (i) (1923–1983): 1923 Goodman and Kay; 1983 **D**

HOUGHTON-LE-SPRING Sunderland
Gaiety Theatre (1911–1929): 1911 J. Davenport; 1929 **D**

HOYLAKE Wirral
Lighthouse Pavilion/Winter Gardens (1911–1922 and 1927–1972?): 1865 built as lighthouse/custom house; 1911 Unknown: converted to theatre; 1933 Unknown: fly tower built; 1999 **D**

HUCKNALL Nottinghamshire
Theatre Royal (1901–1904): 1901 T.V. Woodhouse; n.d. **D**

HUDDERSFIELD Kirklees (West Yorkshire)
Empire (1881–1904): 1881 Unknown; c.1904 **D**
Palace Theatre (1909–1936): 1909 Horsfall and Sons; 1936 **D** (fire)
Theatre Royal (1881–1961): 1881 Entwistle; 1961 **D**

HULL
Alexandra Theatre (1902–1941): 1902 Guest; 1941 bombed
Empire Palace (1897–1939): 1897 Matcham; 1939 bombed
Grand Theatre and Opera House (1893–1935): 1893 Matcham; c.1990 **D**
Hippodrome (c.1895–1913): c.1895 Unknown; 1941 bombed
Palace Theatre (–   ): n.d. **D**
Theatre Royal (–   ): n.d. **D**
Tivoli (–   ): n.d. Smith; 1959 **D**

HUNSTANTON Norfolk
Pier Pavilion (1871–1939): 1871 Wilson; 1939 **D** (fire)

ILFRACOMBE Devon
Pavilion/Victoria Pavilion (1888–1980s): 1888 W.H. Gould; 1915 F.G.M. Chancellor; 1987 **D**

ILKESTON Derbyshire
New Theatre/Royal (1895–1929): 1895 W. Dymock Pratt; 1910 H.S. Hearn; 1990 **D**; fragment remains
Queen's Palace of Varieties (1889–1906): 1889 Unknown; n.d. **D**

ILKLEY Bradford
Bridge Pleasure Gardens Pavilion (–   ): n.d. **D**

INVERNESS Highland
Music Hall (1899–   ): 1899 Reeves and Marbett; n.d. **D**
Theatre Royal (1882–1931): 1882 Unknown; n.d. **D**

IPSWICH Suffolk
Hippodrome (1905–1964): 1905 Matcham; 1984 **D**
Lyceum (1891–1936): 1891 Emden; 1936 **D**

JARROW South Tyneside
Circus of Varieties/Rowland's/Palace Theatre (1889–1915): 1889 Henry Mortimer; 1912 rebuilt after fire; after 1915 **D**
Empire (1912–1977): 1912 Unknown; n.d. **D**
Royal Albert Hall (1883–1910): 1882 Dunn and Hanson; after 1910 **D**
Theatre Royal (1866–1941?) 1866 Unknown; 1894 A.P. Farthing: alterations; 1898 J. Henderson and J. Hall: alterations; 1962 **D**

KEIGHLEY Bradford
Britannia Music Hall (1870–1910): 1870 Unknown: conversion to music hall; after 1974 **D**
Hippodrome (1909–1961): 1909 Unknown; 1961 **D**
Queen's Theatre (1889–1956): 1889 Bailey; 1910 Matcham; 1961 **D**

KENDAL Cumbria
St George's Theatre (1880–c.1930): 1879 John Thompson; 1930s foyer remodelled; 1988 fragmental remains

KETTERING Northamptonshire
Avenue Theatre (1903–1937): 1903 Payne; n.d. **D** (fire)
Victoria Theatre (1888–1933): 1888 Gotch and Saunders; 1936 Unknown: conversion to Odeon; 1970 **D**

KIDDERMINSTER Worcestershire
Alhambra (1868–1870): 1868 Unknown; n.d. **D**
New Theatre (1836–1837): 1836 Unknown; n.d. **D**
Opera House/Playhouse (1903–1968): 1903 Owen and Ward; 1911 Unknown: refurbishment; 1946 W.A. Greenway: refurbishment; 1969 **D**
Royal Oxford Amphitheatre (1868–1876/7): 1868 Unknown: as circus; n.d. **D**
Theatre Royal (i)/Eagle (1867–1870): 1867 Unknown; n.d. **D**
Theatre Royal (ii) (1891–1899): 1891 T. White; 1903 dismantled and re-erected in Cannock

KILMARNOCK East Ayrshire
Opera House (1875–   ): 1875 Ingram; n.d. fragmental remains

KIRKCALDY Fife
Palace (1913–1928): 1913 J.D. Swanston; 1946 **D**

LANCASTER Lancashire
Palace of Varieties (1896–1907): 1896 Unknown; 1907 **D** (fire)

LEAMINGTON SPA Warwickshire
Colonnade (1913–1927): 1913 Unknown; 1978 **D** (fire)
Opera House and Theatre Royal (1882–1935): 1882 Phipps, with Osborne and Reading; 1935 **D** and rebuilt as cinema; 1984 cinema **D**

LEEDS
Empire Palace (1898–1961): 1898 Matcham; 1961 **D**
Hippodrome/Tivoli (1864–1933): 1906 Winn; n.d. **D**
Queen's Theatre (1899–1923): 1899 Hope and Maxwell; n.d. **D**
Theatre Royal (1876–1957): 1876 Moore and Sons; 1957 **D**

LEE-ON-SOLENT Hampshire
Pier Theatre (1885–   ): 1885 Galbraith and Church; 1958 **D**

LEICESTER
Alhambra (1862–1869): 1862 Unknown; after 1869 **D**
Athenaeum (–1908): 1908 **D** (fire)
City of Leicester Working Men's Club and Concert Hall (c.1862–c.1985): c.1862 A. Wakely; 1929 N. Reid; c.1989 **D**
Palace (1901–1959): 1901 Matcham; 1912 Matcham; 1960 **D**
Pavilion Music Hall (1890–1929): 1890 Unknown; 1929 **D**
Royal Opera House (1877–1960): 1877 Phipps; 1960 **D**
Trocadero (1931–1963): 1931 Unknown; 1967 **D**

LICHFIELD Staffordshire
David Garrick (1872–c.1970): 1872 Unknown; c.1988 **D**

LINCOLN Lincolnshire
ABC (1936–1971): 1936 W.R. Glen; 1990 **D**
Alhambra (c.1862–1870): c.1862 Unknown; n.d. **D**
Palace/Empire (1887–1930): 1881 Watkins ; 1887 adapted from Masonic Hall; 1901 Mortimer; 1943 bombed; 1953 **D**
Pavilion/Ginnett's Circus (1878–1883): 1878 Unknown; 1883 **D**

LIVERPOOL
Apollo (1909–1923): 1890s Unknown: as hall; 1909 converted to theatre from County Hall; 1923 reverted to County Hall use; 1941 bombed
Bijou Opera House/Dr Tom's Chapel (1851–1891): 1851 Unknown; 1937 **D**
Coliseum (1909–1941): 1909 Sutton; 1941 bombed
David Lewis Theatre (1906–1977): 1906 Unknown; 1940 Garrison Theatre; 1980 **D**
Haymarket Theatre (1882–1910): 1882 Unknown; n.d. **D**
Kelly's/Royal Colosseum (1850–1916): 1850 Unknown: converted from chapel to music hall; 1904 Unknown: reconstructed; 1941 **D**
Liver (pre-1843–1850): 1843 Unknown; c.1850 **D**
Lyric Theatre (1897–1932): 1897 Unknown; 1940 bombed; 1974 last fragment **D**
Metropole (Bootle) (1911–1941): 1911 Unknown; 1941 bombed; n.d. **D**
New Parthenon (1880–1907): 1880 Unknown; 1962 **D**
Paddington Palace/Coliseum (1890–c.1910): 1890 Unknown; 1990 **D**
Park Palace (1893–1920): 1893 J.H. Havelock-Sutton; 1911 converted to ciné-variety use; 1990 **D**
Parthenon (Moderne) (1845–1908): 1845 Unknown; 1940 **D**
Pavilion (1908–1961): 1908 Alley; 1933 Unknown: refurbishment; 1960 Unknown: stage extended; 1961 Unknown: converted to bingo; 1986 fire (fragmental remains)
Pembroke Music Hall (1874–1907): 1874 Unknown; n.d. **D**
Prince of Wales (Clayton Square) (1861–1896 and 1901–1905):1861 Solomon: conversion of Clayton House; 1912 **D**
Roscommon/Kings (1892–1912): 1892 Unknown; 1915 Unknown: alterations for cinema; 1941 bombed; after 1958 **D**

Rotunda (1860–1930): 1860 Unknown; 1878 Phipps and Davis and Sons; 1941 bombed
Royal Court (i) (1881–1933): 1881 Summers; 1891 Kirby; 1933 **D** (fire)
Royal Hippodrome/Hengler's (1878–1970): 1878 Robinson; 1902 Crewe; 1984 **D**
Royal Muncaster/New Prince's (1890–1921): 1890 H. Pennington; 1964 **D**
Sefton/Royal Sefton (1875–1910): n.d. **D**
Shakespeare (1888–1976): 1888 Ellis Brammall Jr; 1976 **D** (fire)
Stanhope (1894–1906): 1894 converted from chapel; after 1906 **D**
Tivoli Palace (1897–1910): 1906 Crewe; 1978 **D**
Theatre Royal (Breck Road) (1888–): 1888 Unknown; n.d. **D**
Theatre Royal (Garston) (1892–1908): 1892 Unknown; 1908 **D**
Westminster Music Hall (1887–c.1920): 1887 Unknown: conversion; 1941 bombed and **D**

LLANDUDNO Conwy
Astra (–1989): 1989 **D**
Pier Pavilion (1883–1985): 1882 Nelson; 1994 **D**

LLANELLI Carmarthenshire
Royalty/Haggar's/Hippodrome (1892–): 1892 T.P. Martin; 1905 Llewellyn Reeves; 1977 **D**
Vint's Electric Palace (1911–): 1911 W. Bickers; 1973 **D** (fire)

LONDON
Albert Palace (1884–1888): 1884 F. and H. Francis (using shell of 1872 Dublin Exhibition); c.1893 **D**
Albert Palace, Café Chantant (1886–1888): 1886 Frank Matcham; c.1893 **D**
Alhambra Palace (1858–1936): 1854 T. Hayter Lewis: as Panopticon; 1858 Lewis: converted to circus; 1864 J.H. Rowley: converted to music hall; 1866 Rowley; 1881 Perry and Reed; 1883 Perry and Reed: rebuilt after fire; 1888 Edward Clark; 1892 Clark and Pollard; 1897 W.M. Bruton; 1912 Frank Matcham; 1936 **D**; replaced by Odeon Cinema
Alexandra (1897–1950): 1897 Frank Matcham; 1950 **D**
Astleys/Royal Grove/Royal Amphitheatre/Sanger's (1769-1893): 1768 (at Halfpenny Hatch, uncovered area) 1769 (at Westminster Bridge, uncovered area); 1778–9 Unknown: roofed over; 1784 Unknown: roofed circus with stage; 1795 Unknown: rebuilt after fire; 1804 Unknown: rebuilt after another fire; c.1831 Unknown: again rebuilt after fire; 1842 Unknown: rebuilt after fire; 1862 R.W. Griffiths: reconstructed; 1872 J.T. Robinson: reconstructed; 1893 **D**
Bagnigge Wells/Pindar of Wakefield (after 1759–1871): 1759 house and gardens only; after 1759 Unknown: long room built; before 1797 Unknown: long room divided; 1840s Unknown: long room **D**; pub with concert room built; after 1871 **D**
Balham Empire (1900–1909): 1900 Hancock: conversion to theatre; 1974 **D**
Balham Hippodrome (1899–1939): 1899 W.G.R. Sprague; 1960s **D**
Battersea Palace/Washington (1886–1924): 1886 Unknown; 1889 Newton; n.d. **D**
Bedford (before 1840–1959): 1861 Edward Clark; c.1880 Edward Clark; 1898 Bertie Crewe; 1969 **D**
Bohemia (1913–1917): 1913 John Taylor; 1994 **D**

Llandudno, Pier Pavilion

Boltons/Paris Pullman (–): 1986 **D**
Borough/Raglan/Salmon (1846–c.1889): 1846 Unknown; 1871 Unknown: rebuilt after fire; 1887 Unknown: again rebuilt after fire; after 1889 **D**
Bow Palace/Eastern Empire/Palace (1855–1923): 1855 Unknown; 1892 Unknown; 1960 **D**
Bower Saloon/New Stangate (1838–1877): 1838 Unknown; 1875 Philip Phillips; after c.1879 **D**
Britannia, Hoxton (1841–1923): 1841 Sam Lane?: saloon theatre; 1850 Warton; 1858 Finch Hill and Paraire: new theatre; 1940 bomb damaged and **D**
Brixton Theatre (1896–1940): 1896 Frank Matcham; 1940 bomb damaged and **D**
Broadway/Kilburn Empire/Essoldo (1908–1928): 1906 Hingston ; 1908 W.G.R. Sprague: new interior; 1994 **D**
Bycullah Athenaeum (1883–1931): 1883 Unknown; 1931 **D** (fire)
Camberwell Empire/Metropole (1894–1924): 1894 Crewe and Sprague; 1937 **D**
Camberwell Palace (1899–1950s): 1899 E.A.E. Woodrow; 1908 Sharpe; 1955 **D**
Campden House private theatre (1890s): n.d. **D**
Canterbury Hall (1852–1942): 1852 Samuel Field; 1854 Samuel Field: rebuilt; 1858 Samuel Field: enlarged; 1876 E. Bridgman: extensively altered; 1890 Frank Matcham: reconstructed; 1902 Wylson and Long: altered; 1942 bomb damaged ; c.1955 remains **D**
Chelsea Palace (1903–1957): 1903 Wylson and Long; 1957 **D**
Chiswick Empire (1912–1959): 1912 Frank Matcham; 1959 **D**
City of London Theatre (1835–1871): 1835 Sam Beazley; 1871 **D** (Great Central Hall built on site)
Clapton Park/Hackney Theatre (1872–1884): 1872 J.T. Robinson; n.d. **D**
Coal Hole/Wolf Club (c.1815–1862): c.1820 Unknown: concert room; n.d. **D** (site taken in by Terry's Theatre)
Colosseum, Regents Park (1826–1875): 1826 Unknown; n.d. **D**
Cosmotheka/Cosmotheca (1857–1869): 1857 Unknown; after 1876 **D**
Cottrell's Palace (c.1905–1908): 1905 Unknown; 1911 **D**; replaced by cinema
Cremorne Gardens (1840s–1877): 1840s and later Unknown: theatre, circus, dancing platform, etc. built; after 1878 **D**
Cripplegate (c.1896–1931): 1896 Unknown; n.d. **D**
Crouch End Hippodrome/Queen's Hall/Opera House (1896–c.1915): 1896 E. Edmondson: as a public hall; c.1896/7 Frank Matcham: converted to opera house; 1940s bomb damaged and **D**, apart from stage walls

Croydon Grand (1896–1959): 1896 Brough; 1959 **D**

Croydon Hippodrome/Empire Theatre of Varieties/ New Theatre Royal (1800–1930s): 1800 Unknown; 1867 Unknown; 1898 Unknown: new theatre; 1956 **D**

Croydon National Palace of Varieties/North End Circus/Palace/Empire (1895–1953): 1895 Unknown; after 1959 **D**

Crystal Palace Theatre (c.1890–1900): c.1890 Walter Emden; 1936 **D**

Cyder Cellars/Adelphi Club (before 1750–1862): 1834 Sabine: new concert room; 1847 Unknown: improvements; 1940s bomb damaged and **D**

Daly's (1893–1937): 1893 Spencer Chadwick, with C.J. Phipps; 1937 **D**; replaced by Warner Cinema

Davis Theatre (1920s–   ): n.d. **D**

Deacon's/Sir Hugh Myddelton (1830s–c.1890): 1830s crib and long room in pub; 1861 Unknown: new music hall; 1891 **D**

Deptford Broadway (1897–1911): 1897 W.G.R. Sprague; c.1960 **D**

Drill Hall (1870s–1908): 1862 Tupper; 1870s Unknown: converted to theatre; 1909 **D**

Duke of Connaught Coffee Tavern/Smith's Empire/ Palace (1881–after 1900): 1881 W. Rickwood; mid 1980s **D**

Ealing Hippodrome/Ealing Theatre/Lyric Palladium (1899–1958): 1899 Unknown; 1906 Crewe?; 1958 **D**

East Ham Palace (1906–late 1940s): 1906 Wylson and Long; 1958 **D**

East London/Royalty/Royal Brunswick (1787–1828): 1787 Unknown; 1828 Stedman Whitwell: new theatre, following fire; 1828 collapsed and **D** (see Royal Brunswick in gazetteer for extant relics)

Edinboro' Castle (c.1839–c.1872): 1849 James Mullett?: new music hall; after 1873 **D**

Edmonton Empire (1908–1933): 1908 Unknown; 1970 **D**

Edmonton New (?–1910): 1947 **D**

Effingham Saloon/East London/Wonderland/Rivoli (before 1840–1897): before 1840 Unknown; 1846 Palmer (builder): substantial alterations; 1852 J. Hudson: enlargement of gallery; 1854 W. Finch Hill: unexecuted design; 1855 W.J. Lucas: alterations; 1867 John Hudson: largely rebuilt theatre; 1880 Unknown: rebuilt after fire; 1897 **D**; after 1945? cinema on site, **D**

Elephant and Castle (1872–1928): 1872 Dean and Matthews; 1879 J.T. Robinson and Frank Matcham; 1882 Frank Matcham; 1928 **D**; replaced by cinema

Empress, Brixton (1898–1956): 1898 Wylson and Long; 1931 Unknown: radical reconstruction; 1956 David Nye: conversion to cinema; 1993 **D**

London, Fulham Grand (Eric Krieger Collection)

Euston Music Hall/Frampton's/Lord Nelson (1852–1862): 1852 Unknown; 1887 **D**

Euston Palace/Regent/Century (1901–?1940s): 1901 Wylson and Long (with Crewe); 1906 Wylson and Long: alterations; c.1960 **D**

Finsbury Park Empire (1910–1960): 1910 Frank Matcham; 1965 **D**

Forester's Music Hall (before 1870–1917): 1889 Edward Clark; c.1964 **D**

Fulham Grand (1897–c.1950): 1897 W.G.R. Sprague; 1958 **D**

Gables/Hillcroft Theatre (1882–1937): 1882 Alfred Cooper; 1937 **D**

Gaiety (i) (1864–1903): 1864 Bassett-Keeling: as Strand Musick Hall; 1868 C.J. Phipps; 1903 **D**

Gaiety (ii) (1903–1939): 1903 Runtz and Ford, with consultant R. Norman Shaw; 1957 **D**

Gate (i), Floral Street (1925–1926): 1925 Unknown: conversion of warehouse

Gate (ii), Villiers Street (1927–1940): 1927 Unknown, conversion of part of Gatti's Arches and building in forecourt; late 1980s **D**

Gatti's Arches/Players (1867–1910 and 1946–1987): 1867 Unknown conversion of railway arch; 1946 Unknown: reconversion to music hall; late 1980s **D**

Gatti's Palace/Gatti's-in-the-Road (1865–1924): 1865 Bolton?; 1883 Bolton; 1950 **D**

Garrick/Albert, Leman Street (1831–c.1881): 1831 Unknown; 1853 Unknown: rebuilt after fire; 1873 Unknown; 1879 Unknown; after c.1881 **D**

Globe, Strand and Wych Street (1868–1902): 1868 S. Simpson (also attributed to Sefton Parry); 1870 Walter Emden; 1902 **D**

Granville, Walham Green (1898–1956): 1898 Frank Matcham; 1971 **D**

Grecian/Eagle (before 1831–1879): before 1831 Unknown: a large room; c.1832 Unknown: saloon theatre built in pleasure garden; 1841 J.T. Robinson: new theatre; 1877 Unknown: rebuilt; 1899 **D**

Green Dragon Music Hall (1848–1903): 1848 Unknown; n.d. **D**

Greenwich Theatre Royal/Prince of Wales/Morton's (1864–1910): 1864 Noble; 1937 **D**

Hammersmith Palace (1880–1944): 1880 Unknown; 1898 Bruton; 1910 Frank Matcham; n.d. **D**

Harrow Coliseum (   ): n.d. **D**

Highbury Barn/Alexandra/Willoughby's Tea Gardens (C17–1871): after 1785 Unknown: Highbury Farm barn fitted out as a Great Room; before 1835 Unknown: long room built; 1858 Unknown: dancing platform built; 1862 Unknown: new music hall built; 1865 Unknown: music hall converted to theatre; by 1883 **D**

Holborn Empire/Royal/Weston's Music Hall (1857–1941): 1857 Finch Hill and Paraire; 1887 Lander and Bedells; 1897 E. Runtz; 1906 Frank Matcham; 1941 bombed; 1961 **D**

Holborn Theatre Royal (1866–1880): 1866 Finch Hill and Paraire; 1869 Unknown: alterations; 1880–81 **D**

Holloway Empire (1899–1924): 1899 W.G.R. Sprague; 1901 Frank Matcham; c.1976 **D**

Hounslow Empire (1912–1954): 1912 Unknown; 1954 **D**

Ilford Hippodrome (1909–1941): 1909 Frank Matcham; 1941 bombed and **D**

Imperial (i) (1876–1906): 1876 A. Bedborough; 1898 Walter Emden; 1901 Frank Verity: rebuilt interior; 1906 **D**: see Imperial (ii)

Imperial (ii)/Imperial Palace (1909–1931): 1909 Imperial (i) dismantled and moved to Canning Town; 1931 **D** (fire); replaced by cinema

Islington Empire/Philharmonic Hall (1860–1932): 1860 Finch Hill and Paraire; 1870 Finch Hill and Paraire; 1874 Finch Hill and Paraire; 1883 Frank Matcham; 1888 Frank Matcham; 1901 Frank Matcham; c.1962 **D**; 1981 facade **D**

Islington Palace/St Mary's Hall/Mohawks/Blue Hall (in Royal Agricultural Hall) (1869–c.1900): c.1869 probably F. Peck; after 1982 **D**

Karsino, Eel Pie Island (1913–1928): 1913 Frank Matcham; 1971 **D**

Kennington Theatre (1898–1949): 1898 W.G.R. Sprague; 1949 **D**

Kilburn Empire/Carlton/Plaza (1908–   ): 1908 W.G.R. Sprague; 1994 **D**

Kilburn Palace (1886–1909): 1886 Fayer?; 1899 Palgrave, with Wylson and Long; n.d. **D**

King's, Hammersmith (1902–1955): 1902 W.G.R. Sprague; 1963 **D**

Kingsway/Novelty/Folies Dramatiques/Great Queen St Theatre (1882–1940): 1882 T. Verity; 1900 Murray and Foster; 1907 Walker and Foster; 1941 bombed; 1959 **D**

Knightsbridge Hall/Humphrey's Hall/Japanese Village (1883–1890 and 1893–1897): 1883 Unknown; 1890 incorporated Sun Music Hall qv

Lewisham Hippodrome (1911–1950s): 1911 Frank Matcham; 1961 **D**

Little Theatre, Adelphi (1910–1941): 1910 Hayward and Maynard: theatre built within former bank; 1912 Unknown: balcony added; 1920 Hayward and Maynard: rebuilt after bomb damage during First World War; 1941 again bomb damaged; 1949 **D**

Lord Raglan/Raglan Music Hall (1855–1877): 1855 Unknown; 1878 **D**

Lyric Opera House/Lyric Hall (1888–1965): 1888 Isaac Mason: a hall; 1890 F.H. Francis; 1895 Frank Matcham: new theatre behind facade; 1972 **D** (*see* gazetteer entry for Lyric, Hammersmith)

Marlborough Theatre (1903–1919): 1903 Frank Matcham; 1962 **D**

Marylebone Music Hall/Rose of Normandy (1856–c.1900): 1856 Unknown; after 1900 **D**

Metropolitan (c.1836–1962): 1862 Edward Clark: new hall; 1880s Walter Emden: alterations; 1897 Frank Matcham; 1905 Frank Matcham; 1963 **D**

Mile End Empire/Lusby's/Paragon (before 1848–1933): 1885 Frank Matcham: rebuilt; 1937 **D**

Mulberry Music Hall (1865–1903): 1865 Unknown; c.1971 **D**

Music Hall in Cadets' Quarters, Royal Arsenal (1850s/60s): 1850s/60s Unknown; 1970s **D**

New Cross Empire (1899–c.1950/53): 1899 Frank Matcham; 1950s **D**

Odeon/Capitol (1931–1972): 1931 Bertie Crewe; 1982 **D**

Offley's (1830s–1860s): n.d. **D**

Olympic/Royal Olympic (1806–1899): 1806 Unknown: as Olympic Pavilion, a circus; 1811 Unknown: alterations; 1813 Unknown: conversion to theatre; 1818 Lethebridge; 1849 F.W. Bushill: new theatre after fire; 1883 C.J. Phipps; 1890 Crewe and Sprague: rebuilt; 1905 **D**

Opera Comique (1870–1899): 1870 F.H. Fowler; 1876 Unknown: alterations; 1895 Fowler and Hall; 1902 **D**

Oxford Music Hall (1861–1926): 1861 Finch Hill and Paraire; 1869 Finch Hill and Paraire: reinstated after fire; 1873

Edward Paraire: reinstated after fire; 1893 Wylson and Long: rebuilt as theatre; 1926 **D**

Paddy's Goose/White Swan (c.1851–1886): 1851 or earlier Unknown; 1953 **D**

Palace of Varieties, Stonebridge Park (1907–c.1910): 1907 M.T. Saunders; after 1982 **D**

Palaseum (1912 only): 1912 George Billings, Wright and Co.; 1990s **D**

Pantheon/King's Theatre (1772–1814): 1772 James Wyatt: as assembly room; 1791 James Wyatt: converted to opera house; 1791 Crispus Claggett: reconstructed after fire, as concert room; 1812 Nicholas Cundy: conversion to theatre; 1812 John Nash and James Wyatt: repairs; 1813 Nicholas Cundy: reconstructed after fire as opera house; 1834 Sydney Smirke: enlarged and converted to bazaar; 1937 **D**

Park/Alexandra, Camden Town (1873–1890): 1873 J.T. Robinson; after 1890 **D**

Park Hall, Hanwell (c.1890–c.1914): c.1890 Unknown; after 1982 **D**

Parkhurst (1890–1909): 1890 Driver and Perfect; n.d. **D**

Pavilion, Whitechapel (1828–1934): 1828 Unknown; 1856 Simmonds; 1874 J.T. Robinson; 1894 Runtz (with Phipps?); 1940s bomb damaged; 1962 **D**

Peckham Hippodrome (1898–1912): 1898 Ernest Runtz; 1930s **D**; cinema on site

Penge Empire (1915–   ): 1915 W.G.R. Sprague; n.d. **D**

Poplar Hippodrome/New Prince's (1905–c.1925): 1905 Owen and Ward; 1926 Unknown: altered to cinema; c.1950 **D**

Princess's (1840–1902): 1840 T. Marsh Nelson: converted from bazaar; 1842 Unknown: remodelled; 1880 C.J. Phipps; 1931 **D**

Putney Hippodrome (1906–1924): 1906 Hingston; 1975 **D**

Q Theatre (1924–1956): 1924 Unknown: conversion; after 1956 **D**

Queen's, Long Acre (1850–1878): 1850–3 Unknown: as St Martin's Hall for concerts; 1867 C.J. Phipps: theatre built within existing shell; 1879 Unknown: gutted; 1970s last fragments **D**

Queen's Hall/Pictorial Hall 1900–1938): 1900 Unknown; 1986 **D**

Queen's, Hornchurch (1953–1975): 1913 Unknown: built as cinema; 1953 Unknown: converted to theatre; 1976 **D**

Queen's Poplar/Oriental (1865–c.1958): 1865 Unknown; 1867 J.H. Good; 1873 J.T. Robinson: new music hall; 1898 Bertie Crewe; 1922 Bertie Crewe; 1937 Thomas Braddock; 1964 **D**

Railway Tavern, Plumstead (c.1867–1950s): c.1867 probably J.O. Cook: hall at rear of pub; mid 1980s **D**

Regent, Euston/Euston Theatre (1900–c.1932): 1900 Wylson and Long, with Bertie Crewe; 1971 **D**

Regent Music Hall (1861–1879): 1861 Unknown: concert room; 1864 H.S. Ridley: new music hall; after 1879 **D**

Romford Empire (   ): n.d. **D**

Rosemary Branch/Peckham Theatre of Varieties/Lovejoy's (1849–1897): 1849 Unknown; 1890s Unknown: rebuilt; after 1897 **D**; pub remains

Rotherhithe Hippodrome/Terriss's (1889–1940s): 1899 W.G.R. Sprague; c.1950s **D**

Rotunda (1826–c.1885): 1789 Unknown: as a museum; 1806 Unknown: as a lecture theatre; 1826 Unknown: converted to entertainment house; 1940s bomb damaged; after 1951 **D**

Royal Amphitheatre/Alcazar, Holborn (1867–1886): 1867 T. Smith: as a circus; 1873 Unknown: converted to theatre; 1941 bombed and **D**

London, St James's

Royal Artillery Theatre/Garrison Theatre (1863–c.1956): 1863 Noble: converted hall of 1782 by James Wyatt; 1904 Sprague: new interior; after 1956 **D**

Royal Cambridge Music Hall (1864–c.1924): 1864 W. Finch Hill; 1878 J.T. Robinson; 1885 Clarke; 1898 H. Percival; 1936 **D**

Royal County (1897–1912): 1897 J.C. Bourne; 1940 **D**

Royal Pavilion/Royal Victoria Garden/North Woolwich Gardens (1851–1890): 1851 Unknown: hotel and gardens; before 1888 Unknown: concert room, etc.; after 1890 garden buildings **D**

Royal Strand (1832–1905): 1832 Charles Broad: conversion from panorama; 1836 Unknown: enlarged; 1858 S. Reynolds and Samuel Field; 1865 John Ellis; 1882 C.J. Phipps; 1905 **D**

Royal Victor (1867–1903): 1867 Unknown; 1890 Unknown: reconstructed; after 1982 **D**

Royalty/Miss Kelly's, Soho (1840–1938): 1840 Sam Beazley; 1861 Bulot; 1883 Thomas Verity; 1895 William Emden; 1906 Smee and Cobay; 1911 Gissing; 1953 **D**

Ruby Cinema/Imperial/Munts's Hall/Grand Hall (c.1890–1900): c.1890 Unknown: a concert hall; c.1898 Unknown: converted to a music hall; 1985/6 **D**

St George's Hall (1867–1940): 1867 J. Taylor; 1881 Tasker; 1905 Unknown: alterations; 1941 bombed and **D**

St Helena Gardens, Rotherhithe (1770–1878): before 1855 Unknown: long room/music hall built; 1874 Unknown: orchestra and dancing platform added; by 1881 **D**

St James's Theatre (1835–1957): 1835 Sam Beazley; 1869 James Mackintosh; 1879 T. Verity; 1900 A.B. Jackson and J. Emblin-Walker, with Percy Macquoid; 1957 **D**

St Leonard's Hall/Harwood's (i) (c.1852–1870): c.1852 Unknown; 1870 **D**

Sans Souci (i), Strand (1791–1796): after 1796 **D**

Sans Souci (ii), Leicester Place (1797–1835): 1797 William Brooks (builder); 1898 **D**

Scala/Tottenham/Regency/Prince of Wales (1810–1886 and 1904–1969): 1810 Unknown: conversion of concert rooms; 1865 Unknown; 1904 Frank Verity: rebuilt; 1969 **D**

Sebright (1865–1910): 1865 Unknown; 1885 Buckle; 1938 **D**

Shaftesbury (i) (1888–1940): 1888 C.J. Phipps; 1941 bombed and **D** (the present Shaftesbury (ii), on another site, was built in 1911 as the Prince's)

Shakespeare (1896–1923): 1896 W.G.R. Sprague; 1956 **D**

Shelley Theatre (private) (1879–): 1879 Joseph Peacock; after 1896 **D**

Shoreditch Empire/London Music Hall/Griffin (1856–1934): 1856 Unknown; 1894 Frank Matcham; 1935 **D**

Shoreditch Olympia/National Standard/Standard (1837–c.1926): 1837 Unknown; 1867 Unknown: rebuilt after fire; 1876 Unknown: possibly C. Fowler; 1889 Bertie Crewe, with W.G.R. Sprague; 1940 bomb damaged and **D**

South London (1860–1941): 1860 Unknown: conversion of a chapel; 1869 W. Paice: new music hall; 1893 Wylson and Long; 1941 bombed; 1955 **D**

Star, Bermondsey (1867–1919): 1867 Unknown; 1883 Snook and Stock; 1963 **D**

Stoll/London Opera House (1911–1957): 1911 Bertie Crewe; 1958 **D**

Stratford Empire (1899–1940): 1899 W.G.R. Sprague; 1940? bombed and **D**

Streatham Grand/Town Hall Theatre (1890–1903): 1890 Hollands; 1940 **D**

Sun Music Hall (1851–1890): 1851 Unknown; 1884 Edward Clark?; 1885 Spencer Chadwick?; 1893 incorporated into Knightsbridge Hall (qv)

Surrey/Royal Circus (1782–1920): 1782 Unknown: circus with stage; 1800 Rudolphe Cabanel: rebuilt after fire; 1806 Rudolphe Cabanel, with James Donaldson Jr: new theatre after fire; 1809 Unknown: auditorium reconstructed; 1810 Unknown: circus elements removed; 1865 John Ellis: rebuilt after fire; 1904 Kirk and Kirk: converted to a music hall; 1934 **D**

Surrey Zoological Gardens Music Hall (1856–1877): 1856 Horace Jones; 1861 rebuilt after fire; 1877 ceased use as theatre and **D**

Swallow Street Music Hall (before 1860–1903): before 1860 Unknown; 1919 **D**

Terry's (1887–1910): 1887 Walter Emden; 1905 Frank Matcham: alterations; 1910 Unknown: conversion to cinema; 1923 **D**

Tivoli (1890–1914): 1890 Walter Emden; 1891 Frank Matcham; 1900 Walter Emden; 1910 Walter Emden; 1922 **D** (replaced by Tivoli Cinema, itself **D** in 1957)

Toole's/Polygraphic Hall/Charing Cross/Folly (1885–1895): 1855 Unknown: converted from Lowther Rooms; 1869 Arthur Evers: reconstructed; 1876 T. Verity; 1882 J.J. Thompson; 1895 C.J. Phipps: unexecuted rebuilding plan; 1896 **D**

Trevor Music Hall (1854–1889): 1854 Unknown; 1875 George Treacher: alterations; after 1889 **D**

Trocadero/Argyll Subscription Rooms (1882–1895 and 1924–1940s): 1822 Unknown: conversion to entertainment house; 1882 Unknown: conversion to music hall; 1924 F.J. Wills: conversion to cabaret; not clear how much fabric now remains

Uxbridge Savoy (1873–1921): n.d. **D**; replaced by cinema

Uxbridge Theatre (1869–c.1878): 1869 Unknown; 1997 **D**

Variety Theatre/Harwood's (ii) (1870–1910): 1870 C.J. Phipps; 1882 J.G. Buckle; 1887 J.G. Buckle; 1902 Wylson and Long; 1909 Bertie Crewe; 1913 Ward and Ward; 1981 **D**

Vauxhall Gardens (C17–1859): 1859 **D**

Walthamstow King's ( ): n.d. **D**

Walthamstow Palace (1903–1954): 1903 Wylson and Long; 1960 **D**

West London/Pavilion/Marylebone (1832–1912): 1832 Unknown; 1837 Unknown: improvements; 1838 Unknown; 1842 Unknown: enlarged; 1845 Unknown: enlarged; 1868 Unknown; 1883 T. Verity: alterations; 1912 cinema; 1941 bombed; 1974 **D**

White House Theatre (private) (–): n.d. **D**

Willesden Empire proposed 1906 but never built

Willesden Hippodrome (1907–1927): 1907 Frank Matcham; 1940 bomb damaged; 1957 **D**
Winchester/Surrey Music Hall/Grapes/British Saloon/ Grand Harmonic Hall (1840–1878): 1840 Unknown: a concert room; 1846 A.J. Hiscocks: new music hall; 1878 Unknown: alterations; after 1882 **D**; pub remains
Winter Garden/Middlesex/Great Mogul's Head/ Mogul Saloon (c.1836–1960): before 1836 a room in the pub; c.1836 Unknown: new concert room; 1847 Unknown: rebuilt; 1872 Unknown; 1880 Wright; 1891 Unknown; 1911 Frank Matcham: new theatre; 1965 **D**: New London on site
Woolwich Empire/West Kent/Woolwich Theatre Royal/Barnard's (1835–1960): 1835 (a portable theatre); 1836 Unknown: permanent theatre; 1880s J.O. Cook?; 1892 Edward Clark; 1900 Frank Matcham; 1960 **D**
Woolwich Hippodrome (1900–1923): 1900 Bertie Crewe; 1939 **D**; replaced later by cinema
Yorkshire Stingo/Albion Saloon (c.1835–1855): c.1835 Unknown; after 1855 **D**

LONG EATON Derbyshire
Palace (1897–   ): 1897 Unknown; n.d. **D**

LOUGHBOROUGH Leicestershire
New (1896–1901): 1896 Unknown; 1901 **D** (fire)
Theatre Royal/Hippodrome (1905–1953): 1904 Albert E. King; 1972 **D**

LOWESTOFT Suffolk
Hippodrome (1904–1999): 1904 R.S. Cockrill: as circus; 1947 Brown and March: converted to theatre; 1960s Unknown: converted to Bingo; 1999 **D** (fire)
South Pier Pavilion (–   ): n.d. **D**
Sparrow's Nest Theatre (1913–1990): 1913 Unknown; 1991 **D**

LUTON Bedfordshire
Alexandra Theatre (1880–c.1900): 1880 Unknown; 1935 **D**
Grand Theatre (1898–1957): 1898 Stoppe; 1959 **D**

LYE Dudley
Temperance Hall/Palace of Pictures and Variety (1874–c.1930): 1874 Joseph Gethin; 1969 **D**
Victoria (1914–1960s): 1914 Hugh E. Folkes; 1964 **D**

LYMINGTON Hampshire
Jobling's Theatre (1890–1897): 1890 G. Jobling (attributed); c.1960 **D**

LYTHAM ST ANNES Lancashire
Pavilion (1916–1977): 1916 Unknown; after 1977 **D** (fire)
Pier Pavilion (1904–1974): 1904 Unknown; 1974 **D**

MACCLESFIELD Cheshire
Theatre Royal (ii)/Opera House (1882–1931): 1882 Unknown; 1922 A. Clayton: alterations and refurbishment; 1931 interior **D** (fire); 1950s **D**

MAIDENHEAD Windsor and Maidenhead
Hippodrome/New Theatre and Opera House (1911–c.1929): 1911 Unknown; 1990 **D**
Rialto/Pavilion/ABC (1927–c.1936): 1927 Robert Cromie; 1985 **D**

London, Woolwich Hippodrome (Eric Krieger Collection)

MAIDSTONE Kent
Hippodrome (1900–1908): 1900 Unknown; 1908 **D** (fire)
Palace Theatre (1908–1914): 1957 **D**

MANCHESTER
Alcazar/Bridgewater (c.1880–c.1910): c.1880 Unknown; ?1970s **D**
Ardwick Empire/New Manchester Hippodrome (1904–1930): 1904 Matcham; 1935 Unknown: refurbishment; 1964 **D**
Capitol/Horniman (1931–1933, 1948–1950 and 1971–1998): 1931 Peter Cummings; 1933 Peter Cummings; 1998 **D**
Chorlton Pavilion (1904–1916): 1904 Unknown; n.d. **D**
City Theatre/Theatre Royal/Circus (c.1842–1850): c.1842 Unknown; after 1850 **D**
Gaiety Theatre (1884–1922 and 1944–1947): 1884 Darbyshire; 1908 Matcham; 1959 **D**
Harte's Grand Theatre and Fairyland (1894–1899): 1894 Unknown: wooden circus converted to music hall; 1899 **D** (fire)
Hippodrome (1904–1935): 1904 Matcham; 1935 **D**
King's Theatre (1905–1933): 1905 Alley; n.d. **D**
London Music Hall/Queen's Theatre (1862–1911): 1862 Unknown: conversion of hotel; 1870 E. Salomons: reconstructed; n.d. **D**
Metropole Theatre (1898–1938): 1898 Alley; 1962 **D**
Midland Hotel Theatre (1903–1914): 1898 C. Trubshaw; 1914 dismantled
Prince's Theatre (1864–1940): 1864 Salomons; 1869 Darbyshire; 1901 Darbyshire; n.d. **D**
Queen's Park Hippodrome (1904–1952): 1904 Alley; 1966 **D**
Royal Olympic (1838–1841): 1838 Unknown; ?late C19 **D**
Royal Osborne (1896–1935): 1896 Alley; 1958 **D** (fire)
Rusholme Pavilion (1910–   ): 1910 Unknown; 1965 **D**
St James's Theatre (and Exhibition Hall) (1884–1907): 1884 Unknown; 1908 reopened as cinema; n.d. **D**; fragment
Tivoli/Alexandra/Folly (1865–1921): 1865 converted from chapel; 1897 Perceval: reconstructed; 1921 reopened as cinema; 1927 fire; 1936 **D**

MANSFIELD Nottinghamshire
Empire (1914–1960): 1914 W. Willoughby; 1973 **D**
Hippodrome/Opera House (1906–1919): 1906 Unknown; 1991 **D**
Tivoli (–c.1905): 1963 **D**

MARGATE Kent
Hippodrome (1898–1931, 1935–1936 and 1946–1958): 1898 S.F. Davidson; after 1958 **D**

MARLOW Buckinghamshire
County/New County/Odeon/Regal (1938–1980s): 1938 David E. Nye; 1985 **D**

MELTON MOWBRAY Leicestershire
Empire (–1912) ?1912 temporary building **D**

MERTHYR TYDFIL
Empire (1890–   ): 1890 Unknown; n.d. **D**
New/Park (fl 1880s/90s): n.d. **D**

MEXBOROUGH Doncaster
Hippodrome (1893–1939): 1893 G.H. Smith; 1973 **D**

MIDDLESBROUGH
Grand Opera House (1903–1930): 1903 Hope and Maxwell; 1964 **D**
Oxford Palace (1867–1907): 1867 Unknown; 1941 bombed
Theatre Royal (1866–1930): 1866 Blessley; 1900 Hope and Maxwell; 1978 **D**

MIDDLETON Lancashire
Empire/Pardoe's (fl 1910): before 1912 Unknown; after 1912 **D**

MORECAMBE Lancashire
Central Pier Pavilion/Albert (1897–1933): 1897 Unknown; 1933 **D** (fire)
Palace (1910–1950s): 1910 Unknown; 1989 **D**
Royalty (1898–1957): 1898 Matcham; 1957 **D**
Tower Pavilion (1902–1939): 1902 Unknown; c.1960 **D**
West End Pier (1893–1915): 1893 Unknown; 1917 **D** (fire)

MORLEY Leeds
New Pavilion (1911–1913): 1911 Unknown; 1913 **D** (fire)

MOTHERWELL North Lanarkshire
Alhambra (1898–1910): 1898 Unknown; after 1934 **D**
New Century/Motherwell Theatre (1902–1933):1902 Alec Cullen; 1934 Unknown: rebuilt; 1995 **D**
Olympia (1902–1938): 1902 Unknown; n.d. **D**

MOUNTAIN ASH Rhondda Cynon Taff
Rowe's New Theatre (1898–   ): 1898 Unknown; 1995 **D** (fire)

NEATH
Hippodrome (1910–): 1910 Unknown; n.d. **D**
Palace (–   ): n.d. **D**
Vint's Electric Palace (fl 1912): 1932 **D** (fire)

NELSON Lancashire
Majestic (1910–1961): 1910 Unknown; 1926 R. Jaques: rebuilt; 1962 **D**
Tivoli/Marina (1926–1955): 1926 Unknown; n.d. **D**

NEW BRIGHTON Wirral
Palace/Gaiety (1881–1926): 1881 Unknown; 1933 **D**
Pier Pavilion (c.1893–1923): c.1893 Unknown; c.1927 **D**
Tivoli (1914–1955): 1914 Unknown; 1978 **D**

Tower Grand (1898–1969?): 1898 Maxwell and Tuke; 1969 **D** (fire)
Winter Gardens/Alexandra Hall (1907–1936): 1907 Unknown; 1931 Rees and Holt: internal reconstruction; 1936 Unknown: refurbishment to cinema; 1991 **D**

NEWBURY West Berkshire
Plaza/Tufnail's Hall (1925–c.1977): 1925 F.H. Floyd; 1977 Unknown: converted to music hall; 1984 **D**

NEWCASTLE UPON TYNE
Art Gallery Theatre (1892–1900) 1892 Oliver and Leeson, with George Connell; 1897 James T. Cackett Jr; 1900 **D**
Empire Palace (1890–1963): 1890 Oliver and Leeson; 1903 Matcham: theatre rebuilt; 1917 W. and T.R. Milburn: alterations; 1928 W. and T.R. Milburn: alterations; 1933 W. and T.R. Milburn: alterations; 1950–54 E.M. Lawson: alterations; 1963 **D**
Ginnetts Circus (1890–1899): 1890 T.V. Woodhouse and E. Bowman; after 1899 **D**
Grand (Byker) (1896–1954): 1896 William Hope; 1969 **D**
Grand Theatre (1908–1964): 1908 Unknown; n.d. **D**
Hippodrome (1912–1933): 1912 W. and T.R. Milburn; n.d. **D**
Olympia/Opera House (1893–1907): 1893 T.R. Milburn with Oliver and Leeson; 1902 Matcham; 1909 J. Shaw: new theatre (after fire); 1971 **D** (fire)
Oxford Music Hall (1875–1899): 1875 Unknown; 1899 **D** (fire)
Palace (1895–   ): 1895 J.W. Taylor; 1961 **D**
Pavilion (1903–c.1917): 1903 Wylson and Long ; c.1990 **D**
Queen's (1913–   ): n.d. **D**
Tyne Concert Hall (1874–   ): 1874 converted from circus; n.d. **D**
Vaudeville (–1900): 1900 **D** (fire)

NEWPORT Isle of Wight
Medina Hall (c.1890–c.1937): c.1890 Unknown; c.1937 **D**
Odeon (1936–1982): 1936 Andrew Mather; 1983 **D**

NEWPORT (South Wales)
Empire (1899–1942): 1899 Matcham; 1942 **D** (fire)
Little (1937–c.1964): 1966 **D**
Lyceum (1867–   ): 1867 Unknown; 1897 W.G.R. Sprague; 1961 **D**

NORTHAMPTON
Empire (1874–1901): 1874 Unknown: converted from music hall; 1901 **D**
Empire (Palace) (1855–1918): 1855 Unknown; 1863 Unknown: rebuilt; 1919 Unknown: converted to cinema; after 1919 **D**
Grapho's/Winter Garden (c.1910–1914): 1910 Unknown: converted from skating rink; 1914 **D** (fire)
New (1912–1958): 1912 Sprague; 1960 **D**
Palace of Varieties/Vint's (1860–1913): 1860 Unknown; c.1950 **D**

NORTH SHIELDS North Tyneside
Borough (1902–1957): 1900 Woodhouse: as circus; 1902 Simpson: conversion to theatre; 1910 Gibson and Steinlet: new theatre on site; after 1957 **D**
Central Palace of Varieties (1901–   ): 1901 Hope and Maxwell; after 1909 **D**
New Borough (1910–   ): 1910 Unknown; n.d. **D**

Northumberland Music Hall (1874–   ): 1874 Unknown; n.d. **D**
Theatre Royal/Grand (1879–1932): 1879 Unknown; 1939 **D**

NORTHWICH Cheshire
Central (1908–   ): 1908 J.P. Briggs; n.d. **D**
Pavilion (–   ): n.d. **D**

NORWICH Norfolk
Hippodrome (1903–1960): 1903 Sprague; 1966 **D**
Vaudeville (1876–1882): 1876 Lacey; n.d. **D**

NOTTINGHAM Nottinghamshire
Bonington/St Alban's Picturedrome (1912–1957): 1912 W.H. Higginbottom; 1931 George F. Greenwood: conversion to theatre; 1963 **D**
Bulwell Olympia (1915–1932): 1915 Frederick Bull; after 1952 **D**; fragmental remains
Crown and Cushion/Walker's/Coleno's Varieties (1876–1908): 1876 Unknown; n.d. **D**
Empire (1898–1958): 1898 Matcham; 1969 **D**
Grand/Nottingham Repertory (1886–1930): 1886 E. Long; 1930 Unknown: converted to cinema; c.1964 **D**
King's (1878–c.1913): 1878 Unknown: conversion from skating rink; 1993 **D**
Royal Hippodrome (1908–1927): 1908 Crewe; after 1958 **D**

NUNEATON Warwickshire
Royal/Hippodrome/Prince of Wales/New Royal (1895–1926): 1895 H.W. Thomas; 1900 **D** (temporary building); 1900 Owen and Ward (permanent building on same site); 1984 **D**

OLDBURY Sandwell
Gaiety Music Hall (1887–1892?): 1887 Unknown; c.1892 **D**
Grand/Palace/Tivoli (1881–1926): 1881 Unknown; after 1973 **D**

OLDHAM
Adelphi Music Hall (1868–1874): 1868 Ashton; 1875 **D**
Empire (1897–1969): 1897 Sir Sidney Scott; 1981 **D**
Palace (1908–1936): 1908 Bertie Crewe; 1936 Harry Weedon; c.1994 **D**
Palladium (1913–1958): 1913 Thomas Hilton; 1958; Unknown: converted to cinema; 1990 **D**
Royal Court (i) (1892–1906): 1892 Unknown; 1906 **D** (fire)
Royal Court (ii) (1907–1960): 1907 Turner; 1966 **D**
Theatre Royal (1898–1954): 1898 Cook; 1967 **D**
Vento's Palace of Varieties/People's (1891–   ): 1891 Unknown; n.d. **D**

OSWESTRY Shropshire
Empire Pavilion (1911–1920s): 1911 Unknown; n.d. **D**
Garrison (–   ): n.d. **D**
Hippodrome (–   ): n.d. **D**
Playhouse (1864–1939): 1864 Unknown; c.1979 **D**
Theatre of Varieties (–   ): n.d. **D**

OTTERSHAW Surrey
Homewood Theatre (1935–1996): 1935 Unknown; 1996 **D**

OXFORD Oxfordshire
Empire/East Oxford Hippodrome (1902–   ): 1902 Ward: converted from hall; 1982 **D**

New (1886–1933): 1886 Drinkwater; 1908 Sprague; 1933 **D**

PAIGNTON Torbay
Oldway House Theatre (1873–1904): 1873 Bridgman (and possibly Matcham); 1904 dismantled
Pier Pavilion (1879–1919): 1879 Unknown; 1919 **D** (fire)
Summer Pavilion (1938–1966): 1938 Unknown; 1966 **D**
Theatre (–   ): 1890 **D**

PAISLEY Renfrewshire
Hippodrome (1906–1916): 1906 Unknown; 1916 **D** (fire)
Paisley Theatre (1890–1939): 1890 Unknown; c.1960 **D**

PEMBROKE Pembrokeshire
Queen's (1905–   ): 1905 Unknown; n.d. **D**

PENARTH Vale of Glamorgan
Hippodrome (–   ): 1929 **D** (fire)

PERTH Perth and Kinross
Alhambra/Gaumont (1922–c.1929): 1922 A.K. Beaton; 1956 Unknown: rebuilt; 1993 **D** (fire)
Opera House (i) (1845–1895): 1845 Unknown; n.d. **D**
Opera House (ii) (1882–1892): 1882 Unknown; n.d. **D**

PETERBOROUGH
Theatre Royal (1899–1959): 1899 Briggs: conversion from skating rink; 1961 **D**

PLYMOUTH
Grand (1889–1934): 1889 Stoell; 1963 **D**
Palladium (1906–1941): 1906 Unknown; 1941 bombed
People's Palace (fl 1890s) n.d. **D**
Promenade Pier Pavilion (1891–1941): 1891 Unknown; 1941 bombed
Stanton's Theatre of Varieties (–   ): n.d. **D**
Star Hall of Varieties (1896–1918): 1896 Unknown; n.d. **D**
Vauxhall Theatre (fl 1890s): n.d. **D**

POLESWORTH Warwickshire
Palace (1912–1956): 1912 Unknown; 1913 Unknown: balcony added; n.d. **D**

PONTYPOOL Torfaen
Theatre Royal (–   ): after 1912 **D**

PONTYPRIDD Rhondda Cynon Taff
County (1911–1939): 1911 Unknown; 1939 **D**
Hippodrome (1902–   ): 1902 Unknown; n.d. **D**
King's (fl 1911): n.d. **D**
New/Royal Clarence (1890–1912): 1890 Unknown; after 1912 **D**

POOLE
Electric (1911–1927): 1911 Unknown, converted from church; 1927 **D**
Regent (1924–1976): 1927 Unknown; 1977 **D**

PORTH Rhondda Cynon Taff
Palace of Varieties (–   ): n.d. **D**
Porth Opera House (1902–   ): 1902 Unknown; n.d. **D**

PORTSMOUTH
Clarence Esplanade Pier Theatre (1882–1941): 1882 Unknown; 1941 bombed
Empire (1891–1958): 1891 C.J. Phipps; 1913 Unknown: refurbished; 1944 Unknown: refurbished; 1958 **D**
Globe (c.1899–1973): c.1899 Unknown; 1984 **D**
Grecian Saloon/Landport (1843–1850): 1843 Unknown; after 1850 **D**
Hippodrome (1908–1941): 1908 Crewe; 1941 bombed
Prince's (1891–1930): 1891 Matcham; 1924 Unknown: equipped as cinema; 1930 Unknown: rebuilt as cinema; 1941 bombed
Royal Albert/New Princes (1869–1882): 1869 Unknown; 1872 Unknown: renovation; 1882 **D** (fire)
Royal Britannia (1860s–): 1860s Unknown; n.d. **D**
South of England Music Hall/Alhambra (1856–1890): 1856 Unknown; 1890 **D** (fire)
Vento's Temple of Varieties (1884–1910): 1875 Unknown; 1980 **D**

PORT TALBOT Neath Port Talbot
Empire (–): 1938 **D**
Vint's Palace (1911–1972): 1911 Unknown; 1972 **D**

PRESTON Lancashire
Empire (1911–1930): 1911 Bush, Hope and Tasker; 1976 **D**
Hippodrome (1905–1957): 1905 J.J. Alley; 1959 **D**
New King's Palace (1913–1955): 1913 Unknown; 1964 **D**
Prince's/Gaiety (1882–1930): 1882 Unknown; 1900 Mumford; 1964 **D**

RADCLIFFE Bury
Coliseum (–): 1977 **D** (fire)
Grand Opera House (–): n.d **D**

RAMSGATE Kent
Promenade Pier Pavilion (1879–1917): 1917 Collisan?; 1930 **D**
Royal Palace/Amphitheatre (1908–1960): 1883 Latham: amphitheatre; 1908 Matcham: conversion to theatre; 1960 **D**; fragment

RAWTENSTALL Lancashire
Grand/Royal Palace (1898–1937): 1898 Darbyshire and Smith; 1937 **D**

READING
Palace Theatre (1907–1959): 1907 Sprague; 1961 **D**
Royal County Theatre (1895–1937): 1895 Matcham; 1937 **D** (fire)
Theatre Royal and Albert Hall (1871–1894): 1871 Brown; 1877 Unknown: rebuilt; 1894 **D** (fire)
Vaudeville (–): 1957 **D**

REDDITCH Worcestershire
Public Hall/Hippodrome and Circus (1885–c.1921): 1885 John Cotton: as public hall; 1889 Unknown: alterations; 1913 A.H. Robinson: as ciné-variety; 1931 **D**

REDHILL Surrey
Market Hall Theatre (1891–1982): 1860 Unknown: as market hall; 1891 Unknown: enlarged to include theatre; 1903 Unknown: enlarged; 1982 **D**

RETFORD Nottinghamshire
Palace (1911–1930): 1909 Unknown: as skating rink; 1910 Unknown: conversion to theatre; 1930 Unknown: conversion to skating rink; c.1961 **D**

RHOS-ON-SEA Conwy
Playhouse (–): n.d. **D**

RHYL Denbighshire
Gaiety/Pier Amphitheatre (1908–1989): 1908 Unknown; before 1994 **D**
Pavilion (1908–1972): 1908 Maxwell, Tuke and Smith; 1974 **D**
Victoria Bijou (–): n.d. **D**

RINGWOOD Hampshire
Manor House Theatre (1888 –1914): 1888 Unknown; 1914 **D** (fire)

RIPLEY Derbyshire
Empire (1911–1956): 1911 Unknown; 1959 fragment
Victory (c.1920–c.1928): c.1920 Unknown; n.d. **D**

RIPON North Yorkshire
Victoria Opera House (1886–c.1912): 1886 Unknown; n.d. **D**

ROCHDALE
Circus of Varieties (1883–1930): 1908 Hardman; 1920 Cromie; 1970 **D**
Palace (–): n.d **D**
Theatre Royal/Opera House (1865–1895): 1865 Unknown; n.d. **D**

ROTHERHAM
New Hippodrome (1908–1932): 1908 Unknown; 1960 **D**
Theatre Royal (1894–1929): 1894 Platts and Rawmarsh; 1957 **D**

RUGBY Warwickshire
Palace (Vint's) (–): c.1922 **D**
Theatre Royal (1890–1907): 1890 Ward and Hall; 1895 Unknown: internal alterations; 1901 Unknown: new theatre on site; 1907 **D**

RUGELEY Staffordshire
Palace (c.1912–c.1934): c.1912 Unknown; after 1934 **D**

RUNCORN Halton (Cheshire)
Empress (1916–): 1916 Unknown; 1974 **D**
Public Hall/King's (–1932): 1906 Unknown: alterations; 1960 **D**
Theatre Royal (1869–1906): 1869 Unknown; 1906 **D**

RUSHDEN Northamptonshire
Palace (1910–1956): 1910 Unknown; n.d. fragment
Royal Theatre of Varieties (1911 –): 1911 F.E. Preston; 1965 **D**; fragment as part of car showroom

RYDE Isle of Wight
Pier Pavilion (1842–c.1920): 1842 George Moore; after 1920 **D**
Theatre Royal (ii) (1871–1961): 1871 Unknown; 1961 **D** (fire)

ST HELEN'S
People's Palace (1893–1902/3): 1893 William Wesketh; 1902/3 **D**

Theatre Royal (i) (1847–1858): 1847 George Harris; after 1858 **D**

ST PETER PORT Guernsey
St Julian's/Salle St Julien (1876–1931): 1876 Wm Robillard; 1931 Trent and Tully; 1985 **D**
People's Palace/Hippodrome (c.1910–mid 1920s): c.1910 Unknown; n.d. fragment

SALFORD
Devonshire Electric (1913–): 1913 Unknown: conversion; 1970s **D**
Dominion/Essoldo (1930–1947): 1930 J. Gomersall; 1978 **D**
Hippodrome (1904–1962): 1904 Alley; 1962 **D**
Prince of Wales (1882–1929?): 1882 Unknown; 1973 **D**
Regent Theatre and Opera House/Palace (1895–1952): 1895 Matcham; 1919 Unknown: renovations; 1963 **D**

SALISBURY Wiltshire
New (1910–1932): 1910 Unknown; n.d. **D**
Palace/County Hall (1908–1931): 1908 Whitehead; 1910 Butt; c.1990 **D**

SALTCOATS North Ayrshire
La Scala (1913–1960s): 1913 J. Fairweather; after 1960 **D**; only shell remains

SANDGATE Kent
Alhambra (1858–1950): 1858 Unknown; 1950 **D**

SANDOWN Isle of Wight
Pier Pavilion (1895–1934): 1895 Unknown; 1934 **D** (fire)

SCARBOROUGH North Yorkshire
Floral Hall (1910–1980s): 1910 Unknown; 1987 **D**
Londesborough Theatre (1871–1914): 1871 Unknown; 1914 **D**
Pier Pavilion (1889–1915): 1889 Unknown; n.d. **D**

SCUNTHORPE North Lincolnshire
Empire (1896–1942): 1896 Unknown: as public hall; 1942 **D** (fire)

SEACOMBE Wirral
Hippodrome (–1937): n.d. **D**

SEAHAM HARBOUR Durham
Theatre (1873–c.1961): 1873 Unknown; 1901 Unknown: rebuilt; 1975 **D**

SEVENOAKS Kent
Club Hall Theatre (c.1889–1940): c.1889 Unknown; 1940 bombed

SHAFTESBURY Dorset
Savoy (1933–1950s): 1933 E. de Wilde Holding; c.1960 **D**

SHANKLIN Isle of Wight
Pier Pavilion (1909–1982): 1909 Unknown; n.d. **D**

SHEERNESS Kent
Hippodrome (1851–1955): 1851 Unknown; 1970 **D**

SHEFFIELD
Adelphi (–1914): n.d. Hurst and Woodhead; 1865 Hadfield; 1914 **D**
Britannia Music Hall (c.1869–1896): c.1869 Unknown; 1992 **D** (fire)
Ecclesfield Cinema House (1921–1959): 1921 Unknown; after 1959 **D**
Empire (1895–1959): 1895 Matcham; 1963 **D**
Grand/Bijou/New Star (1904–1938): 1904 Unknown; 1938 **D**
Hippodrome (1907–c.1959): 1907 Crewe; 1963 **D**
Palace/Theatre Royal, Attercliffe Road (1896–1961): 1896 Martin and Blomfield Jackson; 1933 Unknown: reconstructed; c.1961 **D**
Playhouse (–c.1958): n.d. **D**
Regent/Gaumont (1927–): 1927 W.E. Trent; after 1985 **D**
Surrey Music Hall (1851–1865): 1851 Unknown; 1865 **D** (fire)
Theatre Royal (–1935): 1901 Matcham; 1935 **D** (fire)

SHERBORNE Dorset
Wessex Theatre (1929–1961): 1929 Satchwell and Roberts; c.1988 **D**

SHILDON Durham
Hippodrome (1911–c.1956): 1911 Unknown; late 1950s **D**

SHIPLEY Bradford
Queen's Palace of Varieties (1907–1913): 1907 Unknown; n.d. **D**

SKEGNESS Lincolnshire
Arcadia (1912–1987): 1912 Frank Tugwell; after 1987 **D**
Gaiety (1938–1960s): 1938 Unknown; 1997 **D**
King's Theatre (1902–1935): 1902 Unknown; 1914 Owen and Ward: alterations; 1954/5 **D**
Pier Pavilion (1881–1940 and 1948–1977): 1881 Clarke and Pickwell; 1929 Unknown: new entrances; 1948 Unknown: reconstruction; 1985 **D** (fire)

SMETHWICK Sandwell (West Midlands)
Bearwood Coliseum (1911–1930): 1911 Bowden; 1948? **D**
Theatre Royal (1897–1932): 1897 Owen and Ward; 1936? **D**

SOUTHAMPTON
Empire (1850–1927): 1877 Mitchell; 1927 **D**
Grand Theatre/New Hippodrome (1898–1959): 1898 Jenkins; 1960 **D**
Hippodrome/Prince of Wales (1883–1939): 1883 J.W. Gordan; 1905 Unknown: alterations; 1940 bombed
Odeon (1899–1993): 1899 Unknown; 1993 **D**
Pier Pavilion (–): n.d. **D**
Royal York/Palace of Varieties (1872–1938): 1872 Unknown; 1890 Emden: rebuilt; 1942 bombed
Theatre Royal (1880–1938): 1880 Unknown; 1940 bombed

SOUTHEND-ON-SEA
Ambassadors (1920–1929 and 1937–1954): 1920 Unknown; 1963 **D**
Garon's Imperial (1911–1920s): 1911 Bertie Crewe; 1920 Unknown: enlarged; 1963 **D**
Hippodrome (1909–1936): 1909 Crewe; c.1960 **D**
Pier Pavilion (1889–1959): 1889 Brunkes and McKerrow; 1959 **D**
Prince's Hall (1896–): 1896 Unknown: conversion; 1931 **D**

Picturedrome Regal/Arcadia (1920–1929 and 1937–1954): 1920 Unknown; 1921 F.G. Bethley; 1963 **D**
Sun Deck Theatre (–   ): n.d. **D**
Talza (mid 1920s–1938): 1920s Unknown; 1970s **D**

SOUTHPORT Sefton (Merseyside)
Empire (fl 1912): 1933 **D**
Opera House (1891–1931): 1891 Matcham; 1931 **D** (fire)
Palladium (1914–1931): 1914 George E. Tonge; 1926 Gray and Evans; 1930 W.E. Trent; 1980 **D**
Pier Pavilion (1902–1933): 1902 R. Knill Freeman and F. Freeman; 1931 Unknown: refurbished; 1933 **D** (fire)
Scala/Winter Gardens (1874–1909): 1874 Maxwell and Tuke; 1905 Unknown: reconstructed; 1962 **D**

SOUTHSEA Portsmouth
Batty's Royal Arena (1860s–   ): 1860s Unknown; after 1900 **D**
South Parade Pier Theatre (i) and (ii) (1879–1904 and 1908–1976): 1879 G. Rake; 1904 destroyed by fire; 1908 Unknown: new theatre built; 1933 Unknown: alterations; 1976 **D** (fire)

SOUTH SHIELDS South Tyneside
Central Palace of Varieties (1901–1927): 1901 Hope and Maxwell; n.d. **D**
Majestic (1918–1919) 1918 Unknown; n.d. **D**
Queen's Theatre (1913–1941): 1913 Gibson and Steinlet; 1941 bombed
Royal Alhambra Music Hall (1866–1868): 1866 Unknown; n.d. **D**
Scala (1890–1919): 1890 Unknown; after 1919 **D**
Siddall's Grand Theatre/Alhambra (1880–c.1885): 1880 J.E. Stout; n.d. **D**
Thornton's Theatre of Varieties (1885–1898): 1885 John Biddick; 1889 Thomas Moore and Sons: alterations; 1898 **D**
Tivoli Palace (1902–   ): 1902 Unknown; n.d. **D**

SPENNYMOOR Durham
Cambridge (1870–1916): 1870 Unknown; after 1916 **D**
Hippodrome (1909 –1909): 1909 **D** (fire)

STAINES Surrey
Majestic (1929–1961): 1929 S.B. Pritlove; 1961 **D**

STALYBRIDGE Tameside
Hippodrome and Grand (1890–1920s): 1890 Unknown; 1964 only facade remains

STANLEY Durham
Theatre Royal (1904–1930): 1904 W. Forster; 1930 **D** (fire)
Victoria Theatre (1893–1922): 1893 Unknown; 1897 W.J. Shell: additions; 1904 T.E. Crossling: new roof; 1933 T.H. Murray: rebuilt as cinema; n.d. **D**

STOCKPORT
Davenport (1937–   ): 1937 Charles Hartley; 1997 **D**
Grand Theatre/Empire/Hippodrome (1869–1951): 1869 Unknown; 1905 Unknown: complete rebuild; 1931 Unknown: remodelled as cinema; 1960 fire, closed; 1965 body of building **D**; 1968 facade **D**
Theatre Royal (1888–1957): 1888 Matcham; 1960 **D**

STOCKTON-ON-TEES
Castle Theatre/Empire (1908–1961): 1908 Hope and Tasker; 1969 **D**
Grand Theatre/Plaza (1875–1936): 1875 Unknown; n.d. **D**
(Royal) Star (1876–1935?): 1876 Unknown; 1891 Matcham and Moses; 1969 **D**
Theatre Royal (1866–1906): 1864 Potts and Son; 1966 **D**

STOKE-ON-TRENT
Alexandra Music Hall (1880–1924): 1880 Unknown; 1960s **D**
Coliseum/Gaumont (Burslem) (1914–1918): 1914 Wood and Goldstraw; 1918 converted to cinema; 1960 **D**
Crown/Gordon/Hippodrome (1897–1918): 1897 Lynam Beckett; 1900 G.F. Ward: rebuilt; 1965 **D**
Empire (1896–   ): 1896 Unknown; n.d. **D**
Empire/Queen's (Longton) (1896–   ): 1888 John Taylor; 1896 Matcham: reconstructed after fire; c.1960s converted to bingo; 1993 **D** (fire); fragments remain
Gaiety/King's/Empire (Hanley) (1873–1925): 1873 Unknown; 1874 Unknown: alterations; 1898 Matcham: rebuilt; 1901 Brearley: extensions; 1925 Grant: converted to cinema; 1956 **D**
Grand Theatre/Grand Theatre of Varieties (Hanley) (1898–1932): 1898 Matcham; 1932 **D** (fire)
Hippodrome/Wedgwood Theatre (Burslem) (1896–c.1940): 1896 G. Francis; 1947 **D**
Imperial/Varieties/People's Hall (Hanley) (1873–c.1908): 1873 T. Rogers; 1909 Unknown: converted to skating rink; 1977 **D**
Music Hall (1914–   ): 1914 Unknown; 1960s **D**
New Queen's Palace/Eagle (c.1880–c.1921): c.1880 Unknown; 1929 **D**
Royal Victoria Theatre (Longton) (1868–1888): 1868 James Rigby; 1949 **D**
Temple of Varieties (Hanley) (–1873): 1873 **D**

STOURBRIDGE Dudley
Alhambra (1870s–1929): 1870s Unknown; c.1975 **D**
Royal (c.1840–   ): c.1840 Unknown; n.d. **D**

STRATFORD-UPON-AVON Warwickshire
Hippodrome (1912–after 1945): 1912 Holmes and Lucas; 1971 **D**

STRETFORD Manchester
Civic Theatre (–   ): n.d. **D**

STROUD Gloucestershire
Empire Theatre (1913–1927): 1913 Baylis Rulaen and Kiddle; n.d. fragment remains

SUNDERLAND
King's/Black's Theatre (1906–1943): 1906 Hope; 1943 bombed; 1954 **D**
Lyceum Theatre (1852–1880): 1852 Joseph Potts; 1880 **D**
Milburn's Varieties (1880–1881): 1880 Unknown; n.d. **D**
People's Palace (1891–1956): 1891 Moore; 1903 W. and T.R. Milburn: alterations; 1924 W. and T.R. Milburn: alterations; 1973 **D**
Roker Variety Theatre (1914–1961): 1914 George R. Smith; 1960s **D**
Star Music Hall (1857–c.1892): 1857 Unknown; 1883 Unknown: rebuilt after fire; 1892 closed; n.d. fragment
Theatre Royal (1855–1933): 1855 G.A. Middlemiss; 1888

Tynemouth, Palace

Thomas Moore and Sons; 1933 Unknown: converted to boxing stadium; 1940 Unknown: converted to cinema; 1994 **D** (fire)
Victoria Hall (1872–1883 and 1906–1941): 1872 Unknown; 1883 rebuilt; 1941 bombed
Wear Music Hall (1871–1902): 1871 Collerford; 1902 **D**

SUTTON-IN-ASHFIELD Nottinghamshire
King's Palace (1904–1920): 1904 L.H. Woodhouse; 1931 **D**
Savoy/Portland (1937–1968): 1937 Alfred J. Thraves; 1991 **D**

SWANAGE Dorset
Grand/Pavilion (1919–1932): 1919 Unknown: conversion; 1960s fragment
Mowlem Institute/Bijou (1900–1960s): 1900 John Mowlem: conversion; 1966 **D**

SWANSEA
Bustin's Concert Room (fl 1850s): n.d. **D**
Empire (1900–1957): 1900 Emden; 1960 **D**
Owen's, Mumbles (–   ): n.d. **D**
Prince of Wales/Circus (1869–after 1911): 1869 Unknown; 1911 rebuilt; n.d. **D**
Royal Standard Music Hall (–   ): n.d. **D**
Star/New (1902–1931): 1973 **D**

SWINDON
Empire/Queen's (1896–1955): 1896 Milverton, Drake and Pizey; 1959 **D**

TAMWORTH Staffordshire
Grand (1915–1929): 1915 Horace G. Bradley; c.1958 **D**
Palace (1910–c.1929): 1910 Clarkson and Fidler; n.d. **D**

TAUNTON Somerset
Lyceum (1913–1998): 1913 H. Walcott Stone and J. Lloyd; 1932 F.C. Mitchell: modernised; 1998 **D**

TEIGNMOUTH Devon
Athenaeum (–   ): n.d. **D**; fragment remains
Pier Pavilion (1890–1970s): 1890 J.W. Wilson; 1975 **D**

TIPTON Sandwell (West Midlands)
Regal Music Hall (1910–1958): 1910 Unknown; 1960 **D**

TON PENTRE Rhondda Cynon Taff
Grand (–   ): n.d. **D**
Lyceum Theatre (1902–1908): 1902 Owen Ward: conversion from town hall; n.d. **D**
Tivoli Music Hall (–   ): n.d. **D**

TONYPANDY Rhondda Cynon Taff
Empire (–   ): n.d. **D**
Theatre Royal (1892–1912): 1892 Unknown; n.d **D**

TOW LAW Durham
Empire Theatre (–   ): n.d. **D**

TREDEGAR Blaenau Gwent
Olympia (fl 1916): n.d. **D**

TREHERBERT Rhondda Cynon Taff
Opera House (1902–   ): 1902 Unknown; after 1912 **D**

TROWBRIDGE Wiltshire
Palace of Varieties (1910–1914): 1910 Albany Ward: converted from skating rink; n.d. fragmental remains
Palace Theatre/New Theatre (1914–1936): 1914 Unknown; 1936 **D**

TYNEMOUTH North Tyneside
Palace-by-the-Sea/Aquarium and Winter Garden (1878–1960s): 1878 Norton and Massey; 1998 **D**

VENTNOR Isle of Wight
Pier Pavilion (1907–1920s): 1907 Unknown; n.d. **D**
Steephill Castle Private Theatre (1833–1950s): c.1833 J. Sanderson; 1963 **D**

WAKEFIELD
City Theatre (fl 1894–   ): n.d. **D**
Empire (–   ): n.d **D**
Hippodrome (1909–1916): 1909 Unknown; n.d. **D**
Queen Street Theatre (–   ): c.1978 **D**

WALSALL
Grand Theatre (1873–1912): 1860 Unknown; 1890 Arnell: rebuild; 1939 **D** (fire)
Her Majesty's Theatre (1900–1933): 1900 Owen and Ward; 1937 **D**
Tivoli Palace (1892–1898?): 1892 Unknown; 1983 **D**

WARMINSTER Wiltshire
Palace (–   ): n.d. **D**

WARRINGTON
Royal Court Theatre (i) (1892–1906): 1892 Bland Darbyshire and Smith; 1906 **D** (fire)
Royal Court Theatre (ii) (1907–1957): 1907 Smith; 1960 **D**

WARWICK Warwickshire
County Theatre (1920–   ): 1920 Baily, Palmer Shipwright; 1922 Unknown: alterations; c.1979 **D**

WASHINGTON Sunderland
Alexandra (1910–late 1960s): 1910 Unknown; n.d. fragmental remains

WEDNESBURY Sandwell (West Midlands)
Hippodrome (1891–1955): 1891 Unknown; 1962 **D**
Rialto (1859–c.1881 and 1918–1927): 1859 Benton Dawes; 1918 Unknown: rebuilt; c.1970 **D**

WELLINGBOROUGH Northamptonshire
ABC/Lyric (1936–1960s): 1936 Edgar Simmons; 1975 **D**
Empire Music Hall (1909–1910): 1909 Unknown; 1910 **D** (fire)
Exchange/Electric (1861–   ): 1861 Bellamy and Hardy: as corn exchange; 1910 Unknown: conversion to cinema; 1920 Unknown: conversion to theatre; after 1959 **D**

WELLS Somerset
Palace (c.1914–c.1935): c.1914 Unknown: conversion; 1998 **D**

WENDOVER Buckinghamshire
Hippodrome (1898–   ): n.d. **D**

WEST BROMWICH Sandwell (West Midlands)
King's/Empire (1914–1927 and 1948–1957): 1914 Wood and Kendrick; 1973 **D**
Olympia/New Hippodrome/Regent (1895–1922): 1895 Unknown: as a temporary theatre; 1906 Unknown: as a permanent theatre; 1922 **D**
Theatre Royal (c.1850–1940): 1896 Owen and Ward: rebuilt; c.1967 **D** (fire)

WESTBURY Wiltshire
Leighton House Private Theatre/Laverton Institute (1888–1911): 1888 Frank Willis; late 1950s **D**

WESTON-SUPER-MARE North Somerset
Grand Pier Pavilion (1904–1930): 1904 Mayoh and Haley; 1930 **D**
Playhouse (i) (1946–1960s): 1946 Unknown: conversion from music hall; c.1961 **D**
Winter Gardens (1882–1942): 1882 Unknown; 1942 **D**

WEYMOUTH Dorset
Jubilee Hall/Regent (1887–1926): 1887 Crickmay and Sons; 1926 W.E. Trent: conversion to cinema; 1989 **D**
Kursaal (1905–1963): 1905 Unknown; 1964? **D**
Theatre Royal (1864–c.1887): 1864 Samuel Jackson; 1884 Samuel Jackson; 1968 **D**

WHITBY North Yorkshire
Empire (1915–   ): 1915 A.E. Young; n.d. **D**
Star (1880s–1920s): 1880s Unknown; 1921 Unknown: conversion to cinema; 1970s Unknown: conversion to bingo; 1997 **D**

WHITEHAVEN Cumbria
Royal Standard Music Hall (1870–1954): 1870 Unknown; 1954 **D**
Shakespeare Hotel Music Hall (c.1860s–c.1900): c.1860s Unknown; n.d. **D**

WHITLEY BAY North Tyneside
Empire (1898–   ): n.d. **D**
Pavilion/Westcliff/Spa (1878–   ): 1989 **D** (replaced)

WHITSTABLE Kent
Theatre (1868–1940): n.d. **D**

WIDNES Halton (Cheshire)
Alexandra (1887–   ): 1887 Unknown; n.d. **D**

WIGAN
Hippodrome (1904–1935): 1904 Owen and Ward; 1909 Thornley; 1956 **D** (fire)

WINCHESTER Hampshire
Regal/Odeon (1933–1969): 1933 Robert Cromie; 1969 **D**

WINDSOR Windsor and Maidenhead
Playhouse (1928–1983): 1928 Robert Cromie; 1984 **D**
Royalty (1910–1935): 1910 Unknown; c.1938 **D**

WOKING Surrey
Central Assembly Halls (1890s–1927): 1890s Unknown; 1927 **D**
Grand Theatre (1895–1935): 1894 town architect; 1962 **D**
Palace (1899–1928): 1899 Unknown; 1906 Unknown: refurbished; 1928 **D**

WOLVERHAMPTON
Empire/Museum/Gaiety/Hippodrome (1870–1956): 1870 Unknown; 1890 John Turner: alterations; 1898 Owen and Ward: new theatre; 1921 Bertie Crew: alterations; 1958 **D** (fire)
Gaumont (1932–1973): 1932 W.E. Trent; after 1973 **D**
Theatre Royal (i) (1845–1894): 1845 Mee; after 1894 **D**
Theatre Royal (ii)/Prince of Wales (1863–1930): 1863 Unknown; 1890 Bradney; 1914 Marcus Brown; 1931 Satchwell and Roberts; 1981 **D**

WORCESTER Worcestershire
Empire Music Hall (1889–1914): 1889 Unknown; 1939 **D**
Royal Alhambra Amphitheatre (1868–1870): 1868 Unknown; n.d. **D**

WORKSOP Nottinghamshire
Empire (1912–1920): 1912 Unknown; n.d. **D**
Music Hall (1843–c.1863): 1843 Unknown; n.d. **D**

WORTHING West Sussex
Pier Pavilion (1889–1926): 1886 Mansergh; 1926 **D**
Theatre Royal (1897–1929): 1897 Cooke; n.d. **D**

WREXHAM
Empire Music Hall (1908–1948): 1908 Unknown; 1956 **D**
St James's (1887–   ): 1887 Unknown; 1903 **D**
Theatre Royal (1891–1914): 1891 Penton; 1964 **D**

YEADON Leeds
Theatre Royal (–   ): n.d. **D**

YEOVIL Somerset
Palace (1920–c.1933): 1920 Unknown; c.1933 **D**

YORK
Hippodrome (–   ): n.d. **D**

YSTRAD AERON Ceredigion
Theatr Felinfach (–   ): n.d. **D**

Appendix 2

Early Theatres

The first edition of *Curtains* established that there are to be seen in Britain very few complete theatres of any kind of an earlier date than 1880, only ten that are wholly or largely earlier than 1837, and, of these, only five with well-preserved pre-Victorian interiors.

This is an extraordinary state of affairs, seen against the fact that theatre is the one art in which the British nations have excelled and frequently led the world for more than 400 years. To see a complete theatre built in Shakespeare's lifetime one must go not to Bankside but to Vicenza. Whilst C17, C18 and early C19 theatres are not uncommon in continental Europe, Britain has no complete, nearly complete or fully restored theatre earlier than the 1760s. Most of the surviving buildings built in the ensuing century are either fragmentary or much altered.

The main reason for this is that theatre in Britain, until well into the C20, was entirely commercial. There was practically no tradition of royal, noble or civic patronage. Commercial pressures meant that successful theatres were rebuilt to accommodate larger audiences, whilst unsuccessful ones were torn down to make way for other developments.

The roofless 'wooden O' playhouses which appeared in the fields beyond the City of London boundaries from 1576 onward, were the first public theatres to be built in Europe since Antiquity. They were crucial to the development of modern English language as well as the English drama and they were arguably the most important single group of theatres ever built.

All of them, the Theatre, Curtain, Newington Butts, Rose, Swan, Globe, Hope, Fortune – and their predecessors at, for example, the Red Lion as well as contemporary indoor theatres at Blackfriars and St Paul's – will eventually have detailed database entries, but they can find no place in this book.[1]

The **Rose** needs to be specially mentioned because the archaeological investigation carried out in 1989 produced the first irrefutable evidence of the physical nature of this immensely important family of buildings. The heated controversy over the preservation and display of the Rose remains was eventually dissipated, but never, in truth, satisfactorily resolved. Nevertheless, the discoveries have been thoroughly documented and are all readily available to the interested reader. So far as this book is concerned, we have followed the rule that, for a theatre to be included, there must be substantial visible and recognisable remains. Throughout, we have treated surviving foundations and isolated fragments of superstructure as demolitions. However important, emotionally as well as evidentially, the surviving fabric may be in this case, it represents only the lowest foot or two (in some places, an inch or two) of the Rose Playhouse and it is all at present (1999) concealed.

The **Globe** has been only partly excavated. The same considerations apply. The sites of the Theatre, the Curtain and other playhouses of the earliest period await physical investigation, if and when the opportunity occurs.

The Wanamaker-inspired reconstruction of the **Shakespeare Globe** is a most impressive building, a scholarly reconstruction based on the best evidence available and an important working

theatre. It is as close as we can now get to the real original, but it is nevertheless 'post-1950' and must be excluded.

Most Great Halls and Guildhalls had theatrical use as 'fit-ups' at some time in their history. We have included only exceptional cases, like the Whitehall Banqueting House which was designed by Inigo Jones with a clear view to its being regularly fitted up as a masquing house, the Great Hall at Hampton Court Palace, which for a very long period had a semi-permanent fit-up, Kings Lynn Guildhall, which at one time contained a permanent Georgian theatre and Middle Temple Hall, whose theatrical associations command attention. We have omitted most town halls, assembly rooms and inns with a record of occasional theatre use, including only a few where the record of regular fit-up seemed particularly worthy of note. It is difficult to be consistent in a way to please everyone and we have undoubtedly left out much that is of interest, but we believe that the ones we have admitted are unarguably worth their place.

Leaving aside the court fit-ups and theatres to which the general public had only occasional access (e.g. Chatsworth 1830, Deal Globe, 1860s and Normansfield, 1879) the earliest substantially complete theatres and music halls noted in this book are:

Bristol, Theatre Royal: 1766 and later
Stamford Theatre: 1768 (exterior)
Bury St Edmunds Theatre (i): 1775 (exterior)
Richmond, Yorkshire, Theatre: 1788
Wisbech, Angles: 1793 (exterior)
London, Drury Lane, Theatre Royal: exterior 1812 to 1831, (parts of interior from 1812, auditorium 1922)
Cambridge, Festival: 1814 and later
Bury St Edmunds Theatre (ii): 1819
London, Haymarket, Theatre Royal: 1821 (exterior)
Bungay Theatre: 1828 (exterior)
Newcastle upon Tyne, Theatre Royal: 1837 (exterior)
London, Royal Opera House: 1858
London, Wilton's Music Hall: 1859 and1878
Glasgow, Britannia: 1859 and later
Canterbury, Alexandra (Penny): before 1860
Bath, Theatre Royal: 1863 (parts of 1805)
London, Hoxton Hall: 1863 and 1867
Leeds, City Varieties: 1865
Brighton, Theatre Royal: 1866 (parts earlier and later)
Newcastle upon Tyne, Tyne Theatre and Opera House: 1867
London, Old Vic: 1871 (parts earlier and later)
Margate, Theatre Royal: 1874 (parts of 1787)
London, Alexandra Palace: 1875
Leeds, Grand: 1878
Glasgow, Citizens: 1878 and later
Scarborough, Spa Theatre: 1879 and later

Other theatres which, although of later date, incorporate recognisable pre-Victorian fabric include Lancaster Grand, York Theatre Royal and London Lyceum. Balmbra's in Newcastle upon Tyne was noted in the 1982 *Curtains!!!* as a music hall of

---

[1] Simon Blatherwick's study of London's *Pre-Restoration Theatres of the Sixteenth & Seventeenth Centuries* English Heritage, 1998, is the most accessible guide to the locations of 23 such early playhouses.

1862 but it is now known that no part of the original hall remains.

All of the theatres noted above have full descriptive entries. We were, however, faced with a problem over small Georgian playhouses, once numerous in country towns, but now reduced to mostly fragmentary remains. These simple, rectangular, almost shed-like rooms, were appearing in numbers by the third quarter of the C18, to serve travelling 'circuit' companies who had previously performed in barns, town halls, inn fit-ups and fairground booths. By the mid C19 most of them were being converted to other uses.

The term 'shed-like' is descriptive, not dismissive. They were elegant in their 'pit, boxes and gallery' simplicity. They not only conformed to a rigidly classical system of proportion but also had to match closely in dimensions on any one circuit, since the company travelled with its scenery and had little time for rehearsal. Most of these small provincial playhouses were in use for only a few weeks of the year (at Christmas, for race weeks, assizes, etc.) and served at other times, with levelled floors, for balls and assemblies.

The disappearance of the circuits and subsequent destruction of scores of these playhouses has left only one in complete condition, that in Richmond, Yorkshire (1788, restored 1963). Several, including those at Penzance (1787), Chichester (1791), Wisbech (1793) and Bungay (1828) are externally complete and their original forms could be fairly accurately deduced. A number of others are still recognisable and all of these have entries in as much detail as seems appropriate to their historic importance. We have not, however, described every remnant, some of which amount to no more than a single wall or have lost all semblance to a theatre, being identified only by local oral tradition. These may be of consuming interest to enthusiasts, but they have neither practical nor museum theatre potential.

James Winston's manuscripts describe 280 theatres existing in 1805 of which a small number only appeared in his published work *The Theatric Tourist*. To inspect the sites of every one of the theatres on his list (which was certainly not itself comprehensive) together with all the similar playhouses built after 1805, in order to see whether any fragment survives would be a Herculean task and we have not attempted it. The following list, however, which notes the 300 or so pre-1837 theatres (most of them 'small Georgians') already entered in the *database*, often by no more than a name and a date, may be found useful. In some cases too little information is at present available to give an informed comment.

The term 'extant' means here that there is substantial recognisable fabric (e.g. a 'readable' exterior). It does *not* imply a fully restorable theatre. Construction date is given but, if this is not known, date(s) given is (are) period when theatre flourished (fl). **D** = demolished. We have included a few items to draw attention to incorrect identifications including one or two which were included in the first edition of *Curtains!!!*. It is only necessary to add that most of the buildings listed below were known simply as 'Theatre'. Some were more substantial houses, holding a patent and properly referred to as 'Theatre Royal'.

A list of this kind will inevitably contain errors and omissions. Corrections and additions based on personal inspection and/or conclusive original research will be welcomed.

Aberdeen, Alhambra: a church in 1794; not a theatre until 1881; gutted as a shop
Aberdeen, Scotts: c.1700?
Aberdeen, Coachie's Playhouse: fl 1780s; **D** about 1818
Aberdeen, Mareschal Street: 1795
Aberystwyth: 1789; possibly in the old Guildhall until 1820
Aberystwyth: 1813; fragmentary
Aberystwyth, Bridge End: c.1818; now a wine bar; some plain brickwork.
Andover, Angel Inn: 1787; possibly a fit-up
Andover: 1803; successor to a fit-up; **D** after 1818
Arundel: 1807; **D** 1836, but parts of side walls may possibly be incorporated into house garden walls
Ashbourne: c.1794; a warehouse by the 1840s; later **D**
Ashby-de-la-Zouch (Lyric): building described in *Curtains* 1982 was never a theatre
Ashby-de-la-Zouch (Royal): 1828; gutted 1867; **D** 1967
Aylesbury: c.1820; **D**
Ayr: 1789; **D**
Ayr: 1815; gutted; now a church
Banbury, Davenport: 1750s; fragmentary (shops)
Banbury: pre 1820; probably a barn fit-up
Banbury, New: 1832; extant, interior gutted, exterior much altered
Barnsley: 1816; **D**
Barnstaple: 1760s; built as successor to fit-up at Bell Inn; **D** c. 1935
Bath, Trim Street: 1705; **D** 1737
Bath, New: 1723; **D** after 1751
Bath, Orchard Street: 1750 extant; *see* entry
Bath, Lindsey's/Harrison's Great Room: 1750s; closed 1770s
Bath, Theatre Royal: 1805 extant; *see* entry
Beaumaris: fl 1801; **D**
Beccles: 1814 building at rear of bank on site needs further investigation
Bedford: c.1780 Inn Yard
Bedford, St Mary's/Hop Pole: c.1820 barn fit-up; closed c. 1850
Belfast, Mill Street: 1768 **D**
Belfast, New, Ann Street: 1778
Belfast, Rosemary Lane: 1783
Belfast, Arthur Street: 1790 **D**
Belfast, Theatre Royal: 1793 C.Sherry; 1881 C.J. Phipps: rebuilt; 1915 Bertie Crewe: converted to cinema; 1961 **D**
Beverley, 90–92 Walkergate: not a theatre; old part was assembly rooms; Regal built on remainder of site
Beverley, Lairgate: 1804; closed 1840; front wall only remains as garden wall
Birmingham, Moor Street: 1740; **D** after 1764
Birmingham, King Street: 1752; became a church c.1779
Birmingham, Theatre Royal, New St: 1774 Saul; 1780 Samuel Wyatt: portico; 1794 Saunders: rebuilt; 1820 Beazley: rebuilt; 1904 Runtz: rebuilt; 1957 **D**
Blandford Forum: 1805; probably closed 1856
Bolton, Mawdsley Street: c.1750; rebuilt in 1859; cellars only in later building (County Court)
Boston, Market Place: 1777; closed c.1820; facade only remains; *see* entry
Boston, Red Lion Square: 1806; **D** 1850
Brecon: 1784; possibly a fit-up; warehouse with mill machinery on site with no evidence of theatre building
Bridlington, Rope Walk: 1789; **D**
Bridgnorth, Old Cockpit: c.1811; extant
Bridgnorth: 1824; **D**

Bridgwater: 1834; closed by 1853

Bridport, East Street: c.1822; **D**

Bridport, Chancery Lane: 1826; much altered as cottages

Bridport, Wykes Court Gardens: c.1836; a conversion; **D**

Brighton, North Street: 1774; **D**

Brighton: 1790; **D**

Brighton, Royal: 1807; rear building and scene door only, facing Bond Street, forms part of present theatre; *see* entry

Bristol, Jacob's Well: 1729; **D**

Bristol: 1744; **D**

Bristol, New/Regency: 1810; built as assembly rooms and converted to theatre

Bungay: 1828; extant; *see* entry

Burton Constable Hall (private theatre): 1830; closed after 1870; **D** before 1927 (important painted scenery remains)

Bury St Edmunds: 1734; extant; *see* entry

Bury St Edmunds, Theatre Royal: 1819; extant; *see* entry

Cambridge: 1808; **D** (*see* entry for Festival Theatre for a note on this theatre)

Cambridge (Festival): 1814; extant; *see* entry

Canterbury (Penny): c.1750; present room probably post 1850; *see* entry

Canterbury, Buttermarket: 1772; **D**

Canterbury, New, Orange Street: 1790; extant exterior; *see* entry

Cardiff, Theatre Royal: 1827; Maddox; 1877 destroyed by fire

Carlisle, Blackfriars: 1813; facade fragment incorporated into later building

Castle Acre: part of only one wall remaining

Chelmsford: 1790; **D** after 1848

Cheltenham, Coffee House Yard: 1774; converted from malthouse; closed c.1782

Cheltenham, New Clarence/Sadlers Wells: c.1795; a house converted to a marionette theatre; fragment

Cheltenham Theatre Royal (i), York Passage/Grosvenor Terrace: 1782; **D**

Cheltenham, New Theatre Royal (ii), Bath Street: 1805; destroyed by fire 1839

Chepstow: 1795; closed 1831; **D** 1936

Chester, Tennis Court Theatre: c.1750; closed c.1768

Chester, Theatre Royal/Music Hall: 1777; within a medieval building; 1855 James Harrison: converted to music hall; 1921 Muspratt and Tonge: converted to a cinema; 1961 retail use

Chesterfield, Theatre Royal: c.17??–c.1780; replaced by New Theatre Royal

Chesterfield, New Theatre Royal: c.1780; last remains **D** in 1982

Chichester: 1764; closed 1790; **D**

Chichester: 1791; extant; *see* entry

Cirencester: 1799; extant, now a house; *see* entry

Colchester: 1765; Thomas Ivory; closed 1812, **D** 1820

Colchester: 1812; the altered Wilkins building largely destroyed in 1918; some external brickwork in modern bus station

Coventry: 1819; **D** before 1906

Dartford: 1789; closed 1845 and **D** (fire)

Daventry, Wheatsheaf: c.1793; inn yard; balconies now filled in

Daventry, New: 1837; became a lecture hall, 1863

Deal, Garrison: ?1794; **D**

Deal, Playhouse: 1798; **D**

Deal, Globe: date given in *Curtains* 1982 is incorrect for this site; present building is entirely post 1860; *see* entry

Derby Theatre Royal: 1773; extant; *see* entry

Dereham: 1816; closed 1912; **D** 1977

Derry, Artillery Street: 1795; extant; converted to a church, *see* entry

Devizes: 1792; **D** 1957

Devonport Dock/Cumberland Theatre: 1762; **D** 1860

Doncaster Playhouse: 1776; 1819 rebuilt by Lindley; **D** 1896

Dorchester, North Square: 1786; fit-up in a riding school; closed 1790; possible fragment in later building

Dorchester, West Back Street: 1793; **D** (1828?); part possibly incorporated into Loyalty Theatre

Dorchester, North Square: 1809; near the earlier North Square theatre; served a variety of later uses and finally **D** c.1990

Dorchester, Loyalty Theatre: 1828; closed 1843; no visible evidence of former theatre in existing building

Dorchester: 1828; little trace of theatre in existing building

Douglas, Isle Of Man: 1788; **D**

Douglas, Isle Of Man, Wellington: 1820

Dover, Clarence: 1790; **D**

Downham Market: ?1829; **D**

Dumfries: 1792; extant; *see* entry

Dundee: 1800; a wooden theatre; **D**

Dundee: 1810; extant: *see* entry (facade only)

Durham, Theatre Royal: building described in *Curtains* 1982 was never a theatre

Durham: 1791; **D** 1869

East Dereham: a fit-up

Eastbourne: 1798; closed 1850

Edinburgh, New (Allan Ramsay's): 1736-7; became a chapel; **D**

Edinburgh, Theatre Royal: 1768 ; 1809 rebuilt; 1828 rebuilt, William Burn; **D** 1859 (fire)

Evesham: fl 1798-1847

Exeter: 1705; a fit-up

Exeter: 1735; closed 1787; **D**

Exeter: 1749; **D**

Exeter: 1787; **D**

Exeter: 1821; **D**

Eye: 1815; there is a building on the site of the Fisher Theatre, but nothing above ground is earlier than the late C19; distinguish from the present Eye Theatre which is a 1980s' conversion of a room behind an old inn

Faversham: 1803; temporary building

Folkestone: 1790s

Framlingham: mid C18; extant, but probably a barn fit-up, *see* entry

Gainsborough: 1772; closed c.1790; **D** 1936

Gainsborough: 1790; closed 1849 and **D**

Glasgow: 1752; temporary theatre; **D**

Glasgow, Alston: 1764; **D** 1788

Glasgow, Theatre Royal, Dunlop Street/Caledonian: 1782; 1802 extended; 1825 reopened; 1829 rebuilt, William Spence; 1840, rebuilt, Spence; 1863 rebuilt; 1869 closed

Cirencester, Theatre (Sally McGrath)

Glasgow, Queen Street: 1805; David Hamilton; **D** after fire in 1829

Gloucester: 1766; **D**

Gloucester, Theatre Royal: 1791; rebuilt 1857 and 1897 (as Palace); *see* entry

Godalming: fl 1802

Gosport: 1796; extant exterior

Grantham: 1757; a fit-up?

Grantham: 1775; **D**

Grantham, Swinegate: 1800; **D**

Grassington: 1790; a barn fit-up; post 1835 a cottage; no trace of theatrical use

Gravesend (Trotter): 1808; **D** 1969

Great Yarmouth: 1832; **D** 1934

Guildford, Market Street: 1804; closed 1828; **D**

Guildford, Theatre Royal: 1830; built as hall; a wall said to be incorporated into Co-op store, 1963

Halesworth: 1793 and 1892; largely rebuilt (as the Rifle Hall); *see* entry

Harrogate (Butler Theatre): 1788; extant; now a house; interior of theatre gone, but front and roof intact; *see* entry

Henley-on-Thames: c.1805; extant; *see* entry

Hereford: 1786; **D** 1856

Hexham: 1823; **D** 1991

Horsham, Denne Road: **D** 1804

Horsham, King's Head: before 1820; Trotter; a fit-up; *see* entry

Horsham: the building described in *Curtains* 1982 seems to have been a cinema, now **D**; probably not on the site of an earlier theatre

Ipswich: C18 theatre, rebuilt 1803; **D**

Kemble: 1758; **D** after 1978

Kendal, New Playhouse: 1758; closed 1789 and radically altered; a Working Men's Institute; extant

Kendal, Shakespeare: 1829; extant; *see* entry

Keynsham: 1770s; inn fit-up

Kidderminster: 1836; probably a fit-up; short-lived

King's Lynn, theatre in Guildhall of St George: after George 1766; some remains; *see* entry

King's Lynn: 1776; **D**

King's Lynn, Theatre Royal: c.1814; **D** 1936

Lancaster, (Grand): 1782; extant: *see* entry

Leamington Spa, Bath Street: 1813; closed 1833 and **D**

Leek: fl 1814

Leicester: 1800; **D** 1836

Leicester, Theatre Royal: 1836; Parsons/Beazley; **D** 1958

Leominster, Burgess Street: 1792; **D** 1883

Lewes: **D**

Lichfield: 1790; **D** 1872; David Garrick Memorial Theatre on site 1953 to 1959

Lincoln: 1732; closed 1764; **D** 1900

Littlehampton, New Theatre: 1807; closed 1852; **D** 1892

Liverpool, Cockpit Yard: c.1600; cockpit used as theatre; **D** c.1820

Liverpool, Old Ropery: 1740; **D**

Liverpool, Drury Lane: 1750; **D** 1829

Liverpool, Theatre Royal (i), Williamson Square: 1772; Sir William Chambers; 1802 Foster rebuilt; 1965 **D**

Liverpool, Christian Street/Adelphi/Queens: 1831; converted from circus; much altered later; became a cinema; **D** 1921

London, Brandenburg House (private theatre): 1792; **D**

London Bridge, Subscription Theatre/Royal Borough/Railroad: 1833; **D** after 1838

London, Croydon: 1779; **D**

London, Croydon: 1800; **D**

London, Deptford, 'One-Sided': before 1840; **D**

London, Edmonton: 1805; **D** 1825

London, Greenwich, Penkethman's: 1710; Unknown; **D** after 1712

London, Greenwich, New Royal Kent: 1834; portable; removed to Woolwich 1835

London, Islington, White Conduit House: before 1745; a large room in 1745, rebuilt as Apollo Room and open-air stage in 1811; **D** completed c.1845

London, Kensington, Royal Kent: 1834; **D** after 1840

London, Peckham: became a school; not clear whether any fabric survives

London, Richmond Hill: 1719; **D** after 1756

London, Richmond Hill: 1733; **D**

London, Richmond: 1765; **D** 1884

London, Uxbridge (Wildman's/Jackmans): **D**

London, Woolwich, Royal Kent: 1810; **D** 1831

Loughborough, Sparrow Hill: 1823; extant; exterior only (*see* entry)

Lowestoft Theatre Royal: 1811; largely rebuilt as Salvation Army Citadel

Lowestoft, Crown Street Hall (ex Theatre Royal): 1812 ; largely **D**; some brickwork incorporated into the present building on the site

Lymington: 1771; literary institute incorporates some old fabric

Macclesfield: closed 1780, and **D**

Macclesfield, Theatre Royal: 1811; closed 1875 and largely rebuilt; **D** c.1993

Maidenhead: late 1790; a fit-up; short lived

Maidenhead: 1796; **D** after 1851

Malling: 1790; ceased operation 1830

Manchester, Marsden Street Theatre: 1753; closed 1755; new theatre 1790; **D** 1869

Manchester: 1775; **D** 1789

Manchester, New Theatre Royal/Queens: 1790; closed 1869 and **D**

Mansfield: c.1788; **D**

Margate, Theatre Royal: 1787; much old fabric incorporated into present theatre; *see* entry

Market Drayton (ex Theatre Royal): 1792; extant; *see* entry

Monmouth: ?1775; probably a fit-up; *see* entry

Newark: 1773; much altered and no longer recognisable as a theatre

Newbury: 1787; fragments remain in modern Arts Centre

Newbury and Speenhamland: 1802; **D** c.1967

Newcastle-under-Lyme: 1787; **D**

Newcastle upon Tyne, Nelson Place: 1787; **D**

Newcastle upon Tyne, Amphitheatre: 1789

Newmarket: 1825; altered exterior; gutted interior

Newport, Isle of Wight: 1790s; **D**

Newport, Shropshire: c.1813; altered shell survives in later shops

Newry, County Down: 1783; **D** 1830s

North Walsham: 1828; closed 1845; **D**

Northallerton: c.1800; extant

Northampton, Marefair: 1806; closed 1807; **D** 1922

Norwich: 1759; **D** (adjoined present Theatre Royal site)

Nottingham: 1760; bombed 1941

Oldham: 1810; closed 1845 and **D**

Oswestry: 1775; extant; *see* entry

Paignton: 1750s; inn fit-up; closed after 1817; **D** 1890

Paisley, Abbey Bridge: 1830; closed 1837

Penzance: 1787; extant; *see* entry

Perth: 1820; extant; facade only

Plymouth, Broad Hoe Lane: 1749; a fit-up; abandoned 1758

Plymouth, Theatre Royal Frankfort Gate: 1758; **D**
Plymouth, George Street: 1793; short-lived temporary building
Plymouth, Theatre Royal : 1813; John Foulston with George Wightwick; theatre **D**; 1937 cinema on site
Plymouth, Globe: 1831; extant; see entry
Poole: 1784; fragment, probably originally a warehouse conversion
Poole, Shatford: 1805; closed 1820
Poole: 1829; ceased use 1832
Portsmouth: 1732; **D**
Portsmouth: 1761; **D** 1856
Portsmouth, Sadler's Wells: 1781; short-lived unlicensed theatre
Preston: 1802; **D** 1955
Pwllheli: extant, possibly a fit-up
Ramsgate, St James's: 1832
Reading, Thornton's: 1788; ceased operation 1815; **D**
Reading: 1801; ceased operation 1865; **D**
Retford: 1789; converted to a chapel in 1841 and **D** 1870
Richmond, North Yorkshire: 1788; extant, carefully restored and operational; see entry
Ripon: 1790; Extant, a bus garage; see entry
Rochdale, Anchor Yard: 1766
Rochester: 1791; much altered internally; behind later building; see entry
Romsey: 1790s
Ryde: 1813; conversion from market house of 1810; closed 1871 and **D**
St Asaph: fl 1806; extant; a first-floor fit-up
St Helier Royal, Jersey (i): 1802; barn fit-up but not **D** until 1947
St Helier Royal (ii): 1828; closed 1863 and **D** (fire)
St Peter Port, Guernsey, Theatre Royal: c.1779; **D** by 1880
Salisbury, Theatre at the Vine: 1745
Salisbury. Playhouse at Sun Inn: 1765; short-lived fit-up
Salisbury, New: 1777; **D**
Salisbury: 1790s **D**
Sandwich: –
Saxmundham: a fit-up
Scarborough, Royal: 1787; **D**
Sheerness: fl 1820s
Shepton Mallet: mid-C18; exterior believed that of Central Hall (now a club)
Shotton Colliery: 1834; much altered by c.1989 when it was **D** after storm damage
Shrewsbury, Theatre Royal: 1791 and 1834; the New Theatre of 1834 (the second theatre on the site) was largely **D** in 1898, some parts of the fabric being incorporated into a new Royal County theatre (see entry); now a retail shop
Shrewsbury, Bridge Place: 1821; opened as a circus; became a theatre; part of a brewery by 1868
Sidmouth: 1803; closed c.1814 and **D**
Skipton, Kendalls Yard: fl 1790
Sleaford: 1825; extant; altered in 1850s; see entry
South Shields: c.1792; closed c.1848
Southampton: 1766; converted from silk mill; **D**
Southampton: 1803; fire 1878
Southend-on-Sea (Trotter): 1804; **D** 1859
Southport: –
Southwell: 1816; two rooms knocked together; irregular shape; extant; no trace of theatre interior
Stafford, Playhouse: 1792; much reconstructed in 1840, 1877, 1894, 1896 and 1912; finally **D** in 1920s

Stamford: 1768; exterior only (still a theatre, but interior not restored to original form); see entry
Stockport: 1823; **D**
Stockport, Theatre Royal/New: 1836; **D** c.1887
Stockton on Tees, Green Dragon Yard: 1766; converted from a barn; extant exterior; see entry
Stourbridge: 1798; **D**
Stroud: 1779; closed c.1800; **D**
Sunderland: 1768; rebuilt in 1828 and again in 1871 as Wear Music Hall; **D** 1902
Swaffham: ?1822; **D**
Swansea: 1807; closed 1898
Tamworth: 1796; much altered as malthouse c.1850, substantially rebuilt as chapel 1870 and now arts centre
Taunton, Shakespeare Inn: 1786; **D** 1799
Taunton, Silver Street: 1800; **D** 1846
Teignmouth, Athenaeum: -
Teignmouth: 1802; closed c.1824; **D**
Teignmouth, Royal Clarence/Circus: 1821; **D** late C19
Tenterden, Royal: –
Tewkesbury: 1762; **D**
Tewkesbury: 1823; **D** after 1838
Thetford: c.1812; facade only
Titchfield: 1809; fit-up
Tonbridge, East Theatre: –
Totnes: 1806; **D** (building in Curtains 1982 was never a theatre)
Truro: 1772; facade only; see entry
Tunbridge Wells: 1802; facade only; see entry
Ulverston, Royal: 1796; fragment existed in 1981
Walsall: 1803; closed c.1845; **D** 1933
Wargrave: 1791; **D**
Warrington: 1773; rebuilt 1884; **D** c.1983
Warrington: 1818; **D** c.1983
Warwick, at Cocksparrow Hall: 1786; **D**
Warwick: 1802; **D**
Wells-next-the Sea: 1812; **D**
Wells: c.1750; **D**
Welshpool: fl 1831
Welshpool, Bear Tavern: fl 1810

Tunbridge Wells, Theatre (Ken Woodward)

Weybridge: c.1757; closed 1810; **D** 1900
Weymouth: 1771; **D** c.1850
Whitehaven: 1769; **D** 1976
Winchester, Market House: c.1620; above butchers' stalls: **D**
Winchester: 1760; temporary garrison theatre; dismantled and removed
Winchester: 1785; **D**; one bay of old facade reproduced in modern building
Windsor: 1706; a booth
Windsor: 1791; barn conversion, closed 1793
Windsor, Thornton's: 1793; closed 1815; became a chapel which was later **D**
Wisbech, Angles: 1793; extant; a theatre, but interior is not a restoration; see entry
Woburn: 1814
Woburn Abbey: c.1820; a fit-up in the Silver Room; use ceased c.1850
Wolverhampton: 1779; **D**
Woodbridge: 1814; extant fragment; see entry
Worcester: 1786; 1869 remodelled; 1875 rebuilt C.J. Phipps; 1878 Phipps; 1903 Rowe; 1960 **D**
Worksop: 1788; **D**
Worthing: 1807; **D** after 1855
Wrexham: c.1824; closed 1873; **D** 1964
York: 1765; extant: see entry

Open-Air Theatres

Open-air theatres are numerous and it has not been possible to be completely consistent about inclusion or exclusion. Where they are buildings of some architectural pretension we have tended to include them. The Singing Theatre at Larmer Tree Gardens, Tollard Royal, for example, is so rare an object that it would have seemed odd to omit it. Those which, however deliberately designed for their purpose they may have been, register on the senses less as buildings and more as garden designs, or which really amount to the theatrical exploitation of landscape features, have been excluded. Some, however, are so important that we cannot leave them completely unmentioned. Amongst the most important examples (which, incidentally, have lengthy database entries) are:

    London, Regent's Park
    Porthcurno, Minack
    Scarborough

We have also omitted (to the regret of some compilers) ancient theatres and arenas which were either earth structures or where architecture, if any ever existed, is now fragmentary or has been conjecturally recreated. These include:

    Caerleon
    City of London, Roman Amphitheatre
    Cliveden
    The Cornish 'Rounds'
    Dorchester
    Verulamium

Concert Halls and Assembly Rooms

A few concert halls and assembly rooms of unusual importance to the theatrical history of a town have been admitted to the book, but major national concert halls, even if occasionally used for dramatic presentation, have been omitted. Thus, there are no entries for London, Royal Albert Hall; Bristol, Colston Hall; or Liverpool, St George's Hall.

Ciné-Variety Theatres

As indicated in the Introduction (Limits of the Survey) ciné-varieties have been a particular problem and the method of selecting them for inclusion *in the book* (the database is omnivorous) will undoubtedly be open to argument.

Physical attributes have been one of the main determinants. An impressive array of the expected features of a live theatre – stage house equipped for flying scenery, get-in doors, adequate dressing rooms, etc. – tends to decide the matter (by this test, Woolwich Granada obviously had to be included, while Woolwich Odeon had no claim for consideration). In less obvious cases we have looked for a clear record of significant theatre use, but with the severe application of the guillotine. We have probably excluded many cinema theatres which others would have included but we have had to focus on the fact that the Trust's main duties are toward dedicated theatres rather than, more broadly, places of public entertainment. Occasionally and paradoxically, a comparatively minor ciné-variety has been included where it happens to represent the best chance for making provision for live theatre in an area denuded of 'classic' theatres.

Serious Gains

When the first gazetteer made its qualitative assessments and identified a number of 'sleeping beauties'[1], the authors had no expectation that they could do more than alert a concerned minority to the existence of hidden (or rather, disregarded) wealth. In the event, the influence of *Curtains!!!, or a New Life for Old Theatres* (a significant subtitle) exceeded all expectations. A wide professional and wider general readership began to refer to 'three-star sleeping beauties' and, although the team's judgements may have been treated with proper caution by listing investigators, planners and politicians, the effect was to help bring a number of fine theatres out of the darkness and into the light. It would be fair to say that most of the sleepers which, in 1982, were unlisted or inappropriately graded have now been given recognition and an impressive number of them have either returned triumphantly to their designed use or have some prospect of doing so (the exceptions are dealt with next, under **Serious Losses**).

Other important influences have been at work over the last 20 years, but *Curtains* played a notable part in giving direction and impetus to a trend toward the more effective safeguarding and exploitation of theatre resources.

Douglas Gaiety, Belfast Grand Opera House, Blackpool Grand, Buxton Opera House, Glasgow Theatre Royal, and Newcastle Tyne Theatre were already showing the way before 1982. Amongst the more notable revivals since then have been:

London, Hackney Empire: perhaps the most unlikely and therefore, most exciting reopening
London, Lyceum: now returned to the centre of West End theatre life after nearly 60 years of slumber
London, Playhouse: another that was so long in non-theatre use that it had almost been forgotten
London, Wilton's Music Hall: programmed opera performances recommenced in 1999; restoration planned at time of writing

---

[1]The term was first used in this sense by Christopher Brereton in 1976 (*Architectural Review*, 160, pp. 216–22, 'Act Now to Save Provincial Theatres')

Manchester, Opera House: now in double harness with the Palace Theatre

Margate, Theatre Royal: not yet completely refurbished, but 'open and on its way'

Sheffield, Lyceum: a magnificent theatre which it is difficult to believe could have been so long disregarded

Wakefield, Opera House: Matcham's smallest touring theatre

York Grand Opera House (or Empire): a building with curious origins which, in 1982, was thought unlikely to return to professional use

In addition to these, a number of theatres which were never really 'Sleepers' but might have been said to be dozing into decline, have been given new life by extensive restoration and improvement works, including Bradford Alhambra, Leeds Grand, and London Richmond Theatre, while the London Savoy which was devastated by fire in 1990 and seemed destined for total demolition, has been meticulously recreated.

At the time of writing some work was under way at Morecambe Victoria Pavilion (Winter Gardens) and some progress was being made on proposals for the restoration and reopening of Swansea Palace.

Remaining 'sleepers' which must be near the top of any priority list include London Normansfield, Coronet, and Clapham Grand, Glasgow Britannia, Aberdeen Tivoli, Boscombe Hippodrome, Brighton Hippodrome, Brighton Imperial, Cambridge Festival and Chatham Theatre Royal, followed shortly by Doncaster Grand, Colchester Hippodrome, Hulme Hippodrome and Playhouse, Liverpool Olympia (a vast and impressive space for which an appropriate live use – not necessarily theatrical – should be found), Plymouth Palace, Salford Victoria, Scarborough Royal Opera House, Bo'ness Hippodrome and Bungay New Theatre.

The Patti Opera House at Craig-y-Nos, Abercrave, and Sir David Salomon's Scientific Theatre at Broomhill, Southborough, are special cases calling for special treatment. Both are of national importance.

Some of these theatres may yet have years to wait, but they are potentially valuable resources and worthy of protection. The often-heard objection that this or that place 'already has a theatre' and 'could not possibly support another' always needs careful examination. The existence of a choice of live entertainment, complementing rather than competing, has been seen to have the effect of creating a keener demand. It is also unwise to write off 'second-bests', where there is no certainty that one's natural first choice is, in fact, secure. If Longton had had second choices of the quality of Southampton Mayflower or Canterbury Marlowe (both long disregarded survivors of the post-war massacre) the recent destruction by fire of Matcham's Empire (see **Serious Losses** below) would have been less damaging to the future cultural life of the town.

Serious Losses

Despite the justified optimism expressed in **Serious Gains** above, some deplorable losses have occurred since the first edition.

Longton Empire (1896 Matcham) was perhaps the most tragic. Described in 1982 as 'a first-class example of Victorian theatre architecture', given a three-star rating and earmarked as a building which could readily be restored and reopened to serve a population of 30,000, it was destroyed by fire on New Year's Eve 1992. This occurred while Stoke-on-Trent Repertory Company were attempting to buy the theatre.

Dunfermline Hippodrome & Opera House (1900 and 1921) was owned by the local authority in a town with no other purpose-built theatre. Despite energetic representations by The Theatres Trust, the Scottish Civic Trust and the Scottish Arts Council, the Secretary of State would not stand in the way of demolition in 1981, urging only that 'dismantling, storing and re-using ... architectural features for use elsewhere' should be considered. In a triumph for theatre architecture and to the shame of Dunfermline, the theatre has been re-erected in the Asolo Centre in Saratoga, Florida, USA, where it is providing the kind of service that could have been enjoyed by its city of origin.

Belfast Royal Hippodrome (1907, Bertie Crewe, much altered) was demolished in 1996, a waste of a building which should have found a use in this vital centre, alongside the restored Opera House.

Few of the other lost 'sleepers' were of vital theatrical importance but they included London Islington Palace (c.1869, a rare minstrel hall), Hanwell Park Hall (c.1890 an unusually ambitious late pub music hall), Bethnal Green Royal Victor (1879/90 pub music hall) and Brixton Empress (1898 and 1931); Blyth Theatre Royal (1900, Hope & Maxwell, demolished to make way for a car park), Birkenhead Music Hall (1862, lost because not listed), Liverpool Pavilion (1908, J.J. Alley, destroyed by fire), Liverpool Royal Hippodrome (1876 and 1902); and Wolverhampton Theatre Royal (1914, in poor condition in 1982).

The demolition of Barnsley Alhambra would scarcely merit notice in this context were it not for the subsequent tragic loss of opportunity to revive the Theatre Royal, now a nightclub. Barnsley, as a result, has been left with no working purpose-built theatre and little prospect of gaining one.

A number of good, potentially recoverable theatres have escaped destruction but have had their chances of revival set back (in some cases by many years) by unhelpful changes of use. London Tottenham Palace was a bingo hall and is to be a church. Middlesbrough Empire and Tunbridge Wells Opera House are both pubs, well restored but now unavailable for return to theatre use for the foreseeable future. The decision to allow the change of use at Tunbridge Wells was particularly regrettable given that the local authority had itself initiated studies directed to re-establishing the Opera House as a theatre of regional significance. Cardiff Prince of Wales, a well-preserved and architecturally unusual theatre was crippled for a decade by a thoroughly ill-advised local authority decision (permitted after call-in) to allow subdivision for a multiplicity of uses. In this case, a later conversion to pub, restoring the auditorium to its original volume, can for once be seen as beneficial. The adjoining Philharmonic, by contrast, has had its interior obliterated in a pub conversion. Gazetteer entries will be found for all of these.

The case of the Brighton Palace Pier (1901) contains lessons for all planning authorities concerning the need for the precise wording of conditions and the close monitoring of performance after permissions have been granted. The Pier is listed Grade II*. Planning permission was given in 1986 for the dismantling of the theatre with a view to its being reinstated as part of a development at the landward end of the pier. The development permission was never implemented and, by the time it expired, the salvaged parts had disappeared. Given the form of the permission there appeared to be no way in which reinstatement could be enforced. In this case, the building lost cannot be dismissed as 'only a pier pavilion'. The Palace Pier theatre, with its oriental arcading and turban domes was one of the best examples of its kind and an exceptionally appropriate ornament for Brighton's seafront.

Appendix 3 • The Principal Architects and Designers

Biographical notes by Victor Glasstone, John Earl, David Wilmore and Bruce Peter. The works of the architects and designers collated by Michael Sell and John Earl with the assistance of the various contributors.

This section introduces the work of the most prolific theatre architects. For reasons of space the list of theatres relating to each architect has been compressed to provide the following information:

(i) the name by which the theatre is likely to be best remembered
(ii) the date the theatre opened

Those theatres appearing in **bold type** are existing buildings with entries in the gazetteer. Some theatres which appear in bold may now retain little of the work of the architects under whose name they appear because a later and major rebuild has obliterated most of their work.

Original architect indicates that the theatre named was either a completely new building or a reconstruction which amounted, for practical purposes, to a new building.

Later architect indicates that alterations, minor or extensive but falling short of total reconstruction, were undertaken to an existing theatre.

The annotation '**D**' is used when the building is known to have been demolished or where the remains are too slight to be of significance. The absence of such an annotation should not be taken as evidence that the building survives.

The lists are as complete as we have been able to achieve for *theatre* works. No claim is made for completeness for those architects who were cinema, rather than theatre, specialists.
Where an entry ends with a note of a number of cinemas, their names and locations are to found on the database.
Some notable interior designers of theatres have been included, with a selection of their works. One or two important interior designers of the cinema era have also been included. The special interest of many cinema theatres derives mainly from decorative inventions which often owe comparatively little to the architect.

John ALEXANDER

Based in Newcastle, Alexander designed a number of small cinemas in the 1920s but for the most of his working life he specialised in the interior design of cinemas. He retired in 1954. A collection of beautifully rendered interior perspectives, recovered after his death, included some of the most highly imaginative inventions of the 1920s and 1930s, not all of which have yet been identified.
Alexander was a creator of interiors in more than one sense, in that, as well as producing the designs, he also manufactured

and modelled the fibrous plaster. Amongst the highlights of his extensive oeuvre were the following, illustrating the extraordinary range of his imagination, from his contribution to the full-blooded classical grandeur of Dundee to the unrestrained Art Deco of Worcester. Only the Northwick now survives intact. Brighton, although severely defaced, is recoverable. *JE*

Interiors only

1936	Dundee, Green's Playhouse (part), **D**	
1938	Worcester, Northwick, listed	
1940	**Brighton, Imperial** (Essoldo)	

J.J. ALLEY

Alley was principally responsible for building the Broadhead circuit. The following list is unlikely to be more than a selection of his work

1896	Manchester, Royal Osborne, **D**	
1898	Manchester, Metropole, **D**	
1901	**Manchester, Hulme Hippodrome**, listed	
1902	**Manchester, Hulme Playhouse**, listed	
1904	**Ashton-under-Lyne, Tameside Hippodrome**	
1904	Manchester, Queen's Park Hippodrome, **D**	
1904	Salford, Hippodrome, **D**	
1905	Manchester, King's, Longsight, **D**	
c.1908	Ashton-under-Lyne, Pavilion	
1908	Liverpool, Pavilion, fragment	
1912	Preston, Royal Hippodrome (attributed), **D**	

Robert ATKINSON, OBE FRIBA (1883–1952)

Atkinson was born in Cumberland. He worked at first in an architectural office in Newcastle upon Tyne and later with John Belcher and C.E. Mallows. A fine draughtsman, he was a Tite prizeman in 1905. After qualifying in 1910 he started a practice in Gray's Inn, working at first as a perspective artist for the projects of other architects. Throughout his life he maintained close involvement with the Architectural Association School. He was a profoundly influential teacher and became, in time, both principal and director of education at the school. Later partners in his private practice were W.T. Benslyn, 1920, and A.F. Anderson, 1924.
There was no single Atkinson style. Although an avowed modernist, he was not a purist. Amongst his major works were hotels, town halls, churches, the Barber Institute of Fine Arts in Birmingham and, in 1931, the entrance foyer to Ellis and Clarke's Daily Express building in Fleet Street. This is unarguably an outstanding Art Deco interior, despite its dismissal by Sir Nikolaus Pevsner as 'sensational Expressionism'.
Atkinson was also a designer of cinemas, with one early unexecuted project of 1906 and a whole series of pre-1914

picture houses. P. Morton Shand described his Brighton Regent, 1921, as 'the first – or anyhow the first notable – cinema to be designed by a qualified architect' (the tone of this observation compares interestingly with Edwin Sachs's disdain for the commercial theatre architects of the 1890s). Atkinson's partner, Benslyn, went on to become a specialist cinema designer.

Brighton Regent, demolished as recently as 1974, is regarded by cinema historian David Atwell as having 'a fair claim to be considered as the first British super cinema to be built .... the first of a long line of fine cinemas in the twenties that paved the way for the talkies and the super cinemas of the thirties'. It should certainly have been listed at a high grade and jealously protected. *JE*

Original architect
1921   Brighton, Regent, **D**
1935   Brighton, Pavilion Theatre (designed as a concert/supper room, attached to the Corn Exchange and Dome, later converted to theatre), listed
1939   London (Ealing), Concert Hall for Municipal Buildings

Later architect
1926   London (Westminster), Vaudeville, part reconstruction of earlier C.J. Phipps theatre, listed
1933   London (Haringey), Crouch End Hippodrome, alterations, **D**
1935   Brighton, Dome, reconstruction of interior, listed
1935   Brighton, Corn Exchange, alterations, listed

Cinemas
Atkinson's work included a number of early picture houses in Aberdeen, Edinburgh and Carlisle, and later cinemas in London and elsewhere.

Samuel BEAZLEY (1786–1851)
The son of an army accoutrements maker of Westminster. He received his architectural training in the office of his uncle, Charles Beazley; fought in the Peninsular War; became the leading theatre architect of his day and a fashionable man about town; was the author of over a hundred operas, farces and plays, many of which he directed himself.

Although Beazley used a variety of styles in his general architecture, his theatres were all neo-classical and Grecian, the most impressive and important being the Lyceum – the splendid portico of which survives, with a later interior by Bertie Crewe, marvellously opulent and vulgar. His 1822 alterations to the auditorium of the Theatre Royal, Drury Lane, introduced to London the Continental fashion of stage boxes framed by a giant Corinthian order. This interior has twice been rebuilt but Beazley's Ionic colonnade in Russell Street is still intact. These two important and irreplaceable fragments are all that remains of his many theatres. The others were on a less monumental scale, but were nonetheless well integrated and intimate Regency/early Victorian commercial theatres, those in the provinces being a great advance on the little home-made Georgian playhouses of his predecessors.

He also designed theatres erected in South America, Belgium and India, but little is known about them. His non-theatre works included country houses, Studley Castle, Warwickshire, libraries, the London Bridge terminus and a number of other railway stations. *VG*

Original architect
1816   London (Westminster), New Theatre Royal English Opera, House replacing earlier Lyceum, **D**
c.1820   Leamington Spa, Royal Assembly Rooms
1821   Dublin, Theatre Royal, Hawkins Street
1820   Birmingham, Theatre Royal, rebuilt after fire, **D**
1834   London (Westminster), Royal Soho (Royalty), **D**
1834   London (Westminster), Lyceum, listed
1836   Leicester, Theatre (possibly with William Parsons), **D**
1836   London (Westminster), St James's Theatre, **D**
1840   London, Leicester Square Casino Promenade Concert Room, unexecuted

Later architect
1822   London (Westminster), Drury Lane Theatre Royal, auditorium (since replaced), listed
1831   London (Westminster), Drury Lane Theatre Royal, colonnade, listed
1840   London (Westminster), Adelphi, rebuilt front, listed

Jonas BINNS (d.1904) **and Sons**
Jonas Binns, described as 'a quiet little man (but) with considerable faculty of speech and definite views', founded one of the leading firms of decorators in the north, Jonas Binns and Sons of Halifax. Binns were among the leading specialists nationally in the decoration of theatres, music halls, churches and other public buildings. They had a prodigious output and were regularly employed to decorate Matcham theatres. Their theatre work ranks with the finest of the 'boom' era (cf Boekbinder and de Jong) including the superb Edinburgh Empire of 1892, Blackpool Grand and Douglas Gaiety. After Jonas's death the business was continued by his three sons. *JE*
    Amongst their many theatrical works were:

Interiors only
1886   Derby, Grand
1889   St Helen's, Opera House, **D**
1891   Southport, Opera House, **D**
1891   Cheltenham, Opera House
1892   Edinburgh, New Empire Palace, listed
1892   Portsmouth, New Princes, **D**
1892   Great Yarmouth, Theatre Royal, **D**
1892   Stoke-on-Trent (Hanley), King's/Empire
1893   Hull, Opera House

Jonas Binns (John Earl Collection)

1894	**Wakefield, Opera House**, listed	
1894	**Blackpool, Grand**, listed	
1895	Salford, Regent, **D**	
1895	Rochdale, Theatre Royal, **D**	
1897	Dublin, Theatre Royal, **D**	
1900	**Douglas, Isle of Man, Gaiety**, listed	
1901	**Halifax, Victoria Hall**, listed	
1903	**Harrogate, Royal Hall, Kursaal**, listed	
1903	**Buxton, Opera House**, listed	

Dates unknown

Ashton-under-Lyne, New Opera House
Bury, Opera House
Halifax, Opera House
Halifax, Town Hall, listed
Halifax, Palace, **D**
Glasgow, New Scotia Music Hall, **D**
Sheffield, Theatre Royal, **D**

J.M. BOEKBINDER
Philip Hunt BOEKBINDER

J.M. Boekbinder's interiors were to be found in many late Victorian theatres (*see also* de Jong and Binns). Little is known about the man, but his work can be seen at its best in, for example, Richmond Theatre (1899) and the front of house at Hackney Empire (1901), both by Matcham.

It is interesting to note that, by 1911, Philip H. Boekbinder (underlined thus in his advertisements) was claiming to be 'the only practising member of the Boekbinder family in business', emphasising that he had 'no association with any other firm trading under the Boekbinder name'. At this time he was producing fibrous plaster, carved wood and stone, mainly for the new cinematograph theatres. Philip also made some elephantine ornaments for the Franco-British Exhibition at White City in 1908. *JE*

John (Priestly) BRIGGS, FRIBA (1869–1944)

Articled to Middleton, Prothero and Philpott, architects at Cheltenham; in private practice in London, 1897–1939; besides theatres also architect to Lloyds Banks (Provincial) and Teddington Memorial Hospital, etc.

Briggs's theatre work neatly spans the boom periods mostly alterations of existing buildings. His stylistic variation in external treatment of new theatres varies enormously; Grand, Doncaster, a delicate 1890s interpretation of Regency; Opera House, Tunbridge Wells, an imposing and very early use of neo-Georgian. Tunbridge Wells has an almost square proscenium opening with decorative infill to top corners; decorated friezes support the ceiling; and there is a nice compactness and busyness, quirky with spiked decoration surrounding the somewhat standard treatment of box and balcony fronts.

Original Architect

1897	St Leonard's, Royal Opera House, **D**	
1899	**Doncaster, Grand**	
1902	Preston, Theatre Royal, **D**	
1902	**Tunbridge Wells, Opera House**	
1908	Northwich, Central, **D**	

Later Architect

1897	**Gloucester, Palace**, rebuilt	
1898	Preston, Theatre Royal, enlarged, **D**	
1899	Peterborough, Theatre Royal, converted from skating rink, **D**	

1901	Colchester, Theatre Royal, reconstruction, **D**	
1902	**York, Grand Opera House/Empire**, converted from Corn Exchange	

James George BUCKLE, ARIBA (1852–1924)

J.G. Buckle set up in practice on his own in 1879, from which time he was architect to the Artisans, Labourers and General Dwelling Company, for whom he claimed to have designed more than a thousand houses in six years. He became ARIBA in 1882. He was not one of the leading theatre designers but, like Ernest Woodrow (Edwin Sachs's collaborator on *Modern Opera Houses and Theatres*) he was a noteworthy figure in the early years of theatre regulation. He collaborated with Woodrow in 1884 on a ground-breaking series of articles on 'Theatre Planning and Construction' published in *Building and Engineering Times* and he produced his own book on *Theatre Construction and Maintenance* in 1888. This contained a set of 'model regulations' and a design for a 'safety theatre'. Like Woodrow, he faded from view at what should have been the height of his career. No work later than 1891, architectural or literary, has so far come to light. *JE*

Original architect

1884	**London (Newham), Stratford Theatre Royal**, listed	
1885	**London (Greenwich), Parthenon (Greenwich Theatre)**, largely rebuilt	

Later architect

1883	London (Hackney), Hoxton Variety Theatre, extension and alterations, **D**	
1884	London (Westminster), Princess's, probably minor alterations, **D**	
1885	London (Tower Hamlets), Sebright Music Hall, major reconstruction, **D**	
1885	London (Westminster), Egyptian Hall, alterations, **D**	
1887	London (Hammersmith), Kensington Olympia, reseating	
1887 and 1891	**London (Newham), Stratford Theatre Royal**, alterations and extension, listed	
1891	**London (Westminster), Royal English Opera House** (Palace Theatre), consultant on sighting, safety, etc. (to Colcutt and Holloway). listed	

Francis Graham Moon CHANCELLOR
also MATCHAM and Co. (post Frank Matcham)

Chancellor was for many years Frank Matcham's chief assistant and job architect on many major projects (e.g. Buxton Opera House). After Matcham's retirement he was in control of the practice and took over completely on his master's death in 1920. The firm thereafter did some moderately interesting work in unchallenging, mildly Art Deco style. All inevitably suffered by comparison with Matcham's turn-of-the-century designs. *JE*

Original architects

1931	**London (Islington), Sadler's Wells**, total rebuild	

Later architects

1913	**Winchester, Theatre Royal**, conversion of hotel to theatre, listed	
1920	**London (Westminster), Drury Lane Theatre Royal**, major alterations (unexecuted), listed	
1928	**London (Lambeth), Old Vic**, alterations including new facade, listed	

1928   **London (Westminster), Empire,** Leicester Square, largely rebuilt (job architect for Thomas Lamb), listed
1934   **London (Westminster), London Pavilion,** internal reconstruction as cinema (with Cecil Masey), listed

also a number of cinemas.

Edward CLARK (d. 1894)
Clark was for more than thirty years quantity surveyor to Trinity House, taking off the quantities for Eddystone, Heligoland, Caldy, Portland, Spurn Head and many other lighthouses. He was also honorary architect to St John's Hospital for Diseases of the Skin, off Leicester Square, and to the RSPCA. His architectural practice was, however, to a great extent, directed toward theatre work. Edward Clark was not an innovative designer and his work (so far as it is now possible to judge) was unexciting, seen alongside that of his contemporaries, Hill and Paraire. Nevertheless, he was an important figure in the first flush of music hall construction in the boom years, 1850–70 and also in the frequent music hall remodellings which occurred in the 1870s and 80s. His Metropolitan design was particularly pleasing in its unassuming way. In later years, as the impact of regulation began to be felt, he pushed himself forward as an expert in negotiating with the controlling authorities. The precise extent and timing of his involvement in each case listed below calls for further research. He was certainly the sole designer of the Metropolitan of 1862 but can have had a minor role only in the modification of the Alhambra and Hoxton Britannia. One of his last works was the radical reconstruction of the 1836 Woolwich Theatre Royal, in 1892. *JE*

?1855	London (Camden), Raglan, **D**
?1860	London (Lambeth), South London Palace, **D**
1861	London (Camden), Bedford, **D**
1862	London (Westminster), Metropolitan, **D**
?1884	London (Kensington and Chelsea), Sun, **D**
1885	London (Tower Hamlets), Royal Cambridge, **D**
1888	London (Westminster), Alhambra, minor works, **D**
1889	London (Tower Hamlets), Forester's, **D**
1892	London (Greenwich), Woolwich Theatre Royal, **D**
n.d.	London (Camden), Royal (Weston's), alterations, **D**
n.d.	London (Westminster), Trocadero
n.d.	London (Westminster), Olympic, **D**
n.d.	London (Hackney), Britannia, **D**
n.d.	London (Hackney), Standard (Olympia), **D**
n.d.	Margate, Hall by the Sea

and a theatre in Lima, Peru.

George COLES (d. 1963)
Arthur ROBERTS (1904–1990)
Coles was one of the most prolific and successful of all cinema architects with many 'supers' to his credit, including the Troxy in Stepney and the immense, 4000-seat Gaumont State in Kilburn, both of which had fully equipped theatre stages. His first cinemas date from the early 1920s. By the end of the decade he was producing designs in a variety of styles from Egyptian (Islington Carlton) to Chinese (Southall Palace). He also made many striking essays in the Art Deco manner, bringing 'the Odeon Style' to perfection with the flowing, uncluttered geometry of the cream faience exterior of Woolwich Odeon, 1937. He has been described as a 'front man' and project

organiser, dependent in many of his best works on the design flair of his partner, Arthur Roberts, who joined the practice in 1927. Roberts, rather than Coles, should probably be credited with at least the interiors of such outstanding designs as the Southall Palace and many of the Odeons, including the Deco brilliance of Muswell Hill, 1936.

Coles died in 1963, but the architectural practice continued until 1979. Roberts left Coles when the cinema building boom collapsed at the outbreak of the Second World War. After the war he was the architect to British Road Services. He died in 1990. *JE*

Original architects

1930	London (Southwark), Trocadero, **D**
1931	London (Ealing), Acton Savoy
1933	**London (Tower Hamlets), Troxy** (with Arthur Roberts), listed
1935	London (Enfield), Enfield Savoy
1937	**London (Brent), Gaumont State, Kilburn,** listed
1937	Bournemouth, Odeon
1939	London (Kingston), Kingston Granada

Later architects

1915	London (Hackney), Kingsland Empire, conversion to cinema (with Percy Adams)
1921	London (Tower Hamlets), Whitechapel Rivoli (with Adams, on site of Wonderland), **D**
1926	London (Tower Hamlets), Forester's, conversion of music hall to cinema, **D**
1934	**London (Newham), Borough (Rex)** reconstruction as cinema
1962	**London (Westminster), Empire,** Leicester Square reconstruction as cinema
1963	**London (Tower Hamlets), Troxy,** internal reconstruction, listed

In addition to these, nearly thirty cinema designs have been noted.

Bertie CREWE (d. 1937)
Architectural education in the office of Clement Dowling, London, and at the Atelier Laloux, Paris, a firm that did the Gare d'Orsay, etc. Matcham claimed that Crewe and Sprague worked at one time for him, something never admitted by either. From Crewe's practice sprang four theatre architects who gained fame in the post-boom period: Robert Cromie, J.C. Derham, Edward Jones and Cecil Masey.

Crewe specialised entirely in theatres and, subsequently, cinemas. One of the most dynamic architects of the 1890s–1900s, with a florid, at times almost wild splendour, coloured by a mannerist Baroque, probably the influence of his time in Paris. His early work with Sprague was tepid by comparison with his later extravagance (e.g. Lyceum, Glasgow Palace, Shaftesbury). Crewe's work is typified by horizontal balconies tied to ranges of stage boxes set in a frame, the whole making a gorgeous and elaborate frontispiece. His decorative features are completely three-dimensional, stunning caryatids, giant elephant heads, seated gods – an invigorating atmosphere for the music halls and melodrama houses which his theatres invariably were. At the Stoll, he designed an opera house, more dignified than his music halls, but exuberantly magnificent in the best Continental mode, with borrowings from American giantism. Unlike Matcham, whom in many ways he resembles, Crewe could produce really competent facades which were convincing in both theatrical and architectural terms. After the First World War he went on to design many cinemas and a few theatres, but his manner became tame and he dwindled into the rounded banalities of the Odeon style. After Crewe's death, his partner, Henry Gordon Kay, continued in practice for some years. *VG*

Original architect

1885	Birmingham, Metropole Theatre, **D**
1889	London (Tower Hamlets), Shoreditch Olympia (with W.G.R. Sprague), **D**
1890	London (Westminster), Olympic Theatre, Wych Street, (with W.G.R. Sprague), **D**
c.1890	Brussels, Alhambra
1892	London (Tower Hamlets), Palace Theatre, Bow, **D**
1893	**Lincoln, Theatre Royal** (with W.G.R. Sprague)
1894	London (Southwark), Camberwell Empire (with W.G.R. Sprague), **D**
1897	**Glasgow, Zoo Hippodrome**
1899	London (Camden), Bedford Palace of Varieties, Camden Town, rebuilt, **D**
1900	**Salford, Victoria**, listed
1900	London (Camden), Euston Palace/Regent (with Wylson and Long), **D**
1900	London (Greenwich), Woolwich Hippodrome, **D**
1904	Glasgow, Palace, **D**
1904	**Glasgow, Pavilion**
1904	Paris, Alhambra
1906	Liverpool, Tivoli Palace, **D**
1906	Coventry, Hippodrome, **D**
1906	Paisley, Hippodrome, **D**
1907	Sheffield, Hippodrome, **D**
1907	Belfast, Royal Hippodrome, **D**
1908	Devonport, Hippodrome, **D**
1908	Portsmouth, Hippodrome, **D**
1908	Nottingham, Royal Hippodrome, **D**
1908	Oldham, Palace, **D**
1908	Accrington, Hippodrome, **D**
1908	London (Edmonton), Empire, **D**
1909	Southend, Hippodrome, **D**
1910	**London (Kingston), Kingston Empire** (with C.J. Bourne)
1911	London (Westminster), Stoll, **D**
1911	**London (Camden), Shaftesbury Theatre** (Prince's), listed
1911	Bristol, Bedminster Hippodrome, **D**
1911	Southend-on-Sea, Garon's Imperial
1913	**Redditch, Palace**
1913	**London (Barnet), Golder's Green Hippodrome**, listed
1913	Aldershot, Hippodrome, **D**
1913	Dublin, The Coliseum, **D**
1913	**Oldham, Hippodrome**
1928	**London (Westminster), Piccadilly** (with Edward Stone)
1930	**London (Camden), Phoenix** (with Sir Giles Gilbert Scott and Cecil Masey), listed
1931	**London (Camden), Saville** (with Bennett and Son), listed

Later architect

1898	London (Tower Hamlets), Queen's Poplar, alterations and facade reconstruction, **D**
1901	**London (Islington), Sadler's Wells**, partly

Left, Bertie Crewe (PGH Kay Collection)

remodelled

1902	Liverpool, Royal Hippodrome, alterations (with A. Skelmerdine), **D**
1904	London (Tower Hamlets), Queen's Poplar/Oriental, alterations, **D**
1904	**London (Westminster), Lyceum**, new auditorium constructed behind Beazley's facade, listed
1906	**Bury St Edmunds, Theatre Royal**, alterations to auditorium, listed
1909	Blackburn, Theatre Royal, rebuilt, **D**
1909	London (Hackney), Hoxton Varieties, alterations, **D**
1911	**Burnley, Empire**
1913	**Manchester, Palace**, auditorium reconstructed, listed
1915	Belfast, Theatre Royal, conversion to cinema, **D**
1921	London (Tower Hamlets), Queen's Poplar, alterations to circle and front of house, **D**
1921	Wolverhampton, Hippodrome, internal alterations, **D**
1922	London (Westminster), Tivoli Cinema, (with Gunton and Gunton), **D**

The Theatre Museum also has a collection of undated theatre designs attributed to Bertie Crewe, some of which were possibly never built. These include London: Anerley New; Dublin: Palace of Varieties; Margate: Palace; Southampton: Prince of Wales; Paris: New Theatre of Varieties.

In addition to his theatres, more than thirty cinema designs have been recorded to date.

Alfred DARBYSHIRE, FSA FRIBA (1839–1908)

Born in Salford, Lancashire, of a Quaker family. He was educated at Friends' School, Ackworth, and at Alderley; articled in 1885 to P.B. Alley; set up in practice in Manchester 1862; travelled on the Continent 1864; President of the Manchester Society of Architects 1901–3; Vice-President of the RIBA 1902–1905; President of the Building Construction and Equipment section of the International Fire Congress organised by Edwin Sachs and held in London in 1903; he was also a member of the British Fire Prevention Council. Ran a successful general practice with F. Bennett Smith, FRIBA (Darbyshire and

Bennett Smith), but was much interested in theatre design and wrote *The Irving Darbyshire Safety Plan*, 1884, *An Architect's Experiences: Professional, Artistic and Theatrical*, 1897 and *The Art of the Victorian Stage*, 1907. The first work advocated the use of an asbestos safety curtain between stage and auditorium; its general principles were subsequently incorporated into his rebuilding of the Exeter theatre after the disastrous fire of 1887, which nearly wrecked Phipps's career. The *Safety Plan* also advocated the elimination of overhanging balconies and stage boxes, and the provision behind the seating of ample colonnades connected directly with the exits. Darbyshire's theatres were characterised by an overall neatness and professionalism, a breadth of vision with no overstatement. Both internally and externally there was a strong flavour of French and German theatres of the 1930s, with echoes of Victor Louis. His most important, the Palace, Manchester (the structure of which remains within Crewe's rebuilding of 1913), was clearly influenced by W.H. Ward's Grand, Birmingham, 1883 with its arcading and related dome over the facade. The Palace probably influenced Phipps's final masterpiece, Her Majesty's 1897. VG

Original architect
1869   Manchester, Prince's, **D**
1884   Manchester, Comedy (later Gaiety), **D**
1887   Crewe, Lyceum, listed
1889   Exeter, Royal, **D**
1891   Manchester, Palace (with F. Bennett Smith), listed
1892   Warrington, Royal Court (with John Bland), **D**
1895   Douglas, Isle Of Man, Derby Castle Theatre, **D**
1898   Rawstenstall, Grand, **D**
1901   Manchester, Princes, **D**

Later architect
1871/73/74 Manchester, Prince's, alterations, **D**
1893?   Crewe, Lyceum, listed
n.d.   Manchester, Theatre Royal
n.d.   London (Westminster), Lyceum, alterations, listed

Unexecuted designs exist for Burnley, Victoria Theatre (with F. Bennett Smith).

EMBLIN WALKER, JONES and CROMIE
Robert CROMIE (dates unknown)
Frederick JONES (dates unknown)
Cromie, who worked for Bertie Crewe between 1910–1914, designed well in excess of forty theatres and cinemas in the 1920s and 1930s, some of them in partnership with Emblin Walker and Frederick Jones. The auditorium of Drury Lane Theatre Royal probably owed its character to Jones rather than either Walker or Cromie. The London Apollo, Hammersmith, has a fine stage with a 63ft proscenium opening and it is likely that many other Cromie cinemas (some of which had imaginative interiors by Mollo and Egan) were well equipped as theatres and had a record of live performance, but further investigation is needed to establish which. Cromie's views on cinema design were succinctly expressed in *Architectural Design and Construction* in 1938 (*see* entry for London Apollo). JE

The following do appear to be of theatrical significance:

Original architects
1927   Maidenhead, Rialto
1928   Windsor, Playhouse, **D**
1928   London (Croydon), Davis, **D**

1929   Epsom, Granada
1929   London (Enfield), Winchmore Hill Capitol, **D**
1931   Dewsbury, Playhouse
1932   London (Kingston), Kingston Regal, listed
1932   Southampton, Plaza
1932   London (Hammersmith), (London) Apollo, listed
1933   Winchester, Regal
1933   London (Merton), Wimbledon Broadway/Regal
1934   Margate, Regal
1937   Scunthorpe, ABC
1937   London (Westminster), Prince of Wales

Later architects
1920   Rochdale, Hippodrome, **D**
1921   London (Hackney), Dalston Theatre, reconstruction as a picture house (with F.E. Jones)
1922   London (Westminster), Drury Lane Theatre Royal, rebuilt auditorium (Emblin, Walker Jones and Cromie), listed
1939   Hull, New (with W.B. Wheatley), converted assembly rooms to theatre

At least twenty-five other, mainly cinema, designs by Cromie are known

Walter EMDEN (1847–1913)
Born in London, Walter Emden was second son of William S. Emden, sometime lessee of the Olympic Theatre. William had another son, Henry (1852–1930), by an Olympic actress. Henry became a leading scenic artist, painting the original act drop for his brother's Trafalgar Theatre in 1892. Walter studied mechanical engineering in the workshops of Maudsley, Sons and Field, Lambeth, and was a civil engineer in the firm of Thomas Brassey. He became an architectural pupil of Kelly and Lawes, FRIBA 1870 in which year he secured his first commission for the re-modelling of the Globe Theatre. He was for a long period a member of the Strand District Board of Works, and for seven years their Chairman. In 1890 he was elected a member of London City Council. He retired 1906, presenting his practice to his four principal assistants, S.H. Egan, W.S. Emden, A.J. Croughton and T.C. Ovenstone, who carried on as Emden, Egan and Co. Besides theatres, Walter Emden was the architect of many hotels, restaurants and similar buildings. Emden exemplified the mid-Victorian laissez-faire attitude to theatre architecture. In his 1870 reconstruction of the Globe (done in his first year of 'studying' architecture) he was already calling himself 'architect'. His lack of formal training shows in his early work: until he started collaborating with Crewe and Phipps, his was the epitome of charming architectural illiteracy. The exterior of Terry's was that of a typical pub of the period, and the famous Tivoli, a glorified fun palace, quite different in manner from the stately colonnade of the Garrick. Internally too, he graduated from simple, delicately decorated balconies supported on slender columns – curtained at the proscenium ends to form stage boxes of the firm elaborate style (still with low-relief ornament) of the Garrick or the Duke of York's, excellent examples of late 1880s–early 1890s Phipps. There is a well-behaved, precise quality to Emden's later work which properly reflects his social achievements in the world of affairs. VG/DW

Original architect
1887   London (Westminster), Terry's, **D**
1888   London (Kensington and Chelsea), Royal Court, listed

1889 **London (Westminster), Garrick** (with C.J.Phipps), listed
1890 London (Westminster), Tivoli, **D**
c.1890 London (Bromley), Crystal Palace Theatre, **D**
1891 Ipswich, Lyceum, **D**
1892 **London (Westminster), Duke of York's,** listed
1893 Sheffield, City (with Holmes)
1897 Southampton, Palace of Varieties, **D**
1898 **Barnsley, Theatre Royal** (with Herbert Crawshaw)
1899 London (Ealing), Ealing Theatre, **D**
1900 Swansea, Empire, **D**

Later architect
1870 London (Westminster), Globe, Newcastle Street, **D**
1871 London (Kensington and, Chelsea), New Chelsea/Court/Belgravia, **D**
1892 **London (Westminster), Palace,** conversion to variety theatre, listed
1895 **Newcastle upon Tyne, Theatre Royal,** reconstruction of auditorium and front of house (with Newcombe), listed
1895 London (Westminster), Royalty, Dean Street, alteration, **D**
1898 London (Westminster), Imperial, alteration to theatre of 1876, by Bedborough, **D**
1906 Reading, Vaudeville (with Emden, Egan and Co.)

Emden also designed cinemas.

John FAIRWEATHER (1867–1942)
John Fairweather was born in 1867 and apprenticed to J.M. Munro, FRIBA, in 1882. Later he attended Glasgow School of Art. He started his own practice in 1895, being joined by his son William John Fairweather in 1938. He designed public buildings, schools and hospitals, but was principally famous as cinema architect for circuits run by show families, the Greens (Glasgow), Bostocks (East Anglia) and Kemps (Saltcoats). He is best known for his ponderous ciné-variety theatres, with breathtaking auditoria lined by soaring classical orders and stacks of boxes. Externally, his facades were less assured, being memorable neither for their grandeur nor their modernity. Between 1921 and 1940, he designed Playhouses at Ayr, Glasgow, Dundee (with a magnificent frontage by Joseph Emberton), Wishaw, Edinburgh and at countless other small ciné-varieties and smaller cinemas. He died in January 1942 in a car accident. *BP*

Original architect
1913 Saltcoats, La Scala
1924 **Ayr, Green's Playhouse**
1927 Glasgow, Playhouse, **D**
1927 Glasgow, Ibrox Capitol
1929 **Edinburgh, Playhouse,** listed
1936 Dundee, Playhouse (with Joseph Emberton), **D**
1929 **Colchester, Playhouse,** listed
1938 **Wigan, Ritz/ABC**
1940 Wishaw, Playhouse

Later architect
1935 **Burton-upon-Trent, Ritz,** total rebuild

FINCH HILL and PARAIRE
William FINCH HILL
Edward Lewis PARAIRE, (1826–1882)
Nothing is known of Finch Hill's early background. He was in

partnership with Paraire (who came of a French family naturalised in Britain) from c.1856–c.1870 about which time the partnership seems to have been dissolved. Both were still in practice in the late 1870s, with separate addresses in the same street. They both described themselves as 'architect and surveyor'. They were famous pub architects; Paraire later also designed churches and banks. Besides their few straight commercial theatres, including the splendid Hoxton Britannia, they were a main link in the pub-into-music hall development. A design for 'a music hall in Covent Garden' (presumably Evans's) was exhibited by Hill at the Royal Academy in 1856. Paraire exhibited the Britannia design in 1859.

Their early music halls were typical of the time: rectangular rooms with a single narrow balcony and a raised platform-stage at the end, set within an alcove. 'Finch Hill was a master of the opulent but never licentious classicism of the 1850s. Audiences knocked back their beer in sumptuous settings designed by an architect who knew the churches of Gibbs, Archer and Hawksmoor' (Mark Girouard). Later theatres were charming and simple: double balconies running round to the proscenium arch, with boxes formed just by curtaining at the ends. The decoration had a crisp fresh quality, quite different from the three-dimensional voluptuousness of the later 1870s and 1880s. Being built before the days of strict building regulations the theatres had almost no street facade, merely thin almost domestic slivers being presented to the street. *VG*

Original architects
1855 **London (Westminster), Evans's Music and Supper Rooms,** (Finch Hill)
1857 London (Camden), Weston's Music Hall (Holborn Empire), **D**
1858 London (Hackney), Hoxton Britannia, **D**
1860 London (Islington), Philharmonic (Empire), **D**
1861 London (Westminster), Oxford Music Hall, **D**
1864 London (Tower Hamlets), Royal Cambridge Music Hall, **D**
1866 London (Camden), Holborn Theatre Royal, **D**

Later architects
1856 London (Tower Hamlets), Effingham Saloon, major reconstruction (Finch Hill), unexecuted
1869 London (Tower Hamlets), Oxford Music Hall, rebuilt, **D**
1870 London (Islington), Philharmonic (Empire), altered, **D**
1873 London (Westminster), Oxford Music Hall, rebuilt, **D**
1874 London (Islington), Philharmonic (Empire), minor works and redecoration, **D**

W.R. GLEN (1884–1954)
William Riddell Glen, MC FRIAS LRIBA studied at Glasgow School of Art and trained with Frank Burnett, Bowson and Carruthers. He started in private practice in 1904, with J.A. Campbell and A.D. Hislop. After the First World War, from 1919 to 1929 he went into partnership with A.V. Gardener, who had already designed cinemas. Glenn was house architect for ABC from 1929 and became one of the most prolific of all cinema architects, being responsible for the design of nearly 100. His interiors were imaginative and extremely varied in character. His larger cinemas had fully equipped stages. *JE*

Original architect
1933 Torquay, Regal, **D**
1935 Southampton, Forum
1936 Exeter, Savoy, **D**

1936	Lincoln, ABC/Savoy, **D**
1937	Bournemouth, Westover
1937	Plymouth, Royal Cinema
1937	Portsmouth, Savoy
1937	Swindon, Savoy/ABC
1937/38	Rochdale, ABC/Regal (with Leslie C. Norton)
1939	Staines, Regal
1939/56	Gloucester, ABC/Regal (designed 1939; completed 1956 by Farrow)
1940	Bristol, Rex, Bedminster

Later architect

1930	**London (Camden), Dominion**, internal alterations, listed
1940s	Winchester, Ritz, redesigned for ABC

In addition to these, nearly sixty cinema designs have been noted

Hubert van HOOYDONK (1859/1860–1940)
Van Hooydonk was born in Breda, the son of a Dutch sculptor. He studied at the Ecole des Beaux Arts, Paris, and was highly regarded as an interior decorator at 20 years old. He worked for the South Audley Street firm of J.D. Jetley but had his own business by the 1890s, decorating aristocratic houses. He also designed furniture and sold easel paintings. In retirement he continued to paint pictures and lacquer screens. *JE*

His known theatrical works, which included at least one interior for Sprague, are:

1881	**London (Westminster), Empire**, Leicester Square, redecoration
1901	**London (Westminster), Apollo Theatre**, design of interior (he personally painted the act drop), listed
1901	Vienna, Volk Theater, interior
1905	**London (Westminster)**, Strand, designed interior, listed

HOPE and MAXWELL
William HOPE (1862–1907)
Joseph Charlton MAXWELL, ARIBA (fl 1885–1926)
A.K. TASKER (from 1908)
Hope set up practice in North Shields at the age of twenty-two in 1884. Joseph C. Maxwell was articled to him during 1885–9, and rejoined the practice as an assistant in 1891 becoming a partner around 1896. Hope's first theatre design in 1894 was for the Wallsend Royalty, though this was never actually built. The design may have been commissioned by Weldon Watts, the local theatre proprietor. Hope then designed in close succession for Watts, Byker Grand, Gateshead Metropole and South Shields Grand. Hope's eclectic architectural manner was based on Queen Anne Revival, in redbrick with gables, corner towers and oeil-de-boeuf windows at high level. Victor Glasstone's summary of his work as 'the architecture of entertainment run riot' encapsulates the mixture of styles which came together to create his extravagant, uninhibited but well-planned provincial theatres.

Hope and Maxwell's first joint theatre venture was the reconstruction of the Scotia Music Hall in Glasgow, renamed the Metropole. They continued to work together, creating amongst others Blyth Theatre Royal, which was built by Arthur Jefferson, the father of Stan Laurel. Its destruction in 1984 was recorded on film as one of the most dramatic, and perhaps one of the last great avoidable losses of its kind. This auditorium like

many of Hope and Maxwell's was decorated with plasterwork supplied by A.R. Dean and Co. of Birmingham, and the balcony fronts were almost identical to those of the Newcastle Palace Theatre (1895 by J.W. Taylor of Newcastle).

The Hope and Maxwell partnership was dissolved towards the end of 1902, and Hope's next theatre, Her Majesty's in Carlisle, was in collaboration with another Newcastle based architect, W.H. Bendle. His final theatre was Sunderland King's Theatre, which opened on Christmas Eve 1906, one week before his death at the early age of forty-four. Externally, the theatre was dominated by an octagonal tower, whilst internally Hope employed the Hennebique ferro-concrete system for the construction of the balcony cantilevers.

The practice, which continued after his death as Hope and Tasker (Andrew Kerr Tasker), designed several other theatres and cinemas including in 1911 the Empire Theatre, Preston, with Bush.

The strength of Hope and Maxwell's work was in its organised chaos. The external treatments were a summation of quotations strung together with charming provincial naiveté, quite unlike the classical pretensions of London based architects like Sprague. Yet the planning of their theatres was workmanlike and methodical and introduced new ideas. It is sad to reflect that only the Swansea Grand remains as a testament to their unquestionable ability to create an auditorium with exceptional theatrical atmosphere. *DW*

Original architects

1890	Newcastle upon Tyne, Theatre of Varieties, Wilfred Street, unexecuted
1894	Wallsend, Royalty, unexecuted
1896	Gateshead, Metropole, **D**, pub remains
1896	South Shields, Grand/Tivoli Theatre of Varieties, **D**
1896	Byker, Newcastle upon Tyne, Grand, **D**
1896	Margate, Hippodrome (with J.C. Maxwell), **D**
1896	Hartlepool, Theatre Royal, unexecuted
1897	**Swansea, Grand**, listed
1898	Southampton, Grand, **D**
1898	Glasgow, Metropole (with J.C. Maxwell), **D**
1899	Leeds, Queen's Palace (with J.C. Maxwell), **D**
1900	Blyth, Theatre Royal (with J.C. Maxwell), **D**
1900	Middlesbrough, Theatre Royal (with J.C. Maxwell), **D**
1900	Newcastle upon Tyne, Theatre, Elswick Road, unexecuted
1901	South Shields, Central Palace of Varieties (with J.C. Maxwell), **D**
1903	Middlesbrough, Grand Opera House (with J.C. Maxwell), **D**
1905	Stockton, Hippodrome, **D**
1905	Carlisle, Her Majesty's (with Bendle), **D**
1906	Sunderland, King's, **D**
1908	Stockton, Castle Theatre/Empire (Hope and Tasker), **D**
1910	Washington, Alexandra Theatre (Hope and Tasker), **D**
1910	Newcastle upon Tyne, Picturedrome (cinema) (Hope and Tasker), **D**
1911	Preston, Empire (Hope and Tasker with Bush), **D**
1912	Gateshead, Shipcote Hall (cinema), **D**

Later architects

1896	Gateshead, Queen's, minor works
1896	Hartlepool, Theatre Royal, alterations for Weldon Watts, unexecuted
1896	Stockton-on-Tees, Theatre Royal, alterations to front of house

1899   West Hartlepool, Alhambra Palace of Varieties, interior
        remodelled, **D**
1902   North Shields, Boro Theatre, plans for reconstruction,
        unexecuted
1904   Tynemouth, Palace by the Sea, alterations, **D**

Felix de JONG

Felix de Jong was possibly the greatest of the theatre decorators (that is, plasterers and artistic painters) operating in the Golden Age, 1880–1900 (but *see also* Binns and Boekbinder). Apart from his dapper, neatly bearded appearance, few personal details are yet known. It would be a major task to identify every one of the scores of theatres and public buildings he embellished for a long list of architects, but it can be said with certainty that he worked so closely with Frank Matcham that they might almost be said to have operated branches of a single design studio. Matcham was known to have exercised total control over every phase of his theatre designs, but the efficiency and speed of delivery of the practice must have been greatly dependent on trusted specialists like de Jong who could translate the master's imaginative compositions (and endless revisions) into brilliant three-dimensional form. A musical parallel might be seen in the creative energy released by the Ellington/Strayhorn partnership.

Matcham's later theatres continued to use elaborate fibrous plaster ornament but, after 1901, de Jong's juicy allegorical paintings were less in demand. Nevertheless, the relationship remained close and, in 1920, de Jong was the executor of Matcham's will.

Matcham occasionally used both de Jong and Boekbinder (qv) in one theatre (e.g. Hackney Empire where de Jong decorated the auditorium and Boekbinder the front of house) probably in order to meet cruel deadlines.

Examples of de Jong's painted interiors can be seen in for example the Tottenham Public House in Oxford Street, London (1892), Portsmouth Theatre Royal (1900) and Hackney Empire (1901). *JE*

Theodore KOMISARJEVSKI (1882–1954)

Komisarjevski, who became a British subject in 1932, was born in Venice of Russian parents. He spent his childhood in St Petersburg and graduated at the Imperial Institute of Architecture, but by 1907 he had entered on a theatre career as a producer and, eventually, manager. After the Revolution he became Director of the Moscow State Theatre but left Russia in 1919 and settled in England where his influence was soon felt in the fields of direction, design and stage lighting. In 1925, for a short but historically important period, he worked under Philip Ridgeway's management at Barnes Theatre (*see* Byfeld Hall). He directed and designed five plays here, with many famous actors and actresses working in the repertory company. Later in life he went to America.

When the Granada circuit was launched in 1930, Komisarjevski was engaged by Sydney Bernstein as house designer. Working frequently with painter Vladimir Polunin, he created some of the most memorable interiors of the supercinema era, combining his skills in architecture and stage design to striking effect. Eclectic in the extreme, his designs were an important part of the excitement of cinema-going, much as Matcham's work had been for the variety theatre audiences of the boom period.

A selection of Komisarjevski's cinema theatre work is given below. *JE*

Felix de Jong
(John Earl Collection)

Interiors only

1925   London (Newham), West Ham Kinema
1927   London (Brent), Willesden Empire
1927   London (Enfield), Rialto
1920   Dover, Granada
1930   London (Camden), Phoenix, listed
1930   London (Waltham Forest), Walthamstow Granada,
        listed
1931   London (Wandsworth), Tooting Granada, listed
1932   London (Ealing), Northfields Avenue/Spanish City
        (attributed), listed
1933   London (Enfield), Edmonton Empire, listed
1934   Shrewsbury, Granada, listed
1935   Manchester, Gaumont, Oxford Street
1936   London (Newham), Granada, Barking Road
1937   London (Harrow), Harrow Granada, listed
1937   London (Greenwich), Woolwich Granada, listed
**1937   London (Wandsworth), Clapham Granada, St
        John's Hill**, listed
1939   London (Kingston), Kingston Granada, listed

MARC HENRI and LAVERDET
Marc HENRI
Gaston LAVERDET

A French firm of decorators who worked closely with Edward Stone and Robert Cromie. Mollo and Egan (qv) started work in their studio. Marc Henri and Laverdet were wholly or largely responsible for the interior design of a number of important theatres. *JE*

Interiors Only

1928   London (Westminster), Piccadilly (Marc Henri)
1929   London (Westminster), Duchess
**1930   London (Westminster), Prince Edward/London
        Casino**
1930   London (Westminster), Whitehall, listed

and many cinemas.

Cecil MASEY (1881–1960)

Cecil Masey was working with his father, Philip E. Masey, ARIBA, by 1896. In 1897 he was with J.P.R. Briggs, FRIBA, then, in 1902, became a draughtsman in Bertie Crewe's office, where he was engaged solely on theatres and music halls. He started his own practice in 1909 and in 1910 worked with Roy Young on the Wimbledon Theatre. From about 1930 he specialised in cinema design.

His cinemas were in a variety of styles but, like Coles, he was often reliant on the skills of other designers to produce his best work. The Woolwich Granada illustrates the curious results sometimes produced. The basic form is, presumably, Masey's. The exterior design by Reginald Uren, is in strikingly modern, Dudok-ish style. The interior, by Komisarjevski, is a dream palace, completely unrelated to the exterior and excelled in imaginative brilliance by few cinema theatres of the period. *JE*

Original architect

1910	**London (Merton), Wimbledon Theatre** (with Roy Young), listed	
1915	London (Bromley), Penge Empire (with W.G.R Sprague), **D**	
1930	**London (Camden), Phoenix** (with Bertie Crewe, Sir G.G. Scott and Komisarjevski), listed	
1931	**London (Wandsworth), Tooting Granada** (with Reginald Uren and Komisarjevski), listed	
1937	**London (Greenwich), Woolwich Granada** (with Slater and Uren, and Komisarjevski), listed	
1937–42	London, National Theatre Projects (with Sir Edwin Lutyens), unexecuted	
1938	**Loughborough, Stanford Hall** (private theatre), listed	

Later architect

1925	London (Lambeth), South London Palace of Varieties, reconstruction, **D**
1928	London (Wandsworth), Balham Palladium, enlarged, **D**
1933	London (Enfield), Edmonton Empire, conversion of music hall to cinema, **D**

At least twenty-four cinema designs by Masey have also been noted.

Frank MATCHAM (1854–1920)
Born in Newton Abbot, Devon, the son of a brewery manager who moved to Torquay after the birth. He attended Babbacombe school there and in 1868 was apprenticed to a local architect and surveyor, George Soudon Bridgeman. In the mid-1870s he joined the London practice of Jethro T. Robinson, consulting theatre architect to the Lord Chamberlain, marrying his daughter in 1877, and taking over his work when Robinson died the following year. 1878 was also important in being the year when the first regulations regarding theatres were enacted, incorporating advice from Robinson.

Henceforth Matcham's success was unbounded and he went on to become the most prolific theatre architect of all time. His work completely spans the boom period, and beyond. Despite his enormous output, he developed a very personal style, instantly recognisable; even his poor and often shoddy external treatment always bears his stamp; yet no two buildings are ever identical. He was the supreme example of the unacademic architect who became a master of his craft. He could always be relied upon to deliver a lively sensuous interior, inexpensively constructed, while remaining acutely aware of the technical difficulties of sight lines, acoustics and construction. Both he and his resident engineer, Robert Alexander Briggs, took out patents for lifts, a concentric cantilever for theatre balconies, etc. Matcham was at his best and most fanciful in the 1890s, with a remarkable grasp of the three-dimensional possibilities of auditorium design, using every trick to achieve maximum effect: dipping balconies, stage boxes step-

ping down and set forwards and backwards to better the sight line; the whole composition awash with a cornucopia of drapery and decoration, often architecturally 'illiterate', but completely convincing and of a piece. After the turn of the century, his style became more restrained, although still brilliantly efficient and thoroughly under control. He also designed pubs. His phenomenal success and popularity both with the public and the great theatrical entrepreneurs was never appreciated by the architectural critics of the day, who, while praising his technical facility 'marked by good seating accommodation, economy on space and cost, and rapidity in execution', damned his aesthetic sense as 'undistinguished'. It is only in recent years that his astonishing theatrical flair has been recognised as near genius. He was the first Victorian theatre architect to receive (in 1980) the accolade of a book devoted to his life and work.

New information is still coming to light on Matcham and no list of works can hope to be exhaustive. Many of the works noted as being to existing buildings will be found to be total or very substantial rebuilds. *VG*

Original architect

1873	Paignton, Oldway House Theatre (as assistant to G.S.Bridgman), **D**
1879	London (Southwark), Elephant and Castle Theatre (completing J.T. Robinson's work), **D**
1885	Glasgow, Hengler's Grand Cirque, **D**
1885	Glasgow, Royalty, **D**
1886	London (Wandsworth), Albert Palace, Café Chantant, **D**
1887	Brighton, Grand/Eden/Ginnett's Circus, **D**
1888	Bolton, Theatre Royal **D**
1888	Stockport, Theatre Royal, **D**
1888	Brighton, Alhambra, **D**
1888	Newcastle upon Tyne, Alhambra
1888	Middlesborough, Royal
1888	London (Greenwich), Woolwich Grand, unexecuted
1889	**Blackpool, Opera House**
1889	**St Helen's, Theatre Royal** (iii)
1889	Halifax, Grand, **D**
1890	Bury, Theatre Royal, **D**
1891	Ashton-under-Lyne, Theatre Royal, **D**
1891	Portsmouth, New Prince's (after destruction of Royal Albert), **D**
1891	**Cheltenham, Everyman Theatre/Opera House**, listed
1891	Southport, Opera House, **D**
1892	**Edinburgh, Empire (Palace)/Festival**, listed
1892	Llandudno, Victoria Palace, unexecuted
1893	Hull, Grand
1894	**Blackpool, Grand**, listed
1894	Bolton, Grand, **D**
1894	**Wakefield, Royal Opera House**, listed
1895	**Belfast, Grand Opera House**, listed
1895	Sheffield, Empire, **D**
1895	Salford, Regent, **D**
1896	London (Lambeth), Brixton Borough Theatre and Opera House, **D**
1896	Cardiff, Empire, **D**
1896	**London (Newham), Stratford Borough**
1897	London (Hackney), Alexandra. Stoke Newington, **D**
1897	Hull, Empire Palace, **D**
1897	**South Shields, Empire/Palace** (with Milburn)
1897	Glasgow, Empire, **D**

1898   Birmingham, Alhambra
1898   Great Yarmouth, Theatre Royal, **D**
1898   Leeds, Empire Palace, **D**
1898   Leeds, County Arcade (adjoined Empire), listed
1898   Morecambe, Royalty, **D**
1898   Stoke-on-Trent (Hanley), Grand, **D**
1898   Nottingham, Empire Palace, **D**
1898   London (Hammersmith), Granville, Walham Green, **D**
c.1899   Huddersfield, Grand (project, never built)
1899   London (Lewisham), New Cross Empire, **D**
1899   London (Richmond), Richmond Theatre, listed
1899   Newport, Empire Palace, **D**
1899   Salford, Broadway
1900   London (Westminster), London Hippodrome,
        listed
1901   London (Hackney), Hackney Empire, listed
1901   Leicester, Palace, **D**
1903   Buxton, Opera House, listed
1903   London (Hammersmith), Shepherd's Bush
        Empire, listed
1903   Harrogate, Royal Hall (with R.J. Beale), listed
1903   London (Islington), Marlborough, **D**
1904   Glasgow, King's, listed
1903   Newcastle upon Tyne, Empire, **D**
1904   Manchester, Ardwick Green Empire, **D**
1904   Manchester, Hippodrome, **D**
1904   London (Westminster), London Coliseum, listed
1905   Aberdeen, His Majesty's, listed
1905   Glasgow, Coliseum
1905   Ipswich, Hippodrome, **D**
1905   Liverpool, Olympia, listed
1906   Aberdeen, His Majesty's, listed
1907   London (Brent), Willesden Hippodrome, **D**
1907   Portsmouth, Southsea King's, listed
1909   London (Redbridge), Ilford Hippodrome, **D**
1910   London (Islington), Finsbury Park Empire, **D**
1911   Brighton, Alhambra Opera House, **D**
1911   London (Lewisham), Lewisham Hippodrome, **D**
1911   Glasgow, Olympia (with George Arthur), facade
1911   London (Westminster), Winter Garden, **D**
1911   London (Westminster), Victoria Palace, listed
1912   Chatham, Empire, **D**
1912   London (Hounslow), Chiswick Empire, **D**
1912   London (Haringey), Wood Green Empire,
        facade
1912   Bristol, Hippodrome (with Crewe), listed
1912   London (Richmond), Karsino, Taggs Island, **D**

Later architect
1879   Glasgow, Royalty Theatre (with Eadie), **D**
1880   Glasgow, Gaiety Music Hall, alterations, **D**
1883   London (Islington), Islington Empire, **D**
1884   London (Lambeth), Astley's, **D**
1884   London (Southwark), Elephant and Castle, **D**
1884   London (Lambeth), Canterbury Theatre of Varieties, **D**
1884   London (Tower Hamlets), Mile End Empire (Paragon), **D**
1886   Blackburn, Theatre Royal, **D**
1887   Stoke-on-Trent (Hanley), Theatre Royal, reconstruction (with C.J. Phipps)
1888   Douglas, Isle of Man, Grand, **D**
1888   London (Islington), Islington Empire (with C. Bell), **D**
1888   Colchester, Grand, reconstruction, **D**
1889   Bristol, Prince's, reconstruction, **D**

Frank Matcham

1889   Rochdale, Theatre Royal and Opera House, alterations, **D**
1890   London (Lambeth), Canterbury Theatre of Varieties, **D**
1891   London (Westminster), Tivoli, alterations, **D**
1892   Bishop Auckland, Eden, **D**
1892   Great Yarmouth, Theatre Royal, **D**
1892   Edinburgh, Empire/Festival, new theatre built, listed
1893   Derby, Grand, alterations
1894   Birmingham, Empire Palace, **D**
1894   Stoke-on-Trent (Hanley), Theatre Royal, major remodelling
1894   London (Hackney), Shoreditch Empire, **D**
1894   Birmingham, Empire Palace, rebuilt, **D**
1894   Manchester, Comedy
1895   London (Hammersmith), Lyric Opera House, **D** and reconstructed
1895   Reading, Royal County, **D**
1895   Bristol, Prince's, alterations, **D**
1896   Liverpool, Empire/Alexandra, reconstructed, listed
1896   Stoke-on-Trent (Longton), Empire, **D**
1896   Manchester, Palace, alterations, listed
1897   London (Haringey), Crouch End Opera House, **D**
1897   Dublin, Theatre Royal, **D**
1897   Nottingham, Theatre Royal, listed
1897   Aberdeen, Tivoli, listed
1897   Glasgow, Empire, **D**
1897   London (Westminster), Metropolitan, rebuilt within old shell, **D**
1897   Lancaster, Grand, alterations
1897   Glasgow, Hengler's Grand Cirque, **D**
1898   Stoke-on-Trent (Hanley), Gaiety, rebuilt, **D**
1899   South Shields, Empire Palace (with Milburn), minor additions
1900   London (Greenwich), Woolwich Empire, major reconstruction, **D**
1900   Keighley, Queen's, **D**
1900   Portsmouth, Theatre Royal, major reconstruction, listed
1900   Derby, Grand Theatre, reconstruction of interior
1900   Douglas, Gaiety, reconstruction, listed
1900   Cardiff, Empire Palace, rebuilt after fire, **D**
1901   London (Islington), Islington Empire, **D**
1901   Brighton, Hippodrome, major reconstruction, listed
1901   St Helens, Theatre Royal, reconstructed after fire
1901   Newcastle upon Tyne, Theatre Royal, Grey Street, reconstruction of interior, listed

1901	Sheffield, Theatre Royal, Tudor Street, alterations, **D**
1902	Hull, Empire Palace, **D**
1902	Bristol, Prince's, remodelling, **D**
1902	Newcastle upon Tyne, Olympia, **D**
1902	**London (Newham), Stratford Theatre Royal**, listed
1903	**Eastbourne, Devonshire Park Theatre**, internal alterations, listed
1903	Glasgow, Empire, **D**
1904	Newcastle upon Tyne, Empire, minor alterations, **D**
1905	London (Camden), Holborn Empire, rebuilt behind Runtz's facade, **D**
1905	London (Westminster), Terry's Theatre, minor alterations, **D**
1906	London (Camden), Holborn Empire, **D**
1907	Birmingham, Grand, alterations (with Essex, Nicol, and Gordon), **D**
1907	Portsmouth, Prince's, alterations
1908	Manchester, Gaiety, **D**
1908	London (Westminster), Metropolitan, **D**
1908	Ramsgate, Royal Palace, converted from New Amphitheatre, **D**
1909	**London (Westminster), London Hippodrome**, listed
1909	**Aberdeen, Tivoli**, listed
1910	Keighley, Hippodrome
1910	London (Hammersmith), Palace of Varieties, **D**
1910	**London (Westminster), London Palladium** (new theatre behind Lewis's facade), listed
1911	Birmingham, Prince of Wales (with Tugwell), **D**
1911	**Blackpool, His Majesty's Opera House**
1911	Castleford, Theatre Royal, **D**
1911 and 1912 Edinburgh, Empire/Festival, partly rebuilt, listed
1912	London (Westminster), Alhambra, alterations, **D**
1912	Castleford, Royal, **D**
1913	Leicester, Palace, **D**

Frank Matcham was also architect to a number of other projects which did not reach fruition (including a European opera house, Woolwich Grand, Beresford Square, a complex in Llandudno, new theatres in Dewsbury, Barrow-in-Furness, Huddersfield (Grand) and Chatham; a new theatre, circus and market in Blackpool and probably many others. Among his non-theatre works were a new wing, designed without charge, for the Variety Artistes' Benevolent Fund at Brinsworth House, the County Arcade in Leeds, the Blackpool Tower Ballroom, and various pubs and shops.

Matcham and Co. designed cinemas in the period after 1912 (see F.G.M. Chancellor).

W. and T.R. MILBURN
William, MBE, FRIBA, FRPS (1858–1935)
Thomas Ridley, FRIBA J (1862–1943)
William (Jr.) FRIBA FRICS (1886–1953)
Stanley Wayman (1887–1961)
William Milburn Sr and Thomas Ridley Milburn were the sons of a shipowner and surveyor, Captain William Milburn, who commanded ships on the River Wear, of both sail and steam. They trained at Sunderland School of Art. William served articles with J. and T. Tillman, FRIBA. Up to 1897 the brothers carried on separate practices, but then joined forces to become W. and T.R. Milburn, one of the largest architectural practices in the North. William's son, William Jr, was RIBA Saxon Snell

prizewinner in 1908 and two years later won the Institute's Godwin Bursary. He subsequently joined the practice, as did Stanley Wayman Milburn, his brother. William Jr, later became principal, but Stanley left in 1947 to form S.W. Milburn and Partners. It has been said that Thomas Ridley Milburn, while he lived, was mainly responsible for the theatre work of the practice. William Sr and William Jr were both sometime Presidents of the Northern Architectural Association. The firm built a number of theatres for the Moss circuit, including the very last of the Moss Empires, that in Southampton, 1928. The Sunderland firm were highly trained architects. Most of their early works have now been demolished, with the exception of Sunderland Empire, 1907, a highly individual design with no obvious precedents or parallels and comparable only to their own later Hartlepool Empire. Its corner entrance tower has been praised as a splendid mannerist conceit, owing much to Wren and Hawksmoor, but the equally unusual box-like slips in the auditorium have been criticised as being over-dominant, distracting attention from the stage.

Their later work was produced at a time when there was a complete lack of direction in theatre design, while cinema design was simultaneously gaining in confidence and striving for evermore spectacular ornamental display. The Milburns' 1920s theatres, which owe little or nothing to the pre-First World War 'boom' theatres and more to North American models, have recently found favour as being amongst the best live theatres of a generally unhappy period.

However much one may regret the loss of fine earlier theatres (like the Matcham Empire in Cardiff, which made way for the Milburns' new theatre) the few remaining Milburn houses are making an important contribution to the theatre life of their cities. The incorporation of their auditorium into the otherwise totally reconstructed Edinburgh Festival Theatre in 1994 was an architectural event of some significance. *DW*

Original architects

1893	Newcastle upon Tyne, Olympia (with Oliver and Leeson), **D**
1897	**South Shields, Empire Palace** (with Matcham)
1901	Sunderland , Palace, **D**
1901	Seaham Harbour, Theatre Royal (ii)
1903	Sunderland, Star Music Hall
1907	**Sunderland, Empire**, listed
1909	Hartlepool, Empire, **D**
1911	Birmingham, New Palace
1911	South Shields, Palace
1912	Seaham Harbour, Empire (attributed)
1912	Newcastle upon Tyne, Hippodrome, **D**
1914	Birmingham, Newtown Palace, **D**
1915	Cardiff, Gaumont (Empire), **D**
1925	**Liverpool, Empire**, listed
1928	**Southampton, Mayflower (Empire)**, listed
1929	**London (Camden), Dominion** (William Jr and T.R. Milburn), listed
1929	South Shields, Empire Palace, alterations
1933	**Oxford, New (Apollo)** (with T.P. Bennett)

Later architects

1890–1901 Sunderland, Avenue Theatre, major alterations
1896	Hartlepool, Alhambra, alterations
1903–1930 Sunderland, People's Palace, alterations,
1911	London (Newham), Stratford Empire, rebuilt, **D**
1914	Birmingham, Empire, rebuilt
1914	Hartlepool, Empire, rebuilt, **D**

1915/16 Cardiff, Empire/Gaumont, rebuilt after fire, **D**
1920 **South Shields, Empire Palace**, alterations
1920 South Shields, Theatre Royal, construction of a bridge to link with Empire Theatre
1921 Hartlepool, Empire, alterations, **D**
1928 **Edinburgh, Empire (Festival)**, rebuilt, listed
1928 Durham, Palladium, **D**
1929 Sunderland, Kings, alterations, **D**
1929 **South Shields, Empire (Palace)**, alterations
1931 Glasgow, Empire, rebuilt, **D**

A number of cinema designs by the Milburns are also known, mainly in the north-east of England.

MOLLO and EGAN
Eugene MOLLO
Michael EGAN (?1908–   )
Mollo and Egan were designers of cinema interiors, providing spectacular inventions for Robert Cromie, Edward Stone, Wimperis, Simpson and Guthrie, David Nye and many other architects. Some of the most striking interiors of the 1930s were actually theirs, although (as with those of John Alexander), rarely credited to them at the time.

Michael Egan was born in France and brought up in Ireland. He became a student at the Architectural Association in 1925 but left before completing the course in order to join Marc Henri and Laverdet in France. Here he met Eugene Mollo. They set up their own firm in 1931. Mollo, the older man, half Russian, was mainly concerned with designing carpets and spray-painted colour schemes. Egan designed the imaginative Art Deco and 'streamlined' decorative plasterwork. A profoundly deaf colleague, the Russian artist, Alexander Bilibin, created fantastic grillwork for Egan's designs. After war service there was little or no cinema work to be done and Egan worked on shoeshop and bank interiors. *JE*

Among many interiors which can be confidently attributed to them are:

1931 **Dewsbury, Playhouse** (with Cromie and Laverdet)
1933 London (Merton), Wimbledon Regal
1934 London (Kingston), Surbiton Odeon
1935 Southend, Astoria
1935 Godalming, Royal
1935 Chelmsford, Ritz
1936 Scarborough, Odeon, Stephen Joseph, listed
1937 Esher, Embassy, listed
1937 Yeovil, Odeon
1937 North Watford, Odeon
1938 Bridlington, Regal

NEATBY, W.J. (fl 1890-1907)
Neatby was a ceramic artist at Doulton's Lambeth Pottery. His significance as a theatre decorator began to emerge only during research for this book. Little is known at present but elements of the following interiors can be definitely attributed to him. *DW*

1896/7 **Blackpool, Winter Gardens**
1898 **Plymouth, New Palace Theatre**
1898 **Newcastle upon Tyne, St Nicholas Hospital Theatre**
1903 London, Gaiety (ii), **D**
1904 Birmingham, Theatre Royal, **D**

OLIVER and LEESON
Thomas OLIVER Jr (1823–1902)
Richard John LEESON (d. 1914)
Oliver and Leeson of Newcastle upon Tyne went into partnership in 1879. As well as working on theatres, they were general practice architects who designed churches, commercial buildings and schools. Their Newcastle Empire was a magnificent example of a music hall, built as an addition to a pub, which although relatively late in date (1890) and with a theatrical stage, retained characteristics of earlier drinking halls, being rectangular in plan with two tiers of balconies on three sides, and mirrors and pictures on the walls. It had a confident Franco-Flemish front. *DW*

Original architects
1890 Newcastle upon Tyne, Empire Music Hall, **D**
1892 Newcastle upon Tyne, Art Gallery Theatre (with George Connell), **D**
1893 Newcastle upon Tyne, Olympia (with T.R. Milburn), **D**

Later architects
1891-3 **Newcastle upon Tyne, Tyne Theatre and Opera House**, addition of grand saloon; also shops and offices adjoining theatre, listed

OWEN and WARD
W.H. WARD
George F. WARD
A successful Birmingham practice who built many theatres, but about whom too little is at yet known. It would appear that W.H. Ward took in Owen and G.F. Ward about 1895 to make the firm of Owen and Ward. Only one of their auditoria, the Darlington Hippodrome (now Civic), remains in anything like its original form. Even early photographs are scarce. Only one, of Her Majesty's, Walsall, has so far come to light. Pronouncements on their architectural style are therefore only tentative. Both these interiors, however, have a neat and competent, unflamboyant quality: horizontal balconies running round to one or two stage boxes, topped by flattened arches, with bulbous fronts flanked by pilasters; the whole composition trimly adjacent to well considered proscenium openings. Externally, judgements are easier to make. The buildings range from W. H. Ward's splendid Birmingham Grand, 1883, the 'Drury Lane of the Midlands', one of the most impressive British theatres of the late C19, to the gingerbread paste-on look of G.F. Ward's Gorden, Stoke-on-Trent, 1900, or Palace, Warrington, 1907. The Civic, Darlington, is in the same idiom, riotous and wonderfully busy – a solidified fairground of shapes and motifs which proudly advertise the building's function as a hippodrome-music hall. These late Owen and Ward theatres are to be compared, internally, with Phipps, externally with Matcham. In fact, they use many of Matcham's themes, arched windows, turrets, broken pediments and onion domes, yet executed with far more verve and conviction. *VG*

Original architects
1878 Wolverhampton, Theatre Royal (W.H. Ward only), **D**
1883 Birmingham, Grand, (W.H. Ward only), **D**
1893 Birmingham, Aston Theatre Royal (W.H. Ward only)
c.1895 Warrington, Parr Music Hall (Owen only)
1897 Smethwick, Theatre Royal, **D**
1898 Wolverhampton, Empire, **D**
1899 Birmingham, Bordesley Imperial Palace, **D**
1900 Nuneaton, Prince of Wales

1900   Stoke-on-Trent, Gorden (G.F. Ward)
1900   Walsall, Her Majesty's, **D**
1901   Birmingham, Alexandra
1903   Kidderminster, Opera House, **D**
1905   London (Tower Hamlets), Poplar Hippodrome, **D**
1906   Carlisle, Palace Theatre of Varieties

Later architects
1896   West Bromwich, Theatre Royal, alterations, **D**
1899   Walsall, Grand, alterations, **D**
1902   Ton Pentre, Lyceum, conversion of Town Hall to theatre
1902/1906   Birmingham, Gaiety Music Hall, internal alterations, **D**
1904   Grimsby, Palace, **D**
1904   Wigan, Hippodrome, **D**
1907   Darlington, Civic, listed
1907   Warrington, Palace (G.F. Ward)
1908   Birkenhead, King's
1908   Middlesbrough, Hippodrome (G.F. Ward)
1908   Seacombe, Kings, reconstruction after fire
1909   Nuneaton, Empire (G.F. Ward)
1911   Doncaster, Palace (Ward and Ball), **D**
1913   London (Hackney), Hoxton Varieties, alterations, **D**
1914   Skegness, Kings, **D**

Charles John PHIPPS, FSA, FRIBA (1835–1897)
Born in Landsdowne near Bath, son of John Rashleigh Phipps. He was articled to Wilcox and Fuller, architects of Bath until June 1857. After a year's travel, he commenced on his own at Bath 1858, then at Cornhill, London 1863–7 and Mecklenburgh Square 1867 to death. FSA 1862, FRIBA 1866, member of Council 1875–6. Advising architect to Theatre Royal, Drury Lane, fifteen years; exhibited seven designs at RA 1863–97; besides theatres designed various business premises, blocks of flats and the Devonshire Club, St James's Street. Also the Carlton Hotel part of the same grand design as Her Majesty's Theatre, which was carried out and modified after his death by his partner and son-in-law, A. Blomfield Jackson (1868–1951), who continued the practice. Phipps's early designs for buildings and furniture were Gothic and ecclesiastical in the style of Godwin and Burges, but after his first theatre he adopted 'a more appropriate classic manner'.

The first of the great Victorian specialists, Phipps was for over thirty years the acknowledged doyen in the field; until recently the only theatre architect of the period to be found in the DNB and one of the few in the standard biographical dictionaries of architects. Fortunately, many of his theatres remain more or less as he designed them. Phipps's most prolific years preceded the flowering of the music hall in the 1890s, and his were primarily straight theatres. Stylistically, his work was much influenced by the great Continental (particularly French) theatres of the C18 and mid-C19, with a solemn, seemingly solid dignity quite different from the slender gimcrack feel of earlier English theatre interiors. The line of his balconies runs horizontally through to stage boxes, which often themselves form the proscenium opening without the intrusion of an elaborate frame surrounding the stage. Decoration in a Phipps theatre is always applied in low relief, and restrained, unlike the integrated high key rumbustiousness of the later Matcham or Crewe theatres at their vibrant best. Externally, too, Phipps had an assured dignified touch, using the customary motifs of classic architecture with confidence; he produced civic buildings with undeniable theatrical character which made an important

C.J. Phipps

contribution to the Victorian street scene. Those that remain such the Theatres Royal, Nottingham and Glasgow, Lyceum, Edinburgh and Her Majesty's still retain their viability in often very altered circumstances. *VG*

Original architect
1865   Nottingham, Theatre Royal, listed
1865   South Shields, Theatre Royal (with T.M. Clemence)
1867   Bristol, Prince's, **D**
1867   Swansea, Royal
1868   London (Westminster), Gaiety, **D**
1870   London (Hackney), Variety Theatre, Hoxton, **D**
1870   London (Westminster), Vaudeville, listed
1871   Dublin, Gaiety
c.1871   Dublin, Leinster Hall
1872   Aberdeen, Tivoli (with J.M. Matthews), listed
1873   Edinburgh, Theatre Royal, **D**
1875   Worcester, Theatre Royal (ii), **D**
1877   Cork, Opera House, **D**
1877   Leicester, Royal Opera House, **D**
1877   Derry, Royal Opera House
1878   Liverpool, Rotunda (with E. Davis and Sons), **D**
1878   Worcester, Theatre Royal, **D**
1879   Liverpool, Alexandra, **D**
1880   Glasgow, Theatre Royal, rebuilt, listed
1881   London (Westminster), Savoy, listed
1881   Belfast, Theatre Royal, **D**
1882   Hastings, Gaiety (with Cross and Wells)
1882   London (Westminster), Strand, **D**
1882   Leamington, Theatre Royal (with Osborne and Reading)
1883   Edinburgh, Lyceum, listed
1883   Eastbourne, Royal Hippodrome
1884   Northampton, Royal Theatre, listed
1884   London (Westminster), Prince of Wales, **D**

1886	Exeter, Theatre Royal, **D**
1888	**London (Westminster), Lyric,** listed
1888	London (Westminster), Shaftesbury Theatre, **D**
1889	**London (Westminster), Garrick** (with W. Emden), listed
1889	Coventry, Royal Opera House (with Essex and Nicoll), **D**
1890	Plymouth, Devonport Empire
1893	London (Westminster), Daly's (with Chadwick), **D**
1894	**Wolverhampton, Grand,** listed
1894	London (Southwark), Camberwell Metropole/ Empire, **D**
1897	**London (Westminster), Her Majesty's,** listed
1897	Dover, Royal Hippodrome, **D**
1899	London (Islington), Holloway Empire, **D**

Later architect

1863	**Bath, Theatre Royal,** listed
1866	**Brighton, Theatre Royal,** listed
1867	London (Westminster), Queen's, Long Acre, **D**
1876	**Dumfries, Theatre Royal,** listed
1876	Dunfermline, Theatre Royal, **D**
1879	**London (Islington), Sadler's Wells**
1880	**London (Westminster), Theatre Royal, Haymarket,** listed
1880	London (Westminster), Princess's Theatre, **D**
1880	**Torquay, Royal Theatre and Opera House,** (alterations)
1882	**Portsmouth, Theatre Royal,** totally rebuilt, listed
1883	London (Westminster), Olympic, **D**
1884	Edinburgh, Theatre Royal, **D**
1884	**Portsmouth, Theatre Royal,** listed
1884/1886	London (Westminster), Hengler's (Palladium site), **D**
1884	**London (Westminster), Lyceum,** part reconstruction, listed
1884	**Nottingham, Theatre Royal,** alterations, listed
1887	**Northampton, Royal Theatre,** reinstated after fire, listed
1887	Darlington, Theatre Royal, rebuilt after fire
1887	**London (Westminster), Vaudeville,** altered, listed
1887	Darlington, Theatre Royal (rebuilt after fire), **D**
1888	**Torquay, Royal Theatre and Opera House**
1890	**Glasgow, Theatre Royal,** listed
1890	**Nottingham, Theatre Royal** (alterations), listed
1890	London (Westminster), Toole's, **D**
1890	**London (Westminster), Vaudeville,** rebuilt, listed
1894	London (Tower Hamlets), Pavilion, Whitechapel (with E. Runtz), **D**
1895	**Glasgow, Theatre Royal,** rebuilt, listed
1897	London (Kingston), Royal County (with Bourne), **D**

Jethro T. ROBINSON, (d. 1878)

Consulting theatre architect to the Lord Chamberlain, he was Frank Matcham's father-in-law. Matcham took over his practice in 1878.

Robinson's interiors make a nice comparison with Phipps's of the same period. Where the latter's were straightforward and sensibly worthy, the former's were fanciful and delicate, with bulbous balcony fronts supported on slender cast-iron columns: all somewhat reminiscent of the 1850s, but running through to jolly little boxes, very much of the 1870s. Robinson's lighthearted touch made him eminently suitable as a designer of circuses and music halls, of which he built quite a few. In the nature of such ephemeral buildings, these have all

disappeared, but we are lucky in still possessing two fine auditoria: the intact Theatre Royal, Margate, and the Old Vic, drastically altered in the 1950s and 1960s but restored to Robinson's design in 1983. *VG*

Original architect

1872	London (Hackney), Hackney Theatre, **D**
1873	London (Camden), Park, Camden Town, **D**
1876	Liverpool, Hengler's Grand Cirque/Royal Hippodrome, **D**
1878	London (Lambeth), Elephant and Castle (completed by Matcham), **D**

Later architect

1871	London (Westminster), Hengler's Grand Cirque, conversion from Corinthian Bazaar (Palladium Site)
1871	**London (Lambeth), Old Vic,** rebuilt interior, listed
1872	London (Lambeth), Astley's, alterations, **D**
1874	**Margate, Theatre Royal,** enlarged and partly rebuilt, listed
1874	London (Tower Hamlets), Whitechapel Pavilion, alterations, **D**
1876	London (Hackney), Grecian, alterations, **D**
1878	London (Tower Hamlets), Royal Cambridge Music Hall, alterations, **D**
1878	Leeds, Theatre (Royal?), alterations, **D**

Ernest RUNTZ, FRIBA (1859–1912)

Sixth son of John Runtz of Stoke Newington and brother of Sir John Runtz. After leaving school he was articled to Samuel Walker, auctioneer, valuer and estate agent, subsequently his partner. He was nearly thirty before commencing a study of architecture at University College, London, obtaining a Donaldson Silver Medal for Fine Art, and, when with Frederick T. Farrow FRIBA, took qualifying examination for RIBA, but was not admitted as Associate because of partnership with Walker. He dissolved the partnership in 1897 and took as partners A.C. Breden, ARIBA, and George Mclean Ford, FRIBA, under the style of Ernest Runtz and Co.; on Breden's death the firm became Ernest Runtz and Ford 1903–09: thereafter Ernest Runtz and Son. In 1909 the RIBA relented and he was invited in as a Fellow. His practice also designed many non-theatrical buildings.

Runtz was a curious figure. Extravagantly praised in his day by Sachs in *Modern Opera Houses and Theatres* (to the detriment of Phipps and Matcham) he appears now to have been only as good as his current partners, and a decidedly lesser figure. Sachs admired Runtz for his facades, which introduced a new Continental civic pomp to the British scene, and because his interiors lacked the vulgar theatrical qualities which we now esteem. In fact, he was always better outside than in! The Empire, Middlesbrough, and the designs for the Opera House, Norwich, (later slightly adapted and built by Sprague) could be Central European Stadt theatres; the Gaiety was Edwardian London at its most impressive and grandiose, but there the facades were designed by R. Norman Shaw acting as consultant. In the Cardiff New, a building which marks the decline of the Victorian and Edwardian tradition the steep balconies (flanked by stark side walls) were completely divorced from the stage boxes, themselves clumsy and heavy (a design flaw which has been recently rectified). *VG*

Original architect

1896	Cambridge, New, **D**
1898	London (Southwark), Peckham Hippodrome, **D**

1899	**Hastings, Hippodrome**
1899	**Middlesbrough, Empire**, listed
1901	Lowestoft, Marina
1902	Halifax, Palace, **D**
1903	London (Westminster), Gaiety (with R. Norman Shaw), **D**
1906	**Cardiff, New** (with Ford), listed

Later architect

1894	London (Tower Hamlets), Pavilion, Whitechapel, part reconstruction (possibly with Phipps), **D**
1897	London (Camden), Holborn Empire, **D**
1901	**London (Westminster), Adelphi**, (with Ford) alterations, listed
1904	Birmingham, Theatre Royal, New Street, **D**

Edwin Otho SACHS (1870–1919)

Edwin O. Sachs is perhaps best remembered in theatrical circles for his definitive 3-volume treatise *Modern Opera Houses and Theatres* (the first volume in collaboration with Ernest A.E. Woodrow). Much of his life was spent working as an organiser and initiator of professional and official bodies. His work in the formation and organisation of The British Fire Prevention Committee, as editor of *Concrete and Constructional Engineering*, as author of *Facts on Fire Prevention* and his organisation of the International Fire Congress held at Earl's Court in 1903 are indicative of his tireless efforts for which he gained national recognition but little financial recompense. His architectural output appears to have been extremely small and few buildings theatrical or otherwise may be attributed to him. *DW*

Works to Theatres

1896–98	London, **Theatre Royal, Drury Lane, stage machinery**
1899	**Llandudno, Grand Theatre** (as consultant to George Alfred Humphreys)
1901	**London, Royal Opera House**, Covent Garden, stage house and auditorium
1907	Cairo, Cairo Opera House, reconstruction (unexecuted project)

W.G.R. SPRAGUE (1865–1933)

Born in Australia, the son of W.A. Sprague and Dolores Drummond, an English actress who gained fame after her return to London in 1874. At sixteen he was articled to Frank Matcham for four years, then to Walter Emden for another three.

Thereafter, well trained in the practicalities of theatre architecture, but uninhibited by the pedantries of an academic education, Sprague set up on his own and designed a large number of theatres. Many fortunately remain as the most elegant smaller houses of the West End. His more extravagant music halls have all disappeared. Unlike his mentors whose knowledge of 'correct' architectural precedent was haphazard (ignorance which they used to great advantage) Sprague gained, through reading and observation, a fine vocabulary of architectural form and detail which he interpreted with a magnificent flair for theatrical atmosphere. As he himself observed, for his 'frontages' he 'liked the Italian Renaissance', but modified and took liberties 'that no architect would ever demur to do so as to get the best effects'. Although his range was less extensive than Matcham's and less dramatically imaginative – both spatially and decoratively – his control was invariably surer. His integration of balconies, boxes and proscenium arch is always masterly and complete. Unlike Matcham, his facades

are 'at one' with his auditoria, and although instantly recognisable as those of a theatre, never obtrude or clash with adjacent buildings, but add a dramatic and well mannered feature to the urban landscape. *VG*

Original architect

1889	London (Tower Hamlets), Shoreditch Olympia (with Crewe), **D**
1890	London (Westminster), Olympic Theatre (with Crewe), **D**
1893	London (Hammersmith), King's, Hammersmith, **D**
1893	**Lincoln, Theatre Royal** (with Crewe), listed
1894	London (Southwark), Camberwell Empire (with Crewe), **D**
1896	London (Wandsworth), Shakespeare, Battersea, **D**
1897	London (Hammersmith), Grand, Fulham, **D**
1897	London (Lewisham), Broadway Theatre, Deptford, **D**
1898	**London (Kensington and Chelsea), Coronet**, Notting Hill Gate, listed
1899	**London (Westminster), Wyndhams**, listed
1899	London (Southwark), Hippodrome, Rotherhithe, **D**
1899	London (Islington), Empire, Holloway, **D**
1899	London (Lambeth), Kennington Theatre, **D**
1899	London (Newham), Stratford Empire, **D**
1899	Bolton, Theatre
1899	Bradford, Empire, **D**
1901	**London (Camden), Camden Theatre**, listed
1901	Southsea, Theatre , unexecuted
1902	London (Wandsworth), Hippodrome, Balham, **D**
1903	Norwich, Hippodrome, **D**
1903	**London (Westminster), Albery**, listed
1904	London (Westminster), Royalty, Dean Street, **D**
1904	London (Greenwich), Royal Artillery, Woolwich, **D**
1905	**London (Westminster), Aldwych**, listed
1905	**London (Westminster), Strand Theatre**, listed
1906	**London (Westminster), Gielgud**, listed
1907	**London (Westminster), Queen's**, listed
1907	Reading, Palace, **D**
1908	**Oxford, New**
1908	London (Westminster), Kilburn Empire, **D**
1908	Paris, Edouard VII
1912	Northampton, New, **D**
1913	**London (Camden), Ambassadors**, listed
1915	London (Bromley), Penge Empire, **D**
1916	**London (Camden), St Martin's**, listed
1929	**London (Lambeth), Streatham Hill**

Later architect

1897	Newport, Lyceum, rebuilt
1897	Coventry, Grand, **D**
1897	**Sheffield, Lyceum** (with E. Holmes), listed
1902	London (Hammersmith), King's, Hammersmith, **D**
1908	Norwich, Hippodrome, **D**
1910	London (Westminster), Kilburn Empire, **D**

Edward Albert STONE, FSI

One of the most successful designers of cinemas and cinétheatres in the 1920s and 1930s, some of which had impressive provision for stage shows. He also designed three of the handful of new theatres built in the West End in that period. He was not an architect and usually entrusted his interiors to accomplished designers like Marc Henri and Laverdet and Mollo and Egan.

Original Architect

1927   London (Westminster), Astoria, conversion of factory to cinema theatre

1929   London (Westminster), Piccadilly (with Bertie Crewe)

1929   London (Lambeth), Brixton Academy/Astoria (with Somerford and Barr), listed

1929/30 London(Westminster), Prince Edward (with Henri and Laverdet)

1930   London (Westminster), Whitehall (with Henri and Laverdet), listed

1930   London (Islington), Astoria/Rainbow, Finsbury Park (with Somerford and Barr), listed

More than a dozen cinema designs have also been noted.

J.D. SWANSTON (1869–1956)
John D. Swanston, TD FRIBA FRICS, had his architectural practice in Kirkcaldy and designed a number of buildings there, public and domestic, many of them in red sandstone,and a few in the Tudor style. He also had a number of important theatres to his credit. Swanston died in Newton Mearns in 1956. *BP*

Original Architect

1904   Kirkcaldy, King's (with William Williamson), listed (facade only)

1906   Edinburgh, King's (with James Davidson), listed

1907   Dundee, Hippodrome

1907   Methil, Gaiety

1913   Kirkcaldy, Palace, **D**

n.d.   Belfast, Alexandra, **D**

Later architect

1921   Dunfermline, Opera House, reconstructed interior, **D**; reconstructed in USA

W.E.TRENT (1874–1948)
William Edward Trent was articled to Henry Poston in 1892 and attended the Architectural Association's evening classes. He started his own practice in 1905 and had made at least one cinema conversion by 1909. He became Chief Architect to Provincial Cinematograph Theatres in 1925 and went on to design more than fifty super cinemas, most of them Gaumont Palaces (Provincial Cinematograph Theatres was taken over by Gaumont British in 1929). Some of his most striking designs with fully equipped theatrical stages are included in the gazetteer.

W.S. TRENT (1903–1944)
William Sydney Trent, the son of W.E. Trent, studied at the Architectural Association school and received the AA diploma in 1923. When his father joined PCT, W.S. Trent took over the private practice. In 1932 he joined Gaumont British to work under his father, whom he predeceased.

In the following list the author is to be understood to be W.E. Trent unless otherwise stated. *JE*

Original architects

1926   Weymouth, Regent, reconstructed Jubilee Hall, **D**

1927   Sheffield, Regent

1929   Stoke-on-Trent (Hanley), Odeon, listed

1929   Bournemouth, Regent (with Seal and Hardy)

1930   London (Westminster), New Victoria (Apollo Victoria) (with E. Wamsley Lewis)

1932   Wolverhampton, Gaumont Palace (with J. Morrison)

1932   London (Lewisham), Lewisham Gaumont Palace (with S. Morrison), **D**

1934   Yeovil, Gaumont Palace

1934   Worcester, Gaumont

1935   Stroud, Gaumont Palace (with W.S.Trent)

1936   Chippenham, Gaumont Palace (with W.S. Trent)

1936   London (Newham), Barking Road Granada (with T. Komisarjevski)

1937   Salisbury, City Hall (with W.S. Trent and R.C.H. Golding)

Later architects

1929 and 1938 London (Hackney), Dalston Theatre

1930   Southport, Palladium, rebuilt auditorium (with Ernest F. Tulley), **D**

1933, 1945 and 1948 London (Camden), Dominion, listed

1938   Leeds, Coliseum, internal reconstruction (with W.S. Trent and Daniel Mackay)

More than thirty other cinema designs have also been noted

VERITY and BEVERLEY
Thomas VERITY, FRIBA (1837–1891)
Francis (Frank) Thomas VERITY, FRIBA (d. 1937)
Thomas Verity was articled to an architect; employed in the architectural office of the War Office, then in South Kensington assisting Captain Fowke in erection of South Kensington Museum, and principal assistant to Major-General Scott in erection of Royal Albert Hall 1867–70, doing all the detailing. Won competition for Criterion Restaurant and Theatre 1870: FRIBA 1878. Consulting architect to Lord Chamberlain 1878 to death. First in partnership with G.H. Hunt, then in later years with his son, Frank Verity. Also designed many non-theatrical buildings.

Francis Thomas Verity was born in London, educated at Cranleigh and articled to his father. He was also a pupil of R. Phene Spiers; studied at Royal College of Art, South Kensington; at University College; the A.A. and R.A. Schools, and in Paris. Gained the RIBA Tite Prize 1889, in which year he was elected ARIBA, becoming Fellow 1896. Continued his father's practice, subsequently building or rebuilding various theatres and, later, innumerable cinemas in London, the provinces and Paris; was European adviser to Paramount and the Union Cinema Company. Many architects, later to become famous, worked in his large and flourishing practice. In his last years he was in partnership with his son-in-law, Sam Beverley, FRIBA.

The Veritys, father and son, were enthusiastic Francophiles and introduced, first, authentic French Second Empire and, later, the grand Beaux Arts tradition to British theatre architecture. Thomas was the more successful in creating a satisfactory theatrical atmosphere, designing interiors which were sensible, warm and intimate, which were amongst the best of the late Victorian. The Criterion and Comedy survive from this period. Frank, whilst reacting against the plush-and-gilt of the Matcham school, launched a theatrical severity of 'correct' classical detailing which gradually declined, via Lillie Langtry's Imperial, and the Scala, into the cinema style of the great balcony and the intimidating side wall. His own cinemas, however, were mostly built in the 1920s, pre-Modernistic therefore, and retaining the trappings of classical decoration, sparsely applied. *VG*

Original architects

1874   London (Westminster), Criterion (Thomas Verity), listed

1881   London (Westminster), Comedy (Thomas Verity), listed

1882   London (Westminster), Novelty, **D**

1884   London (Westminster), Empire/Pandora, Leicester Square (Thomas Verity)

1887   London (Kensington and Chelsea, Knightsbridge Hall (Thomas Verity), **D**

1926   London (Westminster), Plaza Cinema (Frank Verity)

1931   Newcastle upon Tyne, Paramount/Odeon (with Sam Beverley)

1933   Nottingham, Ritz (with Sam Beverley)

1934   Glasgow, Paramount/Odeon (with Sam Beverley)

1936   Horsham, Arts Centre/Ritz (with L.H. Parsons)

1937   Aldershot, Ritz (with Sam Beverley)

1937   Nuneaton, ABC (with Sam Beverley)

1938   Keighley, ABC/Ritz (with Sam Beverley)

late 1930s Winchester, Ritz

1940s   Brighton, Imperial (Sam Beverley)

1960   Weymouth, Pavilion (with Sam Beverley)

Later architects

1876   London (Westminster), Folly/Toole's, reconstruction, **D**

1878 and 1884 London (Westminster), Criterion, extension and partial reconstruction (Thomas Verity), listed

1879   London (Westminster), St James's, **D**

1880   Scarborough, Spa (with Hunt)

1888   London (Westminster), Royalty, **D**

1891   London (Hackney), Dalston Theatre, alterations, not executed (Thomas and Frank Verity)

1893 and 1904 London (Westminster), Empire, Leicester Square, extensive alterations (Frank Verity)

1901   London (Westminster), Imperial, rebuilt interior, **D**

1902   Bath, Theatre Royal

1910–1912 London (Islington), Marlborough Hall, facade reconstruction (Frank Verity)

1912   Windsor, Theatre Royal, interior reconstruction (Frank Verity)

1927   London (Hackney), Dalston Theatre (Frank Verity), organ installed

1928   Bristol, People's Palace, conversion to cinema (Frank Verity)

1939   Dover, King's Hall, reconstruction of former variety theatre as cinema after fire

1967–1968 London (Westminster), Plaza Cinema, reconstruction (Frank Verity), listed

1990   Windsor, Theatre Royal, enlargement (Verity and Beverley)

In addition to the above more than twenty-five cinema designs have been noted.

Albert WINSTANLEY

An architect active mainly in the north-west of England. He had offices in St Anne's-on-Sea, Preston and Manchester (Deansgate). Information about him is sparse. His known works include:

Original architect

1909   Carlisle, Queen's

1909   Fleetwood, Empire, **D**

1909   Whitehaven, Theatre Royal, **D**

1913   Wakefield, Playhouse/Picture House

1934   Manchester (Romiley), Savoy Cinema (ciné-variety)

Later Architect

n.d.   Barrow-in-Furness, Her Majesty's, rebuilt, **D**

1908   Lancaster, Grand, the present facade and interior partly rebuilt, listed

1909   Castleford, Queen's, reconstructed, **D**

1911   Crewe, Lyceum, substantially rebuilt after fire, listed

1911   Bury, Art Theatre

Ernest Augustus Eckett WOODROW (1860–1937)

E.A.E Woodrow was Sachs's collaborator on *Modern Opera Houses and Theatres* but had left the partnership before the second volume was published. He attended the Royal Academy School and served his articles with C.J. Phipps before being elected ARIBA in 1881. By 1885 he was working in the office of the Superintending Architect of the Metropolitan Board of Works, wholly engaged on theatre safety controls in which he established himself as a considerable authority. When the London County Council was formed in 1889 he transferred to the new Theatres Branch and, although he never rose above second-in-command was clearly the most knowledgeable man in the Branch and a major influence on the development of the principles of control operated over the ensuing century. He wrote prolifically and well on theatre subjects in professional and learned journals but, apart from the joint work with Sachs, none of his writings appeared in book form. He went into private practice as a theatre architect in 1895 but was too late on the scene to benefit from the great variety house building boom. Only three theatres can definitely be ascribed to him, (he may have 'ghosted' or acted as consultant on others) two of which were commisssioned by the music hall giants, Dan Leno and Herbert Campbell. The one survivor, the Clapham Grand, is enough to establish him as a designer of skill and imagination whose decision, after 1900, to leave a lifetime's specialisation, is a a matter for great regret. *JE*

Original architect

1897   London (Islington), Collins' Music Hall, new auditorium, **D**

1899   London (Southwark), Camberwell Palace, **D**

1900   London (Wandsworth), Grand, Clapham Junction, listed

E.A.E. Woodrow

WYLSON and LONG
Oswald Cane WYLSON, FRIBA (c.1858–1925)
Charles LONG, ARIBA (d. 1906)

Oswald Cane Wylson was the son of James Wylson, an architect who had worked in the office of Charles Barry and was founder of the association which was to become the Architectural Association. He was also Surveyor to several land societies. Oswald studied at the Royal Academy Schools and University College, London, before being apprenticed to Arthur Cates, architect to the Crown Estate. Wylson was keenly interested in theatre safety. He became hon. deputy chief surveyor of the British Fire Prevention Committee and also sat on the Concrete Research Committee. In both these roles he would have been in regular contact with E.O. Sachs.

Charles Long was a pupil of John Robinson from 1871 and remained with him until he started his own practice in 1881. The Partnership with Wylson first appears in the directories in 1883 when Wylson was 25 and it continued as Wylson and Long after Long's death in 1906.

This firm has been under-rated, largely because little of their best work survives. They were particularly known for their entertainment buildings and restaurants. Their theatres and music halls were in a manner closer to that of Matcham than either Sprague or the Veritys. Styles ranged from a free use of architectural motifs in their earlier work to the classical restraint and consistency shown, for example, in the extant Tottenham Palace.

Sachs considered their Bristol Empire Palace (in oriental style) and their rebuilding of the London Oxford Music Hall in 1893 worthy of inclusion in *Modern Opera Houses and Theatres*.

Their most important work was done in Blackpool with a building on the promenade comprising a variety theatre (Alhambra, later Palace), circus, restaurant and ballroom, all with opulent interiors. Wylson and Long's facades, such as those of the Chelsea and Euston Palaces were splendid piles. It is a great pity that their 1900 interior for the London Pavilion, in elegant French style, has been destroyed, but their Blackpool Winter Gardens Pavilion survives as their most impressive monument. *JE*

Original architects

1893	Bristol, Empire, **D**
1898	London (Lambeth), Brixton Empress, **D**
1899	Blackpool, Palace Ballroom, Circus, etc.
1899	London (Camden), Kilburn Palace (with Palgrave and Son), **D**
1901	London (Camden), Euston Palace (with Bertie Crewe), **D**
1903	London (Kensington and Chelsea), Chelsea Palace, **D**
1903	London (Waltham Forest), Walthamstow Palace, **D**
1903	Newcastle upon Tyne, Pavilion, **D**,
1906	London (Newham), East Ham Palace, **D**
1908	**London (Haringey), Tottenham Palace**, listed

Later architects

1893	London (Westminster), Oxford Music Hall, rebuilt, **D**
1893	London (Lambeth), South London, **D**
1895	**Bath, Palace**, listed
1897	**Blackpool, Winter Gardens Pavilion**, rebuilt auditorium, listed
1898	**London (Hackney), Dalston Theatre**, reconstructed internally
1900	**London (Westminster), London Pavilion**, reconstructed internally, listed
1902	London (Lambeth), Canterbury Theatre of Varieties, **D**
1903	London (Hackney), Hoxton Varieties, alterations, **D**
1906	London (Camden), Euston Palace, alterations, **D**

Bibliography

Books

This list contains regularly consulted references only. Books on individual theatres have not been included. Not listed here are the many books covering theatres and cinemas in defined geographical areas. Among these, Malcolm Webb's *Greater London's Suburban Cinemas 1946–86* Amber Valley, Erdington, 1986 was typical and useful. Place of publication is London unless otherwise stated.

Ashton, Geoffrey and Mackintosh, Iain, *The Georgian Playhouse 1730–1830 – a Catalogue*, Arts Council of Great Britain, 1975

Atwell, David, *Cathedrals of the Movies*, Architectural Press, 1980

Bentham, Frederick, *New Theatres in Britain*, Rank Strand, 1970

Carson, L. (ed.), *The Stage Guide and Directory*, The Stage Offices, 1912

Cheshire, David F., *Music Hall*, David and Charles, 1979

Clegg, Rosemary, *Odeon*, Mercia CSP, 1985

Colvin, Howard, *A Biographical Dictionary of British Architects 1600–1840*, Yale University Press, 3rd edn, 1995

Eyles, Allen, *ABC, The First Name in Entertainment*, Cinema Theatre Association (CTA), 1993

– *Gaumont British Cinemas*, CTA, 1996

Eyles, Allen and Skene, Keith, *London's West End Cinemas*, Keytone, 1984 and 1991

Felstead, Alison, Franklin, Jonathan and Pinfield, Leslie, *Dictionary of British Architects 1834–1900*, Maxwell, 1993

Franchi, Francesca with Hudson, Claire, *Dictionary of Performing Arts Resources*, Society for Theatre Research, 1998

Glasstone, Victor, *Victorian and Edwardian Theatres*, Thames and Hudson, 1975

Gray, A. Stuart, *Edwardian Architecture, A Biographical Dictionary*, Wordsworth, 1985

Gray, Richard, *Cinemas in Britain, One Hundred Years of Cinema Architecture*, Lund Humphries, 1996

Grice, Elizabeth, *Rogues and Vagabonds*, Terence Dalton, 1977

Holden, Michael (ed.), *The Stage Guide*, Carson and Comerford Ltd, 1971

Howard, Diana, *London Theatres and Music Halls 1850–1950*, Library Association, 1970

Leacroft, Richard, *Development of the English Playhouse*, Eyre Methuen, 1973

Mackintosh, Iain and Sell, Michael (eds), *Curtains!!! Or A New Life for Old Theatres*, John Offord, Eastbourne, 1982

Mander, Raymond and Mitchenson, Joe, *Lost Theatres of London*, Rupert Hart Davis, 1968 New English Library, 1976

– *Theatres of London*, Rupert Hart Davis, 1961 and 1963, New English Library, 1975

Mickleburgh, Timothy J., *Guide to British Piers*, Piers Information Bureau, Wirral, 3rd edn, 1998

– *Threatened Piers*, Piers Information Bureau, Hebden Bridge, 1990

Peter, Bruce, *Scotland's Splendid Theatres*, Polygon, Edinburgh, 1999

Richardson, Ruth and Thorne, Robert, *'The Builder' Illustrations Index 1843–1882*, Hutton and Rostron, 1994

Sachs, Edwin O. and Woodrow, E.A.E., *Modern Opera Houses and Theatres* – London 1896–1898, Arno Press NJ, 1968

Senelick, Cheshire and Schneider, *British Music Hall 1840–1923*, Archon, 1981

Shand, P. Morton, *Modern Theatres and Cinemas*, B.T. Batsford, 1930

Sheppard, F. H. W. (ed.), *The Survey of London* (principally from Vol XXIX onwards; the most useful references are listed in Theatres Trust *Newsletter 40*, 1996)

Southern, Richard, *The Georgian Playhouse*, Pleiades, 1948

Strong, Judith, *Encore: Strategies for Theatre Renewal*, The Theatres Trust, 1999

Tolmie, A. W. (ed.), *The Stage Guide*, Carson and Comerford, 1946

Walker, Brian (ed.), *Frank Matcham – Theatre Architect*, Blackstaff Press, Belfast, 1980

[Winston, James] 'a theatric amateur', *The Theatric Tourist*, Woodfall, 1805

Annuals, Journals and Periodicals

Constant use has been made of a variety of learned journals, periodicals and year books and no attempt can be made to list all the important individual articles and references here, although many of them are recorded on the database. One article, however, by Christopher Brereton, stands out as having given Iain Mackintosh the idea for the national survey which culminated in the publication in 1982 of the first *Curtains* gazetteer.

Brereton, Christopher, 'Act Now to Save Provincial Theatres' in *Architectural Review*, October, 1976

A list of the most regularly used sources follows:

The Architect

Architectural Review

British Performing Arts Yearbook, 1988 continuing, Rhinegold, Sheena Barbour (ed.)

The Builder/Building, 1843 continuing

Building News

CTA Bulletin, Cinema and Theatre Association

Era Almanacs and *Era Annual*, 1868–1919

The Era, 1838–1939

Irish Performing Arts Yearbook 1992 continuing (annual)

Kinematograph Year Books, 1913 onward (the 1951 edition was referred to most, since this was a time when many old theatres had survived in cinema use)

Picture House, CTA

Sightline, Association of British Theatre Technicians (ABTT), 1966–1992 (afterwards *ABTT Update*)

The Stage, 1881 continuing

Stage Yearbooks

Tabs, Strand Electric, 1937–1986

Theatre Notebook, Society for Theatre Research (STR), 1945 continuing

Theatre Notebook, Index to Vols 1–25, STR, 1977

Theatre Notebook, Index to Vols 26–40, STR, 1990

Theatres Trust Newsletter, 1985 continuing

Theatres Trust Newsletter Index, 1985–1998, 1998

Notes